FREEDOM, TRUTH, AND HUMAN DIGNITY

Freedom, Truth, and Human Dignity

The Second Vatican Council's Declaration on Religious Freedom

A New Translation,
Redaction History, and Interpretation of
Dignitatis Humanae

David L. Schindler
and
Nicholas J. Healy Jr.

HUMANUM
PONTIFICAL JOHN PAUL II
INSTITUTE SERIES

WILLIAM B. EERDMANS PUBLISHING COMPANY
GRAND RAPIDS, MICHIGAN / CAMBRIDGE, U.K.

Published 2015 by
Wm. B. Eerdmans Publishing Co.
2140 Oak Industrial Drive N.E., Grand Rapids, Michigan 49505 /
P.O. Box 163, Cambridge CB3 9PU U.K.

Printed in the United States of America

21 20 19 18 17 16 15   7 6 5 4 3 2 1

Library of Congress Cataloging-in-Publication Data

Freedom, truth, and human dignity: the Second Vatican Council's Declaration on religious
freedom: a new translation, redaction history, and interpretation of Dignitatis humanae /
David L. Schindler and Nicholas J. Healy, Jr.
pages   cm
Includes bibliographical references and index.
ISBN 978-0-8028-7155-8 (pbk.: alk. paper)
1. Freedom of religion.   2. Catholic Church — Doctrines.
I. Schindler, David L., 1943-   II. Healy, Nicholas J., Jr. (Nicholas John)
III. Vatican Council (2nd: 1962-1965: Basilica di San Pietro in Vaticano).
Declaratio de libertate religiosa.   IV. Vatican Council (2nd: 1962-1965:
Basilica di San Pietro in Vaticano). Declaratio de libertate religiosa. English.

BX8301962.A45 L5365   2015
261.7′2 — dc23

2015004122

www.eerdmans.com

To Joseph Ratzinger/Benedict XVI

Contents

Preface

The Declaration on Religious Freedom, *Dignitatis humanae,* was promulgated by Pope Paul VI on December 7, 1965. In an audience granted to delegates from various countries and international organizations, the pope characterized the Declaration as "one of the greatest documents" of Vatican II.[1] It is perhaps also the most intensely debated document of the Council. Both the drafting of the Declaration on Religious Freedom and the reception of the document within the Church have been characterized by deep disagreements about the nature and ground of religious freedom, the development of the Church's doctrine, and the significance of this teaching for the relationship between the Church and modernity.

"The era we call modern times," writes Joseph Ratzinger, "has been determined from the beginning by the theme of freedom . . . the striving for new forms of freedom."[2] In the Pastoral Constitution on the Church in the Modern World, *Gaudium et spes,* the Council fathers acknowledged the legitimacy of this aspiration for freedom, which goes hand in hand with a recognition of the dignity of the human person: "for authentic freedom is an exceptional sign of the image of God in man" (GS, 17). *Dignitatis humanae* engages modernity in the context of the right to religious freedom.

In his first Encyclical Letter, *Redemptor hominis,* John Paul II emphasized the significance of *Dignitatis humanae* for the mission of the Church. "The Church in our time," he writes, "attaches great importance to all that is stated by the Second Vatican Council in its Declaration on Religious Freedom, both the first and the second part of the document. We perceive intimately that the truth revealed to us by God imposes on us an obligation. We have, in particular, a great sense of responsibility for this truth. . . . The Declaration on Religious Freedom shows us convincingly that, when Christ and, after him, his apostles proclaimed the truth that comes not from men but from God ('My teaching is not mine, but his who sent me,' that is, the Father's), they preserved, while acting with their full force of spirit, a deep esteem for man, for his intellect, his will, his conscience and his freedom. Thus the human person's dignity itself becomes part of the content of this proclamation" (RH, 12).

Guided by these words of John Paul II, the present volume seeks to promote a deeper understanding of the Second Vatican Council's Declaration on Religious Freedom. In addition to presenting a new translation of the finally approved text of the Declaration, the book makes available for the first time in English the five schemas (drafts) of the document that were presented to the Council bishops leading up to this final text. A better awareness of the changes that were introduced into the Declaration in the course of the conciliar debates will enable a better understanding of the document's continuity with and development of earlier Catholic teaching, and the proper sense of its affirmation of the right to religious freedom.

The book is divided into five parts. Part one consists of a new translation of the Declaration on Religious Freedom side by side with the Latin text. This translation remains close to the structure and tenor of the original: first, to facilitate comparison between the English and the Latin, and across successive drafts; second, to ensure consistency between the final Declaration and the preceding versions of the text; and third, to present the meaning of the original document as accurately as possible. Footnotes are also provided that indicate alternative translations of important words or phrases, as found in other published translations.

Part two is an interpretive essay by David Schindler, "Freedom, Truth, and Human Dignity: An Interpretation of *Dignitatis Humanae* on the Right to Religious Freedom." Beginning with an overview of the current state of the question, Schindler develops an extended argument about the meaning of religious freedom, in dialogue especially with John Courtney Murray and Karol Wojtyła/John Paul II.

In part three, "The Drafting of *Dignitatis Humanae*," Nicholas Healy presents the genesis and redaction history of the text. Healy provides a brief overview of each successive draft, and calls attention to the most significant changes incorporated into the final text as a result of the public debate and written observations of the Council fathers.

Part four presents in Latin and English the five successive schemas that were presented and debated at the Council.

Part five places the English of schema 3 side by side with the final text of the Declaration. The two most important turns in the conciliar debate occurred in connection with the drafting of the third schema, which moved the discussion regarding religious freedom from an ecumenical to a civil-political context, and the drafting of the fifth schema, which clarified the ontological link between freedom and truth and established the obligation to truth as the foundation of the right to religious freedom. The juxtaposition of draft 3 and the final text of the Declaration (which changed very little from draft 5) helps to identify more readily the focal points of the debate regarding religious freedom, and the changes that were incorporated as a result.

Included as appendices are, first, the conciliar interventions of Karol Wojtyła regarding the document on religious freedom, and second, the important intervention of Alfred Ancel that was in substance incorporated into draft 5. The study concludes with a select bibliography of works pertinent to the construction, teaching, and interpretation of *Dignitatis humanae.*

The editors wish to thank Fr. Patrick T. Brannan, S.J., and Michael Camacho for their translations in preparation of this book, and the latter as well for his astute and painstaking editing of the book as a whole. We wish also to thank Caitlin Williams for her suggestions and comments on the chapter "The Drafting of *Dignitatis Humanae*," and for her extensive work on the bibliography.

DAVID L. SCHINDLER
NICHOLAS J. HEALY JR.

Notes

1. AAS 58 (1966): 74; cited in Luigi Mistò, "Paul VI and *Dignitatis humanae:* Theory and Practice," in *Religious Liberty: Paul VI and Dignitatis Humanae,* ed. John T. Ford (Brescia: Publicazzioni dell'Istituto Paolo VI, 1995), p. 13.

2. Joseph Ratzinger, *Truth and Tolerance: Christian Belief and World Religions* (San Francisco: Ignatius Press, 2004), p. 236.

Abbreviations

AA	Second Vatican Council, Decree on the Apostolate of the Laity, *Apostolicum actuositatem.*
AAS	*Acta Apostolicae Sedis.* Vatican City: Typis Polyglottis Vaticanis, 1909-.
Abbott	John Courtney Murray, "The Declaration on Religious Freedom," translation and annotation. *The Documents of Vatican II*, ed. Walter M. Abbott, S.J., and Joseph Gallagher. New York: America, 1966.
ADP	*Acta et Documenta Concilio Oecumenico Vaticano II Apparando. Series secunda. (Praeparatio).* 7 vols. Vatican City: Typis Polyglottis Vaticanis, 1964-1969.
Alberigo	*History of Vatican II*, ed. Giuseppe Alberigo and Joseph Komonchak. 5 vols. Maryknoll, NY: Orbis, 1995-2006.
AS	*Acta Synodalia Sacrosancti Concilii Vaticani II.* 34 vols. Vatican City: Typis Polyglottis Vaticanis, 1970-1999.
ASS	*Acta Sanctae Sedis.* 41 vols. Vatican City: Ex Typographia Polyglotta S.C. de Propaganda Fide, 1865-1908.
AV	Philipe André-Vincent, *La Liberté Religieuse: Droit Fondamental.* Paris: Téqui, 1976.
BSS	*Bridging the Sacred and the Secular: Selected Writings of John Courtney Murray, S.J.*, ed. J. Leon Hooper, S.J. Washington, DC: Georgetown University Press, 1994.
CA	John Paul II, Encyclical Letter *Centesimus annus.*
CCC	Catechism of the Catholic Church.
CEP	Joseph Ratzinger, *Church, Ecumenism, and Politics: New Endeavors in Ecclesiology.* San Francisco: Ignatius Press, 2008.
CIV	Benedict XVI, Encyclical Letter *Caritas in veritate.*
Comm.	John Courtney Murray, "Declaration on Religious Freedom: Commentary." *American Participation at the Second Vatican Council*, ed. Vincent A. Yzermans. New York: Sheed & Ward, 1967.

Coventry	John Coventry, S.J., "The Declaration on Religious Freedom," translation. *Decrees of the Ecumenical Councils,* ed. Norman P. Tanner, S.J. Vol. 2. Washington, DC: Georgetown University Press, 1990.
CSD	Compendium of the Social Doctrine of the Church.
De Reg.	Thomas Aquinas, *De Regno.*
De Pot.	Thomas Aquinas, *Quaestiones Disputatae de Potentia Dei.*
De Ver.	Thomas Aquinas, *Quaestiones Disputatae de Veritate.*
DH	Second Vatican Council, Declaration on Religious Freedom, *Dignitatis Humanae.*
DRF	John Courtney Murray, "The Declaration on Religious Freedom." *Vatican II: An Interfaith Appraisal,* ed. John Miller. Notre Dame: Associated Press, 1966.
Dulles	Avery Cardinal Dulles, S.J., "John Paul II on Religious Freedom: Themes from Vatican II," *The Thomist* 65, no. 2 (April 2001): 161-78.
EV	John Paul II, Encyclical Letter *Evangelium vitae.*
GS	Second Vatican Council, Pastoral Constitution on the Church in the Modern World, *Gaudium et spes.*
Hooper	*Religious Liberty: Catholic Struggles with Pluralism,* ed. J. Leon Hooper, S.J. Louisville: Westminster/John Knox Press, 1993.
Idea	Brian Tierney, *The Idea of Natural Rights: Studies on Natural Rights, Natural Law, and Church Law 1150-1625.* Grand Rapids: Eerdmans, 2001.
Journal	Yves Congar, *My Journal of the Council.* Collegeville, MN: Liturgical Press, 2012.
LBC	Josef Pieper, *Leisure: The Basis of Culture.* San Francisco: Ignatius Press, 2009.
LG	Second Vatican Council, Dogmatic Constitution on the Church, *Lumen gentium.*
LTT	Josef Pieper, *Living the Truth.* San Francisco: Ignatius Press, 1989.
MLH	John Courtney Murray, "The Declaration on Religious Freedom: A Moment in Its Legislative History." *Religious Liberty: An End and a Beginning,* ed. John Courtney Murray. New York: Macmillan, 1966.
OL	David L. Schindler, *Ordering Love: Liberal Societies and the Memory of God.* Grand Rapids: Eerdmans, 2011.
Pavan	Pietro Pavan, "Declaration on Religious Freedom." *Commentary on the Documents of Vatican II,* ed. Herbert Vorgrimler. Vol. 4. New York: Herder & Herder, 1969.
Pinckaers	Servais Pinckaers, O.P., *The Sources of Christian Ethics.* Washington, DC: Catholic University of America Press, 1995.
PRF	John Courtney Murray, "The Problem of Religious Freedom." *Religious Liberty: Catholic Struggles with Pluralism,* ed. J. Leon Hooper, S.J.
Regan	Richard J. Regan, S.J., *Conflict and Consensus: Religious Freedom and the Second Vatican Council.* New York: Macmillan, 1967.

Rico   Hermínio Rico, *John Paul II and the Legacy of* Dignitatis Humanae. Washington, DC: Georgetown University Press, 2002.

RH   John Paul II, Enyclical Letter *Redemptor hominis.*

RLDD   Edward Gaffney, "Religious Liberty and Development of Doctrine: An Interview with John C. Murray," *The Catholic World* 204 (February 1967): 277-83.

RM   John Paul II, Encyclical Letter *Redemptoris missio.*

Ryan   Laurence Ryan, "The Declaration on Religious Freedom," translation. *Vatican Council II: The Conciliar and Post Conciliar Documents,* ed. Austin Flannery, O.P. Northport, NY: Costello, 1979.

ST   Thomas Aquinas, *Summa Theologiae.*

TMRF   John Courtney Murray, "This Matter of Religious Freedom," *America* 112 (9 January 1965): 40-43.

TPE   Joseph Ratzinger, *A Turning Point for Europe?* San Francisco: Ignatius Press, 1994.

VS   John Paul II, Encyclical Letter *Veritatis splendor.*

WDD   Josef Pieper, *Wahrheit der Dinge: Eine Untersuchung zur Anthropologie des Hochmittelalters.* Munich: Kösel Verlag, 1947.

WHP   Joseph Pieper, *Was heißt Philosophieren?* Einsiedeln: Johannes Verlag, 2003.

WHTT   John Courtney Murray, *We Hold These Truths.* Garden City, NY: Doubleday Image, 1964.

I.

The Declaration on Religious Freedom

Translated by Patrick T. Brannan, S.J., and Michael Camacho

DECLARATIO DE LIBERTATE RELIGIOSA

Dignitatis humanae

DE IURE PERSONAE ET COMMUNITATUM AD LIBERTATEM SOCIALEM ET CIVILEM IN RE RELIGIOSA

1. Dignitatis humanae personae homines hac nostra aetate magis in dies conscii fiunt,[1] atque numerus eorum crescit qui exigunt, ut in agendo homines proprio suo consilio et libertate responsabili[2] fruantur et utantur, non coercitione commoti, sed officii conscientia ducti. Itemque postulant iuridicam delimitationem potestatis publicae, ne fines honestae libertatis et personae et associationum nimis circumscribantur. Quae libertatis exigentia in societate humana ea maxime respicit quae sunt animi humani bona, imprimis quidem ea quae liberum in societate religionis exercitium spectant. Ad has animorum appetitiones diligenter attendens, sibique proponens declarare quantum sint veritati et iustitiae conformes, haec Vaticana Synodus sacram Ecclesiae traditionem doctrinamque scrutatur, ex quibus nova semper cum veteribus congruentia profert.

Primum itaque profitetur Sacra Synodus Deum Ipsum viam generi humano notam fecisse per quam, Ipsi inserviendo, homines in Christo salvi et beati fieri possint. Hanc unicam veram Religionem subsistere credimus in catholica et apostolica Ecclesia, cui Dominus Iesus munus concredidit eam ad universos homines diffundendi, dicens Apostolis: « Euntes ergo docete omnes gentes baptizantes eos in nomine Patris et Filii et Spiritus Sancti,

THE DECLARATION ON RELIGIOUS FREEDOM

Dignitatis humanae

ON THE RIGHT OF THE PERSON AND OF COMMUNITIES TO SOCIAL AND CIVIL FREEDOM IN RELIGIOUS MATTERS

1. Men and women of our time are becoming more conscious every day of the dignity of the human person.[1] Increasing numbers demand that in acting they enjoy and make use of their own counsel and a responsible freedom,[2] not impelled by coercion but moved by a sense of duty. They also demand that juridical limits* be set to the public power,† in order that the rightful freedom of persons and associations not be excessively restricted.‡ This demand for freedom in human society is chiefly concerned with the goods of the human spirit, first of all those that concern the free exercise of religion in society. Carefully attending to these desires of men's hearts, and proposing to declare to what degree they are in conformity with truth and justice,§ this Vatican Council searches the sacred tradition and teaching of the Church, from which it draws forth new things that are always in harmony with the old.

The sacred Council first professes that God himself has made known to mankind the way in which men are to serve him, and so be saved in Christ and come to blessedness. We believe that this one true religion subsists in the Catholic and apostolic Church, to whom the Lord Jesus committed the task of spreading it among all people, saying to the apostles: "Go, therefore, and make disciples of all nations, baptizing them in the name of the Father

---

* constitutional limits (John Courtney Murray, S.J., trans., in *The Documents of Vatican II*, ed. Walter M. Abbott, S.J. [New York: America, 1966], 675-96, at 679); constitutional limitations (Laurence Ryan, trans., in *Vatican Council II: The Conciliar and Post Conciliar Documents*, ed. Austin Flannery, O.P. [Northport, NY: Costello, 1979], 799-812, at 799); legal bounds (John Coventry, S.J., trans., in *Decrees of the Ecumenical Councils*, vol. II: *Trent to Vatican II*, ed. Norman P. Tanner, S.J. [Washington, DC: Georgetown University Press, 1990], 1001-1011, at 1002)

† the powers of government (Murray, 679; Ryan, 799); government (Coventry, 1002)

‡ in order that there may be no encroachment on the rightful freedom of the person and of associations (Murray, 679); to prevent excessive restriction of the rightful freedom of individuals and associations (Ryan, 799); so that the limits of reasonable freedom should not be too tightly drawn for persons or for social groups (Coventry, 1002)

§ This Vatican Synod takes careful note of these desires in the minds of men. It proposes to declare them to be greatly in accord with truth and justice (Murray, 674); This Vatican Council pays careful attention to these spiritual aspirations and, with a view to declaring to what extent they are in accord with the truth and justice (Ryan, 799); Keenly aware of these aspirations, and wishing to assert their consonance with truth and justice (Coventry, 1002)

docentes eos servare omnia quaecumque mandavi vobis » (*Mt.* 28, 19-20). Homines vero cuncti tenentur veritatem, praesertim in iis quae Deum Eiusque Ecclesiam respiciunt, quaerere eamque cognitam amplecti ac servare.

Pariter vero profitetur Sacra Synodus officia haec hominum conscientiam tangere ac vincire, nec aliter veritatem sese imponere nisi vi ipsius veritatis, quae suaviter simul ac fortiter mentibus illabitur. Porro, quum libertas religiosa, quam homines in exsequendo officio Deum colendi exigunt, immunitatem a coercitione in societate civili respiciat, integram relinquit traditionalem doctrinam catholicam de morali hominum ac societatum officio erga veram religionem et unicam Christi Ecclesiam. Insuper, de hac libertate religiosa agens, Sacra Synodus recentiorum Summorum Pontificum doctrinam de inviolabilibus humanae personae iuribus necnon de iuridica ordinatione societatis evolvere intendit.

I. LIBERTATIS RELIGIOSAE RATIO GENERALIS

2. (*Libertatis religiosae obiectum et fundamentum*). Haec Vaticana Synodus declarat personam humanam ius habere ad libertatem religiosam. Huiusmodi libertas in eo consistit, quod omnes homines debent immunes esse a coercitione ex parte sive singulorum sive coetuum socialium et cuiusvis potestatis humanae, et ita quidem ut in re religiosa neque aliquis cogatur ad agendum contra suam conscientiam neque impediatur, quominus iuxta suam conscientiam agat privatim et publice, vel solus vel aliis consociatus, intra debitos limites. Insuper declarat ius ad libertatem religiosam esse revera fundatum in ipsa dignitate personae humanae, qualis et verbo Dei revelato et ipsa ratione cognoscitur.[3] Hoc ius personae humanae ad libertatem religiosam in iuridica societatis ordinatione ita est agnoscendum, ut ius civile evadat.

Secundum dignitatem suam homines cuncti, quia personae sunt, ratione scilicet et libera voluntate praediti ideoque personali responsabilitate aucti, sua ipsorum natura impelluntur necnon morali tenentur obligatione ad veritatem quaerendam, illam imprimis quae religionem spectat. Tenentur quoque veritati cognitae adhaerere atque totam vitam suam iuxta exigentias

and of the Son and of the Holy Spirit, teaching them to observe all that I have commanded you" (Mt 28:19-20). All men and women are in fact bound to seek the truth, especially in those things concerning God and his Church, and to embrace and hold fast to it once it is known.

The sacred Council likewise professes that these duties touch on and bind the conscience of man. In no other way does truth impose itself than by the strength of truth itself, entering the mind at once gently and with power. Further, since the religious freedom which men and women demand in order to fulfill their duty to worship God concerns immunity from coercion in civil society, it leaves intact the traditional Catholic teaching on the moral duty individuals and society have toward the true religion and the one Church of Christ. In addition, in taking up this issue of religious freedom, the sacred Council intends to develop the teaching of the recent popes on the inviolable rights of the human person and the juridical order of society.

I. THE GENERAL PRINCIPLE OF RELIGIOUS FREEDOM

2. (*The object and foundation of religious freedom*). This Vatican Council declares that the human person has a right to religious freedom. Such freedom consists in this, that all men and women should be immune from coercion on the part of individuals, social groups or any human power, so that no one is forced to act against his conscience* in religious matters, or prevented from acting according to his conscience, in private or in public, whether alone or in association with others, within due limits. In addition, this Council declares that the right to religious freedom has its foundation in the very dignity of the human person, as known from both the revealed word of God and reason itself.[3] This right of the human person to religious freedom must be acknowledged in the juridical order of society,† so that it becomes a civil right.

It is in accord with their dignity that all men and women, because they are persons, endowed with reason and free will and therefore privileged with personal responsibility, are impelled by their nature and bound by a moral obligation to seek the truth, especially the truth concerning religion. They are also bound to hold fast to the truth once it is known, and to order their

---

* in a manner contrary to his own beliefs (Murray, 679); against his convictions (Ryan, 800); against his conscience (Coventry, 1002)

† in the constitutional law whereby society is governed (Murray, 679); in the constitutional order of society (Ryan, 800); in the regulation of law by society (Coventry, 1002)

veritatis ordinare. Huic autem obligationi satisfacere homines, modo suae propriae naturae consentaneo, non possunt nisi libertate psychologica simul atque immunitate a coercitione externa fruantur. Non ergo in subiectiva personae dispositione, sed in ipsa eius natura ius ad libertatem religiosam fundatur. Quamobrem ius ad hanc immunitatem perseverat etiam in iis qui obligationi quaerendi veritatem eique adhaerendi non satisfaciunt; eiusque exercitium impediri nequit dummodo iustus ordo publicus servetur.

3. (*Libertas religiosa et necessitudo hominis ad Deum*). Quae clarius adhuc patent consideranti supremam humanae vitae normam esse ipsam legem divinam, aeternam, obiectivam atque universalem, qua Deus consilio sapientiae et dilectionis suae mundum universum viasque communitatis humanae ordinat, dirigit, gubernat.[4] Huius suae legis Deus hominem participem reddit, ita ut homo, providentia divina suaviter disponente, veritatem incommutabilem magis magisque agnoscere possit.[5] Quapropter unusquisque officium ideoque et ius habet veritatem in re religiosa quaerendi ut sibi, mediis adhibitis idoneis, recta et vera conscientiae iudicia prudenter efformet.

Veritas autem inquirenda est modo dignitati humanae personae eiusque naturae sociali proprio, libera scilicet inquisitione, ope magisterii seu institutionis, communicationis atque dialogi, quibus alii aliis exponunt veritatem quam invenerunt vel invenisse putant, ut sese invicem in veritate inquirenda adiuvent; veritati autem cognitae firmiter adhaerendum est assensu personali.

Dictamina vero legis divinae homo percipit et agnoscit mediante conscientia sua; quam tenetur fideliter sequi in universa sua activitate, ut ad Deum, finem suum, perveniat. Non est ergo cogendus, ut contra suam conscientiam agat.[6] Sed neque impediendus est, quominus iuxta suam conscientiam operetur, praesertim in re religiosa. Exercitium namque religionis, ex ipsa eius indole, consistit imprimis in actibus internis voluntariis et liberis, quibus homo sese ad Deum directe ordinat: huiusmodi actus a potestate mere humana nec imperari nec prohiberi possunt.[7] Ipsa autem socialis hominis natura exigit, ut homo internos religionis actus externe exprimat,

whole life in accord with its demands. They cannot satisfy this obligation in a way that is in keeping with their own nature, however, unless they enjoy psychological freedom as well as immunity from external coercion. The right to religious freedom does not have its foundation in the subjective disposition of the person, therefore, but rather in his very nature. Consequently, the right to this immunity persists even for those who do not satisfy their obligation to seek the truth and to hold fast to it; the exercise of this right is not to be impeded, provided that just public order* is preserved.

3. (*Religious freedom and man's relationship to God*). This becomes even clearer when one considers that the highest norm of human life is the divine law, eternal, objective, and universal, by which God, in the providence of his wisdom and love, orders, directs, and governs the whole world and the ways of the human community.[4] God grants man a share in this law, so that man, under the gentle direction of divine providence, can acknowledge more and more the truth that is itself unchanging.[5] For this reason, each person has the duty, and therefore the right, to seek the truth in religious matters, so that he may prudently form right and true judgments of conscience for himself, using all suitable means.

The truth, however, must be sought in a way proper to the dignity of the human person and his social nature, namely, by means of free inquiry, with the help of instruction or education, communication and dialogue, in which men and women share with one another the truth they have found or think they have found, so as to assist each other in seeking the truth. Once known, however, the truth must be firmly adhered to by means of personal assent.

It is through the mediation of his conscience that man perceives and recognizes the precepts of the divine law; he is bound in all his actions to follow his conscience faithfully, so that he may come to God, his end. He is therefore not to be forced to act against his conscience.[6] Nor is he to be prevented from acting according to his conscience, especially in religious matters. For by its very nature the exercise of religion consists first of all† in interior acts that are voluntary and free, through which man orders himself directly toward God: acts of this kind cannot be commanded or prohibited by any merely human power.[7] Man's social nature itself, however, demands

---

* the just requirements of public order (Murray, 680; Ryan, 801); due public order (Coventry, 1003)

† before all else (Murray, 681); primarily (Ryan, 802); principally (Coventry, 1003)

cum aliis in re religiosa communicet, suam religionem modo communitario profiteatur.

Iniuria ergo humanae personae et ipsi ordini hominibus a Deo statuto fit, si homini denegetur liberum in societate religionis exercitium, iusto ordine publico servato.

Praeterea actus religiosi, quibus homines privatim et publice sese ad Deum ex animi sententia ordinant, natura sua terrestrem et temporalem rerum ordinem transcendunt. Potestas igitur civilis, cuius finis proprius est bonum commune temporale curare, religiosam quidem civium vitam agnoscere eique favere debet, sed limites suos excedere dicenda est, si actus religiosos dirigere vel impedire praesumat.

4. (*Libertas communitatum religiosarum*). Libertas seu immunitas a coercitione in re religiosa, quae singulis personis competit, etiam ipsis in communi agentibus agnoscenda est. Communitates enim religiosae a sociali natura tum hominis tum ipsius religionis requiruntur.

His igitur communitatibus, dummodo iustae exigentiae ordinis publici non violentur, iure debetur immunitas, ut secundum proprias normas sese regant, Numen supremum cultu publico honorent, membra sua in vita religiosa exercenda adiuvent et doctrina sustentent atque eas institutiones promoveant, in quibus membra cooperentur ad vitam propriam secundum sua principia religiosa ordinandam.

Communitatibus religiosis pariter competit ius, ne mediis legalibus vel actione administrativa potestatis civilis impediantur in suis propriis ministris seligendis, educandis, nominandis atque transferendis, in communicando cum auctoritatibus et communitatibus religiosis, quae in aliis orbis terrarum partibus degunt, in aedificiis religiosis erigendis, necnon in bonis congruis acquirendis et fruendis.

Communitates religiosae ius etiam habent, ne impediantur in sua fide ore et scripto publice docenda atque testanda. In fide autem religiosa dissem-

that he express these interior religious acts externally, participating with others in religious matters and professing his religion in a communal way.

It is therefore an injustice to the human person, and to the very order of human existence established by God, for men to be denied the free exercise of religion in society when just public order is preserved.

Furthermore, religious acts, in which men and women privately and publicly order themselves toward God out of a sense of inner conviction, by their nature transcend the earthly and temporal order of things. The civil power,* therefore, whose proper end is the care of the temporal common good,† should in fact acknowledge‡ and show favor to the religious life of its citizens; but this power must be said to exceed its limits if it presumes either to direct or to impede§ religious acts.

4. (*The freedom of religious communities*). The freedom or immunity from coercion in religious matters that belongs to individual persons must also be recognized for them when they act together in community. Religious communities are called for by the social nature of man and of religion itself.

Immunity is therefore due to these communities by right, provided they do not violate the just requirements of public order, so that they may govern themselves according to their own norms, honor the Supreme Being with public worship, assist their members in their practice of religious life, strengthen them by instruction, and promote institutions in which members can join together to order their own life according to their religious principles.

Religious communities likewise have the right not to be impeded, either by legal measures or by administrative action on the part of the civil power, in selecting, educating, appointing, and transferring their own ministers; in communicating with religious authorities and communities in other parts of the world; in erecting religious buildings; or in acquiring and making use of any necessary goods.

Religious communities also have the right not to be prevented from publicly teaching about or witnessing to their faith in speech or in writing.

---

* government (Murray, 681); the civil authority (Ryan, 802); the state (Coventry, 1004)

† the function of [which] is to make provision for the common welfare (Murray, 681); the purpose of which is the care of the common good in the temporal order (Ryan, 802); whose proper purpose is to provide for the temporal common good (Coventry, 1004)

‡ take account of (Murray, 681); recognize (Ryan, 802; Coventry, 1004)

§ to direct or inhibit (Murray, 681); to control or restrict (Ryan, 802); to direct or to prevent (Coventry, 1004)

inanda et in usibus inducendis abstinendum semper est ab omni actionis genere, quod coercitionem vel suasionem inhonestam aut minus rectam sapere videatur, praesertim quando de rudioribus vel de egenis agitur. Talis modus agendi ut abusus iuris proprii et laesio iuris aliorum considerari debet.

Praeterea ad libertatem religiosam spectat, quod communitates religiosae non prohibeantur libere ostendere singularem suae doctrinae virtutem in ordinanda societate ac tota vivificanda activitate humana. Tandem in sociali hominis natura atque in ipsa indole religionis fundatur ius quo homines, suo ipsorum sensu religioso moti, libere possunt conventus habere vel associationes educativas, culturales, caritativas, sociales constituere.

5. (*Libertas religiosa familiae*). Cuique familiae, utpote quae est societas proprio ac primordiali iure gaudens, competit ius ad libere ordinandam religiosam vitam suam domesticam sub moderatione parentum. His autem competit ius ad determinandam rationem institutionis religiosae suis liberis tradendae, iuxta suam propriam religiosam persuasionem. Itaque a civili potestate agnoscendum est ius parentum deligendi, vera cum libertate, scholas vel alia educationis media, neque ob hanc electionis libertatem sunt eis iniusta onera sive directe sive indirecte imponenda. Praeterea iura parentum violantur, si liberi ad frequentandas lectiones scholares cogantur quae parentum persuasioni religiosae non correspondeant, vel si unica imponatur educationis ratio, ex qua formatio religiosa omnino excludatur.

6. (*Cura libertatis religiosae*). Cum societatis commune bonum, quod est summa earum vitae socialis condicionum, quibus homines suam ipsorum perfectionem possunt plenius atque expeditius consequi, maxime in humanae personae servatis iuribus et officiis consistat,[8] cura iuris ad libertatem religiosam tum ad cives tum ad coetus sociales tum ad potestates civiles tum ad Ecclesiam aliasque communitates religiosas spectat, modo unicuique proprio, pro eorum erga bonum commune officio.

Inviolabilia hominis iura tueri ac promovere ad cuiusvis potestatis ci-

In spreading their religious faith and introducing their practices, however, they must always refrain from any kind of activity that would seem to suggest any hint of coercion or dishonest or less than proper persuasion, especially in regard to those less educated or in need. To act in such a way should be considered an abuse of one's own right and a violation of the right of others.

Furthermore, religious freedom entails that religious communities not be prohibited from freely showing the unique value of their doctrine for ordering society and animating all human activity. Finally, there is in man's social nature and in the very nature of religion the foundation for the right by which men and women, moved by their own religious sense, can freely hold meetings and establish educational, cultural, charitable, and social associations.

5. (*The religious freedom of the family*). Each family, as a society in its own original right, has the right to order freely its own domestic religious life, under the guidance of the parents. Parents also have the right to determine the way in which religious instruction will be handed on to their children, in accord with their own religious beliefs. The civil power must therefore acknowledge the right of parents to choose with true freedom among schools or other means of education, and must not unjustly burden them on account of this freedom of choice, whether directly or indirectly. Furthermore, the rights of parents are violated if their children are forced to attend lessons that are at odds with the religious beliefs of their parents, or if a single system of education is imposed that excludes all religious formation.

6. (*The care of religious freedom*). Since the common good of society consists in the sum of those conditions of social life by which men can pursue their own perfection more fully and with greater ease,* it chiefly consists in the protection of the rights and duties of the human person.[8] Care for the right to religious freedom is the responsibility of citizens, social groups, civil powers, the Church, and other religious communities, in virtue of their duty toward the common good, and in the way that is proper to each.

It belongs to the essential duties of every civil power to protect and

---

* The common welfare of society consists in the entirety of those conditions of social life under which men enjoy the possibility of achieving their own perfection in a certain fullness of measure and also with some relative ease (Murray, 683); The common good of society consists in the sum total of those conditions of social life which enable men to achieve a fuller measure of perfection with greater ease (Ryan, 803); The common good of society is made up of those conditions of social living which enable people to develop their own qualities most fully and easily (Coventry, 1005)

vilis officium essentialiter pertinet.[9] Debet igitur potestas civilis per iustas leges et per alia media apta efficaciter suscipere tutelam libertatis religiosae omnium civium, ac propitias suppeditare condiciones ad vitam religiosam fovendam, ut cives revera religionis iura exercere eiusdemque officia adimplere valeant et ipsa societas fruatur bonis iustitiae et pacis, quae proveniunt ex fidelitate hominum erga Deum Eiusque sanctam voluntatem.[10]

Si attentis populorum circumstantiis peculiaribus uni communitati religiosae specialis civilis agnitio in iuridica civitatis ordinatione tribuitur, necesse est ut simul omnibus civibus et communitatibus religiosis ius ad libertatem in re religiosa agnoscatur et observetur.

Denique a potestate civili providendum est, ne civium aequalitas iuridica, quae ipsa ad commune societatis bonum pertinet, unquam sive aperte sive occulte laedatur propter rationes religiosas, neve inter eos discriminatio fiat.

Hinc sequitur nefas esse potestati publicae, per vim vel metum aut alia media civibus imponere professionem aut reiectionem cuiusvis religionis, vel impedire quominus quisquam communitatem religiosam aut ingrediatur aut relinquat. Eo magis contra voluntatem Dei et contra sacra personae et familiae gentium iura agitur, quando vis quocumque modo adhibeatur ad religionem delendam vel cohibendam sive in toto genere humano sive in aliqua regione sive in determinato coetu.

7. (*Limites libertatis religiosae*). Ius ad libertatem in re religiosa exercetur in societate humana, ideoque eius usus quibusdam normis moderantibus obnoxius est.

In usu omnium libertatum observandum est principium morale responsabilitatis personalis et socialis: in iuribus suis exercendis singuli homines coetusque sociales lege morali obligantur rationem habere et iurium aliorum et suorum erga alios officiorum et boni omnium communis. Cum omnibus secundum iustitiam et humanitatem agendum est.

Praeterea cum societas civilis ius habet sese protegendi contra abusus qui haberi possint sub praetextu libertatis religiosae, praecipue ad potestatem civilem pertinet huiusmodi protectionem praestare; quod tamen

promote the inviolable rights of man.[9] The civil power should therefore effectively undertake to protect the religious freedom of all citizens through just laws and other appropriate means, and to provide favorable conditions for fostering religious life,* so that citizens may truly be able to exercise their religious rights and fulfill their religious duties, and so that society itself may enjoy the goods of justice and peace that come from men's fidelity to God and his holy will.[10]

If, in light of a people's particular circumstances,† special civil recognition is granted to one religious community in the juridical order of the state, it is necessary at the same time that the right to freedom in religious matters be acknowledged and observed for all citizens and religious communities.

Finally, the civil power should see to it that the equality of citizens before the law, itself part of the common good of society, is never violated for religious reasons, whether openly or covertly, and that there is no discrimination among citizens.

It follows that it is wrong for the public power to impose by force or fear or any other means the profession or rejection of any religion on its citizens, or to prevent anyone from entering or leaving a religious community. All the more is it against God's will and the sacred rights of the person and the family of nations to use force in any way in order to destroy or repress religion, either in the human race as a whole or in a particular region or in a specific religious group.

7. (*The limits of religious freedom*). The right to freedom in religious matters is exercised in human society, and its use is therefore subject to certain governing norms.

In the use of all freedoms, the moral principle of personal and social responsibility must be observed: in exercising their rights, individuals and social groups are bound by the moral law to keep in mind both the rights of others and their duties toward others, as well as the common good of all. They should act toward all with justice and humanity.

In addition, since civil society has the right to protect itself against abuses that could be committed under the pretext of religious freedom, it belongs especially to the civil power to afford protection of this sort. This

---

* to help create conditions favorable to the fostering of religious life (Murray, 685; Ryan, 804); to ensure favorable conditions for fostering religious life (Coventry, 1005)

† If, in view of peculiar circumstances obtaining among certain peoples (Murray, 685); If because of the circumstances of a particular people (Ryan, 804); If in view of particular demographic conditions (Coventry, 1005)

fieri debet non modo arbitrario aut uni parti inique favendo, sed secundum normas iuridicas, ordini morali obiectivo conformes, quae postulantur ab efficaci iurium tutela pro omnibus civibus eorumque pacifica compositione, et a sufficienti cura istius honestae pacis publicae quae est ordinata conviventia in vera iustitia, et a debita custodia publicae moralitatis. Haec omnia partem boni communis fundamentalem constituunt et sub ratione ordinis publici veniunt. Ceterum servanda est integrae libertatis consuetudo in societate, secundum quam libertas debet quam maxime homini agnosci, nec restringenda est nisi quando et prout est necessarium.[11]

8. (*Educatio ad libertatem exercendam*). Nostrae aetatis homines varia ratione premuntur et in periculum veniunt ne proprio libero consilio destituantur. Ex altera autem parte non pauci ita propensi videntur, ut specie libertatis omnem subiectionem reiciant ac debitam oboedientiam parvi faciant.

Quapropter haec Vaticana Synodus omnes hortatur, praesertim vero eos qui curam habent alios educandi, ut homines formare satagant, qui ordini morali obsequentes legitimae auctoritati oboediant et genuinae libertatis amatores sint; homines nempe, qui proprio consilio res in luce veritatis diiudicent, activitates suas cum sensu responsabilitatis disponant, et quaecumque sunt vera atque iusta prosequi nitantur, operam suam libenter cum ceteris consociando.

Religiosa igitur libertas etiam ad hoc inservire et ordinari debet, ut homines in suis ipsorum officiis adimplendis in vita sociali maiore cum responsabilitate agant.

protection should not be provided in an arbitrary fashion, however, or by unjustly favoring one particular group, but according to juridical norms* that conform to the objective moral order. Such norms are necessary for the effective protection of the rights of all citizens and the peaceful settlement of conflicts of rights, for the adequate care of that genuine public peace that is obtained when men live and work together in true justice, and for the proper guardianship of public morality. All of these constitute a fundamental part of the common good, and come under the category of public order.† For the rest, the customary practice of the fullness of freedom in society should be upheld, ‡ according to which man's freedom should be acknowledged as far as possible, and should not be restricted except when and insofar as necessary.[11]

8. (*Education in the use of freedom*). Men and women of our time are subjected to a variety of pressures and are in danger of losing the use of their own free counsel. On the other hand, not a few seem disposed, under the pretense of freedom, to reject all submission and to make light of the duty of obedience.

For this reason, this Vatican Council urges all men and women, especially those who are responsible for educating others, to be diligent in forming human beings who respect the moral order and are obedient to legitimate authority, and who are lovers of genuine freedom; men and women, that is, who by their own counsel decide matters in the light of truth, who act with a sense of responsibility, and who endeavor to pursue whatever is true and just, cooperating willingly with others in their work.

Religious freedom should therefore also be devoted and ordered to this end, that men and women may come to act with greater responsibility in fulfilling their duties in social life.

---

* juridical norms (Murray, 686); legal principles (Ryan, 805); legal rules (Coventry, 1005)

† These matters constitute the basic component of the common welfare: they are what is meant by public order (Murray, 687); All these matters are basic to the common good and belong to what is called public order (Ryan, 805); These factors together constitute a fundamental part of the common good, and are included in the idea of public order (Coventry, 1006)

‡ For the rest, the usages of society are to be the usages of freedom in their full range (Murray, 687); For the rest, the principle of the integrity of freedom in society should continue to be upheld (Ryan, 805); Nevertheless, that principle of full freedom is to be preserved in society (Coventry, 1006)

II. LIBERTAS RELIGIOSA SUB LUCE REVELATIONIS

9. (*Doctrina de libertate religiosa in revelatione radices tenet*). Quae de iure hominis ad libertatem religiosam declarat haec Vaticana Synodus, fundamentum habent in dignitate personae, cuius exigentiae rationi humanae plenius innotuerunt per saeculorum experientiam. Immo haec doctrina de libertate radices habet in divina Revelatione, quapropter eo magis a Christianis sancte servanda est. Quamvis enim Revelatio non expresse affirmet ius ad immunitatem ab externa coercitione in re religiosa, tamen humanae personae dignitatem in tota eius amplitudine patefacit, observantiam Christi erga hominis libertatem in exsequendo officio credendi verbo Dei demonstrat, atque de spiritu nos edocet, quem discipuli talis Magistri debent in omnibus agnoscere et sequi. Quibus omnibus principia generalia illustrantur super quae fundatur doctrina huius Declarationis de libertate religiosa. Praesertim libertas religiosa in societate plene est cum libertate actus fidei christianae congrua.

10. (*Libertas actus fidei*). Caput est ex praecipuis doctrinae catholicae, in verbo Dei contentum et a Patribus constanter praedicatum,[12] hominem debere Deo voluntarie respondere credendo; invitum proinde neminem esse cogendum ad amplectendam fidem.[13] Etenim actus fidei ipsa sua natura voluntarius est, cum homo, a Christo Salvatore redemptus et in adoptionem filiorum per Iesum Christum vocatus,[14] Deo Sese revelanti adhaerere non possit, nisi Patre eum trahente[15] rationabile liberumque Deo praestiterit fidei obsequium. Indoli ergo fidei plene consonum est ut, in re religiosa, quodvis genus coercitionis ex parte hominum excludatur. Ac proinde ratio libertatis religiosae haud parum confert ad illum rerum statum fovendum, in quo homines expedite possint invitari ad fidem christianam, illam sponte amplecti atque eam in tota vitae ratione actuose confiteri.

11. (*Modus agendi Christi et Apostolorum*). Deus quidem homines ad inserviendum Sibi in spiritu et veritate vocat, unde ipsi in conscientia vinciuntur, non vero coercentur. Rationem enim habet dignitatis personae humanae ab Ipso conditae, quae proprio consilio duci et libertate frui debet. Hoc autem summe apparuit in Christo Iesu, in quo Deus Seipsum ac vias suas perfecte manifestavit. Etenim Christus, qui Magister et Dominus est noster,[16] idemque mitis et humilis corde,[17] discipulos patienter allexit et invitavit.[18] Miraculis utique praedicationem suam suffulsit et confirmavit, ut fidem auditorum excitaret atque comprobaret, non ut in eos coercitionem

II. RELIGIOUS FREEDOM IN THE LIGHT OF REVELATION

9. (*The teaching on religious freedom has its roots in revelation*). The declarations of this Vatican Council regarding man's right to religious freedom have their foundation in the dignity of the person, a dignity whose demands have come to be more fully known to human reason through centuries of experience. What is more, this teaching on freedom has its roots in divine revelation, and for this reason must be observed by Christians all the more faithfully. For although revelation does not expressly affirm the right to immunity from external coercion in religious matters, it nonetheless brings to light the dignity of the human person in all its fullness. It manifests the respect Christ showed for the freedom with which man is to fulfill his duty of believing the word of God, and it educates us in the spirit that the disciples of such a Master should adopt and follow in all things. All of this casts light on the general principles which ground the teaching of this Declaration on religious freedom. Above all, religious freedom in society is fully consonant with the freedom of the act of Christian faith.

10. (*The freedom of the act of faith*). It is a chief tenet of Catholic teaching, contained in the word of God and constantly proclaimed by the Fathers,[12] that man's response to God in faith should be voluntary; no one is to be forced, therefore, to embrace the faith against his will.[13] The act of faith is of its very nature a voluntary act. For man, redeemed by Christ the Savior and called to be an adopted son through Jesus Christ,[14] cannot hold fast to God as he reveals himself unless, drawn by the Father,[15] he offers to God a rational and free submission of faith. It is therefore fully consonant with the nature of faith that in religious matters every kind of coercion on the part of men be excluded. The principle of religious freedom thus contributes in no small way to fostering a state of affairs in which men and women can without hindrance be invited to the Christian faith, embrace it of their own free will, and actively profess it in their whole way of life.

11. (*Christ's and the apostles' way of acting*). God calls men and women to serve him in spirit and in truth, so that they are bound in conscience but are not coerced. For he has regard for the dignity of the human person whom he himself created, who should be led by his own counsel and enjoy his own freedom. This truth appeared in consummate form in Jesus Christ, in whom God perfectly manifested himself and his ways. For Christ, who is our Master and Lord,[16] and at the same time meek and humble of heart,[17] attracted and invited disciples with patience.[18] He supported and confirmed his teaching with miracles in order to awaken and strengthen the faith of his

exerceret.[19] Incredulitatem audientium certe exprobravit, sed vindictam Deo in diem Iudicii relinquendo.[20] Mittens Apostolos in mundum dixit eis: « Qui crediderit et baptizatus fuerit salvus erit; qui vero non crediderit condemnabitur » (*Mc.* 16, 16). Ipse vero, agnoscens zizaniam cum tritico seminatam, iussit sinere utraque crescere usque ad messem quae fiet in consummatione saeculi.[21] Nolens esse Messias politicus et vi dominans,[22] maluit se dicere Filium Hominis qui venit « ut ministraret et daret animam suam redemptionem pro multis » (*Mc.* 10, 45). Sese praebuit ut perfectum Servum Dei,[23] qui « harundinem quassatam non confringet et linum fumigans non extinguet » (*Mt.* 12, 20). Potestatem civilem eiusque iura agnovit, iubens censum dari Caesari, clare autem monuit servanda esse iura superiora Dei: « Reddite ergo quae sunt Caesaris Caesari, et quae sunt Dei Deo » (*Mt.* 22, 21).Tandem in opere redemptionis in cruce complendo, quo salutem et veram libertatem hominibus acquireret, revelationem suam perfecit. Testimonium enim perhibuit veritati,[24] eam tamen contradicentibus vi imponere noluit. Regnum enim eius non percutiendo vindicatur,[25] sed stabilitur testificando et audiendo veritatem, crescit autem amore, quo Christus exaltatus in cruce homines ad Seipsum trahit.[26]

Apostoli, Christi verbo et exemplo edocti, eamdem viam secuti sunt. Ab ipsis Ecclesiae exordiis discipuli Christi adlaborarunt, ut homines ad Christum Dominum confitendum converterent, non actione coercitiva neque artificiis Evangelio indignis, sed imprimis virtute verbi Dei.[27] Fortiter omnibus nuntiabant propositum Salvatoris Dei, « qui omnes homines vult salvos fieri et ad agnitionem veritatis venire » (*1 Tim.* 2, 4); simul autem verebantur debiles etiamsi in errore versabantur, sic ostendentes quomodo « unusquisque nostrum pro se rationem reddet Deo » (*Rom.* 14, 12)[28] et in tantum teneatur conscientiae suae oboedire. Sicuti Christus, Apostoli intenti semper fuerunt ad testimonium reddendum veritati Dei, abundantius audentes coram populo et principibus loqui « verbum Dei cum fiducia » (*Act.* 4, 31).[29] Firma enim fide tenebant ipsum Evangelium revera esse virtutem Dei in salutem omni credenti.[30] Omnibus ergo spretis « armis carnalibus »,[31] exemplum mansuetudinis et modestiae Christi sequentes, verbum Dei praedicaverunt plene confisi divina huius verbi virtute ad potestates Deo adversas destruendas[32] atque homines ad fidem et obsequium Christi reducendos.[33] Sicut Magister ita et Apostoli auctoritatem legitimam civilem agnoverunt: « Non est enim potestas nisi a Deo » docet Apostolus, qui exinde iubet:

listeners, not to exercise coercion over them.[19] He certainly denounced the unbelief of his listeners, but he left the verdict to God in anticipation of the day of judgment.[20] As he sent the apostles into the world, he said to them: "He who believes and is baptized will be saved; but he who does not believe will be condemned" (Mk 16:16). But he himself, acknowledging that weeds have been sown amid the wheat, ordered that both be allowed to grow until the harvest time that will come at the end of the world.[21] He did not want to be a political Messiah or to rule by force,[22] but preferred to call himself the Son of Man who came "to serve and to give his life as a ransom for many" (Mk 10:45). He showed himself to be the perfect Servant of God,[23] who "does not break a bruised reed nor quench a smoldering wick" (Mt 12:20). He acknowledged civil power and its rights when he instructed that tribute be given to Caesar, but he clearly warned that the higher rights of God must be upheld: "Render to Caesar the things that are Caesar's, and to God the things that are God's" (Mt 22:21). In the end, when he completed on the cross the work of redemption by which he achieved for men salvation and true freedom, he brought his revelation to perfect completion. For he bore witness to the truth,[24] yet refused to impose it by force on those who contradicted it. For his kingdom is not claimed by force of blows,[25] but is established by bearing witness to and listening to the truth, and it grows through the love by which Christ, lifted up on the cross, draws men to himself.[26]

Taught by Christ's word and example, the apostles followed the same way. From the very beginnings of the Church they strove to convert men and women to the confession of Christ as Lord, not through coercion or means unworthy of the Gospel, but foremost by the power of the word of God.[27] They steadfastly announced to all the plan of God our Savior, "who desires all men to be saved and to come to the knowledge of the truth" (1 Tim 2:4); at the same time, however, they showed respect for the weak, even though they dwelled in error, thus showing how "each of us shall give account of himself to God" (Rom 14:12)[28] and so far is bound to obey his conscience. Like Christ, the apostles were always intent to bear witness to the truth of God, daring to speak "the word of God with boldness" (Acts 4:31) and in full before the people and their leaders.[29] For with firm faith they held that the Gospel itself is truly the power of God for the salvation of all who believe.[30] Rejecting all "worldly weapons,"[31] therefore, and following the example of Christ's meekness and modesty, they preached the word of God, fully trusting in the divine power of this word to destroy the powers that are opposed to God[32] and to lead men and women to the faith and allegiance of Christ.[33] Like their Master, the apostles also recognized legitimate civil authority: "For

« Omnis anima potestatibus sublimioribus subdita sit; . . . qui resistit potestati, Dei ordinationi resistit » (*Rom.* 13, 1-2).[34] Simul autem non timuerunt contradicere potestati publicae se sanctae Dei voluntati opponenti: « Oboedire oportet Deo magis quam hominibus » (*Act.* 5, 29).[35] Hanc viam secuti sunt innumeri martyres et fideles per saecula et per orbem.

12. (*Ecclesia vestigia Christi et Apostolorum sequitur*). Ecclesia igitur, evangelicae veritati fidelis, viam Christi et Apostolorum sequitur quando rationem libertatis religiosae tamquam dignitati hominis et Dei revelationi consonam agnoscit eamque fovet. Doctrinam a Magistro et ab Apostolis acceptam, decursu temporum, custodivit et tradidit. Etsi in vita Populi Dei, per vicissitudines historiae humanae peregrinantis, interdum exstitit modus agendi spiritui evangelico minus conformis, immo contrarius, semper tamen mansit Ecclesiae doctrina neminem esse ad fidem cogendum.

Evangelicum fermentum in mentibus hominum sic diu est operatum atque multum contulit, ut homines temporum decursu latius agnoscerent dignitatem personae suae et maturesceret persuasio in re religiosa ipsam immunem servandam esse in civitate a quacumque humana coercitione.

13. (*Libertas Ecclesiae*). Inter ea quae ad bonum Ecclesiae, immo ad bonum ipsius terrenae civitatis spectant et ubique semperque servanda sunt atque ab omni iniuria defendenda, illud certe praestantissimum est, ut Ecclesia tanta perfruatur agendi libertate, quantam salus hominum curanda requirat.[36] Haec enim libertas sacra est, qua Unigenitus Dei Filius ditavit Ecclesiam acquisitam sanguine suo. Ecclesiae sane adeo propria est, ut qui eam impugnant, iidem contra Dei voluntatem agant. Libertas Ecclesiae est principium fundamentale in relationibus inter Ecclesiam et potestates publicas totumque ordinem civilem.

In societate humana et coram quavis potestate publica Ecclesia sibi vindicat libertatem, utpote auctoritas spiritualis, a Christo Domino constituta, cui ex divino mandato incumbit officium eundi in mundum universum et Evangelium praedicandi omni creaturae.[37] Libertatem pariter sibi vindicat

there is no authority except from God," the apostle teaches, and for this reason instructs: "Let every person be subject to the governing authorities; . . . he who resists the authorities resists what God has appointed" (Rom 13:1-5).[34] At the same time, however, the apostles were not afraid to speak out against public powers that opposed the holy will of God: "We must obey God rather than men" (Acts 5:29).[35] This is the way that countless martyrs and faithful have followed through the ages and throughout the world.

12. (*The Church follows in the footsteps of Christ and the apostles*). The Church, therefore, faithful to the truth of the Gospel, is following in the way of Christ and the apostles when she acknowledges and supports the principle of religious freedom as consonant with the dignity of man and the revelation of God. Through the ages the Church has carefully protected and handed on the teaching she has received from her Master and the apostles. Although in the life of the people of God as it has made its pilgrim way through the vicissitudes of human history, there have at times appeared ways of acting less in keeping with the spirit of the Gospel, or even opposed to it, the teaching of the Church has nonetheless always stood firm, that no one is to be forced to embrace the faith.

The leaven of the Gospel has long been about its quiet work in the minds of men; to this is due, in large measure, the fact that in the course of time men and women have come to recognize more widely their dignity as persons, and the conviction has grown that in religious matters the person is to be kept immune within civil society from any kind of human coercion.

13. (*The freedom of the Church*). Preeminent among those things that concern the good of the Church and indeed the good of civil society itself on earth, which must always and everywhere be preserved and defended against all harm, is for the Church to enjoy as much freedom in acting as the care of man's salvation may demand.[36] This is a sacred freedom with which the only begotten Son of God endowed the Church whom he purchased with his blood. Indeed, this freedom is so proper to the Church that whoever opposes it acts against the will of God. The freedom of the Church is a fundamental principle* in relations between the Church and the public powers and the whole civil order.

The Church claims for herself freedom in human society and before every public power insofar as she is a spiritual authority, constituted by Christ the Lord, upon whom rests, by divine command, the duty to go throughout the whole world preaching the Gospel to every creature.[37] The

* the fundamental principle (Murray, 693; Ryan, 810); a fundamental principle (Coventry, 1009)

Ecclesia prout est etiam societas hominum qui iure gaudent vivendi in societate civili secundum fidei christianae praescripta.[38]

Iamvero si viget ratio libertatis religiosae non solum verbis proclamata neque solum legibus sancita, sed etiam cum sinceritate in praxim deducta, tunc demum Ecclesia stabilem obtinet et iuris et facti condicionem ad necessariam in missione divina exsequenda independentiam, quam auctoritates ecclesiasticae in societate presse pressiusque vindicarunt.[39] Simulque Christifideles, sicut et ceteri homines, iure civili gaudent ne impediantur in vita sua iuxta conscientiam agenda. Concordia igitur viget inter libertatem Ecclesiae et libertatem illam religiosam, quae omnibus hominibus et communitatibus est tanquam ius agnoscenda et in ordinatione iuridica sancienda.

14. (*Munus Ecclesiae*). Ecclesia Catholica, ut divino obtemperet mandato: « docete omnes gentes » (*Mt.* 28, 19), impensa cura adlaborare debet « ut sermo Dei currat et clarificetur » (*2 Thess.* 3, 1).

Enixe igitur rogat Ecclesia, ut a filiis suis « primum omnium fiant obsecrationes, orationes, postulationes, gratiarum actiones pro omnibus hominibus . . . Hoc enim bonum est et acceptum coram Salvatore nostro Deo, qui omnes homines vult salvos fieri et ad agnitionem veritatis venire » (*1 Tim.* 2, 1-4).

Christifideles autem in sua efformanda conscientia diligenter attendere debent ad sacram certamque Ecclesiae doctrinam.[40] Christi enim voluntate Ecclesia catholica magistra est veritatis, eiusque munus est, ut Veritatem quae Christus est enuntiet atque authentice doceat, simulque principia ordinis moralis, ex ipsa natura humana profluentia, auctoritate sua declaret atque confirmet. Insuper Christiani, in sapientia ambulantes ad eos qui foris sunt, « in Spiritu Sancto, in caritate non ficta, in verbo veritatis » (*2 Cor.* 6, 6-7), lumen vitae cum omni fiducia[41] et fortitudine apostolica, ad sanguinis usque effusionem, diffundere satagant.

Etenim discipulus erga Christum Magistrum gravi adstringitur officio, veritatem ab Eo receptam plenius in dies cognoscendi, annuntiandi fideliter, strenueque defendendi, exclusis mediis spiritui evangelico contrariis. Simul tamen caritas Christi urget eum, ut amanter prudenter patienter agat cum hominibus, qui in errore vel ignorantia circa fidem versantur.[42] Respiciendum igitur est tum ad officia erga Christum Verbum vivificans quod praedicandum est, tum ad humanae personae iura, tum ad mensuram gratiae

Church likewise claims for herself freedom as a society of men and women who enjoy the right to live in civil society according to the precepts of the Christian faith.[38]

Indeed, where the principle of religious freedom is not only proclaimed in words or sanctioned by law but also given sincere and practical application, there the Church maintains a stable condition both in law and in fact, as well as the independence necessary to carry out her divine mission, which is what Church authorities claim in society, ever more insistently.[39] At the same time the Christian faithful, like other men and women, enjoy the civil right of not being prevented from acting according to their conscience. A harmony therefore exists between the freedom of the Church and the religious freedom that must be acknowledged as a right of all persons and communities and sanctioned by juridical law.

14. (*The task of the Church*). In order to obey the divine command: "make disciples of all nations" (Mt 28:19), the Catholic Church should strive with great care "that the word of the Lord may speed on and triumph" (2 Thes 3:1).

The Church therefore earnestly entreats her children, "First of all that supplications, prayers, intercessions, and thanksgivings be made for all men . . . This is good and it is acceptable in the sight of God our Savior, who desires all men to be saved and to come to the knowledge of the truth" (1 Tim 2:1-4).

In forming their conscience, the Christian faithful should carefully attend to the sacred and certain teaching of the Church.[40] For by the will of Christ the Catholic Church is the teacher of truth, and it is her duty to proclaim and authoritatively teach the truth that is Christ, and likewise to declare and confirm with her authority the principles of the moral order that flow from human nature. In addition, as Christians conduct themselves in wisdom toward those outside, "in the Holy Spirit, in genuine charity, in truthful speech" (2 Cor 6:6-7), let them be diligent in diffusing the light of life with all boldness[41] and apostolic courage, even to the shedding of their blood.

The disciple is bound by a grave duty to Christ his Teacher, to know more fully each day the truth received from him, to proclaim it faithfully, and to defend it vigorously, excluding all means contrary to the spirit of the Gospel. At the same time, the love of Christ urges him to deal lovingly, prudently, and patiently with those who dwell in error or ignorance about the faith.[42] He must therefore consider not only his duties toward Christ, the life-giving Word that must be preached, but also the rights of the human

a Deo per Christum tributam homini, qui ad fidem sponte accipiendam et profitendam invitatur.

15. (*Conclusio*). Constat igitur praesentis aetatis homines optare ut libere possint religionem privatim publiceque profiteri, immo libertatem religiosam in plerisque Constitutionibus iam ut ius civile declarari[43] et documentis internationalibus sollemniter agnosci.[44]

At non desunt regimina in quibus, etsi in eorum Constitutione libertas cultus religiosi agnoscitur, tamen ipsae publicae potestates conantur cives a religione profitenda removere et communitatibus religiosis vitam perdifficilem ac periclitantem reddere.

Illa fausta huius temporis signa laeto animo salutans, haec vero deploranda facta cum maerore denuntians, Sacra Synodus Catholicos hortatur, exorat autem homines universos, ut perattente considerent quantopere libertas religiosa necessaria sit in praesenti potissimum familiae humanae condicione.

Manifestum est enim cunctas gentes magis in dies unum fieri, homines diversae culturae et religionis arctioribus inter se devinciri rationibus, augeri denique conscientiam propriae cuiusque responsabilitatis. Proinde ut pacificae relationes et concordia in genere humano instaurentur et firmentur, requiritur ut ubique terrarum libertas religiosa efficaci tutela iuridica muniatur atque observentur suprema hominum officia et iura ad vitam religiosam libere in societate ducendam.

Faxit Deus et Pater omnium ut familia humana, diligenter servata libertatis religiosae ratione in societate, per gratiam Christi et virtutem Spiritus Sancti adducatur ad sublimem illam ac perennem « libertatem gloriae filiorum Dei » (*Rom.* 8, 21).

person, and the measure of grace that God has bestowed through Christ upon those who are invited freely to receive and profess the faith.

15. (*Conclusion*). It is well known that men and women of today desire to be able to profess their religion freely in private and in public. Indeed, religious freedom has already been declared to be a civil right in most constitutions,[43] and is solemnly acknowledged in international documents as well.[44]

Governments are not lacking, however, in which, although freedom of religious worship is acknowledged in their constitutions, the public powers themselves still endeavor to prevent citizens from professing their religion and to make life very difficult and dangerous for religious communities.

Welcoming the former with joy as a favorable sign of the times, while denouncing the latter with sorrow as something to be deplored, this sacred Council urges Catholics and entreats all men and women to consider carefully how necessary religious freedom is, especially in the present condition of the human family.

It is clear that all nations are becoming more united every day, that men and women of different cultures and religions are being bound to one another with closer ties, and that there is a growing consciousness of the responsibility proper to each person. Hence, in order that peaceful relations and harmony may be established and strengthened among mankind, religious freedom must be secured by effective juridical protection* throughout the world, and the highest duties and rights of men and women to lead a religious life freely in society† must be observed.

May God the Father of all grant that the human family, having diligently upheld the principle of religious freedom in society, be led by the grace of Christ and the power of the Holy Spirit to that sublime and everlasting "glorious freedom of the children of God" (Rom 8:21).

---

* be provided with an effective constitutional guarantee (Murray, 696); be given effective constitutional protection (Ryan, 812); be given adequate legal protection (Coventry, 1010)

† the high duty and right of man freely to lead his religious life in society (Murray, 696); that highest of man's rights and duties—to lead a religious life with freedom in society (Ryan, 812); the supreme duties and rights of people in regard to the freedom of their religious life in society (Coventry, 1010)

NOTAE

[1] Cf. IOANNES XXIII, Litt. Encycl. *Pacem in terris,* 11 aprilis 1963: *A.A.S.,* 55 (1963), p. 279, ubi Summus Pontifex ad realitates hodiernas animadvertit: « At hae, de quibus diximus, animorum appetitiones illud etiam manifesto testantur, nostro hoc tempore homines magis magisque fieri dignitatis suae conscios, atque adeo incitari cum ad reipublicae administrationem participandam, tum ad poscendum, ut propria inviolabiliaque iura in publica civitatis disciplina serventur. Neque haec satis; nam homines nunc illud insuper poscunt, ut nempe civitatis auctoritates et ad normam publicae constitutionis creentur, et sua munera intra eiusdem terminos obeant ». Cf. *ibid.,* p. 265: « Illud praeterea humanae dignitas personae exigitur, ut in agendo homo proprio consilio et libertate fruatur. Quocirca, si de civium coniunctione agitur, est profecto cur ipse iura colat, officia servet, atque, in innumeris operibus exercendis, aliis sociam tribuat operam, suo praesertim impulsu et consulto; ita scilicet ut suo quisque instituto, iudicio, officiique conscientia agat, iam non commotus coercitione vel sollicitatione extrinsecus plerumque adductis; quandoquidem, si qua hominum societas una ratione virium est instituta, ea nihil humani in se habere dicenda est, utpote in qua homines a libertate cohibeantur, qui contra ad vitae progressus, ad perfectionemque assequendam apte ipsi incitandi sunt ».

Quod pertinet ad dignitatem illam civilem, secundum quam dignitas humana in publicum prodit, cf. PIUS XII, *Nuntius radiophonicus,* 24 dec. 1944: *A.A.S.,* 37 (1945) p. 14: « In un popolo degno di tal nome il cittadino sente in se stesso la coscienza della sua personalità, dei suoi doveri e dei suoi diritti, della propria libertà congiunta col rispetto della libertà e della dignità altrui ». Hoc loco commendat Romanus Pontifex etiam illud « ideale di libertà e di uguaglianza » (*loc. cit.*), quod in Statu democratico, iuxta sana rationis principia ordinato, obtineat necesse est, quodque postulat, ut hominis ius in societate ad liberum exercitium religionis plene agnoscatur, colatur, defendatur.

[2] Cf. PAULUS VI, *Homilia* Dom. XIV post Pent., *L'Oss. Rom.,* 13-14 sept. 1965.

[3] Cf. IOANNES XXIII, Litt. Encycl. *Pacem in terris,* 11 aprilis 1963: *A.A.S.,* 55 (1963), pp. 260-261: « In hominis iuribus hoc quoque numerandum est, ut et Deum, ad rectam conscientiae suae normam, venerari possit, et religionem privatim publice profiteri ». Cf. PIUS XII, *Nuntius radiophonicus,* 24 dec. 1942: *A.A.S.,* 35 (1943), p. 19, ubi inter « iura fundamentalia personae » hoc etiam collocatur: « il diritto al culto di Dio privato e pubblico, compresa l'azione caritativa religiosa ». Cf. PIUS XI, Litt. Encycl. *Mit brennender Sorge,* 14 martii 1937: *A.A.S.,* 29 (1937), p. 160: «Der gläubige Mensch hat ein unverlierbares Recht, seinen Glauben zu bekennen und in den ihm gemässen Formen zu betätigen. Gesetze, die das Bekenntnis und die Betätigung dieses Glaubens unterdrücken oder erschweren, stehen in Widerspruch mit einem Naturgesetz ». Cf. LEO XIII, Litt. Encycl. *Libertas praestantissimum,* 20 iunii 1888: *Acta Leonis XIII,* 8 (1888), pp. 237-238: « Illa quoque magnopere praedicatur, quam conscientiae libertatem nominant; quae si ita accipiatur ut suo cuique arbitratu aeque liceat Deum colere, non colere, argumentis, quae supra allata sunt, satis convincitur. Sed potest etiam in hanc sententiam accipi, ut homini ex conscientia officii Dei voluntatem sequi et iussa facere, nulla re impediente, in civitate liceat. Haec quidem vera, haec digna filiis Dei libertas, quae humanae dignitatem personae honestissime tuetur, est omni vi iniuriaque maior, eademque Ecclesiae semper optata ac praecipue cara ».

NOTES

[1] Cf. John XXIII, Encyclical Letter *Pacem in terris*, 11 April 1963: AAS 55 (1963), 279, where the pope makes the following observations on present-day realities: "But the aspirations we have mentioned are a clear indication of the fact that men, increasingly aware nowadays of their personal dignity, have found the incentive to enter government service and demand constitutional recognition for their own inviolable rights. Not content with this, they are also demanding the observance of constitutional procedures in the appointment of public authorities, and are insisting that they exercise their office within this constitutional framework." Cf. *ibid.*, 265: "Man's personal dignity requires besides that he enjoy freedom and be able to make up his own mind when he acts. In his association with his fellows, therefore, there is every reason why his recognition of rights, observance of duties, and many-sided collaboration with other men, should be primarily a matter of his own personal decision. Each man should act on his own initiative, conviction, and sense of responsibility, not under the constant pressure of external coercion or enticement. There is nothing human about a society that is welded together by force. Far from encouraging, as it should, the attainment of man's progress and perfection, it is merely an obstacle to his freedom."

Concerning civil dignity, by which human dignity is extended into the public sphere, cf. Pius XII, Radio message, 24 December 1944: AAS 37 (1945), 14: "In a people worthy of the name, the citizen feels within himself a consciousness of his personhood, of his duties and rights, of his own freedom together with respect for the freedom and dignity of others." Here the pope commends also the "ideal of freedom and equality" (*loc. cit.*) that it is necessary to maintain in a democratic state organized according to sound principles of reason, which demands that man's right to the free exercise of religion in society be fully acknowledged, cultivated, and defended.

[2] Cf. Paul VI, Homily, 14th Sunday after Pentecost, *L'Osservatore Romano*, 13-14 September 1965.

[3] Cf. John XXIII, Encyclical Letter *Pacem in terris*, 11 April 1963: AAS 55 (1963), 260-61: "Also among man's rights is that of being able to worship God in accordance with the right dictates of his own conscience, and to profess his religion both in private and in public." Cf. Pius XII, Radio message, 24 December 1942: AAS 35 (1943), 19, where among "the fundamental rights of the person" is also included "the right to worship God privately and publicly, including religious charitable activity." Cf. Pius XI, Encyclical Letter *Mit brennender Sorge*, 14 March 1937: AAS 29 (1937), 160: "The believer has an absolute right to profess his faith and live according to its dictates. Laws that impede this profession and practice of faith are against natural law." Cf. Leo XIII, Encyclical Letter *Libertas praestantissimum*, 20 June 1888: *Acta Leonis XIII*, 8 (1888), 237-38: "Another freedom is widely advocated, namely, freedom of conscience. If by this is meant that everyone may, as he chooses, worship God or not, it is sufficiently refuted by the arguments already adduced. But it may also be taken to mean that every man in the state may follow the will of God and, from a consciousness of duty and free from every obstacle, obey his commands. This, indeed, is true freedom, a freedom worthy of the sons of God, which nobly maintains the dignity of man and is stronger than all violence or wrong—a freedom which the Church has always desired and held most dear."

De conceptu libertatis religiosae, ut ab aliis Christianis intelligitur, cf. documenta Consilii Mundialis Ecclesiarum (World Council of Churches): « *Declaration on Religious Liberty* » (Assembly Amsterdam, 1948), « *Statement on Religious Liberty* » (Assembly New Delhi, 1961).

[4] Cf. S. THOMAS, *Summa theologica*, I-II, q. 91, a. 1; q. 93, a. 1.

[5] Cf. *ibid.*, q. 93, a. 2.

[6] Quoad historiam huius quaestionis cf. J. LECLER, S. I., *Histoire de la tolérance religieuse au siècle de la Réforme*, Paris, Aubier, Editions Montaigne, 1955, tom. II, *fere passim.*

[7] Cf. S. THOMAS, *Summa theologica*, I-II, q. 91, a. 4 c: « De his potest homo legem ferre de quibus potest iudicare. Iudicium autem hominis esse non potest de interioribus actibus, qui latent, sed solum de exterioribus actibus, qui apparent »; cf. II-II, q. 104, a. 5 c: « In his quae pertinent ad interiorem motum voluntatis, homo non tenetur homini oboedire sed solum Deo ». Cf. IOANNES XXIII, Litt. Encycl. *Pacem in terris,* 11 aprilis 1963: *A.A.S.,* 55 (1963), p. 270: « Sed quoniam omnes homines in naturali dignitate sunt inter se pares, tum nemo valet alium ad aliquid intimis animi sensibus efficiendum cogere; quod quidem unus Deus potest, utpote qui unus arcana pectoris consilia scrutetur ac iudicet ». Cf. PAULUS VI, *Nuntius Radiophonicus,* 22 dec. 1964: *A.A.S.,* 57 (1965), p. 181.

[8] Descriptio hic allata *boni communis* invenitur in: IOANNES XXIII, Litt. Encycl. *Mater et Magistra,* 15 mai 1961: *A.A.S.,* 53 (1961), p. 417; *Pacem in terris,* 11 aprilis 1963: *A.A.S.,* 55 (1963), p. 273.

Verba quae sequuntur (« maxime . . . officiis ») desumuntur etiam ex Litt. Encycl. *Pacem in terris,* infra in eadem p. 273.

[9] Cf. IOANNES XXIII, Litt. Encycl. *Pacem in terris,* 11 aprilis 1963: *A.A.S.,* 55 (1963), pp. 273-274: « Verum cum nostra hac aetate commune bonum maxime in humanae personae servatis iuribus et officiis consistere putetur, tum praecipue in eo sint oportet curatorum rei publicae partes, ut hinc iura agnoscantur, colantur, inter se componantur, defendantur, provehantur, illinc suis quisque officiis facilius fungi possit. Etenim "inviolabilia iura tueri, hominum propria, atque curare, ut facilius quisque suis muneribus defungatur, hoc cuiusvis publicae potestatis officium est praecipuum" ». Cf. PIUS XII, *Nuntius radiophonicus,* 1 iunii 1941: *A.A.S.,* 33 (1941), p. 200.

[10] Cf. LEO XIII, Litt. Encycl. *Immortale Dei,* 1 nov. 1885: *A.S.S.,* 18 (1885), p. 161: « Immortale Dei miserenti opus, quod est Ecclesia, quamquam per se et natura sua salutem spectat animorum adipiscendamque in caelis felicitatis, tamen in ipso etiam rerum mortalium genere tot ac tantas ultro parit utilitates, ut plures maioresve non posset, si in primis et maxime esset ad tuendam huius vitae, quae in terris agitur, prosperitatem institutum ». Quod quidem thema, e S. Augustino derivatum, saepe saepius evolvere solebat Leo XIII.

[11] Sic redditur aliis verbis nota regula iuris canonici, ex iure romano quoad sensum deprompta, « Odia restringi et favores convenit ampliari ». Cf. V. BARTOCCETTI, *De regulis iuris canonici* (Angelo Belardetti Editore, Roma 1955), p. 73.

[12] LACTANTIUS, *Divinarum Institutionum,* lib. V, 19: ed. S. Brandt et G. Laubmann, *CSEL* 19, p. 463; *PL* 6, 614 (cap. 20): « Non est opus vi et iniuria, quia religio cogi non potest, verbis potius quam verberibus res agenda est, ut sit voluntas ».

Op. cit.: CSEL 19, p. 464; *PL* 6, 614: «Itaque nemo a nobis retinetur invitus—inutilis est enim Deo qui devotione ac fide caret—et tamen nemo discedit ipsa veritate retinente ».

For an overview of how the concept of religious freedom is understood by other Christians, cf. the documents of the World Council of Churches: "Declaration on Religious Liberty" (Amsterdam Assembly, 1948), and "Statement on Religious Liberty" (New Delhi Assembly, 1961).

[4] Cf. St. Thomas, *Summa theologica*, I-II, q. 91, a. 1; q. 93, a. 1.

[5] Cf. *ibid.*, q. 93, a. 2.

[6] On the history of this question, cf. J. Lecler, S.J., *Histoire de la tolérance religieuse au siècle de la Réforme* (Paris: Aubier, Editions Montaigne, 1955), vol. II, *passim*.

[7] Cf. St. Thomas, *Summa theologica*, I-II, q. 91, a. 4, c: "Man can make laws in those matters of which he is competent to judge. But man is not competent to judge of interior movements, which are hidden, but only of exterior acts, which are apparent." Cf. II-II, q. 104, a. 5, c: "In matters touching the interior movement of the will man is not bound to obey his fellow man, but God alone." Cf. John XXIII, Encyclical Letter *Pacem in terris*, 11 April 1963: AAS 55 (1963), 270: "But since all men are equal in natural dignity, no man has the capacity to force internal compliance on another. Only God can do that, for he alone scrutinizes and judges the secret counsels of the heart." Cf. Paul VI, Radio message, 22 December 1964: AAS 57 (1965), 181.

[8] This description of the common good is found in John XXIII, Encyclical Letter *Mater et Magistra*, 15 May 1961: AAS 53 (1961), 417; *Pacem in terris*, 11 April 1963: AAS 55 (1963), 273.

The words which follow ("it chiefly consists in the protection of the rights and duties of the human person") are also taken from the Encyclical Letter *Pacem in terris*, 273.

[9] Cf. John XXIII, Encylical Letter *Pacem in terris*, 11 April 1963: AAS 55 (1963), 273-74: "It is generally accepted today that the common good is best safeguarded when personal rights and duties are guaranteed. The chief concern of civil authorities must therefore be to ensure that these rights are recognized, respected, co-ordinated, defended and promoted, and that each individual is enabled to perform his duties more easily. For 'to safeguard the inviolable rights of the human person, and to facilitate the performance of his duties, is the principal duty of every public power.'" Cf. Pius XII, Radio message, 1 June 1941: AAS 33 (1941), 200.

[10] Cf. Leo XIII, Encyclical Letter *Immortale Dei*, 1 November 1885: ASS 18 (1885), 161: "The Catholic Church, that imperishable handiwork of our all-merciful God, has for her immediate and natural purpose the saving of souls and securing our happiness in heaven. Yet, in regard to things temporal, she is the source of benefits as manifold and great as if the chief end of her existence were to ensure the prospering of our earthly life." This idea, which derives from St. Augustine, was increasingly developed by Leo XIII throughout his pontificate.

[11] This statement expresses in different words the following well-known rule of canon law, which derives its meaning from Roman law: "Whatever is burdensome should be restricted; whatever is favorable should be increased." Cf. V. Bartoccetti, *De regulis iuris canonici* (Rome: Angelo Belardetti, 1955), 73.

[12] Lactantius, *Divinarum Institutionum*, bk. V, 19: ed. S. Brandt and G. Laubmann, *CSEL* 19, p. 463; *PL* 6, 614 (ch. 20): "There is no need for violence or injury, for religion cannot be forced; the whole matter should be carried on with words rather than whips, so that there might be free will."

Op. cit.: *CSEL* 19, p. 464; *PL* 6, 614: "Therefore we hold no one back against his will—for anyone who is without devotion and faith is of no use to God—and yet no one departs who is held fast by the truth itself."

Op. cit.: *CSEL* 19, p. 465; *PL* 6, 616: « Nihil est enim tam voluntarium quam religio, in qua si animus sacrificantis aversus est, iam sublata, iam nulla est ».

S. AMBROSIUS, *Epistola ad Valentinianum Imp., Ep.* 21: *PL* 16, 1047: « Dei lex nos docuit quid sequamur, humanae leges hoc docere non possumus. Extorquere solent timidis commutationem fidem inspirare non possunt »

S. AUGUSTINUS, *Contra litteras Petiliani*, lib. II, cap. 83: ed. M. Petschenig, *CSEL* 52, p. 112; *PL* 43, 315; cf. C. 23, q. 5, c. 33 (ed. Friedberg, col. 939): « Augustinus respondit: Ad fidem quidem nullus est cogendus invitus; sed per severitatem, immo et per misericordiam Dei tribulationum flagellis solet perfidia castigari ».

S. GREGORIUS MAGNUS, *Epistola ad Virgilium et Theodorum Episcopos Massilliae Galliarum*, Registrum Epistolarum, I, 45: ed. P. Ewald et L. M. Hartmann, MGH Ep. 1, p. 72; *PL* 77, 510-11 (lib. I, ep. 47): « Dum enim quispiam ad baptismatis fontem non praedicationis suavitate, sed necessitate pervenerit, ad pristinam superstitionem remeans in de deterius moritur, unde renatus esse videbatur ».

Epistola ad Iohannem Episcopum Constantinopolitanum, Registrum Epistolarum, III, 52: MGH Ep. 1, p. 210; *PL* 77, 649 (lib. III, ep. 53); cf. D. 45, c. 1 (ed. Friedberg, col. 160): « Nova vero atque inaudita est ista praedicatio, quae verberibus exigit fidem ».

CONC. TOLET. IV, c. 57: MANSI 10, 633; cf. D. 45, c. 5 (ed. Friedberg, col. 161-162): « De Iudaeis hoc praecepit sancta synodus, nemini deinceps ad credendum vim inferre; *cui enim vult Deus misereretur, et quem vult indurat.* Non enim tales inviti salvandi sunt, sed volentes, ut integra sit forma iustitiae: sicut enim homo proprii arbitrii voluntate serpenti oboediens periit, sic vocante gratia Dei, propriae mentis conversione homo quisque credendo salvatur. Ergo non vi, sed liberi arbitrii facultate, ut convertantur suadendi sunt, non potius impellendi . . . ».

CLEMENS III, Litterae Decretales: X, V, 6, 9, ed. Friedberg, col. 774: « . . . Statuimus enim ut nullus Christianus invitos vel nolentes Iudaeos ad baptismum (per violentiam) venire compellat. Si quis autem ad Christianos causa fidei confugerit, postquam voluntas eius fuerit patefacta, Christianus absque calumnia efficiatur: quippe Christi fidem habere non creditur, qui ad Christianorum baptismum non spontaneus, sed invitus cogitur pervenire . . . ».

INNOCENTUS III, *Epistola ad Arelatensem Archiepiscopum*, X, III, 42, 3: ed. Friedberg, col. 646: « . . . Verum id est religioni Christianae contrarium, ut semper invitus et penitus contradicens ad recipiendam et servandam Christianitatem aliquis compellatur . . . ».

[13] Cf. *C.I.C.*, c. 1351; cf. PIUS XII, Alloc. ad Praelatos auditores ceterosque officiales et administros Tribunalis S. Romanae Rotae, 6 oct. 1946: *A.A.S.*, 38 (1946), p. 394, ubi citatur a R. P. *Pro Memoria* Secretarius Status ad Legationem Yugoslaviae ad Sanctam Sedem: « D'après les principes de la doctrine catholique, la conversion doit être le résultat, non pas de contraintes extérieures mais de l'adhésion de l'âme aux verités enseignées par l'Eglise catholique. C'est pour cela que l'Eglise catholique n'admet pas dans son sein les adultes, qui demandent à y entrer ou à y faire retour, qu'à la condition qu'ils soient pleinement conscients de la portée et des conséquences de l'acte qu'ils veulent accomplir ». Idem, Litt. Encycl. *Mystici Corporis*, 29 iunii 1943: *A.A.S.*, 35 (1943), p. 243: «At si cupimus non intermissam eiusmodi totius mystici Corporis conprecationem admoveri Deo, ut aberrantes omnes in unum Iesu Christi ovile

Op. cit.: *CSEL* 19, p. 465; *PL* 6, 616: "For nothing is so voluntary as religion; once the spirit of the one offering sacrifice has turned away, religion is already destroyed, is itself already nothing."

St. Ambrose, *Epistola ad Valentinianum Imp.*, Ep. 21, *PL* 16, 1047: "God's law taught us what to strive for; human laws cannot teach this. Such laws are merely accustomed to extorting a change from the faint of heart; they cannot inspire faith."

St. Augustine, *Contra litteras Petiliani*, bk. II, ch. 83: ed. M Petschenig, *CSEL* 52, p. 112; *PL* 43, 315; cf. C. 23, q. 5, ch. 33 (ed. Friedberg, col. 939): "Augustine replied: No one, indeed, is forced to embrace the faith against his will; but through the severity of God, or rather through his mercy, faithlessness is usually punished by the lashes of tribulation."

St. Gregory the Great, *Epistola ad Virgilium et Theodorum Episcopos Massilliae Galliarium*, Registrum Epistolarum, I, 45: ed. P. Ewald and L.M. Hartmann, *MGH Ep.* 1, p. 72; *PL* 77, 510-11 (bk. I, ep. 47): "For if anyone should have come to the holy baptismal font, not through the persuasion of preaching, but out of compulsion, when he returns to the place of his former superstition he will die the worse for it, having come from a place where he only seemed to have been reborn."

Epistola ad Iohannem Episcopum Constantinopolitanum, Registrum Epistolarum, III, 52: *MGH Ep.* 1, p. 210; *PL* 77, 649 (bk. III, ep. 53); cf. D. 45, ch. 1 (ed. Friedberg, col. 160): "That preaching is indeed new and unheard of, that exacts faith by means of lashing."

Fourth Council of Toledo, ch. 57: Mansi 10, 633; cf. D. 45, ch. 5 (ed. Friedberg, col. 161-162); "Concerning the Jews, the holy synod declared that henceforth force is not to be applied to anyone in order to make them believe; *for God has mercy on whom he wishes, and hardens whom he wishes.* For such men are to be saved not unwillingly but willingly, in order that justice may be perfect: for just as man perished by obeying the serpent through his own free-will, so at the call of God's grace, each man is saved by believing through the conversion of his own mind. Therefore, not by force, but by the free judgment of their own free will are they to be persuaded to convert, rather than compelled . . . "

Clement III, *Litterae Decretales*: X, V, 6, 9, ed. Friedberg col. 774: " . . . For we have decreed that no Christian is to force Jews reluctantly or against their will to approach baptism (by violence). If, however, someone has recourse to Christians on account of his faith, after he has made known his will, let him be made a Christian without dispute; since one who is forced to approach Christian baptism not voluntarily but against his will is not considered to have the faith of Christ . . . "

Innocent III, *Epistola ad Arelatensem Archiepiscopum*, X, III, 42, 3: ed. Friedberg, col. 646: " . . . It is in truth contrary to the Christian religion that anyone ever be forced, against his will and while interiorly opposing it, to receive and keep the Christian faith . . . "

[13] Cf. *Code of Canon Law* [1917], c. 1351; cf. Pius XII, "Allocution to prelate auditors and other officials and administrators of the Tribunal of the Sacred Roman Rota," 6 October 1946: AAS 38 (1946), 394, where the pope cites the *pro memoria* of the Secretariat of State to the Yugoslavian Embassy to the Holy See: "In accordance with the principles of Catholic teaching, conversion should be the result not of external constraints but of the soul's adherence to the truths taught by the Catholic Church. This is why the Catholic Church admits to herself adults who seek to enter or return to her only on the condition that they are fully conscious of the significance and consequences of the act they wish to make." Cf. also the Encyclical Letter *Mystici Corporis*, 29 June 1943: AAS 35 (1943), 243: "Though we desire this unceasing prayer to rise to God from the whole mystical body in common, that all the straying sheep may hasten

quam primum ingrediantur, profitemur tamen omnino necessarium esse id sponte libenterque fieri, cum nemo credat nisi volens. Quamobrem si qui, non credentes, eo reapse compelluntur ut Ecclesiae aedificium intrent, ut ad altare accedant, sacramentaque suscipiant, ii procul dubio veri christifideles non fiunt; fides enim, sine qua "impossibile est placere Deo" (*Hebr.* 11, 6), liberrimum esse debet "obsequium intellectus et voluntatis" (CONC. VAT., *Const. de fide catholica, cap. 3*). Si igitur aliquando contingat, ut contra constantem Apostolicae huius Sedis doctrinam, ad amplexandam catholicam fidem aliquis adigatur invitus, id Nos facere non possumus quin, pro officii nostri conscientia, reprobamus ».

[14] Cf. *Eph.* 1, 5.

[15] Cf. *Io.* 6, 44.

[16] Cf. *Io.* 13, 13.

[17] Cf. *Mt.* 11, 29.

[18] Cf. *Mt.* 11, 28-30; *Io.* 6, 68.

[19] Cf. *Mt.* 9, 28-29; *Mc.* 9, 23-24; 6, 5-6

Cf. PAULUS VI, Litt. Encycl. *Ecclesiam suam,* 6 aug. 1964: A.A.S., 56 (1964), pp. 642-43: «Adeo afuit ut quisquam vi cogeretur venire ad colloquium salutis, ut is magis amoris impulsione invitaretur. Qua invitatione, quamquam grave onus eius animo impositum est, ad quem pertinuit (cf. *Mt.* 11, 21), relicta tamen est ipsi potestas aut veniendi ad colloquium, aut illud fugiendi; quin immo Christus, sive miraculorum numerum (ib. 12, 38 s.), sive eorumdem vim probativam cum ad condiciones tum ad voluntatem audientium aptavit (ib. 13, 13 s.); eo nimirum consilio, ut iidem iuvarentur ad libere assentiendum divinae revelationi, neque exinde suae assensionis praemio carerent ».

[20] Cf. *Mt.* 11, 20-24.

[21] Cf. *Mt.* 13, 30 et 40-41.

[22] Cf. *Mt.* 4, 8-10; *Io.* 6, 15.

[23] Cf. *Is.* 42, 1-4.

[24] Cf. *Io.* 18, 37.

[25] Cf. *Mt.* 26, 51-53; *Io.* 18, 36.

[26] Cf. *Io.* 12, 32.

[27] Cf. *1 Cor.* 2, 3-5; *1 Thess.* 2, 3-5.

[28] Cf. *Rom.* 14, 1-23; *1 Cor.* 8, 9-13; 10, 23-33.

[29] Cf. *Eph.* 6, 20.

[30] Cf. *Rom.* 1, 16.

[31] Cf. *2 Cor.* 10, 4; *1 Thess.* 5, 8-9.

[32] Cf. *Eph.* 6, 11-17.

[33] Cf. *2 Cor.* 10, 3-5.

[34] Cf. *1 Pt.* 2, 13-17.

[35] Cf. *Act.* 4, 19-20.

[36] Cf. LEO XIII, Litterae *Officio sanctissimo,* 22 dec. 1887: A.S.S., 22 (1887), p. 269: «In bonis autem Ecclesiae, quae Nobis ubique semperque conservare debemus, ab omnique iniuria defendere, illud certe praestantissimum est, tantam ipsam perfrui agendi libertate, quantam salus hominum curanda requirat. Haec nimirum est libertas divina, ab Unigenito Dei Filio auctore profecta, qui Ecclesiam sanguine fuso excitavit; qui eam perpetuam in hominibus statuit; qui voluit ipsi ipse praeesse. Atque adeo propria est Ecclesiae, perfecti divinique operis, ut qui contra eam faciunt libertatem, iidem contra Deum et contra officium ». Ut olim Gregorius VII, sic temporibus modernis exstabat LEO XIII propugnator libertatis Ecclesiae. Cf. Litterae

to enter the one fold of Jesus Christ, we still recognize that this must be done of their own free will; for no one believes unless he wills to believe. Hence they are most certainly not genuine Christians who against their belief are forced to go into a church, to approach the altar and to receive the sacraments; for the 'faith without which it is impossible to please God' (Heb 11:6) is an entirely free 'submission of intellect and will' (First Vatican Council, *Constitution on the Catholic Faith*, ch. 3). Therefore, whenever it happens, despite the constant teaching of this apostolic see, that anyone is compelled to embrace the Catholic faith against his will, our sense of duty demands that we condemn the act."

[14] Cf. Eph 1:5.

[15] Cf. Jn 6:44.

[16] Cf. Jn 13:13.

[17] Cf. Mt 11:29.

[18] Cf. Mt 11:28-30; Jn 6:68.

[19] Cf. Mt 9:28-29; Mk 9:23-24; 6:5-6.

Cf. Paul VI, Encyclical Letter *Ecclesiam suam*, 6 August 1964: AAS 56 (1964), 642-43: "No physical pressure was brought to bear on anyone to accept the dialogue of salvation; far from it. It was an appeal of love. True, it imposed a serious obligation on those toward whom it was directed (cf. Mt 11:21), but it left them free to respond to it or to reject it. Christ adapted the number of his miracles (*ibid.*, 12:38ff.) and their demonstrative force to the dispositions and good will of his hearers (*ibid.*, 13:13ff.) so as to help them to consent freely to the revelation they were given and not to forfeit the reward for their consent."

[20] Cf. Mt 11:20-24.

[21] Cf. Mt 13:30 and 40-41.

[22] Cf. Mt 4:8-10; Jn 6:15.

[23] Cf. Is 42:1-4.

[24] Cf. Jn 18:37.

[25] Cf. Mt 26:51-53; Jn 18:36.

[26] Cf. Jn 12:32.

[27] Cf. 1 Cor 2:3-5; 1 Thes 2:3-5.

[28] Cf. Rom 14:1-23; 1 Cor 8:9-13; 10:23-33.

[29] Cf. Eph 6:20.

[30] Cf. Rom 1:16.

[31] Cf. 2 Cor 10:4; 1 Thes 5:8-9.

[32] Cf. Eph 6:11-17.

[33] Cf. 2 Cor 10:3-5.

[34] Cf. 1 Pt 2:13-17.

[35] Cf. Acts 4:19-20.

[36] Cf. Leo XIII, Encyclical *Officio sanctissimo*, 22 December 1887: ASS 22 (1887), 269: "Of the goods of the Church that it is our duty everywhere and always to maintain and defend against all injustice, the first is certainly that of enjoying the full freedom of action she may need in working for the salvation of souls. This is a divine liberty, having as its author the only Son of God, who by the shedding of his blood gave birth to the Church, who established it until the end of time, and chose himself to be its head. This liberty is so essential to the Church, a perfect and divine institution, that those who attack this liberty at the same time offend against God and their duty." Like Gregory VII before him, Leo XIII stands out in the modern

Ex litteris, 7 aprilis 1887: *A.S.S.*, 19 (1886), p. 465: «Nos quidem vel ab initio nostri pontificatus multo et serio cogitare de vobis instituimus, atque, ut ratio Nostri ferebat officii, consilium cepimus omnia conari, si qua ratione liceat, pacatam tranquillitatem cum libertate legitima catholico nomini restituere». In sexaginta fere documentis, quae relationes inter rem sacram remque civilem tractant, octoginta vices occurrit formula verborum, «libertas Ecclesiae», vel formula aequipollens. Ipsi enim Leoni XIII, sicut toti traditioni catholicae, libertas Ecclesiae principium est fundamentale in iis, quae spectant ad relationem inter Ecclesiam et instituta omnia ordinis civilis.

[37] Cf. *Mc.* 16, 15; *Mt.* 28, 18-20.

Cf. PIUS XII, Litt. Encycl. *Summi Pontificatus,* 20 oct. 1939: *A.A.S.*, 31 (1939), pp. 445-46: «Quamobrem Nos, ut eius in terris vices gerimus, qui a sacro vate "Princeps pacis" appellatur (*Is.* 9, 6), civitatum rectores eosque omnes, e quorum opera quovis modo publica res pendet, compellamus vehementerque obtestamur ut Ecclesia plena semper libertate fruatur debita, qua suam possit educationis operam exsequi, ac veritatem impertire mentibus, animis inculcare iustitiam, eosque divina Iesu Christi refovere caritate».

[38] Cf. PIUS XI, Litterae *Firmissimam constantiam,* 28 martii 1937: *A.A.S.*, 29 (1937), p. 196: «Proposita eiusmodi aestimandarum rerum mensura, concedendum sane est, ad christianam vitam explicandam externa quoque praesidia, quae sensibus percipiuntur, esse necessaria, pariterque Ecclesiae tamquam hominum societati opus omnino esse, ad vitae usuram atque incrementum, iusta agendi libertate, ipsosque fideles iure gaudere in societate civili vivendi ad rationis conscientiaeque praescripta».

[39] Cf. PIUS XII, Allocutio *Ci riesce,* 6 dec. 1953: *A.A.S.*, 45 (1953), p. 802, ubi fines clare definiuntur, quos Ecclesia prae oculis habet in ineundis Concordatis: «I Concordati debbono quindi assicurare alla Chiesa una stabile condizione di diritto e di fatto nello Stato, con cui sono conclusi, e garantire ad essa la piena indipendenza nell'adempimento della sua divina missione». Exinde insuper constat, nihil esse in doctrina de libertate religiosa, quod cum praxi hodierna Concordatorum quovis modo pugnat.

[40] Cf. PIUS XII, *Nuntius radiophonicus,* 28 martii 1952: *A.A.S.*, 44 (1952), pp. 270-78, de conscientia christiana efformanda.

[41] Cf. *Act.* 4, 29.

[42] Cf. IOANNES XXIII, Litt. Encycl. *Pacem in terris,* 11 aprilis 1963: *A.A.S.*, 55 (1963), pp. 299-300: «Omnino errores ab iis qui opinione labuntur semper distinguere aequum est, quamvis de hominibus agatur, qui aut errore veritatis aut impari rerum cognitione capti sint, vel ad sacra vel ad optimam vitae actionem attinentium. Nam homo ad errorem lapsus iam non humanitate instructus esse desinit, neque suam umquam personae dignitatem amittit, cuius ratio est semper habenda. Praeterea in hominis natura numquam facultas perit et refragandi erroribus et viam ad veritatem quaerendi. Neque umquam hac in re providentissimi Dei auxilia hominem deficiunt. Ex quo fieri potest, ut si quis hodie vel perspicuitate egeat, vel in falsas discesserit sententias, possit postmodum, Dei collustratus lumine veritatem amplecti».

[43] GIANNINI A., *Le Costituzioni degli Stati del Vicino Oriente,* Roma 1931; PEASLEE AMOS S., *Constitutions of Nations,* New Jersey (USA) 1950; MIRKINE-GUETZEVITCH B., *Le Costituzioni Europee,* Milano 1954; ZAMORA A., *Digesto Constitutional Americano,* Buenos Aires 1958; LAVROFF D. G. ET PEISER G., *Les Constitutions Africaines,* Paris 1963; STRAMACCI M., *Le Costituzioni degli Stati Africani,* Milano 1963; PAVAN P., *Libertà Religiosa e Pubblici Poteri,* Milano 1965.

period as a great defender of the freedom of the Church. Cf. the Encyclical *Ex litteris*, 7 April 1887: ASS 19 (1886), 465: "Indeed, from the beginning of our pontificate we have given much serious thought toward you, and, bearing in mind our office, we resolved to attempt all things possible to restore to the Catholic name peaceful tranquility with lawful freedom." In almost sixty documents that deal with relations between sacred and civil affairs, the phrase "freedom of the Church," or its equivalent, occurs eighty times. Indeed, for Leo XIII himself, as for the whole Catholic tradition, the freedom of the Church is a fundamental principle among those that concern the relationship between the Church and all the institutions of the civil order.

[37] Cf. Mk 16:15; Mt 28:18-20.

Cf. Pius XII, Encyclical Letter *Summi Pontificatus*, 20 October 1939: AAS 31 (1939), 445-46: "Accordingly we, as representatives on earth of him who was proclaimed by the prophet 'Prince of Peace' (Is 9:6) appeal to and vigorously implore the leaders of nations, and those who can in any way influence public life, to let the Church have full liberty to fulfill her role as educator by teaching men truth, by inculcating justice and by inflaming hearts with the divine love of Christ."

[38] Cf. Pius XI, Encyclical *Firmissimam constantiam*, 28 March 1937: AAS 29 (1937), 196: "Once this gradation of values and activities is established, it must be admitted that for Christian life to develop it must have recourse to external and sensible means; that the Church, being a society of men, cannot exist or develop if it does not enjoy liberty of action, and that its members have the right to find in civil society the possibility of living according to the dictates of their consciences."

[39] Cf. Pius XII, Allocution *Ci riesce*, 6 December 1953: AAS 45 (1953), 802, where the limits that the Church has in mind when entering into concordats are clearly defined: "Concordats should therefore assure to the Church a stable condition in right and in fact within the state with which they are concluded, and guarantee to her full independence in fulfilling her divine mission." From this it is evident that there is nothing in the teaching on religious freedom that is at odds in any way with the current practice of concordats.

[40] On the formation of a Christian conscience, cf. Pius XII, Radio message, 28 March 1952: AAS 44 (1952), 270-78.

[41] Cf. Acts 4:29.

[42] Cf. John XXIII, Encyclical Letter *Pacem in terris*, 11 April 1963: AAS 55 (1963), 299-300: "It is always perfectly justifiable to distinguish between error as such and the person who falls into error— even in the case of men who err regarding the truth or are led astray as a result of their inadequate knowledge, in matters either of religion or of the highest ethical standards. A man who has fallen into error does not cease to be a man. He never forfeits his personal dignity; and that is something that must always be taken into account. Besides, there exists in man's very nature an undying capacity to break through the barriers of error and seek the road to truth. God, in his great providence, is ever present with his aid. Today, maybe, a man lacks faith and turns aside into error; tomorrow, perhaps, illumined by God's light, he may indeed embrace the truth."

[43] A. Giannini, *Le Costituzioni degli Stati del Vicino Oriente*, Roma 1931; Amos S. Peaslee, *Constitutions of Nations*, New Jersey (USA) 1950; B. Mirkine-Guetzevitch, *Le Costituzioni Europee*, Milano 1954; A. Zamora, *Digesto Constitutional Americano*, Buenos Aires 1958; D. G. Lavroff and G. Peiser, *Les Constitutions Africaines*, Paris 1963; M. Stramacci, *Le Costituzioni degli Stati Africani*, Milano 1963; P. Pavan, *Libertà Religiosa e Pubblici Poteri*, Milano 1965.

[44] Cf. IOANNES XXIII, Litt. Encycl. *Pacem in terris,* 11 aprilis 1963: *A.A.S.,* 55 (1963), pp. 295-296, ubi, quibusdam defectibus non obstantibus, commendatur Professio Universalis Iurium Humanorum, die 10 dec. 1948 a Foedaratarum Nationum Coetu Generali rata habita: « Nihilominus Professionem eandem habendam esse censemus quemdam quasi gradum atque aditum ad iuridicialem politicamque ordinationem constituendam omnium populorum, qui in mundo sunt. Siquidem ea universis prorsus hominibus solemniter agnoscitur humanae dignitas personae, atque iura cuivis homini asseruntur veritatem libere quaerendi, honestatis sequendi normas, iustitiae officia usurpandi, vitam exigendi homine dignam, alia deinceps cum hisce coniuncta ».

[44] Cf. John XXIII, Encyclical Letter *Pacem in terris*, 11 April 1963: AAS 55 (1963), 295-96, where, certain defects notwithstanding, the pope commends the Universal Declaration of Human Rights, ratified by the General Assembly of the United Nations on December 10, 1948: "Nevertheless, we think the document should be considered a step in the right direction, an approach toward the establishment of a juridical and political ordering of the world community. It is a solemn recognition of the personal dignity of every human being, an assertion of everyone's right to be free to seek out the truth, to follow moral principles, to discharge the duties imposed by justice, and to lead a fully human life. It also recognized other rights connected with these."

Freedom, Truth, and Human Dignity:
An Interpretation of *Dignitatis Humanae* on the
Right to Religious Freedom

David L. Schindler

Catholics are generally aware that a certain approach to the question of religious freedom leading up to the Second Vatican Council emphasized that truth alone had rights, and that error was at best to be tolerated.[1] Catholics are also generally aware that, after the early debates regarding religious freedom, the Council shifted its emphasis from the formal question of truth in its relation to conscience to the rights of the human person. While the vast majority of Council bishops affirmed this shift, it harbored an ambiguity that became the source of intense debate during the further process of redaction. The new approach, with its framing of the question of rights mainly in terms of the dignity of the person (hence *Dignitatis humanae,* the title or *"incipit"* of the final document), so far appeared to involve abstraction from considerations of truth — but in what sense? The Council bishops claimed, not that a person has a right to error as such, but rather that each person has, in relation to others in society and to the state, a *civil* right to exercise his religious freedom, even when he is wrong.

Over time, however, it became clear that the Council bishops did not agree regarding the foundations underpinning the right to religious freedom. Granted that this right is founded in the dignity of the human person, on what does the dignity of the human person itself finally rest, and how does one's conception of these foundations affect the nature of the right? Can one assert a civil right to religious freedom without thereby at least implicitly invoking some claim about the nature of the person, and so far the question of truth? And if rights are not tied in some significant sense to a claim of truth, what assurance can we have that the state will adjudicate justly in the case of conflicting claims of rights, thus avoiding arbitrary repression of one group's rights in favor of another's?

I argue in this interpretive essay that the prevalent readings of DH today, while rightly recognizing the Council's shift of emphasis away from the notion of truth formally considered to the notion of the person, fail for the most part to take note of the profound ways in which the issue of truth emerges once more, *precisely from within this new context centered in the person.* In other words, there are in point of fact not one but *two* significant conceptual shifts that occurred during the course of the conciliar debate. The first occurred in connection with the third draft of the document *(textus emendatus),* when the discussion moved away from the earlier focus on truth and conscience to a focus on the person as the subject of rights. But a second shift also occurred, notable especially in the fifth draft *(textus recognitus),* regarding the concern voiced by some of the Council bishops that the necessary "connection that exists between the obligation to seek the truth and religious freedom itself [had] not yet [i.e., in draft three or four] been made clear."[2] The significance of this second conceptual shift has been largely underestimated in most post-conciliar discussions, despite the fact that the concerns that lay behind the second shift are clearly reflected in the final text of the Declaration. In fact, the controversies regarding *Dignitatis humanae* and religious freedom that have beset the Church since the Council bear on just the issues raised in this second conceptual shift. It is the relationship between these two shifts of emphasis, which emerge especially with schemas 3 and 5, respectively, that I wish to focus upon in this essay.

Let me begin by framing the *status quaestionis* in terms of the following statement by Professor Nicholas Lobkowicz, which summarizes well the prevalent reading of DH on religious freedom:

> The extraordinary quality of the declaration *Dignitatis humanae* consists in the fact that it shifted the issue of religious freedom from the notion of truth to the notion of the rights of a human person. Although error may have no rights, a person has rights even when he or she is wrong. This is, of course, not a right before God; it is a right with respect to other people, the community and the State.[3]

In response to this statement, I would say, first, that the Council did indeed shift the focus of discussion regarding religious freedom from truth as the subject of rights to the person as subject. Second, the Council thus affirmed, not that error has rights, but that the person has rights even when he errs. Third, Professor Lobkowicz nevertheless states, apropos of this shift to the person, that this indicates a shift in "the issue of religious freedom from the notion of truth to the notion of the rights of a human person." This third part of Lobkowicz's statement can, I believe, be reasonably accepted as an accurate summary of the teaching of DH only when qualified further in light of the ambiguity noted above. It was in fact the recognition of this crucial ambiguity by the Council bishops that alone suffices to explain why, with the support of Paul VI, they introduced the changes that they did following schema 3, and why these changes were retained in the final document.

Jesuit Father Hermínio Rico's book *John Paul II and the Legacy of Dignitatis Humanae* helps sharpen the nature of the problem indicated here.[4] Rico poses the question whether, according to DH, human dignity stems finally from the freedom that is inherent in every person, a freedom that can be used well or not, or rather from "the person's relationship with transcendent truth" (142). Rico discusses the first view in terms of John Courtney Murray (and supporters of Murray such as Pietro Pavan), and in terms of what is understood to be the "juridical" approach of the Council bishops from America. He discusses the second view in terms of Karol Wojtyła/John Paul II, and in terms of what is understood to be the "ontological" approach characteristic of the French bishops, an approach reflected in the text from Bishop Ancel cited above. Rico defends the first of these views, arguing that the juridical approach installed in the third draft indicates the essential teaching of DH.[5] Indeed, he argues that Wojtyła's arguments at the Council, and later during his pontificate as John Paul II, while emphatically supportive of the principle of religious freedom, in fact misconstrued the terms of the problem as shaped by Murray's juridical approach, in their insistence on the essential relation of freedom to truth, as well as on the need for appealing to the sources of revelation (cf., e.g., Rico, 113). In this insistence, Rico argues, John Paul II threatened to undermine the genuine achievement of the Declaration in its affirmation of a *universal* right to religious freedom, a right that must continue to be upheld even when persons are in error.

Rico makes a useful contribution to the post-conciliar debate regarding the teaching of DH by drawing into clear relief the fact that, broadly speaking, there are two main approaches to the question of religious freedom — the juridical and the ontological — which emerged, respectively, around schema 3 and schema 5 of the Declaration. He is right as well to focus the discussion of his book above all on the figures of Murray and Wojtyła/John Paul II. As is well known, Murray was the "first scribe" of the crucial third schema.[6] Wojtyła/John Paul II, for his part, made several important interventions during the redactions of the document, supported the changes that were introduced in the later schemas and retained in the final document, and placed the problem of religious freedom and its relation to truth in the forefront of his concerns as pontiff.

Questions regarding what the Council really meant to affirm with respect to the right to religious freedom are thus necessarily linked with how one interprets the significance of the later redactions, especially the fifth and the final, relative to schema 3. As we will see, Murray argued that the changes introduced following schema 3 were not necessary on strictly theoretical grounds, and that the essence of the juridical approach was kept intact in the final text of DH. Indeed, he argued that the juridical approach, with its abstraction of freedom from truth, remains a necessary presupposition for reading the Declaration in a way that can sustain a truly universal right to religious freedom. Those bishops who insisted on the changes introduced in the later schemas argued, on the contrary, that such changes *were* theoretically necessary, and that the juridical approach, if it did not tie freedom in a more integrated way to man's natural relation to the transcendent order of truth, remained so far vulnerable to arbitrariness or abuse in the effort to protect human rights.

My purpose in this essay is to offer a judgment regarding the issue raised here. The argument has nine sections. Section I summarizes (1) Murray's understanding of the so-called juridical approach; (2) Wojtyła's interventions during the course of the redactions; and (3) the principal changes with respect to schema 3 that were introduced especially in schema 5 and that became part of the final Declaration. Section II sets forth Murray's two main criticisms of these changes. Sections III and IV respond to Murray's criticisms, defending the changes — which is to say, the final, officially received Declaration — in the face of these criticisms. The main or "constructive" part of my argument here will be to show the inner coherence of the Declaration. Section V returns to the opening articles of the Declaration in order to show how, in light of the foregoing, the right to religious freedom as a negative immunity is to be properly understood. Section VI shows the coherence of the Declaration in light of the teaching of John Paul II and Benedict XVI. Section VII summarizes the main elements of the preceding argument regarding the proper interpretation of the Declaration. Section VIII then addresses the *status quaestionis* of many important issues connected with the right to religious freedom. Finally, section IX concludes by returning to the central issue, namely, the relationship between freedom and truth and the nature and foundation of the right to religious freedom. This section situates the teaching of the Declaration within the debate regarding the historical emergence and nature of individual rights, as conceived respectively in the ancient-medieval and modern periods.

My intention, in sum, is to demonstrate that the Declaration did indeed center the Church's understanding of religious freedom and rights in the person, and did indeed develop more fully and explicitly her understanding of and commitment to the right to religious freedom. But I argue that the Declaration did so by way of *affirming the person within a new unity of freedom and truth before God.* This is the import of the officially received text of DH, when properly interpreted, especially in light of the changes made to the document in its final redactions. My contention is that it is only when we understand the Declaration's intention to defend the intrinsic unity of freedom and truth, or indeed the notion of the person as himself an integrated order of freedom and truth, that we are able, logically, to see the profound coherence of the doctrine of the right to religious freedom as developed in DH, on the one hand, and in light of the theological anthropology of *Gaudium et spes* and the Council more generally, on the other, as articulated especially in the pontificates of John Paul II and Benedict XVI.[7]

Let me emphasize at the outset: it is not the case that, with the conciliar affirmation of religious freedom, the Church has signaled a new awareness of the importance of freedom *in addition to,* or even *despite,* her traditional emphasis on truth. On the contrary, with this conciliar teaching, rightly understood, the Church rather signals a development in her understanding of the inherent unity of truth with freedom and freedom with truth. While still affirming that the *truth alone* frees, she now affirms at the same time, in a more explicit way, that truth itself presupposes freedom, and that truth *really does free.* My purpose is to demonstrate the sense in which this is so, and how this represents the heart of the teaching undergirding the Declaration's affirmation of the right to religious freedom.

I begin, then, with an overview of Murray and Wojtyła and the redaction process of DH.

I.

(1) *John Courtney Murray and the juridical approach.*[8] (i) According to Murray, the right to religious freedom as defined by *Dignitatis humanae* is "an immunity; its content is negative."[9] This is what is meant in calling religious freedom a "formally juridical concept" (MLH, 27). "The object of religious freedom as a juridical conception," in his words,

is not the actualization of the positive values inherent in religious belief, profession, and practice. These values, as values, are juridically irrelevant, however great their religious, moral, and social significance. The object of the right is simply the assured absence of constraints and restraints on individuals and groups in their efforts to pursue freely the positive values of religion. . . . This is good juridical philosophy. It is of the nature of a juridical formula — in this case, religious freedom — simply to set outside limits to a sphere of human activity, and to guarantee this sphere against forcible intrusion from without, but not to penetrate into the interior of this sphere and to pronounce moral or theological judgments of value on the activity itself. Such judgments exceed the category of the juridical, which is concerned with interpersonal relationships. They likewise exceed the competence of the forces of juridical order — the forces of law and of political authority. (MLH, 28-29)

Murray says that the first to launch such a conception of rights was the United States, and that "the object or content of the right to religious freedom, as specified both in the Declaration and in the American constitutional system, is identical."[10] We can recall here Murray's well-known reading of the First Amendment's religious clauses as "articles of peace," rather than "articles of faith." Articles of faith would express "certain ultimate beliefs, certain specifically sectarian tenets with regard to the nature of religion, religious truth, the church, faith, conscience, divine revelation, human freedom" — would imply, in short, an "ecclesiology" or "religious philosophy."[11] The constitutional order of the state, on the other hand, contains instead only "articles of peace" insofar as this order is understood to "have no religious content" and to "answer none of the eternal human questions with regard to the nature of truth and freedom or the manner in which the spiritual order of man's life is to be organized or not organized" (WHTT, 58). Thus, the juridical or "articles of peace" approach intends to abstract from, or to remain "negative" with respect to, the meaning of man in his transcendent relations to truth and to God, thereby remaining on the "horizontal plane" of man's relationships; while the articles of faith approach makes positive claims with respect to man's transcendent relations to truth and to God, thereby entering into the "vertical plane" of man's relationships.[12] Notice, however, that "negative" is not understood by Murray as a rejection of man's positive relationship to truth and to God, but only as an abstraction from this relationship for purposes of the exercise of civil authority.[13] In Murray's terms, in other words, "negative" implies only a legal-constitutional "indifference," not a substantive "indifferentism," with regard to man's relations to truth and to God.

The key, for Murray, in a word, is that the juridical formula of the First Amendment regarding the free exercise of religion is empty of any "ideology," and that this ideological emptiness is common to both DH and the American Constitution. In neither document does the juridical formula contain a "positive evaluation of the religious phenomenon in any of its manifestations" (DRF, 568).[14]

(ii) To this notion of the right to religious freedom as a negative immunity, Murray says, there corresponds "the constitutional concept of government as limited in its powers" (MLH, 36). This concept of limited government

> yields a more narrow criterion for legal limitation of the free exercise of religion, namely, the necessary exigencies of the public order. . . . Inherent, therefore, in the notion of religious freedom is the notion of government incompetence in matters religious. This latter notion, however, has to be exactly understood. The constitutional provision for religious freedom is a self-denying ordinance on the part of government. That is to say, government denies to itself the competence to be a judge of religious belief and action. But this denial is not an assertion of indifference to the values of religion to man and to society. Nor is it a reassertion of the outworn laicist creed that "religion is a purely private matter." It is simply a recognition of the limited functions of the juridical order of society as the legal armature of human rights.[15] (MLH, 36-37)

Regarding the notion of public order, then, which is essentially tied here to the concept of limited government, Murray says that, "after some hesitation and in spite of some opposition," the Council adopted this notion as its main criterion for the limitation of the right to religious freedom, rather than the traditional notion of the common good, because of the greater precision of the former (DRF, 575; cf. MLH, 34). In adopting the criterion of public order,[16] Murray argues, the Council moved away from the ethical concept of the purpose of political authority characteristic of Leo XIII, and toward the civil concept — the protection of civil rights — that, according to Murray, is more characteristic of Pius XII and John XXIII (MLH, 33).[17] The hallmark feature of this civil concept, "the theory of what we would call 'constitutional government,'" is "the tradition of a free man in a free society," which represents "the essence of the liberal tradition of the West" (RLDD

281). The central principle of this tradition, in Murray's view, is "the political principle of the free society: 'Let there be as much freedom as possible, and only as much restraint as necessary' " (DRF, 573).[18]

The function of government, then, in this conception — which, according to DH as interpreted by Murray, is limited to the securing of public order — becomes more properly "coercive" than "pedagogical" in nature. That is, in contrast with the ancient view of state authority, whose purpose was above all to promote the education and formation of citizen-subjects in and toward the human good, the view adopted by the Declaration, according to Murray, understands the function of the state to be one essentially of ensuring that citizens do not interfere with each other in an intrusive manner.[19]

(iii) Regarding the foundation for the right to religious freedom, Murray says that, in accord with the traditional conciliar custom, the doctrinal authority of the Declaration falls on *what* is affirmed, and not on the *reasons given for* that affirmation, and thus here "upon [DH's] affirmation of the human right to religious freedom, not on the arguments advanced in support of this affirmation" (DRF, 570). In Murray's judgment, the final Declaration leaves intact the juridical notion of rights as defined in schema 3, while it shifts the primary argument given regarding the ground for rights (DRF, 567, 570-71).

With respect to the nature of the foundation of the right to religious liberty as a civil right, then: Murray says first of all that it was necessary that the Declaration propose an argument regarding foundations, in order to demonstrate that "the affirmation was being made in principle" and not as a matter of expediency, that is, of concession to the contingent historical circumstance that the Church no longer exercises the hegemony that she once did in political societies (DRF, 570). Further, in this context, it was important for the Church to show that its argument differed from arguments tied to relativism or religious indifferentism or secularism.

But secondly, Murray says that it is nevertheless "not necessary to believe that the Conciliar argument is the best one that can be made" (DRF, 570). Murray then indicates what he believes is "a more cogent argument," one that he says "can be constructed from the principles of the Declaration itself, assembled into an organic structure." "The mark of man as a person," he says,

is his personal autonomy. Inseparable, however, from personal autonomy is personal responsibility. This is twofold. First, man is responsible for the conformity between the inner imperatives of his conscience and the transcendent order of truth. Second, man is responsible for the conformity between his external actions and the inner imperatives of conscience. . . . Man bears [these responsibilities] as a moral subject, as he confronts, so to speak, his vertical relationship to the transcendent order of truth. However, on the horizontal plane of intersubjective relationships, and within the social order, which is the order within which human rights are predicated, man's fulfillment of his personal responsibilities is juridically irrelevant. The major reason is that no authority exists within the juridical order that is capable or empowered to judge in this regard. . . .

What is juridically relevant, however, and relevant in the most fundamental sense, is the personal autonomy which is constituent of man's dignity. More exactly, resident in man's dignity is the exigence to act on his own initiative and on his own responsibility. This exigence is . . . simply the demand that man should act according to his nature. And this exigence is the basic ontological foundation, not only of the right to religious freedom, but of all man's fundamental rights. . . .[20] (DRF, 571-72)

Thus, "given the exigence of the person to act on his own initiative and responsibility," says Murray, "coercion appears as a thing of no value to the person." Hence "all . . . rights are immunities from coercion" (DRF, 572; cf. also 574-75).

There are two main points to be kept in mind with respect to this argument regarding the foundation for the right to religious freedom. (a) Murray clearly affirms man's responsibilities as a moral subject, in his "vertical relationship to the transcendent order of truth." But he emphasizes that *civil* rights essentially concern, not this vertical plane, but rather the "horizontal plane of intersubjective relationships"; and that they do so, not because man's responsibility to truth is not important, but because it *is*. The burden of a "negative" right, in other words, is solely to create the conditions necessary to enable the person's search for truth.

Now, anyone familiar with the work of Murray knows that the principle operative here is his well-known distinction between state and society. Murray affirms a natural law operative in man that binds and obligates man to a transcendent order of truth, ultimately to God.[21] But man's natural relation and obligation to this order of truth are the proper concern of the institutions of society, such as the family and the Church, *not* of government. The fact that this obligation is *juridically* irrelevant, in other words, does not, according to Murray, make it thereby irrelevant *to man and society as such.*[22] That is just the point of a juridical order conceived in terms of articles of peace: what is relevant in the juridical order is man's nature as exigent to act on his own initiative and responsibility, *not* as obligated to transcendent truth. Murray takes this clean distinction between the two orders, the juridical and the ontological-moral, to be necessary in order to affirm a universal right to religious freedom in a pluralistic society. That is, a civil right that would be truly universal in scope must so far, for Murray, not be tied intrinsically to any particular claim of truth.

In a word: to bring together the nature of freedom as exigent for initiating action and the nature of freedom as obliged to the transcendent order of truth is to unite what Murray insists on keeping apart, as what is, respectively, juridically relevant and juridically irrelevant. A *civil* sense of right must be disjoined from an *ontological-moral* sense of right. As we will see, it is precisely the question of how best to understand the distinction indicated here that drives Murray's criticism of the changes introduced in the later schemas, as well as the Council fathers' decision to make these changes in the first place.

(b) Murray suggests at the same time that how one conceives the foundations of the right to religious freedom is in any case not crucial for determining the nature — the proper object and content — of this right. According to Murray, that is, the "negative" sense of the right to religious freedom remains intact irrespective of whether its primary foundation is the autonomy of the person or the person's obligation to seek the truth. And yet, Murray's own argument would seem to affirm the interlocking, and thus far inseparable, character of the key elements of the juridical approach. Specifically, Murray emphasizes the primacy of the exigence to act on one's own initiative and responsibility *as the reason for* the primacy of a right understood as an immunity: given the primacy of this exigency, it follows that the first thing I demand is that other persons not act toward me in an intrusive manner. That is, according to the juridical approach, a right is first a freedom *from* someone or something, not a freedom *for*.[23] The emphasis on the primacy of the obligation to seek the truth about God and religion, on the contrary, seems to indicate the primacy of a positive relation to another, and thus the priority of freedom *for* another.

We will return to the issues noted here regarding the foundation and the nature of the right to religious freedom. But let us consider now the most important themes that emerge from the interventions voiced by Karol Wojtyła.

(2) *Karol Wojtyła.*[24] (i) First, Wojtyła objected to the purely "negative"

concept of religious freedom as an "immunity from coercion." Such a concept, he thought, lacked an adequate sense of the right to religious freedom as an *intrinsically positive good* owed to all persons.[25] Emphasizing religious freedom only in the negative terms of immunity leaves this right logically vulnerable to indifference in the matter of truth.[26] The "negative" concept abstracts the roots of human dignity from man's positive relationship to God.[27] The right to religious freedom thus has its origins in relation to, and is actually realized only through dependence upon, truth.[28] As Wojtyła put it in an early intervention, "Non datur libertas sine veritate" ("There is no freedom without truth": Intervention 2 [AS III/2, 531]).[29] Again, Wojtyła insisted that one cannot say "I am free" without saying at the same time that "I am responsible" to God and others. "This teaching has its foundation in the Church's living tradition of confessors and martyrs. Responsibility is, as it were, the culmination and the necessary complement of freedom. This should be stressed, so that our Declaration may be seen to be deeply personalistic in a Christian sense, yet not subject to liberalism or indifferentism" (Intervention 4 [AS IV/2, 12]).[30]

(ii) In the related matter of how the political limits to religious freedom are to be conceived, Wojtyła was critical of the statement in the third schema that religious freedom could legitimately be restricted "according to juridical norms determined by the requirements of public order *(secundum normas iuridicas, quae constituunter exigentiis ordinis publici)*" (a. 5b [AS III/8, 433]; cf. schema 4, a. 4b [AS IV/5, 151]). Wojtyła objected that the idea of the exigencies of public order, if not further qualified, could permit limits to the exercise of religious freedom that were *simply* grounded in positive law, and that were thus potentially unjust in light of the God-given nature of this right. According to Wojtyła, rather, "the right to religious freedom, as a natural right (that is, a right having its foundation in natural, and therefore in divine, law) admits of no limitations except on the part of this same moral law. Positive human law cannot impose any limits on this right, except in accord with the moral law. In other words: only a morally evil act, one that is contrary to the moral law, can be considered an abuse of religious freedom" (Intervention 4 [AS IV/2, 12-13]).[31] Juridical limits, in a word, need to be rooted in man's nature and thus include substantively ethical criteria. In light of this, Wojtyła argued, it was "particularly necessary to revise the statements found [in schema 4, a. 4b] on the juridical norm and its power to limit the use of religious freedom, which in many places still do not seem adequate, and which could in fact provide occasion for abuses against true religious freedom" (Intervention 4 [AS IV/2, 13]).

(iii) Wojtyła insisted that, in an ecclesial document on religious liberty, "it would not suffice simply to repeat what has already been said about religious freedom in the civil legislation of many nations, and in international declarations as well" (Intervention 4 [AS IV/2, 11]). The Council should of course take over what is true in those declarations; but at the same time it should make clear the sense in which the Christian teaching on religious liberty has its own distinctive origin and meaning in Scripture and the revelation of Jesus Christ: "The truth is that it is in what has been revealed, indeed in the very fact of revelation, that the true and profound teaching on religious freedom is contained. Men and women are becoming more conscious of this teaching, the more they acknowledge the dignity of the human person in theory and in practice" (Intervention 4 [AS IV/2, 11]).

In this context, Wojtyła thought it important to avoid a conciliar statement that would divide too neatly a doctrine of religious freedom accessible to reason from the richness of what was given in Christian revelation. Wojtyła was critical of earlier schemas of the Declaration on this point.[32] He proposed instead that

> the very concept of religious freedom found in the conciliar document *be presented in essence as a revealed teaching, one that is wholly consonant with sound reason, and yet not separated from it,* as we find in the text. The Council should teach the truth of God, not only the truth of man. If the former is evident to human reason as well, as we see in the contemporary state of affairs in regard to religious freedom, so much the better. Still, the world awaits the Church's teaching on this matter, the revealed teaching, and not simply the repetition of what it is itself already capable of, as we well know. (Intervention 5 [AS IV/2, 293], emphasis original)

Wojtyła's concern here was not that DH had to be tied to an exclusively theological approach, but only that an approach based on reason or philosophy must be conceived as intrinsically open to, and ultimately fulfilled only by, God's revelation in Jesus Christ.[33] Against those who see in religion "nothing more than the alienation of human reason," the Church must "present the human person with complete accuracy. . . . [He] must appear in the real grandeur of his rational nature, and religion must appear as this nature's crown and summit *(culmen)*" (Intervention 2 [AS III/2, 531]). Christian revelation, in other words, must be understood as the *fulfillment* of, and not merely as *an* (arbitrary) *addition to,* what is accessible to reason.

In a word, Wojtyła recognized that the Declaration's teaching regarding religious liberty needed to be accessible to both Christian believers and non-believers alike, but insisted that this must not be understood in a way that would attenuate the distinctive Christian exigence to transform the human person — in Wojtyła's words, to "elevate, animate, and sanctify" him — in his nature and as a subject of rights (Intervention 1 [AS III/3, 767]).

(3) *Redaction history*. Finally, let us note some of the key changes that were made to the Declaration following the third schema *(textus emendatus)*, especially in the fifth schema *(textus recognitus)*, and incorporated into the final authorized text *(textus denuo recognitus)*.[34]

(i) Relating its work to the aspirations of the human spirit, and to the growing awareness in our time of the dignity of the human person (DH, 1), the Declaration states that its purpose is to ponder all of this in light of "the sacred tradition and teaching of the Church." Its intention thus is to draw forth "new things that are always in harmony with the old," in order to "declare to what degree [these modern, human aspirations] are in conformity with truth and justice *(declarare quantum sint veritati et iustitiae conformes)*" (DH, 1).[35] The Declaration thus highlights the fact that the Church intends to take full account of the developments of the present age, genuinely listening to what has been said by other national and international bodies regarding the question of religious freedom, all the while integrating such developments in light of scriptural and doctrinal sources and her own proper ecclesial reality.[36]

(ii) Following this introduction, the Declaration states: "The sacred Council first professes that God himself has made known to mankind the way in which men are to serve him, and so be saved in Christ and come to blessedness," and "that this one true religion subsists in the Catholic and apostolic Church." Taking note of the Church's missionary task — "Go, therefore, and make disciples of all nations . . ." (Matt. 28:19-20) — the Declaration says that "[a]ll men and women are in fact bound to seek the truth, especially in those things concerning God and his Church, and to embrace and hold fast to it once it is known" (DH, 1). Having highlighted this duty, the Declaration stresses that the truth does not impose itself except "by the strength of truth itself," and then states: "since the religious freedom which men and women demand in order to fulfill their duty to worship God concerns immunity from coercion in civil society, it leaves intact the traditional Catholic teaching on the moral duty individuals and society have toward the true religion and the one Church of Christ" (DH, 1).

It is thus within the context of the obligation of all men to seek the truth, especially as it bears on God and the Church of Christ, that the question of religious liberty as an immunity from coercion is situated. This marks a shift from the structure of the third schema, in which the conception of religious freedom as it is "commonly understood today," above all as a juridical right to immunity, is treated at some length already in the first article of the document. In the third schema, the Council's assertion (in a. 3) concerning the "one true religion" which all men are bound to seek comes after its statement regarding freedom as a right to immunity (in a. 1: see AS III/8, 426-27, 429). Schema 4 retained the same structure. Here article 2, "The Declaration," begins with the statement: "This Vatican Council declares that the right to religious freedom has its foundation in the very dignity of the human person. . . . Such freedom consists in this, that men and women should be immune from coercion on the part of individuals, social groups or any human power." The article continues: "This Council also declares that this right must be acknowledged in the juridical order of society, so that it becomes a civil right," and then concludes: "Finally, this Council declares that it does not follow from this affirmation of religious freedom that man has no obligations in religious matters. . . . The principle of religious freedom thus leaves intact the Catholic teaching on the one true religion and the one Church of Christ" (AS IV/1, 146-48). In schema 5 the order of these statements was reversed, so that the Declaration begins with reference to the truth of the Catholic faith, and with man's corresponding obligation to seek the truth in freedom (AS IV/5, 77-78).

It was likewise in the fifth schema that the following paragraph, on the relationship between truth and freedom, was introduced, in article 2. This paragraph, drawing substantially on the intervention of Bishop Ancel referred to above, was retained in the final Declaration:

> It is in accord with their dignity that all men and women, because they are persons, endowed with reason and free will and therefore privileged with personal responsibility, are impelled by their nature and bound by a moral obligation to seek the truth, especially the truth concerning religion. They are also bound to hold fast to the truth once it is known, and to order their whole life in accord with its demands. They cannot satisfy this obligation in a way that is in keeping with their own nature, however, unless they enjoy psychological freedom as well as immunity from external coercion. Nevertheless, religious freedom does not have its foundation in a subjective disposition, but in the very nature of the human person. Consequently, the right to immunity persists even for those who do not satisfy their obligation to seek the truth and to hold

fast to it, provided that legitimate public order is preserved, and that the rights of others are not violated. (AS IV/5, 79)[37]

(iii) Regarding the foundation for the right to religious freedom: affirming with schema 3 that this right consists in immunity from coercion, and likewise that the right derives from the dignity of the human person as endowed with reason and free will, DH, 2 nevertheless links this dignity with men's natural movement *(sua ipsorum natura impelluntur)* and moral obligation to "seek the truth, especially the truth concerning religion," and to "order their whole life in accord with its demands," once it is known. Men cannot satisfy this obligation in keeping with their nature unless they have psychological freedom and are immune from coercion. Because the right to religious freedom is thus founded in the very nature of man *(in ipsa eius natura),* the right is objective and not merely subjective: it is retained by every person regardless of whether he or she lives up to the obligation, "provided that just public order is preserved" (DH, 2). Article 3 adds that "[t]his is clearer when one considers that the highest norm of human life is the divine law, eternal, objective, and universal, by which God, in the providence of his wisdom and love, orders, directs, and governs the whole world and the ways of the human community. God grants man a share in this law, so that man, under the gentle direction of divine providence, can acknowledge more and more the truth that is itself unchanging."

Article 3 then insists, in light of the above, that "each person has the duty, *and therefore* the right *(officium ideoque et ius),* to seek the truth in religious matters" (emphasis added).[38] Given man's social nature, this search for truth must include the right to free inquiry, along with instruction, dialogue, and the like, as well as the right to external expression of man's interior religious acts (DH, 4). Protection of this right is warranted "when just public order is preserved" (DH, 3).

(iv) The term *"just* public order *(iustus ordo publicus)"* is used in articles 2 and 3 of the Declaration, and is an addition made following the third schema. As indicated in our discussion of Wojtyła, the notion of "public order" alone, found in schema 3, articles 4d, 4e, and 5b without further qualification (AS III/8, 432-33), was seen by many Council bishops to be vulnerable to possible abuse by government authorities. This phrase was gradually qualified in the following schemas. In schema 4, the term *legitimus* was introduced in article 6: "Religious communities also have the right not to be prevented from publicly teaching about or witnessing to their faith in speech or in writing, provided they do not violate the legitimate requirements of public order *(legitimis exigentiis ordinis publici)"* (AS IV/1, 153). In schema 5, the term "public order" was more regularly qualified: "provided that legitimate public order is preserved" (a. 2); "when true public order is preserved *(vero ordine publico servato)"* (a. 3); "the legitimate requirements of public order" (a. 4) (AS IV/5, 79, 81, 82). In article 7, moreover, schema 5 says that it pertains to the public power to "afford protection" to civil society "not in an arbitrary fashion . . . but according to juridical norms that are required by the needs of a public order grounded in the objective moral order" (AS IV/5, 85). Finally, in the Declaration itself, public order is consistently qualified with the adjective "just" *(iustus):* "provided that just public order is preserved" (DH, 2), "when just public order is preserved" (DH, 3), "provided they do not violate the just requirements of public order" (DH, 4). In DH, 7 the reference to the demands or needs of public order is dropped. The document states that the public power should provide protection "according to juridical norms that conform to the objective moral order." These qualifiers indicate that the Council bishops recognized that the purely juridical idea of public order needs an explicitly ethical component and so far some intrinsic link to the idea of a positive *good.*[39]

(v) Article 3 of the final text retains reference to the fact that "religious acts, in which men and women privately and publicly order themselves toward God out of a sense of inner conviction, by their nature transcend the earthly and temporal order of things," and that, consequently, control or restriction of such acts exceeds the limits of civil authority.[40] But DH, 3 also eliminates the passage in schema 3, article 4e (AS III/8, 432) (slightly modified and amplified in schema 4, article 3 [AS IV/1, 150]), which frames this restriction in terms of the language of the competence *(competentia)* of civil authority. This competence was understood by Murray to mean that the civil authority's law-giving power excludes caring for souls in any way, and has the essentially negative function of not impeding religious communities from performing their proper tasks of teaching and the like.[41] Article 3 of the Declaration says instead that "[t]he civil power *(potestas civilis)* . . . whose proper end is the care of the temporal common good, should in fact acknowledge and show favor to the religious life of its citizens *(religiosam quidem civium vitam agnoscere eique favere debet)."*[42]

Thus schema 3 and the Declaration in its final form both affirm the transcendence of religious activity vis-à-vis the power of civil government. Schema 3, however, expresses this transcendence in terms of the competence of the state and the state's negative limits where matters of religion are concerned. The final text of the Declaration, in contrast, avoids the language regarding the (negative) competence of the government in matters of religion, and so far also avoids the formal terms of the question regarding the limits of the concerns proper to the state as distinct from religion and the Church. At the same time, the Declaration affirms some principled sense, not precisely defined, of the *government's (potestas civilis),* and not merely of *society's, positive responsibility* to acknowledge and look with favor on the religious life of the citizens.[43] The final document also drops the sentence from the third schema that had affirmed that the "public power completely exceeds its limits if it involves itself in any way *(quovis modo)* in the governing of minds or the care of souls *(in regimen animorum aut in curam animarum)*" (schema 3, a. 4e [AS III/8, 432]).

(vi) Schema 3 had included a long discussion at the beginning of the document on how the historical conditions in which the question of religious freedom is to be framed have changed. Referring to the nineteenth century and the ideology of laicism, with its idea of the absolute autonomy of individual human reason, article 2 of the third schema calls attention to the relativism and indifferentism cloaked within the idea of religious freedom that derives from reason so conceived. However, according to this same article, "it is more clearly affirmed today that the chief function of the public power consists in protecting, nurturing, and defending the natural rights of all citizens" (AS III/8, 429). In other words, according to schema 3, "[i]n the course of history . . . a new kind of question has arisen in regard to religious freedom. For religious freedom today is concerned with observing and upholding the dignity of the human person, and thus with effectively protecting his rights, the first of which is man's right to be free from coercion in religious matters, especially on the part of the public power" (a. 2 [AS III/8, 429]). Schema 3 had thus clearly intended to situate the Council's treatment of the problem of religious liberty within the historical context set by what Murray characteristically referred to as the differences between French or Continental democracy, on the one hand, and Anglo-American constitutional democracy, on the other.[44]

As pointed out in (i) above, the Council bishops certainly understood themselves to be taking account of modern historical developments with respect to human dignity and rights; nonetheless, they eliminated from the final document this long passage from article 2 of the third schema that implied a specific judgment on the different historical approaches to religious freedom and rights in the nineteenth century.

(vii) In schema 4, the Council bishops incorporated a statement pertinent to the question of whether the juridical order of a state may legitimately grant special civil recognition to one particular religious community. This statement was slightly modified in schema 5, and retained in the final document: "If, in light of a people's particular circumstances, special civil recognition is granted to one religious community in the juridical order of the state, it is necessary at the same time that the right to freedom in religious matters be acknowledged and observed for all citizens and religious communities" (DH, 6). The Declaration is thus clear that it is in principle legitimate for a government to privilege a specific religious community in its civil order, provided this government at the same time protects the right to freedom in religious matters on the part of all citizens and of other religious communities.[45]

Needless to say, these seven comments regarding changes that were made in the later drafts and incorporated into the Declaration demand further qualification, and we will therefore have to return to them. Suffice it to say that the changes revolve most basically around the question of the foundation for the right to religious freedom: of how best to conceive the human dignity that grounds such a right, from the perspective of political order. The changes suggest, each in its own way, that this right must be founded on a human dignity intrinsically linked with a transcendent relation and obligation to truth, especially religious truth. This truth is understood to be reasonable and thus accessible in principle to all, Christian believers or not; but it is nevertheless also understood to find its full and proper meaning only in the light of the revelation of Jesus Christ as carried in the sacramental tradition of the Catholic and Apostolic Church.

We will return at a later point to this question of the foundation of the right to religious freedom, and of how the resolution of this question affects the nature of this right. But first we need to consider Murray's criticisms of the changes made in the later redactions of DH indicated here.[46]

II.

Murray's main criticisms can be anticipated from his positive argument as set forth above. He believed, first, that the changes made were unnecessary, and, second, that they risked undermining a principled commitment to the right to religious freedom. He nevertheless insisted that, despite these changes, the "new doctrinal line" that had been adopted in the third schema "remained substantially the same" through the subsequent revisions and was "the line of the definitive declaration, promulgated on December 7, 1965" (MLH, 16). I will first address Murray's two criticisms (in sections III and IV), then assess (in section V) his overarching claim that the definitive declaration essentially sustained the juridical line instituted in schema 3.

Regarding the criticisms, then: Murray first highlights his puzzlement over "the prominence given [in the final document] to man's moral obligation to search for the truth, as somehow the ultimate foundation of the right to religious freedom" (DRF, 570). In the same vein, he questions the statements of DH regarding the responsibility of government to foster the religious life of the people, asserting that the right to religious freedom is "simply an immunity," and that he doesn't know "how you can promote an immunity — making someone more and more immune. This just doesn't make any sense" (DRF, 580).

The source of Murray's puzzlement is clear: the changes, according to him, manifest the Council bishops' failure to appropriate fully the distinction between the Continental-laicist and American liberal traditions. As Murray understands it, while the Continental idea of freedom and rights embodies an ideological or indifferentist and consequently relativist stance vis-à-vis religion, the American idea implies a merely institutional-juridical "indifference" that encourages debate regarding truth, including religious truth, on the part of members of civil society. The American liberal state professes an incompetence in religious matters that implies not secularism, but rather a legitimate secularity whose purpose is to create the free space within society where religion has the possibility to flourish.[47] According to Murray, the Declaration's statements regarding the obligation to truth and the need for the state to foster religion were thus warranted, not on strictly doctrinal grounds, but for a pastoral reason that in fact reflected a mistaken historical judgment. For Murray, this fear of relativism expressed by some of the Council bishops has no theoretical basis, provided one rightly understands that the juridical approach's indifference to truth is only political or methodological, not substantive or ontological. The government's abstraction from truth, rightly-juridically conceived, is for the purpose of creating the free conditions necessary for pursuing the truth. The Council fathers who insisted on the changes in the later drafts missed this distinction, and therefore unnecessarily burdened the final conciliar text with concerns regarding truth.[48]

But this first criticism by Murray is tied to a second: linking the right to religious freedom to the duty to seek the truth fails to yield the necessary political conclusion of a principled universal commitment to this right. Murray suggests that making such a link to truth leads to problematic tendencies that were evidenced in both contemporary Communist and at least some

Catholic governments: namely, "that they already have the truth; that they represent the truth, which is also the good of the people; that, consequently, they are empowered to repress public manifestations of error" (DRF, 571).[49] If freedom is meant for truth, in other words, and if the government is in possession of the truth, then by imposing such truth, the government can be said merely to be assisting freedom to realize its own intrinsic finality. According to Murray, then, binding freedom with truth in the political order leaves the exercise of freedom logically vulnerable to a premature or arbitrary restriction by the government.

Thus Murray's criticisms, in sum: on the one hand, the changes incorporated into the final Declaration assume that the juridical approach, if left unqualified, is logically vulnerable to relativism. But this follows, according to Murray, only if one confuses the history of (Anglo-American) juridical liberalism with the history of (French-Continental) ideological liberalism. At the same time, attaching religious freedom to the duty to seek the truth undermines a consistent commitment to a universal right to religious freedom. That is, a government that takes itself to be responsible in a privileged way for the realization of truth in society will be so far prone to repress groups or persons who are in error, in order to ensure these persons' appropriation of the truth toward which their freedom is in any case already obligated.

The French bishops and many others like Wojtyła who insisted on the changes made were, on the contrary, convinced that joining freedom and rights to the obligation to seek the truth was necessary in order to avoid relativism; and they judged the juridical approach to be problematic on properly philosophical and theological, and not merely (mistaken) historical-pastoral, grounds. Indeed, they were convinced that it is *only in the recognition by government that freedom is intrinsically tied to truth* that the right to religious freedom can be sustained permanently and as a matter of principle for all human beings, whether they are believers or nonbelievers. The Declaration that was approved by the vast majority of the Council bishops, and officially received by the Church, incorporated these changes.

My intention in the remainder of this essay is to defend the inherent reasonableness of this received text of DH in light of the Church's philosophical-theological tradition and in the face of Murray's criticisms. The questions to be answered in this regard are three: First, does a (would-be) purely juridical approach to religious freedom logically entail substantive indifferentism or "neutralism," hence relativism (section III)? Second, does linking freedom with truth yield an enduring, principled commitment to a universal civil right to religious freedom? That is, can a universal right be consistently upheld if we affirm that it is the truth that frees — indeed, that truth alone frees — even-also within the jurisdiction of the legal-constitutional order (section IV)?

Having addressed these two questions, I will then return in section V to the third, overarching question of this essay: Is it the case that, notwithstanding the shift in the conception of the *foundations* for the right to religious freedom in the fifth and final schemas, the juridical understanding of the content of this right still remains essentially intact, as Murray argues? In other words, does the Declaration's conception of the foundation of human dignity — which indeed recognizes the exigence to act on one's own initiative and responsibility, but *only as related to transcendent truth and the obligation to seek this truth* — leave unaffected the primacy accorded by the juridical approach to the negative sense of the right to religious freedom as an immunity? Put more simply, what does the Declaration mean to affirm, in the end, regarding the nature of this right?

III.

In response to Murray's first criticism, then, I will begin (1) by recalling the historical discussion of freedom provided by the late Dominican scholar Father Servais Pinckaers, in order (2) to consider how what Fr. Pinckaers describes as "freedom of indifference," with its relativist consequences, is implicit in the juridical approach to freedom and rights. I will then (3) look at a common objection to this charge of relativism, that the avoidance of relativism is a task that devolves upon society and not the state, before (4) returning to the changes made by the Council bishops and to Murray's criticism that these changes were not theoretically necessary.

(1) In his important book, *The Sources of Christian Ethics,* Pinckaers distinguishes between what he calls "freedom of indifference," on the one hand, and "freedom of excellence" or "freedom of quality" *(liberté de qualité),* on the other.[50] The former expresses the teaching of the nominalists, but is reflected also in a certain stream of modern Scholasticism; the latter expresses the authentic teaching of St. Thomas Aquinas. According to Pinckaers, freedom of indifference is "the most widespread concept of [freedom] today," that which "fills the horizon of [contemporary] thought and experience" — so much so that the alternative view of freedom, freedom of excellence, which prevailed in the patristic and great Scholastic periods, now "necessitates a process of veritable rediscovery" (330).

For St. Thomas and his freedom of excellence, inclinations toward truth and the good, and indeed a desire for a happiness founded in God (335), indicate "the deepest source of that spontaneity which shapes our willing, a primitive élan and attraction that carries us toward the good and empowers us to choose" (402). Such inclinations form the "core of freedom" (332), ordering the human exercise of self-determination from its roots.[51]

The first and decisive point of difference, then, between the modern view and that of St. Thomas, according to Pinckaers, lies in the "breach between freedom and the natural inclinations, which were rejected from the essential core of freedom" (332; cf. 402). The nominalists, and not a few scholastics after them, "exclude[d] natural inclinations from the free act," making these inclinations themselves "subject to choice"; they thereby rendered freedom originally "indifferent" with respect to such inclinations (375), and so far "'indifferent' to nature" itself (333).[52] Freedom on this understanding "has no need . . . of finality, which becomes [merely] one circumstance of actions" (375): "The end was no longer an essential part of the action; it became circumstantial, qualifying it from the outside" (337).[53]

Second, freedom of indifference is understood as "the power to choose between contraries" (375). "[T]he human person's basic dignity lies in the power to act at any given moment in the way he chooses" (338).

Third, the primitive passion underneath freedom of indifference is "the human will to self-affirmation" (338). Freedom is "identified with the will, as the origin of willing and acting, as a power of self-determination" (332).[54] Such a power "corresponds to the Father, for his is the most powerful of acts and it is primary, not being moved, but moving" (331, citing St. Bonaventure). In this view, the "essential note of personality is independence" (337).

Fourth, freedom of indifference insists on the need to take first a negative stand, having as its formula: "against the positive and for the negative." This involves an autonomy that entails "rejection of all dependence" (339), forcing a primitive choice between "my freedom or the freedom of others. The freedom of others appear[s] as a limitation and a threat, since . . . freedom [is] self-affirmation in the face of all others" (350-51). "Freedom is locked within self-assertion, causing . . . the individual to be separated from other freedoms" (375).

Fifth, the will is "no longer defined as an attraction toward the good, exercised in love and desire, as in St. Thomas and the Fathers" (332). Freedom, furthermore, has no need to grow in virtue. Increase or decrease in freedom is a matter, not of interior growth, but simply of the reduction or expansion of exterior limitations (337).

In light of our concern with religious freedom, we may summarize the fundamental problems regarding freedom of indifference as follows. First, the natural inclinations to truth and the good and to God become what Pinckaers calls "objects of circumstance," and thus matters of a choosing that is contingent and arbitrary because empty of any original or natural information by truth and goodness. Here is the root of the relativism to which, according to Pinckaers, freedom of indifference logically leads.

Second, on this account freedom is a power that moves before it is moved, or again a power of self-determination that recognizes no anterior dependence. It is, so to speak, a more originally spontaneous (*sponte,* of one's own self or will) than originally re-sponsive power.

Third, freedom of indifference emphasizes the individual's autonomy, such that the freedom of others is viewed first as a potential limit upon, or as an intrusive threat to, one's own freedom. One's own freedom becomes set, at the most primitive level, in potential competition with that of others. The movement of freedom in the first instance abstracts from (and so far treats as absent), rather than affirms (and so far accepts as already present), the naturally given order of relations to God and others and to truth and the good that bind freedom in love, from within freedom's own deepest élan.

Each of these three problematic features stems from a common failure to grasp what is entailed by the fact that inclinations to the true and the good, and the desire for a happiness that is founded in God, are naturally constituent of the person, and so are "*the deepest source* of that spontaneity which *shapes* our willing" and which "*engenders* all our choices" (402, 353, emphasis added).

In all of the above ways, freedom of indifference stands in contrast with freedom of excellence or of quality, which *already within its reflexivity as a free act* is an *ordered relation* to the true and the good and God. Freedom of excellence is an *act of choice* only as initially integrated into this *naturally given order.* Such freedom is thus a matter of self-determination only as itself always already "determined" or bound in love; spontaneous *(sponte)* only as re-sponsive; and in-dependent only as a dependent participant. Finally, freedom of quality is a positive act before it is negative: at its deepest level it cannot but begin by affirming (however implicitly) the dynamic relation to another — to a truth and a good rooted in God — within which it originally discovers itself.[55]

(2) My contention is that what is described by Fr. Pinckaers as freedom of indifference is (unintentionally) presupposed in the juridical ap-

proach to freedom and rights defended by Murray. To be sure, Murray insists that the articles of peace proper to the constitutional order are to be undergirded by substantive articles of faith generated by members of civil society. It is this restriction of the constitutional order to "articles of peace," however — to freedom *from* — that marks the problem in the juridical approach. This latter approach is established as juridical, in other words, precisely by its exclusion of articles of faith, or by its abstraction of man's exigence for acting on his own initiative and responsibility from the order to transcendental truth, for all purposes of the administration of legal power. But it is just this abstraction of freedom from the order of truth — which abstraction renders truth so far extrinsic to freedom — that, according to Pinckaers, transforms freedom into freedom of indifference. Hence the main premise of my argument regarding Murray's first criticism: the fact that the initial abstraction of freedom from its ordering in and toward truth is intended exclusively for legal-political purposes does not mean that freedom of indifference is thereby avoided; *it means merely that it is freedom of indifference alone* (as distinct from freedom of quality) *that is privileged for legal-political purposes.*

Recalling Pinckaers's description, then, we can indicate the metaphysical features of human being and action that are logically, if unintentionally, privileged in Murray's conception of juridical order: freedom as the power to choose between contraries *(est ad opposita)*; the will as first moving, not moved, as "sponsive," not re-sponsive; freedom as a matter most primitively of potential intrusiveness and competition between individuals — freedom thus as first a "negative" act relative to the non-self; freedom as an act ordered in the first instance not by love or desire but by external, hence "coercive," constraints; finally and most comprehensively, a human act whose ends are no longer natural but circumstantial — an idea of the human act, that is, which is rightly seen as open to relativism.

Murray's abstraction of freedom from truth and God thus does not leave the juridical order empty of a definite idea of the nature of freedom, of some implicit articles of faith regarding the nature of freedom vis-à-vis truth and God. The juridical approach implies, not *no* claim of truth about the nature of freedom, but rather a definite ("substantive") claim on behalf of freedom of indifference. This originally indifferent sense of freedom reconfigures the primitive nature of both freedom and truth, and thus bears the same range of metaphysical implications as freedom of excellence, only different ones. The entire order of transcendent truth and good and the dynamic relation to God that on St. Thomas's understanding are *naturally given at the core of freedom* now become *contingent objects of choice,* for all purposes of the enforcement of civil law.[56]

Again, let us be clear: although claims of truth about the nature of the good and of religion are considered irrelevant with respect to the legal power of the *state,* a properly understood juridical approach at the same time encourages individuals and groups *in society* to develop and defend just such claims. The problem, however, is that the juridical state, insofar as it would act consistent with its own inner logic, must always treat such natural claims, *for all legal-constitutional purposes,* as contingent objects of choice. However much these truth-claims might be proposed by individual citizens or groups as natural to man, such claims can logically be considered by the state only as arbitrary additions to the free-intelligent human act, insofar as the latter is subject to the constitutional authority of the state. Truth-claims made by members of *society* regarding what they take to be *natural to man* will, *eo ipso,* be (mis-)represented by the *state* as *simple objects of choice.* Rights claims defended in the name of juridically conceived legal power, in a word, can and will be evaluated only as competing exercises of arbitrary choice. We arrive thus at (procedural) relativism.

Now, in its conventional usage, relativism signals the absence of any normative standards or claims to truth rooted in nature. The term thus calls attention to the arbitrariness of such claims in the way just indicated. But notice the paradox implied here. The relativism implicit in the juridical approach is in fact driven by freedom of indifference; and freedom of indifference, as we have seen, despite its vaunted purely formal character, its apparent *a priori* emptiness of any metaphysical claim of truth, hiddenly expresses a *single* or *unitary claim* regarding the *nature* of the human act. The work of Pinckaers makes this clear: the abstraction of truth and of the desire for God from the original sense of freedom leaves us, not with no metaphysics of freedom, but only with the alternative metaphysics of freedom of indifference. As we have seen, Murray himself in fact understands the exigence for exercising initiative as *that aspect of man's nature* that alone is pertinent to human dignity in the latter's grounding of the civil right to religious freedom.

The point, then, is that the apparently arbitrary character of the juridical state in the face of any given claim of rights masks what is always in advance a monolithic (a single: *monos,* and stone-like, hence rigid: *lithos*) claim on behalf of the truth of freedom of indifference. The would-be formlessness characteristic of relativism is a *metaphysical* formlessness: relativism hiddenly embodies the *paradoxically "substantive" formlessness of freedom of indifference.* The consequence is twofold: on the one hand, the articles of peace that supposedly characterize the juridical approach *do not exist and cannot exist as such.* Such articles of peace, of their (masked) inner logic, express the metaphysical articles of faith summed up in freedom of indifference. But this is just to say, on the other hand, that the *fiction* of articles of peace implies the *reality* of articles of faith, which, expressing freedom of indifference, so far (hiddenly) dictate relativism — or better, a relativistic monism.

Recognition that this is so is crucial, because it removes in advance what is typically the trump card played in the debates regarding the juridical approach: namely, that this approach alone can succeed in rendering justice in principle to *all* groups in society, with their variant claims of truth, because, unlike all non-liberal approaches to constitutional order, it avoids the question of *any* truth about man. The nature of the debate changes, however, when we recognize the simple but crucial fact that the would-be purely juridical approach to government and civil-human rights is as fraught with a metaphysics of human being and action as any other approach to government and civil-human rights, except that the juridical approach tends of its essence to hide this fact.

Consider the core implications of this paradoxically monolithic vision of relativism for the problem of rights. Civil rights are meant to apply to every person, regardless of his or her peculiar claims of truth about the good or about God and religion. Given the negative-juridical approach, however, these rights will be attached to all persons *only qua original agents,* or *original choosers,* as distinct from *original-natural receivers of,* or *participants in,* truth. Here is the neuralgic point: for purposes of the exercise of legal-constitutional authority, each person's claim of rights will be evaluated in terms of a freedom in regard to which the truth and the good are understood to be first enacted or constructed, as distinct from naturally given.[57] For the purposes of the defense of juridically protected rights, freedom will be assumed to be voluntaristic in nature; intelligence to be a matter most basically of technical skill and strategic management exercised in the service of claims that are not inherently reasonable but arbitrary; and religious truth to be a function of positivistic election. Natural communities such as the family, and any religious communities that understand themselves to be rooted in naturally given relations to God, will be treated by the juridical state as essentially voluntary communities. The maximum openness to all worldviews assumed by the juridical approach to rights, by virtue of which this approach claims to be uniquely able to accommodate the pluralism of modern societies, is thus an illusion. This illusory openness masks, and so far hiddenly imposes, a monism that transforms all would-be diverse claims of truth into surface manifestations of a single claim of truth: one that at root always, even if unwittingly, regards its content as contingently elected by way of an originally indifferent free-intelligent human act.[58]

In a word, the (would-be purely) juridical approach to government hiddenly, if unintentionally, imposes *a priori* a thoroughgoing logic of repression with respect to all those human beings who would tie their rights claims to naturally given relations to the truth and the good and the Creator. Civil rights are logically restricted to nominalistically conceived individuals demanding protection of their liberty from intrusion by other such individuals; which is to say, such rights are granted only to those citizens who are willing to make the case for their civil liberty in such nominalistic terms, or who will have their case rendered in such terms regardless.[59]

(3) In the face of the typical rejoinder of the juridical approach, that its state-society distinction provides the necessary principle for resisting such relativism, there are two possible responses. (i) On the one hand, one can continue to insist that a robust civil society which permits and indeed encourages each group to make its best case for truth and religion provides all that is necessary for resisting relativism. The problem of relativism, in other words, on this view, stems not from the *de jure* logic of the juridical approach but only from the *de facto* failure of citizen groups themselves to make their case adequately.

Such a response, however, misses the subtle but crucial core of the foregoing argument. Let us imagine, for example, that a liberal society inherited a given set of assumptions regarding the human person and human dignity: regarding the worth of embryonic life, the gender distinction, marriage and family, the reality and cultural implications of God as Creator and Redeemer, and the like. Suppose a majority of citizens takes such assumptions to be natural to man, to be structured into the human creature by virtue of the act of creation, and thus to be somehow always already a *given* for him. As long as a majority of citizens holds such a set of assumptions consciously or unconsciously, there would appear to be no principled reason why a liberal society would drift toward relativism. But here is the problem: the juridical approach, which is the hallmark of the liberal state brought into being by a liberal society, remakes any and all possible natural truths about man before God into voluntary claims. In this way, it (hiddenly) builds freedom of indifference into the law, such that this freedom becomes the single truth in and through which all other truths claimed in society have their legal-juridical relevance.

Insofar as any of the basic natural assumptions noted above become subject to the jurisdiction of legal-constitutional authority, then, they are recast, *eo ipso*, in terms of a civil unity ordered around freedom of indifference. Efforts by citizens to have or keep such truths enshrined in law will be subject to the dynamic of a homogenizing logic that remakes the content of such truths into objects of (arbitrary) choice, when and insofar as these truths become disputed in society and juridical protection is sought for those who hold them. Citizens may indeed retain the legal right to hold such truths, but the truths themselves have relevance to the legal order only as matters of "opinion," not as naturally true and inherently reasonable; only as matters, thus, that are to be adjudicated exclusively on the basis of a justice conceived as formal fairness between various competing individual interests. Different claims of truth will and can be adjudicated only in terms of competing exercises of freedom of indifference, under the logic of proceduralism that such indifference implies. Here, then, is where would-be robust debate in a liberal society that is informed by the juridical approach to government will, and logically must, given enough time, come to an end: in a civil society that characteristically invites debate even as it is always already hiddenly "dictating" a unity enforced juridically in terms of a relativistic monism.

Thus, in the name of maintaining a clear distinction between society and state, by inviting debate regarding all possible claims of truth about the nature of the human being and his freedom, the juridical state in fact absorbs society, for all of the state's legal-political purposes, into the single truth of freedom of indifference that defines the juridical state. The truth of this argument is verified historically, in that there exists no liberal society today whose legal-constitutional order has not over time evolved in just this direction of relativistic monism, with respect to the anthropological-ontological claims noted above regarding the nature and dignity of the human being.[60]

(ii) On the other hand, then, there is the response of those who recognize that robust debate in a liberal civil society, and so a principled freedom to conduct one's own search for the truth and to present the fruit of this search to others, is logically impossible over the long term insofar as such a society organizes itself constitutionally in terms of the juridical approach. This response recognizes in at least some implicit way that defenders of the juridical approach, by abstracting freedom from truth for legal purposes, do not succeed thereby in avoiding a claim of truth about freedom or indeed about the nature of the truth itself. Such a response recognizes that this abstraction of freedom from truth makes truth extrinsic to freedom: truth becomes a simple object of freedom rather than a natural end providing freedom with its original order *as* freedom. What those who follow this second response see, in a word, is that the juridical approach's reading of the state-society distinction rests upon and is mediated by freedom of indifference, and thus by a freedom conceived so far to be related first extrinsically and not intrinsically to truth. But it is just this extrinsicist conception of the relation between freedom and truth that evacuates in advance any genuine search for truth and, *a fortiori,* drains societal debates regarding the truth, especially about religion, of any real rational vigor.

(4) My contention is that it was the Council bishops' grasp of the link between an extrinsically conceived relation between freedom and truth, on the one hand, and the logic of relativism, on the other, that prompted the main qualifiers with respect to the juridical approach that these bishops incorporated into the final Declaration. Note that this does not mean that the bishops rejected the distinction between society and state; it means only that this distinction needed to be (re-)conceived in terms of an intrinsic relation between freedom and truth. Indeed, the bishops recognized that the society-state distinction could be rightly sustained *only* on the basis of this intrinsic relation, such that freedom and truth each require the other for their own integrity.

Now, in making this claim, I do not mean to suggest that the Council bishops developed a fully articulated theory with respect to the problems attendant upon the juridical approach and the relation between freedom and truth presupposed therein. I have only wished to show, drawing on the Church's tradition of thought regarding freedom as articulated by Pinckaers, that there is abundant justification for what was the intuitive conviction of a majority of the Council fathers: that the would-be merely "institutional indifference" claimed by the juridical approach is as a matter of its inmost logic a *metaphysical* and not merely "methodological" indifference, and thus what is properly termed "indifferentism" or "neutralism." That is why the majority of the Council fathers, including Wojtyła, judged it reasonable and important to tie the Declaration's argument regarding the civil right to religious liberty to a more explicit anthropological and theological framework: to the human person's obligation to seek the truth about God, and to the indissoluble relation between freedom and truth. There is, in a word, objective warrant for the anthropological revisions that the Council bishops, by a vast majority, approved for inclusion in the final Declaration.

The burden of my argument with respect to Murray's first criticism, then, is that the juridical approach he proposes lands him in a fundamental dilemma. On the one hand, defense of the juridical approach implies the legal enshrinement of a metaphysics of an originally indifferent human freedom and intelligence, and so far the relativism feared by the Council bishops who supported the changes to the Declaration made in the later schemas. On the other hand, rejection of such a relativistic notion of political-constitutional order requires tying the juridical order in some principled way to the obligation to seek the truth. Or, to use the language of articles of peace and articles of faith: on the one hand, Murray's would-be articles of peace imply articles of faith consisting in a definite idea of freedom (freedom of indifference) that carries within it a definite idea of the nature of truth (truth as simply a matter of choice: relativism); and this definite idea of freedom and truth undermines what is the legitimate intention of articles of peace, namely, a principled affirmation of a universal right to religious freedom. But this is to say, on the other hand, that if Murray would realize the legitimate intention of articles of peace, he would have to develop articles of faith that in fact sustain this intention, by replacing freedom of indifference with a more adequate notion of freedom as bound intrinsically to truth.[61]

Either way, Murray's first criticism, that the changes made in the later schemas were introduced without genuine warrant, does not and cannot stand. His own affirmation of a universal right to religious freedom demands of its inner logic acceptance of just the sorts of additions made by the Council fathers following the third schema of the Declaration. The Council fathers, then, were right on properly theoretical grounds that the changes they proposed were necessary. The merely *civil* right to religious freedom asserted by Murray had to be tied in principle to an *ontological-moral* — indeed ultimately *theological* — right, or, more precisely, had to be tied to some form of an ontology of freedom of excellence as distinct from freedom of indifference.

But this leaves us still with the need to address the burden of Murray's second criticism: if the civil right needs such an ontological-moral ground, needs so far to be tied in principle to the truth about human being and agency in relation to God, how can such a right be sustained as *universal?* In what sense can a person who is in error still be considered a subject of rights? The foregoing argument, in other words, even if it succeeds in responding to one part of Murray's concerns, may seem only to return us to a version of the old terms of the problem: whether the truth has rights. It is to Murray's second criticism, then, and to this problem, that I now turn.

IV.

The second question is thus whether the final text of DH, in binding religious freedom with the obligation to seek the truth about God, and thus with relation to truth and to God, is still able consistently to affirm a universal civil right to religious freedom: in other words, whether binding freedom to truth in this way yields the necessary political consequence of a principled commitment to the right to immunity. In asking this question, it is essential to keep in mind the premise to which the foregoing argument has brought us: that there is no way of defending the right to religious freedom that does not, at least implicitly, invoke some claim of truth that grounds human dignity, and thereby impart to such a right its most basic meaning. We have seen that the juridical view purports to avoid such a claim of truth, but in fact succeeds only in proposing a hidden claim on behalf of freedom of indifference as the foundation for human dignity.

The Council bishops who supported the changes in the final Declaration recognized, on the contrary, that it is not the supposed absence of a view, but only an adequate view, of the truth about man and his freedom in relation to God that alone can sustain rights for every human being with objective moral consistency. Indeed, these bishops mean to say both that this *truth alone* frees, and that this truth *really does free*. My task in regard to Murray's second criticism, then, is not to establish *that* some claim of truth is necessary to ground and give initial definition to the meaning of freedom and rights, since some such truth-claim will always be operative regardless. The task, rather, is to show how the explicit ontological unity of truth and freedom endorsed by the majority of Council bishops, and incorporated in the final Declaration, succeeds in defending consistently the universal right to religious freedom that is excluded by the juridical approach.[62]

The heart of the Declaration's argument in this connection is expressed in article 2, which, as we have seen, was an addition made in schema 5:

> It is in accord with their dignity that all men and women, because they are persons, endowed with reason and free will and therefore privileged with personal responsibility, are impelled by their nature and bound by a moral obligation to seek the truth, especially the truth concerning religion. They are also bound to hold fast to the truth once it is known, and to order their whole life in accord with its demands. They cannot satisfy this obligation in a way that is in keeping with their own nature, however, unless they enjoy psychological freedom as well as immunity

from external coercion. The right to religious freedom does not have its foundation in the subjective disposition of the person, therefore, but rather in his very nature. Consequently, the right to this immunity persists even for those who do not satisfy their obligation to seek the truth and to hold fast to it; the exercise of this right is not to be impeded, provided that just public order is preserved. (DH, 2)

The argument is thus that the right to immunity from coercion in matters of religious truth resides in every person because it is rooted in the "very nature" of the person *(non . . . in subiectiva personae dispositione, sed in ipsa eius natura ius . . . fundatur)*. Human persons are naturally endowed with reason and free will even as they are naturally moved by *(sua ipsorum natura impelluntur)*, and morally bound to seek, the truth, especially with respect to religion.

Now, it is important to see that the position enunciated in this text from DH finally presupposes, and demands completion in light of, the revelation of God in Jesus Christ as emphasized in the second part of the Declaration. That Jesus Christ is the ultimate and most basic foundation for an integrated view of freedom and truth was repeatedly stressed by Archbishop Wojtyła, as we have seen. DH states that, "[a]lthough revelation does not expressly affirm the right to immunity from external coercion in religious matters," it nonetheless "manifests the respect Christ showed for the freedom with which man is to fulfill his duty of believing the word of God," and thereby clearly directs us to the "general principles which ground the teaching of this Declaration on religious freedom" (DH, 9). Furthermore, article 10 says that it is one of the key truths in Catholic teaching that "man's response to God in faith should be voluntary":

> The act of faith is of its very nature a voluntary act. For man, redeemed by Christ the Savior and called to be an adopted son through Jesus Christ, cannot hold fast to God as he reveals himself unless, drawn by the Father, he offers to God a rational and free submission of faith. It is therefore fully consonant with the nature of faith that in religious matters every kind of coercion on the part of men be excluded. (DH, 10; cf. the texts cited in DH 10, n. 12, from the history of the Church)

And further:

> [God] has regard for the dignity of the human person whom he himself created, who should be led by his own counsel and enjoy his own

freedom. . . . For Christ, who is our Master and Lord, and at the same time meek and humble of heart, attracted and invited disciples with patience. He supported and confirmed his teaching with miracles in order to awaken and strengthen the faith of his listeners, not to exercise coercion over them. (DH, 11)

We will return in section VIII to the question of the role played by Christian revelation in the argument regarding human dignity and religious freedom. It is important, however, to take account here of the Declaration's appeal to the *nature* of the human being, which is made not only for pastoral reasons — that is, because this ecclesial document is meant to speak not only to Christians but to all of humanity — but for reasons intrinsic to truth itself. In article 2, the claim to a right is tied to human dignity, and this dignity is tied to a view of the human person who, properly conceived as free and intelligent, is naturally inclined, and hence morally obliged, to seek the truth. The right to religious freedom, in other words, is rooted in the person's natural inclination to seek the truth, but this inclination is rightly realized only via the freedom and intelligence that define his human nature. The human person is by nature a truth-seeker and a truth-knower, but only as exigent for acting — reasoning and choosing — on his own initiative and responsibility. Truth makes one free; at the same time, there is no truth without freedom. The argument from revelation in part II of the Declaration takes over and deepens this double claim set forth in article 2. Indeed, this seems to me the core claim of DH, the claim that alone accounts adequately for the changes introduced in the final drafts.

As we have noted, it is not the responsibility of a conciliar document to provide a sustained constructive argument in these matters. My main purpose here is to indicate the warrants for the position taken by the Declaration, in light of the ancient-classical thought carried in the teaching of the Church. As in the previous section, with the help of Fr. Pinckaers, we exposed the problems inherent in the modern understanding of freedom against the backdrop of the ancient-medieval idea of freedom, so now, with the help of philosophers Kenneth Schmitz and Josef Pieper, we will (1) demonstrate similar problems in the modern idea of (human) nature and truth against the background of the ancient-medieval idea of (human) nature and truth, in order (2) to respond to Murray's second criticism, that a right tied to truth cannot be genuinely universal.

(1) My contention is that it is the modern presupposition of an originally extrinsic relation between truth and freedom — of an original indif-

ference of each to the other — that *alone justifies the claim that entering into the truth necessarily involves the lessening of freedom.* I will show on the contrary why, on the medieval view, the movement into truth presupposes and demands freedom, even as freedom itself presupposes the movement into truth. My argument addresses four points, regarding: (i) the nature of nature; (ii) the spirituality of human nature: the *anima forma corporis;* (iii) the originally "transcendental" nature of truth; and (iv) the nature of man as inherently religious.

(i) *Nature.* An adequate idea of truth presupposes an adequate idea of nature. The first thing to note is that, on a proper reading of nature, relations between one natural entity and another are not primarily mechanical, but organic. Organic relations of their essence involve dimensions of immanent or interior order, and thus cannot be reduced to extrinsic and forceful-mechanical activity. The difference indicated here is that between the ancient-medieval idea of nature, on the one hand, and the modern idea to which we have become accustomed, on the other. Thus Aristotle says that everything constituted by nature "has within itself the principle of movement and rest (ἐν ἑαυτῷ ἀρχὴν ἔχει κινήσεως καὶ στάσεως)" (*Physics,* bk. II, ch. 1, 192b14-15). According to this understanding, the defining features of nature are three: (a) ἀρχή: beginning, origin, or first cause, hence what has an original principle or source within itself; (b) κίνησις: movement, from the verb κινέω, to move or set in motion, or indeed to cause; and (c) στάσις: standing, or standing still, stationariness, from the verb ἵστημι, to make stand, or stop, or stay. As we will see, each of these features of Aristotle's concept of nature, or better, all of them together as understood in relation to each other, are essential for the classical understanding of truth and indeed of the relation between truth and freedom.

Key for Aristotle in his understanding of nature, says Professor Schmitz, is form.[63] Form implies immateriality: natural things, insofar as they are informed, bear this feature of immateriality. There are for the ancients and medievals many "modes, kinds, and degrees of immateriality, beginning with the simplest forms of primitive material composites and building in complexity, unity, and power towards the human intellectual form and beyond it" (169).

In this classical conception, the main characteristics of form are as follows. First, "formal principles manifest a kind of eidetic autonomy: they are what it is they are, and the composites of which they are forms are what they are by virtue of their formal principles" (170). The point is that the conception of form in traditional philosophy includes at its heart the principle of self-identity: in the first instance, immateriality is "inseparable from a sort of self-possession and self-definition" (170).

Second, form in medieval philosophy is a principle of activity. The radical self-determinateness of form manifests itself as "self-determination." But it is important to see that form "carries out its self-determination by a certain reflexivity that is rooted in the very nature of form and its self-determinateness. This primitive reflexivity lies deeper than self-conscious reflection, deeper even than the great cycle of organic activity. It is inseparable from all action" (170).

The most basic kind of activity for the ancients and medievals, thus, is not activity that is simply directed outward, or what is termed "purely transitive activity." On the contrary, purely transitive activity is a kind of "limit-concept that is most closely approximated only by minute particles that dissolve themselves in their own ephemeral activity" (170). Which is to say, purely transitive activity would be a characteristic only of an instance of matter that is utterly without form. In sum, "the formal element may . . . be said to *dwell within* the sphere of power originating from its own activity," and so is characterized above all by what is termed *immanent* activity (170, emphasis added). This reflexive-immanent activity, furthermore, "is the active basis upon which the principle of reciprocity [among things] is built" (170). Reflexive-immanent activity, in other words, is what enables each thing to enter into genuine relations with other things: into relations, that is, which are not simply extrinsic and thus forceful, and which so far protect the integrity of the nature of the things *in* relation and *as* related. Form so far bears a certain "generosity" (171).

Our summary point regarding the classical idea of nature, in light of Schmitz's reflections, is that it is this immanent or interior activity of natural things, which always exists *within* their transitive or outward-directed activity, that permits genuine reciprocity among things. Relations among things of nature are not at root primarily matters of external force: of two things acting merely in an outward direction with respect to each other, as in the prevalent modern conception of nature. Nor is the capacity of one entity to receive from another a matter of simple passivity with respect to that other. Each thing of nature actively appropriates its environment in a way that at root involves immanent or interior activity, thus "prefiguring" the freedom of the human spirit. All of this, suggests Schmitz, follows from the immateriality of form that is fundamental for the classical understanding of nature.[64]

(ii) *The spirituality of human nature: anima forma corporis.* Our idea of nature is deepened immeasurably when we move from the immateriality of form in natural things to the spirituality of the human soul as the form of the body. Consistent with the argument of Schmitz, Josef Pieper, in his *Wahrheit der Dinge,* "The Truth of Things,"[65] says that "'having an intrinsic existence' corresponds to 'being able to relate'" so that "the higher the form of intrinsic existence, the more developed becomes the relatedness with reality" (LTT, 81-82). This is because "the inside (*das Innere:* inwardness or interiority) is the power by virtue of which a relation to something external is possible [or, is that by which a thing is able to relate itself to something outside it: *sich in Beziehung zu setzen zu einem Aussen*]"; interiority is thus "the capacity to establish relations and to communicate."[66] This inwardness finds its perfection in spirit. Spirit thus needs to be understood not simply as incorporeality, but as the capacity to relate, indeed as "the capacity to relate itself to the totality of being" (LBC, 98; cf. LTT, 83). "To have spirit, or to be spirit, means to exist in the midst of the whole of reality and before the whole of being, the whole of being *vis-à-vis de l'univers*" (LBC, 99). As St. Thomas says, "the higher the power [of the soul], the more comprehensive is the sphere of objects toward which it is ordered" (LTT, 83; cf. ST I, q. 78, a. 1). This view, according to Pieper, represents "the tradition of Western philosophy" (LBC, 99). Thus Aristotle, for example, says that the human soul, the spiritual form of the human-natural body, "is, fundamentally, everything that is" (LBC, 99; cf. *De Anima,* bk. III, ch. 8, 431b20: ἡ ψυχὴ τὰ ὄντα πώς ἐστι πάντα). The same idea is expressed in the medieval axiom, "*anima est quodammodo omnia,* the soul is in a certain sense all things" (LBC, 99). Again, the spiritual soul, according to Aquinas, "is meant to fit in with all being *(convenire cum omni ente)*" (LBC, 99; cf. De Ver. I, 1).[67]

> To the philosophers of the past — to Plato, Aristotle, Augustine, and Thomas Aquinas — the belonging together of "spirit" and "world," in the sense of the whole of reality, is strictly and deeply anchored in both terms *(ist sogar die Zusammengehörigkeit der Begriffe 'Geist' und 'Welt' — im Sinne von Gesamtwirklichkeit — so eng und so tief in beiden Gliedern verankert).* . . . [T]hey formulated that relation in such precise terms that we scarcely dare to take them at their word. Not only, they said, is it of the nature of the spirit for its frame of reference to be the totality of existing things; but it is also of the nature of existing things for them to lie within spirit's frame of reference. (LBC, 100, translation slightly altered; WHP, 43)

Pieper emphasizes here that he is not referring "to some vague abstract 'spirituality' *(Geistigkeit)* but to a personal spirit, to an immanent power of establishing relationships" (LBC, 100; WHP, 44). He is referring above all to the creator God, but also to "limited, created human spirit" (LBC, 100).[68]

(iii) *The transcendental meaning of truth.* Furthermore, the inner relation between spirit and the world as conceived by St. Thomas, says Pieper, implies the medieval proposition "*omne ens est verum* — all that is, is true" (LTT, 91). That is, being and truth are interchangeable concepts, because and insofar as everything that is is known (by the Creator) and knowable (by the created human spirit) (LTT, 91).[69] "[T]he world of all existing things 'is placed between two knowing minds,' the mind of God and the mind of man," and thus all things are true (LTT 98; cf. De Ver. I, 2). Aquinas therefore calls truth a "transcendental": that is, "a *mode of being* . . . that 'pertains to every being as such'" (LTT, 30; cf. De Ver. I, 1: *modus generalis consequens omne ens*).[70]

(iv) *Man's nature as a naturally religious being (homo religiosus).* Pieper's Thomistic reading of spirit and of the originally transcendental nature of truth shows, finally, that the human being is by nature, and most profoundly, religious: open to and interiorly oriented, at the core of his being, toward God. Dominican Father Philipe André-Vincent, in his book on the Council and religious freedom, *La Liberté Religieuse: Droit Fondamental,* echoes Pieper here.[71] According to André-Vincent, the free-intelligent human act "cannot be defined negatively," in terms of what is first a negative relation, or "freedom from." Rather the human act is defined first as the "spontaneity of a nature which is finally . . . determined by the Absolute Being only, of a will which beyond all goods and through them tends to the Sovereign Good; of an intelligence which through all truth and beyond all truth adheres to the Primordial Truth" (AV, 214). Thus the act of religion is the fundamental act of man: "it embraces the whole of man and of the universe" (AV, 191). "Every man finds in the religious act the meaning of his life. He is so ordered by his nature, whatever his religion or irreligion. [An] 'ontological obligation,' it has been called: that is, a religious obligation written into the nature of the human being, into his ontological structure. That structure founds religious freedom" (AV, 215-16).[72]

This overview of the ancient-medieval tradition in light of the work of Kenneth Schmitz and Josef Pieper yields three profoundly relevant points with respect to the relation between truth and freedom, the claim that truth and freedom can be realized only simultaneously, in an original unity with one another.

First of all, regarding spirit: in its correspondence to the totality of being, spirit is also the highest form of inwardness, what Goethe called *"wohnen in sich selbst"* — dwelling in oneself. The more embracing the power with which to relate oneself to objective being, the more deeply that power needs to be anchored in the inner self of the subject so as to counterbalance the step it takes outside. And where this step attains a world that is in principle complete (with totality as its aim), the reflective [or free] self, characteristic of spirit, is also reached. (LBC, 102)

Again:

[T]o have (or to be) an "intrinsic existence" means "to be able to relate" [or, to be capable of relation: *beziehungsfähig sein*] and "to be the sustaining subject at the center of a field of reference." The hierarchy of existing things, being equally a hierarchy of intrinsic existences, corresponds on each level to the intensity and extension of the respective relationship in their power, character and domain. Consequently, the spirit-based self, the highest form of being and of intrinsic existence as well, must have the most intensive power to relate and the most comprehensive domain of relatedness: the universe of existing things. These two aspects, combined — dwelling most intensively within itself ["the capacity of living in oneself, the gift of self-reliance and independence": LBC, 102], and being *capax universi,* able to grasp the universe — together constitute the essence of the [human] spirit *(das Wesen des Geistes).* Any definition of "spirit" will have to contain these two aspects as its core. (LTT, 83; WDD, 87-88)

The most intensive power to relate and the most comprehensive domain of relatedness have "in the philosophical tradition of Europe . . . always been regarded as the attributes of the human person, of being a person" (LBC, 102).[73]

Thus it is characteristic of the human being, by virtue of his spiritual soul, to be and to act from within himself, "intrinsically" or intensively and interiorly, and thus independently; but to act thus only as *already ordered by and toward the world and ultimately God,* thus only as *already standing in the truth as implied by creation.* To separate the intensive, self-reflexive, free-intelligent human act from its standing in the truth is, *eo ipso,* to drain this act of its original meaning as spiritual. It is to drain the human act of the inner depth and breadth and order indicated in its reality as *capax universi,* a capacity for receiving the other: the world and God. It is to lose what is peculiar to the spiritual soul of man, indeed, what is present already (analogically) in the immaterial (non-spiritual) form of natural entities: namely, a *unity* of immanent and transitive activity. In light of such a separation, the immanent character of the free-intelligent human act becomes a matter of empty (merely "subjective": formless, arbitrary) inward activity, while its transitive character becomes a matter of simply outward-directed (merely "objective": surface, extroverted) activity.

Second, regarding truth: for the medievals, each instance of knowledge of the truth presupposes this already-given reciprocal reference of, or transcendental relation between, mind and reality. This is why Aquinas says that "knowledge is in a certain sense the offspring *(Frucht)* of truth" (LTT, 63; WDD, 65; cf. De Ver. I, 1: *Cognitio est quidam veritatis effectus*). That is, each instance of knowledge as an adequation of mind and reality *(adequatio intellectus et rei)* presupposes an originally-"transcendentally" given relation between the mind and all of reality, a true relation that has its origin and end in God.[74] In a word, it is not knowledge that first produces truth; rather, it is truth — as a transcendental — that first enables knowledge.

The point here is that the free-intelligent human act is from its roots *disposed toward,* and so far *already initially ordered by,* this relation. Human intelligence of its nature already stands in the truth and tends toward or desires truth. We recall again the words of Pieper: "The human mind, by its nature and created structure, *finds itself* in this preordained orientation toward the universe in the same way and at the same moment it finds its own existence" (LTT, 91; emphasis added).[75]

Third, regarding man's relationship to God: this understanding of the originally given relation of the human spirit to the world presupposes an original relation to God. The free, intelligent human act is best understood, in its primitively given nature and most profound depths, as an order or orientation toward the truth about God. To separate the human act from its inner ordering by and toward this truth is to evacuate this act of its essential character as spiritual.

In sum: we cannot separate the free human act from its ordering in and toward the truth of things and God, or man's "truthing" of things from his own reflexive, interiorizing act, without thereby doing violence simultaneously to the nature both of spirit (human freedom and intelligence) and of truth (about things and about God). Such is the import of the Aristotelian concept of nature, deepened by the medieval (Thomistic) understanding of the spiritual nature of the human soul, the transcendental convertibility of being and truth, and the natural, always-already given, relation to God implied in this convertibility.

(2) In responding to Murray's second criticism, then, that a right to freedom tied to truth cannot be universally sustained, we can begin by noting Pieper's claim that modern thinkers characteristically fracture the indissoluble unity between the mind's interior, self-reflexive ordering toward things, on the one hand, and the inherent knowability and truth of things, on the other. Such fracturing stems from, and in turn reinforces, modernity's inadequate understanding of the spiritual nature of man's soul, the transcendental nature of truth, and the natural religiosity of man. The arguments we have presented thus point us back to the problem identified by Pinckaers, regarding a freedom (or human act) originally indifferent to the order of truth given by the Creator. The discussion in this section has covered much of the same ground covered already in terms of Pinckaers, though in terms now of the question of truth in its relation to spirit (the free, intelligent act).

Thus, Pieper says that Bacon, Hobbes, and Descartes, for example, deny that there is "truth in all things" (cf. LTT, 15-16). Descartes assumes an external relation between mind and things: between a human act that is originally indifferent to the world of things, and a world of things each of which bears an identity with itself that is originally indifferent to its being known or related to others. The human act, in its original reflexivity as free, is interiorly empty of relation, which is to say, is not already ordered toward and by the world. Things are not recognized to be standing in the truth already by virtue of their being as creatures *(verum qua ens)*. Rather, they first become true by virtue of man's initiating activity *(verum quia factum)*.[76]

Thus, on the Cartesian view, we have a free-intelligent human act that is no longer fraught of its inmost essence as spiritual with an openness to and ordering by the totality of things, and ultimately God. In other words, we have a free-intelligent act that is no longer understood to be of its essence an original participant in the (transcendental) truth of things as established by the creative act of God. The consequence of such a view is an inability to grasp that an ever-deepening appropriation of the truth of things, on the one hand, and an ever-deepening appropriation of one's own spiritual nature as free and intelligent, on the other, *occur only at the same time, each in direct proportion to the other.*

Now I am not suggesting that Murray, in his argument regarding the root of human dignity and the nature of (religious) freedom, follows this Cartesian position in an obvious or deliberate manner. As indicated, Murray clearly affirms, from within the Scholastic tradition, the human act's relation to the transcendent order of truth and to God. The point, however, as also indicated, is that for all legal-juridical purposes, and consistent with a certain strain of Scholasticism in modernity as described by Pinckaers, Murray abstracts the free-intelligent human act from its original relatedness to this order.[77] For purposes of constitutional order, the human act is conceived as a reflexive act of freedom and intelligence that is primitively empty, to which truth is logically something always yet-to-be-added. Truth is thereby first simply an object of this primitively empty act. The human act, considered from the perspective of the juridical order, is first empty; and truth thus becomes, *from that same juridical perspective,* adventitious, something that, as such, cannot but logically burden the free-intelligent human act by arbitrarily limiting and closing what is considered by government, for legal or public purposes, to be simply open, or abstracted from all (metaphysical-religious) content. Freedom and truth in this conception stand in a basic tension with each other, such that each threatens the original integrity of the other.

The problem I am raising here with respect to Murray thus repeats and amplifies the problem identified earlier in terms of freedom of indifference. Murray's approach effectively overlooks, for purposes pertinent to the exercise of constitutional power, the spiritual nature of the human act (as *capax universi et Dei*), the transcendental nature of truth *(verum qua ens),* and the fundamental relatedness to God implicit in this spiritual human act and transcendental truth. But it is just the overlooking of these three features regarding the nature of the human spirit and of transcendental truth that informs, and alone justifies, Murray's second criticism of the Declaration: namely, that its linking of freedom with truth weakens rather than strengthens the right to religious freedom. His criticism, in other words, is that a government claiming to know the truth about the human being will be logically inclined to short-circuit the freedom of its citizens. But this assumes that linking freedom with truth, bringing them into intrinsic relation with each other, constitutes a principled threat to the integrity of freedom as well as to the right that is a function of this freedom. Such a claim presupposes that freedom and truth have their integrity only as first extrinsic to each other, rather than as interiorly open to one another, in such a way that each has its original integrity only as already given form by the other.

The paradoxical problem in Murray's position here is seen more clearly when we compare it with that of another group of Council bishops, comprised in the end of a small minority. This group was also critical of the final position taken by the Declaration, though from a direction opposite to that of Murray. I have in mind here the Council fathers centered around Archbishop Marcel Lefebvre. Lefebvre opposed the final Declaration because he took its affirmation of an intrinsic right to religious freedom to set in place in government a dynamic that would lead to the undermining of truth in civil society. As much as Murray believed that tying freedom to truth risked undercutting (or at least prematurely limiting) freedom, in other words, Lefebvre believed that opening truth in principle to freedom risked undercutting truth.

The opposition between Murray and Lefebvre appears to be, and in a crucial sense is, fundamental. However, it is important, if we would understand properly what the Declaration intended in its final affirmation regarding religious freedom, to see how this opposition is nonetheless dialectical in nature. That is, *what is (otherwise) the deep difference between the Murrayite and Lefebvrite positions is driven by a common assumption:* both positions imply that freedom and truth stand by nature (at least as conceived for juridical purposes) in an originally extrinsic relation to each other.

That this is so for Lefebvre can be seen in the central distinction that guides his criticism of the Declaration. Regarding the question of the foundation of the right to religious liberty, Lefebvre says that we must distinguish "between the *ontological* dignity and the *operative* dignity of man."[78] The former "consists in the intellectuality of his nature, that is, the nobility of a nature endowed with intelligence and free will. Man is essentially called to know God" and "is capable of the beatific vision" (19). Thus it can be said that the "ontological dignity of man consists mainly in a transcendental orientation to God and is . . . a 'divine call' which is the foundation in man of the duty to search for the True God and the true religion to which, once found, man must adhere" (19). In this sense, "the ontological dignity of the human person is the same in everyone and can never be lost" (19). The problem, however, Lefebvre argues, is that "original sin profoundly wounded human nature in its faculties, most especially in its capacity to know God. The natural dignity of man has suffered, as a consequence, a universal degradation that not even the grace of baptism can heal completely in Christians" (20). The upshot is that there are "radical inequalities among people in the concrete natural dignity of persons," which "require unequal treatment from both divine and human authority" (20). Furthermore, the fact that a soul in error may be said to be *searching* for God and truth means that he is only "*potentially* 'connected'" to these, not actually in acceptance of them: man's dependence on God, in other words, is in this case not yet "effective" (36-37, emphasis added).

Regarding the operative dignity of man, Lefebvre says that it "is the result of the exercise of his faculties, essentially intelligence and will" (20). "To the perfection of nature is added to man a supplementary perfection which will depend on his actions" (20). Man's operative dignity, thus, "will consist in *adhering in his actions to truth and goodness*" (20). It follows for the Archbishop that "if man fails to be good or, if he adheres to error or evil, he loses his dignity" (20). In a word, for Lefebvre the dignity of the human person, in the operative sense, "does not consist in liberty apart from truth. . . . Liberty is good and true to the extent to which it is ruled by truth" (22).

Lefebvre's problem with the teaching of *Dignitatis humanae,* in sum, is that it roots the right to religious freedom not in this operative dignity of man, which consists in "the actual adherence of the person to the truth," but rather in the ontological dignity of man, which "refers only to his free will" made in the image of God (33). In the view of the Declaration, "any man, regardless of his subjective dispositions (truth or error, good or bad faith), is inviolable in the actions by which he operates his 'relation' to God" (31). But, according to Lefebvre, this is false: "when man cleaves to error or moral evil, he loses his operative dignity, which therefore cannot be the basis for anything at all" (33).[79]

Thus, regarding the logic of Lefebvre's and Murray's positions with respect to each other: on the one hand, Lefebvre recognizes that there is in man a "transcendental relation to God" and a "divine call" that founds man's duty and dignity, and hence his right to search for the truth. But this relation and call have been profoundly affected by sin, to the extent that man's original natural orientation to truth and God are now conceived as only "potential," not yet in any proper sense actual or effective. Hence the operative dignity of man, the dignity that truly qualifies him as a subject of the right to religious freedom, is for Lefebvre tied to the exercise of his faculties of freedom and intelligence in the actual realization of truth and goodness in relation to God. Murray, on the other hand, locates human dignity, for purposes relevant to man's being recognized as a subject of the right to religious freedom, in man's exigence for exercising initiative, abstracted from man's relation to the transcendent order of truth.

The upshot is that both Lefebvre and Murray in their different ways — one stressing freedom's need to actualize relation to truth and God, the other freedom's original abstraction from truth for purposes of civil rights — presuppose a free-intelligent human act that is *originally disjoined from,* and thus *yet-to-be-related to,* truth and God. Both so far overlook the spiritual nature of the free-intelligent human act: that this act is *indissolubly both* self-reflexive and interiorly intensive, on the one hand, *and* actually oriented toward and by the world and God *(capax universi et Dei),* on the other. In a word, both fail to integrate the classical (Thomistic) understanding of the spiritual human act and of transcendental truth into their respective approaches to the problem of the foundations and nature of the right to religious freedom. The result is that both see an original and basic *tension* between truth and freedom, such that an emphasis on one somehow threatens the integrity of the other (at least for purposes of juridical order).[80]

Again, Murray and Lefebvre approach this tension with opposing emphases. Lefebvre, viewing freedom as a potential threat to truth, insists that truth needs in principle to be enshrined in law and that citizens' exercise of freedom is to be limited in light of truth so understood.[81] Murray, on the other hand, concerned to protect citizens' freedom and the rights that are a function of this freedom, defends the juridical approach to the law that would bracket the truth, all the while transferring to citizens and civil institutions the responsibility for generating the truth necessary to provide foundations for the juridical order.

Murray's appeal to freedom in abstraction from truth in the juridical order, however, hides what is already a claim of truth. This hidden claim of truth, which in fact is *not true* and *does not free,* logically deflects in advance any effort to integrate into the exercise of juridical power the different claim of truth implied by the spiritual nature of the human act and the transcendental nature of truth, and thus by the nature of man as *capax universi et Dei.* Indeed, Murray's would-be purely juridical approach, which embeds the single truth of freedom of indifference, leads logically, against Murray's own deepest intention, to just the sort of relativism feared by Lefebvre.

My point, in sum, is that Murray and Lefebvre, while emphasizing freedom and truth, respectively, in their approaches to the juridical order, nevertheless share an original extrinsicism between freedom and truth that precludes, *a priori,* any recognition that the integrity of each *is realized only within* their original unity. But this unity of freedom and truth is just the burden of the Council's inclusion of article 2 in the Declaration: only such a unity of freedom and truth permits a principled defense of a universal right to religious freedom. Here, in the indissoluble unity between the person in his interior, self-determining activity, and the person in his standing always already inside the truth of things, lies the foundation of the person as at once a subject of the right to freedom *and* as a participant in truth, finally in the truth about God: a participant obliged to seek ever-deeper participation in this truth, and to embrace it once found. In a word, man is a subject of the right to freedom only as already a participant in the original truth of things; and he is a participant in the original truth of things only as at once a subject of the right to freedom.

The Declaration thus *takes over the essential concerns of both Murray (freedom, rights) and Lefebvre (truth, duty),* while nevertheless *transforming the basic terms in which their respective arguments are articulated.* The Declaration is able to affirm an original unity between freedom and truth, such that it is right to say both that the *truth alone* frees and that the truth alone *really does free,* because of the Declaration's (implicitly) presupposed ancient-medieval view regarding the spirituality of the free-intelligent human act and the transcendentality of truth, both of which imply relation to the Creator. All persons have the right to seek the truth, ultimately about God, *in freedom, because all persons share in the spiritual nature of the human act ordered to the transcendental nature of truth, and are (thereby) obliged to seek the truth about God.* This means that there can be no entry into truth, rightly understood, no legitimate promotion of the person's movement toward truth, that does not presuppose and demand respect for the interior self-determining, hence free, activity proper to the spiritual nature of the person. Murray's criticism of this argument of the final Declaration, therefore, as well as Lefebvre's opposing criticism, are in the end warranted only if the ancient-medieval tradition's idea of the spirituality of the free-intelligent human act and of the transcendentality of truth is false.[82]

This response to Murray's second criticism, however, leaves us still with the third question indicated above. Murray insists that, notwithstanding the two deficiencies in the argument of the Declaration that he identifies, the Declaration in its final form understands the right to religious freedom in the primarily negative terms of immunity from coercion. According to Murray, in other words, the juridical approach as first proposed in the third schema remains essentially intact in the final document. What does the foregoing defense of the Declaration against the criticisms of Murray imply regarding this claim?

V.

The principal terms of the answer to this question can, again, be found in a proper reading of the first three articles of the Declaration. I will begin by citing extensively from these three articles, <u>underlining</u> some of the key wording and passages introduced in the fifth and final drafts.

It is in article 2 that we find the statement that the right to religious freedom means "that all men and women should be immune from coercion on the part of individuals, social groups or any human power, so that no one is forced to act against his conscience in religious matters, or prevented from acting according to his conscience, in private or in public, whether alone or in association with others, within due limits." Following this statement, article 2 indicates that "the right to religious freedom has its foundation in the very dignity of the human person, as known from both the revealed word of God and reason itself," and that "[t]his right of the human person to religious freedom must be acknowledged in the juridical order of society, so that it becomes a civil right." The Declaration then elaborates further the roots of human dignity and thereby of the right to religious freedom in a paragraph that was inserted in the fifth schema, drawing largely on the intervention of Bishop Ancel, as indicated above.

> It is in accord with their dignity that all men and women, because they are persons, endowed with reason and free will and therefore privileged with personal responsibility, are impelled by their nature and bound by a moral obligation to seek the truth, especially the truth concerning religion. They are also bound to hold fast to the truth once it is known, and to order their whole life in accord with its demands. They cannot satisfy this obligation in a way that is in keeping with their own nature, however, unless they enjoy psychological freedom as well as immunity from external coercion. The right to religious freedom does not have its foundation in the subjective disposition of the person, therefore, but rather in his very nature. Consequently, the right to this immunity persists even for those who do not satisfy their obligation to seek the truth and to hold fast to it; the exercise of this right is not to be impeded, provided that just public order is preserved. (DH, 2)

Article 3 proceeds to place the foregoing statements within a more comprehensive framework:

> This becomes even clearer when one considers that the highest norm of human life is the divine law, eternal, objective, and universal, by which God, in the providence of his wisdom and love, orders, directs, and governs the whole world and the ways of the human community. God grants man a share in this law, so that man, under the gentle direction of divine providence, can acknowledge more and more the truth that is itself unchanging. For this reason, each person has the duty, and therefore the right, to seek the truth in religious matters, so that he may prudently form right and true judgments of conscience for himself, using all suitable means.

The truth, however, must be sought in a way proper to the dignity of the human person and his social nature, namely, by means of free inquiry, with the help of instruction or education, communication and dialogue. . . .

It is through the mediation of his conscience that man perceives and recognizes the precepts of the divine law; he is bound in all his actions to follow his conscience faithfully, so that he may come to God, his end. (DH, 3)

Man "is not to be forced to act against," nor "prevented from acting according to," his conscience, "[f]or by its very nature the exercise of religion consists first of all in interior acts that are voluntary and free, through which man orders himself directly toward God" (DH, 3).

Article 3 states further that the free exercise of religion in society cannot be denied "when <u>just</u> public order is preserved." To deny this free exercise is to do "injustice to the human person, and to the very order of human existence established by God. . . . Furthermore, religious acts, in which men and women . . . order themselves toward God out of a sense of inner conviction, by their nature transcend the earthly and temporal order of things. The civil power, therefore, <u>whose proper end is the care of the temporal common good</u> *(bonum commune temporale),* should in fact acknowledge and show favor to *(agnoscere eique favere)* the religious life of its citizens;[83] but this power must be said to exceed its limits if it presumes either to direct or to impede religious acts."

Turning to the first article of the Declaration, then, we find the opening statement that

> Men and women of our time are becoming more conscious every day of the dignity of the human person. Increasing numbers demand that in acting they enjoy and make use of their own counsel and <u>a responsible</u> freedom, not impelled by coercion but moved by a sense of duty. They also demand that juridical limits be set to the public power, in order that the rightful freedom of persons and associations not be excessively restricted. This demand for freedom in human society is <u>chiefly</u> concerned with <u>the goods of the human spirit</u> *(animi humani bona),* first of all those that concern the free exercise of religion in society. Carefully attending to these desires of men's hearts, <u>and proposing to declare to what degree they are in conformity with truth and justice</u> *(declarare quantum sint veritati et iustitiae conformes),*[84] this Vatican Council searches the sacred

tradition and teaching of the Church, from which it draws forth new things that are always in harmony with the old. (DH, 1)

Article 1 then stresses that "God himself has made known to mankind the way in which men are to serve him, and so be saved in Christ and come to blessedness. We believe that this one true religion subsists in the Catholic and apostolic Church, to which the Lord Jesus committed the task of spreading it among all people. . . . All men and women are in fact bound to seek the truth, especially in those things concerning God and his Church, and to embrace and hold fast to it once it is known."

The article states further that "these duties touch on and bind the conscience of man. In no other way does truth impose itself than by the strength of truth itself, entering the mind at once gently and with power." The point, then, is that, "since the religious freedom which men and women demand in order to fulfill their duty to worship God concerns (*respiciat:* regards, depends upon, looks for help to)[85] immunity from coercion in civil society, it leaves intact the traditional Catholic teaching on the moral duty individuals and societies have toward the true religion and the one Church of Christ."

My purpose in citing at length these statements from articles 1-3, many elements of which (as the underlined text indicates) were introduced in the later schemas, is to call attention to how frequently, clearly, and emphatically the Declaration refers to truth, especially concerning God, as the foundation of human dignity, thereby indicating the ground of the right to religious freedom. The claim of truth sets the basic and positive context within which the right to religious freedom is affirmed in its negative content as an immunity. The fact that this is so is acknowledged in some way by almost everyone involved in the debate regarding the proper meaning of religious freedom as declared by the Council. The main point of contention arises rather over whether this positive context *internally* affects the original meaning of the right identified in article 2 in the negative terms of immunity. Is this negative meaning understood by the Declaration to be informed, at least implicitly, by the human act's positive élan toward, and initial order of relation to, truth and God? The argument of the proceeding sections has shown why an affirmative answer to this question is warranted on "systematic" grounds, and indeed why the answer *must be* affirmative if the coherence of the Declaration's argument regarding a universal right to religious freedom is to be sustained as a matter of principle. Here our purpose is to show more explicitly, in terms of the language of articles 1-3, the sense in which this positive framework of truth operates inside the negative definition and gives to the latter its original and proper, or actual-concrete, meaning.

(1) Consider the following two statements: (i) "This right of the human person to religious freedom must be acknowledged in the juridical order of society, so that it becomes a civil right *(hoc ius personae humanae ad libertatem religiosam in iuridica societatis ordinatione ita est agnoscendum, ut ius civile evadat)*" (DH, 2); (ii) "For this reason, each person has the duty, and therefore *(ideoque)* the right, to seek the truth in religious matters, so that he may prudently form right and true judgments of conscience for himself, using all suitable means" (DH, 3). The first sentence clearly refers to the right to religious freedom as something that pertains to man in his intrinsic reality as man. It is the right to religious freedom that pertains to *man as such,* in other words, that is *to be recognized in the constitutional order* such that (*ita:* in order that) this natural right will become a *civilly recognized* right. Thus this first sentence distinguishes between a right proper to man in his moral nature as such, and a right in its civil sense; at the same time, the natural, and so far ontological and moral, right to religious freedom is understood to be *operative within* the civil right to religious freedom, precisely as the inner ground for affirming this right in its *distinctly civil or juridical sense.*[86]

Immediately preceding the first sentence cited here, sentence (i), are the statements that the right to religious freedom "consists in this, that all men and women should be immune from coercion," and that this right "has its foundation in the very dignity of the human person, as known from both the revealed word of God and reason itself" (DH, 2). Immediately following sentence (i), the Declaration indicates the nature of this foundation: that persons — beings endowed with reason and free will and bearing personal responsibility — are impelled by nature and also bound by a moral obligation to seek the truth, especially religious truth. For this reason, the second sentence cited above, sentence (ii), from article 3, refers to the *right (ius)* to seek the truth in religious matters precisely as a *consequence (ideoque)* of the nature-based *duty (officium)* to seek this truth.[87] This second sentence, furthermore, declares this right to be *for the sake of (ut)* forming judgments that are right and true *(recta et vera).*[88] In sum, the person's immunity from coercion that is affirmed in the Declaration, as articulated in articles 2 and 3, takes its bearings, its original meaning as negative, *from a freedom understood to be already positively tied to truth and ordered toward the search for truth, especially religious truth.*

In the terms used earlier in this study, the "freedom *from*" intrusive activity by others characteristic of a right already presupposes and is ordered in terms of "freedom *for*" the truth, especially about God. I have a right to be free *from* coercion *because* I am made *for* truth and God, *for the purpose of* seeking the truth and God. To remove the act of freedom from this original *"for"* is, according to the Declaration, to remove from the person the very dignity that warrants this claim to the right of freedom *from* coercion in the first place. Freedom *from* is indeed essential to the meaning of a right; but this essential negative meaning has its integrity as negative only as founded in and initially informed by the human act's positive movement toward, as well as obligation to seek, the truth, especially about God.

In a word, as Ancel concisely put it in his intervention: "Not only is there no opposition between religious freedom and the obligation to seek the truth, . . . but in fact religious freedom has its foundation in this obligation itself, and the obligation to seek the truth in turn requires religious freedom." Indeed, Ancel says that "the very heart of the Declaration *(nucleum declarationis)*" can be found here (AS IV/2, 17).[89]

(2) In his comments accompanying his translation of the Declaration, however, Murray provides a different interpretation of the above. He says that "in assigning a negative content to the right to religious freedom," the Declaration is "making [the right] formally a 'freedom from' and not a 'freedom for,'" and that in this "the Declaration is in harmony with the sense of the First Amendment of the American Constitution" (Abbott, 674n5). Consistent with what we said earlier, Murray indicates that it was important for the Council to make an argument supporting the principle of religious freedom, but that it was nonetheless "not the intention of the Council to affirm that the argument, as made in the text, is final and decisive" (680n7). Regarding the nature of the Council's argument, then, Murray makes two points. First, he states that "the simple essence of the matter is that man, being intelligent and free, is to be a responsible agent. Inherent in his very nature, therefore, is an exigency for freedom from coercion, especially in matters religious" (680n7). This argument of DH, 2, he says, provides "the objective foundation of the right to religious freedom . . . in terms that should be intelligible and acceptable to all men, including non-believers."[90]

Second, Murray says that the Declaration also includes further arguments in article 3 that are meant to "appeal to those who believe in God, in the objective order of truth and morality, and in the obligation to seek the truth, form one's conscience, and obey its dictates. To the man who so believes, it will be evident that no one is to be forced or constrained to act against his own conscience" (680n7). Murray also notes in this connection what he takes to be the different approaches of the American theorists, on the one hand, and the Declaration itself, on the other. The former ground religious freedom in political terms, relating it to "a general theory of constitutional government, limited by the rights of man, and to the concept of civic equality," while the latter "lays less stress on this political argument than it does on the ethical foundations of the right itself."

There are difficulties with respect to the line of interpretation that Murray offers here, however. He concludes by stating that the Declaration leaves one "free to construct the argument [undergirding the right to religious freedom] in the form which may seem more convincing" (Abbott, 68on7). This claim is highly ambiguous. Murray recognizes that the Declaration does in fact affirm a distinct argument regarding the right to religious freedom. However, this argument is not the one that Murray prefers, that is, the argument based on personal autonomy, which Murray takes to be the only argument capable of sustaining this right universally and in its essentially negative meaning. What Murray means, then, is that the argument *actually made by* the Declaration is inadequate; and that we are free to make alternative arguments, *so long as these alternative arguments succeed in grounding the right to religious freedom in its negative sense as immunity from coercion, as "freedom from" and not "freedom for."*

In a word, Murray understands his interpretation as a defense of what he takes to be the core teaching of the Declaration, namely, the right to freedom as primarily and most properly a negative right. And he takes his argument based on personal autonomy to be necessary to sustain a right so understood, even as he criticizes the Declaration's argument based on truth for its supposed inability to sustain this right in a principled manner. The point, then, is that Murray's apparent openness to different arguments regarding the foundation of the right to religious freedom is rigged in advance. On the one hand, the suggestion of openness presupposes his view of foundations that logically entails the simple primacy of a negatively conceived right; on the other hand, the suggestion begs the fact that the changes made in the final drafts of the Declaration were for the express purpose of *correcting* Murray's juridical view, by way precisely of tying the negative right to immunity to man's positive obligation to seek the truth, an obligation that according to the Declaration is rooted in man's nature.

I have already shown the problems with Murray's argument, as well as the soundness in principle of the Declaration's argument, on the basis of the Christian philosophical tradition. Here I would like briefly to go over the same ground in terms of the opening articles of the Declaration, read now in light of Murray's interpretation of the negative meaning of the right vis-à-vis the question of the foundation of that right.

On the one hand, Murray ties his defense of a primarily negatively conceived right to religious freedom to the human person's exigence to act on his own initiative and his own responsibility. In Murray's own argument, in other words, the demand for the right to religious freedom *to be recognized* is linked logically to the demand that this right *be conceived first and most basically in the negative terms of immunity.* Thus in regard to DH, 2, Murray writes in his commentary that "man, being intelligent and free, is to be a responsible agent. Inherent in his very nature, *therefore,* is an exigence for freedom from coercion" (Abbott, 680n7; emphasis added). Murray's primarily negative right, in a word, presupposes some version of a primarily negative freedom, of a freedom first related to truth extrinsically, not intrinsically.

On the other hand, the Declaration makes the opposite claim: because every person is positively impelled by nature to seek the truth, every person has a right to seek the truth. It was precisely the juridical approach's initial abstraction of freedom from truth which provoked the concern on the part of many Council bishops regarding the risk of relativism, and which alone accounts adequately for the changes proposed in the later drafts of the Declaration. The very point of these changes, in other words, was to clarify and emphasize *the internal relation between freedom and truth:* to insist that there *actually exists no freedom outside of its naturally given movement toward truth and toward God.* But if the free-intelligent human act is intrinsically related to the order of truth and to God, then this act evidently cannot be related first extrinsically, hence negatively, to truth, even for exclusively legal-political purposes. Freedom cannot be negatively related to truth without thereby changing the primitive nature of the freedom upon which the right to religious freedom rests. The changes incorporated into the final text of the Declaration, then, by expressly tying freedom with truth, thereby involve taking over the negative meaning of the right to religious freedom, *all the while simultaneously infusing this negative meaning with the positive meaning that derives from freedom's original-dynamic order toward truth.* In a word, the right to religious freedom, on a proper reading of the Declaration, bears a unity of negative and positive meanings, within an ontological (not temporal) priority of the positive.[91]

In sum: just as Murray's argument regarding the foundations for the civil right to religious freedom is logically tied to a freedom conceived in abstraction from truth and God, *and therefore to a primarily negative right,* so is the Declaration's argument regarding foundations logically tied to a freedom already related to truth, *and therefore also to a negative right, but only as already infused with a positive movement toward and ordering by truth and God.*

(3) Four final comments will further clarify my argument regarding the Declaration's teaching on the right to religious freedom. (i) First, as indicated, Murray suggests that the Declaration's argument based on the obligation to seek the truth, especially in religious matters, is not *per se* "intelligible and acceptable to all men, including non-believers" (Abbott, 680n7). But this suggestion contradicts the express intention and meaning of the text. Article 3 to be sure begins by acknowledging that further light is shed on the subject of religious freedom by the recognition that "the highest norm of human life is the divine law." The precise burden of articles 2 and 3, however, is to underscore that the movement toward the truth and the obligation to seek the truth in religious matters are rooted in the *very nature* of the human being, and that it is just because of this *rootedness in nature* that the right to religious freedom can in principle never be abandoned, even with respect to nonbelievers. These articles of the Declaration underscore this fact while simultaneously acknowledging that a deeper sense of the rootedness of the law of nature *in the divine law* will help us to enter into a deeper understanding of the law of nature itself. This indeed expresses exactly the spirit (and letter) of Wojtyła's interventions regarding the reasonable, vis-à-vis theological, nature of the Declaration. Wojtyła argued not that the Declaration needed to be simply theological in its method, but that the reasonable (philosophical) arguments it makes on behalf of nature needed themselves to be open to final integration in light of Scripture and the revelation of God in Jesus Christ.[92] Indeed, Murray's comment here, that in article 3 "an argument is suggested that will appeal to those who believe in God, in an objective order of truth and morality, and in the obligation to seek the truth" (Abbott, 680n7), implicitly overlooks a central part of the Catholic-Thomistic natural law tradition, within which the inclination to do good and to seek the truth about God are essential ingredients of human nature itself, and thus in principle available to reason.[93]

In a word, the Declaration clearly does not understand its reference to believing in God, to an objective order of truth and morality, and to the obligation to seek the truth to be a function simply of theological faith. Nor does it understand such a reference to be apt only with respect to those who have actually succeeded in living with fidelity this belief in God and truth and the obligation to search for the truth.[94] On the contrary, the text is explicit: such a recognition of the movement toward God and of a moral obligation to seek the truth, especially religious truth, "does not have its foundation in the subjective disposition of the person, . . . but rather in his very nature" (DH, 2). *That is why "the right to this immunity persists even for those who do not satisfy their obligation to seek the truth and to hold fast to it"* (DH, 2, emphasis added). This does not mean that all human beings are *explicitly conscious* of the movement toward, or obligation to seek, God and truth, but only that human beings cannot be aware of themselves, of their own nature as human, without thereby being aware at least implicitly of this movement and obligation.[95]

(ii) Second, we should recall here once more that most commentators, including those who support Murray's reading of DH, acknowledge that the Declaration did not accept his argument regarding foundations. Most of these commentators also follow Murray in his claim that the Declaration's view of this foundation is not integral to the Declaration's understanding of the nature of this right as (in Murray's view) primarily negative. Now, the foregoing reflections have shown that the Declaration's argument regarding foundations is indeed integral to its understanding of the nature of the right to religious freedom. But we should point out that not a few of these same commentators also tend to assume that the shift of the Declaration's argument regarding foundations away from the juridical approach was in an important sense due to Murray's health problems during discussion of the final drafts of the Declaration.[96]

As indicated, Murray suffered a collapsed lung requiring time in the hospital, thus forcing him to miss important subcommittee meetings that dealt with the revision of schema 4 of the Declaration. I mention this again only to note the fact that such an appeal to Murray's absence does not suffice as an adequate hermeneutic for interpreting a conciliar text. Deciphering the authentic meaning of such a text is not a matter of ascertaining the sum of the subjective dispositions and intentions of the Council bishops, or indeed of balancing competing arguments in terms, say, of political strategies or unforeseen health conditions. While reviewing the detail of these strategies and health conditions may be interesting, and while careful historical study of the evolution of a text through its stages of redaction has an indispensable role to play, neither suffices for an authentic Catholic hermeneutic.

An authentic hermeneutic assumes the sacramental nature of the teaching office of the Church, and begins with a final text received in faith. The proper way of proceeding is to look for the meaning of the text that accounts best, that is, most coherently, for all the elements of the text while also disclosing (and, where indicated, drawing out further) the faith of the

Church that originates with Jesus Christ and is handed on by the apostles via the creedal-magisterial tradition of the Church. It is not that historical events like Murray's ill health are not important and do not need to be taken into account. On the contrary, belief in a sacramental Church with a sacramental teaching office, rightly understood, implies belief in a divine providence that allows and indeed demands honest examination of such events, precisely because divine providence itself works through them, however fortuitous they may seem. The crucial point is that divine providence is never outwitted by such events. What must be recognized, in a word, is that providence works its positive will not (only) despite, *but more fundamentally within and through,* the vicissitudes of health problems or even political posturings of members of the Council.

The upshot is that commentators are able rightly to interpret the conciliar document in an authentically Catholic manner only insofar as they take this document to bear a meaning that has an objectivity and integrity *in se,* one that of course emerges in and through historical circumstances but nevertheless also transcends them.

(iii) Third, as indicated already, I do not mean to suggest by my argument that DH developed a fully integrated theory in defense of this ontological unity of freedom and truth characteristic of the person in relation to God. The point is simply that the key elements for such an integrated theory are to be found in the text itself. The text, in other words, bears a unity of meaning, one that, I have argued, consists in its affirmation of an intrinsic relation between freedom and truth, and of this positive relation as the internal context for the negative meaning of the right to religious freedom. My contention is that it is such an affirmation that alone can bring together the two overarching concerns voiced during the course of the redactions of the Declaration: to affirm *both* the intrinsic good of the right to religious freedom *and* the integrity of the human person in his natural ordering toward and in truth, in relation to God. To be sure, the final text of the Declaration, approved by the vast majority of the bishops, bears signs of the debate between the two dominant, and significantly different, approaches to the question of the relation between freedom and truth vis-à-vis political authority in civil society. In the end, however, the Council clearly rejected the juridical approach's claim of an originally empty act of freedom in favor of a freedom understood to exist actually only within an ordered relation to truth and God, a freedom fraught with an obligation to seek the truth, especially religious truth, and to embrace that truth when found with the whole of one's being. To be sure, and again emphatically: in approving this freedom, the bishops did not develop a well-rounded reasonable/philosophical or scriptural/theological theory on its behalf. However, it is not the proper task of a Council to resolve such philosophical or theological debates, except to the extent necessary to establish the parameters for future understanding in the Church, in a way that both is faithful to the apostolic teaching of the Church and reaches to the natural depths of the human heart. In the words of André-Vincent, the redacting process of the Declaration itself invites a further "prolongation" (*prolongement*: AV, 203), one that ponders further the nature of the realities engaged in the received text of the Declaration, in light of this text itself.[97]

Thus qualified, I believe the positive vision of the Declaration and of the principles that set essential boundaries for future discussion among Catholics is summed up in the following two statements.

First, Bishop Ancel explains as follows the reason for the crucial intervention he offered during the redaction of schema 5, the substance of which was incorporated into article 2 of the Declaration:

> [T]he connection that exists between the obligation to seek the truth and religious freedom itself has not yet [in schemas 3 and 4] been made clear. To be sure, we have often heard that man has an obligation to seek the truth; likewise, we have heard that religious freedom presents no obstacle to this obligation; but at no time, unless I am mistaken, has the positive connection between these two been made clear. Thus, in a few words, I would like to indicate what this ontological foundation is, and in this way to show the necessary connection that exists between the obligation to seek the objective truth and religious freedom itself. My proposition is as follows: the obligation to seek the truth is itself the ontological foundation of religious freedom, as set forth in our text. (AS IV/2, 17)

Second, a decade later, in 1976, André-Vincent, in summarizing the teaching of *Dignitatis humanae*, says that

> the mother-idea *(l'idée-mère)* [of DH] appears with the foundation of the right to religious freedom: the ontological bond of the person with truth, a natural bond grounding a natural obligation to search for the truth and to adhere to it, grounding at the same time a right to the freedom necessary to realize that obligation. The ontological bond of freedom to truth is the mother-idea of the Declaration. (AV, 203-4)[98]

(iv) A fourth and final point: as indicated at the outset of this essay, Rico argues that Pope John Paul II, especially as the years of his pontificate advanced, retreated from the fullness of the Declaration's teaching, downplaying its appreciation of the individual person and its embrace of the primarily negative-juridical idea of the right to religious freedom.[99] In the face, for example, of what he perceived to be a growing secularism and indifferentism in society, according to Rico, John Paul II attempted to restore a more traditional, pre-conciliar emphasis on truth, indeed on the revelation of Jesus Christ, as alone providing the sufficient conditions for a rightful exercise of freedom. The fact of the matter, however, is that the pontificate of John Paul II confirms, while to be sure clarifying further, the authentic teaching of the Declaration that he supported already in his work as Archbishop of Kraków at and immediately after the Council.[100] My purpose in the next section, then, will be to summarize, in terms of representative texts from the writings of John Paul II and his successor Benedict XVI, how these pontificates assume while developing the Council's authentic teaching on religious freedom. The effort will be to show how these writings sharpen the basic terms in which the foundation and nature of the right to religious freedom must now be framed, if we are to promote an integrated reception of the teaching enunciated by the Declaration.

VI.

(1) *Religious freedom within the missionary task of the Church.* The importance of *Dignitatis humanae* and the issue of religious freedom for John Paul II's pontificate is signaled in the prominence he gives this document already in his first encyclical, *Redemptor hominis.* Placing discussion of the Declaration within the context of the Church's "missionary attitude," John Paul says that "the Church attaches great importance to all that is stated by the Second Vatican Council in its Declaration on Religious Freedom, both the first and the second part of the document. We perceive intimately that the truth revealed to us by God imposes on us an obligation. We have, in particular, a great sense of responsibility for this truth" (RH, 12). He continues:

the Church, because of her divine mission, becomes all the more the guardian of this freedom, which is the condition and basis for the human person's true dignity. Jesus Christ meets the man of every age, including our own, with the same words: 'You will know the truth, and the truth will make you free' (Jn 8:32). These words contain both a fundamental requirement and a warning: the requirement of an honest relationship with regard to truth as a condition for authentic freedom, and the warning to avoid every kind of illusory freedom, every superficial unilateral freedom, every freedom that fails to enter into the whole truth about man and the world. (RH, 12)

Notable here is the fact that, for John Paul II, respect for religious freedom is an expression of the Church's mission to make known the truth about Jesus Christ. This mission imposes on us a responsibility for this truth, even as that responsibility itself demands respect for the dignity of the human being and thus for the freedom that is foundational for that dignity. The obligation imposed by the Church's missionary attitude, in other words, is not merely that we respect the freedom of every human being, but that we do so *by virtue of our very obligation to the truth*. The demand to respect the freedom of all human beings flows organically from the positive demand to seek and proclaim the truth, even as these two demands are indissoluble: neither is merely instrumental or functional in relation to the other.

(2) *The necessary bond between the right to religious freedom and truth and the natural law.* The missionary task of the Church indicates the framework for the unwavering link John Paul II makes between the right to religious freedom, on the one hand, and truth, human nature, and natural law, on the other. Thus in *Centesimus annus,* the pope refers to "the transcendent dignity of the human person, who, as the visible image of the invisible God, is therefore by his very nature the subject of rights which no one may violate — no individual, group, class, nation or state" (CA, 44). Furthermore, he says, "in constantly reaffirming the transcendent dignity of the person, the Church's method is always that of respect for freedom" (CA, 46). In his address to the United Nations in 1979, John Paul II cites from the important articles 2 and 3 of DH as a "contribution to respect for man's spiritual dimension." All human beings, "endowed with reason and free will and therefore bearing personal responsibility, are both impelled by their nature and bound by a moral obligation to seek the truth, especially religious truth." The practice of religion thus "of its nature consists [in] voluntary and free internal acts."[101]

Benedict XVI for his part reinforces these statements by John Paul II in his own address to the United Nations almost thirty years later. Human rights, he says, are based on the natural law inscribed on human hearts and present in different cultures and civilizations. Removing human rights from this context would mean restricting their range and yielding to a relativistic conception, according to which the meaning and interpretation of rights could vary and their universality would be denied in the name of different cultural, political, social, and even religious outlooks. This great variety of viewpoints must not be allowed to obscure the fact that not only rights are universal, but so too is the human person, the subject of those rights.[102]

Furthermore, in his 2011 "Message for the Celebration of the World Day of Peace," Benedict states the following:

Openness to truth and perfect goodness, openness to God, is rooted in human nature; it confers full dignity on each individual and is the guarantee of full mutual respect between persons. Religious freedom should be understood, then, not merely as immunity from coercion, but even more fundamentally as a capacity[103] to order one's own choices in accordance with truth. (n. 3)

The right to religious freedom is rooted in the very dignity of the human person (DH, 2), whose transcendent nature must not be ignored or overlooked. God created man and woman in his own image and likeness. For this reason each person is endowed with the *sacred right* to a full life, also from a spiritual standpoint. . . . Our nature appears as openness to the Mystery, a capacity to ask deep questions about ourselves and the origin of the universe, and a profound echo of the supreme Love of God, the beginning and end of all things, of every person and people. The transcendent dignity of the person is an essential value of Judeo-Christian wisdom, yet thanks to the use of reason, it can be recognized by all. This dignity, understood as a capacity to transcend one's own materiality and to seek truth, must be acknowledged as a universal *good,* indispensable for the building of a society directed to human fulfillment. (n. 2)[104]

The texts cited here spell out more fully the unity between truth and the person's right to religious freedom, by affirming that the truth of the person as ordered to the transcendent is the foundation of this right. John Paul II and Benedict XVI unequivocally affirm a principled, or universal, right to religious freedom, even as they bind this universal right with a universal human nature and dignity conceived in terms of relation to God. Such dignity is understood in terms of freedom and intelligence, to be sure, but a freedom and intelligence that is intrinsically and dynamically ordered to "the whole truth about man and the world," which means finally to the truth about God as revealed in Jesus Christ (RH, 12). Rights are universal, in a word, not because they are abstracted from truth-claims about nature and natural law, which would make rights a matter primarily and most basically of immunity from coercion, but because they are, on the contrary, rooted in the truth which every human being on earth participates in, *by nature,* and which, *as a consequence* (ontological, not temporal) demands the human being's immunity from coercion.

(3) *The right to religious freedom as the foundation and premise for all other rights.* John Paul II stresses that "freedom of conscience and of religion . . . is a primary and inalienable right of the human person; what is more, insofar as it touches the innermost sphere of the spirit . . . it upholds the justification, deeply rooted in each individual, of all other liberties."[105] In his 1988 "Message for World Day of Peace," he says, again, that "religious freedom, insofar as it touches the most intimate sphere of the spirit, sustains and is as it were the raison d'être of other freedoms. And the profession of a religion, although it consists primarily in interior acts of the spirit, involves the entire experience of human life, and thus all its manifestations" (n. 3). In *Redemptoris missio,* he says that the Church is "obliged to do everything possible to carry out her mission in the world and to reach all peoples. And she has the right to do this, a right given her by God for the accomplishment of his plan. Religious freedom, which is still at times limited or restricted, remains the premise and guarantee of all the freedoms that ensure the common good of individuals and peoples" (RM, 39).

It is not uncommon today for the right to religious freedom to be claimed as the most basic human right and indeed the foundation of all other rights. What is not so common, however, is to make explicit, as John Paul II does, the sense in which such a claim rests on an ontological judgment regarding the nature of religion or the natural religiosity of man (man as *homo religiosus*). It is because religion goes to the innermost depths of the human person and comprehends the whole of his life and experience that the right to freedom in matters of religion has priority over all other rights. Loss of the depth and comprehensiveness of the relation to God that is structured into man's original nature as a creature would, *eo ipso,* undermine the warrant for speaking of the right to religious freedom as the most fundamental right.

(4) *The indissolubility of freedom with truth and of truth with freedom.*

The question regarding the link between freedom and truth runs through all of the preceding points, and was also, as we have seen, the basic question driving the debate over religious freedom at the Council. In his writings as pope, John Paul II gives more precision to the nature of this link. In *Veritatis splendor,* for example, he says that freedom, rightly understood, is "never freedom 'from' the truth but always freedom 'in' the truth" (VS, 64). Later in this same encyclical, he says that the "essential bond between Truth, the Good, and Freedom has been largely lost sight of by present-day culture. As a result, helping man to rediscover it represents nowadays one of the specific requirements of the Church's mission" (VS, 84). Again, in *Evangelium vitae,* he says that "freedom . . . possesses an inherently relational dimension *(libertatem . . . essentialem necessitudinis rationem secum fert),*" and an "essential bond with the truth *(constitutivum veritatis vinculum)*" (EV, 19). Also in *Veritatis splendor,* John Paul states:

> [Man's] freedom is real but limited: its absolute and unconditional origin is not in itself, but in the life within which it is situated. . . . Human freedom belongs to us as creatures; it is a freedom which is given as a gift, one to be received like a seed and to be cultivated responsibly. It is an essential part of that creaturely image which is the basis of the dignity of the person. Within that freedom there is an echo of the primordial vocation whereby the Creator calls man to the true Good, and even more, through Christ's revelation, to become his friend and to share his own divine life. It is at once inalienable self-possession and openness to all that exists, in passing beyond self to knowledge and love of the other. Freedom, then, is rooted in the truth about man, and it is ultimately directed towards communion. (VS, 86; cf. 85, 87)

Note the echo of Pieper (and Pinckaers) found in this last citation: the self-possessing activity of the human subject is simultaneous with, and inseparable from, his openness to all that exists. Man's self-possessiveness or freedom is not first indifferent to the world, but always already informed by an openness to, and thus positive capacity for, the world. This is the implication of the pope's statement that freedom is intrinsically related to truth. A freedom that is intrinsically related to truth is one that *is ordered by truth in its original constitution **as** free.* What such a view of freedom excludes is the sort of primitively *extrinsic* relation to truth that would construe truth as first *consequent* upon the act of freedom, such that the act of freedom is originally indifferent to truth.

An intrinsic *(constitutivum)* relation between freedom and truth alone accounts for the letter and the spirit of the above statements by John Paul II, as well as the interventions by Karol Wojtyła regarding religious freedom at the time of the Council. This intrinsic relation enables us to understand the root meaning of John Paul's statement in *Fides et ratio* that "truth and freedom either go together hand in hand or together they perish in misery" (FR, 90).

(5) The intrinsic relation between freedom and truth implies an intrinsic relation between man qua man and man qua citizen: between man as subject of a moral right to religious freedom and man as subject of a distinct civil right to religious freedom. *Dignitatis humanae* states that "the right to religious freedom [which] has its foundation in the very dignity of the human person . . . must be acknowledged in the juridical order of society, so that it becomes a civil right *(in iuridica societatis ordinatione ita est agnoscendum, ut ius civile evadat)*" (DH, 2). In other words, as we have indicated above, it is the *naturally or ontologically rooted moral right to religious freedom proper to the human person as such* that is to be recognized *also as a civil right.* The language here thus supports a unity simultaneous with distinction between these respective orders of rights. It is because all men are *ontologically* moved by nature to seek the truth, especially religious truth, that they have a *moral* duty and right to religious freedom; and this *moral right* demands distinct recognition as a *civil right.*[106]

This position, supported by Wojtyła at the Council, is characteristic of the pontificate of John Paul II. It is only such a position that accounts adequately for the many texts of John Paul cited above which clearly insist that the ontological truth about man, which grounds his moral right, be recognized also civilly, in the juridical order.[107]

Such a uniting of the ontological-moral with the juridical is likewise implied in Benedict's *Caritas in veritate,* which insists that the concerns proper to cultural institutions such as the family — concerns like the truth of love — need to be included within the concerns proper to the economy and the state, in order that we might move beyond the binary logic of market-plus-state.[108] Finally, the intrinsic relevance of the ontological meaning of man generally for civil government is nicely summed up in John Paul II's *Catechism of the Catholic Church:*

> Every institution is inspired, at least implicitly, by a vision of man and his destiny, from which it derives the point of reference for its judgment, its hierarchy of values, its line of conduct. Most societies have formed

their institutions in the recognition of a certain preeminence of man over things. Only the divinely revealed religion has clearly recognized man's origin and destiny in God, the Creator and Redeemer. The Church invites political authorities to measure their judgments and decisions against this inspired truth about God and Man. (CCC, 2244)

The point here, of course, is not that John Paul II does not recognize the distinction between the ontological-moral and civil-juridical orders, but that he affirms an intrinsic rather than extrinsic relation between these. It is because freedom and truth, especially the truth about God, bear an intrinsic relation to each other that this relation cannot be fractured — that is, reduced to an extrinsic relation — *even for purposes of a (would-be) purely juridical order,* without thereby distorting the original nature of each. The juridical approach that separates freedom and truth logically involves juridical enforcement of just the reductive sense of freedom and of truth, and consequently the arbitrary rights, that Karol Wojtyła/John Paul II consistently opposed over a lifetime.

(6) How, then, do we best frame the issue that most profoundly governs the argument of the Second Vatican Council's Declaration on Religious Freedom, in light of John Paul II's and Benedict XVI's reading of this document? For a summary answer to this question, I return to two terms that are basic to Servais Pinckaers and Josef Pieper.

Pinckaers emphasizes the difference between freedom of indifference and freedom of quality. As pointed out earlier, the latter bears a dual meaning that can give rise to significant ambiguity. On the one hand, freedom of quality calls attention to the original ordering of freedom by and toward truth and the good, an ordering that implies the natural desire for God. On the other hand, it signals the virtuous acting into which freedom is able to grow, and refers thus to what is *logically yet to be accomplished.* Translating *liberté de qualité* as "freedom *for* excellence" reinforces this second meaning in a way that disposes us to overlook the first, and thus to miss the crucial point, both for Pinckaers and for the argument regarding religious freedom developed in this essay.[109]

There is also the term "capacity" used by Josef Pieper,[110] and indeed by Benedict XVI in the texts cited above. "Capacity" can be read as an originally neutral space for containing something, an empty (or originally "indifferent") container that is logically yet to be filled. But for Pieper, in the spirit of Pinckaers, it also carries the positive sense of what is already, in its original structure, apt or fit for what is meant to fill it.

The respective arguments of Pinckaers and Pieper draw attention to the original dynamic ordering of the human act toward the truth and the search for God. They thus highlight the modern failure, often even within Catholicism, to grasp that the free-intelligent human act is *initially, by nature,* ordered within, and so far by, a truthful ontological relation to the world and its Creator. Human freedom, in its self-reflexivity as free and in its own deepest logic, cannot but love implicitly the good and the true and God. Human freedom, in its inmost élan as free, is never neutral toward these.

In this context, we showed above that Lefebvre and Murray, from their opposite directions, both fail to integrate adequately just this original natural ordering of freedom by truth into their respective approaches to the question of the right to religious freedom. We have, on the one hand, a human dignity tied to an exercise of freedom *abstracted from* truth (Murray); and, on the other, a human dignity tied exclusively to an exercise of freedom that *has realized* truth (Lefebvre). In neither case do we have a human dignity, and hence a human right, tied to a freedom that is at once originally ordered toward truth ("already") and still to be fully realized ("not yet"). In neither case, in other words, do we have a right to religious freedom rooted in a human dignity characterized in terms of an initial, *natural-ontological,* unity of freedom and truth.

My argument has been that it is this "already" coincident with the "not yet" of the free-intelligent human act's relation to the world and God that is affirmed by both Pinckaers and Pieper. The human being, as a creature, stands in an original relationship of truth with the world and with God, a *naturally given* relationship that he is called to freely and intelligently *realize* over a lifetime. My contention is that this is also the position implied in the important text of DH, 2: that, because they are persons — beings endowed with reason and free will — all men are impelled by nature and so far originally ordered (and bound by a moral obligation) to seek the truth, especially as that truth bears on religion.

In a word: *what the Declaration, consistent with the Catholic tradition, understands as proper to the meaning of the human person, namely, reason and free will,*[111] **bears the further implication of a true relation to the world and God that is always first given.** The pontifical writings of John Paul II and Benedict XVI accentuate this implication of relation to the world and to God in their understanding of the nature and dignity of the human person. What characterizes both the Declaration and the writings of these pontificates, albeit in distinctly developed ways, is the centrality given to relation to God (in Christ) and others (the world) in the constitution of the human person and the human act.[112] The question, finally, regarding the Council's teaching in the matter of religious freedom, is whether this relation is originally given to the person ("transcendentally"), or originally enacted by the person ("categorially"). Does the free and intelligent human actor dwell already by nature within the truth of the world and God that he is at the same time yet to realize? In short, what, in light of such questions, do we make of John Paul II's statement quoted above:

> Human freedom . . . is an essential part of that creaturely image which is the basis of the dignity of the person. Within that freedom there is an echo of the primordial vocation whereby the Creator calls man to the true Good. . . . It is at once inalienable self-possession and openness to all that exists, in passing beyond self to knowledge and love of the other. Freedom then is rooted in the truth about man, and it is ultimately directed towards communion. (VS, 86)

The burden and the cogency of the Declaration's argument regarding the nature of the civil right to religious freedom (is the right primarily negative or positive?), and the nature of freedom and truth as pertinent to the legal constitutional order (is truth originally bound with freedom or simply an object of freedom?), hinge on the response to this question regarding the nature of the relation between the human subject, on the one hand, and the world and God, on the other, and the spiritual character of the human act that this relation entails.

VII.

Before turning to the many further issues that are implicated in the interpretation of *Dignitatis humanae* I have presented here, let me first summarize the main elements of the foregoing argument:

(1) There is an originally given, intrinsic relation between freedom and truth.

(2) This is best conceived in light of the ancient-medieval understanding of the spiritual nature of the human being and human act *(anima forma corporis),* and the transcendental nature of truth, as recovered in distinct ways by Pinckaers (freedom) and Pieper (spirit, knowledge, and truth, especially in relation to God).

(3) The Declaration's teaching regarding the right to religious freedom

presupposes and (implicitly) takes over this earlier teaching, in terms of the human person as *subject of rights*. The Declaration does not develop this understanding of the person in a thematic way. Its intention, rather, is to arrive at an adequate notion of a right, and this involves attending in a particular way to the *subjectivity* of the person, which it affirms while simultaneously securing *the intrinsic link between that subjectivity and the order of truth,* especially religious truth. But this process evidently involves the Declaration in drawing out more fully and explicitly the interiority traditionally understood to be proper to the human act, an interiority fraught with an originally given true relation to the world (all that exists) and to God. Human subjectivity or interiority, in other words, is first positively, not "negatively" (or "indifferently"), related to the world and to God, and is necessarily presupposed by this relation.

(4) The Declaration thus ties the meaning of rights to a human subjectivity understood to be originally "truthed" by the world and, implicitly and more profoundly, by relation to the Creator. The right to religious freedom is an immunity from coercion only inside, and by virtue of, this *naturally given positive relation to God and others.* On the Declaration's view, what is primary in the self's relation to the other is *a positive letting be.* On the juridical view, by contrast, what is primary is *the self's negative immunity from constraint or intrusiveness by the other.*

(5) This position affirmed by the Declaration, even if not developed in an integrated fashion, exposes the root problem of the prevalent "juridical" interpretation, which holds that the right to religious freedom is primarily negative. This negative sense is indeed essential to the right's proper meaning as conceived by the Declaration, but is understood to take its inner dynamic from within the human being's original true and positive relation to God and to other human creatures. This latter positive relation, indeed, discloses how a right conceived primarily in negative terms is so far individualist and constructivist in nature. Granting priority to a singular human act conceived first in abstraction from its relation to the world and to God makes that relation into something first enacted or constructed by the self (thus implying a nominalistic view of the human being). It is this implied individualism and constructivism that logically gives rise to relativistic monism.

(6) The pontificates of John Paul II and Benedict XVI confirm the foregoing interpretation of religious freedom in *Dignitatis humanae,* while developing in a more integrated way the notion of the person undergirding this interpretation. They develop further the *relationality to truth and God* implied in the medieval conceptions of the spiritual, interior-subjective

nature of the human act, and of this act's original-transcendental ordering *toward* and *by* the world. John Paul II and Benedict XVI, in other words, affirm the *modern emphasis on the subjective dimension of the person*, by way of taking over and drawing out the further meaning already implicit in *the medievals' objective notions of the human spirit and truth*.

VIII.

The core claim of the juridical reading of *Dignitatis humanae*, then, is that the civil right to religious freedom is primarily negative, and that this right is tied to a human dignity conceived in abstraction from the person's relation to truth. As indicated in the course of our argument, this juridical under-standing involves its own approaches to several other issues that bear on religious freedom and the Church's relationship to modernity. In light of my task of interpreting the Declaration, it is incumbent upon me to show how my argument regarding the nature and foundation of the right to religious freedom can accommodate the concerns raised by the prevalent juridical reading of the Declaration in regard to these issues. This accommodation, however, as we will see, involves reconfiguring the terms in which the issues are customarily approached today. My purpose here, then, is not to provide a fully articulated response to any of these issues, but only to say enough to clarify the *status quaestionis* demanded by the Declaration in its rightful understanding.

Development of doctrine. The Church's affirmation of the right to religious freedom in *Dignitatis humanae* does indeed signal a genuine development of doctrine. But this development is not rightly understood simply as a matter of the Church coming to recognize the legitimacy of a freedom that has already been given its proper form in modern culture, to which the Church then adds her own distinctive theological framework. The development lies, rather, in drawing out the depths of meaning regarding the human person that are rooted in the ancient-medieval notions of the human spirit and truth, and are indeed required already by the gospel of Jesus Christ. Recog-nizing modernity's legitimate demand for freedom, the Church clarifies the terms in which this demand is rightly understood in light of the gospel and the laws of human nature.[113]

The Declaration thus draws out the implications of the interiority of the human person in his transcendent openness to the truth of being and of God. Entry into the truth realizes the subjective-interior free act of man which *by nature is made-for-truth,* even as the realization of truth takes place only *via this subjective-interior free act.* The development of doctrine in *Dignitatis humanae* thus consists in a deepened sense of *the demand of truth itself* for freedom, as the inner condition and form of truth's own proper realization. It consists also in a deepened sense of *the human person:* of the person's proper rational and free act as a primitive unity of subjectivity-interiority, on the one hand, and ordering toward and in objective truth, on the other.

In a word, the Declaration affirms the modern emphasis on freedom and the civil right to religious freedom, in its affirmation that the truth regarding the person in relation to God *itself demands freedom,* and *really does free.* Any rightful claim of a development of doctrine in the matter of religious freedom needs to recognize a growth in the Church's understanding of the mutual implication of truth and freedom, and of the human dignity that flows from this mutual implication.[114]

"*A new dogmatic orientation*" or "*a new orientation for the Church's social doctrine*"? The current dominant juridical reading of the Declaration, largely set in place by Murray, understands the Church's development of doctrine in the matter of religious freedom differently. A significant contemporary example is provided by Martin Rhonheimer in his recent collection of essays, *The Common Good of Constitutional Democracy.*[115] In what follows, we will consider Rhonheimer's understanding of the development of doctrine regarding religious freedom, as he unfolds this in relation to Benedict XVI's "hermeneutic of reform."

In an essay originally published in 2009, titled "Benedict XVI's 'Hermeneutic of Reform' and Religious Freedom," Rhonheimer makes a twofold claim. First, he insists that Vatican II's teaching on religious freedom is essentially concerned, not with religious truth-claims or the nature of the Church and its faith, but rather with the mission and function of the state.[116] The teaching of DH, in other words, does not signal "a new dogmatic orientation"; it signals rather "a new orientation for the Church's social doctrine" (432). Second, Rhonheimer claims that, with the Declaration, the Church has come to recognize that modern constitutional democracy affirms a strictly *civil* right to religious freedom, which, rightly understood, so far avoids the implication of religious or metaphysical truth.

Rhonheimer invokes Benedict XVI in support of his proposal. In his 2005 Christmas Address to the Roman Curia, Benedict emphasized the need to understand the Second Vatican Council not primarily in terms of "discontinuity," but in terms of "reform," which involves elements of both continuity and discontinuity. Benedict used the language of "different levels" to distinguish between permanent principles of the Church, on the one hand, and "the practical forms that depend on the historical situation and are therefore subject to change," on the other. For Benedict, then, when interpreting the Council, it is necessary to distinguish between a continuity of principles and a discontinuity in concrete historical situations. True reform, he says, consists in just this "combination (*insieme:* whole, harmony, ensemble) of continuity and discontinuity." Rhonheimer, in his interpretation of Benedict, highlights the latter's language of "different levels," interpreting this difference as "precisely" a "separation": between the level of religious truth and the Church, on the one hand, and that of the state-political or civil-legal order, on the other. Indeed, according to Rhonheimer, Benedict "made precisely that separation of the 'different levels' that the preconciliar Magisterium . . . had been unable to accomplish," due to its confusing questions regarding "religious truth and . . . [the] true Church" with those regarding "the state political order and the civil legal order" (430-31).

For Rhonheimer, then, in affirming the right to religious freedom, the Church acknowledges what she takes to be a new *political* development, as distinct from a new deepening in her understanding of truth in relation to freedom: "[T]he Church has modified its conception of the function of the state and of its duties toward the true religion, a conception that in reality is not at all of a purely theological nature; nor has it to do with the nature of the Church and its faith, but it concerns the nature of the state and its relationship with the Church. So, at the most, this is a question concerning an aspect of the social doctrine of the Church" (440). For this reason, says Rhonheimer, the discontinuity with earlier Church teaching "arises only at the level of the assertion of the civil right, and is therefore only of the political order" (442).[117]

Now Rhonheimer clearly acknowledges that the right to religious freedom is "based on the very nature of the human person" (442). Thus it is "correct to say that the Second Vatican Council considers religious freedom as part of natural law." However, "[t]he perspective of Vatican II is . . . not simply and solely that of natural law, but is always also that of religious freedom 'as a civil right,' meaning, in the final analysis, as the right to freedom of worship" (442). For Rhonheimer, it was just this sense of a *civil* right to religious freedom that Pius IX condemned in his 1864 encyclical *Quanta Cura*. The discontinuity between Vatican II, on the one hand, and the preconciliar magisterium represented by Pius IX, on the other, concerns not the *interpretation* of natural law, properly speaking, but only its *application*. For this reason, natural law is "not at all affected by the discontinuity that is in question here. The contradiction arises only at the level of the assertion of the civil right, and is therefore only of the political order. The doctrine of Vatican II and the teaching of *Quanta Cura* with its *Syllabus errorum* are therefore in contradiction not at the level of the natural law, but at the level of natural law's legal-political application in situations and in the face of concrete problems" (442).

According to Rhonheimer, in sum, while Pius IX understood his condemnation of the civil right to religious freedom as "a necessity of the dogmatic order" (444), this was only because the pope thought recognition of this right entailed acceptance of religious indifferentism and relativism. This condemnation, in other words, was due to a misplaced understanding of the state as "the guarantor of religious truth," such that "the Church possesses the right to make use of the state as its secular arm to ensure its pastoral responsibilities" (445). In point of fact, however, Rhonheimer argues, "such a conception of the state did not rest in the slightest on the principles of Catholic doctrine on faith and morality" (445). What Pius IX judged to be a *dogmatic* error, in other words, derived from what was merely a mistaken *historical judgment* regarding the nature of the modern liberal state. In a word, the difference between the twentieth-century conciliar Church and the nineteenth-century Church is a difference, not in the Church's self-understanding in the dogmatic sense, but in her understanding of the state and the temporal order (453).[118]

Rhonheimer's argument, however, misses the fact that the Council indicated a deepened sense of the mutual relation between truth and freedom, and that this newly retrieved "dogmatic" integration of truth and freedom was itself what demanded a corresponding deepening in her understanding of the state. But my concern here is limited to Rhonheimer's reading of Benedict as interpreter of the Council: has he understood accurately Benedict's sense of the Church's "reform" in the matter of religious freedom as an *insieme* of continuity and discontinuity?

My own argument regarding DH has been that there can be no exercise of religious freedom or the right to religious freedom that is neutral with respect to the human person in his relation to God and thus with respect to the ultimate nature and dignity of the person.[119] Every defense of the right to religious freedom, even that of Rhonheimer on behalf of a *distinctly civil* right, one purportedly innocent of metaphysical-religious claims, inevitably invokes some notion of the relation between truth and freedom, and thus some notion of the human being and the nature of his relation and obligation to what is ultimately true. Every such argument will therefore implicate, however unconsciously, some understanding of the Church's dogmatic doctrinal tradition and its development. This of course does not mean that the Council's affirmation of a civil right to religious freedom does not entail also a doctrine of the state and its relation to the Church. The point, rather, is that the Church's doctrine of the state and its relation to the Church *is itself, simultaneously and at a more fundamental level, an expression of her understanding of the nature of truth in its inner relation to freedom:* of the nature of truth as open to freedom, and freedom to truth, in the *inmost ontological structure of each,* hence in a way that cannot but bear intrinsic implications for the mutual relation of truth and freedom *also in the political order.* In a word, it is the Church's deepened understanding of truth that itself carries in its wake a deepened doctrine of the state.

My contention is that this understanding, which is the burden of this present essay's reading of DH, lies also at the heart of Benedict's 2005 remarks regarding the Council's affirmation of a right to religious freedom.[120]

The center of the Council's concern, Benedict says in this address, is the question of man and of the relationship between the Church and the modern world: "In the great dispute about man which marks the modern epoch, the Council had to focus in particular on the theme of anthropology. It had to question the relationship between the Church and her faith on the one hand, and man and the contemporary world on the other. . . . The question becomes even clearer if, instead of the generic terms 'contemporary world,' we opt for another that is more precise: the Council had to determine in a new way the relationship between the Church and the modern era." Benedict indicates three areas where this question of the relation between the Church's faith and the modern world is especially important: faith and modern science, the relationship between the Church and the state, and the question of religious tolerance, or the Church's relationship with world religions. All of these involve new historical circumstances in which the permanent principles of the faith need to be thought anew. At the heart of the Council, then, is also the relationship between faith and reason: "The steps the Council took towards the modern era, which had rather vaguely been presented as 'openness to the world,' belong in short to the perennial problem of the relationship between faith and reason that is re-emerging in ever new forms."

Benedict's reference to the teaching of *Dignitatis humanae* is thus situated within the context of the dialogue between faith and (modern) reason. Here, as Rhonheimer indicates, Benedict affirms that the Council "recogniz[es] and mak[es] its own an essential principle of the modern state with the Decree on Religious Freedom." Indeed, Benedict says further that, in so doing, the Council "has recovered the deepest patrimony of the Church," and "can be conscious of being in full harmony with the teaching of Jesus himself (cf. Mt 22:21), as well as with the Church of the martyrs of all time. The ancient Church naturally prayed for the emperors and political leaders out of duty (cf. Tim 2:2), but while she prayed for the emperors, she refused to worship them and clearly rejected the religion of the state." How are we to understand this statement? What is the precise nature of the "essential principle of the modern state" that the Church has now recognized and made her own?

According to the pope, "[t]he martyrs of the early Church died for their faith in the God who was revealed in Jesus Christ, and for this very reason they also died for freedom of conscience and the freedom to profess one's own faith — a profession no state can impose but which, instead, can only be claimed with God's grace in freedom of conscience." As this last sentence makes clear, Benedict's point is that the martyrs rejected "the religion of the state" because the God they worshiped *transcended* the state, while the state refused to recognize this transcendence. The martyrs' rejection of "state religion," in other words, did not lie first in the fact that the Roman state favored religion, but that, in so doing, it identified the state with its particular religion in such a way that the state refused to recognize the freedom of those not practicing this religion to worship and fulfill their positive obligation to the transcendent God. Benedict is thus making a statement about the Roman state that bears in the first instance not on the nature of the state, but on the nature of the Christian faith and its transcendent order of truth. Or better: his statement bears on the nature of the state, but *only as bearing more basically on the truth of the faith professed by the Christian martyrs.*

Again, Benedict says that "[t]he Second Vatican Council, with its new definition of the relationship between the faith of the Church and certain essential elements of modern thought, has reviewed or even corrected certain [of her] historical decisions, but in this apparent discontinuity it has actually preserved and deepened her inmost nature and true identity." The Church's development, in other words, signals *a preservation coincident with a deepening of her own inmost reality qua Church.* The apparent discontinuity in this development both preserves and deepens the truths of the faith, on the one hand, and does so in terms of the "inmost nature and true identity of the Church herself," on the other. To be sure, this development in the Church is elicited through political developments in the modern state. But the ecclesial development neither consists first in, nor reduces essentially to, the recognition of an external political development. Rather, the Council's recognition of "certain essential elements of modern thought" involves *"making [these] its own"* (emphasis added), in a way that recovers "the deepest patrimony of the Church . . . in full harmony with the teaching of Jesus himself." The point, in other words, is that the Church's recognition of certain essential elements of the modern state is due first and above all to fidelity to her own tradition, reaching back to Jesus Christ, a fidelity that calls for further deepening in light of the concrete "historical situation" presented by the new "practical form" of the modern constitutional state. The Church's making an essential element of modern thought her own, in a word, means *affirming* that element *all the while reconfiguring it where necessary in light of her own tradition.*

Thus, at the heart of this *rediscovery of and fidelity to her faith* in light of this *new historical situation* lies the Church's recognition of religious freedom, not as "an inability to discover the truth," in a sense implying metaphysical relativism, but rather as a freedom that "derives from human coexistence (*convivenza humana:* human living together, human community), or rather, as an intrinsic consequence of the truth that cannot be externally imposed but that the person must adopt solely through the process of conviction." The Church affirms religious freedom, in other words, by virtue of her deepened understanding that freedom truly conceived arises from within human community and indeed as an intrinsic consequence of the inner nature of truth itself, which can never be externally imposed but must always be appropriated freely. She affirms religious freedom, in sum, by way of the (re-)discovery of the roots of her own tradition, which insist on the communal nature of the human being and on a truth that presupposes and demands — on grounds of both faith and reason — the interiority and thus freedom of the human subject.

It is not the case, then, that the Church maintains a simple continuity *within herself* coupled with a discontinuity accounted for *simply in terms of a new "extrinsic" relation to the state, due to changes in the state itself.* On the contrary, the "discontinuity" in the Council's teaching derives most basically from within the Church's *own continuity,* indeed her self-identity, as the Church originated with Jesus Christ. That is why, for Benedict, the proper way to interpret the conciliar developments regarding religious freedom and the modern state is in terms of what he calls a "hermeneutics of *reform*": because the continuity *as well as* the discontinuity have their roots in one and the same source, namely, the Church in her faithful understanding of the right relation between faith and reason, vis-à-vis the truth of the revelation of God in Jesus Christ. Herein lie the permanent principles that have been deepened and developed further in light of "the practical forms that depend on the [current] historical situation."

Thus we may say that Benedict's 2005 address confirms what has been argued earlier in this essay: that the essential element of modernity embraced by the Church consists in modernity's growing awareness of the subjectivity or interiority of the human person, coincident with the demands of this growing awareness in the realm of modern politics with respect to the right to religious freedom. But the Church embraces this subjectivity, and the right to freedom which it implies, first by way of a (re-)discovery of the further depths of her own tradition, a rediscovery that, again, is elicited from, and thought through in light of, the distinct historical development of the modern constitutional state. The Church in her Declaration on Religious Freedom signals a deeper appreciation of the fact that *truth itself implies an interiorizing subject and so far a free subject,* even as freedom finds itself always already within the order of being, an order that is true and good and that points finally to the creative freedom and intelligence of God. All of this reaches back to Aquinas himself, and to the ancient sources on which he drew, and receives its deepest anchoring in the life and teaching of Jesus Christ.

The reason why the ancient Church refused to worship the emperors, then, and why it rejected the ancient religion of the state, is that this worship and this religion of the state *denied the human-Christian act's positive transcendence toward God.* The ancient Christians' refusal of this worship and rejection of this religion are *the logical (ontological) consequence* of their understanding of the dynamics of the human act in light of faith in Jesus of Nazareth. In this light, the Council's teaching is best read as a development of theological doctrine in the proper sense, and only thus also, at the same time, a development in the Church's social doctrine.[121]

Reason and revelation. As indicated earlier, Wojtyła insisted in his conciliar interventions on religious freedom that the Church needed to be clear that her teaching in this matter was rooted in the revelation of Jesus Christ, and that arguments based on reason should therefore not be separated too much from those based on the gospel. Changes were made in the fifth and final texts, however, that answered Wojtyła's main concern, which was that arguments made primarily on the basis of reason be recognized to be clearly open to, consistent with, and intrinsically fulfilled by arguments based on the gospel. It is therefore inaccurate to construe Wojtyła's interventions at the

Council, or indeed his explicit recommendation later in *Redemptor hominis,* 12, that *both parts* of *Dignitatis humanae* be read together, to imply that he wanted the Declaration to take a theological *rather than* philosophical approach. What he wanted, on the contrary, was that the approach adopted be properly integrated: that the philosophical-rational elements of the argument be integrated, or at least readily integrateable, with the truth of God's definitive revelation in Jesus Christ.

The Declaration's argument, properly interpreted, does indeed presuppose the revelation of Jesus Christ as its origin and end. The shift that was increasingly made in the later drafts of the Declaration toward an argument for the right to religious freedom based on man's relation to the truth, especially religious truth, implies awareness of this larger theological context. Once again, we may question whether the connection between the philosophical and theological-scriptural components of the argument is adequately developed in theoretical terms. But what the Declaration actually does is sufficient for its purposes. Neither, on the one hand, does the Declaration take its emphasis on rational elements to compromise the turn to Jesus Christ (in part II); nor, on the other hand, does the Declaration take its presupposed faith in Jesus Christ to preempt the distinctly rational elements (in part I).

Society and state; the limited state. As we have seen, in rejecting the formal-juridical approach to the civil right to religious freedom, the Declaration rejects an extrinsic relationship between truth and freedom. But this implies that the Declaration also rejects an extrinsic relation between society and state, according to which society, on the one hand, is held to be exclusively responsible for securing the truth, while the state, on the other hand, is responsible solely for securing the (negative) right to religious freedom. However, this does not mean that the Declaration thereby rejects *the principle of a distinction* between society and state. On the contrary, it takes this distinction to be necessary in order to avoid a totalitarian state. Protection against totalitarianism can nevertheless be secured only insofar as both society and state bear a unity of purpose within their distinctness: the *state,* in its exercise of constitutional authority on behalf of the right to religious freedom, should be ordered internally in light of the truth about man, a truth that is properly secured by the institutions of *society,* and by the state itself as the legal-constitutional authority *of* society.

The point here, as it concerns the nature of a distinction, can be clarified with reference to the difference between a Cartesian and a Catholic-Thomistic pattern of thinking. Cartesians believe that what is distinguished maintains its integrity only if the two referents are external to one another: the soul and the body, for example, each retain their proper integrity only as outside each other. Thomists, in contrast, insist that the integrity of what is distinguished is maintained only from within an anterior unity: the soul and the body each keep their proper integrity only as first shaped from within (in different, asymmetrical ways) by the other.[122]

The contemporary language of society and state, at least in its liberal usage, inclines us to think of these in Cartesian fashion as two "things," each with its own independent reality and responsibility. In truth, however, the state is but society's way of organizing itself politically, of society providing itself with legal-constitutional order. In its very distinctness as a legal-constitutional order, the state remains essentially subordinate to the common good of those natural communities, above all those rooted in religion and family, that make up the society of which the state is itself a natural "prolongation."

The proposal of this essay, then, yields two principles with respect to the state-society distinction, apropos of our interpretation of the Declaration. First, the state remains always and everywhere subordinate to the end of the person as he exists in his original relation to the Creator through the family, and so far subordinate to the end of society itself that is rooted in such naturally given community. Because of, and *within,* this subordination to society, the state shares a common end with society, and so far a common responsibility for the mutual relation of truth and freedom that is necessary for the realization of this end. Second, the state bears this common responsibility *in its own distinct way.*[123] The nature of this distinct responsibility for truth on the part of both state and society will be clarified further below in connection with questions regarding the competence of the state, the Church-state distinction, and the secularity of the state and society.

It is in light of this distinction-within-unity between state and society that we can understand properly the idea of a limited state, the kind of state implicit in a rightly conceived "free society." The Declaration does indeed demand a limited state, but not in the formal-juridical sense discussed earlier. The authority of the state is limited not first in light of the *negative freedom* of individual persons' exercising their logically indifferent freedom of choice, but rather in light of the *positive freedom* of persons who are originally ordered by nature to God through the family. The purpose of governmental authority is always and everywhere to *assist,* not *replace,* the authority of this community that begins in the nature of the human being. Indeed, that is the burden of what we showed earlier in terms of DH: it is the very demand for the state's positive assistance of citizens in their relation to this original community that requires the state's principled recognition of citizens' right to freedom in the negative sense of immunity.

Benedict XVI's 2011 address to the German Bundestag helps to clarify the rightful sense of the distinction between state and society that I have indicated here.[124] Reflecting on the foundations of law *(Recht)*, Benedict refers in this address to the story of God's invitation to Solomon upon the latter's accession to the throne: What will the young ruler ask for? Passing over success, wealth, long life, and the destruction of his enemies, Solomon asks "for a listening heart, so that he may govern God's people, and discern between good and evil." This story indicates the "fundamental criterion and the motivation for [the] work of the politician," which according to Benedict must be "a striving for justice *(Gerechtigkeit)*," that justice which alone establishes "the fundamental preconditions for peace." Even today, then, "Solomon's request remains the decisive issue facing politicians and politics." While most political matters can be decided by the principle of the majority, this principle does not suffice when "the dignity of man and of humanity" are at stake. This is obvious in the face of overtly totalitarian regimes like the Nazis. But it is not so easy to see in the case of "the decisions of a democratic politician": "In terms of the underlying anthropological issues, what is right *(recht)* and may be given the force of law is in no way simply self-evident today. The question of how to recognize what is truly right and thus to serve justice *(Gerechtigkeit)* when framing laws has never been simple, and today, in view of the vast extent of our knowledge and our capacity, it has become still harder."

How then are we to judge regarding what is right? Benedict responds: "Unlike other great religions, Christianity has never proposed a revealed law to the state and to society, that is to say, a juridical order derived from revelation *(Rechtsordnung aus Offenbarung)*. Instead, it has pointed to nature and reason as the true sources of law — and to the harmony of objective and subjective reason, which naturally presupposes that both spheres are rooted in the creative reason of God." Benedict highlights the significance of the fact that "Christian theologians aligned themselves against the religious law associated with polytheism and on the side of philosophy, and that they acknowledged reason and nature in their interrelation as the universally valid source of law." Indeed, he says that in this they were following the lead of St. Paul: "'When Gentiles who have not the Law (the Torah of Israel) do by nature what the law requires, they are a law to themselves . . . , they show that what the law requires is written on their hearts, while their conscience also bears witness . . .' (Rom 2:14f). Here we see the two fundamental concepts of nature and conscience, where conscience is nothing other than Solomon's listening heart, reason that is open to the language of being *(der Sprache des Seins)*."[125] This idea of natural law, however, is "today viewed as a specifically Catholic doctrine, not worth bringing into the discussion in a non-Catholic environment." This is due above all to a positivist understanding of nature that "has come to be almost universally accepted." According to this understanding, "nature — in the words of Hans Kelsen — is viewed as 'an aggregate of objective data linked together in terms of cause and effect.'" Ethics and religion are thus consigned to "the subjective field," remaining "extraneous to the realm of reason in the strict sense." Benedict says that this is "a dramatic situation which affects everyone, and on which a public debate is necessary." Indeed, "an essential goal of [his] address is to issue an urgent invitation to launch" such a debate.

Here Benedict introduces a striking metaphor. A "positivist reason which recognizes nothing beyond mere functionality," he says, "resembles a mere bunker with no windows," and in this case it is we ourselves who must "provide the lighting and atmospheric conditions, being no longer willing to obtain either from God's wide world. And yet we cannot hide from ourselves the fact that even in this artificial world, we are still drawing upon God's raw materials, which we refashion into our own products. The windows must be flung open again, we must see the wide world, the sky and the earth once more and learn to make proper use of all this." In this context, Benedict asks how reason can "rediscover its true greatness," and how nature can "reassert itself in its true depth, with all its demands, with all its directives." Referring to recent ecological developments stressing the need to "listen to the language of nature," the pope says that "there is also an ecology of man. Man too has a nature he must respect and that he cannot manipulate at will. Man is not merely self-creating freedom. Man does not create himself. He is intellect and will, but he is also nature, and his will is rightly ordered if he respects his nature, listens to it and accepts himself for who he is, as one who did not create himself. In this way, and in no other, is true human freedom fulfilled." Here Benedict refers again to the German philosopher Kelsen, who claimed that ethical norms "can only come from the will," and that "nature could only contain norms . . . if a will had put them there. But this, [Kelsen] says, would presuppose a Creator God, whose will had entered into nature. 'Any attempt to discuss the truth of this belief is utterly futile,' he observed." Benedict responds: "Is it really? . . . Is it really pointless to wonder whether the objective reason that manifests itself in nature does not presuppose a creative reason, a *Creator Spiritus?*"

The conviction that there is a Creator God is what gave rise to the idea of human rights, the idea of the equality of all people before the law, the recognition of the inviolability of human dignity in every single person and the awareness of people's responsibility for their actions. Our cultural memory is shaped by these rational insights. To ignore this or dismiss it as a thing of the past would be to dismember our culture totally *(eine Amputation unserer Kultur insgesamt)* and rob it of its wholeness *(ihrer Ganzheit berauben)*. The culture of Europe arose from the encounter between . . . Israel's monotheism, the philosophical reason of the Greeks and Roman law. This three-way encounter has shaped the inner identity of Europe. In the awareness of man's responsibility before God and in the acknowledgment of the inviolable dignity of every single human person, it has established criteria of law; it is these criteria that we are called to defend at this moment in our history.[126]

According to Benedict, then, it is the encounter between Israel's monotheism, the philosophical reason of the Greeks, and Roman law, mediated via the Christian Middle Ages, which provided the framework within which the juridical culture of the West was born.[127]

Benedict's Bundestag address concludes by returning to the discussion of God's invitation to King Solomon: "even today, there is ultimately nothing else [law-makers] could wish for but a listening heart — the capacity to discern between good and evil, and thus to establish true law *(wahres Recht)*, to serve justice and peace."

I cite this 2011 address at length in order to make four points vis-à-vis the distinction between state and society and the idea of a limited state. (1) In past works, Joseph Ratzinger has referred to the well-known claim advanced by Ernst-Wolfgang Böckenförde that the state " 'is dependent on other powers and forces for its own foundations and maintenance.' In other words, it lives on the basis of presuppositions 'that it cannot guarantee for itself.' This means that there is something 'indispensable' for a pluralistic democracy that is not established within the political sphere."[128] Note, however, what is implied in Ratzinger's reading of Böckenförde's statement in light of Benedict's Bundestag address. First, the state is distinct from society, that is, from the communities (e.g., religious and familial) that are most immediately and properly responsible for the foundations and maintenance of true law. These foundations are nonetheless understood to be *intrinsic* to the nature and functioning of law and the juridical-political order. That is, the dependence of the law on a proper idea of what is truly right, and thus of what truly serves justice, is to be understood as intrinsic to law as such. The rulers responsible for framing the law must *listen* to "the language of being," to a nature and a natural law that finally bear witness to "a creative reason, a *Creator Spiritus.*"

The burden of Benedict's/Ratzinger's argument, then, is that *the law is an intrinsic mediator* of the language of being, of nature and natural law, indeed of these finally in their presupposition of a creative source in the Creator God. The law bears intrinsic witness to what is true and good. But this emphatically is not to say that the law is the source or final arbiter regarding the truth and the good. Nor does it yet say anything about the nature of the law's right to "coerce" citizens vis-à-vis the truth, the good, and the Creator. It *is* to say, nonetheless, that the state and its juridical procedures bear a *pedagogy* regarding these.[129] My first point, then, is that the state bears a principled responsibility for the truth (including the ultimate ground of truth), not as the primary source or guarantor of this truth, but still inescapably as a mediator of such a vision. In this sense, the state remains irreducibly distinct from society, even as it shares a principled unity of concern with society. The relevant distinction, in a word, is not between an intrinsic concern for the truth (on the part of society) versus no intrinsic concern for the truth (on the part of the state). It is rather between distinct ways of bearing intrinsic responsibility for the truth.

(2) Second, Benedict conceives the state's necessary subordination to a transcendent order of truth, rooted finally in the creative reason of the Creator God, to be first positive, not negative, in nature. In other words, it is precisely because the state recognizes a transcendent source of truth and good beyond itself, and a human dignity positively founded on this, that the state must recognize a universal right of every human being to freedom in the "negative" sense as an immunity from coercion by others. It is because of the primacy of this positive recognition of man as made for and in a truth rooted in the creative reason of God, and of man as so far responsible to this truth, that the "negative" claim of each person's right to an uncoerced freedom in the exercise of this responsibility demands protection, always and everywhere. It is *the primacy of this positive sense* of man, in a word, that *essentially demands his "negative" right.*

(3) Third, Benedict's argument implies that there can be no neutrality on the part of the state and its governors vis-à-vis the idea of nature or natural law, and, by implication, regarding the ultimate source and foundation of these.[130] Either our laws recognize "a creative Reason, a Creator God," which alone can sustain the idea of nature and natural law necessary for the realization of genuine justice, including just notions of human rights and the equality of all people before the law. Or our laws, lacking this recognition, will

necessarily incline toward an understanding of man as a kind of "self-creating freedom" which has *no inner need first to listen* to the language of being; and incline as well toward dissolving the very idea of nature or natural law, and of the creative Reason that natural law ultimately implies, such that the justice mediated by the state becomes by definition arbitrary, and thus open in principle to totalitarianism. For Benedict/Ratzinger, then, the inevitable non-neutrality of the state is non-neutrality in a specifically ontological and indeed finally theological sense. The state in its juridical procedures will inescapably, however unconsciously and against its own express intentions, be guided by some vision regarding the nature of reality before God: regarding the nature of the human person, of natural law, of truth and the good, and finally regarding whether these ultimately have a creative-reasonable foundation in a logos-bearing Creator. "Fairness" can never be adjudicated in a purely formal way, in the sense of being able to avoid invoking the implication of some ontological vision of the nature of the human person before what is ultimately true and good. To employ language used earlier in this essay, any would-be "articles of peace" appealed to by the state are for Benedict always fraught with articles of ontological and ultimately theological "faith."[131]

(4) Fourth, Benedict insists strongly on the integrity of reason and nature and natural law in relation to faith. Indeed, he takes recognition of this integrity to indicate a kind of shared synthesis of the great ethical intuitions of mankind (Israel, the Greeks, Roman Law) that is given a distinctive center in Christianity. This synthesis, according to Benedict, as understood in Christian faith, involves affirmation of a "rationally formed turning to the one God who is seen to be the reason at work at the origin of all things and as creative love" (TPE, 158). What is important to see, then, is that, for Benedict, reason bears an ontological structure, which, followed in its inner dynamism, leads to "an ethos that listens to the reason of creation and finds in this an echo of the reason of the Creator" (TPE, 158). But it is equally important to see that Benedict/Ratzinger affirms this strong sense of reason in terms at once of reason's inner openness to revelation, and indeed while affirming reason's need for Christian faith for the right exercise of reason in the concrete order of history (TPE, 36).[132] As we will see, this double claim regarding both the integrity of reason and its concrete need for faith is important for a proper understanding of the Church-state problem.

The public order and the common good; freedom as "the political method par excellence." The sense in which the Church, in DH, has embraced the notion of public order, as distinct from what is traditionally understood as the common good, is bound up with the nature of the distinction between truth and freedom, and society and state. Public order is rightly conceived as a distinct end of the state's juridical power only insofar as it is tied to the true common good. In a word, the idea of public order, with its *"negative"* limit, is rightly demanded by freedom, but only as itself *positively related* to the true good of the human being.

This interpretation alone explains why the Declaration's references to public order in schema 3 were qualified in later drafts by terms such as *iustus, verus, legitimus,* and the like, all of which qualify public order in terms of a substantive order of justice or moral truth.[133] This duality-within-unity between public order and common good implies two things. On the one hand, it signals a greater recognition by the Church that freedom is an intrinsic good of the person: freedom is *not merely instrumental* to the realization of a common good conceived first without any inner reference to this freedom. On the other hand, it signals the Church's recognition that freedom bears its intrinsic worth *as freedom* only as initially formed by the fuller truth about the goodness of the person as positively open toward God.

Thus, in and through the Declaration, we are able to see a new meaning in the traditional Thomistic view that the law is concerned with what is good for human beings. The Declaration deepens this traditional view by taking into account more explicitly *the subjectivity of persons,* while at the same time avoiding the relativistic implications of a subjectivity (and public order) abstracted from what is the true common good.[134]

Commenting on the criterion of public order as it appears in DH, 7, Murray claims that "freedom is the political method par excellence, whereby the other goals of society are reached," and that "freedom is an end or purpose of society, which looks to the liberation of the human person." Referring to the concluding statement of this article of the Declaration — "For the rest, the customary practice of the fullness of freedom in society should be upheld, according to which man's freedom should be acknowledged as far as possible, and should not be restricted except when and insofar as necessary" — Murray says that "experts may well consider this to be the most significant sentence in the Declaration," insofar as it is (according to him) a "statement of the basic principle of the 'free society'" (Abbott, 687n21).

Murray is not wrong to claim that freedom is the political method par excellence, and that it is an intrinsic end or purpose of society. For the Declaration, however, this principle is properly understood *only insofar as freedom is conceived as itself bound with the truth,* in the ways we have indicated. That is why the sentence to which Murray refers here begins with the word *ceterum* ("for the rest"). This sentence in fact follows upon a detailed listing of the norms to which the exercise of freedom is subject. All men are "bound by the *moral law* to keep in mind both the rights of others *and their duties toward others, as well as the common good of all,*" and to act toward all with *justice and humanity (secundum iustitiam et humanitatem).* The civil authority, in turn, is to act according to juridical norms that "conform to *the objective moral order*" and that are concerned with both the care of that *genuine* public peace *(honestae pacis publicae)* that comes about when men live together in *true justice (vera iustitia),* and the care of public morality *(publicae moralitatis)* (DH, 7, emphasis added). Finally, in the sentence immediately preceding the one cited above and highlighted by Murray, article 7 states: "All of these [matters] constitute a fundamental part of the common good, and come under the category of public order *(Haec omnia partem boni communis fundamentalem constitutunt et sub ratione ordinis publici veniuntur)*."[135] The Council's appeal to public order thus implies that the Church does indeed affirm freedom as the basic method of political order, but *in the sense of a freedom already informed with truth* (the common good, true justice, the objective moral order, and the like) as indicated in the rest of article 7.[136]

For the Declaration, then, the only political method that really frees (that is, in a non-arbitrary way) is one that recognizes freedom's immanent-natural ordering from and toward the truth and the universal good. It is this ordering that alone frees freedom in its integrity. The Declaration, in a word, does affirm "the basic principle of the 'free society,'" but not as conceived in liberal terms.[137]

It is important to see in this context that the exercise of the right to religious freedom as affirmed in the Declaration is subject to limitation, not only in terms of the disruption of a public peace comprised of externally ordered behavior, but also, as a matter of principle, in terms of disorder in claims of truth regarding the human person. We will return to this issue below. It suffices here simply to point out that the absence of truth itself, given the indissoluble unity of freedom and truth, will, *eo ipso,* involve the lessening of freedom.[138]

The competence of the state in religious matters. It is widely assumed, following Murray's juridical reading, that the Declaration rejects the idea of the competence of the state in matters of religion. It is true that the Declaration did use the language of competence and incompetence in its earlier drafts.[139] Nevertheless, the final text of the Declaration omits the language of competence, in favor of statements such as the following:

[R]eligious acts, in which men and women privately and publicly order themselves toward God out of a sense of inner conviction, by their
nature transcend the earthly and temporal order of things. The civil
power *(postestas civilis),* therefore, whose proper end is the care of the
temporal common good, should in fact acknowledge and show favor to
the religious life of its citizens *(religiosam quidem civium vitam agnoscere
eique favere debet);* but this power must be said to exceed its limits if it
presumes either to direct or to impede religious acts. (DH, 3)

Later, in article 6, the Declaration says also that the civil authority should
"effectively undertake . . . to provide favorable conditions for fostering religious life, so that citizens may truly be able to exercise their religious rights
and fulfill their religious duties, and so that society itself may enjoy the goods
of justice and peace that come from men's fidelity to God and his holy will."

What, then, in light of our earlier argument, did the Council mean to
affirm in the matter of the political authority's competence regarding religious matters?

The state has no right to interfere with the exercise of religion provided this exercise observes the just requirements of public order. But the
reason is clear from the argument of our previous section: the state has no
right *because it is of the very nature of religion to transcend the earthly and
temporal order.* The implication, then, is twofold. On the one hand, for the
Declaration, the civil authority as such is not and cannot be the first or final
arbiter of religion and religious truth and practice, and in this sense remains
incompetent in religious matters. On the other hand, recognition by the state
that this is so is tied to a positive recognition of the transcendent nature
of religion. The negative prohibition implied by "incompetence," in other
words, necessarily presupposes and is based upon the positive recognition
of the transcendent nature of religion that is owed by the state: the negative
prohibition has its warrant *only in terms of this positive recognition.*[140]

When the Declaration says that the state must create conditions favorable to the fostering of religious life, it therefore means just that. The
free conditions to be secured are not simply "negative," or empty of positive
implication, because in this case legal protection would be secured only
for the exercise of a logically indifferent freedom, with the law *allowing for*
public support for religion, but only insofar as the latter is conceived in voluntaristic terms and subject to the formal justice of a "negatively"-conceived
public order.[141] On the contrary, these conditions are *for the sake of fostering
religious life.* According to the Declaration, in a word, the political authority

may not interfere with religion precisely because, and by virtue of, its *positive responsibility to recognize the nature of religion in its integrity as transcendent, and so far in its integrity* **as religion.**

The claim here is a strong one, because it implies a demand that government somehow recognize a claim of truth regarding the nature of religion. We will return to this question in more sustained fashion below. Here let us only recall that the juridical approach itself, in granting primacy to the negative in its assertion of the state's religious incompetence, thereby, contrary to its own intentions, implies a definite judgment regarding the nature of religion. The religion that alone is sanctioned in a juridically conceived state is one whose transcendent reference, for purposes pertaining to the state's constitutional authority, is understood to be first *posited* rather than *naturally given.* From the legal-political point of view, the human person is considered *by nature* neutral, hence logically indifferent, to transcendence, and so far religiously "silent." The person is treated by the state as *naturally a-gnostic* in matters of religion: whether he believes or does not believe, his theism or a-theism is in any case a matter essentially of choice. In either case, religion is considered, from the legal point of view, something logically yet-to-be-added. It is taken to involve only a part, or fragment, of man's life, as distinct from comprehending the whole of man and reaching to his depths and shaping all of his cultural, economic, political, and intellectual activities, after the manner of the historic religions of the world that recognize man to be by nature *homo religiosus.*[142]

Recognizing the paradox exposed here is essential for a proper reading of religious liberty as understood by *Dignitatis humanae.* On the one hand, the juridical state claims simple incompetence in matters of religion, and in so doing thereby renders the state competent enough (even if not consciously, or *de jure,* so) to treat positivistic religious groups as alone subjects of the right to religious freedom, to the exclusion of those religions explicitly rooted in nature — except insofar as these latter behave like positivistic religions for purposes of legal-constitutional order. On the other hand, the state implicitly supported by the Declaration claims a competence in matters of religion, even as, in so doing, it includes individuals of all religions (both "natural" *and* positivistic) as subjects of the right to religious freedom. The state affirmed by the Declaration also recognizes positivistically conceived religions because it takes the choices of these religions to express at root, even if unconsciously, a natural religious sense, which, insofar as it is natural, can never be repressed. This state recognizes the importance of such choices for the whole reality of each person, even in those cases where the person himself understands religion to involve only a part of his reality — for example, when he reduces religion to moral behavior or takes religion to refer only to something "outside" the temporal order. In a word, the state called for by the Declaration takes all persons and groups to be subjects of the right to freedom vis-à-vis religion, because it recognizes that the acts of the human person, of their very nature internal and voluntary and conscientious (DH, 3), are rooted in and express the dignity of all persons as "impelled by their nature and bound by a moral obligation to seek the truth, especially the truth concerning religion" (DH, 2).

The proper question regarding the state's competence in religious matters, in sum, is not *whether* government will be competent, at least by implication, in such matters, but rather *what sort of* competence government will exercise regardless, consciously or unconsciously. Recognition of the state's inevitable "competence" with respect to the integrity of religion leads to the question of how, from the point of view of the Declaration, we are to understand properly the question of the "establishment" of a particular religion.

The "establishment" of religion. Immediately following the sentence in article 6 regarding the duty of the state to "provide favorable conditions for fostering religious life," *Dignitatis humanae* says: "If, in light of a people's particular circumstances, special civil recognition is granted to one religious community in the juridical order of the state, it is necessary at the same time that the right to freedom in religious matters be acknowledged and observed for all citizens and religious communities" (DH, 6). How is this statement to be understood?

First, the Declaration rejects the idea that it is problematic in principle for a society to grant special civil recognition to a particular religious community in its constitutional order. What is required is only that this special recognition involve a consistent affirmation of the right of all persons and religious communities to religious freedom.

Second, as indicated above, no society will, or can, avoid privileging some definite form of religion in its constitutional order. The claim to avoid such privileging implies the privileging only of religious communities of a positivistic, or naturally a-gnostic, sort.

Third, given these two points, the pertinent question becomes that of determining which sort of legal preference most consistently sustains the universal right to religious freedom. As we have seen, the juridical state claims that it uniquely secures such a right. But it does so by virtue of its privileging, for all legal purposes (logically, if not explicitly in its constitutional law), persons or groups that take religion to be essentially an object of individual choice. We have shown that such preference leads toward legal imposition of a relativistic monism in matters of religion.

Fourth, the argument of the Declaration, on the contrary, shows that a genuinely universal right to religious freedom can be consistently affirmed only insofar as freedom is recognized by the state to be intrinsically tied to (religious) truth, and religious life to be of its very nature ordered to transcendence.

Fifth, it follows (a) that every state will of necessity "establish" or "confess" some claim of truth, implicit or explicit, regarding the nature of religion; and (b) that only that state which "establishes" or "confesses" a claim of truth on behalf of a transcendent religious sense rooted in nature can with logical consistency affirm a right to religious freedom for all human beings without exception. Only that state which shows favor to religious life in its natural integrity can also truly recognize religious life that is conceived voluntaristically. It is important to keep both of these points in mind.[143]

This double claim, however, leaves us still with the more specific question of Catholic religiosity and the Catholic Church. I will treat this question in two steps: first, in terms of the historical principle, or what Murray terms the distinction between classical and historical consciousness; second, in terms of the relation between Church and state.

The historical principle: the distinction between classical consciousness and historical consciousness, and the thesis-hypothesis approach. There are three main points to be made in regard to this issue. (1) Those who hold the juridical reading of the Declaration typically interpret the statement about "establishment" of religion in article 6 to mean that, if the circumstances *happen* to favor civil recognition of one religious community in the constitutional order of the state, that is fine, so long as the right to all citizens and groups to religious freedom is respected. But a different and stronger sense of the historical principle is warranted in light of the argument of the Declaration as a whole, and indeed in light of the ancient-medieval philosophical tradition as articulated above.

I have argued that only the state that favors a religiosity ordered by nature to transcendent truth can protect with consistency a universal right for all citizens and groups. What the historical principle, rightly interpreted, adds to this is that there is an *intrinsic reason,* or indeed an *objective warrant,* for a state favoring such religion to come into existence, *on the assumption that it does in fact secure this universal right.* Here, then, is the neuralgic point: such a state can rightfully come into existence only through means that respect all persons' dignity and right to religious freedom. Thus persons who seek such a state *must begin from where they find themselves histori-cally*: either in historical circumstances that already favor a religion ordered by nature to transcendent truth and to the Creator, or in circumstances that are less favorable or even hostile to such a religion. These persons are reasonably-morally permitted — indeed, in light of the Declaration, *are called and thus morally bound to seek* — to bring into being a state that favors a religion ordered by nature to transcendent truth and to God. The indispensable requirement is that they respect the conditions of history, that is, the historical conditions of the men and women who together constitute society at a given time and place. In the phrase made famous by John Paul II in *Redemptoris missio:* Christians are to *propose, not impose* the truth.[144]

What the Declaration demands first of all, then, is that Christians follow both sides of this injunction simultaneously: they are not to impose the truth, even as they are really to propose it. But, secondly, this demand of the Declaration implies endorsement of the ancient-medieval conceptions of man as spiritual and of truth as a "transcendental," in the sense articulated by Pieper. It is indeed the very truth of this medieval, or classical, conception that itself requires recognition of the subjective, and so far also historical, conditions of the person whereby truth is realized.[145] "Classical consciousness" and "historical consciousness," in other words, presuppose each other. These forms of consciousness are at root not opposed; on the contrary, each has its original and proper meaning only as qualified in relation to the other.

(2) The argument here can helpfully be placed in light of the well-known *thesis-hypothesis* approach to the question of religious freedom that dominated the pre-conciliar discussion, and that indeed continued in significant, if often unconscious, ways to shape the background of the discussion during the course of the conciliar debate itself.

According to this approach, there are two principles that govern the question of religious establishment and the right to religious freedom. On the one hand, if historical circumstances favor a religion embodying the truth about man in his creatureliness, the state should establish such a religion and its truth ("thesis"), while rejecting the religious freedom of other religions (legal institution of intolerance: "error has no rights"). On the other hand, if historical circumstances do not favor a religion naturally rooted in the truth about man, the state should concede the religious freedom of all religions ("hypothesis").[146]

Those who follow the juridical view take the conflict between these different principles of approach to be resolved by an appeal to the historical principle, conceived differently from what is implied by the Declaration. The juridical argument is that the establishment of a particular religion by the state is acceptable as long as the state finds itself in historical circumstances favoring that religion, and as long as it recognizes the religious freedom of other religions. Otherwise, however, given the religiously pluralistic situation that prevails in modern societies, only that sort of state is legitimate which supports the right to religious freedom in abstraction from truth. Thus, state establishment of a particular religion is acceptable *only when contingent historical circumstances permit it;* while the pervasive pluralistic conditions of modern societies make *the normal, indeed normative, circumstance to be one in which the state restricts itself to the protection of religious freedom in abstraction from truth.*[147]

This resolution to the problem posed by the thesis-hypothesis schema, however, is unsatisfactory from the point of view of the Declaration, rightly understood.

To see why this is so, let us consider the difference between Murray's reading of the thesis-hypothesis approach, and of the distinction between classical and historical consciousness which it involves, and that presupposed by the Declaration. The problem with classical consciousness, according to Murray, is "its fallacy of a false 'objectivism,' as if truth could somehow be divorced from the possession of truth" (TMRF, 41).[148] Classical consciousness starts with "the abstract or ideological," in contrast to historical consciousness, which begins with "the factual and historical." The appeal of the latter "is to the fact that today man is growing more and more conscious of his own dignity, personal and civil" (TMRF, 41). Murray argues that the discussions at the Council "made it clear that, despite resistance in certain quarters, classicism is giving way to historical consciousness" (BSS, 195). He says that we can see this development in the Council's intentional decision to call itself "pastoral." This pastoral concern does not eliminate the traditional or "classic" doctrinal concern for truth. The point, rather, is that the pastoral concern

is illuminated by historical consciousness: that is, by concern for the truth not simply as a proposition to be repeated but more importantly as a possession to be lived; by concern, therefore, for the subject to whom the truth is addressed; hence, also, by concern for the historical moment in which the truth is proclaimed to the living subject; and, consequently, by concern to seek that progress in the understanding of the truth demanded both by the historical moment and by the subject who must live in it. (BSS, 195)

In the argument that he himself proposed to the Council, Murray thus states, in reference to the thesis hypothesis distinction:

> Religious freedom is not thesis; neither is it hypothesis. [The juridical argument] abandons these categories of systematization. It does not accept, as its basic systematic notion, the abstract notion of the exclusive rights of truth, which creates the disjunction, thesis and hypothesis. Instead, it posits, as the basis for a systematic doctrine of religious freedom, the concrete exigencies of the personal and political consciousness of contemporary man — his demand for religious freedom, personal and corporate, under a limited government. This demand is approved by reason; it ought to be approved by the authority of the Church. Hence [the juridical view] affirms the validity of an order of constitutional law in which the public care of religion is limited to public care of religious freedom. . . .
>
> In negative terms, [the juridical view] rejects the opinion that public care of religion necessarily means, per se and in principle, a political and legal care for the exclusive rights of truth and a consequent care to exterminate religious error. In positive terms, it holds that public care of religion is provided in both necessary and sufficient measure when the constitutional order recognizes, guarantees, and protects the freedom of the Church, both as a religious community and as a spiritual authority, at the same time that it gives similar recognition, guarantee, and protection to the general religious freedom — personal, ecclesial, associational, practical — of the whole body politic. Within the new perspectives of today, the Church does not demand, per se and in principle, a status of legal privilege for herself. The Church demands, in principle and in all situations, religious freedom for herself and religious freedom for all men. (PRF, 146)[149]

Murray's argument here begs the burden of what the Declaration proposes in its final text, even as it also fails to resolve the key problem presented by the thesis-hypothesis approach. Murray insists that his juridical view eludes the categories of thesis-hypothesis. Yet his view privileges freedom — for the Church and for all persons — as alone relevant in our changed historical circumstances, for the limited purposes of the legal-constitutional order. Murray argues that the Council does not attenuate concern for the truth, except insofar as truth is abstractly conceived in terms of an "objectivism" that divorces it from its need to be possessed and lived, thereby turning truth into an ahistorical proposition. But Murray proposes this argument in the context of claiming that classical consciousness has today given way to historical consciousness. For him this means that, relative to the proper concerns of government, the basis for a doctrine of religious freedom now lies, not in "the abstract notion of the exclusive rights of truth," but in "the concrete exigencies of the personal and political consciousness of contemporary man." In excluding the "abstract" notion of truth as the basis for the right to religious freedom, Murray focuses per se and in principle on the "historicity" of the human subject in his progress in time toward truth. For Murray, then, it is the freedom of the human subject in his movement toward truth, as not yet having attained the truth itself in any principled way, that alone is relevant to the question of the civil right to religious freedom.

This proposal, however, does not so much elude the categories of thesis-hypothesis as effectively make the "hypothesis" itself into the "thesis." Murray's proposal privileges — in light of what he regards as the religious pluralism peculiar to the historical conditions of modernity — the right to religious freedom in abstraction from the question of truth. As shown earlier in a different context, Murray conceives truth as an object yet-to-be-realized by freedom, and so far as irrelevant to the proper concerns of the legal-juridical order.[150] Murray's proposed resolution of the thesis-hypothesis problem thus leaves intact what gives rise to the disjunction between thesis and hypothesis in the first place: the presupposition of an external relation between truth, on the one hand, and the human subject or the subjective free-intelligent human act, on the other. Murray leaves this disjunction intact, while granting primacy to freedom instead of truth. He thus seeks to disestablish truth in favor of establishing freedom, making the constitutionally sanctioned unity of society into something exclusively "civil," not "religious."[151]

Here, then, is the problem with Murray's appeal to the distinction between classical consciousness and historical consciousness as a way of resolving the thesis-hypothesis problem. As we have shown, a state that is "unified" around a freedom considered to be primitively empty of truth hides its own claim of truth on behalf of freedom of indifference, which entails monist-relativist consequences.[152] This solution, in other words, however much against its own intentions, effectively turns freedom into freedom of indifference, which now itself becomes, paradoxically, a "timeless essence" (an ever-empty act) that for all legal purposes has always not yet realized objective truth, such that the human subject becomes a subject that is ever-on-the-way to realizing his object. Murray's argument thus in fact espouses an ahistorical truth (monism), albeit in the name now of a would-be empty freedom, with the consequence that any "truth" chosen by the free subject at any given historical moment becomes, *eo ipso,* arbitrary (relativism). The paradoxical result is a truth that is simultaneously "objectivist" (qua formal act of choice) and "subjectivist" (qua object of empty, arbitrary act of choice). Both aspects come together in a monistic relativism consisting in a "trans-historical historicism."

In contrast, the ancient-medieval tradition is able to accommodate the historical-subjective nature of the human act without lessening concern for (objective) truth. According to this tradition, as we have seen, "worldly" truth always and everywhere is realized only in and through the subjectivity-interiority of the person. The medieval tradition builds awareness of the historical subjectivity of the human person into the person's original onto-logical relation to the transcendent order of truth. Truth and subjectivity thus presuppose each other, in the ways described earlier.[153] Both need to be emphasized, in the *distinctness* between them that at once *presupposes and demands their original unity.* The consequence is that the free human act cannot be rightly understood except in light of its immanent-dynamic order toward and in the truth; and that truth cannot be rightly understood except in light of its presupposition of the spiritual subjectivity-interiority of the free human act.

The difference between Murray's juridical view and the view presupposed in the Declaration, then, does not lie in the fact that the juridical view recognizes the historical subjectivity of the human person, while the Declaration does not. It lies rather in the fact that the Declaration's argument, unlike the juridical one, recognizes that the human person in his historical subjectivity is originally made for, and already stands initially within, the transcendent order of truth. In a word, Murray's juridical approach reflects the modern account of subjectivity, in relation to which truth is *first an object* (of choice), while the Declaration's approach is anchored in the medievals' metaphysical subjectivity, which discovers itself only as already *a participant in objective truth.*[154]

(3) Relative to the question of religious establishment, the point is thus that *both* the approach of Murray *and* that of the thesis-hypothesis tradition he opposes presuppose an external relation between truth and freedom. The approach recommended by the Declaration, on the other hand, insists on an

original integration of truth and freedom, in a way that resolves the dialectical tension between "thesis" (truth) and "hypothesis" (freedom). The Declaration insists on holding thesis and hypothesis together, so to speak, in *every historical situation.* Thus, whether the conditions of society favor the religious understanding of man as transcendentally ordered to the truth about the Creator or not, those who understand man in this way must seek and affirm this truth while protecting the freedom of others, *even as* they emphasize the freedom of others while seeking and affirming the truth. To be sure, prudential political judgments will differ significantly in cases where the historical conditions are favorable and where these conditions are unfavorable or even hostile. But the principle remains consistent: the burden of both "thesis" (truth) and "hypothesis" (freedom) is to be realized even as the reality of each is restored in a new way, with truth itself including freedom and freedom truth. If the state favors a transcendent religious truth in its constitutional law, it must do so *while protecting a right to freedom in religious matters on the part of all citizens* (as long as the demands of a truly just public order are observed). And if the state is unfavorable or even hostile to a transcendent religion rooted in nature, those citizens who hold this view of religion and transcendent truth must nonetheless seek to open the state's constitutional order to such a view, in a way, again, that respects the dignity hence right to freedom of all other citizens.[155] In a word, the principle enunciated by John Paul II holds for citizens also when they organize their government: it is always the case that truth is to be proposed, not imposed. Rightly understood, this means neither that proposing the truth legitimates imposing it, nor that not imposing the truth legitimates not really proposing it.

Church and state. We turn, then, to the church-state question as it bears on the link between religious truth and the right to religious freedom, specifically in light of the Catholic faith and the revelation of the gospel of Jesus Christ that provide the basic framework for *Dignitatis humanae.*

(1) First of all, my argument has made it clear that no state, including the juridical state, can avoid the implication of an ontology and indeed a theology, in the sense of some definite understanding, however unconscious, of the relation between time and eternity, or the world and God, with implications for what Catholics understand as the supernatural revelation of God in Jesus Christ.[156] Although this point has been made in different ways in the course of my argument, it bears repeating yet again in the context of the separation of church and state claimed by the juridical state. This "separation," as we have shown, implies in fact a "union" between a *certain kind*

of state and a *certain kind of church,* and thus implies support for one kind of church to the exclusion of another kind.

The juridical state presupposes a definite conception of the distinction between the person as citizen and the person as religious. The distinction is made in such a way that it requires these two realities to be fragmented for all legal-public purposes, even if the person elects to unite them privately. If the person elects to unite them publicly, this will be understood for legal purposes only in terms of a moral intention that of its very nature remains "private," having so far no juridical relevance.[157] Thus this distinction, juridically conceived, of its inner logic prevents a person from being able consciously to *form* his acts *qua citizen and subject of rights* in the *truth of what he believes.*[158]

Any argument regarding the church-state distinction that would meet the demands of reason needs to come to terms with the paradox implied here. The juridical state demands fragmenting the person's reality as citizen from his reality as religious, such that the state claims *de jure* neutrality with respect to the latter by virtue of its (supposed) clean bracketing of his civic reality from his religious reality. At the same time, the juridical state, in so doing, still (unwittingly) conceives citizenship as internally united with a kind of "religiosity," albeit now of a positivist sort. The juridical state's vaunted separation of church and state of its inner logic (con-)*fuses* a definite kind of state — the juridical-liberal state — with a definite kind of church — a positivist, e.g. "congregationalist," church. Legally, then, and in fact, if not explicitly, the state *grants freedom unequally* to positivistic churches, at the expense of non-positivistic churches, or of those which understand the human person to be by his very nature, and thus *also in his public-civil activity,* a *capacity **for** God.*

In the face of the question regarding church and state, it is therefore imperative to keep in mind the totalizing nature of liberalism's religiously positivistic juridical state. The fact that this state *ex officio* brackets any explicit religious dimension in the person, insofar as he is a subject of the right to religious freedom, does not mean that the state thereby exercises its authority in a way that bears only on the *earthly-temporal part* of the person. On the contrary, such a state, in bracketing this religious dimension, divides the earthly and the heavenly dimensions of the person's being into *fragments* that can now be related, for all public-legal purposes, only in terms of the *external relation of addition.* The juridical state, despite its official intention to *abstract* the earthly-temporal dimension of the person from his heavenly-eternal dimension, inevitably renders judgments that legally protect the *"whole"* of the person, but now only qua *the sum of two* — earthly and (possibly) heavenly — *fragments*.

(2) It is in light of this paradoxical sense of a union of church and state presumed by the juridical state that any attempt at a proper reading of the Declaration in the matter of the church-state distinction must be approached. As we have shown, the Declaration understands the unity between freedom and truth to be not only pertinent to but foundational for the civil right to religious freedom, while insisting at the same time that human beings "are also bound to hold fast to the truth once it is known, *and to order their whole life in accord with its demands (totam vitam suam iuxta exigentias veritatis ordinare)*" (DH, 2; emphasis added). The Declaration also says that the civil authority needs to recognize and show favor to the religious life of citizens (DH, 3). Furthermore, and more closely related to the question of the relationship between church and state, the Declaration states that the "one true religion subsists in the Catholic and apostolic Church," and that all persons "are in fact bound to seek the truth, especially in those things concerning God and his Church, and to embrace and hold fast to it once it is known" (DH, 1). The Council fathers of course see no contradiction between these claims, including the last one, and the Declaration's defense of a universal right to religious freedom. But they also do not understand this last claim merely as a contingent add-on, a compromise, for example, made to accommodate a conservative minority of Council fathers. On the contrary, each of these claims is consistent with and necessary for the integrity of the position of the Declaration, rightly understood.

I showed earlier, in metaphysical terms, that the intrinsic link of freedom with truth, ultimately with the transcendent order of truth originating in God, does not undercut but in fact establishes the very idea of human dignity which alone is able to sustain a universal right to religious freedom in a principled manner.[159] I also pointed out texts from part II of the Declaration that indicate the biblical roots of the unity of freedom and truth in Jesus Christ.[160] But we need to return to the question of the biblical and theological roots of this unity, now in terms of the question of church and state. Does the Church, or indeed *must* the Church, pursue a certain privileging by the state, even to the extent of seeking legal recognition as the "established" church? And if so, what is the self-understanding of the Church whereby such establishment might nonetheless be shown consistently to demand the principle of a genuinely universal right to religious freedom?

First of all, the fact that it is not in principle problematic for the Church to seek privileging by the state, even to the point of legal establishment, follows from my argument regarding the juridical state. The juridical state, which, uniquely among all states, claims no legal privileging and, *a fortiori*, no establishment of any religion or church, in fact organizes itself legally (if only implicitly so) around a definite claim of positivist religious truth, and thus "establishes" those religious communities or churches which hold to such a truth. In making the claim for establishment, then, the Catholic Church would so far in principle be unexceptional, except that its claims would be explicit, not hidden. I have also argued that the metaphysical understanding of freedom and truth carried in the Catholic tradition entails a principled defense of the universal right to religious freedom. The task remains, however, to show how this metaphysics is sustained in the Church's teaching regarding Jesus Christ and indeed regarding the nature of the Church herself. Needless to say, it is beyond the scope of the present study to attempt a comprehensive statement in these matters. It will suffice to record two central principles defended by the Council. The first indicates the sense in which the revelation of God in Christ legitimates the autonomy of the human creature, and so also his freedom, from within the heart of the union with Christ for which the creature was made. The second shows that this autonomy-for-union, indeed autonomy-*in*-union, which is characteristic of the creature in his wholeness — even-also as he engages the world, including its political structures — is demanded by the Church's own self-understanding as indicated by the Council.

(i) Regarding the first, it will suffice to point to the hypostatic union of Christ as defined by the Council of Chalcedon and stated anew and in more concrete terms in *Gaudium et spes,* 22. In Jesus Christ, we find the full and distinct integrity of the divine *and* human natures, in the unity of the single divine person. In God's incarnation in Jesus Christ, human nature was *assumed (assumpta),* even as it was not *absorbed* or *preempted (non perempta).* To be sure, there is only one hypostatic union. But what the Church's understanding of this union shows, as clarified further in GS, 22, is that the divine life, in which every human being is graciously called by God to participate from the first moment of his created existence, *fulfills and opens up in an infinitely new way* human nature itself, even as it simultaneously *releases that nature into its deepest integrity and autonomy* — its "otherness" — *as human and natural.*[161] The (paradoxical) dual nature of the principle indicated here is just the point. The life of grace brought about in Jesus Christ, via baptism into his Church, makes man truly a *participant in divine life* even as it simultaneously thereby reaffirms and deepens the otherness of man in the integrity of his *nature* as human.

The point, as it concerns the dignity of the human being and the unity of freedom and truth, is twofold: on the one hand, union with Christ is understood by the Council to deepen, not weaken, the freedom that is characteristic of man's nature as man. On the other hand, and at the same time, every human being has been invited to this union with Christ from the beginning of his existence, a union for which man was created and which therefore fulfills him as man. But note that this fulfillment never takes place in an extrinsic way, as if the supernatural reality of Christ were superadded to human nature, and completed the latter as if coming simply from "outside." On the contrary, the fulfillment is intrinsic, in the sense that the invitation has already been extended to the creature in his original constitution as a creature. In Christ, the human person comes more deeply into possession of his natural self, even as he moves ever more deeply into the reality of God. The creature, in other words, always somehow "anticipates," *within the completeness of his own natural finality* as a creature, a further completion in and by the love of God revealed in Christ, without being able either to grasp what this anticipation is intended for or to bring about its realization himself.[162]

The crucial implication of this Christology, then, is first, that it confirms and deepens the natural integrity of the human being in his freedom as ordered to the transcendent truth, ultimately about God. And second, that the union with Christ to which each creature is called *truly fulfills the creature's nature,* his nature as ordered to truth, in a way that the creature himself already *by nature desires,* even if not in a fully conscious way. Note the paradox entailed by this double claim: the integrity of nature as nature, on the one hand, and the gratuitous fulfillment of nature as called to participate in the life of Christ, on the other, are not opposed or indifferent to each other. Man's union with Christ, in light of the teaching of Chalcedon as developed further in GS, 22, requires the completeness of man's nature as such, even as it affirms that man is already positively open, from within this completeness, to being taken up into union with Christ by means of his grace.

This double claim thus sustains and clarifies further the argument of the Declaration as I have presented it: the union with Christ called for by Christian faith presupposes and demands as a matter of principle the integrity of every human person in his freedom as he searches for truth; and this union at the same time fulfills this freedom and this search intrinsically, in a way that every man by nature, in his inmost depths, desires.[163] The Christological claim, in a word, shows how the human creature is ordered to giving the gift of his entire self to Jesus Christ in faith, precisely *from inside* his autonomous exercise of freedom as a creature, in a way that indeed reveals what is finally the true nature of that autonomy — as an act of love.

(ii) The second point regards the self-understanding of the Church, in its implications for the question of establishment and Church-state relations. It will suffice here to highlight a single central principle: the *communio* ecclesiology developed at the Council in *Lumen gentium*.[164] This ecclesiology entails the affirmation of a positive distinction between the orders of laity and priesthood in the Church, a distinction that may be seen as a theological correlate to the political distinction between society and state in the secular order.

There are two points to be made in this connection. (a) First of all, the Church has of course always affirmed a distinction between laity and priests. What is newly emphasized in the notion of *communio* is the Council's integration of the laity into the essential meaning of the Church. This integration implies a renewed sense of the universal call to holiness in its distinctively lay form. The laity are called to live the full arc of holiness, and they are to do so in their reality *as lay,* and not simply as extensions of the priestly-clerical-institutional Church. The *Catechism of the Catholic Church* expresses most succinctly the root of this claim, in its statement that Mary goes before us all in holiness, and that in this respect "the 'Marian' dimension of the Church precedes the 'Petrine'" (n. 773). The pontificates of John Paul II and Benedict XVI have drawn out more fully this sense of the priority of Mary and so far also of the lay dimension of the Church.[165] This priority involves a greater integration of Mary and the laity into the meaning of the Church, and, in this sense, also a deeper understanding of the "spousal" relation that exists between Mary/the laity and the priesthood of Peter, even as it affirms at the same time the continued priority of Peter as sacramental-hierarchical office.[166] There is in fact a mutual but asymmetrical priority of each in relation to the other. The crucial point is that this integration of the lay-Marian dimension indicates a new understanding of the distinctive role of the laity, not only in the Church, but also by implication in terms of the Church's relation to the world.

What this means can be seen in the difference it entails with respect to the more customary pre-conciliar understanding of the laity, in which the "worldly" activity proper to the laity was conceived essentially as a function or extension of the priestly-institutional dimension of the Church. In obedience to the hierarchical Petrine office, the laity were understood to enter into the world in order to help temporal structures and processes realize their (autonomous) temporal ends. This task was understood in moral-social terms, as bringing about the "humanization" of "terrestrial life" in service to the Church.[167] The upshot is that the laity had an essentially temporal-social task in the world, one that was morally-spiritually inspired. Any reference to an explicitly ecclesial presence in the world was understood exclusively in reference to the Church as Petrine office or institution.[168]

By contrast, according to Vatican II, the holiness of the Church includes the laity *in their properly lay character as present in the world.* To be sure, all holiness in the Church expresses the sacrament of Jesus Christ, whose "official-objective" bearer is Peter. But the burden of the Council's *communio* ecclesiology is that this office is originally born in the "lay-subjective" holiness of Mary (even as Mary's holiness remains in turn subordinate, in its own way, to Petrine office). Thus the laity, in their proper reality as lay, are meant to bear "subjectively" the "objective" sacramental reality of the Church into the world. Which is to say, they are to form the temporal structures and processes of the world, as far as possible, in and through the Eucharist: to order the temporal ends of "worldly" structures to their integrity at once as temporal-natural and as themselves open further to the reality of God in Jesus Christ, sacramentally embodied in the Church's Eucharist.[169]

This "worldly" responsibility of the laity remains essentially ecclesial, therefore, because it involves, in its task of forming the world, *proposing the sacramental reality of the Eucharist in its integrity.* The laity, integrated into the sacramental-Eucharistic meaning of the Church (via participation in the Petrine institution that bears this sacramental meaning by way of office), have the distinct task of making this Eucharistic reality present in the world, *from within the world itself* and in a way that realizes the world's natural integrity.[170]

Thus the one Church, in her distinct meaning as at once hierarchical priestly office and lay, is responsible for both the eternal or heavenly order, revealed in and through the sacramental reality of the Church, on the one hand, and the temporal or earthly order, on the other. Both the Petrine office and the laity are responsible for the unity within distinctness of the eternal and the temporal. The Petrine office secures this unity properly through its responsibility for the eternal order as such, in its objectively ecclesial-sacramental realization, an eternal order understood to bear the final meaning of the temporal order. The (Marian) laity, on the other hand, secure this unity properly through their responsibility for the temporal order, albeit as this temporal order is already turned toward and initially formed by the eternal order (sacramentally realized in the Church).

(b) This *communio* ecclesiology has specific implications regarding the relation between church and state. Here I will identify three:

First, the Church in her lay-Marian reality[171] is meant to remain *present in the world,* seeking to open *from within* all the temporal structures and processes of civil society, including the *state structures* that are a distinct but integral expression *of* civil society, to eternal reality as revealed in Jesus Christ (and as objectively-sacramentally present in the Church). It is the Church in her lay reality that thus properly seeks to inform the state. The state, in a word, is to remain intrinsically lay, even as, like all other societal institutions, it is meant to be transformed as far as possible in light of the true end of the human being and the human community.

Second, Catholics believe that the truth of human existence lies in the God of Jesus Christ, who remains sacramentally present in the teaching office and Eucharistic liturgy of Peter. The Church in her lay-Marian reality and worldly task thus retains her inner reference to Peter, even as this reference itself demands a principled distinctness between the lay and the Petrine dimensions of the Church. The Church-lay, as part of its task of forming worldly structures, so far rightly seeks favored status for the Church-Peter, in a sense that may include even privileged recognition in the constitutional order. At the same time, the Church-lay, in seeking to inform the structures of civil society, including those of the state, with the truth that is ultimately Eucharistic love, insists that the Church as a Petrine reality remain *distinct* as a transcendent, objective-sacramental reference point *for* society and the state. The church-state relation, properly understood, thus calls for a permanent distinction between the state and the Church as *sacerdotium:* requires, that is, that the state always and as a matter of principle remain lay, and never be fused institutionally with the Petrine Church.

Third, the foregoing is to be understood in terms of the mutual but asymmetrical priority that exists in the relation of the laity and the Petrine office, with respect to the world, as indicated above. The Church-lay and the Church-Petrine are *both* intrinsically responsible for both the temporal order and the eternal order, but each retains a distinct priority within this common responsibility. In regard to direct and proper responsibility for the eternal order, qua eternal, the Church-lay remains subordinate to the Church-Petrine; in regard to direct and proper responsibility for the temporal order, qua temporal, the Church-Petrine remains subordinate to the Church-lay.[172]

In all of this, the Church, in both her lay-Marian and Petrine dimensions, is to observe the principles established earlier regarding the rightful autonomy of human nature demanded by Christology, respect for the right to religious freedom of all persons of all faiths or of no explicit faith at all,

and recognition of the historical principle, which requires that human beings be met first where the concrete conditions of their history have brought
them.[173]

EXCURSUS

Let me add here three comments that will assist in clarifying the church-state
problem as framed in the foregoing discussion. Each of these comments is
best understood in light of Benedict's Bundestag address, with its emphasis
on the intrinsic need for the ruler or lawmaker to *listen* to nature and to
the echoes of the Creator revealed therein. (1) First, D. C. Schindler, in a
recent essay,[174] provides a helpful summary in connection with the point I
have wished to make, in terms of the well-known fifth-century dictum of
Pope Gelasius I: "Two there are . . . whereby this world is ruled by sovereign
right, the sacred authority *(auctoritas)* of the priesthood and the royal power
(potestas)."[175] Emphasizing the distinction between authority and power,
Schindler suggests an analogy "between the effective power in the political
realm and the authority that transcends that realm but informs it" (608n50).

> Interpreted according to the principle of analogy, to say as Gelasius does
> that the state has *"potestas"* rather than *"auctoritas"* means that the state
> is not the *author* of the realities it governs in the temporal sphere, but or-
> ders them according to their truth, according to the meaning they have
> as given, *prior* to the state's judgments and thus as defining the scope and
> character of the state's power. The state's competence is limited in this
> respect by received meanings. The church, by contrast, is the *authority,*
> which means it is her role to bear witness to the truth of things, but she
> does not effectively regulate them directly in the political sphere. The
> state, for example, does not define religion, or freedom, or the human
> person, marriage, and so forth, but receives these definitions from the
> authority responsible for and to the truth of these things, and determines
> the best way to preserve, protect, and promote these realities, as defined
> in the common life of the political community. Here is a "separation" of
> church and state, but without any extrinsicism. (608)

Schindler goes on to deal with the question of a "'confessional state' in the
sense of a nation with a 'state-established church'" (609). He concludes by
arguing that Catholicism has greater resources for religious pluralism than

liberalism does, that indeed the analogy indicated here "actually strengthens and elevates" the autonomy of the state, because "the authority of the Church is essentially generous: it establishes the state precisely by allowing the state to establish itself" (610).

It is important to see, for reasons that are indicated in Schindler's text and developed further in what follows, that the assigning of the definition of religion to the authorities responsible for the truth of religion does not preclude, but on the contrary demands, the state's own distinctive responsibility for transposing this definition of religion into a properly political form.

It needs to be emphasized here, then, that legal privileging as recognized in the preceding paragraphs means that the state should seek to order the temporal sphere as far as possible in terms of the truth about man's end, freedom, rights, marriage, and the like, but should do so by virtue of lay persons working from inside all temporal structures and processes (including the law, as qualified earlier in light of the historical principle and of Aquinas) to move them toward their true natural ends as open to the revelation of God in Jesus Christ, in a way that respects the freedom and dignity of all persons. In a word, the privileging of the Church indicated in the preceding paragraphs is a privileging of the *authority* of the Church as the *sacrament* of man's ultimate end and meaning; and of the Church as exercising *political power* only in the form of the initiatives of the lay Church operating from within temporal structures and processes.

(2) Second, Henri de Lubac, in an article written prior to the Council in the early 1930s, provides helpful historical insight regarding the longstanding question as to whether the Church exercises direct authority in the political order, as well as the principles necessary for resolution of the question.[176] He says that "the Church acts on the State only by addressing herself to the consciences of the citizens. Thus, her power is never either directly or 'indirectly' a *power over the temporal*. It is rather a power *in temporal matters*" (213). Thus, on the one hand, de Lubac rejects the idea that the Church has direct power over the state, in the sense of direct jurisdiction over temporal matters: acting as a temporal power, "ordering temporal measures, deposing and legislating" (209). He argues further in this connection that the theory of "indirect power," formulated by Robert Bellarmine, is ambiguous, leading in the end back to "direct power." Were a pope to seek to depose a prince for a spiritual reason, for example, the deposition would nonetheless remain "directly intentional, directly aimed for, directly brought about." It would involve, in other words, direct action of a temporal-political sort, while "bring[ing] about, indirectly, a spiritual end" (229).

On the other hand, having thus argued against what he terms "the remaining fragments of theocracy," de Lubac turns to the opposite error of liberalism, and proposes what he takes to be a "very simple *principle*" whereby we rightly affirm Church "interventions that can have temporal repercussions" (230).

> The authority of the Church . . . is exercised openly on consciences. But it does not follow that there are areas of thought or human activity that ought to be, *a priori,* closed to it. Because there is no activity, however profane it may appear, where the Faith and morality guarded by the Church cannot in one way or another . . . be involved. Christianity is universal not only in the sense that all men have their Savior in Jesus Christ but also in the sense that *all of man* has salvation in Jesus Christ. Since the destinies of Christianity were placed in the hands of the Church, the Church is catholic — that is, universal — in that nothing human can remain alien to her. And it is hard to see why "politics" should be an exception to this principle. As we have said, this was the teaching of Leo XIII in *Immortale Dei,* and, in general, it suffices to justify the Church's interventions in response to a certain "liberalism." But again the *nature* of these interventions and the *conditions* in which they are legitimate must be specified.
>
> As we have seen, the authority of the Church intervenes only by acting on consciences. There is no question of constraint. Just as grace does not come from outside to diminish and mutilate human nature but, on the contrary, affects it from the interior so that it is elevated and transfigured, the Church, messenger of Christ's grace, influences humanity and, in particular civil society, from within. She does not become society's guardian. Rather, she ennobles it, inspiring it to become Christian — and thus, more human. (230-31)

De Lubac goes on to say that the most important action of the Church, in light of the above, is that "by her very essence and through all of her faithful members, she reveals the ideal introduced into humanity by the Christian revelation" (231). But her legitimate action can also include the proclaiming of *"non licet"*: for example, condemning an act by a state or political party that undercuts the good of religion. The principle operative here, however, would be that the measure taken by the Church "directly concerns" the good of religion or the spiritual, and only concomitantly the temporal order.[177]

De Lubac's argument seems to me to anticipate, while being qualified and further illuminated by, both the Second Vatican Council's *communio* ecclesiology, which deepens the distinction (within unity) of the Church-lay and the Church-Petrine, and the Council's Christology, which protects the integrity of human nature (and reason) by way of opening into an ever-deeper integration of that nature into the Eucharistic reality of Jesus Christ. De Lubac's argument is also further illuminated by Schindler's reading of the distinction between *auctoritas* and *potestas*. There are three points to be made, then. First, it is the Church-Petrine that is denied proper jurisdiction over temporal affairs. Second, it nevertheless remains true that the Church rightfully exercises authority over consciences, in a way that concerns not only all men but all of man, and thus also man in his exercise of political power. Thus the Church-Petrine exercises proper authority, or "directive power," over the *conscience* of the laity *in* the latter's exercise of political power, even as the laity's "worldly" presence includes the effort to order all temporal reality in light of the ultimate end of human existence as revealed by God in Jesus Christ. And this ordering includes not only *societal* structures, but the structures of *the state and its law* as well. The laity therefore retain their proper autonomy in the exercise of political power, relative to the Church-Petrine, in the ways indicated above. That is, the Church-Petrine makes no jurisdictional claim regarding the state and its law qua political power *(potestas)*. But she continues to exercise her authority *(auctoritas)* over the consciences of the laity as they go about the "worldly" tasks that are properly theirs, including the task of statecraft.

The crucial point, thirdly, is that the laity are to work to inform the law as far as possible with the truth about the ultimate meaning and end of man in relation to God. This lay effort to inform the law with the truth about man is to be guided by a rightly understood historical principle, a principle that recognizes the right of every human being to realize in freedom the truth to which he or she is already bound (and bound to seek) by nature, and that, in this recognition, takes account of the concrete conditions in which human beings find themselves at any given point in history. Assuming this guidance by the historical principle, the laity are meant to order the political or legal-constitutional power of the state as far as possible in the truth about man: in the truth of his nature as created, as at once *open to* the truth of this nature as revealed by God in Jesus Christ.

(3) Finally, despite its language, which is strange to contemporary readers, Thomas Aquinas's *De Regimine Principium*, or *De Regno*,[178] provides principles that enable us to qualify and illuminate further the approach to

the church-state relation affirmed in the preceding paragraphs and implied by my reading of *Dignitatis humanae*.

> If the ultimate end of man were some good that existed in himself, then the end of the multitude to be governed would likewise be for the multitude to acquire such good, and persevere in its possession. If such an ultimate end . . . were a corporeal one, namely, life and health of body, to govern would then be a physician's charge. If that ultimate end were an abundance of wealth, then knowledge of economics would have the last word in the community's government. . . . It is, however, clear that the end of a multitude gathered together is to live virtuously. For men come together for the purpose of living well together, a thing which the individual man living alone could not attain, and the good life is the virtuous life. . . . Yet through virtuous living man is further ordained to a higher end, which consists in the enjoyment of God, as we have said above. Consequently, since society must have the same end as the individual man, it is not the ultimate end of an assembled multitude to live virtuously, but through virtuous living to attain to the possession of God. (De Reg. I, 15)

> If this end could be attained by the power of human nature, then the duty of a king would have to include directing men to it. . . . But because man does not attain his end, which is the possession of God, by human power but by divine power, according to the words of the Apostle (Rom 6:23): "By the grace of God life everlasting," therefore the task of leading him to that last end does not pertain to human but to divine government. Consequently, government of this kind pertains to that king who is not only a man, but also God, namely, our Lord Jesus Christ, who by making men sons of God brought them to the glory of Heaven. . . . Thus, in order that spiritual things might be distinguished from earthly things, the ministry of this kingdom has been entrusted not to earthly kings but to priests, and most of all to the chief priest, the successor of St. Peter, the Vicar of Christ, the Roman Pontiff. (De Reg. I, 15)

> Now anyone on whom it devolves to do something which is ordained to another thing as to its end is bound to see that his work is suitable to that end: the armorer so fashions the sword that it is suitable for fighting, for example, and the builder should so lay out the house that it is suitable for habitation. Therefore, since the beatitude of heaven is the end of that

virtuous life which we live at present, it pertains to the king's office to promote the good life of the multitude in such a way as to make it suitable for the attainment of heavenly happiness, that is to say, he should command those things which lead to the happiness of heaven and, as far as possible, forbid the contrary. But what conduces to true beatitude and what hinders it are learned from the law of God, the teaching of which belongs to the office of the priest. (De Reg. I, 16)

Five comments will enable a proper understanding of the continued relevance of this argument by Aquinas, in light of the statements of Schindler and de Lubac above, as well as Benedict's Bundestag address, and indeed in light of our interpretation of the Declaration as a whole. First, the subjection of earthly rulers (kings) to priests ("most of all to the chief priest, the successor of St. Peter") is to be understood as a subjection to the latter in the form of heeding his *auctoritas,* not *potestas civilis.* In accord with the proposal of de Lubac, this means that the Church possesses authority *in* all temporal affairs as these bear implications for man's ultimate end, but that this authority is never properly a matter of the Church's *direct political jurisdiction over* temporal affairs.

Second, the Church's direct political jurisdiction *(potestas)* over temporal affairs is essentially a matter of lay and not priestly (Petrine) responsibility. The development of doctrine indicated in the Declaration, relative to Aquinas's argument, is thus to be found in the Church's *communio* ecclesiology, which affirms the intrinsically ecclesial reality of the laity in (mutual-asymmetrical) subordination to Petrine office. This development sustains a proper sense of the abiding authority of the Church *in* the temporal, including the political, order, which has always been a rightful concern of the Church, despite her sometimes-illicit recourse to direct temporal-political power. It also presupposes a proper sense of the historical principle, which demands respect for the subjectivity, hence rights, of the human person, at once as essentially ordered by the truth and as affected by the changing, and sinful, conditions of history. Indeed, respect for the subjectivity of the human being in its legitimate meaning finds its proper roots in Aquinas's own metaphysical anthropology.

Third, in their efforts to invest law with the truth about the human being, the laity must remain mindful that the truth that is built into man's nature and that is thus, at least in principle, universally accessible to human reason, itself opens finally to a revealed truth that is recognized only through supernatural faith in Jesus Christ. The laity's efforts to realize the truth about man in their exercise of political power will therefore seek, in a principled way, to direct attention to the authority of God himself as source of all truth, and this will involve inviting attention also to the authority of God's own truth as revealed in Jesus Christ and sacramentally present in the Church. The laity must themselves take responsibility for the jurisdiction of truth in the constitutional-legal order, while resting on the principles (not specific political policies) drawn from the authority of the Word of God, whose sacramental-"official" bearer is the Petrine Church. As stated in the older language of Aquinas, the king (earthly ruler) is to form the multitude in the virtuous living that is finally "learned from the law of God, the teaching of which belongs [sacramentally] to the office of the priest."

Fourth, we should recognize in all this what is implied in the statements of de Lubac and the argument of Aquinas, and indeed in the whole of my interpretation of the Declaration as it bears on the problem of the state (in relation to the Church): namely, that Plato's dictum that the state is "the soul writ large" remains in its core true.[179] The state, in other words, in its legal-political order, is informed by a definite view of the human being vis-à-vis ultimate truth, which finally, even if unconsciously, gives the state its political unity. This definite view, however much it is generated by human beings, *simultaneously informs* them. Indeed, it orders their way of life analogously to the way in which the soul informs the body.[180] The liberal society with its juridical state has created the illusion that it can successfully avoid what is implied in this analogy. But in fact, as my argument regarding the Declaration makes clear, *the liberal-juridical state merely embodies a different kind of soul,* filled with different ends: those mostly of success and comfort, or reductively conceived wealth and poverty and freedom and intelligence, rather than virtue and wisdom and indeed holiness — that is, for all purposes of political order.[181]

Fifth, it is important, in light of the foregoing, to bear in mind the principle enunciated earlier that the Church, while proposing principles that reach to the heart of political authority, nevertheless has no authority in terms of making definitive pronouncements regarding any particular historical form of government (for example, democracy, monarchy, and the like). Properly speaking, that is, the Church, in her sacramental-Petrine office, no more endorses liberal democracy than she does liberal capitalism, qua political or economic institutions; nor can she do so without violating the principles set forth in the preceding paragraphs and earlier sections of this essay. Nor for that matter does she, properly speaking, endorse socialism: for example, the socialisms that are today mostly dialectical inversions of liberal democracy and liberal capitalism. This does not mean that the Petrine Church remains neutral with respect to any or all particular historical, political, or economic institutions. It means merely that the Church's Petrine authority lies in articulating the ontological, anthropological, and theological principles operating at least implicitly in each such institution, and judging and defending the right understanding of these principles (or indeed in pronouncing her *non licet* insofar as any institution violates these principles).[182] Thus we can say, for example, that the Petrine Church, in supporting the inherent dignity of each human person, and thus the right of each person to freedom in the realization of the truth to which he is obligated by nature, will so far demand the presence of democratic elements in the order of the state. And we can say at the same time that the Church, in supporting a definite vision of the human person that gives a society its civil unity, to the exclusion of contrary visions, will demand hierarchical, and so far "monarchical," elements in the order of the state. It is for the laity, however, to give concrete order to political and economic institutions in terms of these principles, working from within the institutions of society and state to bring them to the integrity of their natural ends as open to God, and correcting them when necessary.

Needless to say, the foregoing statement of principles in regard to the church-state relation leaves much to sort out in theological and prudential-historical terms. It nonetheless suffices for my present purpose, which is to indicate the *status quaestionis* of the problem. These principles must be understood, once again, in light of the fact that the juridical state is itself always "a soul writ large," albeit an empty or positivist soul that differs from that presupposed in the argument of the Declaration, a state that thus grants favored legal status, however unconsciously, to those churches that lend support to such a positivist soul. The pertinent question, then, once again, is not *whether* some definite truths regarding God and human destiny, and so far some church or religion, will be legally privileged (at least by logical implication), even in liberal democratic states, but rather *which privileged truths,* and *privileged churches,* are able to affirm with the most consistency the truth about the universal dignity of the human person, and thereby afford also the most complete and just protection of the right to religious freedom of every person. My answer, proposed in terms of the Declaration, has been that the positivistic religions (churches) legally favored *de facto* by the juridical state cannot, as a matter of principle, sustain this dignity and right, while

Catholicism is able to sustain this dignity and right and is committed as a matter of principle to doing so.[183]

Secularity and the freedom of the Church. The foregoing sections have implied a response to many of the questions that arise in connection with the problem of secularity and the freedom of the Church. Let me nonetheless clarify further how this problem is to be understood in light of the Declaration, and indeed in light of the terms that Murray adopts in his discussion of the matter, at the Council and afterwards.

In an article on the Declaration published in 1966, Murray argues that, with the writings of Leo XIII, the Church finally made clear "that there are two distinct societies, two distinct orders of law, as well as two distinct powers. This was the ancient affirmation[184] in a new mode of understanding — an authentic development of doctrine" (BSS, 192). Murray says that, on the basis of this development, Leo adds a second: "[H]e reiterated that the essential claim which the Church makes on civil societies and their governments is stated in the ancient formula, 'the freedom of the Church.'" According to Murray, however, "[i]t was not possible for [Leo] to complete these two developments with a third — the affirmation of the freedom of society and of the duty of government toward the freedom of the people" (BSS, 192). Nevertheless, Leo XIII's work prepared the way "for further progress in understanding the rightful secularity of society and state, as against the ancient sacral conceptions," a progress that "reaches its inevitable term" in *Dignitatis humanae*. In the Declaration, Murray argues,

> The sacrality of society and state is now transcended as archaistic. Government is not *defensor fidei.* Its duty and rights do not extend to what had long been called *cura religionis,* a direct care of religion itself and of the unity of the Church within Christendom or the nation-state. The function of government is secular: that is, it is confined to a care of the free exercise of religion in society — a care therefore of the freedom of the Church and of the freedom of the human person in religious affairs. The function is secular because freedom in society, for all that it is most precious to religion and the Church, remains a secular value — the sort of value that government can protect and foster by the instrument of law. Moreover, to this conception of the *state* as secular, there corresponds a conception of *society* itself as secular. *It is not only distinct from the Church in its origin and finality; it is also autonomous in its structures and processes.* Its structural and dynamic principles are proper to itself

and proper to the secular order — the truth about the human person, the justice due to the human person, the love that is the properly human bond among persons and, not least, the freedom that is the basic constituent and requirement of the dignity of the person. (BSS, 192-93; emphasis added)

According to Murray, then, "the highest value that both state and society are called upon to protect and foster is the personal and societal value of the free exercise of religion. . . . Not nostalgic yearnings to restore ancient sacralizations, not futile efforts to find new forms of sacralizing the terrestrial and temporal order in its structures and processes, but the purification of these processes and structures and the sure direction of them to their inherently secular ends — this is the aim and object of the action of the Church in the world today" (BSS, 193). Murray concludes:

> The Declaration is an act in that lengthy process known today as *consecratio mundi*. The document makes clear that the statute of religious freedom as a civil right is, in reality, a self-denying ordinance on the part of the government. Secular government denies to itself the right to interfere with the free exercise of religion, unless an issue of civil offense against the public order arises (in which case the state is acting only in the secular order, not in the order of religion). On the other hand, the ratification of the Declaration by Vatican Council II is, with equal clarity, a self-denying ordinance on the part of the Church. To put the matter simply and in historical perspective, the Church finally renounces, in principle, its long-cherished historical right to *auxilium brachii saecularis* [the help of the secular arm]. . . . The secular arm is simply secular, inept for the furtherance of the proper purposes of the People of God. More exactly, the Church has no secular arm. In ratifying the principle of religious freedom, the Church accepts the full burden which is the single claim she is entitled to make on the secular world. Thus a lengthy, twisting, often tortuous development of doctrine comes to a term. (BSS, 193-94)

My comments in response to this reading of secularity are three. First and most simply, and to state the obvious: what Murray proposes regarding secularity and the development of doctrine assumes his own juridical reading of the Declaration, and indeed his own reading of Leo XIII and John XXIII as precursors of the juridical approach.

148

Second, as we have seen, Murray's interpretation of secularity is governed by his emphasis, in matters pertaining to religion, on freedom in abstraction from truth, and so far on freedom of indifference. Striking in the present context, however, is his emphasis on the abstraction of freedom from truth in terms of the functions of *society,* and not only of the state. According to Murray, what the Church seeks from society is only the freedom of its citizens, abstracted from freedom's positive capacity for truth, and what the Church seeks from the state is only the protection of this freedom. In his continued insistence on freedom's abstraction from truth, Murray now draws out more explicitly his understanding of freedom's abstraction from man's ultimate (religious) end, as this is given by nature, and also by grace through the supernatural revelation of God in Jesus Christ. What the Church rightly demands, with respect to both civil society and civil governmental authority, is only protection for the exercise of freedom of choice.

Third, Murray says that "the sacrality of society and state is now transcended as archaistic"; that "the government is not *defensor fidei,*" and its duty does not include "a direct care of religion itself." The function of government, rather, is secular, that is, confined to a care of "the freedom of the Church and of the freedom of the human person in religious affairs." To this secular conception of the state, then, there corresponds a secular conception of society. Here we come to Murray's crucial point in the matter of secularity and sacrality: that society is "distinct from the Church in its origin and finality," and "autonomous in its structures and processes."

What Murray understands here as the *"either-or"* of secular and sacral is understood by the Council rather in terms of a paradoxical *"both-and."* According to the Council, the secular is truly confirmed in its autonomy, and indeed in its completeness as secular, even as it is open to further fulfillment by the sacral, or the divine life of Christ. Thus the Church, through her laity, is to enter society always and everywhere in terms of this dual principle: to move the structures and processes of society to the ends *proper to their nature,* while seeking *in* this very activity to open these structures ever more fully to the Eucharistic love revealed in Jesus Christ and sacramentalized in the Church. She is to carry out this task in respectful dialogue with all members of society.[185]

Regarding the following key terms of Murray's understanding of secularity, then: first, the truth about the person and his freedom in the secular order lies in the exigency of freedom, not abstracted from truth, but already ordered toward and by transcendent truth. The justice due to the human person is determined by the criterion of public order, but only as this order is informed by the true common good of man. Finally, the love which according to Murray is society's proper concern is indeed that which lies in the bond among persons, but only as this bond is already open to the transcendent order of truth. The concern of society with regard to each of these — the human person, justice, and love — is properly conceived, in a word, only when intrinsically tied to the ultimate end of the human being, an end which, in its integrity as terrestrial and temporal, is itself open to the heavenly and eternal that is itself concretely embodied in the revelation of God in Jesus Christ.

Murray's summary claim that the aim of the Church today is to direct society's structures and processes to "their inherently secular ends" in "the terrestrial and temporal order" is thus question-begging. The claim misses the fact that for the Council, rightly understood, the integrity of the earthly-temporal itself presupposes an inner opening to the heavenly-eternal, and so far an original and abiding unity between temporal and eternal. Murray begs the question of the sense in which the supernatural revelation of God in Jesus Christ (re-)affirms, even as it transforms, what is ultimately meant by this unity (within distinctness) of time and eternity. The Declaration on Religious Freedom, when seen in light especially of *Gaudium et spes* and other conciliar documents, does indeed involve a movement toward the *consecratio mundi,* but this "consecration" involves a deepening of the autonomy of the world that is *simultaneous* with opening the world as far as possible to its heavenly destiny, already here and now. Finally, the Church, in the Declaration, does not in fact relinquish her right to "the help of the secular arm," insofar as we rightly understand this help in terms of a *communio* ecclesiology and the distinct call to a holiness in the world on the part of the laity, as qualified in the previous section.[186] The secular arm — that is, secular institutions or worldly structures — are rather to be formed by the laity, for "the furtherance of the proper purposes of the People of God" who are endowed with the task of being the loving soul of the world, which demands working from within the structures of the world as well as inherent respect for the freedom of all.[187]

Murray's reading of the Council in the matter of secularity, as expressed here, leads logically to *privatizing* the reality of the Church in its engagement with the world. The Catholic faith, on his understanding, is permitted relevance in the public world of modern civilization only as a moral-intentional *inspiration* that remains hidden, and not as an *informing and transforming presence.*[188] Finally, on Murray's reading, the Church can have a legitimate presence in the public world only insofar as she is content to assist in moving temporal structures and process to their temporal ends in abstraction from, and so far in logical indifference to, the (transcendent, eternal) reality of God.[189]

Pluralism and modern democratic societies. We have been occupied with the problem of pluralism often, even if only implicitly, throughout the course of this essay. Pluralism is assumed to be that feature of modern democratic societies which warrants the juridical approach to government and constitutional order, because this approach alone appears logically capable of supporting a "civil," as distinct from "substantive" metaphysical or religious, unity, and thus of affirming an equality of rights for adherents of all religions as well as for those who have no explicit faith at all.

The problem, as we have shown, is that the pluralism claimed for modern democratic societies is deceptive. The juridical approach rests on the assumption that we can abstract for legal-public purposes the purely formal meaning of freedom from the truth by which freedom is naturally ordered. The assumption is that we can abstract freedom from truth without thereby reconstituting the nature of freedom as freedom of indifference. The juridical freedom of indifference, however, implies a definite metaphysics that displaces the ancient-medieval freedom at the heart of the Catholic tradition.

The point, thus, once again, is that the juridical approach implies a metaphysical *monism* of freedom of indifference. The logical consequence is that modern democratic societies, insofar as they are guided by the assumptions of the juridical approach, are in principle not more pluralistic, or less metaphysically unified, than pre-modern societies, in terms of their support for one type of religious anthropology or religious life. On the contrary, modern societies and governments are only unified *differently* from traditional societies and government, and in a manner that is more blind and less conscious, and indeed, in this sense, *more profoundly repressive, albeit in a more subtle manner.*

To be sure, in asserting this, I do not mean to deny the obvious and extreme pluralism of modern societies, with their abundant diversity of religious faiths, lifestyles, modes of dress, and the like. Nor do I mean to deny the violence used in the imposition of unity characteristic of many pre-modern, including Catholic, societies. I wish only to highlight again how modern democratic societies and governments, hiddenly, and contrary to their own express intentions, "dictate" religious-anthropological unity, in the name *precisely of not doing so.* My concern in this respect has been with the problem of religious freedom, and I have thus focused on these societies' implied freedom of indifference and the "negative" rights it entails. But the case regarding an implicit monism underlying what is a more obvious and explicit pluralism could be made as well, for example, in terms of the patterns of economic life (notions of wealth and poverty) or of academic-scientific life (notions of knowledge and truth and "critical method") that are dominant in modern liberal societies.[190]

The point, then, is that we can approach the problem of the right to religious freedom properly only insofar as all parties to the discussion come to terms with the metaphysical monism that operates hiddenly within and tacitly controls what appears to be, and in certain respects is, a societal pluralism otherwise fostered by the liberal-juridical state.

Religious freedom and the question of dialogue. My argument in this essay has been that the Council did *not* remove the question of truth from the political-constitutional order. On the contrary, the Council affirms that the right to religious freedom that is the hallmark concern of the modern constitutional-democratic government can be sustained in a principled way only insofar as this right is rooted in the truth about man in relation to God. Those responsible for making laws and administering justice realize the constitutional-democratic state's intention of securing the right to religious freedom, not by avoiding metaphysical-religious questions, but on the contrary only by facing them with listening hearts and minds.

But a certain irony becomes evident here, in view of the history of the Council's Declaration. As discussed by Nicholas Healy in his historical overview of the redactions of the Declaration, the problem of religious freedom was first situated in an ecumenical context.[191] In the third redaction, the discussion was moved to a political context. This change of context was of course legitimate: the question with which the document was specifically concerned, after all, was that of a *civil* right. As we have now seen, however, the bishops recognized that the question of truth reemerges in terms of the civil order itself. Every free-intelligent act of the human being bears in its depths a desire for the true and indeed ultimate meaning of things that alone fulfills his nature. According to the bishops, human dignity and the claim of the right to religious freedom rest on this order. That is why the pontificates of John Paul II and Benedict XVI have repeatedly insisted, in the name of the conciliar teaching, that questions regarding metaphysical and religious truth be kept alive *at the heart of the legal-political order, as an essential condition for protecting this right.*

Hence the reason for reintroducing here the matter of interreligious dialogue. Recall DH's statement that the civil authorities should "create conditions favorable to the fostering of religion" (DH, 6; cf. DH, 4). Creating such conditions involves a principled concern with truth on the part of the civil authorities, and this implies the further responsibility of the latter to foster awareness among citizens of the question regarding the nature of the human being and the ultimate foundation for his dignity, *as well as to promote dialogue in society where differences exist in the face of this question.* Three comments will help to clarify what this means.

First, the dialogue indicated may be said to realize the literal meaning of the term *ecumenical:* what is universal, including every church body or religious view. Because of its metaphysical-religious nature, however, this dialogue differs from ecumenical or interreligious dialogue in its more usual sense as occupied primarily with questions of overtly religious doctrines that are, or appear to be, of immediate concern only to explicit adherents of religion. Also due to its metaphysical-religious, and thus radical, nature (radical because it goes to the root [*radix*] of things), the dialogue envisioned is not of a sort that is best conducted via programs, meetings, commissions, and gatherings of experts. On the contrary, the questions making up its content are ontological, opening up to the religious and involving the breadth and depth of human life in its destiny before God; and the questions thus become in principle the responsibility of every human being. In this context, the civil authorities' creation of "conditions favorable to the fostering of religion" needs to take the form of assisting those communities to flourish that are most properly fitted by nature for forming persons in the truth about man before God — namely, familial and religious communities, and educational institutions given their form and end in organic relation with such communities — while respecting the integrity of each person's search for this truth.

Second, the dialogue implied by the teaching of DH in the present cultural situation calls above all for *reawakening* the very questions regarding the meaning and truth of man that the prevalent liberal-juridical ethos systemically ignores, and insists must be ignored for the sake of peace and equal justice in the matter of rights. This task of reawakening the questions bears simultaneously a positive and a critical dimension.[192] On the one hand, the effort must be to show how each human act bears by nature the desire for what is ultimately true and good, and thus for God; and in this connection to assist as far as possible in exhibiting the truth about man and God, *showing that man's very freedom and right to search is itself fully liberated only by this truth.* Notice, in other words, that the end of the religious dialogue to be fostered is not merely to share in a search for truth to the exclusion of arriving at truth. It is rather more properly to seek indeed to arrive at the truth about God, *in the context simultaneously* of showing (also) how *this very truth* affirms the intrinsic, hence abiding, goodness of the search itself.[193]

On the other hand, this positive effort needs to be accompanied by the critical task of showing that the liberal-juridical state's would-be official agnosticism in matters of metaphysical-religious truth is in fact not such. On the contrary, this putative agnosticism hiddenly harbors a claim of truth regarding the nature of the human act, taking this act for all legal-public purposes to be a structurally formal exercise of freedom that, as we have seen, transforms all metaphysical-religious truth-claims into options. The civil authorities of the juridical state, in other words, hiddenly govern on the basis of a truth-claim regarding religion, while the nature of this hidden truth-claim is such that it drains religious inquiry and dialogue of any public metaphysical substance or seriousness. Any religious dialogue that the civil authorities of the juridical state could consistently foster can, *eo ipso,* have no other terminus than that of talking without end. Or better, such dialogue will always, and from the outset, have structured into it the conclusion that religious truth is finally but an object of nonrational choice.

The dialogue envisioned by the Council, then, both recognizes *the truth about religion,* and does so while insisting that *this truth itself demands continued inquiry and respect for every person's right to inquiry;* while the dialogue envisioned by the juridical state hiddenly imposes the monist relativism of a dogmatic agnosticism regarding religious truth, even as it thereby empties inquiry of its raison d'être and reduces dialogue to the exchange of subjective preferences.

Finally, the reason for this fostering of religious dialogue by religious authorities, according to the logic of the Declaration, is not merely or primarily to secure *civil* unity. Rather it is to secure unity in terms of truth itself, in the context of showing that it is this very unity in truth that demands inquiry after truth, and respect for the right to such inquiry, as goods intrinsic to truth: to secure unity thus in terms of a truth that itself permits and indeed demands its own legitimate sort of pluralism.[194] The burden of the bishops' concern, in a word, is that the civil authorities recognize that religious truth and inquiry and dialogue are essential features of the societal common good to which the state stands in service, even as this recognition will entail coming to terms with the juridical state's rejection of religious truth (on the basis of that state's own hidden truth-claim regarding the nature of religious truth), and its consequent elimination of inquiry and dialogue, rightly conceived in their substantive seriousness. Affirming the freedom and rights that are the genuine aspiration of liberalism, civil authorities will need to come to terms with the paradox of the vacuous metaphysical "substance," or "substantive" metaphysical vacuity, hidden within the logic of the would-be purely juridical state.

In the words of Cardinal Ratzinger: "In any question concerning man and the world, the question about the Divinity is always included as the preliminary and really basic question. No one can understand the world at all, no one can live his life rightly, so long as the question about the Divinity remains unanswered. Indeed, the very heart of the great cultures is that they interpret the world by setting in order their relationship to the Divinity."[195] My suggestion is that Cardinal Ratzinger's statement remains pertinent also in the liberal-juridical context of the question regarding a universal right to religious freedom.

IX.

I conclude by situating the teaching of the Declaration within the ongoing debate regarding the historical emergence and nature of individual rights, as conceived respectively in the ancient-medieval and modern periods.[196] The issues here are vast; I focus them only in terms of what is the over-arching question that occupied the bishops at Vatican II in their discussion of the right to religious freedom: namely, what is the relation between the subjective right claimed *by* the individual and the objective demand made *on* the individual, in the constitution of the right to religious freedom, and of rights more generally.[197] In *Dignitatis humanae*, the Church makes her own the concern for rights characteristic of the modern constitutional state, by affirming a right to religious freedom while situating its negative meaning as an immunity inside its anterior and more basic objective structure as a positive call to respond to others in truth, as ordered from and toward the Creator. Where does this teaching place the Council in terms of the historical discussion regarding the relative continuity or discontinuity that exists between the ancient-medieval and modern traditions?

Professor Brian Tierney, in his well-known historical studies on the theory of rights, defends a basic continuity between these traditions (for example, from Thomas Aquinas through Ockham up to Locke).[198] Discovering rights language used already in twelfth-century canonists' juridical writings, Tierney criticizes those authors, such as Leo Strauss and Michel

Villey, who argue that a profound shift occurs in the modern idea of rights. According to such critics, the modern idea of rights, centered in the individual's negative claim of freedom with respect to others, undermines the ancient-medieval idea of a natural right or law whereby the individual is first positively bound by nature to others and to a transcendent ground. Modern rights, in other words, are self-centered and arbitrary in a way that the natural law (right) of the ancients and medievals is not. Tierney insists otherwise. On the one hand, he says, "The metaphysical 'moderate realism' of Aristotle and Aquinas affirmed the primary existence of individual entities" and this is "not incongruous with an emphasis on individual rights" (Idea, 31). On the other hand, "Ockham's more radical criticism of a realist theory of universals did not exclude a concern with rights relationships" (Idea, 31). Indeed "an emphasis on community as well as on individual rights persisted even in Locke" (Idea, 233n80). Tierney summarizes his argument as follows: "The doctrine of individual rights was not a late medieval aberration from an earlier tradition of objective right or of natural moral law. Still less was it a seventeenth-century invention of Grotius or Hobbes or Locke. Rather . . . it was a characteristic product of the great age of creative jurisprudence that, in the twelfth and thirteenth centuries, established the foundations of the Western legal tradition" (Idea, 42). "The idea of natural rights in its earlier formulations was not one of 'atomic individualism'; it was not necessarily opposed to the communitarian values of traditional societies" (Idea, 347). "In fact one finds natural rights regarded as correlative with natural law at every stage in the history of the doctrine — in the twelfth-century renaissance of law, in the eighteenth-century Enlightenment, and still in twentieth-century discourse" (Idea, 33-34).

Tierney, then, argues that individual rights, on the one hand, and the demands of community, on the other, can be understood as complementary, not necessarily opposed. We need rely neither on a particular metaphysical theory — are human beings best conceived simply as individuals (nominalistically) or in terms of a universally shared nature? — nor on the caring God of religious faith. It is enough to see that humans display "certain relevant characteristics like rationality and free will," (Idea, 5) and (accordingly) to believe "in the value and dignity of human life" (Idea, 347). The latter is "[t]he one necessary basis for a theory of human rights" (Idea, 347).

This claim by Tierney, however, avoids the root question pressed by the bishops at the Council in their redactions of *Dignitatis humanae*. Tierney says that the rights claims of one individual need not conflict with the demands of the community, and he is in principle correct in this. But this raises the crucial question: On what reasonable, non-arbitrary grounds do we properly adjudicate competing claims when conflicts do arise? Rights claims are by definition matters of securing *justly ordered* relations between individuals and the community, above all in the hardest cases, when the most powerful stand on one side and the weakest and most defenseless stand on the other. On the basis of whose freedom and dignity do we resolve conflicting claims in such cases, when both groups claim dignity and thus an equal right to freedom? Tierney's sense of a historical continuity in the matter of rights presupposes, and depends upon, his leaving this question unresolved. Or, more precisely, his argument is that we need no particular metaphysical or theological grounds for adjudicating conflicting rights claims in a truly just manner. What he offers in the face of such a conflict is the assertion of a principled complementarity between individual rights claims and the demands of the community, which rests on the recognition by all sides of a human dignity rooted in features like reason and free will.[199] The Council bishops, in contrast, recognized that the issue raised here is just the one that must be answered. The issue is not whether the rights claims of individuals and the community can *at root* and *in principle* be complementary — that is granted. The issue concerns the principled basis for resolving these respective claims in a truly just, non-arbitrary, manner, when they do in fact conflict. Recognizing that this is the question most needing an answer, the bishops responded by tying rights — specifically, the right to religious freedom — to a human nature ordered toward and by the truth about God.[200]

The point to which I wish to draw attention, then, is that the bishops' response implicitly transforms the terms of Tierney's argument. Indeed, a profound irony emerges that in a crucial sense turns his argument on its head. On the one hand, the teaching of the Declaration affirms, consistent with thinkers like Strauss and Villey, that natural law (the objective basis for rights) must have priority: the subjective right of each individual arises inside the objective demands of the other — of truth and the good — as ordered toward and by the Creator. On the other hand, the Declaration, recognizing a subordination of right in its "negative"-subjective sense to right in its "positive"-objective sense, at the same time affirms a *unity* between the subjective and the objective meanings of right. In so doing, the Declaration does indeed, so far, affirm an important principle of historical continuity in the matter of classical-medieval and liberal modern rights — *but not in Tierney's sense.* The continuity lies in the fact that right in its objective meaning is indissoluble with right in its subjective sense: as we have seen, the bishops affirm the right to immunity precisely *by virtue of the call built into man's nature to seek the truth about God.* But it is just this sense of continuity that leads the bishops to reject the conception of the right to freedom that would separate — or fail to affirm an intrinsic relation between — freedom's *immunity from,* on the one hand, and *what freedom is for and is already interiorly ordered by,* on the other. The continuity affirmed by the bishops is therefore a continuity first on ancient-medieval terms, *not* modern terms.

But let us clarify further. First, the bishops' implicit affirmation of an essential principle of historical continuity in the matter of rights recognizes the problems characteristic of the dominant modern theories of rights. Indeed, the later redactions of the Declaration are responses to just such problems, and thus to the ambiguity resident in Tierney's sense of historical continuity, which insists that the question of the *relative priority* of objectivity and subjectivity in individual rights claims need not be pressed. In fact, the nature of the individual self vis-à-vis his or her relations and obligations to others and ultimately to God (thus the metaphysical question of nominalism) is exactly the burden of concern in the bishops' revisions.

Second, in pressing this question regarding the relative priority of objectivity and subjectivity, and in giving priority to the former, the Declaration takes over while reconfiguring the principle of subjectivity that is the hallmark feature of modern rights. It is important to understand here, however, that the bishops' assertion of the priority of objective right does not reduce right in its "negative"-subjective sense as an immunity to a mere *instrument* for the realization of truth — as though the subjectivity of the individual could be dispensed with once the truth were secured. That would be the case only if the subjective right were not an interior demand of the objective right itself. In fact, the indissoluble unity affirmed by the bishops, between the individual's subjective freedom, on the one hand, and the objective demand generated by truth and the call of God, on the other, secures the individual's subjective right to freedom as an intrinsic and not merely instrumental good.[201]

Thus, in stressing that the subjective right arises on the basis of the objective order of right, the Declaration makes subjectivity an intrinsic, albeit distinct, feature of objective right itself. The very objective order to which right in its negative-subjective meaning is subordinate itself demands the interiority — and so far distinct center requiring immunity from coercion (by others) — of the one in whom this objective right inheres.

Finally, in relating objectivity and subjectivity organically, simultaneously with subordinating the latter to the former, the bishops develop and deepen the meanings of both objectivity and subjectivity as customarily conceived. They grant primacy to objectivity while opening it to its implied dimension of subjectivity; and they affirm subjectivity while integrating it from the beginning with objective form. The key here is to recall the *personal* context in which the bishops frame the question of the right to religious freedom. The subjective right to freedom is claimed by a human person even as the objective context in which that right first emerges is set by the call of a personal God. The objective demand made on the human person is therefore not most basically that of an impersonal law — some sort of categorical imperative, for example, or even the objectivity of truth as conceived in certain streams of Scholasticism, which fail to recognize truth's inner openness to subjectivity or the interiority of a subject.[202] Nor, on the other hand, is the person's subjective claim of a right amorphous, or without form, as though the objective force of this claim emerges simply as a function of the person's originally unordered initiative. More simply put, the bishops, in holding together the subjective right of the individual self and the objective demand of the other, avoid the collapse into what may be termed either subjectivist arbitrariness, on the one hand, or objectivist rigorism, on the other.

The Council thus recognizes a unity of objective and subjective dimensions in the constitution of rights, simultaneous with its subordination of subjective to objective, and in so doing affirms what is rightly termed a continuity-within-discontinuity of ancient-medieval and modern approaches. The sort of principled continuity-within-discontinuity indicated here is a theoretical possibility not considered by Tierney in his account of the historical data in the matter of the evolution of rights.[203]

In sum, the Church at the Council points toward a distinctive integration of the achievements of the ancient-medieval and modern periods in the matter of objective and subjective right: in a way that affirms the ancient-medieval priority of an objective, naturally given, transcendent order, even as it affirms at the same time the intrinsic and not merely instrumental goodness of the subjective right intended by the moderns. The Church does all of this in recognition of the absolute priority of God in Jesus Christ, and thus in terms that are faithful above all to her biblical-creedal roots. I do not, of course, mean to suggest that the Declaration provided a fully worked-out theory in these matters. I am proposing merely that the burden of the late redactions, and final text, of the Declaration is to anchor the *subjective* right to religious freedom in the *objectivity* of a human *nature* bound ontologically to *truth*, finally to the truth of *the Creator God*. It is this nature in its very objectivity that demands a subjective right.

But here we see why it is important to place the teaching of the Declaration within the broader teaching of the conciliar documents as a whole, indeed as this has been developed and deepened in the pontificates of John Paul II and Benedict XVI, even as we situate all of this in light of the Church's entire magisterial-creedal tradition. Key again is the notion of the person, the anthropology developed in light of the Council's ecclesiological and Christological teachings. Boethius has given us a classical definition of the person as "an individual substance of a rational nature," and this definition is an indispensable foundation for any adequate notion of individual rights. As we have seen in light of the medieval tradition and the thought of Aquinas as retrieved by Pieper, the notion of rationality is developed in the tradition in terms of the *spirituality* of the human, intelligent-free act. This spirituality implies an interiority characteristic of the human person that is open to all that is *(anima est quodammodo omnia)*. Such spirituality so far implies relationality to the world, and implicitly to God as the source of the truth and goodness of the world. God's creation consists in the creative act of knowledge and love that establishes all being as respectively true and good in itself ("transcendentally"), as always first given to man and not first enacted or constructed by him.

John Paul II and Ratzinger/Benedict XVI, in interpreting the teaching of the Council as a whole, deepen the notion of the person as intrinsically related above all to God and, inside relation to God, to all others, thus deepening the notion of the person as "communional." The human person is a singularity originally constituted through and in a communion of persons.[204] The idea of the human person that derives from and best integrates the developments indicated here, we may say, is that of the person as *gift*. The truth of the human being lies in his reality as gift: as *good qua given* by God in God's intelligent and free act of creation. It is within the person's objective meaning as gift that the person's subjective rights claim emerges: the objective meaning and the subjective claim are indissoluble. I can claim my right as an individual only *qua the truth of my being as given* by God through and with others — especially other human beings, but also the cosmic beings that otherwise make up the world. It is because I am by nature a gift that I rightfully, always and as a matter of principle, claim immunity from coercion by others. But it is because I am by nature a gift that this rightful claim to immunity also always presupposes, and emerges only inside, what is my anterior debt in love to the truth and goodness of God and others.

The Declaration on Religious Freedom, understood in light of the teaching of the Council as a whole, thus leads to a kind of paradox. On the one hand, we are to affirm the negative right to religious freedom in a principled way, and not as a matter simply of accommodation to a good already realized in modern liberal constitutional government, or of compromise and concession in the face of the historical difficulties presented by modern pluralism. Indeed, this intrinsic affirmation of rights in their "negative"-subjective sense reaches beyond prevalent rights theories today in its radicality and its comprehensiveness — because subjective rights, on the Council's reading, are rooted in the human person *qua given* (by God), and not as otherwise qualified in terms of potential usefulness or burdensomeness, and the like.

On the other hand, we are to affirm this "negative"-subjective right only as bound to and understood in light of the objective demands of love as carried in the notion of the human person as gift — of the person thus in his constitution as from and for God, and in a principled sense also from and for others in God. The subjective right affirmed by the Church, in other words, takes its primitive meaning as "negative" only as always already taken up into the reality of the self as *given,* as *gift from* another that is of its deepest nature, and thus in its root structure, *positively responsive to* the other.

It follows from this twofold affirmation that the Church is to embrace from her depths the principle of subjective rights that is arguably the central concern of the modern social-political order. She is nonetheless called at the same time, in light of the prevalent juridical-liberal understanding of subjective rights, to transform these rights from the inside out, by reconfiguring the original meaning of subjectivity to include positive reference to the anteriorly given truth and goodness of others under God. Indeed, it is just *the radical and comprehensive nature* of the Church's embrace of the principle of a subjective right *that itself establishes the demand for a profound transformation* of the prevalent liberal-juridical understanding of such a right. It is not the case that rights can be adequately treated first as simply "negative" immunities, the foundations of which can vary without affecting the original meaning of immunity. On the contrary, on the Council's reading, the meaning of rights as immunities takes its original form from inside the human subject's positive "obligatory" objective ordering toward God and others.[205]

The Church's embrace of rights, in a word, can be properly understood only when tied to, and situated within, her comprehensive Christological and anthropological mission to the contemporary world: within the call to form a "civilization of love" open finally to the God revealed in Jesus Christ. This, it seems to me, is the comprehensive burden of the teaching of the Council on the right to religious freedom.[206]

Notes

1. Cf., e.g., the chapter "On the Relations Between Church and State and On Religious Tolerance" in the early schema *De Ecclesia,* proposed by Cardinal Alfredo Ottaviani and the Theological Commission (ADP II/4, 657-72).

2. Bishop Alfred Ancel, oral intervention of 22 September 1965 (AS IV/2, 17) A signif icant portion of Bishop Ancel's intervention was incorporated into the final text of *Dignitatis humanae,* as I will discuss more at length as we proceed. For a fuller discussion of the six re-dactions of the Declaration, see the historical overview by Nicholas J. Healy, Jr., "The Drafting of *Dignitatis Humanae,"* in this volume.

3. Nicholas Lobkowicz, "Pharaoh Amenhotep and Dignitatis Humanae," *Oasis,* 4, no. 8 (December 2008).

4. Hermínio Rico, *John Paul II and the Legacy of Dignitatis Humanae* [= Rico] (Washington, DC: Georgetown University Press, 2002).

5. According to Rico, the approach that ultimately "prevailed in the overall structure of the declaration and in the basic conceptual definitions . . . was personified in John Courtney Murray" (29). Rico nonetheless also affirms that, regarding "the [specific] arguments advanced to ground the right, Murray actually found himself on the losing side of the dispute" (47).

6. Richard J. Regan, S.J., *Conflict and Consensus: Religious Freedom and the Second Vatican Council* (New York: Macmillan, 1967), 95. Cf. J. Leon Hooper, S.J., ed., *Religious Liberty: Catholic Struggles with Pluralism* (Louisville: Westminster/John Knox Press, 1993), 127. According to Jan Grootaers, in October 1964 Murray became *"la cheville ouvrière,"* or what Regan and Hooper term the "first scribe" (literally, the "mainspring" or "kingpin") in the subsequent reformulation of the text: see Jan Grootaers, *Actes et acteurs à Vatican II* (Leuven: Leuven University Press, 1998), 65.

7. Rico indicates, correctly, that John Paul II emphasized the relation between freedom and truth throughout his papacy. But reading the Council as essentially ratifying the juridical approach, Rico wrongly understands the pope's insistence on the intrinsic relation between freedom and truth as a backing away from DH's teaching regarding religious freedom. On the contrary, what John Paul II affirmed regarding religious freedom throughout the course of his papacy was in essence just what he had repeatedly affirmed in his interventions as Archbishop of Kraków during the redactions of DH, namely, that there is an essential, mutual binding of freedom and truth. My argument will show that it is this view alone that can account adequately for the final form of the Declaration.

8. What Murray calls the juridical approach to religious freedom was introduced at the Council in the third schema *(textus emendatus)* of what became the Declaration. This draft, as well as the slightly emended fourth schema *(textus reemendatus),* were written with Murray as their "first scribe," as mentioned. Due to health issues, Murray was not organically involved in the subcommittee discussions regarding the decisive fifth schema, which was largely carried over into the finally approved document. It was in the fifth draft that many significant changes were added pertinent to the question of the foundations of the right to religious freedom and the duty to seek the truth about God. Cf. Hooper, 127: "A fifth text (the *textus recognitus*) was written while Murray was out of circulation because of a collapsed lung. The fifth text was presented to the Council on 25 October 1965, during the fourth session (September to December, 1965). After the incorporation of several proposed amendments, a final text was approved and

promulgated on 7 December 1965, as a conciliar declaration. The main argument of the fifth and final texts was grounded on the human right to search after the truth and to embrace the truth once found. Murray's principal line of argument entered the text . . . as an addendum." Cf. also Regan, 158: "[T]he *textus recognitus* integrated the argument from man's right and duty to follow conscience and the argument from the social nature of man and religion under the primacy of the argument from man's right and duty to seek truth; the constitutional argument was simply appended as a further consideration." In a footnote to this passage, Regan notes that "On October 5 Murray suffered a lung collapse, which forced him to the sidelines of subsequent Secretariat deliberations on drafting the *textus recognitus*. Murray discounts as highly improbable that he would have had much influence on the *textus recognitus* even if he had been present at all the Secretariat deliberations. In any event, Murray did return to action in time to consider the petitions for final revision of the Declaration" (Regan, 168n15). On the question of the hermeneutical significance of Murray's absence relative to the final form of the Declaration, see section V.3.ii.

9. John Courtney Murray, "The Declaration on Religious Freedom: A Moment in Its Legislative History" [= MLH], in *Religious Liberty: An End and a Beginning,*" ed. John Courtney Murray (New York: Macmillan, 1966), 15-42, at 27-28. Cf. also Edward Gaffney, "Religious Liberty and Development of Doctrine: An Interview with John C. Murray" [= RLDD], *The Catholic World* 204 (February 1967): 277-83, at 279: "Fundamentally, religious freedom is a freedom from something; it is an immunity from coercion."

10. Murray, "Declaration on Religious Freedom: Commentary" [= Comm.], in *American Participation at the Second Vatican Council,* ed. Vincent A. Yzermans (New York: Sheed & Ward, 1967), 668-76, at 668. Cf. also Murray, "The Declaration on Religious Freedom" [= DRF], in *Vatican II: An Interfaith Appraisal,* ed. John Miller (Notre Dame: Associated Press, 1966), 565-76, at 568; and MLH, 28.

11. Murray, *We Hold These Truths* [= WHTT] (Garden City, NY: Doubleday Image, 1964), 58, 60.

12. For further discussion of this distinction between articles of peace and articles of faith, see n. 61 below.

13. As Pietro Pavan puts it in his commentary on the text of DH, "there is [in the Declaration] no question of the relations between the person and truth or between the person and God, but of the interpersonal relations in human and political society" ("Declaration on Religious Freedom," in *Commentary on the Documents of Vatican II,* vol. 4, ed. Herbert Vorgrimler [New York: Herder & Herder, 1969], 58). Or, as he puts it elsewhere, "Religious freedom . . . does not concern the relation of the person to truth, but the mutual relationships between physical as well as moral persons" (63-64). According to Pavan, this is what is indicated by the change in the subtitle made in the fifth schema, where *libertas* was qualified as *socialis et civilis libertas.*

14. Thus, according to Murray, the American Constitution distinguishes between "a right as an immunity and a right as a positive claim" (Comm., 668). It considers a right not as a claim upon, but as an assurance against, the government, and this negative character is what defines rights as properly "political" or "civil." Though Murray affirms an essential identity between DH and the American Constitution in the matter of the "negative" content of the right to religious freedom, he also states that "the Declaration is not as correct and clear as the [American] Constitution . . . that the statute of religious freedom is essentially a self-denying ordinance on the part of the government" (Comm., 669).

15. Elsewhere Murray defines the idea of public order as follows: "The public order is that limited segment of the common good which is committed to the state to be protected and maintained by the coercive force that is available to the state — the force of law and of administrative or police action" ("This Matter of Religious Freedom," [= TMRF] *America*, 112 [9 January 1965]: 40-43, at 40). Cf. also MLH, 35: "The underlying distinction here is between what is necessary for the sheer coexistence of citizens within conditions of elemental social order, and what is useful in promoting their collaboration toward more perfect conditions of social welfare. . . . The category of the necessary is the category of public order. The wider category of the useful covers the more comprehensive concept of the common good." Finally, on the distinction between the common good and public order, see Murray, "The Problem of Religious Freedom" [= PRF] in *Religious Liberty: Catholic Struggles with Pluralism*, 127-97, at 145. This essay was written by Murray before and during the third session of the Council; according to Hooper, it presents the central argument of schema 3 (PRF, 127).

16. Cf., e.g., the reference to "the exigencies of public order" as that which determines juridical norms in schema 3, aa. 5b and 4e (AS III/8, 432-33). This earlier schema places an emphasis on the negative duties of the state (aa. 7 and 9) and favors conditions for exercising choice (a. 4e).

17. Cf. Murray, "The Declaration on Religious Freedom," in *Bridging the Sacred and the Secular: Selected Writings of John Courtney Murray, S.J.* [= BSS], ed. J. Leon Hooper, S.J. (Washington, DC: Georgetown University Press, 1994), 187-99, at 194-99. Cf. also Murray's statements in *Council Daybook*, vol. 3: Vatican II, Session 4, Sept. 14 to Dec. 8, 1965 (Washington, DC: National Catholic Welfare Conference, 1965), 14-17. According to Murray, "Leo XIII's dominant conception of government was paternal; it was adapted to the historical conditions of his time," namely "the historical fact of the formless 'illiterate masses'" (14). As a consequence, "in Leo XIII the traditional distinction between society and state is largely lost from view." Pius XII, on the contrary, understood that "government is simply political; it represents a return to tradition (to St. Thomas, for instance)." Pius thus returns to the traditional idea of "'the people,' a structured concept, at whose root stands 'the citizen (who) feels within himself the consciousness of his own personality, of his duties and rights, of his proper freedom as joined with a respect for the freedom and dignity of others' (Radio Discourse, Christmas 1944)" (14). Pius likewise revives the distinction between society and state, making it "a pillar of his . . . concept of the juridical state" (15). There is in Pius XII, then, and still more fully in John XXIII, an affirmation of "the truth of the juridical nature of the state — its primary commitment to the protection of the exercise of man's rights and to the facilitation of the performance of his duties. There is, finally, the truth of the limitation of the powers of government by a higher order of human and civil rights, which John XXIII elaborated, again in dependence on Pius XII, but with greater detail and emphasis" (15). For further discussion of the tradition from Leo XIII to John XXIII, see PRF, 155-78.

18. Cf. Murray's commentary on DH in *The Documents of Vatican II* [= Abbott], ed. Walter M. Abbott, S.J. and Joseph Gallagher (New York: America, 1966), 679-96, at 687n21.

Regarding the Church's development of doctrine in the matter of religious freedom, Murray says that the Church gave formal expression in DH to an awareness that had long been developing already in modern culture, and that was given its distinctive juridical-"doctrinal" formulation especially in the founding documents of America. He affirms in this regard that DH was "an exercise in *aggiornamento* in the strict sense. Its achievement was simply to bring the Church abreast of the developments that have occurred in the secular world" (DRF, 565).

Murray's conception of public order and his understanding of freedom as the political method par excellence, as well as the question of the Church's development of doctrine in DH, will be treated at greater length in section VIII.

19. Cf. Murray, "On Religious Liberty," *America* 109 (November 1963): 704-6. On the importance of this article for the course of the Council discussion, see Walter Kasper, *Wahrheit und Freiheit: Die 'Erklärung über die Religionsfreiheit' des II. Vatikanischen Konzils* (Heidelberg: Carl Winter, 1988), 20-21. On the relationship between the coercive and the pedagogical functions of government, see n. 144 below.

20. Cf. DRF, 574: "The truth about the human person is that his fundamental exigence is to act on his own initiative and responsibility"; and DRF, 572: "[T]he basic exigence of the person is for immunity from coercion." There are of course many slightly variant expressions of Murray's notion of the foundations of human dignity as articulated here. See, e.g., RLDD, 282: "The Declaration takes its stand on the notion of the dignity of the human person. This notion is, of course, known through human reason, but it is also known through revelation, where man is clearly proclaimed to have been created in the 'image of God'; that is to say, man is a creature of intelligence and free will called upon to have dominion over his actions and to be the one who directs the course of his own life."

21. See, e.g., WHTT, ch. 1, "*E Pluribus Unum:* The American Consensus," 27-43; ch. 4, "The Origins and Authority of the Public Consensus: A Study of the Growing End," 97-124; and ch. 13, "The Doctrine Lives: The Eternal Return of Natural Law," 295-336.

22. See Murray's extensive discussion regarding the important question of "the spiritual substance of a free society" in WHTT, 192, 210.

23. Cf. Abbott, 675n5: "It is further to be noted that, in assigning a negative content to the right to religious freedom (that is, in making it formally a 'freedom from' and not a 'freedom for'), the Declaration is in harmony with the sense of the First Amendment to the American Constitution."

24. On Wojtyła's interventions regarding religious freedom, see, *inter alia,* Avery Cardinal Dulles, S.J., "John Paul II on Religious Freedom: Themes from Vatican II" [= Dulles], *The Thomist* 65, no. 2 (April 2001): 161-78; Rico, 103-16; Kasper, *Wahrheit und Freiheit,* 26-31.

25. See Wojtyła, Intervention 1 (AS III/3, 766): "[T]he authors of the schema . . . state that religious freedom is immunity from external coercion. Again, on page 5, they give the following definition: 'religious freedom, or the person's right not to be prevented by others from observing and proclaiming his public and private duties to God and to men, both individually and collectively, as these duties are manifested by conscience.' Both of these definitions seem to be partial and negative, and concerned with religious tolerance rather than with freedom. . . . Thus I propose that this definition and understanding of freedom in our schema be supplemented with a definition and understanding in which the importance for freedom of the objective truth itself — not only of subjective truth — is made more clear."

26. In the words of Avery Dulles, interpreting Wojtyła, "the merely negative definition could easily be exploited to promote unacceptable forms of liberalism or indifferentism" (Dulles, 165). In this regard, Wojtyła calls for the Council to emphasize not only the *right* to religious freedom, but also the *responsibility* that is entailed in such a right: see Wojtyła, Intervention 4 (AS IV/2, 12).

27. "It was imperative . . . to work with a positive conception of religious freedom, rooted in a theological understanding of the dignity of the person in relationship with God" (Dulles, 165).

28. "On the one hand, freedom exists for the sake of truth; on the other hand, without truth, freedom cannot achieve its own perfection" (Intervention 2 [AS III/2, 531]). In a set of written observations on the third schema, Wojtyła proposed that the document state in its opening article: "this sacred Council declares that this Catholic teaching on the one true religion is in no way opposed to human freedom; for the human person's obligation to follow the truth, once it is known, is not opposed to his free will. On the contrary, it is here that the true dignity of the human person is made manifest, which corresponds intimately to the teaching of the Gospel, and is at the same time drawn from the font of reason itself" (Intervention 3 [AS, Appendix, 606]). Dulles points out that Wojtyła voiced this concern for the recognition of freedom's intrinsic dependence upon truth in his first intervention at the Council (Dulles, 166).

29. The immediate context of this statement regards what Wojtyła calls "religious freedom . . . in the ecumenical sense," which he distinguishes here from religious freedom "in the civil sense." This distinction reflects the fact that what became the Declaration on Religious Freedom was originally a chapter of the Decree on Ecumenism. In ecumenism, Wojtyła argues, dialogue should arise from the very heart of one's faith and should be ordered toward the fullness of truth: "The relationship of freedom to truth is of the utmost importance [here] . . . for the aim of [ecumenism] is nothing less than the liberation of the whole of Christianity from schism, which cannot be fully achieved until the union of Christians is made perfect in truth. For this reason it is not enough, in our interactions with other Christians, to propose the principle of religious freedom as simply a principle of tolerance" (Intervention 2 [AS III/2, 531]).

On the other hand, Wojtyła says, "When the discussion concerns religious freedom in . . . the civil sense, then, to be sure, the principle of tolerance enters into the question" (531). "Nevertheless," he continues, "we should consider" that many in the political sphere, especially atheists operating in Communist regimes, "are inclined to see in all religion nothing more than the alienation of human reason. . . . When speaking about religious freedom [in the civil sense], therefore, we must present the human person with complete accuracy." Precisely in the civil context, then, "The human person must appear in the real grandeur of his rational nature, and religion must appear as this nature's crown and summit. For religion consists in the human mind holding fast to God in freedom, in a way that is wholly personal and conscientious, arising from a desire for the truth. . . . The Council, therefore, in the light of faith and of sound reason, should declare the full and genuine truth about man, who in religion is in no way alienated, but rather achieves his own perfection." In this way, "The [civil] right to freedom in the exercise of religion is connected with those rights of the person which concern the truth" (531-32).

While it is right to distinguish between the ecumenical and the political contexts, then, it is clear all the same that for Wojtyła not only the former but also the latter is concerned with the truth about man. "It is in the truth that the human person achieves his own proper perfection, for the truth corresponds to his rational nature and constitutes the firmest foundation for true freedom" (Intervention 1 [AS III/3, 766]). Acknowledging that "we need to bring together in a better way the rights of the person and the rights of the truth itself," Wojtyła insists that "*the civil right* [to religious freedom] has its foundation not only in the principle of tolerance . . . but *also in the natural right of every person to know the truth*" (766, emphasis added). For more on the relationship between the ecumenical and the political, see the end of section VIII.

30. "Civil powers should strictly and meticulously observe the religious freedom of persons and communities also for this reason, that is, on account of the responsibility incumbent upon each and every human person in this matter, or, in other words, out of respect for the

profound significance that religion has for man. . . . [B]y emphasizing the responsibility that corresponds to freedom, we might also express in this way, at least indirectly, the significance and objective force of religion. The right itself is indeed subjective — that is, the right of a subject, a person — and it is a right to freedom; but since with freedom comes great responsibility, and with a right a serious obligation, then — even within the perspective of the subject, which seems in some ways to be characteristic of our schema — there nevertheless appears most clearly the objective value of religion, *which ultimately comes from the truth itself*" (Intervention 4 [AS IV/2, 12], emphasis original).

31. Cf. Intervention 5 (AS IV/2, 292-93). According to Wojtyła, "No human being or human power has the right to use coercion on a person who arrives at an erroneous conclusion, if this erroneous conclusion is not itself opposed either to the common good, or to another's good, or to the good of the person in error. If it is, in fact, opposed to one or more of these, then it is clear that legitimate superiors, such as parents or those responsible for the common good, can exercise a kind of coercion on the one in error, lest by acting on his error he cause proportionately grave evil either to others or to himself" (Intervention 1 [AS III/3, 768]). Wojtyła elsewhere says that "In the case of an erroneous conscience, even one that is invincibly erroneous, respect for the person does not exclude the possibility of persuading him of the truth by means of arguments in support of it. Any remote or immediate physical pressure or physical or social coercion, however, is excluded" (Intervention 3 [AS, Appendix, 607]).

32. See Intervention 1 (AS III/3, 767), where Wojtyła expresses dissatisfaction with a passage in the first schema in which "it seems that the Christian moral order, consisting in supernatural charity, is superimposed upon *(superaedificari)* the purely natural order, which flows from the dignity of the human person in the order of nature. It would be better to say: the Christian moral order contains within itself the moral order of nature and all the rights of the human person; at the same time, it elevates, animates, and sanctifies these. . . ." According to Dulles, the changes made in the final document appeared to accommodate Wojtyła's concerns (Dulles, 163-64).

Cf. also, in this regard, Wojtyła, Intervention 4 (AS IV/2, 11): "See how that teaching that is found in parts II and III [of schema 4] is one and the same teaching of the Church; it is presented in part III in a more scriptural, or positive, way, and in part II in a more speculative way. Still, it would seem better not to separate reason and revelation so much in these sections, at least as they appear to be from their titles." In this earlier schema, part II was titled "The teaching on religious freedom derived from reason," and part III "The teaching on religious freedom in the light of revelation." In the following, fifth schema, as well as in the final document, a new division was introduced, which included only two major headings: part I, "The general principle of religious freedom," and part II, "Religious freedom in the light of revelation."

33. Once we recognize this, we see why, for Wojtyła, anchoring the right to religious freedom ultimately in revelation itself allows for, and indeed presupposes, a certain priority of reason's grounding of this right, which further anchors the universality of the claim to this right by all persons, believers and nonbelievers. Cf. in this connection *Fides et ratio,* 76, on the sense in which the light of the gospel first opens reason to new concepts — such as the notion of a free and personal God, of the reality of sin, of the person as a spiritual being, or of history as event — which subsequently enrich the operations of reason in its own concrete historical exercise as such.

34. For a more detailed account of the redaction history, see the essay by Nicholas

Healy in this volume, as well as the side-by-side presentation of the third schema and the final document.

On the morning of September 21, 1965, Pope Paul VI called a meeting to ensure that the vote on schema 4 of the Declaration would not be postponed. The resolution voted on that day was unusually phrased: "whether the *Textus reemendatus* on religious freedom should be taken as the basis for the definitive Declaration *(tamquam basis definitivae Declarationis)*, to be further perfected in accordance with Catholic teaching on the true religion *(ulterius perficiendae iuxta doctrinam catholicam de vera religione)*, and with the amendments proposed by the Fathers in the course of the discussion, to be approved according to the norms of Council procedure" (AS IV/1, 434). According to Gilles Routhier, the general formulation for the vote regarding a future revision was suggested to Paul VI by Cardinal Augustin Bea the evening before. The pope gave his written consent, while adding in parentheses "while reaffirming the teaching on our true religion" (cf. *The History of Vatican II*, ed. Giuseppe Alberigo and Joseph A. Komonchak [= Alberigo], vol. 5: *The Council and the Transition*, [Maryknoll, NY: Orbis, 2006], 100n198, 105n219).

Bishop Émile De Smedt provides an important note from an audience with Paul VI a few days later, on September 30, 1965, summarizing the pope's instructions to the committee charged with revising schema 4: "to emphasize the obligation of seeking the truth; to present the traditional teaching of the ecclesiastical magisterium; to avoid basing religious freedom solely on freedom of conscience; to state the doctrine in such a way that the lay state would not think itself dispensed from its obligations to the Church; to specify the authority of the declaration (doctrinal, dogmatic, juridical, or practical?)" (cited in Alberigo, vol. 5, 111n239).

The committee was thus instructed to leave the basic framework of schema 4 intact, on the one hand, and to make the several additions indicated in De Smedt's summary, on the other. Paul VI's interventions are interesting, then, for two reasons. First, they help explain why, as many interpreters have noted, the final Declaration does not seem to contain a *fully integrated* theory of religious freedom: that is, because the changes the pope called for — above all in response to the intervention by Bishop Ancel in the name of the French bishops — were not to alter the existing framework as set in schema 4. Second, the instructions clearly map the changes to schema 4 which the pope nonetheless thought important.

Pope Paul's actions to be sure had the twofold purpose (also) of gaining the support of both sides in the Council fathers' debate regarding a document on religious freedom and the approach to be taken in this matter. On the one hand, he accommodated the concerns of those who feared that a decision to postpone a vote on schema 4, in order to take account of the new interventions, could result in a failure by the Council to produce any document on religious freedom at all. On the other hand, his instructions to De Smedt accommodated what the pope himself agreed were the important concerns raised by those who thought the ontological link between freedom and truth had not yet been made sufficiently clear. The pope thus ensured both that the Council would issue a Declaration on Religious Freedom, and that this Declaration would contain a clear statement regarding the link between freedom and truth.

35. In this sentence of the opening paragraph, as in general, the text available through the Vatican website follows Murray's translation: "This Vatican Council takes careful note of these desires in the minds of men. It proposes to declare them to be greatly in accord with truth and justice. To this end, it searches into the sacred tradition and doctrine of the Church . . ." (cf. Abbott, 674). The Latin reads: "Ad has animorum appetitiones diligenter attendens, sibique proponens declarare quantum sint veritati et iustitiae conformes, haec Vaticana Synodus sac-

ram Ecclesiae traditionem doctrinamque scrutatur. . . ." The use of the subjunctive and the term *quantum* here *(quantum sint)* seems to call for a different translation. Rather than making a declarative statement in this regard ("It proposes to declare them to be greatly in accord . . ."), the Declaration is rather posing an indirect question (the Council "propos[es] to declare to what degree they are in conformity . . ."). In this regard, the translation of Laurence Ryan better captures the sense of the original text: "This Vatican Council pays careful attention to these spiritual aspirations and, with a view to declaring *to what extent* they are in accord with the truth and justice, searches the sacred tradition and teaching of the Church . . ." (*Vatican Council II: The Conciliar and Post Conciliar Documents,* ed. Austin Flannery, O.P. [Northport, NY: Costello, 1979], 799, emphasis added).

Cf. the last of Wojtyła's written observations, on schema 4, which concludes: "By means of such changes, the overall character of the document will be improved in this sense, that the Council will produce a revealed teaching *on the moral and indeed fundamental issue of religious freedom (de re morali et quidem fundamentali, qualis est libertas religiosa),* using to this end arguments derived from reason also, since the subject matter fully admits them" (Intervention 5 [AS IV/2, 293], emphasis original). The task of the Council bishops, as Wojtyła saw it, was not simply to presuppose the secular sense of religious freedom that is prevalent in modernity, but to ponder this sense in light of the Church's own teaching and tradition.

36. The final text of DH bears the subtitle, "On the right of the person and of communities to social and civil freedom in religious matters," followed by two parts, titled respectively, "I. The general principle of religious freedom" (aa. 2-8), and "II. Religious freedom in the light of revelation" (aa. 9-15). The first of these parts replaced what was termed in schema 3 "The teaching on religious freedom derived from reason." The point of this shift, already indicated above in our discussion of Wojtyła, was to prevent a reading of the document that would harden the teaching of its first and second parts into a dichotomy between reason and faith. For more on the relationship between reason and revelation, see section VIII.

37. Cf. DH, 2. In a short speech on 22 September 1965 (referred to in n. 2 above) which concerned "the connection that exists between the obligation to seek the truth and religious freedom," Bishop Ancel proposed that "the obligation to seek the truth is itself the ontological foundation of religious freedom":

> For in fact every man, because he is a human being, endowed with reason and free will, is bound to seek the objective truth, and to hold fast to it and order his whole life according to its demands. . . . [B]ecause it does not have its foundation in any subjective disposition, but in the very nature of man, this principle has a strictly universal validity. . . . Nevertheless, in order for man to be able to satisfy this obligation in the way God wills, that is, in a way consistent with his nature, he must enjoy not only psychological freedom but also immunity from all coercion. Not only is there no opposition between religious freedom and the obligation to seek the truth, therefore, but religious freedom in fact has its foundation in this obligation itself, and the obligation to seek the truth in turn requires religious freedom. Finally, venerable Fathers, please note that many people, whether Christians or not, will look especially to what is said in article 2 of our text. Indeed, this article constitutes the very heart of the declaration. I would therefore like for this ontological foundation to find a place in this article, and for the connection that exists between religious freedom and the obligation to seek the truth to be clearly stated there. (AS IV/2, 17)

Regan indicates that three days later, on 25 September 1965, Bishop Carlo Colombo (who, as private theologian of Paul VI in the first session of the Council, was "attentively listened to") emphasized once more that the right to religious freedom has its foundation above all in "the obligation of every man to seek truth" (Regan, 84-85). According to Regan, the argument "from man's right and duty to seek truth was proposed by Colombo and Ancel, introduced into the third and fourth texts in a subordinate position, and given primacy in the fifth and final texts" (173). Cf. schema 3, a. 4b (AS III/8, 431); schema 4, a. 3 (AS IV/1, 148-49); and n. 38 below.

38. The nature of the connection between man's duty and his right in this regard — i.e., that man has a right to religious freedom *because of* his duty to seek the truth — was made clearer in the fifth schema, which introduced the term *ideoque* ("and therefore") between *officium* and *ius* (AS IV/5, 80). The statement that "Man has the duty and the right to seek the truth *(Homo habet officium et ius quarendi veritatem)*" could be found already in schema 3, a. 4b (AS III/8, 431).

39. It needs to be clear, in other words, that public order, rightly understood, bears a substantively just, and not merely negative-juridical, content. Thus the final text of the Declaration states that any limitation of the right to religious freedom by the civil power is legitimate only insofar as it is undertaken in accord with

> juridical norms that conform to the objective moral order. Such norms are necessary for the effective protection of the rights of all citizens and the peaceful settlement of conflicts of rights, for the adequate care of that genuine public peace that is obtained when men live and work together in true justice, and for the proper guardianship of public morality. All of these constitute a fundamental part of the common good, and come under the category of public order. For the rest, the customary practice of the fullness of freedom in society should be upheld, according to which man's freedom should be acknowledged as far as possible, and should not be restricted except when and insofar as necessary. (DH, 7)

The final text of the Declaration thus situates what Murray understands as the central principle of the liberal tradition — "as much freedom as possible and only as much restraint as necessary" (DRF, 573) — explicitly within a public order understood to include the features of objective moral order and true justice that are characteristic of the common good. Murray's consistent translation of *bonum commune* as "common welfare" risks obscuring this fact. On this last, cf. n. 89, below. Regarding public order and the common good, see also section VIII.

40. Cf. Wojtyła, Intervention 2 (AS III/2, 532): "No secular arm may insert itself into this relationship [between God and man], because religion of its very nature transcends all secular matters."

41. Cf. the following changes in this article beginning with the third schema through the final document:

Schema 3, a. 4e: "Religious acts, in which men and women privately and publicly order themselves toward God out of a personal, intimate conviction, transcend the temporal and earthly order of things. In performing these acts, therefore, man is not subject to the civil power, whose competence, on account of its end, is restricted to the earthly and temporal order, and whose legislative power extends only to external actions. The public power, therefore, since it cannot pass judgment on interior religious acts, likewise cannot coerce or impede the public exercise of religion, provided that the demands of public order are preserved. Man's freedom should be acknowledged as far as possible and should not be restricted except insofar as it is necessary. The public power completely exceeds its limits if it involves itself in any way in the governing of minds or the care of souls" (AS III/8, 432).

Schema 4, a. 3: "Furthermore, religious acts, in which men and women privately and publicly order themselves toward God out of a sense of inner conviction, by their nature transcend the earthly and temporal order of things. The competence of the civil power, however, on account of its proper end — which today is more accurately perceived and described in terms of the demands of the dignity of the person and his rights — is restricted in its purpose to the earthly and temporal order, in order that human persons can strive toward their final end more easily and freely, according to their conscience. The civil power must therefore be said to exceed its limits if it involves itself in those matters that concern the very ordination of man to God. Nor can it be said to be deprived in any way of its inherent worth, provided it performs its duty toward the community, restricting itself to secular matters, and in this way acknowledging and serving the human person" (AS IV/1, 150).

Schema 5, a. 3: "Furthermore, religious acts, in which men and women privately and publicly order themselves toward God out of a sense of inner conviction, by their nature transcend the earthly and temporal order of things. The civil power, therefore, must be said to exceed its limits if it either impedes or directs those matters that by their nature transcend the earthly and temporal order of things" (AS IV/5, 81).

DH, 3: "Furthermore, religious acts, in which men and women privately and publicly order themselves toward God out of a sense of inner conviction, by their nature transcend the earthly and temporal order of things. The civil power, therefore, whose proper end is the care of the temporal common good, should in fact acknowledge and show favor to the religious life of its citizens; but this power must be said to exceed its limits if it presumes either to direct or to impede religious acts."

42. And again, in DH, 6, it is said that the civil power should "provide favorable conditions for fostering religious life *(propitias suppeditare condiciones ad vitam religiosam fovendam)*, so that citizens may truly be able to exercise their religious rights and fulfill their religious duties, and so that society itself may enjoy the goods of justice and peace that come from men's fidelity to God and his holy will."

43. As indicated, the final text also, to be sure, says that the civil power "must be said to exceed its limits if it presumes either to direct or to impede *(dirigere vel impedire)* religious acts" (DH, 3). Note however that the final text affirms in this context the positive *obligation* of the *civil authority* (state) to acknowledge and show favor to the religious life of its citizens *(agnoscere eique favere debet)* (DH, 3). Schema 3, in contrast, makes reference rather to the need for civil *society (societas civilis)*, not the state, to provide *favorable conditions* for spreading the truth and fostering religious life *(propitias suppeditat condiciones ad veritatem divulgandam vitamque religiosam fovendam)*, that is, as distinct from showing favor to religious life itself (schema 3, a. 6 [AS III/8, 434]). Schema 3 also states, as we have indicated, that the "public power completely exceeds its limits if it involves itself *in any way (quovis modo)* in the governing of minds or the care of souls *(in regimen animorum aut in curam animarum)*" (a. 4e [AS III/8, 432], emphasis added).

Regarding the sense in which civil authorities should recognize and favor religion, Murray comments that "it would seem to be in the sense of the Declaration to say that governmental favor of religion means favor of the freedom of religion. Similarly, conditions favorable to religious life should be understood to mean conditions favorable to the free profession and practice of religion. Government does not stand in the service of religious truth, as an instrument for its defense or propagation. Government, however, must somehow stand in the service of religion, as an indispensable element of the common temporal good. This duty of service is discharged by service rendered to the freedom of religion in society" ("The Issue of Church and State at Vatican Council II," in *Religious Liberty: Catholic Struggles with Pluralism*, 199-227, at 217). For Murray, then, given his juridical approach, the function of the state with regard to religion is limited to creating *free conditions* wherein religion might be fostered, as distinct from fostering religion itself. Murray's choice of terms in his translation of DH, 3, regarding the positive role of government toward religion, is in keeping with this understanding: whereas Ryan, for example, renders *agnoscere* here as "to recognize" ("the civil authority . . . must recognize and look with favor on the religious life of the citizens" [Ryan, 802]), Murray uses a more neutral "to take account of" ("Government . . . ought indeed to take account of the religious life of the people and show it favor" [Abbott, 681]). Murray does, however, translate *agnoscere* as "to recognize" when it is a matter of the state's obligation toward the individual's right to religious freedom: "This right of the human person to religious freedom is to be recognized in the constitutional law whereby society is governed. Thus it is to become a civil right" (DH, 2, Abbott, 679; cf. also Murray's translation of DH, 4, 5, 6). For more on the sense of the need for government to foster religion, see section VIII.

44. See, e.g., DRF, 568-69.

45. Murray interprets this paragraph to mean that "the Declaration disavows the legal institution of state religion that in various ways was characteristic of the sacral society. The disavowal is discreet but firm: 'If, in view of peculiar circumstances obtaining among people, special civil recognition is given to one religious community in the constitutional order of society. . . .' The statement regards legal establishment of religion as hypothetical, as a matter of circumstances, not of doctrine. Thus, again, the notion of the sacral society is dismissed into history, beyond recall. The free society of today is recognized to be secular" ("The Declaration on Religious Freedom: Its Deeper Significance," *America* 114 [23 April 1966]: 592-93, at 593). Thus, according to Murray, the only thing that the Church seeks in the political realm is "the freedom of the Church: this is the fundamental principle in what concerns the relations between the Church and governments and the whole civil order" (593). He interprets this as the Church's "final farewell to the sacral society and to the situation of legal privilege in it that she had bought at the price of her own freedom" (593). Regarding the Declaration's disavowal of the sacred function of the state according to Murray, see also "The Issue of Church and State," in Hooper, 206. The relationship between Church and state, and Murray's interpretation of this relationship, will be discussed further in section VIII.

46. As Rico points out, Murray "finally . . . concede[d] the wisdom of the conciliar [position]. It was more prudent to let the political principle take secondary position and give primacy to religious arguments" (Rico, 50). The reason for this, Rico says, citing Murray, is largely the "vast confusion and opposition . . . [that] would have arisen if the major political argument for religious freedom — from the principle of equality before the law — had been pressed. Minds and emotions conditioned by the Continental experience of nineteenth-century laicism would surely have seen it as a concession to, if not an outright embrace of, the indifferentist principle of the equality of all religions before God" (Rico, 50; see Comm., 673). However, if it is true that in the end "Murray settles for the declaration as we have it," according to Rico this is ultimately because

the efforts of Anglo-American bishops, nevertheless and in spite of opposition, enabled the inclusion in the text of an explicit statement of the principle of equality before the law, "the essential basis of religious freedom" [Comm., 672] in American constitutional history. Murray gladly welcomes this inclusion, not just because it is a sound principle but especially because in this way "the commentator on the Vatican Declaration can find a footing in the text from which to enlarge its argument and to make a more balanced and convincing case for religious freedom by appealing to political as well as to religious or moral principles" [Comm., 673]. This sentence describes with precision the whole hermeneutical strategy of Murray's commentaries and interpretations of *Dignitatis humanae.*

. . . His commentaries in the near aftermath of Vatican II kept the focus on the workings of the political-juridical argument. . . . Because of the difficulties the correct understanding of the declaration was facing, Murray insists on the explanation of the core issue, perhaps purposely avoiding distractions of further explorations until the essential point had reached such widespread acceptance and clear comprehension that it could be considered to be above challenge. This effort to attract all the attention to the simple, fundamental doctrinal statement of the document may also explain his apparently lessening comments on the importance and reach of *Dignitatis humanae*: "[A] document of very modest scope," dealing with "the lesser issue of the free exercise of religion in civil society," "in itself minor," whose "achievement was simply to bring the Church abreast of the developments that have occurred in the secular world." (Rico, 50-51)

The point here is that while Murray's juridical interpretation has largely been taken for granted as the proper hermeneutic for reading the Declaration — such that Rico, for example, feels justified in accusing John Paul II of backpedaling in his own teaching regarding the Declaration, emphasizing the link between rights and truth, rather than resting them simply on a civil-juridical basis — it is actually the case that both Murray and Rico themselves recognize that the final document gives pride of place *not* to the political argument but rather to the "religious" one, that is, to the grounding of man's (religious) freedom in his ordination by nature to truth, and ultimately to God.

47. The Declaration's statements that government should show religion favor (DH, 3, 6) are thus for Murray best understood as warranted because "society itself may benefit from [such favor] in terms of justice and order, and so on. Therefore, the duty of government to favor religion in society does not derive from the rights to religious freedom, but from another root. So at least I understand the matter" (DRF, 580).

48. Murray distinguishes four general approaches among the Council fathers regarding the foundation of the right to religious freedom: (1) some thought that the whole matter was too complex and that the Council should stick to short, practical statements on the matter; (2) some argued that the foundation was to be found in the right and duty to follow conscience; (3) others, such as Murray, argued for the juridical approach; (4) lastly, there was the approach of the French with its focus on truth. According to Murray, the difference between (3) and (4) had "not a little" to do with the postponement of the vote on 19 November 1964, the culmination of what became known as "Black Week." See Murray, "Religious Freedom," in *Freedom and Man,* ed. John Courtney Murray (New York: P. J. Kenedy, 1965), 131-40. Cf. also TMRF, 42: while the Americans considered religious freedom a "problem . . . in the legal and

juridical order," so as to be "formally and in the first instance a juridical notion," to the French "this view of the matter seemed 'superficial' (I heard the adjective often)." The issue at stake here was not the affirmation of religious freedom as a human right, which all agreed upon, but rather the nature and foundation of this right.

49. Apropos of Murray's criticism of the argument from the obligation to seek the truth, see also his "Arguments for the Right to Religious Freedom," in Hooper, 229-44, at 234-36. Cf. Regan, 173: "A fourth line of argument, from man's right and duty to seek truth, was . . . given primacy in the fifth and final texts. But this argument will not establish the right of all men to religious freedom if it is not fixed in a social and political context, since it must conclude to the right to communicate what is in fact false, or even known to be false, and to the right of a complacent man to communicate his religious views, whether true or false. To be convincing, the argument must rely on the fact that [the] search for truth, as social dialogue and exchange, requires the political condition of freedom. Only in this context may *every* man claim, within the limits of public order, a right to immunity in all expression that concerns the order of truth, and religious truth in particular." As I will argue further on, this argument is sound only if one fails to see that truth itself, properly understood, already requires freedom as a matter of truth's inner logic as true.

50. Servais Pinckaers, O.P., *The Sources of Christian Ethics,* trans. Sr. Mary Thomas Noble, O.P. (Washington, DC: Catholic University of America Press, 1995), 327-78. The French *"liberté de qualité"* suggests a more subtle range of meaning than the English translation "freedom for excellence." The problem with translating *liberté de qualité* as "freedom for excellence" is that it tends to blur the difference between the two freedoms that Pinckaers presents, by failing to indicate adequately the way in which freedom of quality implies an *ordering in relation to truth* already in its *original constitution* as freedom. "Freedom *for* excellence" shifts emphasis toward freedom's need to grow in virtue, in a way that often overlooks freedom's primitive ordering *toward* and *by* the good and the true. It is not merely the case that freedom has to grow in virtue, but that it does so *because* the inclination to the good and the true is present already at freedom's *very source,* and hence orders freedom in its first actuality as such. In what follows, therefore, I will translate this phrase as either "freedom *of* excellence" or "freedom of quality." For more on the ambiguity of "freedom for excellence," see section VI.6.

51. Thus for St. Thomas, "natural law was the expression, in the form of precepts, of our natural inclinations, which were guided by our inclinations to goodness and truth" (404). Ockham's freedom of indifference set freedom in opposition to these natural inclinations, and in this way "demolished what we might call the capstone of St. Thomas's doctrinal edifice and overturned the structure of moral theology" (405).

52. "All natural inclinations, summed up in the inclination toward goodness or happiness, were . . . uprooted from the will's depths, to be placed before it, beneath it, and subjected to its choice. They were no longer a part of the essence of freedom" (333).

53. Although freedom of indifference has its origins in the nominalists, it also became characteristic of the scholastic tradition, represented especially by the theologian Charles Billuart (1685-1757), who according to Pinckaers "played the role of classical author" for this tradition in the eighteenth and nineteenth centuries (352). For Billuart, freedom was best defined as freedom of indifference because "it was applied to contraries *(est ad opposita),*" and was "free from all necessity, including every natural instinct and all determination to any 'one thing,' which would cancel the power to choose between contraries" (353). "Even among Thomists," then, "freedom of indifference was accepted, though it had caused the relativism against which

they were fighting" (352). "Apparently it did not occur to Billuart to wonder how St. Thomas could place the natural inclination to the good and to happiness at the very source of human freedom, as the inclination that wins us our final end and engenders all our choices" (353).

54. This contrasts with the view of St. Thomas that freedom is "a faculty proceeding from reason and will," which only in their unity make the act of choice (331).

55. Cf. also the following statements of Pinckaers: "freedom . . . presupposes natural inclinations and takes root in them so as to draw forth the strength needed for their development. . . . In this we discover the true, specifically moral meaning of the famous principle of ancient philosophy, *sequi naturam,* 'follow nature,' so frankly adopted and christianized by the Fathers of the Church. This 'nature' does not restrain human freedom; it is essentially liberating" (357-58). "Thus founded on a natural sense of goodness and truth, freedom is no longer characterized by indifference, but rather by the spontaneous attraction and interest experienced in regard to all that is true and good" (359). Freedom thus bears "a natural openness to the truth and the good" (377); it is "the outcome *(le produit)* of the mind's inclination to truth and the will's inclination to goodness" (381). In this way one could say that our natural "instinct for truth and goodness, which is at bottom an instinct for God . . . creates freedom, which can neither exist nor develop without it" (404).

56. The simple but crucial point I mean to introduce here is that the (putative) purely formal freedom that establishes juridical rights in their merely negative sense is in fact not innocent of a "positive" metaphysical conception of the human person. A freedom viewed first as structurally empty of relation to God, and so far as silent or neutral with respect to God, does not thereby cease to embed *a kind of relation* to God, one with definite implications regarding a transcendent order of truth or goodness. On the contrary, such a freedom implies that man's relation to God — insofar as God is believed to exist — is one that is logically yet-to-be-enacted by a conscious act of choice, thus one that is so far, in this sense, *extrinsic* to freedom in the latter's primitive constitution as such. Such a freedom implies, *eo ipso,* a definite idea regarding the nature of man as a creature and God's nature as Creator. It follows that the (would-be) purely formal freedom and negative rights of a (would-be) purely juridical political order have the same range of metaphysical implications as a freedom innerly fraught with an order of positive relations to God and others, and to truth and goodness, *only implications of a different sort.* To use the contemporary jargon, the juridical idea of rights, in its purported metaphysical "thinness," is rather, of its inner logic, metaphysically "thick," albeit in a peculiarly hidden sense.

Thus it is not the case that the two freedoms, the freedom abstracted from truth (juridical-political) and the freedom ordered to truth (societal-ontological), each represent, as it were, one half of the whole of freedom. On the contrary, Pinckaers's point is that the original act of choosing, rightly understood in light of St. Thomas, already embeds a desire or love for truth and God: in the *very reflexivity that constitutes its reality as an act,* freedom *is moved by, hence already initially "formed" with respect to,* the reality of truth, the good, and God. The original act of choosing is already affected from within its inmost depths by this desire for and "form" of truth. Murray's argument implies a failure to see this. It implies that the relation between the act of choosing, on the one hand, and the truth (or God) that is chosen, on the other, is a matter of adding content to an act conceived as initially empty or purely formal. This expresses the essence of an ontology of freedom as indifference.

57. Cf. Joseph Ratzinger, *Introduction to Christianity* (San Francisco: Ignatius Press, 2004), 58-66, on the difference between the ancient-medieval conception of truth, according

to which a thing is true or good already *in itself,* insofar as *it is,* having received being via the creative intellect of God *(verum* or *bonum qua ens);* and the modern conception of truth, according to which a thing is true only insofar as we ourselves have made or shaped it *(verum* or *bonum quia factum).*

58. For further reflection on the monism hidden within liberal pluralism, see my "Civil Community Inside the Liberal State: Truth, Freedom, and Human Dignity," in *Ordering Love: Liberal Societies and the Memory of God* [= OL] (Grand Rapids: Eerdmans, 2011), 65-132, at 65-88.

59. On this, see my "The Repressive Logic of Liberal Rights: Religious Freedom, Contraceptives, and the 'Phony' Argument of the *New York Times,*" *Communio* 38 (Winter 2011): 523-46.

60. The relationship between a liberal state and a liberal society is mutually reinforcing. On the one hand, a liberal state arises out of a liberal society, insofar as the state represents society's way of organizing itself legally. The existence of a liberal state therefore presupposes the kind of society that (unwittingly) privileges a "neutral" or "indifferent" freedom. On the other hand, the liberal state will in turn reinforce precisely this understanding of freedom, *also* within society. This is because, within a liberal society, the state represents the authority common to all the various groups that make up this society. The one authoritative unity that overarches all of these groups is that provided by the state. This state therefore *de facto* represents the highest unifying truth of society, even when it claims incompetence in regard to truth claims. Within a liberal society, the *only* "truth" which is common to all members of this society is that of state neutrality or juridical liberalism, which, as I have shown, enforces freedom of indifference.

61. Several commentators have raised questions regarding the coherence of Murray's distinction between articles of peace and articles of faith, and the place of this distinction in his overall argument. Gerard Bradley, for example, asks whether the distinction does not, contrary to Murray's intention, logically involve a privatization of all claims linked with religion, and so far imply endorsement of the "proceduralist" democracy that Murray meant to avoid (see Bradley's "Beyond Murray's Articles of Peace and Faith," in *John Courtney Murray and the American Civil Conversation,* ed. Robert P. Hunt and Kenneth L. Grasso [Grand Rapids: Eerdmans, 1992], 181-204). Bradley suggests that a way of resolving Murray's problem, at least for purposes of American constitutional law, is to maintain an "originalist" reading of the First Amendment, according to which "'nonestablishment' would . . . mean an equality among religious groups (but imply no hostility toward fostering religion generally)" (204). I agree strongly with the burden of what Bradley wants to affirm. My own argument insists only that sustaining the kind of commitment to equality that Bradley envisions involves the integration of articles of faith into the fairness intended (but not realized!) by articles of peace. And this integration can be brought about only on the basis of an adequate view of the *nature* of the human being in relation to truth and to God. This, I argue, is the approach adopted in the final text of *Dignitatis humanae.*

Kenneth Craycraft proposes that Murray's appeal to "articles of peace" is best interpreted as ironic, a kind of "myth" that would be helpful in persuading Catholics to accept the American regime, whose meaning is otherwise likely to be conceived in terms of some amalgam of Protestantism and the Enlightenment (see *The American Myth of Religious Freedom* [Dallas: Spence Publishing, 1999]).

Robert Hunt argues that Murray's appeal to "a political 'articles of peace'" can be protected from proceduralism, or an "antiperfectionist 'negative liberty,'" only if these political articles of peace are supported by "a societal 'articles of faith' that is open to religion as an aspect of human flourishing" (Hunt, "Two Concepts of Religious Freedom," in *Catholicism and Religious Freedom: Contemporary Reflections on Vatican II's Declaration on Religious Liberty,* ed. Grasso and Hunt [Lanham, MD: Rowman & Littlefield, 2006], 19-42, at 37). Hunt thus reads the distinction between "articles of peace" and "articles of faith" in terms of Murray's distinction between state and society, which for Murray, and Hunt, lies at the heart of the modern Western constitutional state and its hallmark limited government.

I share these commentators' concerns regarding the need to qualify Murray's distinction between articles of peace and articles of faith. The difficulty nonetheless, as we will see, is that Murray insists, in his reading of the Council's Declaration on Religious Freedom, on the "juridical irrelevance" of man's transcendent relation to truth, even as he criticizes the final redactions of the Declaration that tied the right to religious freedom to this transcendent truth. This commits him to a continued embrace of the dichotomy between (juridical-legal) "articles of peace" and (societal) "articles of faith" that logically involves a proceduralist state. As I will argue, the concerns of these commentators can be adequately addressed, in a way that realizes the legitimate intention of both "peace" and "faith," only by recognizing, also for juridical-legal purposes, the nature of freedom as originally ordered to the truth and to God. What this implies in terms of the Declaration itself will be clarified as we proceed. For a helpful reading of the articles of peace/articles of faith distinction as pertinent to my argument, cf. especially David Crawford, "The Architecture of Freedom: John Paul II and John Courtney Murray on Religious Freedom," in *Catholicism and Religious Freedom: Contemporary Reflections,* 195-221; and also Adrian Walker, "Whose New Horizon?" *Catholic Social Review* 3 (1998): 63-68.

62. The problem with the use of the term "juridical approach" without a qualifier is that it implies that such an approach actually exists. As we have seen, however, any approach claiming to be (simply) juridical — absent of a definite view regarding the nature of freedom — thereby tacitly enshrines freedom of indifference. It is important then to understand that even when the term "juridical" is employed in this essay without the necessary qualifier "would-be purely" — to avoid repetition of a clumsy phrase — the qualifier is still implied.

63. Kenneth L. Schmitz, "Immateriality Past and Present," in *The Texture of Being: Essays in First Philosophy* (Washington, DC: Catholic University of America Press, 2007), 168-82, at 172.

64. Due to this intrinsic immateriality, "The forms of material things . . . escape the strict circumscription of space and time and outstrip determinate indexing. They are trans-indexical just because they are principles of order that are replicable in the many spatially and temporally distinct individuals that instantiate them. . . . [T]he formal principles, even of material things, are not exhausted in their formation of a single spatially and temporally indexed distinct individual. Form, if we may so speak, radiates beyond any determinately indexed instance of it" (171). This immateriality of nature rooted in form enables material things to be known without being essentially distorted. Knowledge of these things consists in giving them a sort of "second nature through and in which the thing[s] [can] be present to the knower" (171). Hence the "generosity" inherent in nature: by virtue of their formal and so far immaterial character, natural things are able to be known truly, are capable, as it were, of lending their being to be known in its eidetic integrity by others. And the human knower, on the other hand, by virtue of his immanent-transcendent activity, is able generously to let the thing be cognitionally as it really is in itself. The real relation between the knower and the thing known that consists in the genuine knowledge called truth, in other words, presupposes

immaterial form in the thing (in nature) and spiritual form in the knower (in human nature). But all of this will be discussed further in connection with the work of Josef Pieper.

65. *Wahrheit der Dinge: Eine Untersuchung zur Anthropologie des Hochmittelalters* [= WDD] (Munich: Kösel Verlag, 1947). This text is available in English as the first part of a two-part work: cf. Josef Pieper, *Living the Truth* [= LTT] (San Francisco: Ignatius Press, 1989), 11-105. I will cite primarily from this translation, with some alterations or indications from the German where noted.

66. Josef Pieper, "The Philosophical Act," in *Leisure the Basis of Culture* [= LBC] (San Francisco: Ignatius Press, 2009), 75-143, at 94. Cf. Pieper, *Was heißt Philosophieren?* [= WHP] (Einsiedeln: Johannes Verlag, 2003), 34: "Das Innere ist die Kraft eines Wirklichkeit, Beziehung zu haben, sich in Beziehung zu setzen zu einem Aussen; 'Innen' heisst Beziehungs- und Einbeziehungskraft." This interiority capable of relation with the whole involves the whole human person qua human. Here I am not interested in distinguishing between the faculties of intellect and will, but am concerned rather with the spiritual act as such, that is, the intelligent-free human act. Cf. Pinckaers on the unity of intellect and will in the thought of St. Thomas: "St. Thomas explained freedom as a faculty *proceeding from* reason and will, which unite to make the act of choice" (331). "St. Thomas's analysis of choice was unique in that it united and maintained in close relationship two dimensions that were later to be separated as a consequence of nominalism. One dimension related to the intellect. . . . The other dimension applied mainly to the will. . . . These two dimensions together [for St. Thomas] constituted freedom and its exercise" (383).

67. It is important to note that this "most comprehensive ability to relate — namely, the power to 'conform to all that is' — implies at the same time also the highest form of intrinsic existence, of selfness" (LTT, 81). It is both of these elements combined, "dwelling most intensively within itself, and being *capax universi*" that "together constitute the essence of the spirit" (LTT, 83). There is an asymmetrical order here, however: I can only know myself in knowing something else. It is only simultaneously in relation to the world and above all to God that I discover the depths of my own interiority. Or, as Aquinas puts it: "Our intellect cannot know itself by being immediately aware of itself; but by being aware of something else it comes to know itself" (LTT 136; cf. De Ver. X, 8).

68. The human spirit is understood by the medievals to be open to the infinite *and* simultaneously to be the form of the body. Thomas Aquinas says, for example, that "the soul united with the body is more in the image of God than when separate; for [in this union] it realizes its own essence more perfectly" (LTT, 94; cf. De Pot. V, 10).

69. Cf. Ratzinger, *Introduction to Christianity*, 59: "For the ancient world and the Middle Ages, being itself is true, in other words, apprehensible, because God, pure intellect, made it, and he made it by thinking it. To the creative original spirit, the *Creator Spiritus*, thinking and making are one and the same thing. His thinking is a creative process. Things are, because they are thought. . . . Conversely, this means that since all being is thought, all being is meaningful, *logos*, truth. It follows from this traditional view that human thinking is the rethinking of being itself, rethinking of the thought that is being itself. Man can rethink the *logos*, the meaning of being, because his own *logos*, his own reason, is *logos* of the one *logos*, thought of the original thought, of the creative spirit that permeates and governs his being."

70. Thus, "'To be true' means the same as 'to manifest and reveal being'" (LTT, 61; cf. De Ver. I, 1: *Verum est manifestativum et declarativum esse*). This is contrasted with the Enlightenment idea of truth, polemicized by Kant, according to which "truth means: each thing

is what it is" — an "entirely degenerated concept" that considers "reality's intrinsic orientation toward nothing but itself" (LTT, 67). This same loss of the medieval understanding of the transcendental meaning of truth is also reflected in the common Enlightenment conception of the world as existing "outside" God. Pieper contrasts this with "the conception held by the great Christian thinkers of the High Middle Ages," such as St. Thomas, who "maintained . . . that the archetypes of all things, and the things themselves, are in God, while God 'is necessarily in all things, in the most intrinsic manner *(intime).*' Thomas Aquinas would never speak of an 'outside' God. It is one thing to affirm that Creator and creation are not identical. . . . But to speak of a *Deus extramundanus* is not the Christian language; it is the deistic language of the Enlightenment" (LTT, 48).

71. Philipe André-Vincent, *La Liberté Religieuse: Droit Fondamental* [= AV] (Paris: Téqui, 1976).

72. Indeed, André-Vincent says that it is the fact of man's nature as fundamentally religious that alone establishes the right to religious freedom as the first and most basic of all human rights. This connection between the person and truth, ultimately the primordial truth who is God, establishes the relation between natural law and the gospel that is necessary to show that the second part of the Declaration is not merely a juxtaposition or superimposition with respect to the first part. "Religious freedom grounds itself on the personal relationship of the spirit to the truth, of man to God. This evidence obtained by the labor of natural reason is reinforced by the light of revelation" (AV, 191).

73. "The human mind, in the very core of its nature, is receptivity, readiness, openness for all reality. . . . The human mind is ultimately the pure receptor of all that is" (LTT, 83n12; citing A. Rohner, "Das Grundproblem der Metaphysik," in *Philosophia Perennis,* ed. J. von Rintelen [Regensburg: Josef Habbel, 1930], 1083).

74. Cf. Kenneth Schmitz, *The Gift: Creation* (Milwaukee: Marquette University Press, 1996), 111-12: "[T]he world is not some thing apart from its creatures: it does not have its own *act* of being. Still, it does have its own *mode* of being. The world is not an individual. Nor is it a mere collection, a network of relations resting upon non-worlded and private individuals. Nor is it the System of which they are mere members. Rather, the world is that which is built into its creatures, and they into it. For they are built-up in and for and with regard to the world within which they have their being. The world is a sort of compossibility grounded in the mutual existence of creatures. The creator's regard for creatures' being-in-the-world is not restricted to ordinary categorial relations, but is directed fundamentally to a distinctive kind of transcendental interrelationship. For the mode of the world is that it have its being in the acts of its creatures."

The point here is that relationality is already something given ("transcendentally"), not simply first established by "categorial" relations between things, that is, by relations enacted by various entities. While the worldly community does not exist except in and through such individuals and their relations, at the same time these individuals and their relations do not exist except by virtue of the (transcendent) relationality built into their being by the Creator in the very act of creation. Needless to say, "transcendental" is here understood in its classic-metaphysical sense, rather than its modern-Kantian (or indeed "transcendental Thomist") sense. Transcendental truth has its roots in the *esse commune* implied by the act of creation, rightly understood; it is not something that is first a function of the human mind. Cf. Adrian Walker, "Personal Singularity and the *Communio Personarum:* A Creative Development of Thomas Aquinas' Doctrine of *Esse Commune,*" *Communio* 31 (Fall 2004): 457-79.

75. Pieper continues: "And the mind's inborn ability to 'reach the whole' is actuated already in each single instance of cognition; for the light that makes any individual object intelligible is the same light that permeates the universe. All this, then, is the anthropological meaning, the affirmation about the nature of man, contained in the principle: *omne ens est verum* — all that is, is true."

76. See n. 57 above, on Ratzinger's distinction between the *verum qua ens* of the ancients-medievals and the *verum quia factum* of the moderns. The latter need not of course imply absolute idealism, such that the mind creates reality. It implies only that the mind is understood to be precipitously constructive in relation to the world: constructive in a way that overlooks the original givenness of things to the mind and as fit for the mind, and the anterior receptive-immanent activity on the part of the mind that must be presupposed in accommodating this original givenness.

77. Apropos of our argument in this section, we should note the importance of Murray's rejection of what he terms "the fallacy of a false 'objectivism,' as if truth could somehow be divorced from the possession of truth" (TMRF, 42). For Murray, the truth really becomes true for man when he possesses it. Such a claim seems so far in keeping with Pieper's claim that the subject's growth in inwardness is integral to his growth in truth. The problem is that Murray's emphasis on the importance of the self's inner-subjective possession of truth is not informed sufficiently by the self's *originally given, anterior ordering in and by* the truth.

Thus Murray is right, in connection with the problem of "objectivity," to take note of modernity's growing historical consciousness, with its greater awareness of the dignity of the human subject. He is right also that the Declaration reflects this awareness. The problem, however, is that he fails to integrate these claims with the medieval understanding of the spirituality of the human subject and the transcendentality of truth. The result is that the human subject to which he appeals is not sufficiently ordered objectively by nature.

I will return later, in Section VIII, to Murray's discussion of the distinction between what he calls classical consciousness and historical consciousness. My concern here is simply to point out that Murray's emphasis on the importance of the self's possession of the truth is legitimate only insofar as this self-possession is placed within the self's inner-original ordering in and by the truth. When not so conceived, the freedom of the human subject, on the one hand, and the truth, on the other, tend to collapse into matters of "subjectivism" and "objectivism," respectively.

78. Archbishop Marcel Lefebvre, *Religious Liberty Questioned* (St. Louis: Angelus Press, 2002), 19.

79. In this connection, Lefebvre cites a text from Yves Congar in support of Murray: "What is new in [*Dignitatis humanae*] compared to the teachings of Leo XIII, and even of Pius XII, . . . is the determination of the *proper and proximate* foundation of this liberty, established not on the objective truth of religious or moral goodness but on the ontological quality of the human person" (32; citing Congar, bulletin "Études et documents du Secrétariat de l'épiscopat français," n. 5, 15 June 1965, 5).

This statement by Congar manifests the same sort of problematic assumption indicated earlier in the case of Murray, regarding the original ontological unity between truth and the human subject in his nature as free and intelligent. The "ontological quality of the human person," on the one hand, and "objective truth," on the other, cannot be abstracted from one another without falsifying the proper nature of both. Nor, contra Lefebvre, does sin affect this order of reality so profoundly that it can no longer be said truly to represent the enduring objective *natural* order of reality. Congar, then, like Murray, makes the mistake of originally *juxtaposing* objective truth and the dignity of the human subject.

To be sure, the question of the sense in which the (subjective) acts of the human person affect his situation, pertinent to his reality qua subject of a right to religious freedom, demands further commentary, and we will return to this issue in section VIII. It suffices here to underscore the fact that the position affirmed by the Declaration, as we have interpreted it, incorporates the concerns of both objective truth and the ontological quality of the human person, while reconfiguring the nature of both as originally-transcendentally united with each other. This original indissoluble unity between the objective order of truth and the human subject is not drained of its essential natural integrity by sin, and thus it founds the human dignity warranting affirmation of a right to religious freedom for every human being, subject only to the demands of a true and just public order.

Closely related to Lefebvre's argument here is his suggestion that the Declaration, in referring to the human being who is "searching" for God and the truth, confuses the orders of actuality and potentiality. Thus, a soul in error may be said to be searching for God and truth, but this means that he is still only "potentially 'connected' to [these]. . . . To be searching is at the most a potential acceptance of the truth only and therefore cannot be the basis for rights due solely to the actual acceptance of said truth. Only the effective dependence on God and His revealed truth confers on man dignity and thus a right to liberty of action" (36-37).

This argument, however, misses the burden of the medieval understanding of both the spiritual nature of the human act and the transcendental nature of truth, which demands a view of the human subject searching for God and truth as more than merely "potentially 'connected' " to these. The human subject who is searching, in other words, does not exist only as a negative capacity for, or empty container waiting to be filled by, God and truth. Rather, the human subject is already actually (transcendentally, if not yet categorially) related to God and truth from the beginning of his existence. Cf. in this connection D. C. Schindler, "Freedom Beyond Our Choosing: Augustine on the Will and Its Objects," *Communio* 29 (Winter 2002): 618-53. I will return in section VI.6 to this question of the sense in which man's searching, or original capacity, for the truth is only a "potential" relation.

80. Of course, insofar as they are distinct, there is always a kind of tension between freedom and truth. The point is that this tension exists within an original unity, and thus avoids both dialectic and indifference (which ultimately presuppose each other). Such a tension is instead *fruitful* and *dramatic*. But I cannot go into this further here.

81. We will return to this idea in section VIII.

82. Murray's concern regarding governments that claim to be in possession of the truth that freedom seeks, and that therefore feel justified in imposing the truth in order to aid freedom's search, presupposes a truncated vision of truth. He fails to grasp that freedom is an inherent dimension *of* truth, and thus is to be respected always and everywhere, *by virtue of* the defense of truth itself. Indeed, truth cannot be received *as* truth unless it is received in freedom, that is, for its own sake. If the truth is not received freely but instead "imposed," whether overtly or subtly, then it is no longer received as truth, but rather becomes reconstituted as an instrument in the service of power. Of course, it is important to understand that not imposing the truth does not rule out, for example, the importance of good laws that assist primarily in the education of freedom, in keeping with the demands of a public order tied intrinsically to the common good.

83. On Murray's translation of this passage, see n. 43 above.

84. Regarding Murray's translation of this phrase, see n. 35 above.

85. Both Ryan and Murray translate *respiciat* as "has to do with." The point, in any case, is that the term scarcely entails that immunity is the *exclusive* meaning of religious freedom.

86. This contrasts with Pavan's view, cited in n. 13 above, that "there is [in the Declaration] no question of the relations between the person and truth or between the person and God, but of the interpersonal relations in human and political society." On the contrary, for the Declaration in its rightful understanding as articulated in these texts, the relation between persons implies relation to the truth and to God.

87. On the addition of the important qualifier *ideoque,* see n. 38 above.

88. Cf. Wojtyła, Intervention 1 (AS III/3, 766), cited above: in regard to the negative definition of religious freedom as immunity from coercion ("the person's right not to be prevented by others from observing and proclaiming his public and private duties to God and to men . . . as these duties are manifested by conscience"), Wojtyła comments that this definition "seem[s] to be partial and negative, and concerned with religious tolerance rather than with freedom. To be sure, everyone is permitted to follow a sure *(certam)* conscience, even if it is invincibly erroneous; but there is another principle that should be set before this one, namely: we should follow a sure and true *(certam et veram)* conscience." The statement that man has the duty to seek the truth in order to form for himself sure *(certa)* judgments of conscience, found in schemas 3 and 4 (AS IV/1, 148), was changed to right *(recta)* judgments in schema 5 (AS IV/5, 80) and to right and true *(recta et vera)* judgments in the final Declaration.

89. It is this integration of the positive roots of freedom into freedom's "negative" meaning that alone adequately accounts for two further changes made in the final drafts of the Declaration, as indicated above. First, there is the qualification of the concept of public order as the criterion for determining when the exercise of the right to religious freedom might be properly limited. The term *iustus (ordo publicus)* is added in order to protect against a merely "procedural" sense of this public order, whereby justice would consist essentially in a balancing of competing interests (see section I.3.iv). Second, since the "religious acts, in which men and women privately and publicly order themselves toward God . . . by their nature transcend the earthly and temporal order of things," the civil government, *whose proper end is the care of the common good (bonum commune) on earth,* should in fact *acknowledge and show favor to (agnoscere eique favere) the religious life of its citizens"* (DH, 3, emphasis added). The use of the term "common good" implies a reference to some positive good held (naturally) in common by citizens; the indication of the government's responsibility to recognize and favor the religious life of the citizens within this context of the common good implies a positive recognition by government of religion itself as *good,* and not merely a recognition by government of the conditions of freedom that make religion possible, although of course also the latter. The point is that the changes indicated here, which involve affirmation of the essential link of freedom with truth (and the good) as the ground of the human dignity that alone warrants the claim of rights, are explicable only as efforts to ensure *positive recognition* of freedom *for* (truth, especially about God) as integral to, and as able to account consistently for the universality of, the right to religious freedom in the first place.

90. As stated earlier, this is for Murray the "more cogent argument" that "can be constructed from the principles of the Declaration itself, assembled into an organic structure" (DRF, 571-72).

91. It should be noted that this does not make freedom merely functional or instrumental with regard to truth. To think this would be to miss the nub of the point being made,

which is that truth and freedom mutually presuppose each other, asymmetrically: each simultaneously depends upon the other, with the self-reflexive act of freedom "first" presupposing a transcendent relation to its object as true.

Incidentally, this is one way of stating the basic flaw governing the argument of Rico's book: he thinks that granting priority to truth entails the instrumentalization of freedom. Indeed, Rico takes this to characterize the essence of the classical approach to the problem of the relation between truth and freedom. In response, I would say that, however much it may be true that Christians at various times in the political history of Europe took truth to permit the denial of freedom, the fact remains that the anthropological-ontological heart of the Christian tradition, as indicated above via Pinckaers and Pieper (Aquinas), affirms that truth and freedom are at root two dimensions of the same ontological reality.

92. See my earlier discussion of Wojtyła, and the texts cited there (section I.2.iii). Interpreters repeatedly suggest, in contrast to what I am proposing here, that Wojtyła wanted only a theological approach. Cf., e.g., in this connection, Regan's claim that "the role of rational argumentation was progressively de-emphasized and less space accorded to it in the successive texts" (Regan, 159).

93. Natural law is a staple of Murray's thought, of course. My point is that he seems here to relegate awareness of God to the theological order, while this is clearly not the intention of the Declaration.

94. The book by Rico is particularly egregious in its mischaracterization on both points, especially as they concern the work of Wojtyła/John Paul II.

95. Cf. Ratzinger's comments on the "ontological dimension" of conscience, which "consists in the fact that something like an original memory of the good and true ... has been implanted in us, that there is an inner ontological tendency within man, who is created in the likeness of God, toward the divine.... This anamnesis of the origin, which results from the god-like constitution of our being, is not a conceptually articulated knowing, a store of retrievable contents. It is, so to speak, an inner sense, a capacity to recall, so that the one whom it addresses, if he is not turned in on himself, hears its echo from within" ("Conscience and Truth," in *On Conscience* [San Francisco: Ignatius Press, 2007], 32). Cf. also, in this connection, the statement of Aquinas in De Ver. XXII, 2, ad 1: "All cognitive beings ... know God implicitly in any act of knowing."

There is a widespread tendency among interpreters of DH, especially defenders of Murray, to take the Declaration's affirmation of an intrinsic relation between freedom and truth and an objective moral order as implying a conscious conviction of this relation on the part of those who would be proper subjects of the right, that is, as a condition of their being accorded a right. Such a reading, as noted, is characteristic of Rico (cf., e.g., Rico, 64). But this reading confuses the Declaration's appeal to the *nature* of human beings with an appeal to their actual, explicitly conscious, existential condition at a given moment in their history. DH, 2 clearly avoids such a mistake.

96. As indicated in n. 8 above, Murray became seriously ill and was hospitalized as work began on the fifth draft of the Declaration. Some 200 written interventions from the Council bishops had been submitted for consideration by the members of the redacting committee for the fifth text. Interpreters often note the significance of Murray's absence during this crucial penultimate redaction. Gilles Routhier, for example, says that "Murray's absence led to a shifting of the tone of the text, as the theological dimension received greater emphasis at the expense of the more strictly juridical or rational argument proposed

by Murray [earlier]" ("Finishing the Work Begun: The Trying Experience of the Fourth Period," in Alberigo, vol. 5, 114). Donald Pelotte, in his *John Courtney Murray: Theologian in Conflict* (New York: Paulist Press, 1975), claims that the final revisions to the text were "altogether unnecessary," concurring with Routhier regarding the effect of Murray's absence: "These changes, however, weakened the Declaration and left it somewhat ambiguous. In all likelihood many of the last-minute changes would never have been made had Murray not been ill" (99).

97. André-Vincent acknowledges a significant ambiguity that remains in the final document: "Without a doubt, the intention of the Fathers and the objective sense of the text refer to the traditional notion of natural right" (AV, 155-56). But the final text, he suggests, is nonetheless not sufficiently clear regarding the difference between a traditional natural law theory (which is objective) and a "modern natural right" theory (which is dominated by subjectivism): "The Declaration formulates an objective requirement of natural law as it founds religious freedom in human nature; but it does so in the optic of modern natural right."

My own argument supports André-Vincent's claim regarding an ambiguity that remains in the text, but differs from his argument on two points: first, on any adequate reading of the redaction process leading to the final document, and of the final document itself, the Declaration clearly does reject a (subjectivist) modern rights theory, even if not on the basis of a fully theoretically integrated conception of rights of its own. In other words, contrary to André-Vincent's suggestion that in the end DH holds that religious liberty is a negative right, I argue that this right is in fact essentially *also* negative, but not *primarily* so — or in other words, that it is only negative as initially informed by man's positive dynamic ordering by truth in relation to God. Second, contrary to what André-Vincent seems to suggest, I believe there is a legitimate development in the text in terms of the incorporation of the subjectivity of the subject of rights, an incorporation that is implied already in the objective meaning of nature and spirit and transcendental truth in the ancient-medieval tradition. This was the burden of my argument in section IV regarding Murray's second criticism.

98. Cf. in this connection Rico's comment: "As the similarity of language and coincidence of emphases have made obvious, [John Paul II's] reading of the document, in what concerns the relationship between freedom and truth, follows the approach of a line of reconstruction of the doctrine of *Dignitatis humanae* illustrated . . . by the work of André-Vincent. This interpretation tends to present freedom and truth in competition one against the other" (Rico, 221). Rico is right that John Paul II appears to follow in a significant sense André-Vincent's line of argument, though not without important differences: notably, John Paul II's greater emphasis on and development of the intrinsic mutual relation of human subjectivity and truth — his view that an adequate appreciation for the integrity of either of these entails recognition of the original mutual, albeit asymmetrical, openness of each to the other. Rico's charge of a "line of reconstruction," however, and his assertion that there is a competition between freedom and truth on John Paul II's reading beg the question on both scores. In fact, the Council rejected the juridical approach; and the heart of that rejection lay exactly in its insistence on an original unity between freedom and truth, a unity which the Council judged to be alone sufficient to keep freedom *from undermining its own natural integrity as free.* But this has already been dealt with at length in the body of my argument.

99. To cite but one expression of the burden of Rico's argument: "While John Paul II unequivocally underscores the priority of the duty toward the truth, the Declaration, in turn, has affirmed even more forcefully the dignity and autonomy of the individual person and

the respect for each one's way and pace of forming his or her own conscience in the personal search for truth" (Rico, 177).

100. Recognition of profound continuity, of course, does not entail denial of differences and development, due, for example, to John Paul II's growing awareness of and dealings with the different cultural situations presented earlier by Communism and later by the liberal countries of the West.

101. John Paul II, "Address to the 34th General Assembly of the United Nations," 2 October 1979, n. 20.

102. Benedict XVI, "Address to the Members of the General Assembly of the United Nations," 18 April 2008.

103. While there does not appear to be an official language version of this text, the French *(capacité)* and Italian *(capacità)* indicate that what is intended here has a more positive meaning than a merely neutral "ability." On the significance of the term "capacity," see section VI.6.

104. Cf. Benedict XVI, Angelus message of 4 December 2005: "The Second Vatican Council dedicated an attentive reflection . . . to the relationship between truth and freedom. In particular, the Council bishops approved, precisely 40 years ago, a Declaration on the question of religious liberty, that is, the right of persons and of communities to seek the truth and to profess their faith freely. The first words that give this document its title are *Dignitatis humanae*: religious liberty derives from the special dignity of the human person, who is the only one of all the creatures on this earth who can establish a free and conscious relationship with his or her Creator. . . . [T]he Second Vatican Council reaffirms the traditional Catholic doctrine which holds that men and women, as spiritual creatures, can know the truth and therefore have the duty and the right to seek it (cf. DH, 3). Having laid this foundation, the Council places a broad emphasis on religious liberty, which must be guaranteed both to individuals and to communities with respect for the legitimate demands of the public order."

105. John Paul II, "Letter to the Madrid Conference on European Security and Cooperation," 1 September 1980, n. 5; cf. also nn. 1, 3.

106. The point here is not an identity but an intrinsic relation between the natural and the moral that allows for the legitimate integrity of each. This suffices to avoid what is termed the naturalistic fallacy. An intrinsic relation between the nature of the person and his claim of rights, or again between what a person *is* and what he *is obliged* or *has a right to do,* does not entail that the latter is a matter of simple inference from the former.

107. Thus, to cite but one example, the pope says in *Centesimus annus* that "authentic democracy is possible only in a State ruled by law, and on the basis of a correct conception of the human person *(in recta personae humanae notione consistit).* . . . It must be observed in this regard that, if there is no ultimate truth to guide and direct political activity *(nulla si sit postrema veritas quae quidem politicam actionem dirigat et moderetur),* then ideas and convictions can easily be manipulated for reasons of power. As history demonstrates, a democracy lacking foundations [or first principles: *principiis*] turns into open or hidden totalitarianism" (CA, 46).

108. Cf. CIV, 39: "My predecessor John Paul II . . . in *Centesimus annus* . . . spoke of the need for a system with three subjects: the *market,* the *State* and *civil society.* He saw civil society as the most natural setting for an *economy of gratuitousness* and fraternity, but did not mean to deny it a place in the other two settings. Today we can say that economic life must be understood as a multi-layered phenomenon: in every one of these layers, to varying degrees and in ways specifically suited to each, the aspect of fraternal reciprocity must be present. In

DAVID L. SCHINDLER

the global era, economic activity cannot prescind from gratuitousness. . . ." Benedict goes on to argue that "[t]he exclusively binary model of market-plus-State is corrosive of society, while economic forms based on solidarity, which find their natural home in civil society without being restricted to it, build up society." Indeed, Benedict here criticizes interpretations of *Centesimus annus*, which, in rightly calling attention to the three distinct "sectors" of society/ culture, economy, and state, fail to see that the concerns proper to culture regarding truth and love are intrinsic and not merely extrinsic to the proper concerns of economy and state. Cf. also CIV, 38, 41; and my "Beyond the Binary Logic of Market-Plus-State: A Sane Social Order for the Global Liberal Age," in *The Beauty of God's House: Essays in Honor of Stratford Caldecott*, ed. Francesca Aran Murphy (Eugene, OR: Wipf & Stock, 2014), 149-88.

109. The following description of freedom for excellence indicates the problem with how the term is usually understood: "Freedom . . . is a matter of gradually acquiring the capacity to choose the good and to do what we choose with perfection" (George Weigel, "A Better Concept of Freedom," *First Things* 121 [March 2002], 14-20, at 16). To be sure, this statement makes an essential point regarding freedom of excellence. The point, however, is that it is just the *originally given* positive capacity, or aptness, of freedom *for the good* that inclines freedom's movement toward, and choice of, the good in the first place. Recall here, for example, the following statements of Pinckaers: "St. Thomas place[s] the natural inclination to the good and to happiness *at the very source* of human freedom" (353, emphasis added; cf. 375); freedom, rightly understood, "grows like a living organism," the wholeness of whose specific order is present from the outset (362); and *"finality is a principal element of* free action" (375).

110. Cf., e.g., WDD, 85: "die Begriffe 'ein Innen haben' und *'beziehungsfähig* sein' einander entsprechen" ("the concept of 'having an interiority' corresponds to *'being capable* of relation' " [LTT, 81; translation modified and emphasis added]). Pieper also uses *Beziehungskraft* (WDD, 88), "the power to relate," which implies a *positive* aptness *for;* and *Vermögen* (WHP, 46), which again implies a positive power or capacity to do something.

111. Cf., e.g., the classic Boethian definition of the person as "an individual substance of a rational nature" (*Liber de Persona et Duabus Naturis: Contra Eutychen et Nestorium*, ch. 3).

112. Cf. the strong statements in the *Compendium of the Social Doctrine of the Church:*

> *The likeness with God shows that the essence and existence of man are constitutively related (costitutivamente relazionate) to God in the most profound manner.* This is a relationship that exists in itself, it is therefore not something that comes afterwards and is not added from the outside. The whole of man's life is a quest and a search for God. This relationship with God can be ignored or even forgotten or dismissed, but it can never be eliminated. Indeed, among all the world's visible creatures, only man has a "capacity for God" *("homo est Dei capax")* (cf. GS 12; EV 34). The human being is a personal being created by God to be in relationship with him; man finds life and self-expression only in relationship, and tends naturally to God (cf. EV 35). (CSD, 109)
>
> *The relationship between God and man is reflected in the relational and social dimension of human nature.* Man, in fact, is not a solitary being, but "a social being, and unless he relates himself to others *(sine relationibus aliis)* he can neither live nor develop his potential" (GS, 12). (CSD, 110)

Notice that the translation of this last sentence from *Gaudium et spes,* 12 evokes the issue we have been concerned with in this article. While the original Latin indicates only that man cannot live without relations to others (relations which, as rooted in nature, are so far already in some significant sense *given*), the English translation renders this "unless he relates [himself] to others," thereby implying a conflation of the person's natural socialness, or being-in-relation, with a relationality that is first effected by the subject.

113. The Declaration's position, in my opinion, satisfies the marks of an authentic development of doctrine as indicated in Blessed John Henry Newman's *An Essay on the Development of Christian Doctrine* (Notre Dame: University of Notre Dame Press, 2010). See especially Part II, chapter V.

114. The Church's development regarding the mutual implication of freedom (subjectivity, interiority) and truth (objectivity) entails a development in her understanding of the relation between the positive and negative meaning of the right to religious freedom. As we will see, recognition of this mutual implication also entails a development in the Church's understanding of the relation between the traditional ethical state and the modern juridical state; between the common good and public order; and so on. Murray understands the Church's development of doctrine to consist in her increased recognition of "negative" rights, the juridical state, and public order, which he takes to coincide with less concern for rights in their anteriorly "positive" meaning, the ethical state, and the common good. This reading presupposes his claim that the Declaration signals the Church's growing recognition of freedom and subjectivity, *alongside* her traditional recognition of (objective) truth. My argument, on the contrary, is that the Declaration signals rather a new *integration* of truth and freedom: a deepened recognition that *the truth itself* bears *the distinct feature of freedom*. This integration of truth and freedom implies in turn its own distinct way of expanding the meaning of rights in their "positive" meaning, the ethical state, and the common good, so as to include, while reconfiguring, what is affirmed in "negative rights," the juridical state, and public order. The Church's doctrinal development regarding the mutual implication of truth and freedom, then, implies development with respect to each of the issues treated in this section, all of which are bound up with this question of the relation between truth and freedom.

115. Martin Rhonheimer, *The Common Good of Constitutional Democracy: Essays in Political Philosophy and on Catholic Social Teaching,* ed. William F. Murphy, Jr. (Washington, DC: Catholic University of America Press, 2013).

116. "The council's doctrine on religious freedom is essentially a doctrine on the functions and limits of the state, as well as on a fundamental civil right — a right of persons, not of truth — involving a limitation in the sovereignty and competence of the state in religious matters. It is also a doctrine on the Church's freedom . . . to exercise its salvific mission without hindrance, even in a secular state — a right that also belongs to every other religion. Finally, it is a doctrine on the state's responsibility to encourage, in a neutral and impartial way, the creation of the necessary conditions in the public and moral order within which religious freedom can flourish and citizens can fulfill their religious duties" (433).

117. Rhonheimer says that "Vatican II . . . situated the limits of freedom of opinion [and similar freedoms] in the rights of citizens, legally defined and juridically enforceable, and in the requirements of public order and morality. These limits correspond fully with the logic of secular, liberal, constitutional, and democratic state, which is neutral with respect to religious truth claims, and have nothing — repeat *nothing* — to do with the 'defense of religious truth' . . ." (434). We should note that Rhonheimer says elsewhere in his book that the neutrality of the state is a myth. But he qualifies this as follows: "Of course, I am not referring here to the equal procedural justice of the state under the rule of law, rightly desired by all, nor to the procedural legitimacy of the democratic decision-making process, both of which possess substantial

ethical-political value. That neutrality *is* a myth, however, which consists in the claim that both the theory and the practice of justice of a democratic constitutional state must limit themselves to purely procedural and formal aspects; also a myth is the opinion that such a state can avoid declaring, as part of its juridical public order, specific content-laden conceptions that are bind ing for all, and promoting specific conceptions of life, thus privileging them juridically" (169). The question focused in the present study is that of the sense in which what Rhonheimer terms the "specific content-laden conceptions" that guide the theory and practice of democratic justice are metaphysical-religious in nature (even if unconsciously so). Rhonheimer says elsewhere, for example, that "[t]he modern democratic constitutional state is also an order of truth and virtue, even if this is so in a very different way than in the classical ethic of the *polis*" (89). The difference consists in the fact that the modern democratic state's order of truth and virtue is "mediated by the functionality of institutional praxis that limits, restricts, and conditions political praxis ac cording to criteria of peace, freedom, and justice" (89). The question raised in the present study, again, is whether the order of truth and virtue indicated by Rhonheimer here, and the criteria of peace, freedom, and justice to which he refers, do or do not turn finally (intrinsically, even if unconsciously) on metaphysical-religious questions regarding the nature of the intelligent-free human act in its relation to the truth about God, or what is ultimate — whether such questions are not unavoidable even in the exercise of what Rhonheimer understands as public reason, and thus in the administration of legal-constitutional order. Rhonheimer's argument regarding Benedict's reading of Vatican II and religious freedom, as well as his argument with respect to Pius IX, indicates a response to this question that follows Murray in its essentials. Our discus sion regarding Rhonheimer in these matters, however, is restricted here to his interpretation of Benedict, which is our primary concern.

118. In light of our own interpretation of DH, it must be said that the Second Vatican Council, rightly interpreted, does not in fact reject Pius IX's fundamental concern: truth is a proper concern of statecraft, such that the state properly seeks to safeguard the truth about the human being before God. The Council, however, affirms this concern in a way that now recognizes a new implication in the nature of truth itself. The conciliar Church insists that the affirmation of truth itself demands principled recognition of the right to religious freedom. The "discontinuity" that makes room for freedom as an inherent dimension of truth itself, in other words, *grows organically out of the very concern for truth defended by Pius IX.*

Thus we may say, contra Rhonheimer, that the Church at Vatican II has in fact con firmed Pius IX's concern for the truth, indeed for truth as essential to a properly understood legal-political order, while correcting Pius's exclusion of freedom and the right to religious freedom from this concern. At the same time, however, the Church has also rejected an un derstanding of religious freedom that would exclude metaphysical and religious truth from the inner meaning of freedom, and from the right to religious freedom, and so far also from the concerns of the legal-political order. If Pius IX's understanding of truth did not take sufficient account of the subjectivity and interiority of the human subject that is demanded by the nature of truth itself, Rhonheimer's concern for the rights that flow from human subjectivity does not take sufficient account of this subjectivity's inner participation in the truth of things as created by God. Analogous to the relation between Lefebvre and Murray indicated earlier, we may say that Pius IX ignores truth's demand for human subjectivity, while Rhonheimer ignores human subjectivity's implication of truth. The Church of the Council rejects the exclusion of freedom from truth, as well as the exclusion of truth from freedom, affirming instead the mutual inner-relation of truth and freedom.

119. Cf. n. 117 above regarding Rhonheimer's understanding of neutrality.

120. Benedict's 2005 Christmas Address to the Roman Curia needs to be read also in light of his more recent statements on religious freedom, especially his 2011 address to the German Bundestag, which will be treated in our consideration of the state-society distinction and the nature of the limited state.

121. We should note here that Benedict's 2005 address (rightly) affirms a difference between the model of the modern state offered in the American Revolution and "the theoretical model with radical tendencies that had emerged during the second phase of the French Revolution." In connection with this, see our comments in n. 205 below, and section IX generally.

122. For more on the question of "distinction," see my "Modernity and the Nature of a Distinction," OL, 350-82, especially 360-65.

123. Indeed, in a way that demands certain subordination to the state itself on the part of the societal institutions rooted in family and religion. Cf. here the statement of Aquinas: "As one man is a part of the household, so a household is a part of the state: and the state is a perfect community. . . . And therefore, as the good of one man is not the last end, but is ordained to the common good, so too the good of one household is ordained to the good of a single state, which is a perfect community" (ST I-II, q. 90, a. 3 ad 3).

124. "The Listening Heart: Reflections on the Foundations of Law," Address to the German Bundestag, Reichstag Building, Berlin, 22 September 2011.

125. It is important to understand that conscience for Benedict/Ratzinger is not simply an inner act, such that it could rightly be understood in an individualistic sense. On the contrary, conscience implies mission to and for the world, indeed implies responsibility for the whole of creation and for him who made it. Cf. here Ratzinger's discussion of Reinhold Schneider and Bartolomé de Las Casas in the essay "Conscience in Its Time," in *Church, Ecumenism, and Politics: New Endeavors in Ecclesiology* [= CEP] (San Francisco: Ignatius Press, 2008), 163-72, especially 164. Cf. also Ratzinger, "Difficulties Confronting the Faith in Europe Today," *Communio* 38 (Winter 2011): 733-34: "[C]onscience is not some individualistic . . . calculation; rather it is a 'con-sciens,' a 'knowing along with' creation and, through creation, with God the Creator. . . . [M]an's greatness . . . [lies] in the fact that his being allows the highest wisdom, truth itself, to shine through. . . . [M]an is so much the greater the more he is capable of hearing the profound message of creation, the message of the Creator. . . . [H]armony with creation, whose wisdom becomes our norm, does not mean a limitation upon our freedom but is rather an expression of our reason and our dignity."

126. Ratzinger recognizes that there is a fundamental "ambivalence" in the modern doctrine of rights, especially in our "post-metaphysical age," in which "the unknowability of the true and man's incapacity for the good seem to have become absolute certainties," with the consequence that rights have their ground only in political authority and utility (*A Turning Point for Europe?* [= TPE] [San Francisco: Ignatius Press, 1994], 52-53). Nonetheless, according to Ratzinger "[t]here is a sound core to the idea of human rights," such that it can "continue to be a guide to the truth and a protective barrier against positivism" (53). This can happen only when we recognize that rights, and so law, are grounded in our common human nature, not in a "hypertrophied" freedom: "The law is molded, not created, by us. In other words, there can be no foundation for law without transcendence. When God and the basic pattern of human existence laid down by him are ousted from public consciousness and relegated to the private, merely subjective realm, the concept of law dissolves into thin air and, with it, the foundation of peace" (53-54).

127. In his earlier work, Cardinal Ratzinger puts the same point in a slightly different way: the concept of a universal common good "behind and above all good things has been formulated in the European tradition on a basis that Europe did not give itself but received from a higher tradition: in the Ten Commandments, in which Israel and Christianity, moreover, communicate with the oldest and purest traditions of mankind as a whole. The Ten Commandments also contain the essential core of what the early modern period formulated under the concept of human rights; these in turn are the basis of the distinction between the totalitarian state and the state that imposes limits on itself. . . . [T]he doctrine of human rights is based on the conviction that man is made in the image of God." It is for this reason, Ratzinger says, that Europe "must hand on, not only its rationality, but also the inner origin of this rationality and the foundations that make it meaningful — the recognition of the Logos as the foundation of all things, a glimpse of the truth that is also the criterion of the good. Then Europe will bring together the great traditions of mankind . . ." (TPE, 140-42). Indeed, as Ratzinger says elsewhere in TPE, the Christian faith is a "synthesis of the great ethical intuitions of mankind from a new center that holds them all together" (37).

128. "A Christian Orientation in a Pluralistic Democracy?," in CEP, 193-208, at 194. Cf. also here "That Which Holds the World Together: The Pre-political Moral Foundations of a Free State," in *The Dialectics of Secularization* (San Francisco: Ignatius Press, 2006), 53-85. Regarding the source of the statement by Böckenförde, see his *State, Society and Liberty: Studies in Political Theory and Constitutional Law* (New York: Berg, 1991), 45: "[T]he liberal, secularised state is nourished by presuppositions that it cannot itself guarantee. That is the great gamble it has made for liberty's sake. On the one hand, it can only survive as a liberal state if the liberty it allows its citizens regulates itself from within on the basis of the moral substance of the individual and the homogeneity of society. On the other hand, it cannot attempt to guarantee those inner regulatory forces by its own efforts — that is to say, with the instruments of legal coercion and authoritative command — without abandoning its liberalness and, at a secularised level, lapsing into that pretension to totality out of which it led the way into the denominational civil wars. The prescribed state ideology, the revival of the Aristotelian *polis* tradition, and the proclamation of an 'objective System of values' all do away with the very split out of which public liberty is constituted. There is no way back across the threshold of 1789 that does not destroy the state as the order of liberty."

129. In this connection, let me say that statements like that of Böckenförde — that "[t]he prescribed state ideology, the revival of the Aristotelian polis tradition, and the proclamation of an 'objective system of values,' all do away with the very split [between religion and the political order] out of which public liberty is constituted" (Böckenförde, 45) — are at the least profoundly misleading and beg for qualification. On the one hand, they fail to take account of the distinction between the pedagogical and the coercive functions of law that is in fact basic to the classical tradition (Aristotle, Aquinas). Indeed, the idea of law as something primarily or essentially coercive signals a departure from a genuinely classical conception of political order, at least in its Aristotelian-Thomistic sense. On the other hand, such statements beg the fundamental question of whether the liberal state itself does not inevitably imply, however unconsciously, a definite vision of what is true and good, and indeed of man's relation to the Creator. Indeed, that has been my claim throughout: liberalism's defense of rights implies not no vision of the nature of truth and the good and the human person in relation to God, but on the contrary a deeply fragmented vision of this nature. And even a fragmented vision of nature — of truth and the good and man's relation to God — as I have pointed out, implies a

claim about the essence, and thereby the whole, of what each of these consists in. Furthermore, insofar as such a defense is carried out without acknowledgment of its own (implicit) vision of nature, it becomes itself coercive in an objectionable sense. On the relationship between the pedagogical and coercive purposes of law, see n. 144 below.

130. Regarding non-neutrality, see CEP, 129, 219. According to Ratzinger, if the sphere of what is "above" is lost, criteria will inevitably come from "below" (CEP, 225).

131. This is what Benedict's Bundestag address means when it affirms that the state, in its framing of laws and administration of legal justice, needs to "rediscover [reason] in its true greatness," so that nature might "reassert itself in its true depth, with all its demands, with all its directives." Law, in other words, needs to be a fundamental image of justice (CEP, 210).

132. According to Ratzinger, it is faith alone that sets reason free to perform its own work fully in the concrete order weighted by sin (TPE, 36; cf. CEP, 153, 219). Ratzinger also says that politics is the sphere of the ethical, not the theological — but that ethics can be given a full and rational basis only in theology (CEP, 216).

133. See section I.3.iv.

134. I have in mind here, for example, Aquinas's recognition that human law needs to "take account of many things, as to persons, as to matters, and as to times" (ST I-II, q. 96, a. 1); and that law therefore does not seek to repress every vice (q. 96, a. 3) or prescribe every virtue (q. 96, a. 4), but rather must take into account "the changed condition of man, to whom different things are expedient according to the difference of his condition" (q. 97, a. 1) — which includes taking account of "custom" (q. 97, a. 3). I take the argument of Aquinas here to involve an implicit appeal to the subjectivity of persons, and thus to the historical principle as discussed further on in this section. It needs to be stressed in this connection, however, that, in this implied recognition of subjectivity, Aquinas never relinquishes the intrinsic ordering of law to the good, and thus does not follow the principle of public order understood in the juridical sense.

135. That is, they belong to public order as an integral part of, and not as extrinsic to, the common good. See in this connection our earlier discussion regarding the primacy of a "negative" right to religious freedom and the primacy of public order it entails. Murray's translation — that "[t]hese matters constitute the basic component of the common *welfare*: they are what is meant by public order" (Abbott, 687; emphasis added) — is ambiguous on the point raised here, regarding the Declaration's affirmation in article 7 of what Murray calls the "basic principle of the 'free [i.e., liberal] society.'"

136. With reference to this article of the Declaration, the *Catechism of the Catholic Church* states: "Freedom is exercised in relationships between human beings. Every human person, created in the image of God, has the natural right to be recognized as a free and responsible human being. All owe to each other this duty of respect. The right to the exercise of freedom, especially in moral and religious matters, is an inalienable requirement of the dignity of the human person. This right must be recognized and protected by civil authority within the limits *of the common good* and public order (cf. DH 2, 7)" (CCC, 1738; emphasis added).

137. For the Declaration, rightly interpreted, truth and freedom mutually include each other, such that an increase in one entails a proportionate increase in the other, in an asymmetrical manner: freedom's positive ordering toward truth — freedom *for* — provides the inner dynamic form for freedom in its negative sense as freedom *from*. Rightly understood, then, this intrinsic link between freedom and truth does not undercut the claim that freedom is the proper method of political order, because truth of its essence demands freedom. As

Pieper shows, there is no truth in the medieval (Thomistic) tradition whose realization does not presuppose the interiorizing activity of a subject. Limiting the exercise of freedom by a truth that is itself understood to involve freedom, therefore, can never be said *in principle* to restrict freedom. To be sure, limiting the exercise of freedom by truth may be (and is) rightly qualified in given instances on the prudential-political grounds indicated by Aquinas (see n. 134 above). The crucial point nonetheless is that the state's method of proceeding on such grounds remains tied to the truth and is so far non-arbitrary; while the juridical state's limiting of freedom is of its nature so far arbitrary.

138. It is helpful to recall again that, for St. Thomas, the exercise of freedom proceeds from a unity of reason and will (see n. 66 above), and that some understanding of truth will play an intrinsically dispositive (not deterministic) role in every act of choice (cf., e.g., ST I, q. 82, a. 4, ad 1, on the mutual-asymmetrical unity of intellect and will, truth and the good). But if truth always disposes freedom, a false, or indeed "heretical," understanding of truth cannot but dispose freedom in the wrong way, indeed in a way that will tend to enslave freedom. Recall here also that the freedom of indifference that is presupposed in the juridical state's criterion of public order is not no claim of truth. Rather, this freedom embeds a claim of truth that hiddenly disposes the juridical state toward exclusion ("excommunication") of the contrary view of truth expressed in freedom of quality, in the exercise of political justice.

It thus follows from our earlier argument that the question regarding the governmental right to repress false claims of truth (that is, to repress "heresy," or heterodox religious views) does not disappear in the case of a juridically conceived state. On the contrary, the inner logic of such a state begs this question, all the while disenfranchising all non-positivist moral or religious claims (qua non-positivist). We can thus see in this connection that Murray's early claim that there is no theological or political principle that justifies "a governmental right to repress heterodox religious opinions" needs to be revisited and qualified (see Murray's "Governmental Repression of Heresy," in *Proceedings of the Third Annual Convention of the Catholic Theological Society of America* [Bronx, NY: Catholic Theological Society of America, 1948], 26-98, at 95). Murray's argument does not take account of the fact that every civil government will inevitably, even if unconsciously, both offer a pedagogy regarding, and exercise "coercive" power in supporting, some religious claims of truth while rejecting others, and that *this includes liberal-juridical government.* The pertinent question in the matter of "repressing heresy," given the argument of the Declaration, is thus whether a given state, in its inevitable endorsement (conscious or unconscious) of some religious views over others, will endorse those views that protect with consistency the right of all citizens to religious freedom, subject to the demands of a truly just public order integrated in light of a true and just common good.

139. Cf. schema 4, a. 3: "The competence of the civil power, however, on account of its proper end — which today is more accurately perceived and described in terms of the demands of the dignity of the person and his rights — is restricted in its purpose to the earthly and temporal order, in order that human persons can strive toward their final end more easily and freely, according to their conscience. The civil power must therefore be said to exceed its limits if it involves itself in those matters that concern the very ordination of man to God" (AS IV/1, 150). Cf. also schema 3, a. 4e (AS III/8, 432).

140. That is why the Declaration, immediately following its affirmation of the right to religious freedom coincident with the transcendent nature of religious life, says that "the civil power, *therefore (igitur),* whose proper end is the care of the temporal common good, should in fact acknowledge and show favor to the religious life of its citizens" (DH, 3, emphasis added).

141. Note, then, that, as stressed by Murray, the Declaration emphasizes the state's inability to judge the interior movements of the will in religious activity (cf. DH, 3, with its citation of Aquinas in n. 7). The point is that the state nevertheless cannot avoid a judgment, implicit or explicit, regarding the nature, or *the objective logic,* of religion. Cf. in this connection the following statement of Murray, which emphasizes government's responsibility to care for the *free exercise* of religion, rather than for religion itself: "[I]n what concerns religion in society, government has a duty that is twofold. The first duty is to acknowledge the human right to religious freedom, and effectively to protect it and vindicate it against violation. The second duty derives from the general duty of government to assist the people in the performance of their duties; in this case, it is to show a general and undiscriminating favor toward religion in society . . . and to assist in the creation of conditions that will help, not hinder, the people in the exercise of their religious rights and in the performance of their religious duties" (Abbott, 684n14). Regarding Murray's emphasis on fostering the freedom of conditions for the exercise of religion, as distinct from religion itself, see n. 43 above, and the discussion on secularity and freedom of the Church in section VIII. Cf. also here Aquinas's acceptance of Isidore of Seville's statement that human law should "foster religion," and that law "is called virtuous because it fosters religion" (ST I-II, q. 95, a. 3).

142. A religion that conceives man as naturally religious of course does not exclude choice as also essential for the realization of this religiosity. It implies only that this choice is already informed from within by a natural inclination to search for God and indeed to rest in him once found. This natural inclination also does not exclude the supernatural origin of religion: it implies only that man is somehow ordered by nature to this supernatural religion. I am by nature apt for seeking God because in each of my free-intelligent acts God is somehow always remembered, inside my natural inclination to the true and the good. On this last point, cf. n. 95 above.

143. The assumption here is that man has a nature that implicitly seeks God and is therefore somehow tacitly, from its depths, aware of God and nature's destiny in God. On this, see Aquinas, De Ver. XXII, 2, ad 2; and Joseph Ratzinger, *On Conscience,* cited in n. 95 above. Cf. also, more generally, Henri de Lubac, *The Discovery of God* (Grand Rapids: Eerdmans, 1996). To be sure, this does not mean that all persons explicitly recognize the truth of nature or natural law, or, *a fortiori,* that this truth frees. The point is that human law, rightly understood in light of the Declaration, should seek to convey this truth, precisely as a way of securing a principled right to religious freedom. In this connection, see the discussion at the end of section VIII, regarding the need for genuine ecumenical and interreligious dialogue as an essential condition for a truly free and justly conceived juridical order.

144. "On her part, the Church addresses people with full respect for their freedom. Her mission does not restrict freedom but rather promotes it. *The Church proposes; she imposes nothing.* She respects individuals and cultures, and she honors the sanctuary of conscience. To those who for various reasons oppose missionary activity, the Church repeats: *Open the doors to Christ!*" (RM, 39). "Proposing," of course, entails also, with respect to the juridical order, making good laws, laws that are primarily "pedagogical," but also, secondarily, "coercive."

In the modern age, government authority is typically conceived as essentially "coercive" in nature, in the sense that its exclusive function is the negative one of protecting persons' immunity from the intrusive behavior of others. While of course not denying this coercive function, the Declaration implicitly affirms, consistent with the ancient-medieval view, that law is primarily pedagogical in nature. Cf. Aquinas, ST I-II, q. 92, a. 1: "The proper effect of law is to lead its subjects to their proper virtue: and since virtue is that which makes its subject good, it follows that the proper effect of law is to make those to whom it is given, good. . . . Wherefore the Philosopher says . . . that lawgivers make men good by habituating them to good works." According to Aquinas, the coercive force of law applies more to those who are vicious, but nonetheless to the same end, namely, education in virtue: "But since some are found to be depraved, and prone to vice, and not easily amenable to words, it was necessary for such to be restrained from evil by force and fear, in order that, at least, they might desist from evil-doing, and leave others in peace, and that they themselves, by being habituated in this way, might be brought to do willingly what hitherto they did from fear, and thus become virtuous" (q. 95, a. 1). Cf. q. 98, a. 6: "[E]very law is imposed . . . on some men who are hard-hearted and proud, whom the law restrains and tames; and it is imposed on good men, who, through being instructed by the law, are helped to fulfill what they desire to do."

On the biblical and Christological roots of the need to propose the truth while simultaneously respecting the historical conditions of the one to whom the truth is being proposed, see, *inter alia*, DH, 11.

145. I do not mean to imply here that the terms "subjective" and "historical" are synonymous in meaning. I mean only that "subjectivity" in the classical sense carries with it the implication of "historical" singularity and uniqueness, a singularity that develops in time and thus bears a distinctly temporal dimension.

146. Murray summarizes the thesis-hypothesis distinction as follows: "The thesis states the ideal — the care of religion that constitutional law ought to provide, per se and in principle. The hypothesis states the concessions that may have to be made to circumstances — the care that constitutional law may provide, per accidens and in view of circumstances" (PRF, 132). According to the "thesis," Murray says, false religions have no right, either divine or human, to public existence and action within society. On the other hand, when the "hypothetical" situation obtains, the Church "gives no positive approval to the . . . constitutional situation." On the contrary, such a situation remains evil, but may be regarded as a lesser of possible evils, and, as such, "tolerated, per accidens and in practice" (134).

147. Cf. Murray's comments on the paragraph of DH, 6 dealing with establishment: "This paragraph is carefully phrased. The Council did not wish to condemn the institution of 'establishment,' the notion of a 'religion of the state.' A respectable opinion maintains that the institution is compatible with full religious freedom. On the other hand, the Council did not wish to canonize the institution. A respectable opinion holds that establishment is always a threat to religious freedom. Furthermore, the Council wished to insinuate that establishment, at least from the Catholic point of view, is a matter of historical circumstance, not of theological doctrine. For all these reasons the text deals with the issue in conditional terms" (Abbott, 685n17).

148. Cf. also BSS, 194-95, and "Appendix: Toledo Talk" (1967) in BSS, 334-42. Murray's appeal to the distinction between historical and classical consciousness appears to have its origin in an early draft of Bernard Lonergan's essay "The Transition from a Classicist World View to Historical-Mindedness." Cf. BSS, 334n2, and Lonergan, *A Second Collection*, ed. William F. J. Ryan, S.J. and Bernard J. Tyrrell, S.J. (Philadelphia: Westminster, 1974), 1-10.

149. What I call the "juridical view" in my citation Murray calls the "Second View," in contrast to the "First View" that he is criticizing. According to Hooper, Murray wrote this article "before and during the third session, while he was also drafting the *textus emendatus*"

(PRF, 127). The article thus articulates the argument regarding religious freedom that Murray defended in his work on schemas 3 and 4 of the Declaration.

150. See section IV.2.

151. For Murray's most important account of the distinction between civil unity and religious unity, see WHTT, ch. 2, "Civil Unity and Religious Integrity: The Articles of Peace."

152. See section III.2.

153. See, e.g., section IV.1.ii-iv.

154. Regarding the related question of whether truth has rights: the proper subject of rights is the human person. It follows from the foregoing reflections, however, that rights will necessarily be tied to some claim of truth about the nature of the human dignity that founds those rights and thereby gives them their primary meaning. The traditional question of whether truth has rights therefore reappears, though now in a renewed form shaped by a deeper awareness of the subjectivity presupposed in the tradition's own metaphysics of truth and the human act. Once we understand that the human subject is by nature made for and primitively ordered by the truth of the world in relation to God, we see that the rights demanded for this subject cannot be detached from this original order. For it is indeed, once again, the freedom of the subject as naturally-dynamically bound up with this order that founds the dignity of the subject which warrants rights in the first place.

155. Cf. here nn. 134, 138, 141, and 144 above, regarding the nature of human law and the fostering of the good, virtue, and religion.

156. A view of nature as originally structurally indifferent to the supernatural revelation of Jesus Christ itself implies some sense, however unconscious, of nature and the supernatural, and the relation between them. An originally "negative" relation, in other words, is not no relation, but a relation already fraught with quite definite implications regarding the nature of man and God.

157. Thus a religious believer is permitted to propose any view regarding morality, economics, politics, or the like, as long as this view meets the criteria of the "secular" as understood in the dominant liberal culture. Any reference to religious truth, in other words, or reference indeed to any truth seen to be intrinsically affected in its content by religious faith, is *eo ipso* disallowed. One's religious faith may in fact *motivate* the truth one proposes, but the *content* of that truth must remain "secular" in the prevailing liberal sense.

158. For a paradigmatic articulation of the nature of the distinction between the person qua citizen and the person qua religious, as conceived along liberal-juridical lines, cf. John Locke, *A Letter Concerning Toleration* (Indianapolis: Hackett, 1983), 26-33: "I esteem it above all things necessary to distinguish exactly the Business of Civil Government from that of Religion, and to settle the just Bounds that lie between the one and the other. . . . [T]he Power of Civil Government relates only to Mens Civil Interests, is confined to the care of the things of this World, and hath nothing to do with the World to come. . . . The End of a Religious Society . . . is the Publick Worship of God, and by means thereof the acquisition of Eternal Life. All Disciples ought therefore to tend to that End, and all Ecclesiastical Laws to be thereunto confined. Nothing ought, nor can be transacted in this Society, relating to the Possession of Civil and Worldly Goods. . . . [T]he Church it self is a thing absolutely separate and distinct from the Commonwealth. The Boundaries on both sides are fixed and immovable. He jumbles Heaven and Earth together, the things most remote and opposite, who mixes these two Societies; which are in their Original, End, Business, and in every thing, perfectly distinct, and infinitely different from each other."

159. See, *inter alia*, section IV.2.

160. See the beginning of section IV.

161. Cf. John Paul II, *Fides et ratio*, 80:

> The mystery of the Incarnation will always remain the central point of reference for an understanding of the enigma of human existence, the created world and God himself. The challenge of this mystery pushes philosophy to its limits, as reason is summoned to make its own a logic which brings down the walls within which it risks being confined. Yet only at this point does the meaning of life reach its defining moment. The intimate essence of God and of the human being become intelligible: in the mystery of the Incarnate Word, human nature and divine nature are safeguarded in all their autonomy, and at the same time the unique bond which sets them together in mutuality without confusion of any kind is revealed (cf. Ecumenical Council of Chalcedon, *Symbolum, Definitio: DS* 302).

Cf. also the Decree on the Apostolate of the Laity, *Apostolicam actuositatem*:

> All that goes to make up the temporal order: personal and family values, culture, economic interests, the trades and professions, institutions of the political community, international relations, and so on, as well as their gradual development — all these are not merely helps to man's last end; they possess a value of their own, placed in them by God, whether considered individually or as parts of the integral temporal structure: "And God saw all that he had made and found it very good" (Gen 1:31). This natural goodness of theirs receives an added dignity from their relation with the human person, for whose use they have been created. And then, too, God has willed to gather together all that was natural, all that was supernatural, into a single whole in Christ, "so that in everything he would have the primacy" (Col 1:18). Far from depriving the temporal order of its autonomy, of its specific ends, of its own laws and resources, or its importance for human well-being, this design, on the contrary, increases its energy and excellence, raising it at the same time to the level of man's integral vocation here below. (AA, 7)

162. It is not my intention to enter further into the theological issues implied here. Suffice it to say that the invitation given in creation renders the creature no longer indifferent or neutral to the revelation of God in Jesus Christ, even as it leaves the creature unable to anticipate, or bring about on his own, participation in the reality of this revelation, which occurs only in baptism. The point, in a nutshell, is that the creature experiences himself as gift, and so far always anticipates generosity, even as such anticipation of its inner essence *awaits* the surprise of any further gift.

163. Cf. Joseph Ratzinger, *Values in a Time of Upheaval* (New York: Crossroad, 2005), 92: "[The] *anamnesis of the Creator, which is identical with the foundations of our existence,* is the reason that *mission* is both *possible* and *justified.* The Gospel may and indeed must be proclaimed to the pagans, because this is what they are waiting for, even if they do not know this themselves (see Isa. 42:4)" (emphasis original).

164. Cf. the Final Report of the 1985 Extraordinary Synod of Bishops, *The Church, in the Word of God, Celebrates the Mysteries of Christ for the Salvation of the World,* part II, section C, 1: "The ecclesiology of communion is the central and fundamental idea of the Council's documents."

165. Cf., e.g., John Paul II, *Redemptoris mater* and *Mulieris dignitatem;* Joseph Ratzinger,

An Interpretation of Dignitatis Humanae

Daughter Zion (San Francisco: Ignatius Press, 1993) and, together with Hans Urs von Balthasar, *Mary, the Church at the Source* (San Francisco: Ignatius Press, 2005).

166. Cf. the Congregation for the Doctrine of the Faith, "Letter to the Bishops of the Catholic Church on Some Aspects of the Church Understood as Communion" (28 May 1992).

167. Cf. Murray's article on lay theology, "Towards a Theology for the Layman: The Problem of Its Finality," *Theological Studies* 5 (March 1944): 43-75, at 73-74:

> The ministerial priesthood is to mediate the Holy Spirit to the soul of man; the lay priesthood is to mediate the Christian spirit to the institutions of civil society. The former exercises its mediation in the wholly spiritual order in which the very life of God mysteriously flows into the human soul, to effect its divinization; the latter exercises its mediation in that borderland of the spiritual and temporal, wherein the life of the Church makes vital contact with the terrestrial life of man, to effect its humanization. The former, as the instrument of Christ, is to bridge the gap created by sin and ignorance between man and God, his Father; the latter, as the instrument of the hierarchy, is to bridge the gap created by secularism between the profane activity of man and the life of the Church, his Mother. The former is instrumentally to rescue man from sin and the peril of losing his soul in hell; the latter is instrumentally to rescue man from social injustice and the peril of losing his humanity on earth.
>
> Perhaps these formulas sharpen the distinction. But, as a matter of fact, the Church herself in these latter days has wished to sharpen the distinction between spiritual and temporal, in order the better and the more organically to unite them without danger of confusion. Correlatively, and for the same purpose, it is necessary to sharpen the distinction between the ministerial and lay priesthoods.

This is to be sure an early statement by Murray regarding the laity, and his views in this matter continue to develop until the end of his life. He is in fact critical of "Catholic Action" insofar as, while emphasizing the work of the laity in the world, it continues to understand the laity as simple extensions of the hierarchy. The point here is simply that Murray conceives the purposes of priests and laity to differ from each other as concerned properly with the order of "divinization," on the one hand, and the order of "humanization," on the other. Murray consistently stresses in his life-work the distinct importance of the lay vocation in the world, as more than simply an extension of the hierarchy, and he so far anticipates developments at the Council. The difficulty, as we will see in our discussion of secularity, is that through the course of his work at the Council he retains this emphasis on the difference between the finalities of the priestly (eternal, supernatural) and the lay (temporal, natural), in such a way that the ecclesial, or Christian, task of the lay person in the world is to work for the integrity of a temporal order conceived first in abstraction from the eternal order revealed by God in Jesus Christ. The task of the lay person, in other words, does not include opening temporal structures and processes to their natural end *as itself open* to the revelation of God in Christ. This contrasts with the Council's *communio* ecclesiology, which recovers a unity within the distinct finalities of the temporal and the eternal. Cf. also in this connection n. 169 below.

168. It is interesting to note in this context the traditional language often used in discussing the Church-state distinction: namely, the Church as *sacerdotium* (priesthood) and the state as *imperium* (empire, political authority, or sovereignty).

169. The Church herself, of course, is officially present in the world as an institution for the confecting of sacramental life. It is the laity, on the other hand, who are to form the

academy, the economy, and the polity eucharistically. It is the laity, in other words, who are meant to draw all worldly structures and processes (all civil, political, economic, academic, and cultural institutions) toward their ultimate Eucharistic reality, *from within the inner temporal finalities of each of these structures and processes.* Cf. John Paul II, *Christifidelis laici,* 15, where the pope, citing the words of Paul VI, says:

> the Church "has an authentic secular dimension, inherent to her inner nature and mission, which is deeply rooted in the mystery of the Word Incarnate, and which is realized in different forms through her members" (AAS 64 [1972], 208). The Church . . . is sent to continue the redemptive work of Jesus Christ, which "by its very nature concerns the salvation of humanity, and also involves the renewal of the whole temporal order" (AA, 5).
>
> Certainly *all members* of the Church are sharers in this secular dimension but *in different ways.* In particular the sharing of the *lay faithful* has its own manner of realization and function, which, according to the Council, is "properly and particularly" theirs. Such manner is designated with the expression "secular character" (LG, 31). . . . [The lay faithful] are persons who live an ordinary life in the world: they study, they work, they form relationships as friends, professionals, members of society, cultures, etc. However, the Council considers their condition not simply an external and environmental framework, but as a reality *destined to find in Jesus Christ the fullness of its meaning.* . . .
>
> They are not called to abandon the position that they have in the world. Baptism does not take them from the world at all, as the apostle Paul points out: "So, brethren, in whatever state each was called, there let him remain with God" (1 Cor 7:24). On the contrary, he entrusts a vocation to them that properly concerns their situation in the world. The lay faithful, in fact, "are called by God so that they, led by the spirit of the Gospel, might contribute to the sanctification of the world, as from within like leaven, by fulfilling their own particular duties. Thus, especially in this way of life, resplendent in faith, hope and charity they manifest Christ to others" (LG, 31). Thus for the lay faithful, to be present and active in the world is not only an anthropological and sociological reality, but in a specific way, a theological and ecclesiological reality as well. In fact, in their situation in the world God manifests his plan and communicates to them their particular vocation of "seeking the Kingdom of God by engaging in temporal affairs and by ordering them according to the plan of God" (LG, 31).
>
> Precisely with this in mind the Synod Fathers said: "The secular character of the lay faithful is not therefore to be defined only in a sociological sense, but most especially in a theological sense. The term *secular* must be understood in light of the act of God the creator and redeemer, who has handed over the world to women and men, so that they may participate in the work of creation, free creation from the influence of sin and sanctify themselves in marriage or the celibate life, in a family, in a profession and in the various activities of society." (*Propositio* 4)

170. Cf. my "Liturgy and the Integrity of Cosmic Order: The Theology of Alexander Schmemann," OL, 288-309, especially 296-302.

171. Or lay-common priesthood: cf. *Lumen gentium,* 10 and 34. What I am proposing is that Vatican II's *communio* ecclesiology demands a distinction between a common or lay priesthood (originating in baptism) that bears the sacramental meaning of the Church in a "subjective"-Marian way, on the one hand, and a hierarchical-ministerial priesthood (origi-

nating in Holy Orders) that bears the sacramental meaning of the Church in an "objective"-Petrine way, on the other.

172. This is why the Church consistently affirms that she has an intrinsic mission in worldly (say, economic) affairs, in terms of shaping societal life in light of "integral human development," all the while insisting at the same time that, in so doing, she offers no explicit alternative model (no "third" kind of *economic* or *political-legal* proposal). The Church-Petrine, that is, speaks "officially" regarding the principle of "integral human development," while at the same time remaining subordinate to the Church-lay in the latter's framing these principles from within, and in terms of the concrete economic structures of the world. Again, John Paul II made clear the Church's official opposition to the political principles of Communism and Nazism (and indeed also those of Western "totalitarian democracy"), but at the same time demanded that priests not hold political office. Needless to say, these two examples leave open many questions. The principle affirmed here is clear, however, even if its concrete understanding in any given historical situation essentially involves prudential judgments. Cf. my discussions of this in "The Anthropological Vision of *Caritas in Veritate* in Light of Economic and Cultural Life in the United States," OL, 430-49, especially 434-41; and "Beyond the Binary Logic of Market-Plus-State."

173. Note that the historical principle is to be understood here as set forth above, and thus in a way that presupposes that reference to truth and to man's end is always implicated in the concrete conditions of every man's history.

174. D. C. Schindler, "Liberalism, Religious Freedom, and the Common Good: The Totalitarian Logic of Self-Limitation," *Communio* 40 (Summer-Fall 2013): 577-615, especially 605-15.

175. Pope Gelasius, "Letter Twelve to Emperor Anastasius" (494); cited in Hugo Rahner, *Church and State in Early Christianity* (San Francisco: Ignatius Press, 1992), 174.

176. Henri de Lubac, *Theological Fragments* (Ignatius Press: San Francisco: 1989), 199-234. The first part of this article, pp. 199-222, was published as "Le pouvoir de l'église en matière temporelle," *Revue des Sciences Religieuses* 12 (1932): 329-54, and is reproduced in *Theological Fragments* with several slight modifications; the second part, "Supplement," pp. 223-34, was a lecture given at the *Union d'études catholiques sociaux,* Lyon, in 1931.

177. It should be noted that de Lubac refers to the problem of a "separated philosophy" in connection with the foregoing discussion, stating that, although this separation was a misfortune for the Church, it nevertheless helped her see more "the character and rights of rational speculation" (216). The point, in other words, is that grace, while operating within nature and reason, respects the integrity of these even as it elevates and transfigures them.

178. Regarding Aquinas's authorship, see *Aquinas: Political Writings,* ed. R. W. Dyson (Cambridge: Cambridge University Press, 2002), xix.

179. See Plato, *Republic,* 368d-e.

180. Cf. De Reg. I, 13: "Therefore let the king recognize that such is the office which he undertakes, namely, that he is to be in the kingdom what the soul is in the body, and what God is in the world."

181. Patrick Deneen is quite right in his argument that the liberal state, having set virtue aside as a legitimate purpose of government, invariably accommodates for the absence of virtue by way of an ever-increasing appeal to legal force and control (see Deneen's "Unsustainable Liberalism," *First Things* 225 [August/September 2012], 25-31). I would only emphasize here that this inevitable precipitous recourse to legal control itself embodies a distinctive kind of "virtue"

or "soul." The liberal-juridical state, in replacing the good of the human being effectively with the good of debate and procedures without end, informs itself thereby merely with the paradox of a *small* "soul writ large." See in this connection Alasdair MacIntyre, *Whose Justice? Which Rationality?* (Notre Dame: University of Notre Dame Press, 1988), 335-48.

182. Cf., in this connection, nn. 108 and 172 above.

183. Reference to any kind of legally privileged subordination of the state to the Church inevitably sounds jarring to contemporary readers. This is so first of all because contemporary readers tend to take for granted the idea that the liberal state bears no such subordination to a church; whereas the liberal state, however unconsciously, legally privileges churches of a definite (positivistic) kind. Furthermore, rightly concerned about the violence committed in many pre-modern societies in the name of legally privileged religious belief, contemporary readers often fail to take note of the violence characteristic of modern liberal societies (e.g., the massive killing of the unborn innocent that is legally permitted in such societies), a violence that is tied to an idea of rights ultimately rooted in a positivistic freedom that is itself in a basic way the logical fruit of modern religion. The idea of a legally privileged Church sounds jarring, finally, because of the failure by Catholics to distinguish appropriately, in accord with the Council's *communio* ecclesiology, between the lay and the Petrine dimensions of the Church; and to distinguish properly between *auctoritas* and *potestas civilis*.

184. Cf. the principle of Gelasius referred to in n. 175 above (cited in BSS, 192).

185. Cf., e.g., DH, 11 and 14.

186. The "negative" right to "freedom of the Church," in other words, is to be understood in light of her positive freedom to carry out her divine mission in the world, as indicated, for example, in DH, 13.

187. Cf. Balthasar, "The Council of the Holy Spirit," in *Explorations in Theology,* vol. 3: *Creator Spiritus* (San Francisco: Ignatius Press, 1993), 245-67, with its brief discussion of the "Letter to Diognetus" (c. 190 A.D.) at 247f.

188. Note that statements by Murray such as the following appear to contradict this claim: "This frank profession of Catholic faith, at the outset of the Declaration on Religious Freedom, is in no sense at variance with the ecumenical spirit, any more than it is at variance with full loyalty to the principle of religious freedom. Neither the spirit of ecumenism nor the principle of religious freedom requires that the Church refrain from stating publicly what she believes herself to be. The demands of truth are no more opposed to the demands of freedom than they are opposed to the demands of love" (Abbott, 679n3). "Implicitly rejected [in DH, 4] is the outmoded notion that 'religion is a purely private affair.' . . . Religion is relevant to the life and action of society. Therefore religious freedom includes the right to point out this social relevance of religious belief" (Abbott, 683n11). Statements such as these, however, presuppose the terms of Murray's argument as a whole. Thus the Church is free to state publicly what she believes herself to be, but only in a sense that disallows any effort by her to shape the public order, other than by assisting it to realize its own temporal ends, in abstraction from man's ultimate end. Again, the Church is relevant to society, but only in terms of its *social* relevance. The Church is not to inform the structures of society in terms of her proper reality as Church, in the sense of *communio* as developed above. Thus Murray's view of the secular mission of the laity as expressed in the preceding paragraph, which means to accentuate and expand the importance of this secular mission, in fact paradoxically *reduces* this importance, by excluding from all worldly structures the new substance introduced by the gospel that informs these structures by leavening them from within.

Cf., in light of the above, the following statement of Christopher Dawson: "[T]he contribution of Christianity to culture is not merely the addition of a new religious element; it is the process of re-creation which transforms the whole character of the social organism" (*The Crisis of Western Education* [Garden City, NY: Doubleday, 1965], 143). See also *Christifidelis laici*, 15, cited in n. 169 above.

189. It is significant in this context that Murray rarely mentions the fact that the need to suffer the Cross is integral to the Christian's "worldly" presence. The demand for a *realistic Christian* presence in the world that would seek transformation of the world in a way involving the need to suffer is absent from his arguments regarding religious freedom. On the need for a witness in "diffusing the light of life" in the world, to the point of "shedding blood," see DH, 14; and also DH, 11.

190. Those in America who are overly impressed with the pluralism of liberal societies tend, for example, to extol the differences among the churches, temples, and synagogues, and the contents of belief which they preach, while overlooking the extent to which these churches treat beliefs, in line with the dominant culture and its legal-constitutional order, as matters most basically of free choice, and indeed the way in which, in so doing, they conform their public behavior to the liberal disjunction of the temporal and eternal orders, in contrast to the historic religions' opening of the temporal to the eternal. They are impressed with the vast pluralism in the claims of the knowledge produced in liberal societies, while overlooking the extent to which arguments for such claims that would be reasonable and thus publicly relevant must be conceived in terms of quantitative control of the abstractions called empirical "facts," as opposed to being rooted in human experience, rightly interpreted philosophically and theologically (on this, see my chapter "Living and Thinking Reality in Its Integrity," OL, 310-27). Finally, they are impressed by what seem to be the rights accorded in principle to every person in a liberal society, while overlooking what is in reality the restriction of principled protection of rights to those who are capable of taking the action sufficient to claim these rights (e.g., to fully functioning adult individuals), to the exclusion of those who are not capable of doing so (e.g., the unborn or those who are at the end of a terminal illness).

The point being made here can be put in the words of the eminent twentieth-century cultural historian, Christopher Dawson: "We have seen that every social culture is at once a material way of life and a spiritual way of life. Culture as a common way of life is inseparable from culture as a common tradition of language and thought and a common inheritance of knowledge, and this in turn involves an organized attempt to co-ordinate human action with the transcendent divine power which rules the world and on which man's life depends" (Dawson, *Religion and Culture* [Washington, DC: Catholic University of America Press, 2013], 150). This statement by Dawson holds true also for modern liberal societies and not only for traditional societies. The difference, and it is a profound albeit paradoxical one, is that modern liberal societies embody the truth of the statement while expressly denying it, and thereby embody it in an unconscious and, so far, more dangerous sense. Cf. again Dawson: "[M]odern culture is not pluralistic in character, as some social scientists have assumed; on the contrary, it is more unitary, more uniform and more highly centralized and organized than any culture that the world has known hitherto" (*The Crisis of Western Education* [Garden City, NY: Doubleday-Image, 1965], 118).

191. Cf. Healy, "The Drafting of *Dignitatis Humanae*," sections II-III.

192. Cf. in this connection the following statement by Benedict XVI, "Address to Representatives of Other Religions," at the Pope John Paul II Cultural Center, 17 April 2008:

Religious freedom [and] interreligious dialogue . . . aim at something more than a consensus regarding ways to implement practical strategies for advancing peace. The broader purpose of dialogue is to discover the truth. What is the origin and destiny of mankind? What are good and evil? What awaits us at the end of our earthly existence? Only by addressing these deeper questions can we build a solid basis for the peace and security of the human family. . . .

We are living in an age when these questions are too often marginalized. Yet they can never be erased from the human heart. . . . Spiritual leaders have a special duty, and we might say competence, to place the deeper questions at the forefront of human consciousness, to reawaken mankind to the mystery of human existence, and to make space in a frenetic world for reflection and prayer.

. . . While always uniting our hearts and minds in the call for peace, we must also listen attentively to the voice of truth. In this way, our dialogue will not stop at identifying a common set of values, but go on to probe their ultimate foundation.

For further discussion of this address, see my "Cultural Implications of Religions in Public Life: Recuperating the Deeper Questions," in OL, 26-33. Cf. also Ratzinger, *Truth and Tolerance* (San Francisco: Ignatius Press, 2004), 79:

Christianity has more in common with the ancient cultures of mankind than with the relativistic and rationalistic world that has cut loose from the fundamental insights of mankind and is thus leading man into a vacuum, devoid of meaning, which risks being fatal for him unless the answer to it comes to him in time. For the knowledge that man must turn toward God, and toward what is eternal, is found right across all cultures. . . . It is not relativism that is confirmed; rather, it is the unity of the human condition and its common experience of contact with a truth that is greater than we are.

193. The assumption here is that truth or dogma and mystery are not mutually exclusive but, rightly understood in light of the Catholic tradition, mutually imply each other. Entry into truth does not lessen one's sense of mystery but opens one to deeper dimensions of the mystery. Truth therefore never in principle forecloses searching and inquiry but rather intensifies these.

194. The ultimate sense of and ground for pluralism in Christianity lies in its doctrine of the Triune God. Though of course it is beyond present purposes to develop the point, what this doctrine implies is that unity, in its deepest Christian understanding, opens to plurality — without sacrificing unity.

195. Joseph Ratzinger, *Truth and Tolerance*, 61. Cf. also Benedict XVI, "Meeting with Representatives from the World of Culture," 12 September 2008, *Collège des Bernardins*, Paris, France: "Our present situation differs in many respects from the one that Paul encountered in Athens, yet despite the difference, the two situations also have much in common. . . . God has truly become for many the great unknown. But just as in the past, when behind the many images of God the question concerning the unknown God was hidden and present, so too the present absence of God is silently besieged by the question concerning him. *Quaerere Deum* — to seek God and to let oneself be found by him, that is today no less necessary than in former times. A purely positivistic culture which tried to drive the question concerning God into the subjective realm, as being unscientific, would be the capitulation of reason, the renunciation of its highest possibilities, and hence a disaster for humanity, with very grave consequences.

An Interpretation of Dignitatis Humanae

What gave Europe's culture its foundation — the search for God and the readiness to listen to him — remains today the basis of any genuine culture."

196. For an overview of the Church's teaching on human rights, see J. Brian Benestad, *Church, State and Society: An Introduction to Catholic Social Doctrine* (Washington, D.C.: Catholic University of America Press, 2011), 35-80.

197. As the language here suggests, when I use the terms "subjective right" and "objective right" in what follows, I refer, on the one hand, to the subjective meaning of a right insofar as it indicates a claim made *by* the human subject *on* others, and, on the other hand, to the objective meaning of a right insofar as it indicates a call or demand made *on* the subject *by* others. These two dimensions of a right, correctly understood, are indissoluble, even as they remain distinct. The Latin terms *ius* (from *iungere*, "to join"; hence, "that which is binding") and *iustitia* (right, justice, law), as well as the German *Recht*, carry this double meaning of (subjective) right and (objective) order or justice. And indeed the terms "natural law," "natural right," and "natural rights" all reflect different emphases with respect to this range of meaning. I do not want to enter into the linguistic issues here, however, but rather keep the discussion focused on the relative place of subjective and objective demands in the constitution of rights as framed in the earlier sections of this study.

198. *The Idea of Natural Rights: Studies on Natural Rights, Natural Law, and Church Law 1150-1625* [= Idea] (Grand Rapids: Eerdmans, 2001 [first published in 1997]); "Historical Roots of Modern Rights: Before Locke and After," in *Rethinking Rights: Historical, Political, and Philosophical Perspectives*, ed. Bruce P. Frohnen and Kenneth L. Grasso (Grand Rapids: Eerdmans, 2009); "The Idea of Natural Rights — Origins and Persistence," *Northwestern Journal of International Human Rights* 2, no. 1 (Spring 2004): 1-13. This last article presents in summary fashion the author's argument in *The Idea of Natural Rights*.

199. It is important to take note of Tierney's argument regarding the universality of rights. First of all, having set aside any notion of human nature as an "abstract essence" inhering in all individuals, Tierney conceives this universality after the manner of something that begins in a particular region (e.g., Western culture), and then eventually extends its influence into other regions of the world (cf. Idea, 346-47). Unawares, Tierney thus reads into the (supposed) universality of human nature the heart of a nominalistic metaphysics, according to which universality is something that starts out simply in a particular people, in a particular time and place, and, through *extension of influence*, eventually conditions most or all other people. Secondly, Tierney says that "if natural rights are inherent in human beings as such, they must always have existed; and this seems contradicted by the lack of such rights throughout the course of history" (Idea, 5). He responds by arguing that "the idea of rights is a moral one." That is, "it does not refer to the rights that people can actually exercise in any given society but to rights that ought to be recognized in all societies because they are necessary for the fulfillment of some basic human needs and purposes" (Idea, 5). But this response merely intensifies the original question: On the basis of what do we determine which needs and purposes are basic and universal, such that they "ought to be recognized in all societies"?

Tierney answers that, while "we in the West tend to exaggerate the range of rights that should be considered truly universal . . . , if we continue to cherish a few core rights that really do respond to the common needs of humanity we might still hope to ameliorate, to some extent, the condition of human kind in the coming centuries" (Idea, 347). Tierney insists that rights claims are most likely to emerge and be effective when people face things like "gross political oppression," especially in an age like ours which has been "so fertile in the invention of new forms of tyranny" (Idea, 347). In the face of such situations, he says, people become more conscious of the fact that rights need to be extended in their reach. He cites as an example the European discovery of America and the resultant colonialism and oppression, which called forth a newly emergent understanding of rights, in a way exemplified above all in Bartolomé de las Casas, who asked whether rights inhered not only in civilized people like the Spaniards, but also in "idol-worshippers, cannibals, naked savages even" ("The Idea of Rights — Origins and Persistence," 4). In sum, Tierney seems assured that some genuinely universal sense of rights will survive, since "surely in all societies, humans have preferred life to death, freedom to servitude, . . . dignity to humiliation" (Idea, 347). For this reason, it is not necessary to root rights in "some outmoded metaphysical theory of essences," nor necessarily to rest them on religious faith. On the contrary, it is enough to see that humans display "certain relevant characteristics" like "rationality and free will," and thus to believe "in the value and dignity of human life" ("The Idea of Natural Rights — Origins and Persistence," 12). If we do so, Tierney claims, when faced with the emergence of severe forms of oppression and tyranny, we will effectively call forth the rights claims that are needed.

Again, the difficulty in Tierney's argument is that it begs the crucial question. Furthermore, Tierney's relative optimism is not supported by current history. It is not true that "surely all societies have preferred life to death" and "freedom to servitude" — that is, in the hardest cases where the lives and freedom of certain *others* are, or seem to be, particularly burdensome to *our own* lives and freedom. One thinks, for example, of one of contemporary culture's newest forms of rights claims, increasingly endorsed by those liberal societies for whom human rights are fundamental: namely, the legal right to kill the unborn. On any legitimate criterion of numbers of deaths, or grossness of violence imposed on the very weakest of human beings, there is scarcely a more significant example of tyranny, even among the most brutal regimes of the twentieth century.

Needless to say, there is much needing argument here. My point regarding Tierney's argument is that it amounts in the end to little more than an assurance that reasonable people will eventually come to recognize the human dignity of the oppressed based on their rationality and free will, and will do so especially in the face of the grossest forms of tyranny and oppression. This assurance, however, presumes ideas of "reasonable," and of rationality and free will, which, on Tierney's own explicit terms, can express no "abstract essence" of the human being but only what the people of a particular historical time and place (for example, in modern Western liberal societies) take to be reasonable, rational, and free. Liberal societies that affirm the legal right to kill unborn human beings judge the rationality and free will actually exercised by an adult agent to have greater dignity, and thus to warrant a deeper claim to rights, than what such societies deem to be the embryo's merely potential capacity to exercise rationality and free will. How, then, do we adjudicate justly in such a case?

Tierney's claim of a basic continuity between ancient-medieval ideas of right ("rights") and modern ideas of rights thus rests on his failure to come to terms with the precise question on which the debate between the medieval and the modern approaches to rights turns: On the basis of what principle do we adjudicate when rights claims conflict, above all in the hardest cases? In the face of this question, Tierney takes it to suffice merely to assert a complementarity between individual rights and the demands of the community, regardless of whether we subscribe to a more "nominalist" or more "realist" understanding of the individual (and of community), or indeed whether we support this understanding with belief in God. Those who hold that a profound shift occurs in the modern conception of rights, on the contrary, argue that only recognition of the truly *social nature* of the human being (the so-called "realist" understanding), a recognition rooted in God or a transcendent order of truth, suffices to avoid arbitrariness in the adjudication of rights claims.

In a word, Tierney's claim regarding a continuity between medieval and modern approaches to rights begs the question, even as this question-begging is itself a function of an (unconscious) nominalism. Indeed, it is a function of the sort of nominalism that, according to the medievals, renders it impossible to resolve rights claims non-arbitrarily, precisely at the juncture when protection of such claims is most urgently needed — that is, in the hardest cases, such as that illustrated by abortion.

200. Recall here the statement of Bishop Ancel, the substance of which was inserted into article 2 of the fifth (and the sixth-final) text of the Declaration: "My proposition is as follows: the obligation to seek the truth is itself the ontological foundation of religious freedom" (AS IV/2, 17).

201. Cf. Bishop Ancel: "[R]eligious freedom has its foundation in this obligation itself, and the obligation to seek the truth in turn requires religious freedom.... [T]his ... constitutes the very heart of the Declaration *(nucleum declarationis)*" (AS IV/2, 17). Regarding the language of *negative*-subjective, perhaps we should note that, as indicated in the preceding sentence, and as discussed in the earlier sections of this essay, a subjective right is never simply or primarily negative. While this negative dimension is necessary, it does not exhaust the full meaning of "subjective right," which indeed receives its first meaning from freedom's positive, originally responsive movement toward the (objective) other.

202. This is why the language of duty or obligation, while of course indispensable, must nonetheless be understood, in a rightly conceived Catholic context, as an obligation whose basic foundation and form *is love.*

203. Indeed, as indicated earlier, it was the failure to recognize the possibility of this sort of continuity-within-discontinuity based on the unity-within-distinction of subjective right and objective right that drove the vigorous debate during the Council between the Lefebvrites and the defenders of the juridical approach.

We may recall in this connection the statement by Council historian Joseph Komonchak: "Those who see the Council's achievement as a naïve capitulation to modernity often fail to distinguish not only between the particular social reform Catholicism adopted in the last century and a half and the permanent essence of the church but also between the liberal political structures of modern democracies and the liberal ideology which often legitimates them. Those who celebrate the Council as a long-overdue accommodation to modernity often focus on its acceptance of many of the liberal structures of the day but ignore or play down the Council's insistence on the substantive relevance of religion to society. If the one group tends to demonize modernity, the other tends to deify it; and it is not hard to see why they encourage one another's simplicities" ("Vatican II and the Encounter Between Catholicism and Liberalism," in *Catholicism and Liberalism: Contributions to American Public Philosophy,* ed. R. Bruce Douglass and David Hollenbach [Cambridge: Cambridge University Press, 2002], 76-99, at 95).

Komonchak is quite right that the Council's teaching regarding religious liberty did not rely on easy certainties regarding either liberalism or anti-modern Catholicism: it neither demonized nor deified modernity. In fact, *Dignitatis humanae* retrieved what is most true about modernity (its emphasis on subjectivity and the dignity of the human subject), in terms of what lies at the heart of the ancient-medieval tradition (its understanding of the spiritual nature of human subjectivity and the transcendental nature of truth, in light of an adequate doctrine of creation). The difficulty regarding Komonchak's statement emerges only when we see that he follows Murray in affirming that the Council endorsed the distinction between a *constitutional* indifference of the state (or liberal political *structures*), on the one hand, and a *substantive cultural* indifference to questions of truth and value (or liberal *ideology*), on the other. The problem, in other words, is that the claim on behalf of a constitutional indifference that would avoid a substantive "ideological" indifference itself privileges a subjective human act that is originally lacking objective ordering by truth. Murray's juridical interpretation of the Declaration, in other words, presupposes a reductive sense of modern subjectivity even as it implies a defective grasp of ancient-medieval notions of the free-intelligent human act and of truth, as implied by a right understanding of creatureliness. The Council bishops, on the other hand, recognized that constitutional indifference entailed substantive indifference; this alone accounts for why they voted to make explicit in schema 5 the ontological relation between freedom and truth.

204. Cf. John Paul II, *Man and Woman He Created Them: A Theology of the Body*, trans. Michael Waldstein (Boston: Pauline Books and Media, 2006):

> The concept of original solitude includes both self-consciousness and self-determination. The fact that man is "alone" contains within itself this ontological structure.... This man, about whom the account of the first chapter [of Genesis] says that he has been created "in the image of God," is manifested in the second account *as a subject of the covenant* ... and "partner of the Absolute." *Man is "alone": this is to say that through his own humanity,* through what he is, he is at the same time set into a *unique, exclusive, and unrepeatable relationship with God himself.* (151)

> In the biblical account, solitude is the way that leads to the unity that we can define, following Vatican II, as *communio personarum* (*Gaudium et spes*, 12).... *[M]an became the image of God not only through his own humanity, but also through the communion of persons,* which man and woman form from the very beginning. (162-63)

See also Joseph Ratzinger, "The Dignity of the Human Person," Commentary on *Gaudium et spes*, Part I, Chapter I, in *Commentary on the Documents of Vatican II, vol. 5: Pastoral Constitution on the Church in the Modern World,* ed. Herbert Vorgrimler (New York: Herder & Herder, 1969):

> With Augustine (*De Trinitate,* XIV, 8, 11) the image of God is interpreted as capacity for God, qualification to know and love God. That is what for Augustine gives the idea of man as the image of God its dynamic aspect.... [D]ominion over the world is only the consequence, not the content, of likeness to God, and consequently points beyond itself back again to the image of God. (121)

> The conciliar text ... brings[s] the existence of humanity as man and woman into undefined connection with human likeness to God. And on that basis it describes man as a social being who essentially exists in relationships.... [But] (as in the case of work already mentioned) the likeness to God in sexuality is prior to sexuality, not identical with it. It is because the human being is capable of the absolute Thou that he is an I who can become a Thou for another I. The capacity for the absolute Thou is the ground of the possibility and necessity of the human partner. Here too, therefore, it is most important to pay attention to the difference between content and consequence. (122-23)

205. I have made no mention in this interpretive essay regarding America's understanding of rights, as formulated above all in the founding documents of the Declaration of Independence and the Constitution. As mentioned earlier, Benedict XVI recognizes in a positive way the distinctness of the American regime, even as he signals the ambivalence in modern rights theories. Evidently, this issue is vast. I would only affirm here a general principle, and make two points in its regard. The fundamental question to be posed in light of the Council's teaching on rights is the one addressed throughout this essay: What is the nature of the human being and the foundation of his dignity; and what follows from this regarding the nature of rights? More specifically, how is the relation between the individual self and others, ultimately God, understood: first in extrinsic (contractualist-social) terms, or first in intrinsic (natural-social) terms)? Are rights in this context understood primarily as "negative" or positive? How, in a word, are subjective right and objective right related in the person; and what follows for the nature of the right to life, liberty, and the pursuit of happiness?

The two points I would propose in connection with these questions are these. On the one hand, the Declaration of Independence clearly affirms that subjective rights are rooted in nature, and indeed in a nature that is created by God. In this sense, the claim regarding the positive distinctiveness of America within modern rights theories is in principle warranted. On the other hand, the American Declaration's approach to rights remains highly ambiguous with respect to the questions posed and addressed in this essay. That is, rights as articulated in the Declaration are on their face conceived as demands made by individual selves on others. The Creator is viewed most basically as an *ensurer* of such rights, an ensurer, that is, of my individual autonomy. Rights, in a word, are first "negative," not positive — they are immunities lacking the anterior positive form implied by freedom's originally responsive relation to the truth and goodness of others, and to God as creative source of this truth and goodness.

The nature of the ambiguity indicated here can be illustrated in the work of John Locke, who takes the individual self to be the proper subject of rights, such that the right to life is most basically an individual's right to self-preservation. To be sure, each individual recognizes that other individuals have this same right. The individual is obliged to respect this right in others, however, only insofar as the assertion of others' rights does not enter into competition with the individual's own assertion of rights (cf., e.g., his *Second Treatise on Government*, ch. 2, §6: "Every one, as he is bound to preserve himself, and not to quit his station wilfully, so by the like reason, *when his own preservation comes not in competition*, ought he, as much as he can, to preserve the rest of mankind, and may not, unless it be to do justice on an offender, take away, or impair the life, or what tends to the preservation of the life, the liberty, health, limb, or goods of another" [emphasis added]). The ambiguity in America's founding documents is also indicated in the language of James Madison, who states that what needs most to be developed in a well-constructed union is "its tendency to break and control the violence of faction" (*The Federalist,* N. 10). Madison defines a faction as "a number of citizens, whether amounting to a majority or minority of the whole, who are united and actuated by some common impulse of passion, or of interest, adverse to the rights of other citizens, or to the permanent and aggregate interests of the community" (*The Federalist,* N. 10).

Thus both Locke and Madison recognize a community of rights, but this community is constituted in the first instance "negatively," as an aggregate of individual selves bound together most basically for the self-preservation and the self-interests of each individual. Note that I do not mean to suggest here that the teachings of either Locke or Madison exhaust the meaning of rights expressed in America's founding documents. Indeed, I take for granted that the idea of rights affirmed in these documents draws implicitly on a much broader English tradition that reaches back to the Magna Carta and that is operative in the long history of English common law, as well as on the natural common sense of human beings. My point is simply that the documents nonetheless bear an ambiguity that can scarcely be avoided in an eighteenth-century Anglo-Saxon political document, namely, the ambiguity discussed above in terms of the work of Tierney, regarding the relative priority of subjective right and objective right. As we have seen, what the Second Vatican Council demands in this context is the priority of objective right coincident with the union of objective right and subjective right. Contrary to the position taken by Tierney, this teaching of the Council demands recognition of the profound difference between factions ordered in terms of (subjective, individual) interests, on the one hand, and a community ordered in terms of (objective, communally shared) truth and goodness, on the other. Life, liberty, and the pursuit of happiness are rights of the individual only as these are at once bound to the life, liberty, and happiness of others, as originally and positively *formed* by this binding relation to others, and to the Creator.

Rights adequately understood presuppose a community of persons, the *truth* of whose *goodness* — and thus dignity — is *originally given*. It is this truth of the goodness, and hence the dignity, of all human persons in their givenness or, more properly, *giftedness*, that alone finally sustains rights in the sense required by the teaching of the Council.

What I wish to say regarding America's founding documents is thus, in a word, that the Church's conciliar teaching invites us to affirm these documents' anchoring of rights in a human nature created by God, while deepening and transforming the documents' understanding of nature, nature's God, and the relation of nature to God. This conveys what I take to be the sense of Benedict's (justified) positive recognition of the distinctiveness of American liberalism, while at once identifying the ambivalence that Benedict sees in modern rights theories more generally. Illuminating in this latter context is the summary statement of Ratzinger:

> Men cannot really be united by a common interest but only by the truth: in this way, freedom and justice are brought to realization in their inherent unity. Here we can state with a fair amount of precision what the distinction is between a large group of robbers and a genuine state: merely pragmatic criteria, which are thereby necessarily the criteria of a party, determined by the group, are essentially the constitutive factor of structured robber societies. Something other than these — that is, something other than a large group that regulates itself only in accordance with its goals — exists only when a righteousness comes into play that is measured, not by the interest of the group, but by a universal criterion. Only this do we call the 'justice' that constitutes the state. It includes the Creator and creation as its points of orientation. (TPE, 131-32)

206. Cf. John Paul II, *Redemptor hominis,* 12:

> In this unity in mission, which is decided principally by Christ himself, all Christians must find what already unites them, even before their full communion is achieved. . . . It also enables us to approach all cultures, all ideological concepts, all people of good will. We approach them with the esteem, respect, and discernment that since the time of the Apostles has marked the *missionary* attitude, the attitude *of the missionary*. . . . The *missionary* attitude always begins with a feeling of deep esteem for "what is in man," for what man has himself worked out in the depths of his spirit concerning the most profound and important problems. It is a question of respecting everything that

has been brought about in him by the Spirit, which "blows where it wills." The mission is never destruction, but instead is a taking up and fresh building, even if in practice there has not always been full correspondence with this high ideal. And we know well that the conversion that is begun by the mission is a work of grace, in which man must fully find himself again.

For this reason the Church in our time attaches great importance to all that is stated by the Second Vatican Council in its Declaration on Religious Freedom, both the first and the second part of the document. We perceive intimately that the truth revealed to us by God imposes on us an obligation. We have, in particular, a great sense of responsibility for this truth. By Christ's institution the Church is its guardian and teacher, having been endowed with a unique assistance of the Holy Spirit in order to guard and teach it in its most exact integrity. . . . The Declaration on Religious Freedom shows us convincingly that, when Christ and, after him, his Apostles proclaimed the truth that comes not from men but from God ("My teaching is not mine, but his who sent me," that is, the Father's), they preserved, while acting with their full force of spirit, a deep esteem for man, for his intellect, his will, his conscience and his freedom. Thus the human person's dignity itself becomes part of the content of that proclamation, being included not necessarily in words but by an attitude towards it. This attitude seems to fit the special needs of our times. Since man's true freedom is not found in everything that the various systems and individuals see and propagate as freedom, the Church, because of her divine mission, becomes all the more the guardian of this freedom, which is the condition and basis for the human person's true dignity.

Jesus Christ meets the man of every age, including our own, with the same words: "You will know the truth, and the truth will make you free."

III.

The Drafting of *Dignitatis Humanae*

Nicholas J. Healy Jr.

The debate on religious liberty will in later years be considered one of the most important events of a Council already rich enough in important events.

Joseph Ratzinger

I. Introduction

In the apostolic constitution *Humanae salutis,* which officially convoked the Second Vatican Ecumenical Council, Pope John XXIII indicated the basic concern of the upcoming Council:

Today the Church is witnessing a crisis underway within society. While humanity is at the threshold of a new age, tasks of immense seriousness and breadth await the Church, as in the most tragic periods of her history. It is a question in fact of bringing the modern world into contact with the perennial life-giving energies of the Gospel, a world which exalts itself with its technical and scientific conquests, but also bears the effects of a temporal order that some have wanted to reorganize by excluding God.[1]

For John XXIII and the Council fathers that gathered in Rome from 1962 to 1965, the program of "bringing the modern world into contact with the . . . Gospel" involved a twofold task: First, a renewed *traditio* or handing-on of the faith of the Church. "The greatest concern of the Ecumenical Council," said John XXIII in his opening address, "is this: that the sacred deposit of Christian doctrine should be guarded and taught more efficaciously. . . . [A]uthentic doctrine should be studied and expounded through the methods of research and literary forms of modern thought."[2] The second requirement was a discernment of the "signs of the times" that acknowledged both the positive developments of modernity as well as a pervasive forgetfulness of God, or what Pope Paul VI would describe as a tragic "split between the Gospel and culture."[3]

Looking back at the Council from a distance of forty years, Pope Benedict XVI reflected on the guiding vision of John XXIII and the significance of the Council's achievement:

> In the great dispute about man which marks the modern epoch, the Council had to focus in particular on the theme of anthropology. It had to question the relationship between the Church and her faith on the one hand, and man and the contemporary world on the other. The question becomes even clearer if, instead of the generic term "contemporary world," we opt for another that is more precise: the Council had to determine in a new way the relationship between the Church and the modern era.[4]

These words shed light on why the Declaration on Religious Freedom is rightly considered "one of the major texts of the Council."[5] As John Courtney Murray argues, "[F]ormally, it settles only the minor issue of religious freedom. In effect, it defines the Church's basic contemporary view of the world — of human society, of its order of human law and of the functions of the all too human powers that govern it. . . . Therefore the declaration . . . lays down the premise, and sets the focus, of the Church's concern with the secular world."[6]

Murray's claim regarding the importance of *Dignitatis humanae* invites further reflection and elaboration. First, the teaching on religious freedom needs to be situated within the larger context of the trinitarian Christ-centeredness that is the centerpiece of the Council's approach to the relationship between the Church and the modern world.[7] What Murray describes as "the Church's concern with the secular world" finds its source and measure in the life, death, and Resurrection of the Incarnate Son of the Father. In the words of *Gaudium et spes,*

> [The Church] holds that in her most benign Lord and Master can be found the key, the focal point and the goal of man as well as of all hu-

man history. The Church also maintains that beneath all changes there are many realities which do not change and which have their ultimate foundation in Christ, who is the same yesterday, today, and forever (cf. Heb 13:8). Hence, under the light of Christ, the image of the unseen God, the firstborn of every creature (cf. Col 1:15), the Council wishes to speak to all men in order to shed light on the mystery of man and to cooperate in finding the solution to the outstanding problems of our time. (GS, 10)

Secondly, the suggestion that the issue of religious freedom has been "settled" is complicated by the deep disagreements over the nature and ground of religious freedom that divided the proponents of *Dignitatis humanae* and that have accompanied its reception.[8] These differences came to light during the debates on the Council floor and within the subcommission responsible for drafting the Declaration. Between November of 1963 and December of 1965, six distinct drafts of a text on religious freedom were presented to the Council fathers. Two public debates were held, during which some 120 fathers spoke. In addition, over six hundred written interventions were sent to the Secretariat for Promoting Christian Unity, which was responsible for drafting and revising the schema.

There exist several well-documented accounts of the conciliar debates and the redaction history of the Declaration on Religious Freedom.[9] My limited aim in what follows is to provide a brief overview of each successive draft, and to call attention to the some of the important changes introduced into the final text as a result of the public debate and written observations of the Council fathers.

II. The Preparatory Phase

On Pentecost Sunday, June 5, 1960, Pope John XXIII instituted the various commissions that would have responsibility for drafting the texts for the Second Vatican Council.[10] In addition to ten preparatory commissions that roughly corresponded to the ten congregations of the Roman Curia, he established a "Secretariat for Promoting Christian Unity" (SCU) with Cardinal Augustin Bea as its first president. Initially the SCU's purpose was to help other Christians "to follow the work of the Council and to find more easily that path by which to arrive at the unity Jesus Christ sought from his heavenly Father."[11] Under the direction of Bea, and with the encouragement of John XXIII, the Secretariat's role was expanded to include the preparation of schema or draft texts to present to the Council.[12] At the first plenary meeting of the SCU in November of 1960, a subcommission chaired by Bishop Émile De Smedt of Belgium was charged with drafting a document on religious freedom. On December 27, 1960, at a meeting in Fribourg, Switzerland, De Smedt presented a paper that was accepted as a basis for further reflection and elaboration. In the months that followed, the "Fribourg text" was discussed at a plenary session of the SCU and, after further revision, given the title *"Schema Constitutionis de liberatate religiosa."*[13] The document was formally approved at the SCU's meeting of August 26-September 2, 1961 and forwarded to the Central Preparatory Commission.[14] The key affirmation reads as follows:

> The Catholic Church has never admitted and cannot admit the state positively to propose the doctrine of religious indifferentism which states that all religions are of the same value, but it quite approves modern civil societies when, in the practical ordering of civic life, they establish by law that religious freedom and political equality should be granted to the adherents of every religion.[15]

Independently of the work of the SCU, the Theological Commission, headed by Cardinal Alfredo Ottaviani, also drafted a document that touched on the theme of religious freedom. The schema on the Church, *De Ecclesia,* included a chapter titled "On the Relations Between Church and State and On Religious Tolerance."[16] This document, very different in character from the proposal of the SCU, reiterated the traditional idea of the duties of the state toward the Catholic faith:

> The civil power cannot be indifferent with regard to religion. . . . The civil power also, and not only each of the citizens, has the duty of accepting the revelation proposed by the Church itself. Likewise, in its legislation, it must conform itself to the precepts of the natural law and take a strict account of the positive laws, both divine and ecclesiastical, intended to lead men to supernatural beatitude. . . . It devolves seriously upon the civil power to exclude from legislation, government, and public activity everything it would judge to be capable of impeding the Church from attaining its eternal end.[17]

The schema acknowledged that the application of these principles will differ depending on historical circumstances. In a state whose citizens profess the

Catholic faith, "the civil power can regulate and moderate the public manifestations of other cults and defend its citizens against the spreading of false doctrines."[18] At the same time, the common good of the Church and the common good of the state may call for a "just tolerance" of other religions. Thus in "states where a great part of the citizens do not profess the Catholic faith . . . the authorities should concede civil liberty to all forms of worship that are not opposed to natural religion."[19]

The texts of the SCU and of the Theological Commission were submitted for review to the Central Preparatory Commission at the same time, thus "provok[ing] the most dramatic confrontation witnessed by that body."[20] Cardinal Ottaviani sharply criticized the doctrinal content of the *"Schema Constitutionis de liberatate religiosa"* as a departure from Catholic tradition. In addition he questioned whether the SCU had the competence to propose a schema dealing with relations between Church and state.[21] As a result of the clash between Ottaviani and Bea, the issue was remanded to the pope, who created a special mixed commission charged with harmonizing the respective texts of the Theological Commission and the SCU. The proposed commission never met. The SCU continued to revise its own document on religious freedom while unsuccessfully seeking input from the Theological Commission.[22]

During the first session of the Council the bishops were informed of the preparatory work of the SCU on religious freedom along with "a note that spoke of the need to harmonize the text with the section on tolerance in the schema of the Theological Commission."[23] In fact, Cardinal Ottaviani and other members of the Doctrinal Commission (successor to the preparatory Theological Commission) seemed intent on removing the issue of religious freedom from the Council's agenda.[24] In order to ensure that the SCU's schema on religious freedom would survive, the Coordinating Commission approved a decision to incorporate the text into the schema on ecumenism, with the understanding that the Doctrinal Commission would review the document prior to its distribution. Despite repeated requests by the SCU and the Coordinating Commission, the Doctrinal Commission refused to formally review the SCU's text on religious freedom.

In September of 1963, Cardinal Spellman of New York sent a letter in the name of the United States episcopate to the Council moderators asking that the subject of religious freedom be reintroduced to the Council's agenda.[25] Spellman also appealed directly to Pope Paul VI, who responded by admonishing the Doctrinal Commission to complete its work in a timely manner. The Doctrinal Commission acquiesced and scheduled a plenary meeting for November 11, 1963 to discuss the SCU's text on religious freedom. Following a contentious debate, the Commission voted 18 to 5 to allow the text to be distributed to the Council bishops.[26]

III. The First Text (*De Oecumenismo,* Caput V: De Libertate Religiosa)

The first text on religious freedom was presented to the Council fathers on November 19, 1963 as chapter five of the schema on ecumenism. In a lengthy address that introduced the text, Bishop De Smedt offered four principal reasons for the Council to affirm the right to religious freedom:

(i) Truth: The Church must teach and defend the right to religious freedom because of the question of truth, the care of which was committed to her by Christ.

(ii) Defense: The Church cannot remain silent today when almost half of mankind is deprived of religious freedom by atheistic materialism of various kinds.

(iii) Peaceful Social Life: Today in all nations of the world, men, who adhere to different religions or who lack all religious belief, must live together in one and the same human society.

(iv) Ecumenism: Many non-Catholics harbor an aversion against the Church or at least suspect here a kind of Machiavellism because we seem to them to demand the free exercise of religion when Catholics are in a minority in any nation and at the same time refuse and deny the same religious freedom when Catholics are in the majority.[27]

De Smedt proceeded to differentiate the document's affirmation of religious freedom from religious indifferentism or doctrinal relativism: "What therefore is meant in the text by 'religious freedom'? Positively, religious freedom is the right of the human person to the free exercise of religion according to the dictates of conscience. Negatively, it is immunity from all external force in his personal relations with God."[28]

The first draft grounded the right to religious freedom on freedom of conscience and the free character of the act of faith: "For the human person, endowed with conscious and free activity, can fulfill the will of God only to the extent that he perceives the divine law by means of the dictates of his conscience; for this reason, he cannot attain his final end unless he prudently forms judgments of conscience for himself and faithfully follows their dictates."[29] In a key passage, the implication of freedom of conscience for the social and political orders is explained as follows:

> This personal freedom is not truly and effectively acknowledged if it is not permitted to engage in external and public action. In human communities and within civil society, therefore, no one can be deprived of the external exercise of his freedom, provided the rights of others remain secure as well, as demanded by the common good.[30]

Addressing what would become a contentious issue, the first draft indicated that religious freedom may be limited or justly impeded only if it "contradicts the common good, or that objective order that consists in both the rights of God, Creator and Savior, and the inalienable rights and freedoms of the human person."[31]

Due to time constraints, the chapter on religious freedom was not formally discussed during the second session. However, the general discussion on the schema on ecumenism exposed some of the fault lines of the upcoming debate on religious freedom. Several Spanish bishops objected to the content of chapter five on grounds that it was "inopportune" and would expose Catholic faithful to the dangers of proselytism and indifferentism.[32] Cardinal Joseph Ritter of St. Louis and Cardinal Albert Meyer of Chicago, speaking on behalf of the United States episcopate, expressed strong approval of the entire schema on ecumenism, especially the chapter on religious freedom.[33]

IV. The Second Text *(Declaratio prior)*

At the conclusion of the second session on December 2, 1963 Cardinal Bea noted with regret that there had been insufficient time to discuss chapter five of the schema on ecumenism. He requested that written observations and emendations be sent to the SCU by the middle of February 1964. Some 380 written observations were received and examined first by a subcommittee and then at a plenary session of the SCU that met from February 27 to March 7, 1964.[34] Acceding to the request of several bishops, the second draft became a quasi-independent declaration appended to the schema on ecumenism and identified as *Declaratio prior*.[35] It was sent to the Council fathers on April 27, 1964.

The changes introduced into the second draft can be summarized as follows.[36] First, there was an attempt to provide a clearer definition of religious freedom by inserting a new paragraph into the opening section:

> Men and women, made in the image of God and called to fellowship with the divine nature, have both the duty and the honor to follow the will of their Creator and Savior in religious matters, according to the dictates of their conscience. From this derives the right to religious freedom in society, by which men and women are able to practice their religion in private and in public, and cannot be prohibited from practicing it by any kind of coercion. This religious freedom requires that the necessary conditions be promoted in human society in order to enable all men and women, whether individually or within religious groups, to respond to their divine vocation freely and fully.[37]

Second, there was a more explicit statement of the right of groups or communities to religious freedom. Third, drawing on John XXIII's account of the common good in *Mater et magistra* and *Pacem in terris,* the revised draft further elaborated the proper limits to religious freedom: "The exercise of this right to religious freedom cannot be limited except when it seriously contradicts the end of society, which consists in the complex of those conditions of social life by which men and women are able to pursue their own perfection more fully and with greater ease."[38] Fourth, the *Declaratio prior* included new language regarding the incompetence of the state in religious matters: "Civil powers have no direct capacity or competence to determine or regulate the relationship between citizens and their Creator and Savior."[39] Fifth, there was a more explicit treatment of the objective nature of divine laws and the "divine vocation" as the ground of human dignity. Finally, the text concluded with a reflection on the present situation of humanity and the need for peaceful coexistence.

During the opening weeks of the third session, the second draft of the Declaration was formally presented by De Smedt and debated in the Council hall from September 23 to 25, 1964. Forty-three fathers spoke, many in the name of large groups of bishops. Giovanni Miccoli describes the charged atmosphere: "The scholastic technicalities that at times made the course of the debate wearisome did not obscure the real issue or the passionate involvement in the subject; it was an open and at times intensely dramatic clash."[40] The Spanish bishops, supported by key members of the Curia, were united in their fundamental opposition to the text. The core argument put forward by the opponents of the schema was that truth alone has a right to freedom, while error may be "tolerated" for the sake of avoiding a greater evil. Since the Catholic Church is the authentic depository of truth, she alone has the right to complete religious freedom. In an ideal situation, the state should acknowledge the rightful claims of the Catholic Church.[41] Drawing on magisterial teaching from popes Pius IX through Pius XII, several Council bishops argued that key aspects of the text, such as the claim that the state is incompetent in matters of religion, represented a sharp departure from authoritative Catholic teaching.

The question over whether the text on religious freedom represented a genuine development of doctrine or a break with the preceding tradition would remain one of the most contentious issues of the Council.[42] According to John Courtney Murray, *Dignitatis humanae* was "the most controversial document of the whole Council, largely because it raised with sharp emphasis the issue that lay continually below the surface of all the conciliar debates — the issue of the development of doctrine. The notion of development, not the notion of religious freedom, was the real sticking point for many of those who opposed the Declaration even to the end."[43]

The American hierarchy was virtually unanimous in voicing their support of the text. On the first day of the debate, Cardinal Cushing of Boston spoke "in the name of almost all of the bishops of the United States," indicating his "praise and approval" of the schema: "The substance of the doctrine as we have it here is true and solid. . . . [T]he Declaration must remain intact as to its essential meaning."[44] Cardinal Meyer of Chicago spoke of the opportuneness of the text. The people of our time, he said, are awaiting the Church's approval of religious freedom.[45]

Also supporting the text were several Council fathers representing countries with repressive Communist governments. Cardinal König of Vienna called attention to the tragic situation in countries behind the iron curtain, where governments promote atheism and where religious freedom is effectively denied.[46] He urged the Council not to be silent in the face of this injustice.

The intervention of Bishop Dubois of Besançon articulated a core concern of the French episcopate. While generally supportive of the text, Dubois criticized its overly juridical conception of religious freedom.[47] He argued that the Church's affirmation of religious freedom should be based on religious principles drawn from Scripture and the fathers of the Church.

On the final day of the debate, Bishop Karol Wojtyła sounded a theme that would become increasingly important in future redactions of the text:

When dealing with religious freedom in the first sense, the ecumenical sense, we need to emphasize more strongly the connection that exists between freedom and truth. On the one hand, freedom exists for the sake of truth; on the other hand, without truth, freedom cannot achieve its own perfection. Hence the words of our Lord, which sound so clearly for every man: "The truth will set you free." There is no freedom without truth.[48]

The substance of Wojtyła's intervention was supported by Bishop Carlo Colombo of Milan, who had recently served as the private theologian of Pope Paul VI. Like Wojtyła, Colombo indicated that he was in favor of an affirmation of religious freedom, but he wanted a "profound revision of the text, in order to prepare the ground psychologically for it."[49] Given the importance of the theme — religious freedom is the *punctum saliens* for a dialogue between the Church and thinking people of our time — Colombo argued that the teaching on religious freedom needed to be grounded and explained in terms of immutable doctrinal principles such as the obligation and natural right of every human being to seek the truth.

V. The Third Text *(Textus emendatus)*

Following the debate of 23-25 September 1964, the SCU commissioned a subcommittee to revise the text.[50] The committee's work soon was interrupted by an attempt on the part of opponents of the Declaration to remove the issue of religious freedom from the competency of the SCU.[51] In the end a compromise was reached whereby (i) the text on religious freedom would remain under the jurisdiction of the SCU; (ii) the document would be studied by a group of experts chosen from the SCU and the Doctrinal Commission; and (iii) at the appropriate time the text would be sent to the Doctrinal Commission for review.

By the end of October 1964, a new draft had been completed with John Courtney Murray acting as "first scribe." The third draft or *Textus emendatus* was presented as an independent schema bearing the title "Declaration on Religious Freedom or On the Right of the Person and of Communities to Freedom in Religious Matters." The substantially revised text (80 percent new) was structured in four parts: I. The General Principle of Religious Freedom; II. The Teaching on Religious Freedom Derived from Reason; III. Practical Consequences; and IV. The Teaching on Religious Freedom in the Light of Revelation. Whereas the first and second drafts had grounded the right to religious freedom on freedom of conscience, the third draft approaches the idea of religious freedom as a formally juridical concept.[52] Religious freedom is described as "a true right, having its foundation in human dignity, a right that should be acknowledged in the juridical and political structure of society, so that it becomes a civil right."[53] The key premise for the juridical or constitutional argument concerns the total incompetence of the state in religious matters:

> Religious acts, in which men and women privately and publicly order themselves toward God out of a personal, intimate conviction, transcend the temporal and earthly order of things. In performing these acts, therefore, man is not subject to the civil power, whose competence, on account of its end, is restricted to the earthly and temporal order, and whose legislative power extends only to external actions. The public power, therefore, since it cannot pass judgment on interior religious acts, likewise cannot coerce or impede the public exercise of religion, provided that the demands of public order are preserved. Man's freedom should be acknowledged as far as possible and should not be restricted except insofar as it is necessary. The public power completely exceeds its limits if it involves itself in any way in the governing of minds or the care of souls.[54]

Whereas earlier drafts had discussed the proper limits of religious freedom in terms of the "common good" or "the end of society," the *Textus emendatus* introduces the idea of "public order" as the limiting principle: "The exercise of religion in society should be immune from the coercive intervention of the state, except when such exercise seriously harms the public order, either by disturbing the public peace, by violating public morality, or by offending the civil rights of others."[55]

The third draft also includes an annotated overview of the historical development of the Church's teaching on religious freedom, from the nineteenth-century papal condemnations of liberalism through John XXIII's *Pacem in terris*. Faced with new challenges, "the Church has continued to unfold a more ample teaching on social and civil matters, from principles that remain always the same in their meaning and purpose, bringing forth from out of her treasury things both new and old."[56] The principal novelty undergirding the development of the Church's teaching is "[t]he fact that the human person is and must be the foundation, end, and subject of all social life," which is "asserted more strongly today in the teaching of the Church."[57] Coincident with this focus on the human person is a new understanding of the nature and purpose of government: "[I]t is more clearly affirmed today that the chief function of the public power consists in protecting, cultivating, and defending the natural rights of all citizens."[58]

Finally, under the heading "The Teaching on Religious Freedom in the Light of Revelation," the *Textus emendatus* affirms the importance of the freedom of the Church and the free character of the act of faith. Arguing that religious freedom "has deep roots in the word of God," the text includes a reflection on the example of Christ and the Apostles who "strove to convert men and women to God, not through coercion or by dishonest means, but by the power of the word of God."[59]

On the day the *Textus emendatus* was presented, the Secretary General of the Council announced that a vote on the schema would take place in two days on November 19, 1964. However, a number of Council bishops requested that the vote be delayed in light of the fact that the proposed Declaration on Religious Freedom was not simply an amended text but a substantially new document. More time was needed to study the new schema. On November 19, Cardinal Tisserant announced that, due to the concerns raised by several fathers, the Council of Presidents had decided against holding a vote. This announcement, which forms part of the so-called "Black Week" of the third session, provoked a strong reaction within the Council hall.[60] The majority feared that the postponement of the vote represented an illegitimate maneuver on the part of a minority that was irreconcilably opposed to religious freedom. Proponents of the Declaration immediately began to gather signatures to petition Pope Paul VI that a vote take place the following day.[61] Paul VI declined to intervene, but he did assure Cardinals Meyer, Ritter, and Léger (who presented the petition signed by several hundred Council fathers) that the Declaration on Religious Freedom would be the first item on the agenda at the start of the fourth and final session.

VI. The Fourth Text — *Textus reemendatus*

When he announced the decision to postpone the vote on religious freedom, Cardinal Tisserant indicated that observations on the schema should be sent to the SCU by January 31, 1965. By mid-February, SCU had received

218 written observations.[62] The subcommittee tasked with reviewing these interventions included Msgrs. Cantero, De Smedt, Primeau, and Shehan, with Congar, Feiner, Hamer, Murray, Pavan, Stransky, and Thijssen serving as experts.[63] In March of 1965, a revised schema or *Textus reemendatus* was approved at a plenary session of the SCU and sent to the Doctrinal Commission for review. After further revision, the text was distributed to the Council fathers in May of 1965, together with a report that recalled the origins of the Declaration, elaborated on the method and principles of the schema, and anticipated possible objections.[64]

The fourth draft maintained the basic structure of the preceding text while changing the headings of the four parts. Among the more significant changes introduced into the fourth draft are the following:

(i) The lengthy historical narrative on the practice of religious freedom in the nineteenth and twentieth centuries, and the teaching of the Church in response to this practice, was replaced with a summary statement that "attending anew to her divinely inspired tradition of teachings, [the Church] draws forth from out of her treasury things both old and new."[65]

(ii) In order to address the persistent criticism that the schema represented a departure from the Church's established doctrine, the *Textus reemendatus* affirmed that "the principle of religious freedom . . . leaves intact the Catholic teaching on the one true religion and the one Church of Christ."[66]

(iii) In response to a concern that the limiting principle of "public order" was open to abuse in the hands of repressive regimes, the fourth draft further elaborated this concept:

> Civil society has the right to protect itself against abuses that could be committed in the name of religious freedom. It belongs especially to the civil power to afford protection of this sort, not in an arbitrary fashion, but according to juridical norms that are required by the needs of public order. Public order is that good of society that concerns the adequate care of public peace, the due preservation of public morality, and the effective protection of the equal rights of all citizens and the peaceful settlement of conflict of rights. This good is in fact so necessary to the whole society that any acts that inflict serious injury upon it must be suppressed. The exercise of religion in society, therefore, cannot be legitimately prohibited by the coercive intervention of the civil power unless such exercise disturbs the public peace, violates public morality, or offends the rights of others.[67]

(iv) New language was inserted addressing the delicate issue of the official state recognition or "establishment" of Catholicism as codified in the concordats between the Holy See and various predominantly Catholic countries such as Italy, Portugal, Spain, and the Dominican Republic:

> This practice of religious freedom does not prevent one religious community from being granted special recognition in the juridical order of the state, in light of the historical circumstances of the people, provided that at the same time the right to freedom in religious matters be acknowledged and observed for all citizens and religious communities.[68]

(v) Finally, the *Textus reemendatus* expanded the section titled "The Teaching on Religious Freedom in the Light of Revelation," with a reflection on how religious freedom is exemplified in salvation history. The text affirms that religious freedom "also has roots in divine revelation, through which the dignity of the human person first began to be made manifest in all its fullness."[69] In addition, new material was added to the conclusion regarding the promotion of genuine freedom:

> Religious freedom should therefore be devoted and ordered to this end, that men and women may be able to pursue more easily that noble freedom to which they are called by God. For this reason, this Vatican Council urges all men and women, especially those who are responsible for educating others, to be diligent in forming human beings who are obedient to legitimate authority and who are lovers of genuine freedom; men and women, that is, who by their own counsel decide matters in the light of truth.[70]

As promised, the Declaration on Religious Freedom was the first item on the agenda for the final session of the Council. Following a brief report by De Smedt, the debate began on Wednesday, September 15 and would continue through Tuesday, September 21. The first speaker was Cardinal Spellman, who declared his unqualified support for a Declaration that meets the needs of modern times: "[T]oday mankind is united in wanting to give full recognition to the dignity of the human person."[71] In the days to follow, seven other fathers from the United States echoed and amplified Spellman's strong endorsement of the Declaration, with a series of interventions planned and coordinated by John Courtney Murray.[72]

The opposition renewed their criticism of the text on multiple fronts.

Cardinal Ruffini argued that the *Textus reemendatus* failed to distinguish between true and false religions and that it ignored or undermined the duty of public authorities to render worship to God and to favor the Catholic Church.[73] The Spanish episcopate, together with curial Cardinals Ottaviani and Browne, continued to make the case that the Declaration did not accord with the received teaching of the Church. For example, Msgr. Modrego y Casáus declared that "the teaching in the schema certainly contradicts . . . the explicit teaching of the Roman pontiffs up to and including John XXIII."[74] Cardinal Ottaviani concurred and accused the text of offering solutions to disputed questions that are "contrary to common teaching."[75] Ottaviani argued that, in order to bring the text "in accord with the earlier teaching of the Catholic Church," the document should open with a solemn proclamation that "the Catholic Church has a true, innate, objective right to its freedom, because it has a divine origin and a divine mission."[76] Finally, several fathers objected to the selective use of scriptural citations to support the idea of religious freedom.

As with the first debate in the preceding session, the Council bishops from countries with Communist governments indicated their strong support for the Declaration. Cardinal Slipyj of Lviv, Cardinal Šeper of Zagreb, Cardinal Wyszyński of Warsaw, and Cardinal Beran of Prague spoke from experience regarding the evil effects of the denial of religious freedom. Josef Beran, who was imprisoned by the Germans at Dachau and then by the Communist Czechoslovakian regime from 1949 until 1963, was speaking at the Council for the first time and his words made a strong impression. After recalling the wounds inflicted by the denial of religious freedom in his native land (e.g., the burning of Jan Hus and the imposition of Catholicism by the Habsburgs after the Battle of White Mountain), he concluded: "Thus history, too, warns us that at this Council the principle of religious freedom and freedom of conscience must be set forth clearly and without any restriction flowing from opportunistic considerations."[77] At the same time, several bishops from behind the iron curtain, especially the Polish episcopate, reiterated their concern that the limiting principle of "public order" was open to abuse by Communist governments.

Meanwhile, a parallel debate was unfolding behind the scenes among the Council moderators over the question of whether to hold a vote on the schema on religious freedom. Opponents of the Declaration were opposed to the idea of voting, proposing instead that the document be returned to the SCU or preferably to a new mixed commission for further revision. On September 20, the governing bodies of the Council (moderators, Council of Presidents, and Coordinating Commission) held a meeting where it was decided against holding a vote. Only the direct intervention of Paul VI, who summoned the moderators to a meeting on the morning of September 21, ensured that a vote would be held.[78]

On September 21, after five days of discussion, the debate was closed and the following resolution was placed before the fathers: "Is it agreeable to the Fathers that the *Textus reemendatus* on religious freedom should be taken as the basis for a definitive declaration, still needing to be further perfected in accordance with Catholic doctrine concerning the true religion and proposed amendments which will be subsequently approved according to the norms of Council procedure?"[79] The unusual language of the resolution, which bears witness to the concerns of the schema's critics, was chosen to ensure the largest possible majority. The result of the voting exceeded the expectations of those in favor of the Declaration: with 2,222 fathers present, the resolution received 1,997 votes in favor *(placet)* and 224 against *(non placet)*. "This week," wrote Bishop Colombo, "will remain famous in the history of the Council as the week in which the great majority of the fathers gave their substantial approval to the schema on religious freedom."[80]

The day following the vote witnessed two key interventions that would guide the final revisions to the text. According to the rules of the Council, oral interventions were permitted after the close of debate only when an individual was speaking in the name of more than seventy fathers. Karol Wojtyła, speaking in the name of the bishops of Poland, noted the lack of integration between Part Two, "The Teaching on Religious Freedom Derived from Reason," and Part Three, "The Teaching on Religious Freedom in the Light of Revelation." "It seems better, therefore, not to separate reason and revelation so much in the titles of these sections. This kind of separation remains too steeped in scholastic methods. The truth is that it is in revelation that the true and profound teaching on religious freedom is contained."[81] Thus, "it would not suffice simply to repeat what has already been said about religious freedom in the civil legislation of many nations, and in international declarations as well."[82] Instead, the Church's teaching on religious freedom should be drawn from Revelation, and "at the same time [be] in harmony with sound reason."[83] Secondly, Wojtyła noted the fundamental importance of the concept of "responsibility," which is "the culmination and the necessary complement of freedom."[84] Developing his earlier intervention on the relationship between freedom and truth, Wojtyła suggested that an explicit reflection on each individual's responsibility before God would help bring to light "the objective value of religion, which ultimately comes from the truth itself."[85]

Bishop Ancel of Lyons, speaking in the name of one hundred French bishops and thirty-one Indonesian bishops, emphasized the need to explain more clearly the connection between the obligation to seek the truth and religious freedom itself. Gilles Routhier notes that this intervention "made a deep impression on Paul VI and would win Ancel membership in the commission that would revise the text."[86] In light of its importance for the final redaction of the Declaration, Ancel's intervention is worth citing at length:

> Several times the request has been made that the *ontological foundation* of religious freedom be set forth. For the argument stemming simply from the dignity of the human person seems to some to be insufficient.
>
> Moreover, the connection that exists between the obligation to seek the truth and religious freedom itself has not yet been made clear. To be sure, we have often heard that man has an obligation to seek the truth; likewise, we have heard that religious freedom presents no obstacle to this obligation; but at no time, unless I am mistaken, has the positive connection between these two been made clear.
>
> Thus, in a few words, I would like to indicate what this ontological foundation is, and in this way to show the necessary connection that exists between the obligation to seek the objective truth and religious freedom itself.
>
> My proposition is as follows: the obligation to seek the truth is itself the ontological foundation of religious freedom, as set forth in our text.
>
> For in fact every man, because he is a human being, endowed with reason and free will, is bound to seek the objective truth, and to hold fast to it and order his whole life according to its demands.
>
> All those who seek truth and justice with their whole heart, even non-believers, can agree with us on this principle.
>
> On the other hand, because it does not have its foundation in any subjective disposition, but in the very nature of man, this principle has a strictly universal validity.
>
> Ultimately, this principle is explicitly affirmed by Scripture in countless ways and in different forms.
>
> Nevertheless, in order for man to be able to satisfy this obligation in the way God wills, that is, in a way consistent with his nature, he must enjoy not only psychological freedom but also immunity from all co-

ercion. Not only is there no opposition between religious freedom and the obligation to seek the truth, therefore, but in fact religious freedom has its foundation in this obligation itself, and the obligation to seek the truth in turn requires religious freedom.

> ... In this way, moreover, the opinion of those who have been more open to religious freedom will be supported, while greater assurance will also be given to those who have been apprehensive in this regard, and not without reason in this time of growing indifferentism and subjectivism.[87]

At an audience with De Smedt on September 30, 1965, Paul VI offered guidelines for revision. Routhier summarizes the content of a handwritten note of De Smedt titled "instructions de Paul VI pour la révision du texte": "to emphasize the obligation of seeking the truth; to present the traditional teaching of the ecclesiastical magisterium; to avoid basing religious freedom solely on freedom of conscience; to state the doctrine in such a way that the lay state would not think itself dispensed from its obligations to the Church; to specify the authority of the declaration (doctrinal, dogmatic, juridical, or practical?)."[88] Each of these concerns would be addressed in the final stage of revision.

VII. The Fifth Text — *(Textus recognitus)*

Following the debate and vote of September 21, the SCU returned the text to an expanded subcommission, which began its work of reviewing some 200 written interventions.[89] The commission worked at a furious pace. On October 5, Murray became seriously ill and had to desist from working;[90] Congar too was exhausted to the point of illness.[91] By October 11, a new draft was ready for review by the SCU and, following further revision, circulated to select members of the Doctrinal Commission for study. Pope Paul VI showed a particular interest in the work of the subcommittee charged with revising the text.

The fifth draft, identified as the *Textus recognitus* and bearing the slightly revised subtitle "On the Rights of the Person and of Communities to Social and Civil Freedom," was distributed to the Council fathers on October 22, 1965. The text is divided into a Preface (a. 1); Part One, "The General Principle of Religious Freedom" (aa. 2-8); Part Two, "Religious Freedom in the Light of Revelation" (aa. 9-14); and a "Conclusion" (a. 15).

Among the more significant changes introduced into the fifth draft are the following:

(i) An affirmation in the opening article that the "one true religion subsists in the Catholic and apostolic Church, to whom the Lord Jesus committed the task of spreading it among all people. . . . Since all men and women are bound to seek the truth, especially in those things concerning the worship of God, and to embrace and hold fast to it once it is known, they are also bound by a sacred duty to embrace and profess the Catholic faith, insofar as they are able to acknowledge it."[92]

(ii) Following the suggestions of Msgrs. Ancel, Colombo, and Wojtyła, new language was introduced grounding the right to religious freedom in the obligation to seek the truth:

> It is in accord with their dignity that all men and women, because they are persons, endowed with reason and free will and therefore privileged with personal responsibility, are impelled by their nature and bound by a moral obligation to seek the truth, especially the truth concerning religion. They are also bound to hold fast to the truth once it is known, and to order their whole life in accord with its demands. They cannot satisfy this obligation in a way that is in keeping with their own nature, however, unless they enjoy psychological freedom as well as immunity from external coercion. Nevertheless, religious freedom does not have its foundation in a subjective disposition, but in the very nature of the human person. Consequently, the right to immunity persists even for those who do not satisfy their obligation to seek the truth and to hold fast to it, provided that legitimate public order is preserved, and that the rights of others are not violated.[93]

As a result of these revisions, the principal argument for religious freedom shifted away from the juridical principle regarding the incompetency of the state in religious matters towards an anthropological and theological account of the human person's relationship to truth.[94] The "negative" aspect of religious freedom, i.e., immunity from coercion, is a consequence of the human person's natural ordination to the truth (and ultimately to God). Conversely, participation in the truth requires freedom.[95]

(iii) Regarding the nature and purpose of government: The sentence in the preceding draft that had restricted the competency of the civil power to "the earthly and temporal order" was deleted. Furthermore, the corollary claim that civil authority would "exceed its limits if it involves itself in those matters that concern the very ordination of man to God" was revised to read: "The civil power must therefore be said to exceed its limits if it either impedes or directs those matters that by their nature transcend the earthly and temporal order of things."[96] Finally, whereas the preceding draft had admonished "civil society" to provide favorable conditions for religion, the *Textus recognitus* clarifies that it is the responsibility of the state *(potestas civilis)* to "provide favorable conditions for fostering religious life."[97]

(iv) In response to concerns that the limiting principle of "public order" was vulnerable to misuse, the *Textus recognitus* inserted new language regarding limits that are determined by "the needs of a public order *grounded in the objective moral order.*"[98]

(v) The much-disputed passage treating the legal recognition of religion was qualified with a conditional "if": "*If*, in light of a people's historical circumstances, special civil recognition is granted to one religious community in the juridical order of the state, it is necessary at the same time that the right to freedom in religious matters be acknowledged and observed for all citizens and religious communities."[99]

(vi) Addressing the concern to avoid a false separation of reason and revelation, the fifth draft replaced the heading "The Teaching on Religious Freedom Derived from Reason" with "The General Principle of Religious Freedom." The fifth draft also elaborated the relationship between religious freedom and revealed truth:

> [A]lthough revelation does not expressly affirm the right to immunity from external coercion in religious matters, it nonetheless brings to light the dignity of the human person in all its fullness. It manifests the respect Christ showed for the freedom with which man is to fulfill his duty of believing the word of God, and it educates us in the spirit that the disciples of such a Master should adopt and follow in all things. All of this casts light on the general principles which ground the teaching of this Declaration on religious freedom.[100]

Voting on the fifth schema took place on October 26 and 27, 1965, according to the customary method of first ascertaining basic approval or disapproval of sections of the text with a vote of *placet* or *non placet*. This was followed by a second round of votes that allowed the fathers to express reservations by voting *placet, non placet,* or *placet juxta modum*. The results are listed below, with the first round in the left hand column and the second round on the right:

Article 1 (1st vote):
   placet   2031
   non placet 193

Articles 2-3 (2nd vote):
   placet   2000
   non placet 228

Articles 4-5 (3rd vote):
   placet   2026
   non placet 206

Articles 6-8 (4th vote):
   placet   2034
   non placet 186

Articles 9-10 (7th vote):
   placet   2087
   non placet 146

Articles 11-12 (8th vote):
   placet   1979
   non placet 254

Articles 13-15 (9th vote):
   placet   2107
   non placet 127

Articles 1-5 (5th vote):
   placet   1539
   non placet   65
   placet juxta modum 534

Article 6-8 (6th vote)
   placet   1715
   non-placet   68
   placet juxta modum 373

Articles 9-12 (10th vote):
   placet   1751
   non placet   60
   placet juxta modum 417

Articles 13-15 (11th vote):
   placet   1843
   non placet   47
   placet juxta modum 307

VIII. The Official Declaration *(Textus denuo recognitus)*

The voting on October 26 and 27 revealed that a strong majority (about 90 percent) was in favor of the Declaration. At the same time, a significant number of fathers wished to introduce revisions or modifications. The subcommittee of the SCU patiently worked through numerous proposals to amend the Declaration while resisting attempts to recast a schema that had been approved as a whole and in each part by the required two-thirds majority.[101] The final text, *textus denuo recognitus,* was completed on November 6 and approved at a plenary session of the

SCU on November 8 and 9. Among the changes introduced into the sixth and final text:

(i) In the opening paragraph, a sentence from the third draft was re-inserted, linking the deepened sense of the dignity of the human person in our time and the demand for religious freedom: "They also demand that juridical limits be set to the public power, in order that the rightful freedom of persons and associations not be excessively restricted."[102]

(ii) Language regarding "the Catholic teaching on . . . the moral duty individuals have toward the Church" was revised to "the traditional Catholic teaching on the moral duty individuals *and society* have toward the true religion and the one Church of Christ."[103]

(iii) The sixth draft introduced new language regarding the purpose or end of government as well as the state's responsibility for religion. Where the preceding draft had asserted that the "civil power must therefore be said to exceed its limits if it either impedes or directs those matters that by their nature transcend the earthly and temporal order of things," the text was revised to read:

> The civil power, therefore, whose proper end is the care of the temporal common good, should in fact acknowledge and show favor to the religious life of its citizens; but this power must be said to exceed its limits if it presumes either to direct or to impede religious acts.[104]

In an important *relatio* introducing the *Textus denuo recognitus,* De Smedt indicated that these revisions were added in order to address the underlying concern of some fathers that the teaching of the Declaration represented a departure from earlier Catholic teaching:

> [W]hile the papal documents up to Leo XIII insisted more on the moral duty of public powers toward the true religion, the recent Supreme Pontiffs, while retaining this doctrine, complement it by highlighting another duty of the same powers, namely, that of observing the exigencies of the dignity of the human person in religious matters, as a necessary element of the common good. The text presented to you today recalls more clearly (see numbers 1 and 3) the duties of the public power toward the true religion *(Textus hodie vobis praesentatus officia potestatis publicae erga verum religionem claris recalit);* from which it is manifest that this part of the doctrine has not been overlooked.[105]

The revisions to the final text on the state's responsibility for religion, read in light of De Smedt's official *relatio,* demonstrate a decisive shift away from John Courtney Murray's understanding of the incompetency of the state in religious matters.

(iv) Acknowledging the concerns of Cardinal Wyszyński and the Polish episcopate, the final text further qualified the limiting principle of "public order" in terms of the objective moral order. Whereas the preceding draft described "legitimate public order" and "true public order," both of these texts were replaced with "*just* public order."[106]

The *textus denuo recognitus* was distributed to the fathers on November 17 and a vote was scheduled for November 19. After a series of votes on each section of the text, there was a vote on the text as a whole: the result was 1954 *placet* and 249 *non placet.* All that remained was a final vote at a public session of the Council. On December 7, 1965, the day before the conclusion of the Council, the Declaration on Religious Freedom was formally approved with 2308 positive and 70 negative votes.

IX. Conclusion

In an essay submitted to the Ante-preparatory Commission in December of 1959, the young auxiliary bishop of Kraków, Karol Wojtyła, expressed a hope that the upcoming Council would focus its attention on the mystery of the human person as created in the image of God and redeemed in Christ.[107] The crucial issue of our time, Wojtyła suggested, is the human person, a unique being who participates in the material cosmos but who also has intense spiritual longings — a being who is destined to participate by grace in the very life of the Trinity. According to Wojtyła, not only the faithful, but the entire world wanted to hear from the upcoming Council what the Church had to say about the human person and about the distinctiveness of "Christian personalism."[108]

Wojtyła's request found a surpassing answer in the theological vision of Christian humanism outlined in the major texts of the Second Vatican Council, especially the Pastoral Constitution on the Church in the Modern World and the Declaration on Religious Freedom. In the opening words of *Dignitatis humanae,* the Council fathers noted that "[m]en and women of our time are becoming more conscious every day of the dignity of the human person."[109] What is the ultimate ground of this dignity, and in what sense does this dignity require an acknowledgment of the intrinsic good of human freedom in the social order?

"Search[ing] the sacred tradition and teaching of the Church," the

Council fathers sought to "develop the teaching of the recent popes on the inviolable rights of the human person."[110] The human person has a right to religious freedom: "[N]o one is [to be] forced to act against his conscience in religious matters, or prevented from acting according to his conscience, in private or in public."[111] This right to religious freedom "has its foundation in the very dignity of the human person, as known from both the revealed word of God and reason itself."[112]

This solemn declaration of an ecumenical council was the fruit of what John Courtney Murray described as "the greatest argument on religious freedom in all history."[113] From the draft text prepared by the Secretariat for Promoting Christian Unity in 1961 through the six versions of the schema presented to the Council fathers, the Declaration on Religious Freedom faced steep challenges and objections. Among those who supported the Declaration, significant differences emerged regarding the meaning and ground of religious freedom, the relationship between freedom and truth, and the nature and purpose of the political authority. As a result of the conciliar debate, the final document was significantly enriched and deepened. Perhaps the most important revision concerns the relationship between freedom and truth. In the seminal words of Bishop Ancel, "[T]he obligation to seek the truth is itself the ontological foundation of religious freedom."[114] Or, as stated by Bishop Wojtyła, "[T]here is no freedom without truth."[115]

Fifty years later, the teaching of *Dignitatis humanae* has lost none of its importance for the Church's encounter with the modern world. The affirmation of religious freedom bears witness to the transcendent dignity of the human person and the unity of truth and freedom that is ultimately grounded in the mystery of Christ. There is no freedom without truth. Interpreting and developing the teaching of *Dignitatis humanae*, Pope Benedict XVI agrees wholeheartedly and adds *there is no truth without freedom*. The truth, he writes,

> cannot unfold except in an otherness open to God, who wishes to reveal his own otherness in and through my human brothers and sisters. Hence it is not fitting to state in an exclusive way: "I possess the truth." The truth is not possessed by anyone; it is always a gift which calls us to undertake a journey of ever closer assimilation to truth. Truth can only be known and experienced in freedom; for this reason we cannot impose truth on others; truth is disclosed only in an encounter of love.[116]

Openness to truth and perfect goodness, openness to God, is rooted
In human nature; it confers full dignity on each individual and is the
guarantee of full mutual respect between persons. Religious freedom
should be understood, then, not merely as immunity from coercion,
but even more fundamentally as an ability to order one's own choices in
accordance with truth.[117]

The great achievement of *Dignitatis humanae* is to affirm and uphold the
dignity of the human person who is created in love and called to live in
communion with the truth.

Notes

1. AAS 54 (1962), 6.
2. John XXIII, "Opening Address of the Second Vatican Council," October 11, 1962.
3. Paul VI, *Evangelii nuntiandi,* 20.
4. Benedict XVI, "Address to the Roman Curia," December 22, 2005.
5. Paul VI, "Closing Message of the Council," December 8, 1965 (AAS 58 [1966], 10).
One day earlier, during an audience granted to delegates from various international organizations, Paul VI said:

> In a declaration that will undoubtedly remain one of the greatest documents of the
> Council, the Church echoes the aspiration to civil and social freedom in religious
> matters, so universally felt today; i.e., that no one should be forced to believe; that no
> longer should anyone be prevented from believing or professing his or her faith, since
> it is a fundamental right of the human person. (AAS 58 [1966], 74)

6. John Courtney Murray, "The Declaration on Religious Freedom," in *Bridging the
Sacred and the Secular: Selected Writings of John Courtney Murray, S.J.,* ed. J. Leon Hooper, S.J.
(Washington, DC: Georgetown University Press, 1994), 193. As reported by Yves Congar in *My
Journal of the Council* [= *Journal*] (Collegeville, MN: Liturgical Press, 2012), 795, Pope Paul VI
had a similar view of the significance of *Dignitatis humanae.* In his diary entry of October 1,
1965, Congar writes: "De Smedt gave an account of the fifty-minute audience he had had [with
Paul VI] yesterday. The Pope said to him: this is a major document. It establishes the attitude
of the Church for several centuries. The world is waiting for it."
7. In his "Opening Address" at the start of the second session on 29 September 1963,
Pope Paul VI confirmed the Christocentric orientation of the Council:

> From what point, dear brethren, do we set out? . . . What is the road we intend to follow?
> What is the goal we propose to ourselves? These three very simple and at the same time
> very important questions have, as we well know, only one answer, namely that here
> at this very hour we should proclaim Christ to ourselves and to the world around us;
> Christ our beginning, Christ our life and guide, Christ our hope and our end. . . . Let
> no other light be shed on this Council, but Christ the light of the world! Let no other

truth be of interest to our minds, but the words of the Lord, our only Master! Let no other aspiration guide us but to be absolutely faithful to him!

8. It should be noted that there were, in a large sense, three distinct positions among the fathers regarding religious freedom: (i) those who opposed the Council's issuing a document on religious freedom; (ii) those who supported such a document, but insisted that the document tie the right to religious freedom to the human person's relation and obligation to God (freedom as ordered to truth); and (iii) those who supported religious freedom, but thought this right should rather be conceived in juridical terms. In *John Paul II and the Legacy of Dignitatis Humanae* (Washington, DC: Georgetown University Press, 2002), Hermínio Rico compares and contrasts the two main positions within the conciliar majority that supported the Declaration on Religious Freedom: the so-called "French" and "American" schools (ii. and iii. in the above schema). For an account of the metaphysical and theological issues embedded in these two distinct approaches to religious freedom, see the essay by David L. Schindler, "Freedom, Truth, and Human Dignity: An Interpretation of *Dignitatis Humanae* on the Right to Religious Freedom," in the present volume.

9. Cf. *inter alia, History of Vatican II,* vols. 1-5, ed. Giuseppe Alberigo (Maryknoll, NY: Orbis, 1995-2006); Dominique Gonnet, *La Liberté Religieuse à Vatican II: La contribution de John Courtney Murray* (Paris: Cerf, 1994); Jérôme Hamer, "Histoire du Texte de la Déclaration," in *La Liberté Religieuse* (Paris: Cerf, 1967); Pietro Pavan, "Declaration on Religious Freedom," in *Commentary on the Documents of the Second Vatican Council,* vol. 4, ed. H. Vorgrimler (New York: Herder & Herder, 1969), 49-86; Richard Regan, *Conflict and Consensus: Religious Freedom and the Second Vatican Council* (New York: Macmillan, 1967); Silvio Scatena, "Lo Schema Sulla Libertà Religiosa: Momenti e Passaggi dalla Preparazione del Concilio all Secondo Intersessione," in *Experience, Organizations and Bodies at Vatican* II (Leuven: Biliotheek van Faculteit Godgeleerdheid, 1999), 387-417; Jan Grootaers, "Paul VI et la déclaration conciliaire sur la liberté religieuse *Dignitatis humanae,*" in *Paolo VI e il rapporto Chiesa-mondo al Concilio* (Brescia: Istituto Paolo VI, 1991), 85-125.

10. Cf. John XXIII, *Superno Dei nutu* (AAS 52 [1960], 433-37). For a detailed account of the history of the various preparatory commissions, see the chapter by Joseph Komonchak, "The Struggle for the Council During the Pre-Preparation of Vatican II," in Alberigo, vol. 1, 167-356.

11. AAS 52 (1960), 436.

12. Cf. Thomas Stransky, "The Foundation of the Secretariat for Promoting Christian Unity," in *Vatican II Revisited by Those Who Were There,* ed. Alberic Stacpoole (Minneapolis: Winston Press, 1986).

13. Cf. Hamer, "Histoire du texte," 53-60; M. Lamberigts, "Msgr Emiel-Jozef De Smedt, Bishop of Bruges, and the Second Vatican Council," in *Experience,* 431-69.

14. ADP II/4 676-84. Cf. Alberigo, vol. 1, 298.

15. ADP II/4, 680.

16. ADP II/4, 657-72.

17. ADP II/4, 658-59.

18. ADP II/4, 660.

19. ADP II/4, 660.

20. Alberigo, vol. 1, 299. The meeting to discuss these two texts was held on June 18, 1962.

21. The issue of the competency of the SCU would only be resolved during the first

session of the Council, when John XXIII raised the Secretariat to the same rank as the Council commissions, thereby empowering it to submit the various schema that it had prepared.

22. Cf. Alberigo, vol. 1, 299-300; vol. 3, 275-88.

23. Alberigo, vol. 3, 277.

24. Cf. Regan, *Conflict and Consensus,* 30-36; Alberigo, vol. 3, 279-81.

25. Cf. Alberigo, vol. 3, 280; also, Pelotte, *John Courtney Murray,* 82f.

26. Congar, who did not attend the meeting, provides the following account of the discussion: "[T]he experts who spoke were Gagnebet, K. Rahner, Häring, Murray, and Lio. . . . Cardinal Browne, Ottaviani, and, at the beginning Parente, attacked the text violently. But in the end . . . the vote gave a majority of 18 in favour, with 5 against and one abstention. . . . It is a fact: every time there is a vote, the result is favourable!" (*Journal,* 420).

27. AS II/5, 485-95; cited in *Council Daybook: Vatican II, Sessions 1 and 2,* ed. Floyd Anderson (Washington, DC: National Catholic Welfare Conference, 1965), 277-78.

28. AS II/5, 485-95.

29. *Caput* V, 3 (AS II/5, 434).

30. *Caput* V, 5 (AS II/5, 435).

31. *Caput* V, 5 (AS II/5, 436).

32. See, for example, Cardinal de Arriba y Castro, AS II/5, 530-31.

33. AS II/5, 536-38 (Ritter); AS II/5, 597 (Meyer).

34. For an analysis of these written interventions, see Hamer, "Histoire du Texte"; and Regan, *Conflict and Consensus,* 53-72.

35. In the spring of 1964, the Central Commission decided that chapters four and five of the schema on ecumenism should become independent declarations. Chapter four, *"De Judaeis,"* became the *Declaratio altero.* Chapter five, *"De libertate religiosa,"* became the *Declaratio prior.*

36. In a *Relatio* introducing the *Declaratio prior* (AS III/2, 345-46), the SCU summarized the criteria that guided the revision of the text. Several of the changes noted here are based on this *Relatio super declarationem de liberate religiosa,* as summarized in Alberigo, vol. 4, 104.

37. *Declaratio prior,* 26 (AS III/2, 317).

38. *Declaratio prior,* 29 (AS III/2, 320).

39. *Declaratio prior,* 30 (AS III/2, 321).

40. Alberigo, vol. 4, 108-9.

41. The words of Bishop Ortiz of Tuy-Vigo can be taken as representative of the concerns of the Spanish episcopate: "When a state declares itself to be Catholic . . . it is simply showing in solemn manner its obedience to the divine law, its determination publicly to offer God the worship owed to him, and its obligation to aid the Church by its own actions" (AS III/2, 438).

42. Yves Congar, a firm proponent of religious freedom, records his uneasiness in his diary entry of September 24, 1964:

> I spend the afternoon . . . studying the *De libertate religious* and the reactions it has aroused. I remain uneasy. This text is, in the end, premature. It sweeps the place entirely clean of what had been there, that is, of the manner in which this matter has been spoken of hitherto, and replaces all that with something else. This can perhaps be done, but it should be done only after mature reflection. But there has not been time for sufficient reflection. There is some truth in the objections raised against the text, in the criticisms

of Fr. de Broglie. What is required is addition, *augere vetera novis* [to augment the old by means of the new], not substitution pure and simple. But, on the other hand, in the former position, there is something of the "theologico-political treatise," closely connected to the times, to Christendom and its after-effects, that must also be subjected to criticism and from which we need to be set free. (*Journal*, 592)

43. *The Documents of Vatican II*, ed. Walter M. Abbott, S.J., and Joseph Gallagher (New York: America, 1966), 673.

44. AS III/2, 361-62.

45. AS III/2, 366-68.

46. AS III/2, 468-70.

47. AS III/2, 505-7.

48. Wojtyła, Intervention 2 (AS III/2, 530-32). For an account of how Wojtyła conceived the connection between religious freedom in an ecumenical context and religious freedom "in the civil sense," see Schindler's essay in the present volume, section I.2.i.

49. AS III/2, 554-57.

50. Subcommittee members included De Smedt, Hamer, Murray, Pavan, and Willebrands.

51. See Alberigo, vol. 4, 166-93. On October 9, 1964, Cardinal Bea received a letter from the Archbishop Felici, the secretary general of the Council, informing him that, by wish of the Holy Father, the text on religious freedom would be rewritten by a new mixed commission. Four members from the Doctrinal Commission were announced as members of the new mixed commission: Cardinal Michael Browne, Msgrs. Marcel Lefebvre and Carlo Colombo, and Rev. Aniceto Fernandez. Three of the four members of the proposed mixed commission were outspoken opponents of the SCU's text on religious freedom. Fearing that the Declaration was being removed from the jurisdiction of the SCU, several Cardinals gathered at the residence of Cardinal Frings on the afternoon of October 11 to draft a letter of protest and petition to Pope Paul VI. On October 13, a letter signed by at least thirteen Cardinals was presented to Paul VI (cf. AS VI/3, 440f.). The letter begins: "Not without great distress, we have learned that the Declaration on Religious Freedom, although it is in utter agreement with the wishes of the majority of the fathers, is to be sent back to some sort of mixed commission, to which, it is said, four members have already been appointed, three of whom seem to be against the direction taken in the Council on the subject." The letter goes on to request "most insistently" that the Declaration "be left to the usual procedure of the Council and dealt with according to the regulations provided, lest the result be very great harm done to the entire people of God." The controversy over the status of the Declaration was resolved on October 16 by means of a letter from the Secretary of State, Cardinal Cicognani, to Felici:

> It has been decided that: 1. There is no question of a new commission or of a mixed commission, but rather of a group of experts who will study the new schema prepared by the Secretariat for Christian Unity; 2. The topic remains within the province of the same Secretariat . . . the text will at the right moment be sent on to the two commissions: that is, the secretariat and the commission for doctrine on faith and morality. (Alberigo, vol. 4, 191)

52. In an essay titled "This Matter of Religious Freedom," published soon after the close of the third session, Murray explains the new doctrinal line of the third draft:

The advocates of religious freedom were divided among themselves. This has happened not seldom within the so-called "progressive" majority of the Council. To understand the division, one would have to note the difference in methodology and focus of argument between the first two drafts of the Declaration and the third draft. The first two drafts followed a line of argument common among French-speaking theologians. The argument began, not in the order of historical fact, but in the order of universal truth. The truth is that each man is called by God to share the divine life. This call is mediated to man by conscience, and man's response to it is the free act of faith. The essential dignity of man is located in his personal freedom of conscience, whereby he is truly a moral agent, acting on his own irreducible responsibility before God. Thus religious freedom was conceived to be formally and in the first instance an ethical and theological notion. The effort then was made to conclude, by inference to the juridical notion of religious freedom, to man's right to the free exercise of religion in society. The trouble was that this structure of argument seemed vulnerable to the advocates as well as to the adversaries of religious freedom. It is not obvious that the inference from freedom of conscience to the free exercise of religion as a human right is valid. Nevertheless, many French-speaking theologians and bishops considered their view to be richer and more profound. They were therefore displeased by the third draft of the Declaration, which relinquished their line of argument in favor of a line more common among English and Italian-speaking theorists. This line, as I have indicated, addresses the problem where it concretely exists — in the legal and political order. It considers religious freedom to be formally and in the first instance a juridical notion, whose validity, however, is to be established by a convergence of theological, ethical, political and legal argument. To the French-speaking school, this view of the matter seemed "superficial" (I heard the adjective often). This division of opinion was not, indeed, regarding the affirmation of religious freedom as a human right, but rather the manner of making the case for the affirmation. (TMRF, 42)

For a presentation of the philosophical and theological differences underlying the American and French approaches to religious freedom, see the essay by Schindler in the present volume.

53. *Textus emendatus,* 1 (AS III/8, 426).

54. *Textus emendatus,* 4e (AS III/8, 432).

55. *Textus emendatus,* 5b (AS III/8, 433).

56. *Textus emendatus,* 2 (AS III/8, 428). Cf. *Caput* V, n. 1 (AS II/5, 437-39); *Declaratio prior,* n. 1 (AS III/2, 322-23).

57. *Textus emendatus,* 2 (AS III/8, 428).

58. *Textus emendatus,* 2 (AS III/8, 429).

59. *Textus emendatus,* 12 (AS III/8, 438, 439).

60. Congar recalls the atmosphere of November 19, 1964: "[T]he majority is very worked up. . . . Immediately five stations were set up where a petition to the Pope could be signed, asking that the vote intended for this morning should take place tomorrow. . . . Ritter and Léger went to the Pope, carrying a petition covered with more than eight-hundred signatures asking *instanter, instantissime* [urgently, most urgently] that the vote should be taken before the end of this Session, that is to say: tomorrow" (*Journal,* 689).

61. AS V/3, 89-91. The text of the petition in the *Acta* includes 456 signatures; other accounts suggest as many as 800 or even 1,000 signatures.

62. AS IV/1, 605-881.

63. Congar's Council journal records the "difficult and muddy" work of the committee. On February 27, 1965, he writes: "Our work as experts is more or less finished. A text will be offered to the Fathers of the Commission. There will still be THEIR discussion, that of the Council, the revision of the text, its being put to the vote, the *modi*. . . . Not to mention its being read and assessed by the Pope. He is, it appears, very favourable to the text. But I am sure he will be subjected to terrible pressures. It will be represented to him that, in sanctioning the text, he will contradict the teaching of predecessors, put the Church at risk, favour indifferentism and individualistic and anarchic relativism. Now, it is true that there is a danger along those lines. But the text should be taken together with the entire work of the Council, which is on the brink of a powerful revitalisation of the Catholic Church and its dynamism. This does not prevent me questioning myself this evening. Have we done our best, have we done well?" (*Journal*, 736).

64. See AS IV/1, 168-99.

65. *Textus reemendatus*, 1 (AS IV/1, 146).

66. *Textus reemendatus*, 2 (AS IV/1, 148).

67. *Textus reemendatus*, 4b (AS IV/1, 151).

68. *Textus reemendatus*, 5 (AS IV/1, 152).

69. *Textus reemendatus*, 8 (AS IV/1, 154).

70. *Textus reemendatus*, 14 (AS IV/1, 161-62).

71. AS IV/1, 200.

72. A letter of Murray to Cardinal Ritter, August 13, 1965, outlines the following sequence of interventions: Spellman (freedom); Cushing (freedom as a positive value); Cushing (development of doctrine); O'Boyle (religious freedom is not indifferentism but a true image of the Church); Primeau (religious freedom and Christian freedom within the Church); Hallinan (religious freedom and schema XIII) (Murray papers, 18, 1001; cited in Alberigo, vol. 5, 66, n. 54).

73. AS IV/1, 204-7.

74. AS IV/1, 255.

75. AS IV/1, 299.

76. AS IV/1, 299.

77. AS IV/1, 393-94; cf. Alberigo, vol. 5, 91.

78. Cf. Alberigo, vol. 5, 96-101.

79. AS IV/1, 434: "Utrum textus reemendatus de libertate religiosa placeat Patribus tamquam basis definitivae declarationis ulterius perficiendae iuxta doctrinam catholicam de vera religione et emendationes a Patribus in disceptatione propositas et approbandas ad normam Ordinis Concilii?"

80. *L'Italia*, September 26, 1965; cited in Alberigo, vol. 5, 106-7.

81. Wojtyła, Intervention 5 (AS IV/2, 293).

82. Wojtyła, Intervention 4 (AS IV/2, 11).

83. Wojtyła, Intervention 4 (AS IV/2, 11).

84. Wojtyła, Intervention 4 (AS IV/2, 12).

85. Wojtyła, Intervention 4 (AS IV/2, 12).

86. Cf. Alberigo, vol. 5, 108, n. 230.

87. AS IV/2, 16-20.

88. Alberigo, vol. 5, 111, n. 239.

89. Members included Ancel, Cantero, Charriére, Colombo, Degrijse, De Smedt, Her-

maniuk, Lorsheider, Premeua, and Willebrands. The experts were Becker, Benoit, Congar, Feiner, Hamer, Medina, and Murray.

90. Routhier notes that "Murray's absence led to a shifting of the tone of the text, as the theological dimension received greater emphasis at the expense of the more strictly juridical or rational argument proposed by Murray" (Alberigo, vol. 5, 114). Cf. Pelotte, *John Courtney Murray: Theologian in Conflict* (New York: Paulist, 1975), 99, who claims that the final revisions to the text were "altogether unnecessary," and concurs with Routhier regarding the effect of Murray's absence: "These changes, however, weakened the Declaration and left it somewhat ambiguous. In all likelihood many of the last-minute changes would never have been made had Murray not been ill."

91. On October 5, the same day that Murray was taken to the hospital, Congar records the following diary entry: "For myself, today I can't stand up — yes, simply stand up — except with great difficulty. . . . I have not the least strength. I am always, and every day, without vitality and strength" (*Journal*, 801).

92. *Textus recognitus,* 1 (AS IV/5, 77-78). Cf. *Textus emendatus,* 3 (AS III/8, 429); *Textus reemendatus* 2 (AS IV/1, 148).

93. *Textus recognitus,* 2 (AS IV/5, 79).

94. Philipe André-Vincent describes the ontological bond of freedom to truth as the "mother-idea" of the entire Declaration:

> [T]he mother-idea appears with the foundation of the right to religious freedom: the ontological bond of the person with truth, a natural bond grounding a natural obligation to search for the truth and to adhere to it, grounding at the same time a right to the freedom necessary to realize that obligation. The ontological bond of freedom to truth is the mother-idea of the Declaration. (*La Liberté Religieuse: Droit Fondamental* [Paris: Téqui, 1976], 203-4)

95. Cf. Schindler's essay in the present volume.

96. *Textus recognitus,* 3 (AS IV/5, 81).

97. *Textus recognitus,* 6 (AS IV/5, 83).

98. *Textus recognitus,* 7 (AS IV/5, 87) (my italics).

99. *Textus recognitus,* 6 (AS IV/5, 84) (my italics).

100. *Textus recognitus,* 9 (AS IV/5, 86).

101. Congar writes on November 5, 1965: "Michalon, then Feiner, arrived for the modi of the *De libertate.* I would never have thought this work could be so tedious and so tiring. It is awful: there is no intellectual object to be pursued, but simply attention has to be given successively to a litany of disparate comments. Each time, one has to refer to the text, weigh or assess the reasons; these raise new questions, to which, however, one can give neither satisfaction nor even a following up, because it is not our job to rewrite the text" (*Journal*, 833).

102. DH, 1.

103. DH, 1 (my italics).

104. DH, 3. Pavan notes that "[t]his addition was meant to remove the doubts of some fathers who still believed that the neutralistic character of the state was implicitly asserted in the document" (Pavan, "Declaration on Religious Freedom," 61).

105. AS IV/6, 719. I am indebted to Rev. Brian Harrison for calling attention to the significance of De Smedt's *relatio* presenting the *Textus denuo recognitus.* Cf. Brian W. Harrison, "John Courtney Murray: A Reliable Interpreter of *Dignitatis Humanae?*" in *We Hold These*

Truths and More: Further Reflections on the American Proposition, ed. Donald J. D'Elia and Stephen M. Krason (Steubenville, OH: Franciscan University Press, 1993), 134-65.

106. DH, 2, 3.

107. ADP II/2, 741-48.

108. ADP II/2, 742.

109. DH, 1.

110. DH, 1.

111. DH, 2.

112. DH, 2.

113. Abbott, 672.

114. AS IV/2, 19.

115. Wojtyła, Intervention 2 (AS III/2, 531).

116. Benedict XVI, Post-Synodal Apostolic Exhortation *Ecclesia in Medio Oriente,* 27.

117. Benedict XVI, "Message for the Celebration of the World Day of Peace," 1 January 2011, 3.

IV.

The Five Conciliar Schemas

Translated by Patrick T. Brannan, S.J., and Michael Camacho

SCHEMA DECRETI DE OECUMENISMO

CAPUT V
DE LIBERATATE RELIGIOSA

(*Acta Synodalia* II/5, 433-41)

Huius capitis momentum ac necessitas neminem fugit, qui considerare velit, quantum recta libertatis religiosae consideratio conferat ad contactus et relationes sereno et pacato animo instaurandos sive inter christianos, sive generatim in ordinata hominum societate.[1]

Ecclesia catholica omnes et singulos homines, qui in adoptionem filiorum Dei praedestinati sunt, instanter hortatur ut in praesentibus culturae et morum circumstantiis omnia studia sua convertant ad defendendum honorem Dei et dignitatem personae humanae ab Eo creatae et redemptae. Quapropter, reiecto vetere discordiae fermento, in novis azymis sinceritatis et caritatis, aestiment et promoveant veritates et valores inter ipsos communes. Sed insimul, quod spectat ea in quibus unanimis consensus nondum attingitur, non tantummodo attendant ad Sacra et absoluta Dei iura necnon ad veritates seu obiecta quae semper observanda sunt, sed etiam ad iura et officia personarum seu subiectorum quibus veritati adhaerendum est. Haec omnia Dei dona in Verbo hominibus tributa sunt ut in hoc saeculo inveniatur tutamentum mentis et corporis ab omnibus qui a Spiritu Sancto moventur ut ad domum Patris communis libere accedant.

1. Ecclesia Catholica, ut divino obtemperet mandato: « docete omnes gentes ... docentes eos servare omnia quaecumque mandavi vobis » (*Mt.* 28, 19-20), infatigabili cura elaborare debet « ut sermo Dei currat et clarificetur » (2 *Thess.* 3, 1) et omnes « unanimes, uno ore honorificent Deum et Patrem Domini nostri Iesu Christi » (cf. *Rom.* 15, 6).

Hac de causa adiurat filios suos « primum omnium fieri obsecrationes, postulationes, gratiarum actiones pro omnibus hominibus ... Hoc enim bonum est ... coram Salvatore nostro Deo, qui omnes homines vult salvos fieri et ad agnitionem veritatis venire » (1 *Tim.* 2, 1-4). Sed praeterea ipsos adhortatur ut, in sapientia ambulantes ad eos, qui foris sunt (cf. *Col.* 4, 5),

Schema 1: *On Ecumenism,* **Chapter 5: On Religious Freedom**
(November 19, 1963)

DRAFT OF THE DECREE ON ECUMENISM

CHAPTER 5
ON RELIGIOUS FREEDOM

(Acta Synodalia II/5, 433-41)

The importance of and the need for this chapter are inescapable to those willing to consider how much an honest consideration of the issue of religious freedom may contribute to restoring a spirit of peace and tranquility to human relationships, both among Christians and within human society in general.[1]

The Catholic Church earnestly urges each man and all men, who have been predestined for adoption as children of God, to direct all their energy in the present circumstances of culture and customs to defending the honor of God and the dignity of the human person created and redeemed by him. Therefore, may all men and women, rejecting the old ferment of discord, in the new unleavened bread of sincerity and charity esteem and promote the truths and values they have in common between them. At the same time, since this matter of religious freedom concerns things about which a unanimous consensus has not yet been reached, let them consider not only the sacred and absolute rights of God and those truths or objects that must always be observed, but also the rights and duties of persons or subjects who must hold fast to the truth. All these gifts of God have been bestowed on men in the Word, so that all those who are moved by the Holy Spirit to come freely to the house of their common Father may find in this world a means of protection for both mind and body.

1. In order to obey the divine command "Make disciples of all nations . . . teaching them to observe all that I have commanded you" (Mt 28:19-20), the Catholic Church should strive tirelessly "that the word of the Lord may speed on and triumph" (2 Thes 3:1) and that all "together with one voice may glorify God the Father of our Lord Jesus Christ" (cf. Rom 15:6).

For this reason the Church implores her children "First of all that supplications, prayers, intercessions and thanksgivings be made for all men . . . This is good . . . in the sight of God our Savior who desires all men to be saved and to come to the knowledge of the truth" (1 Tim 2:1-4). But she also urges them, as they conduct themselves in wisdom toward those outside (cf.

« in Spiritu Sancto, in caritate non ficta, in verbo veritatis » (2 *Cor.* 6, 6-7) lumen vitae diffundere satagant mediis naturae et gratiae quibus ipse Dominus usus est, praedicatione nempe doctrinae, exemplo vitae et testimonium perhibendo veritati (cf. *Io.* 18, 37) usque ad proprii sanguinis effusionem.

[434] 2. Quamdiu tamen sunt in statu viae, discipuli Christi cum officio veritatem annuntiandi et defendendi semper et ubique coniunctam habebunt obligationem amanter, prudenter et patienter agendi cum hominibus qui nondum ad plenam Evangelii cognitionem pervenerunt. Etenim usque ad consummationem saeculi errores circa fidem spargentur et fideles indesinenter videre debebunt ne quis eos seducat (cf. *Mt.* 24, 3-15). Praeterea ab ipsis agnoscendus et admittendus est modus progressivus et humanus quo Deus homines ad suam veritatem et suum amorem allicit. Respiciendum igitur est non tantum ad officia erga verbum vivificans quod praedicandum est, sed etiam ad iura et mensuram gratiae quae personae ad fidem libere admittendam invitatae a Deo tribuuntur.

Haec est ratio cur Ecclesia filios suos hortatur ut veritatem facientes in caritate (cf. *Eph.* 4, 15), dum homines ad fidem veram adducere conantur, semper curent ut ab ipsis, qui ad imaginem Dei creati sunt (cf. *Gen.* 1, 27), assensus ne detur nisi cum plena libertate et non reprehendente corde eorum (cf. *1 Io.* 3, 21). In annuntiatione veritatis ab omni coactione abstinendum est.[2] Error reiiciendus est, veritas praedicanda, persona errantis circa fidem ad veritatem allicienda.[3] Attamen quamdiu in errore invincibili versatur, haec persona humana aestimatione digna est atque eius libertas religiosa ab Ecclesia agnoscitur et vindicatur.[4]

Et revera haec libertas religiosa, seu immunitas ab externa coactione natura actus fidei postulatur. Nam homo a Salvatore redemptus et « in adoptionem filiorum per Iesum Christum » *(Eph.* 1, 5) vocatus, revelationi divinae adhaerere non potest nisi ex una parte Pater traxerit eum (cf. *Io.* 6, 44) et ex altera parte rationabile ac liberum Deo praestiterit fidei obsequium. His de causis Ecclesia Catholica praecipit et mandat: « ad amplexandam fidem catholicam nemo invitus cogatur » (*C.I.C.,* can. 1351).

3. Eadem libertas religiosa non tantum a christianis, sed ab omnibus et singulis hominibus et a communi hominum conviventia observanda est.[5]

Humana enim persona, activitate conscia et libera praedita, cum voluntatem Dei tantummodo adimplere possit prout lex divina mediante dictamine conscientiae percipitur, finem suum ultimum obtinere nequit nisi

Col 4:5), that "in the Holy Spirit, in genuine charity, in truthful speech" (2 Cor 6:6-7) they be diligent in diffusing the light of life, using the means of nature and grace that the Lord himself employed, namely, the preaching of doctrine, the example of their life, and bearing witness to the truth (cf. Jn 18:37) even to the shedding of their own blood.

[434] 2. Nevertheless, as long as they are on this pilgrim way, Christ's disciples have the obligation always and everywhere to deal lovingly, prudently, and patiently with those who have not yet arrived at the full knowledge of the Gospel, together with the duty to proclaim and defend the truth. For errors will be sown about the faith until the end of the world, and the faithful must vigilantly take care that no one lead them astray (cf. Mt 24:3-15). They must also recognize and accept the gradual and human way in which God attracts men and women to his truth and his love. They should therefore consider not only their duties toward the life-giving word that must be preached, but also the rights and measure of grace that God has bestowed upon those persons who are invited freely to receive the faith.

For this reason the Church urges her children, as they live the truth in charity (cf. Eph 4:15), that, while striving to lead men and women to the true faith, they always take care that those who were created in God's image (cf. Gen 1:27) give their assent with full freedom and an uncondemning heart (cf. 1 Jn 3:21). In proclaiming the truth, all coercion must be avoided.[2] Error is to be rejected, the truth to be preached, and the person in error about the faith to be drawn toward the truth.[3] Nevertheless, as long as he remains in invincible error, this person retains his dignity, and his religious freedom is acknowledged and defended by the Church.[4]

This religious freedom, or immunity from external coercion, is in truth demanded by the very nature of the act of faith. For man, redeemed by the Savior and called "to be an adopted son through Jesus Christ" (Eph 1:5), cannot hold fast to divine revelation unless on the one hand he is drawn by the Father (cf. Jn 6:44), and on the other he offers to God a rational and free submission of faith. For these reasons, the Catholic Church teaches and commands that "No one may be forced to embrace the Catholic faith against his will" (*Code of Canon Law* [1917], can. 1351).

3. The same religious freedom must be observed not only by Christians but by each and every man and community of men who live and work together.[5]

For the human person, endowed with conscious and free activity, can fulfill the will of God only to the extent that he perceives the divine law by means of the dictates of his conscience; for this reason, he cannot attain his

iudicium conscientiae prudenter efformando eiusque dictamen fideliter exsequendo. Ideo homo qui conscientiae suae sincere obedit, ipsi Deo, etsi quandoque confuse vel inscie, obedire intendit et honore dignus aestimandus est.

Hanc rationem profundius scrutando prae oculis habenda est sequens consideratio:

[435] In unoquoque actu morali ponendo homo observare debet duas sequentes exigentias:

1) Unica datur Veritas quae est ipse Deus. Iura Dei sunt absoluta et unusquisque homo semper et ubique sese submittere debet sacrae voluntati Dei.

2) Deus qui hominem ad imaginem suam liberum creavit, ab ipso petit submissionem liberam, i. e. ex perspecta voluntate divini imperatam obedientiam.

In omni actu morali ponendo personae humanae problema aliquod obicitur. Ipse personaliter sub Dei lumine et adiutorio, adhibitis omnibus mediis informationis (pro homine christiano hoc est i. a. doctrina Ecclesia) et ratione habita iurium aliorum videre debet quid Dei voluntas a sua libertate exigat. Ex natura rei in hoc problemate solvendo nec ullus alius homo, nec ulla humana potestas sese ipsi substituere valet.

Quae cum ita sint, si, non obstantibus omnibus suis conatibus ad recte videndum quid Deus in concreto problemate ab ipso petat, persona humana erroneam solutionem admittit, nec ullus homo, nec ulla humana potestas ius habet sese huic conscientiae erranti substituendi a. v. in ipsam coercitionem exercendi.

Ecclesia catholica intolerantiam religiosam summo gradu odiosam atque offensivam erga personam humanam esse declarat.[6] Ipsa enim homo privatur libertate sua in observandis iis dictaminibus conscientiae suae quae ipsi etiam bona fide erranti ut suprema et sacratissima apparent.

4. In materia religiosa praedicta externae coactionis exclusio ab Ecclesia catholica vindicatur non ut mera « libertas opinionis » nec ut mera « libertas adimplendi ritus propriae religionis », sed ut vera « libertas religiosa » seu ius personae ne ab aliis impediatur quominus observet et proclamet officia sua publica et privata erga Deum et erga homines, singulariter vel collective sumptos, prout conscientia manifestantur. Ecclesia catholica affirmat talem libertatem religiosam competere tum singulis personis humanis tum

final end unless he prudently forms judgments of conscience for himself and faithfully follows their dictates. The man who sincerely obeys his conscience therefore intends to obey God himself, although at times in a confused way or unknowingly, and should be considered worthy of respect.

In entering further into this reasoning, the following consideration should be kept in mind:

[435] In every moral act that he performs, man should observe the following two demands:

1) There is only one truth which is God himself. The rights of God are absolute, and every single man, always and everywhere, should submit himself to the sacred will of God.
2) God, who created man free in his own image, seeks from him free submission, that is, the obedience that comes from a clear perception of the divine will.

In every moral act that he performs, some problem is presented to the human person. He himself personally, under God's light and assistance, using every means of knowledge (for a Christian this means, among other things, Church teaching), and taking into account the rights of others, should see what it is that the will of God demands of his freedom. By its very nature, in resolving this problem, no other man and no other human power can take his place.

Since this is the case, if the human person, despite all his efforts to see truly what God is asking of him in this concrete situation, arrives at an erroneous conclusion, no human being and no human power has the right to take the place of this erring conscience, or in other words to exercise coercion over it.

The Catholic Church declares that religious intolerance is hateful and offensive to the human person in the highest degree.[6] Such intolerance deprives man of his freedom to observe the dictates of his conscience, which appear to him as supreme and most sacred even when he errs in good faith.

4. In this religious matter, the Catholic Church upholds the exclusion of all external coercion. In doing so, she defends no mere "freedom of opinion" or "freedom of worship," but true "religious freedom," or the person's right not to be prevented by others from observing and proclaiming his public and private duties to God and to men, both individually and collectively, as these duties are manifested by conscience. The Catholic Church declares that such religious freedom belongs both to the individual human person

coetibus hominum, qui exigentiis suae conscientiae adducuntur ut collatis viribus vitam religiosam ducant vel promoveant.[7]

5. Haec libertas personalis realiter et effective non agnoscitur si in activitate externa et publica implicari non potest. Quare in humana convivientia et in societate civili nemo externo exercitio suae libertatis privari potest, dummodo, sicut bono communi exigitur, iura quoque aliorum salva remaneant.[8]

[436] Ideo in vita publica exercitium externum libertatis conscientiae impediri non potest nisi contradicat bono communi seu ordini obiectivo iurium Dei Creatoris et Salvatoris et inalienabilium iurium et libertatum personae humanae.[9]

Pro omnibus civibus in materia exercitii libertatis illud « minimum » in tuto esse debet sine quo ex una parte essentialis autonomia humanae personae non illaesa remaneret, et ex alter a parte humana societas, constans ex conviventibus hominibus qui, peccato originali eiusque sequelis contaminati, errare possunt, de facto impossibilis redderetur.

Hac de causa haec Sacra Synodus solemniter declarat et inculcat conatus ad religionem ipsam sive in toto genere humano, sive in determinato coetu religioso penitus exstinguendam manifestissime et gravissime laedere iura Creatoris et Salvatoris hominum, iura quoque sacratissima conscientiae humanae et familiae gentium.

Potestas publica nequit imponere civibus professionem determinatae religionis tamquam conditionem ut pleno et integro iure vitae nationali et civili participare valeant. Potestas humana debet iustitiam et aequitatem observare erga omnes qui in re religiosa dictamini suae conscientiae obediunt.

Haec libertas religiosa pariter offenditur praeprimis damnatione mortis propter rationes religiosas, sed praeterea religionis causa peractis spoliatione bonorum, privatione eorum quae ad vitam decentem requiruntur, abnegatione aequalitatis socialis vel civilis, nationalitatis, competentiae ad actus civiles, exercitii eorum iurium fundamentalium quae concorditer a nationibus agnoscuntur.[10]

Reprobanda quoque est discriminatio, quae homini vel nationi iniuriam vel vexationem facit propter originem, colorem vel sanguinem.

Sacra Synodus solemniter affirmat ius ad libertatem conscientiae in re religiosa externe exercendam, salvo bono communi, semper et ubique valere et ab omnibus agnoscendum esse.

Nostris autem temporibus ubique terrarum libertas religiosa speciali

and to groups of men and women who are moved by the promptings of their conscience to lead or promote a joint religious life.[7]

5. This personal freedom is not truly and effectively acknowledged if it is not permitted to engage in external and public action. In human communities and within civil society, therefore, no one can be deprived of the external exercise of his freedom, provided the rights of others remain secure as well, as demanded by the common good.[8]

[436] In public life, therefore, the external exercise of freedom of conscience cannot be impeded unless it contradicts the common good, or that objective order that consists in both the rights of God, Creator and Savior, and the inalienable rights and freedoms of the human person.[9]

In the exercise of their freedom, this "minimum" should be guaranteed to all citizens. Without this guarantee, the essential autonomy of the human person would not remain intact; on the other hand, human society would be rendered impossible *de facto*, since it consists of men and women who live and work together and who, affected by original sin and its consequences, can err.

For this reason, the sacred Council solemnly declares and insists that attempts to abolish religion completely, either in the human race as a whole or in a specific religious group, manifestly and gravely violate the rights of the Creator and Savior of mankind, as well as the most sacred rights of the human conscience and of the family of nations.

The public power cannot impose on citizens the profession of a particular religion as a condition for the full and complete right to participate in national and civil life. This power should observe justice and equity toward all those who obey the dictates of their conscience in religious matters.

Religious freedom is likewise offended when anyone is condemned to death for religious reasons; it is also offended when, on account of their religion, citizens are unjustly deprived of their goods, refused those things necessary for a decent life, or denied social or civil equality, nationality, competency for civil activity, or the exercise of those fundamental rights that are internationally acknowledged and agreed upon.[10]

Discrimination that causes injury or hardship to a human being or a nation on account of origin, color, or race must also be condemned.

This sacred Council solemnly declares that the right to exercise freedom of conscience in religious matters in an external way is always and everywhere valid, provided the common good is secured, and that it must be acknowledged by all people.

In our time, however, religious freedom must be promoted everywhere

modo urgenda est quia in dies frequentiores fiunt relationes quibus homines disparis cultus et diversae religionis inter se connectuntur.[11]

6. Quum grassante materialismo hodierno fundamenta omnis religionis et societatis corrodantur, Ecclesia catholica nuncupata vota facit ut quicumque christiano nomine honorantur, quantum fieri potest secundum exigentias sanae rationis, ordinem naturalem et depositum vitae christianae consertis precibus et viribus tueantur et promoveant, immo ut omnes homines bonae voluntatis, sive credentes sive nullam religionem [437] profitentes, simul operam dent ad ordinandam societatem secundum normas morales ex ipsa dignitate personae humanae profluentes.[12]

7. Quae normae quamvis fundamentum commune ad instaurandum ordinem vere humanum praebeant, a Christifidelibus tamen non ut unica et suprema norma considerandae sunt. Fide constat hominem ad imaginem Dei factum et in Dei adiutorem constitutum, in vita sua dirigenda et in labore suo perficiendo, regi posse ac debere praecepto caritatis, quo munus perficiendae creationis (*Gen.* 1, 28; 2, 5 et 15) et servitium sociale, quod omni activitati bona culturae humanae producenti intrinsecum est, in aedificationem Ecclesiae (*1 Cor.* 24, 5) et in gloriam Dei (*1 Cor.* 10, 31) ordinantur.

NOTAE

[1] Modo suo oecumenico decretum proponit altam doctrinam Ioannis Pp. XXIII in Litt. Encycl. *Pacem in terris.* Duo sunt praecipua capita doctrinae:

1) «In hominis iuribus hoc quoque numerandum est, ut et Deum, ad rectam conscientiae suae normam, venerari possit, et religionem privatim publice profiteri » (*A.A.S.*, 55, 1963, p. 260);

2) huic iuri officium respondet illud agnoscendi et colendi; quod officium incumbit *a)* omnibus aliis hominibus (*ibid.*, p. 264), et maxime *b)* rei publicae curatoribus (*ibid.*, pp. 273-74).

Doctrinam hanc sui praedecessoris fel. record. apertis verbis sanxit Paulus VI glor. regn.: « Ob huiusmodi dolores quanta afficimur tristitia, et quam vehementer dolemus, cum cernimus in quibusdam territoriis religiosam libertatem, sicut alia praecipua hominis iura, opprimi eorum principiis et artibus, qui opiniones a suis diversas de re politica, de hominum stirpibus, de cuiusvis generis religione non tolerant. Dolemus praeterea tot adhuc iniurias alicubi iis esse illatas, qui religionem suam honeste ac libere profiteri velint » (Allocutio ad Patres Concilii Oecumenici Vaticani II, 29 septembris 1963, Typis Polyglottis Vaticanis, p. 36).

in a special way, because relationships in which men and women of different cultures and diverse religions are united to one another are becoming more common every day.[11]

6. With the advance of modern materialism, the foundations of every religion and of society itself are wearing away. For this reason, the Church that is called Catholic prays that everyone who is honored with the Christian name may, as far as possible and in accordance with the requirements of right reason, protect and promote with united prayers and efforts both the natural order and the deposit of Christian life. The Church prays also that all men and women of good will, whether believers or those who profess no religion, **[437]** may work together to order society according to the moral norms that flow from the very dignity of the human person.[12]

7. Although such norms offer a common foundation for building up a truly human order, the Christian faithful should nonetheless not consider them to be the sole and supreme norm. By faith we know that man, made in the image of God and established as God's helper, can and ought to be governed by the rule of charity as he directs his life and carries out his work. By this rule the task of perfecting creation (Gen 1:28; 2:5, 15) and the service to society that is intrinsic to every activity that promotes the goods of human culture are ordered to the building up of the Church (1 Cor 24:5) and to the glory of God (1 Cor 10:31).

NOTES

[1] In its own ecumenical way, this decree proposes the lofty teaching of Pope John XXIII, expressed in the Encyclical Letter *Pacem in terris*. Two points are particularly central to this teaching:

1) "Also among man's rights is that of being able to worship God in accordance with the right dictates of his own conscience, and to profess his religion both in private and in public" (AAS 55 [1963], 260);

2) There corresponds to this right the duty to acknowledge and care for it; this duty is the responsibility of *a)* all other men (*ibid.*, 264) and especially *b)* government leaders (*ibid.*, 273-74).

Paul VI expressly sanctioned this teaching of his predecessor: "On account of such sufferings we are afflicted with much sorrow, and grieve exceedingly, when we see that in certain lands religious freedom, like certain other rights of man, is suppressed by the principles and practices of men who do not tolerate opinions that differ from their own concerning political affairs, man's origin, or religion of any kind. In addition, we grieve that so many injuries have been inflicted thus far anywhere against those who wish to profess their religion honestly and freely" ("Address to the Fathers of the Second Vatican Council," 29 September 1963, Vatican Polyglot Press, 36).

Haec porro doctrina proponitur ut terminus hodiernus longioris evolutionis tum in doctrina catholica de dignitate personae humanae tum in Ecclesiae pastorali sollicitudine pro hominis libertate. In hac evolutione principium continuitatis est ipsa haec doctrina atque sollicitudo. Principium vero progressus est duplex distinctio, quae ab Ecclesia lentius facta est, quaeque a Ioanne Pp. XXIII clare tandem est affirmata. Primo, distinguendum est inter falsas ideologias, quas vocant, et incepta atque instituta, quae ordinem civilem et politicum contingunt ut haec, quatenus cum rectae rationis praeceptis congruant, probari possint, illis ideologiis falsis constanter reiectis (cf. *ibid.*, p. 300). Deinde, distinguendum est inter errores religiosos et personam humanam bona fide errantem, ut iura, quae ad dignitatem libertatemque humanam pertineant, adhuc agnosci et coli debeant, illis ipsis erroribus immutabiliter denegatis (cf. *ibid.*, pp. 299-300).

His accedit, quod rerum eventus continuo mutabilis occasionem praebuit veri nominis progressus in doctrina Ecclesiae in eiusque sollicitudine pastorali, ut his [438] diebus ad amplissimum humanae libertatis patrocinium suscipiendum Ecclesia obstringatur, quod est explendum et doctrina magisteriali et omnium fidelium actuositate (cf. *ibid., fere passim*). Etenim Ioannes Pp. XXIII, una cum veritate, iustitia, caritate, etiam libertatem effert, utpote quae est his nostris temporibus omnis bene ordinatae civitatis necessaria consuetudo (cf. pp. 266, 268, 279, 297, 301). Quod utique est in documentis Ecclesiae simul novum quid, simul traditioni alte catholicae quid consentaneum quam maxime.

Enimvero sicut olim, ita hodie, ab Ecclesia damnatur libertas conscientiae illa, quam praedicaverunt rationalismi fautores, hoc fundamento innixi, quod individual conscientia exlex est, ut nullis sit normis obnoxia divinitus traditis. Damnatur etiam hodie, sicut olim, libertas cultus illa, cuius principium est indifferentismus religiosus, ex radice relativismi doctrinalis deducta. Neque minus hodie, quam olim, damnatur illa separatio Ecclesiae a Statu, quae dicitur, quam proponit theoria rationalistica de iuridica omnicompetentia Status, secundum quam Ecclesia intra ipsum organismum Status incorporetur necesse est, ut sit potestati statali subiecta. Integram plenamque vim suam retinent hae damnationes olim latae, quia inconcussum manet earum principium, quod est doctrina catholica de hominis dignitate et sollicitudo catholica pro veri nominis libertate. Dignitas enim hominis in hoc reponitur, quod soli Deo vivo et vero serviat, et libertas hominis in hoc maxime manifestatur, quod hoc servitium sit liberum, ad rectam normam propriae conscientiae praestitum.

Ast hoc idem principium nostris his temporibus ad novas ducit conclusiones, quas efformare coeperunt Romani Pontifices recentiores. Periculum enim non iam adest, ne falsi nominis libertas dignitati humanae iniuriam faciat, quod olim accidit. Novum adest periculum, ne libertatis humanae omne genus nova quadam tyrannide obruatur, pereunte primo libertate religiosa quod absit. Pro sua ergo aucta sollicitudine curaque erga hominis dignitatem, doctrinam traditionalem novo modo, nostris temporibus accommodato, aptaverunt recentiores Romani Pontifices. Collocant enim inter iura hominis praecipua ius ad liberum exercitium religionis in societate, iuxta dictamina conscientiae rectae, sive vera sit conscientia sive errore veritatis aut impari rerum sacrarum cognitione bona fide capta (cf. *Pacem in terris, A.A.S.,* 55, 1963, p. 299). Eamdem doctrinam eamdemque, quae ei subest, sollicitudinem proponit praesens *Decretum de Libertate Religiosa.*

² Cf. PIUS XII, Alloc. ad Praelatos auditores ceterosque officiales et administros Tri-

Schema 1: On Ecumenism, Chapter 5: On Religious Freedom

This teaching is proposed as the current terminus of a rather long evolution, both in Catholic teaching on the dignity of the human person and in the Church's pastoral concern for human freedom. In this evolution, the principle of continuity itself constitutes this teaching and concern. In truth, the principle of progress contains a two-fold distinction that has been made by the Church rather slowly, but that has in the end been clearly declared by Pope John XXIII. First, the distinction must be made between what may be called false ideologies, on the one hand, and the undertakings and institutions that are connected with the civil and political order, on the other; the latter, to the extent that they are in harmony with the precepts of right reason, can be accepted, while the former false ideologies must be consistently rejected (cf. *ibid.*, 300). Second, the distinction must be made between religious error and the human person who errs in good faith; the rights that belong to human dignity and freedom should continue to be recognized and respected, while the errors themselves must be constantly rejected (cf. *ibid.*. 299-300).

In addition, the continually changing nature of things affords the occasion for true progress in the Church's teaching and in its pastoral concern, so that **[438]** today the Church is obliged to undertake the fullest defense of human freedom, which is to be carried out both in magisterial teaching and in the actions of all the faithful (cf. *ibid., passim*). Indeed, Pope John XXIII proclaimed freedom also, along with truth, justice, and charity, to be a necessary element of every well-ordered state in our times (cf. 266, 268, 279, 297, 301). Undoubtedly, in the writings of the Church this is something new and at the same time altogether consistent with the depths of the Catholic tradition.

To be sure, just as she has in the past, the Church condemns also today that freedom of conscience that is proclaimed by proponents of rationalism, who claim that the individual conscience is beyond the law, and so not liable to any divinely given norms. Also today, as in the past, the Church condemns that freedom of worship that has its origins in a religious indifferentism rooted in doctrinal relativism. No less today than formerly does the Church condemn the so-called separation of Church and state proposed by the rationalistic theory of a juridically omnicompetent state, according to which the Church must necessarily be incorporated within the organization of the state itself, in order to be subjected to its power. These former condemnations retain their full and complete force because their principle remains unshaken, namely, the Catholic teaching on the dignity of man and the Catholic concern for true freedom. For the dignity of man is found in serving the living and true God alone, and the freedom of man is most fully revealed in the fact that this service is to be free, offered in accordance with the right precepts of his own conscience.

But in our time this same principle leads to new conclusions, which the recent popes have begun to formulate. For the danger today is not that a false kind of freedom should harm human dignity, as happened formerly. A new danger is arising, namely, that every kind of human freedom might be overthrown by a new kind of tyranny, with religious freedom perishing first of all. In keeping with their growing concern and care for the dignity of man, the recent popes have therefore adapted the traditional teaching in a new way that is accommodated to our times. For among the particular rights of man they include also the right to the free exercise of religion in society, according to the dictates of an upright conscience, whether this conscience be true or in good faith overcome by error or an inadequate understanding of sacred matters (cf. *Pacem in terris,* AAS 55 [1963], 299). The same teaching and the same underlying concern is proposed by the present *Decree on Religious Freedom.*

[2] Cf. Pius XII, "Allocution to the prelate auditors and other officials and administrators

bunalis S. Romanae Rotae, 6 oct. 1946: *A.A.S.*, 38, 1946, p. 394, ubi citatur a R. P. Pro Memoria Secretariae Status ad Legationem Yugoslaviae ad Sanctam Sedem: « D'après les principes de la doctrine catholique, la conversion doit être le résultat, non pas de contraintes extérieures mais de l'adhésion de l'âme aux verités enseignées par l'Eglise catholique. C'est pour cela que l'Eglise catholique n'admet pas dans son sein les adultes, qui demandent à y entrer ou à y faire retour, qu'à la condition qu'ils soient pleinement conscients de la portée et des conséquences de l'acte qu'ils veulent accomplir ». Idem, Litt. Encycl. *Mystici Corporis,* 29 iunii 1943: *A.A.S.*, 35, 1943, p. 243: «At si cupimus non intermissam eiusmodi totius mystici Corporis conprecationem admoveri Deo, ut aberrantes omnes in unum Iesu Christi ovile quam primum ingrediantur, profitemur tamen omnino necessarium esse id sponte libenterque fieri, cum nemo credat nisi volens. Quamobrem si qui, non credentes, eo reapse compelluntur ut Ecclesiae aedificium intrent, ut ad altare accedant, sacramentaque suscipiant, ii procul dubio veri [**439**] christifideles non fiunt; fides enim, sine qua " impossibile est placere Deo " (*Hebr.* 11, 6), liberrimum esse debet " obsequium intellectus et voluntatis " (Conc. Vat., *Const. de fide catholica,* cap. 3). Si igitur aliquando contingat, ut contra constantem Apostolicae huius Sedis doctrinam, ad amplexandam catholicam fidem aliquis adigatur invitus, id Nos facere non possumus quin, pro officii nostri conscientia, reprobamus ».

[3] Cf. IOANNES XXIII, Litt. Encycl. *Pacem in terris,* 11 apr. 1963: *A.A.S.*, 55, 1963, pp. 299-300: « Omnino errores ab iis qui opinione labuntur semper distinguere aequum est, quamvis de hominibus agatur, qui aut errore veritatis aut impari rerum cognitione capti sint, vel ad sacra vel ad optimam vitae actionem attinentium. Nam homo ad errorem lapsus iam non humanitate instructus esse desinit, neque suam umquam personae dignitatem amittit, cuius ratio est semper habenda. Praeterea in hominis natura numquam facultas perit et refragandi erroribus et viam ad veritatem quaerendi. Neque umquam hac in re providentissimi Dei auxilia hominem deficiunt. Ex quo fieri potest, ut, si quis hodie vel perspicuitate egeat, vel in falsas discesserit sententias, possit postmodum, Dei collustratus lumine, veritatem amplecti ».

[4] Cf. PIUS XII, Alloc. *Vous avez voulu,* 7 sept. 1955: *A.A.S.*, 37, 1955, p. 679: «Aux non catholiques l'Eglise applique le principe repris dans le Code du Droit Canon, " Ad amplexandam fidem catholicam nemo invitus cogatur " (canon 1351), et estime que leurs convictions constituent un motif, mais non toutefois le principal, de tolérance ».

[5] Cf. IOANNES XXIII, Litt. Encycl. *Pacem in terris,* 11 apr. 1963: *A.A.S.*, 55, 1963, pp. 260-261: « In hominis iuribus hoc quoque numerandum est, ut et Deum, ad rectam conscientiae suae normam, venerari possit, et religionem privatim publice profiteri ». Cf. PIUS XII, *Nuntius radiophonicus,* 24 dec. 1942: *A.A.S.*, 35, 1943, p. 19, ubi inter « iura fundamentalia personae » hoc etiam collocatur: « il diritto al culto di Dio privato e pubblico, compresa l'azione caritativa religiosa ». Cf. PIUS XI, Litt. Encycl. *Mit brennender Sorge,* 14 martii 1937: *A.A.S.*, 29, 1937, p. 160: « Der gläubige Mensch hat ein unverlierbares Recht, seinen Glauben zu bekennen und in den ihm gemässen Formen zu betätigen. Gesetze, die das Bekenntnis und die Betätigung dieses Glaubens unterdrücken oder erschweren, stehen in Widerspruch mit einem Naturgesetz ». Cf. LEO XIII, Litt. Encycl. *Libertas praestantissimum,* 20 iunii 1888: *Acta Leonis XIII,* 8, 1888, pp. 237-238: « Illa quoque magnopere praedicatur, quam conscientiae libertatem nominant; quae si ita accipiatur ut suo cuique arbitratu aeque liceat Deum colere, non colere, argumentis, quae supra allata sunt, satis convincitur. Sed potest etiam in hanc sententiam accipi, ut homini ex conscientia officii Dei voluntatem sequi et iussa facere, nulla re impediente, in civitate liceat. Haec quidem vera, haec digna filiis Dei libertas, quae humanae

of the Tribunal of the Sacred Roman Rota," 6 October 1946: AAS 38 (1946), 394, where the pope cites the *pro memoria* of the Secretariat of State to the Yugoslavian Embassy to the Holy See: "In accordance with the principles of Catholic teaching, conversion should be the result not of external constraints but of the soul's adherence to the truths taught by the Catholic Church. This is why the Catholic Church admits to herself adults who seek to enter or return to her only on the condition that they are fully conscious of the significance and consequences of the act they wish to make." Cf. also the Encyclical Letter *Mystici Corporis*, 29 June 1943: AAS 35 (1943), 243: "Though we desire this unceasing prayer to rise to God from the whole mystical body in common, that all the straying sheep may hasten to enter the one fold of Jesus Christ, we still recognize that this must be done of their own free will; for no one believes unless he wills to believe. Hence they are most certainly not genuine Christians who against their belief are forced to go into a church, to approach the altar and to receive the sacraments; [439] for the 'faith without which it is impossible to please God' (Heb 11, 6) is an entirely free 'submission of intellect and will' (First Vatican Council, *Constitution on the Catholic Faith*, ch. 3). Therefore, whenever it happens, despite the constant teaching of this apostolic see, that anyone is compelled to embrace the Catholic faith against his will, our sense of duty demands that we condemn the act."

³ Cf. John XXIII, Encyclical Letter *Pacem in terris*, 11 April 1963: AAS 55 (1963), 299-300: "It is always perfectly justifiable to distinguish between error as such and the person who falls into error—even in the case of men who err regarding the truth or are led astray as a result of their inadequate knowledge, in matters either of religion or of the highest ethical standards. A man who has fallen into error does not cease to be a man. He never forfeits his personal dignity; and that is something that must always be taken into account. Besides, there exists in man's very nature an undying capacity to break through the barriers of error and seek the road to truth. God, in his great providence, is ever present with his aid. Today, maybe, a man lacks faith and turns aside into error; tomorrow, perhaps, illumined by God's light, he may indeed embrace the truth."

⁴ Cf. Pius XII, Allocution *Vous avez voulu*, 7 September 1955: AAS 37 (1955), 679: "The Church applies to non-Catholics that principle found in the Code of Canon Law, 'No one may be forced to embrace the Catholic faith against his will' (canon 1351), and deems that the convictions of non-Catholics constitute a reason, even if not the principal reason, for tolerance."

⁵ Cf. John XXIII, Encyclical Letter *Pacem in terris*, 11 April 1963: AAS 55 (1963), 260-61: "Also among man's rights is that of being able to worship God in accordance with the right dictates of his own conscience, and to profess his religion both in private and in public." Cf. Pius XII, Radio message, 24 December 1942: AAS 35 (1943), 19, where among "the fundamental rights of the person" is also included "the right to worship God privately and publicly, including religious charitable activity." Cf. Pius XI, Encyclical Letter *Mit brennender Sorge*, 14 March 1937: AAS 29 (1937), 160: "The believer has an absolute right to profess his faith and live according to its dictates. Laws that impede this profession and practice of faith are against natural law." Cf. Leo XIII, Encyclical Letter *Libertas praestantissimum*, 20 June 1888: *Acta Leonis XIII*, 8 (1888), 237-38: "Another freedom is widely advocated, namely, freedom of conscience. If by this is meant that everyone may, as he chooses, worship God or not, it is sufficiently refuted by the arguments already adduced. But it may also be taken to mean that every man in the state may follow the will of God and, from a consciousness of duty and free from every obstacle, obey his commands. This, indeed, is true freedom, a freedom worthy of the sons of God, which nobly maintains the

dignitatem personae honestissime tuetur, est omni vi iniuriaque maior, eademque Ecclesiae semper optata ac praecipue cara ».

[6] Iuri ad libertatem religiosam, sicut ceteris naturae iuribus, respondet officium in aliis hominibus: cf. IOANNES XXIII, Litt. Encycl. *Pacem in terris*, 11 apr. 1963: *A.A.S.*, 55, 1963, p. 264: « Quibus probatis, consequens est etiam, ut in hominum consortione unius hominis naturali cuidam iuri officium aliorum hominum respondeat; officium videlicet ius illud agnoscendi et colendi ». Hoc officio praecipue tenetur potestas publica: « Verum cum nostra hac aetate commune bonum maxime in humanae personae servatis iuribus et officiis consistere putetur, tum praecipue [440] in eo sint oportet curatorum rei publicae partes, ut hinc iura agnoscantur, colantur, inter se componantur, defendantur, provehantur, illinc suis quisque officiis facilius fungi possit » (*ibid.*, pp. 273-274). Et citatur PIUS XII, *Nuntius radiophonicus*, 1 iunii 1941: *A.A.S.*, 33, 1941, p. 200: « Inviolabilia iura tueri, hominum propria, atque curare, ut facilius quisque suis muneribus defungatur, hoc cuiusvis publicae potestatis officium est praecipuum ».

[7] Commemoranda est hoc loco expositio constitutionalismi, qui dicitur, a Ioanne XXIII data in Litt. Encycl. *Pacem in terris*, 11 apr. 1963: cf. *A.A.S.*, 55, 1963, pp. 278-279, in contextu totius documenti. Est enim huiusmodi constitutionalismus, qui sane religioni christianae plurimum debet, doctrina de iuridiciali et politica civitatis compositione secundum quam « potestas publica suapte natura ad tutandum communitatis bonum spectat, cuius princeps officium est agnoscere honestos libertatis fines eiusque iura sarta tecta servare » (*ibid.*, pp. 285-286). Immo ad constitutionalismum vero sensu christianum pertinet illud quod praedicavit Leo XIII, Litt. Encycl. *Sapientiae christianae*, 10 ian. 1890: *A.S.S.*, 22, 1889-90, p. 396: « Dubitari vero salva fide non potest, istiusmodi regimen animorum Ecclesiae esse assignatum uni, nihil ut in eo sit politicae potestati loci; non enim Caesari, sed Petro claves regni caelorum Iesus Christus commendavit ». Agit igitur ultra vires, et rem sacram, quae homo est, maxime violat potestas publica, quando sese regimini animorum vel curae animarum immiscet.

[8] Quod pertinet ad dignitatem illam civilem, secundum quam dignitas humana in publicum prodit; cf. PIUS XII, *Nuntius radiophonicus*, 24 dec. 1944: *A.A.S.*, 37, 1945, p. 14: « In un popolo degno di tal nome il cittadino sente in se stesso la coscienza della sua personalità, dei suoi doveri e dei suoi diritti, della propria libertà congiunta col rispetto della libertà e della dignità altrui ». Hoc loco commendat Romanus Pontifex etiam illud « ideale di libertà e di uguaglianza » (*loc. cit.*), quod in Statu democratico, iuxta sana rationis principia ordinato, obtineat necesse est, quodque postulat, ut hominis ius in societate ad liberum exercitium religionis plene agnoscatur, colatur, defendatur, provehatur.

[9] Quod attinet ad intolerantiam religiosam ex parte potestatis publicae, suprema principia tradit Pius XII, Alloc. *Ci riesce*, 6 dec. 1953: *A.A.S.*, 45, 1953, pp. 798-799: « Può darsi che in determinate circostanze Egli (Dio) non dia agli uomini nessun mandato, non imponga nessun dovere, non dia persino nessun diritto d'impedire e di reprimere ciò che è erroneo e falso? Uno sguardo alla realtà dà una risposta affermativa ». Et, allato exemplo divinae providentiae, pergit: « Quindi l'affermazione: Il traviamento religioso e morale deve essere sempre impedito, quanto è possibile, perchè la sua tolleranza è in se stessa immorale, non può valere nella sua incondizionata assolutezza. D'altra parte, Dio non ha dato nemmeno all'autorità umana un siffatto precetto assoluto e universale, nè in campo della fede nè in quello della morale. Non conosco un tale precetto ne la comune convinzione degli uomini, nè la coscienza cristiana, nè le fonti della rivelazione, nè la prassi della Chiesa ».

dignity of man and is stronger than all violence or wrong—a freedom which the Church has always desired and held most dear."

[6] As with the other rights of nature, there corresponds to the right to religious freedom a duty toward other men: cf. John XXIII, Encyclical Letter *Pacem in terris*, 11 April 1963: AAS 55 (1963), 264: "Once this is admitted, it follows that in human society one man's natural right gives rise to a corresponding duty in other men; the duty, that is, of recognizing and respecting that right." The public power is especially bound by this duty: "It is generally accepted today that the common good is best safeguarded when personal rights and duties are guaranteed. The chief [**440**] concern of civil authorities must therefore be to ensure that these rights are recognized, respected, co-ordinated, defended and promoted, and that each individual is enabled to perform his duties more easily" (*ibid.*, 273-274). Here there is a reference to Pius XII, Radio message, 1 June 1941, AAS 33 (1941), 200: "To safeguard the inviolable rights of the human person, and to facilitate the performance of his duties, is the principal duty of every public power."

[7] One must keep in mind here the explanation of constitutionalism provided by John XXIII, in the Encyclical Letter *Pacem in terris*, 11 April 1963: cf. AAS 55 (1963), 278-79, within the context of the entire document. This kind of constitutionalism, which in fact owes much to the Christian religion, is a doctrine that concerns the juridical and political composition of the state, according to which "the whole raison d'etre of the public power is to safeguard the interests of the community. Its sovereign duty is to recognize the noble realm of freedom and protect its rights" (*ibid.*, 285-86). Indeed, Leo XIII's statements in the Encyclical Letter *Sapientiae christianae*, 10 January 1890: ASS 22 (1889-1890), 396, concern Christian constitutionalism in the true sense: "No one can, however, without risk to faith, foster any doubt that the Church alone has been invested with such power of governing souls as to exclude altogether the civil authority. In truth, it was not to Caesar but to Peter that Jesus Christ entrusted the keys of the kingdom of heaven." The public power therefore exceeds its powers and completely violates sacred matters, of which man himself is a part, when it involves itself in the governing of minds or the care of souls.

[8] Concerning man's civil dignity, by which human dignity is extended into the public sphere, cf. Pius XII, Radio message, 24 December 1944: AAS 37 (1945), 14: "In a people worthy of the name, the citizen feels within himself a consciousness of his personhood, of his duties and rights, of his own freedom together with respect for the freedom and dignity of others." Here the pope commends also the "ideal of freedom and equality" (*loc. cit.*) that it is necessary to maintain in a democratic state organized according to sound principles of reason, which demands that man's right to the free exercise of religion in society be fully acknowledged, cultivated, defended, and promoted.

[9] Concerning religious intolerance on the part of the public power, the primary principles were indicated by Pius XII, Allocution *Ci riesce*, 6 December 1953: AAS 45 (1953), 798-99: "Is it possible that in certain circumstances God may not give men any mandate, may not impose any duty, may not even communicate the right to impede or repress what is erroneous and false? One glance at reality indicates that the answer is yes." After giving an example of divine providence, the pope continues: "Hence the assertion: 'religious and moral error should always be impeded as much as possible, because tolerating them is in itself immoral,' cannot be valid absolutely and unconditionally. God has not granted to human authority such an absolute and universal command in matters of faith or morals. I know of no such command, nor does the common conviction of mankind, the Christian conscience, the sources of revelation, or the practice of the Church."

[10] Cf. IOANNES XXIII, Litt. Encycl. *Pacem in terris*, 11 apr. 1963: *A.A.S.*, 55, 1963, pp. 295-296, ubi, quibusdam defectibus non obstantibus, commendatur Professio Universalis Iurium Humanorum, die 10 dec. 1948 a Foederatarum Nationum Coetu Generali rata habita: « Nihilominus Professionem eamdem habendam esse censemus quemdam quasi gradum atque aditum ad iuridicialem politicamque ordinationem constituendam omnium populorum, qui in mundo sunt. Siquidem ea [441] universis prorsus hominibus solemniter agnoscitur humanae dignitas personae, atque iura cuivis homini asseruntur veritatem libere quaerendi, honestatis sequendi normas, iustitiae officia usurpandi, vitam exigendi homine dignam, alia deinceps cum hisce coniuncta ».

[11] Cf. PIUS XII, Alloc. ad Praelatos auditores ceterosque officiales administros Tribunalis S. Romanae Rotae, 6 oct. 1946: *A.A.S.*, 38, 1946, p. 393: « I sempre più frequenti contatti e la promiscuità delle diverse confessioni religiose entro i confini di un medesimo popolo hanno condotto i tribunali civili a seguire il principio della "tolleranza" e della "libertà di coscienza". Anzi vi è una tolleranza politica, civile e sociale verso i seguaci delle altre confessioni, che in tali circostanze è anche per i cattolici un dovere morale ». Insuper, ad communitatem internationalem quod attinet, cf. PIUS XII, Alloc. *Ci riesce*, 6 dec. 1953: *A.A.S.*, 45, 1953, p. 797: « Gli interessi religiosi e morali esigeranno per tutta la estensione della Comunità (dei popoli) un regolamento ben definito, che valga per tutto il territorio dei singoli Stati sovrani membri di tale Comunità delle nazioni. Secondo le probabilità e le circostanze, è prevedibile che questo regolamento di diritto positivo verrà enunciato così: Nell'interno del suo territorio e per i suoi cittadini ogni Stato regolerà gli affari religiosi e morali con una propria legge; nondimeno in tutto il territorio della Comunità degli Stati sarà permesso ai cittadini di ogni Stato-membro l'esercizio delle proprie credenze e pratiche etiche e religiose, in quanto queste non contravvengano alle leggi penali dello Stato in cui essi soggiornano ». Secundum Romanum Pontificem, cives catholici et Status catholici moderatores possunt ex conscientia eiusmodi legi consentire.

[12] Cf. PIUS XI, Litt. Encycl. *Caritate Christi compulsi*, 3 maii 1932: *A.A.S.*, 24, 1932, pp. 178, 184; Litt. Encycl. *Divini Redemptoris*, 19 mart. 1937: *A.A.S.*, 29, 1937, p. 102; PIUS XII, Epist. Encycl. *Sertum Laetitiae*, 1 nov. 1939: *A.A.S.*, 31, 1939, p. 644; *Nuntius radiophonicus*, 24 dec. 1939: *A.A.S.*, 32, 1940, p. 11; *Nuntius radiophonicus*, 1 sept. 1944: *A.A.S.*, 36, 1944, p. 251. Et iam olim LEO XIII, Litt. *Nous ne voulons pas*, 22 iunii 1892: *A.S.S.*, 25, 1892-93, pp. 69-70.

[10] Cf. John XXIII, Encyclical Letter *Pacem in terris*, 11 April 1963: AAS 55 (1963), 295-96, where, certain defects notwithstanding, the pope commends the Universal Declaration of Human Rights, ratified by the General Assembly of the United Nations on December 10, 1948: "Nevertheless, we think the document should be considered a step in the right direction, an approach toward the establishment of a juridical and political ordering of the world community. It is [441] a solemn recognition of the personal dignity of every human being; an assertion of everyone's right to be free to seek out the truth, to follow moral principles, to discharge the duties imposed by justice, and to lead a fully human life. It also recognized other rights connected with these."

[11] Cf. Pius XII, "Allocution to prelate auditors and other officials and administrators of the Tribunal of the Sacred Roman Rota," 6 October 1946: AAS 38 (1946), 393: "The increasingly frequent contact and co-mingling of different religious confessions within the borders of the same nation have led civil courts to follow the principles of 'tolerance' and 'freedom of conscience.' There is, in fact, a political, civil and social tolerance toward those of other faiths which in certain circumstances is a moral obligation for Catholics also." In addition, regarding the international community, cf. Pius XII, Allocution *Ci riesce*, 6 December 1953: AAS 45 (1953), 797: "The interests of religion and morality will require for the whole extent of the community of nations a well-defined rule, one that will hold throughout the territory of each individual sovereign member state of the community of nations. Depending on the circumstances, it is likely that this rule of positive law will be set forth as follows: within its own territory and for its own citizens, each state will regulate religious and moral affairs according to its own laws; nevertheless, throughout the whole territory of the community of states, the citizens of every member state will be allowed to exercise their own beliefs and ethical and religious practices, as long as these do not contravene the penal laws of the state in which they are residing." According to the pope, Catholic citizens and leaders of Catholic states can in good conscience consent to such a law.

[12] Cf. Pius XI, Encyclical Letter *Caritate Christi compulsi*, 3 May 1932: AAS 24 (1932), 178, 184; Encyclical Letter *Divini Redemptoris*, 19 March 1937: AAS 29 (1937), 102; Pius XII, Encyclical Epistle *Sertum Laetitiae*, 1 November 1939: AAS 31 (1939), 644; Radio message, 24 December 1939: AAS 32 (1940), 11; Radio message, 1 September 1944: AAS 36 (1944), 251; Leo XIII, Encyclical *Nous ne voulons pas*, 22 June 1892: ASS 25 (1892-93), 69-70.

SCHEMA DECRETI DE OECUMENISMO

Declaratio prior

(*Acta Synodalia* III/2, 317-27)

DE LIBERTATE RELIGIOSA
SEU
DE IURE PERSONAE ET COMMUNITATUM
AD LIBERTATEM IN RE RELIGIOSA

25. Huius declarationis momentum neminem fugit, qui attendere velit, quantum recta libertatis religiosae consideratio conferat ad contactus et relationes sereno et pacato animo instaurandos inter christianos; huiusmodi enim consideratio est condicio omnino necessaria ut dialogus oecumenicus haberi possit.

26. (*Natura libertatis religiosae describitur*). Homines ad imaginem Dei formati et ad consortium divinae naturae vocati officium et honorem habent ut, secundum dictamen conscientiae, voluntatem Creatoris et Salvatoris in re religiosa sequantur. Inde exoritur ius ad libertatem religiosam in societate, vi cuius homines religionem suam privatim et publice exercere valent nec ulla coactione ab ea exercenda prohiberi possunt. Haec libertas religiosa postulat ut in humana societate condiciones [318] necessariae promoveantur, in quibus omnes, vel singillatim vel in coetibus religiosis coniuncti, vocationi divinae libere et integre respondere possint.

Per libertatem religiosam homo a Dei potestate nullo modo emancipatus est, quasi falsum et verum posset aequae aestimare, vel ab omni erga Summum Numen obligatione solutus esset, vel ipsi officium non incumberet rectam sibi de rebus religiosis conscientiam formandi, vel sibi pro libito statuere valeret utrum et in qua religione Deo servire velit.

His prae oculis habitis, Sacra Synodus, dum hominum a Deo dependentiam affirmat, libertatem simul in societate circa res religiosas ab omnibus ubique terrarum agnoscendam et observandam esse hac declaratione manifestare intendit.[1]

Schema 2: *Prior Declaration* (April 27, 1964)

DRAFT OF THE DECREE ON ECUMENISM

Prior Declaration

(*Acta Synodalia* III/2, 317-27)

ON RELIGIOUS FREEDOM
OR
ON THE RIGHT OF THE PERSON AND OF COMMUNITIES
TO FREEDOM IN RELIGIOUS MATTERS

25. The importance of this declaration is inescapable to those willing to reflect on how much an honest consideration of the issue of religious freedom may contribute to restoring a spirit of peace and tranquility to relationships among Christians. Indeed, a consideration of this kind is an altogether necessary condition for being able to engage in ecumenical dialogue.

26. (*A description of the nature of religious freedom*). Men and women, made in the image of God and called to fellowship with the divine nature, have both the duty and the honor to follow the will of their Creator and Savior in religious matters, according to the dictates of their conscience. From this derives the right to religious freedom in society, by which men and women are able to practice their religion in private and in public, and cannot be prohibited from practicing it by any kind of coercion. This religious freedom requires that the necessary conditions [318] be promoted in human society in order to enable all men and women, whether individually or within religious groups, to respond to their divine vocation freely and fully.

Religious freedom in no way frees man from God's power, as though he could equally value what is false and what is true, as though he were released from all obligations toward the Supreme Being, as though he no longer had the duty to form for himself a right conscience in religious matters, or as though he could determine for himself at will whether or in which religion he wished to serve God.

Bearing these things in mind, this sacred Council, while affirming man's dependence on God, intends at the same time to make clear by means of this declaration that freedom in society concerning religious matters must be acknowledged and observed by all men and women throughout the world.[1]

27. (*Munus Ecclesiae*). Ecclesia catholica, ut divino obtemperet mandato: « docete omnes gentes . . . docentes eos servare omnia quaecumque mandavi vobis » (*Mt.* 28, 19-20), impensa cura adlaborare debet « ut sermo Dei currat et clarificetur » (*2 Thess.* 3, 1) et omnes unanimes, uno ore honorificent Deum et Patrem Domini nostri Iesu Christi.[2]

Obsecrat igitur Ecclesia a filiis suis « primum omnium fieri obsecrationes, orationes, postulationes, gratiarum actiones pro omnibus hominibus . . . Hoc enim bonum est et acceptum coram Salvatore nostro Deo, qui omnes homines vult salvos fieri et ad agnitionem veritatis venire » (*1 Tim.* 2, 1-4). Insuper ipsos hortatur ut, in sapientia ambulantes ad eos, qui foris sunt,[3] « in Spiritu Sancto, in caritate non ficta, in verbo veritatis » (*2 Cor.* 6, 6-7) lumen vitae diffundere satagant auxiliis naturae et gratiae quibus ipse Dominus usus est, praedicatione nempe doctrinae, exemplo vitae et testimonio perhibito veritati,[4] etiam usque ad sanguinis effusionem.

28. (*Ad amplectendam fidem nemo cogatur*). Dum vero discipuli Christi in statu viae sunt, cum officio veritatem annuntiandi et defendendi coniunctam semper et ubique habent obligationem agendi amanter, prudenter et patienter cum hominibus qui in erroribus circa fidem versantur. Etenim ab ipsis agnoscendus et admittendus est modus suavis et humanae naturae aptatus, quo Deus homines sensim ad suum amorem allicit.Respiciendum igitur est et ad officia erga verbum vivificans, quod praedicandum est, et ad iura personae et ad mensuram gratiae, quae a Deo tribuuntur homini qui ad fidem libere admittendam invitatur.

Haec est ratio cur Ecclesia filios suos hortatur ut, veritatem facientes [319] in caritate,[5] semper curent ut, dum homines ad fidem veram adducere conantur, ab ipsis assensus ne detur nisi cum plena libertate et sine animi reprehensione. Error reiciendus est, veritas praedicanda, intellectus illustrandus.[6] In annuntianda autem veritate ab omni directa vel indirecta coactione abstinendum est.[7]

Ecclesia catholica praecipit ne ullus invitus cogatur ad amplexandam fidem catholicam. Quae traditionalis norma Ecclesiae[8] pro unaquaque persona valet et ab ipsa natura actus fidei postulatur. Homo enim a Salvatore redemptus et « in adoptionem filiorum per Iesum Christum » (*Eph.* 1, 5) vocatus, revelationi divinae adhaerere non potest nisi ex una parte Pater traxerit eum[9] et ex altera rationabile ac liberum Deo praestiterit fidei obsequium.

29. (*Religiosa personae libertas in societate*). Libertatem religiosam

27. (*The task of the Church*). In order to obey the divine command "Make disciples of all nations . . . teaching them to observe all that I have commanded you" (Mt 28:19-20), the Catholic Church should strive with great care "that the word of the Lord may speed on and triumph" (2 Thes 3:1), and that all together with one voice may glorify God the Father of our Lord Jesus Christ.[2]

The Church therefore entreats her children, "First of all that supplications, prayers, intercessions, and thanksgivings be made for all men . . . This is good and it is acceptable in the sight of God our Savior, who desires all men to be saved and to come to the knowledge of the truth" (1 Tim 2:1-4). In addition she urges them, as they conduct themselves in wisdom toward those outside,[3] that "in the Holy Spirit, in genuine charity, in truthful speech" (2 Cor 6:6-7) they be diligent in diffusing the light of life, using the resources of nature and grace that the Lord himself employed, namely, the preaching of doctrine, the example of their life, and bearing witness to the truth,[4] even to the shedding of their blood.

28. (*No one may be forced to embrace the faith*). While Christ's disciples are on this pilgrim way, they have the obligation always and everywhere to deal lovingly, prudently, and patiently with those who dwell in error about the faith, together with the duty to proclaim and defend the truth. For they must recognize and accept the gentle way, adapted to human nature, in which God gradually attracts men to his love. They must therefore consider both their duties toward the life-giving word that must be preached, and the rights of the person and the measure of grace that God has bestowed upon those who are invited freely to receive the faith.

For this reason the Church urges her children, as they live the truth [319] in charity,[5] that, while striving to lead men and women to the true faith, they always take care that these men and women give their assent with full freedom and without interior reservation. Error is to be rejected, the truth to be preached, and man's intellect to be enlightened.[6] In proclaiming the truth, however, all direct or indirect coercion must be avoided.[7]

The Catholic Church teaches that no one may be forced to embrace the Catholic faith against his will. This traditional precept of the Church[8] is valid for each and every person and is demanded by the very nature of the act of faith. For man, redeemed by the Savior and called "to be an adopted son through Jesus Christ" (Eph 1:5), cannot hold fast to divine revelation unless on the one hand he is drawn by the Father,[9] and on the other he offers to God a rational and free submission of faith.

29. (*The religious freedom of the person in society*). The Catholic Church

non tantum a christianis et pro christianis, sed ab omnibus et pro omnibus hominibus et coetibus religiosis in societate humana observandam esse Ecclesia catholica asserit.[10]

Vocatio enim divina, quae homini iter ad Deum et ad salutem in Deo assequendam aperit atque praescribit, maximam revera personae humanae dignitatem constituit. Quapropter in sociali convictu libertas sequendi hanc vocationem sine ulla imposita vel impediente coactione cum maximum et unicuique proprium bonum tum aliarum libertatum fundamentum ac tutelam constituit, atque ideo ab unoquoque tamquam verum strictumque ius erga eos quibuscum vitam degit habenda et observanda est.

Huius autem vocationis hominis seu integrae necessitudinis ad Deum norma est lex divina, quae est aeterna, obiectiva, absoluta, universalis. Unusquisque ergo tenetur ad hanc Dei ordinationem omni studio recte cognoscendam ut se libere ei conformare valeat.

Homo tamen dum his in terris vitam degit, voluntati Dei obtemperare potest tantummodo prout legem divinam sui ipsius conscientiae dictamine percipit, et finem suum ultimum obtinere nequit nisi iudicium conscientiae sibi prudenter efformando eiusque dictamen fideliter sequendo. Ideo qui conscientiae suae sincere oboedit, ipsi Deo, etsi quandoque confuse vel inscie, oboedit et honore dignus aestimandus est. Si quis igitur, quantumvis conatus sit recte videre quid Deus in concreto ab ipso petat, in erroneam interpretationem incidat, nullus homo nec ulla humana potestas ius habet illum inducendi ad operandum contra suae conscientiae dictamen.

Quum libertas religiosa elemento essentiali privaretur et inanis evaderet, si publice exerceri non posset, ab Ecclesia catholica vindicatur non [320] tantum libertas opinionis, nec tantum libertas adimplendi ritus propriae religionis, sed verum propriumque personae ius ad servanda et testanda officia sua privata et publica erga Deum et homines, sive singulares sive collective sumptos, ad totam scilicet vitam suam secundum postulata suae religionis ordinandam in re familiari, educativa,culturali, sociali, caritativa et in aliis humanae vitae activitatibus.[11]

Exercitium iurium in re religiosa propter naturam socialem hominis limitatum est et eam mensuram excedere non potest sine qua nec dignitas essentialis personae humanae illaesa maneret, nec re vera possibilis esset societas hominum qui, utpote libero arbitrio praediti et sequelis peccati originalis contaminati, errare possunt. Id exercitium limitari non licet nisi in quantum graviter contradicit fini societatis, qui constat complexu earum

declares that religious freedom must be observed not only by Christians and for Christians, but by all men and for all men and religious groups in human society.[10]

For the divine vocation, which reveals and prescribes for man the path he is to follow toward God and toward salvation in him, in truth constitutes the highest dignity of the human person. For this reason the freedom to follow this vocation in society without any imposed or impeding coercion constitutes both the greatest and the most proper good of each person, and is the foundation and protection of other freedoms. It must therefore be regarded and observed by each person as a true and strict right of those with whom he lives.

The norm governing this vocation of man, or this integral relationship to God, is the divine law, which is eternal, objective, absolute, and universal. Each person is therefore bound to come to know this decree of God with all diligence, so that he can conform himself to it freely.

Nevertheless, while he passes this life on earth, man can obey God's will only to the extent that he perceives the divine law by means of the dictates of his own conscience, and he cannot attain his final end unless he prudently forms judgments of conscience for himself and faithfully follows their dictates. The one who sincerely obeys his conscience therefore obeys God himself, although at times in a confused way or unknowingly, and should be considered worthy of respect. If anyone, therefore, striving to see truly what God is asking of him in a concrete situation, arrives at an erroneous conclusion, no human being and no human power has the right to force him to act against the dictates of his conscience.

If religious freedom could not be exercised publicly, it would be deprived of an essential dimension and end up devoid of meaning. For this reason, the Church defends not [320] simply freedom of opinion or freedom of worship, but the true and proper right of the person to observe and bear witness to his private and public duties to God and to men, both individually and collectively. The Church defends man's right, that is, to order his entire life according to the demands of his religion, in matters familial, educational, cultural, social, and charitable, as well as in other activities of human life.[11]

The exercise of one's rights in religious matters is limited on account of man's social nature. If it were to go beyond this limit, the essential dignity of the human person would not remain intact, nor would a society of persons in fact be possible, since men and women, endowed with free will and affected by the consequences of original sin, can err. The exercise of this right to religious freedom cannot be limited except when it seriously contradicts the

vitae socialis condicionum, quibus homines suam ipsorum perfectionem possunt plenius et expeditius consequi[12] ac simul fideliter observare inalienabilia iura a Deo hominibus in communi tributa.

Si igitur in sensus religiosi manifestationibus usus inveniantur perversi, qui personae dignitati et iuribus aliorum clare noceant, populorum rectores secundum prudentiae regulas iis obstent oportet.[13]

Contra vero, publicae rei moderatoribus nefas est imponere civibus professionem vel reiectionem cuiuscumque religionis tamquam condicionem, qua plene vel partialiter vitae nationali et civili participare possint. Pariter haec libertas religiosa offenditur damnatione ad poenas propter rationes religiosas; atque etiam laeditur quando, religionis causa, peragitur spoliatio bonorum, privatio rerum quae ad vitam decentem requiruntur, negatio aequalitatis socialis et nationalitatis, recusatio accessus ad actus civiles et exercitii iurium fundamentalium quae, hodie praesertim, concorditer et universaliter agnoscuntur.[14]

Publicae rei moderatores ex alia parte tenentur ius personae ad libertatem in re religiosa efficaciter tueri ipsumque apte promovere.[15] Reipublicae enim proprium est personae iura non tantum agnoscere et observare, sed etiam eorum exercitium facilius reddere et impedire quominus hominibus huiusmodi iura exercentibus difficultates ponantur.[16]

30. (*Libertas coetuum religiosorum in societate*). Ius ad libertatem religiosam, quod singulis personis competit, etiam coetibus agnoscendum est. Hi enim constituuntur libera personarum voluntate, imperante conscientia; praeterea requiruntur sociali hominum natura et dignitate, ut ipsi religionem revera vivere possint.

Ipsis igitur, intra supra dictos limites a fine societatis imponendos, ius competit ut secundum proprias leges sese regant, Deum cultu publico honorent, membra sua in vita religiosa exercenda adiuvent et doctrina [321] sustentent easque insitutiones promoveant, in quibus membra inter se adiuvent ad vitae activitates secundum sua principia religiosa ordinandas.

Homines ergo qui, iuxta dictamen conscientiae suae in Ecclesia catholica fidem suam profiteri volunt, a rei publicae moderatoribus exspectare possunt et debent ut suae Ecclesiae libertas religiosa agnoscatur. Ipsi enim ius habent vivendi in societate quam libera voluntate elegerunt, quaeque ex

end of society, which consists in the complex of those conditions of social life by which men and women are able to pursue their own perfection more fully and with greater ease,[12] and at the same time observe more faithfully the inalienable rights that God has bestowed on all.

If, therefore, in certain manifestations of man's religious sense, perverse practices are discovered that clearly harm the dignity of the person and the rights of others, government leaders must oppose these practices, in accord with principles of prudence.[13]

On the other hand, it is wrong for government leaders to impose on citizens the profession or rejection of any religion as a condition for being able to participate in national and civil life, either in full or in part. Religious freedom is likewise offended when anyone is punished for religious reasons. It is also violated when, on account of their religion, citizens are unjustly deprived of their goods, refused those things necessary for a decent life, denied social equality or nationality, refused access to civil activities, or denied the exercise of those fundamental rights which, especially today, are universally acknowledged and agreed upon.[14]

On the other hand, government leaders are bound to protect the person's right to freedom in religious matters effectively and to promote it in a fitting way.[15] For it is proper to the state not only to acknowledge and uphold the person's rights, but also to facilitate their exercise, and to prevent obstacles from being put in place for men and women in their exercising rights of this kind.[16]

30. (*The freedom of religious groups in society*). The right to religious freedom that belongs to individual persons must be recognized for groups as well. For these are established by the free will of persons, under the direction of their conscience. Furthermore, such groups are called for by the social nature of men and their dignity, so that they may truly be able to live out their religion.

These groups therefore have the right, within the limits imposed by the end of society, as stated above, to govern themselves according to their own laws, to honor God with public worship, to assist their members in their practice of religious life, to strengthen them by instruction, [321] and to promote institutions in which members can assist one another in ordering the activities of their life according to their religious principles.

Therefore, men and women who wish to profess their faith in the Catholic Church according to the dictates of their conscience can and should expect government leaders to acknowledge the religious freedom of their Church. For they have the right to live in a community that they have cho-

ipsorum animi persuasione, a Deo volita et a Christo fundata est tamquam institutio sine qua integra vita christiana dari non potest, quandoquidem ad essentiam vitae christianae pertinet ut vivatur in populo seu in communitate instrumentis salutis praedita.

His perpensis, haec Sacra Synodus declarat vim quamlibet ad religionem ipsam delendam sive in toto genere humano, sive in aliqua regione, sive in determinato coetu religioso, manifestissime et gravissime laedere voluntatem Creatoris et Salvatoris hominum, atque ipsa sacra personae humanae et familiae gentium iura.

Ius pariter coetibus religiosis competit ut sincerae honestaeque propagationi seu annuntiationi religionis studeant, vitato tamen « proselytismo » quippe qui mediis impropriis et inhonestis utatur. Illi coetus impediri nequaquam possunt quominus rationes suae religionis proponant, ut apud auditores persuasio religiosa oriatur, qua moti sese libere eorum Communitati adsocient.

Civiles potestates nullam directam capacitatem et competentiam ad determinandas vel moderandas relationes civium cum Creatore ac Salvatore suo possident, ideoque non possunt Communitates religiosas temporalibus finibus reipublicae subordinare. Quo magis autem societas civilis propitias suppeditat condiciones ad vitam religiosam fovendam, eo magis ipsa fruetur bonis quae undequaque proveniunt ex fidelitate hominum erga vocationem suam divinam.

31. (*Libertas religiosa praesenti aetate*). Postquam Sacra Synodus hac sua declaratione affirmavit personae humanae et Ecclesiae aliarumque Communitatum religiosarum ius ad libertatem religiosam in societate ubique et ab omnibus observandum esse, omnes huius aetatis homines denique adprecatur ut considerent quantopere libertas religiosa in praesentibus adiunctis agnoscenda et defendenda sit.[17]

Manifestum enim est genus humanum magis magisque in dies unum fieri, arctiores fieri relationes quibus homines diversae culturae et religionis inter se connectuntur, augeri apud omnes conscientiam propriae cuiusque responsabilitatis, rem publicam ob ipsam etiam iuridicam sui regiminis configurationem ineptam esse ad iudicia de veritate circa rem [322] religiosam ferenda. Pacifica cohabitatio et iusta concordia in Familia humana hodie ut cum maxime dari non possunt, nisi ubique terrarum suprema et sanctissima Dei vocatio atque suprema hominum iura et officia ad vitam religiosam libere in societate ducendam observentur. Faxit igitur Deus et Pater omnium

sen with free will and out of inner conviction, a community that has been willed by God and founded by Christ as that institution without which one cannot live an integral Christian life; indeed, it belongs to the essence of the Christian life that it be lived out among this people or community, which has been given as the instrument of salvation.

Having weighed these considerations, this sacred Council declares that any use of force intended to destroy religion itself, either in the human race as a whole or in a particular region or in a specific religious group, manifestly and gravely violates the will of the Creator and Savior of mankind and the sacred rights of the human person and of the family of nations.

Religious groups likewise have the right to sincerely and honestly spread or preach their religion, while avoiding any "proselytism" that would make use of improper or dishonest means. These groups cannot be impeded in any way from proposing reasons for their religion in order to inspire religious conviction among their listeners, so that the latter, moved by this conviction, may freely join their community.

Civil powers have no direct capacity or competence to determine or regulate the relationship between citizens and their Creator and Savior, and therefore cannot subordinate religious communities to the temporal ends of the state. The more that civil society provides favorable conditions for fostering religious life, however, the more it will enjoy those goods that come forth everywhere from men's fidelity to their divine vocation.

31. (*Religious freedom in the present time*). Finally, having proclaimed in this declaration the right to religious freedom in society, a right that belongs to the human person, to the Church, and to other religious communities, and that must be observed everywhere by all persons, this sacred Council implores all men and women of our time to consider how necessary it is for religious freedom to be acknowledged and defended in the present circumstances.[17]

It is clear that mankind is becoming more and more united every day; that men and women of different cultures and religions are being joined to one another with closer ties; that there is a growing consciousness by all of the responsibility proper to each person; and that the state, on account of the juridical structure of its government, is considered unfit to pass judgment on truths that concern [322] religious matters. Peaceful coexistence and just harmony cannot be fully achieved within the human family today, however, unless the supreme and most holy calling of God and the supreme rights and duties of men and women to lead a religious life freely in society be ob-

ut Familia humana, diligenter servata sociali libertate religiosa in societate, per gratiam Christi et virtute Spiritus Sancti adducatur ad superiorem illam ac perennem libertatem « qua Christus nos liberavit » (*Gal.* 5, 1).

NOTAE

[1] Modo suo oecumenico decretum proponit altam doctrinam IOANNIS PP. XXIII in Litt. Encycl. *Pacem in terris.* Duo sunt praecipua capita doctrinae:

1) «In hominis iuribus hoc quoque numerandum est, ut et Deum, ad rectam conscientiae suae normam, venerari possit, et religionem privatim publice profiteri» (*A.A.S.*, 55 [1963], p. 260);
2) huic iuri officium respondet illud agnoscendi et colendi; quod officium incumbit
   a) omnibus aliis hominibus (*ibid.*, p. 264), et maxime *b)* rei publicae curatoribus (*ibid.*, pp. 273-74).

Doctrinam hanc sui praedecessoris fel. record. apertis verbis sanxit PAULUS VI glor. regn.: « Ob huiusmodi dolores quanta afficimur tristitia, et quam vehementer dolemus, cum cernimus in quibusdam territoriis religiosam libertatem, sicut alia praecipua hominis iura, opprimi eorum principiis et artibus, qui opiniones a suis diversas de re politica, de hominum stirpibus, de cuiusvis generis religione non tolerant. Dolemus praeterea tot adhuc iniurias alicubi iis esse illatas, qui religionem suam honeste ac libere profiteri velint » (*Allocutio* ad Patres Concilii Oecumenici Vaticani II, 29 sept. 1963: *A.A.S.*, 55 [1963], pp. 855-856).

Haec porro doctrina proponitur ut terminus hodiernus longioris evolutionis tum in doctrina catholica de dignitate personae humanae tum in Ecclesiae pastorali sollicitudine pro hominis libertate. In hac evolutione principium continuitatis est ipsa haec doctrina atque sollicitudo. Principium vero progressus est duplex distinctio, quae ab Ecclesia lentius facta est, quaeque a IOANNE PP. XXIII clare tandem est affirmata. Primo, distinguendum est inter falsas ideologias, quas vocant, et incepta atque instituta, quae ordinem civilem et politicum contingunt ut haec, quatenus cum rectae rationis praeceptis congruant, probari possint, illis ideologiis falsis constanter reiectis (cf. *ibid.*, p. 300). Deinde, distinguendum est inter errores religiosos et personam humanam bona fide errantem, ut iura, quae ad dignitatem libertatemque humanam pertinent, adhuc agnosci et coli debeant, illis ipsis erroribus immutabiliter denegatis (cf. *ibid.*, pp. 299-300).

His accedit, quod rerum eventus continuo mutabilis occasionem praebuit veri nominis progressus in doctrina Ecclesiae in eiusque sollicitudine pastorali, ut his diebus ad amplissimum humanae libertatis patrocinium suscipiendum Ecclesia obstringatur, quod est explendum et doctrina magisteriali et omnium fidelium actuositate (cf. *ibid., fere passim*). Etenim IOANNES PP. XXIII, una cum veritate, iustitia, caritate, etiam libertatem effert, utpote quae est his nostris temporibus omnis bene ordinatae civitatis necessaria consuetudo (cf. pp. 266,

served everywhere on earth. May God the Father of all therefore grant that the human family, having diligently upheld social religious freedom within society, be led by the grace of Christ and the power of the Holy Spirit to that superior and everlasting freedom "for which Christ has set us free" (Gal 5:1).

NOTES

[1] In its own ecumenical way, this decree proposes the lofty teaching of Pope John XXIII, expressed in the Encyclical Letter *Pacem in terris*. Two points are particularly central to this teaching:

1) "Also among man's rights is that of being able to worship God in accordance with the right dictates of his own conscience, and to profess his religion both in private and in public" (AAS 55 [1963], 260);

2) There corresponds to this right the duty to acknowledge and care for it; this duty is the responsibility of *a)* all other men (*ibid.*, 264) and especially *b)* government leaders (*ibid.*, 273-74).

Paul VI expressly sanctioned this teaching of his predecessor: "On account of sufferings of this kind we are afflicted with much sorrow, and grieve exceedingly, when we see that in certain lands religious freedom, like other particular rights of man, is suppressed by the principles and practices of men who do not tolerate opinions that differ from their own concerning political affairs, the origin of men, or religion of any kind. In addition, we grieve that so many injuries have been inflicted thus far in any land against those who wish to profess their religion honestly and freely" ("Address to the Fathers of the Second Vatican Council," 29 September 1963: AAS, 55 [1963], 855-56).

This teaching is proposed as the current terminus of a rather long evolution, both in Catholic teaching on the dignity of the human person and in the Church's pastoral concern for human freedom. In this evolution, the principle of continuity itself constitutes this teaching and concern. In truth, the principle of progress contains a two-fold distinction that has been made by the Church rather slowly, but that has in the end been clearly declared by Pope John XXIII. First, the distinction must be made between what may be called false ideologies, on the one hand, and the undertakings and institutions that are connected with the civil and political order, on the other; the latter, to the extent that they are in harmony with the precepts of right reason, can be accepted, while the former false ideologies must be consistently rejected (cf. *ibid.*, 300). Second, the distinction must be made between religious error and the human person who errs in good faith; the rights that belong to human dignity and freedom should continue to be recognized and respected, while the errors themselves must be constantly rejected (cf. *ibid.*, 299-300).

In addition, the continually changing nature of things affords the occasion for true progress in the Church's teaching and in its pastoral concern, so that today the Church is obliged to undertake the fullest defense of human freedom, which is to be carried out both in magisterial teaching and in the actions of all the faithful (cf. *ibid., passim*). Indeed, Pope John XXIII proclaimed freedom also, along with truth, justice, and charity, to be a necessary element of every well-ordered state in our times (cf. 266, 268, 279, 297, [**323**] 301). Undoubtedly, in the

268, 279, 297, [323] 301). Quod utique est in documentis Ecclesiae simul novum quid, simul traditioni alte catholicae quid consentaneum quam maxime.

Enimvero sicut olim, ita hodie, ab Ecclesia damnatur libertas conscientiae illa, quam praedicaverunt rationalismi fautores, hoc fundamento innixi, quod individual conscientia exlex est, ut nullis sit normis obnoxia divinitus traditis. Damnatur etiam hodie, sicut olim, libertas cultus illa, cuius principium est indifferentismus religiosus, ex radice relativismi doctrinalis deducta. Neque minus hodie, quam olim, damnatur illa separatio Ecclesiae a Statu, quae dicitur, quam proponit theoria rationalistica de iuridica omnicompetentia Status, secundum quam Ecclesia intra ipsum organismum Status incorporetur necesse est, ut sit potestati statali subiecta. Integram plenamque vim suam retinent hae damnationes olim latae, quia inconcussum manet earum principium, quod est doctrina catholica de hominis dignitate et sollicitudo catholica pro veri nominis libertate. Dignitas enim hominis in hoc reponitur, quod soli Deo vivo et vero serviat, et libertas hominis in hoc maxime manifestatur, quod hoc servitium sit liberum, ad rectam normam propriae conscientiae praestitum.

Ast hoc idem principium nostris his temporibus ad novas ducit conclusiones, quas efformare coeperunt Romani Pontifices recentiores. Periculum enim non iam adest, ne falsi nominis libertas dignitati humanae iniuriam faciat, quod olim accidit. Novum adest periculum, ne libertatis humanae omne genus nova quadam tyrannide obruatur, pereunte primo libertate religiosa quod absit. Pro sua ergo aucta sollicitudine curaque erga hominis dignitatem, doctrinam traditionalem novo modo, nostris temporibus accommodato, aptaverunt recentiores Romani Pontifices. Collocant enim inter iura hominis praecipua ius ad liberum exercitium religionis in societate, iuxta dictamina conscientiae rectae, sive vera sit conscientia sive errore veritatis aut impari rerum sacrarum cognitione bona fide capta (cf. *Pacem in terris, A.A.S.*, 55 [1963], p. 299). Eamdem doctrinam eamdemque, quae ei subest, sollicitudinem proponit praesens *Decretum de Libertate Religiosa*.

[2] Cf. *Rom*. 15, 6.

[3] Cf. *Col*. 4, 5.

[4] Cf. *Io*. 18, 37.

[5] Cf. *Eph*. 4, 15.

[6] Cf. IOANNES XXIII, Litt. Encycl. *Pacem in terris*, 11 aprilis 1963: A.A.S., 55 (1963), pp. 299-300: « Omnino errores ab iis qui opinione labuntur semper distinguere aequum est, quamvis de hominibus agatur, qui aut errore veritatis aut impari rerum cognitione capti sint, vel ad sacra vel ad optimam vitae actionem attinentium. Nam homo ad errorem lapsus iam non humanitate instructus esse desinit, neque suam umquam personae dignitatem amittit, cuius ratio est semper habenda. Praeterea in hominis natura numquam facultas perit et refragandi erroribus et viam ad veritatem quaerendi. Neque umquam hac in re providentissimi Dei auxilia hominem deficiunt. Ex quo fieri potest, ut, si quis hodie vel perspicuitate egeat, vel in falsas discesserit sententias, possit postmodum, Dei collustratus lumine, veritatem amplecti ».

[7] Cf. PIUS XII, Alloc. ad Praelatos auditores ceterosque officiales et administros Tribunalis S. Romanae Rotae, 6 oct. 1946: A.A.S., 38 (1946), p. 394, ubi citatur a R. P. *Pro Memoria* Secretariae Status ad Legationem Yugoslaviae ad Sanctam Sedem: « D'après les principes de la doctrine catholique, la conversion doit être le résultat, non pas de contraintes extérieures mais de l'adhésion de l'âme [324] aux verités enseignées par l'Eglise catholique. C'est pour cela que l'Eglise catholique n'admet pas dans son sein les adultes, qui demandent à y entrer

writings of the Church this is something new and at the same time altogether consistent with the depths of the Catholic tradition.

To be sure, just as she has in the past, the Church condemns also today that freedom of conscience that is proclaimed by proponents of rationalism, who claim that the individual conscience is beyond the law, and so not liable to any divinely given norms. Also today, as in the past, the Church condemns that freedom of worship that has its origins in a religious indifferentism rooted in doctrinal relativism. No less today than formerly does the Church condemn the so-called separation of Church and state proposed by the rationalistic theory of a juridically omnicompetent state, according to which the Church must necessarily be incorporated within the organization of the state itself, in order to be subjected to its power. These former condemnations retain their full and complete force because their principle remains unshaken, namely, the Catholic teaching on the dignity of man and the Catholic concern for true freedom. For the dignity of man is found in serving the living and true God alone, and the freedom of man is most fully revealed in the fact that this service is to be free, offered in accordance with the right precepts of his own conscience.

But in our time this same principle leads to new conclusions, which the recent popes have begun to formulate. For the danger today is not that a false kind of freedom should harm human dignity, as happened formerly. A new danger is arising, namely, that every kind of human freedom might be overthrown by a new kind of tyranny, with religious freedom perishing first of all. In keeping with their growing concern and care for the dignity of man, the recent popes have therefore adapted the traditional teaching in a new way that is accommodated to our times. For among the particular rights of man they include also the right to the free exercise of religion in society, according to the dictates of an upright conscience, whether this conscience be true or in good faith overcome by error or an inadequate understanding of sacred matters (cf. *Pacem in terris*, AAS 55 [1963], 299). The same teaching and the same underlying concern is proposed by the present *Decree on Religious Freedom*.

[2] Cf. Rom 15:6.

[3] Cf. Col 4:5.

[4] Cf. Jn 18:37.

[5] Cf. Eph 4:15.

[6] Cf. John XXIII, Encyclical Letter *Pacem in terris*, 11 April 1963: AAS 55 (1963), 299-300: "It is always perfectly justifiable to distinguish between error as such and the person who falls into error—even in the case of men who err regarding the truth or are led astray as a result of their inadequate knowledge, in matters either of religion or of the highest ethical standards. A man who has fallen into error does not cease to be a man. He never forfeits his personal dignity; and that is something that must always be taken into account. Besides, there exists in man's very nature an undying capacity to break through the barriers of error and seek the road to truth. God, in his great providence, is ever present with his aid. Today, maybe, a man lacks faith and turns aside into error; tomorrow, perhaps, illumined by God's light, he may indeed embrace the truth."

[7] Cf. Pius XII, "Allocution to prelate auditors and other officials and administrators of the Tribunal of the Sacred Roman Rota," 6 October 1946: AAS 38 (1946), 394, where the pope cites the *pro memoria* of the Secretariat of State to the Yugoslavian Embassy to the Holy See: "In accordance with the principles of Catholic teaching, conversion should be the result not of external constraints but of the soul's adherence [324] to the truths taught by the Catholic Church. This is why the Catholic Church admits to herself adults who seek to enter or return

ou à y faire retour, qu'à la condition qu'ils soient pleinement conscients de la portée et des conséquences de l'acte qu'ils veulent accomplir ». IDEM, Litt. Encyl. *Mystici Corporis,* 29 iunii 1943: *A.A.S.,* 35 (1943), p. 243: «At si cupimus non intermissam eiusmodi totius mystici Corporis conprecationem admoveri Deo, ut aberrantes omnes in unum Iesu Christi ovile quam primum ingrediantur, profitemur tamen omnino necessarium esse id sponte libenterque fieri, cum nemo credat nisi volens. Quamobrem si qui, non credentes, eo reapse compelluntur ut Ecclesiae aedificium intrent, ut ad altare accedant, sacramentaque suscipiant, ii procul dubio veri christifideles non fiunt; fides enim, sine qua « impossibile est placere Deo » (*Hebr.* 11, 6), liberrimum esse debet « obsequium intellectus et voluntatis » (CONC. VAT., *Const. de fide catholica,* cap. 3). Si igitur aliquando contingat, ut contra constantem Apostolicae huius Sedis doctrinam, ad amplexandam catholicam fidem aliquis adigatur invitus, id Nos facere non possumus quin, pro officii nostri conscientia, reprobamus ».

[8] LACTANTIUS, *Divinarum Institutionum,* lib. V, 19: ed. S. Brandt et G. Laubmann, *CSEL* 19, p. 463; *PL* 6, 614 (cap. 20): « Non est opus vi et iniuria, quia religio cogi non potest, verbis potius quam verberibus res agenda est, ut sit voluntas ».

Op. cit.: CSEL 19, p. 464; *PL* 6, 614: « Itaque nemo a nobis retinetur invitus—inutilis est enim Deo qui devotione ac fide caret—et tamen nemo discedit ipsa veritate retinente ».

Op. cit.: CSEL 19, p. 465; *PL* 6, 616: « Nihil est enim tam voluntarium quam religio, in qua si animus sacrificantis aversus est, iam sublata, iam nulla est ».

S. AMBROSIUS, *Epistola ad Valentinianum Imp.,* Ep. 21: *PL* 16, 1047: « Dei lex nos docuit quid sequamur, humanae leges hoc docere non possunt. Extorquere solent timidis commutationem, fidem inspirare non possunt ».

S. AUGUSTINUS, *Contra litteras Peliliani,* lib. II, cap. 83: ed. M. Petschenig, *CSEL* 52, p. 112; *PL* 43, 315; cf. C. 23, q. 5, c. 33 (ed. Friedberg, col. 939): « Augustinus respondit: Ad fidem quidem nullus est cogendus invitus; sed per severitatem, immo et per misericordiam Dei tribulationum flagellis solet perfidia castigari ».

S. GREGORIUS MAGNUS, *Epistola ad Virgilium et Theodorum Episcopos Massilliae Galliarum,* Registrum Epistolarum, I, 45: ed. P. Ewald et L. M. Hartmann, *MGH Ep.* 1, p. 72; *PL* 77, 510-11 (lib. I, ep. 47): « Dum enim quis piam ad baptismatis fontem non praedicationis suavitate, sed necessitate pervenerit, ad pristinam superstitionem remeans inde deterius moritur, unde renatus esse videbatur ».

Epistola ad Iohannem Episcopum Constantinopolitanum, Registrum Epistolarum, III, 52: *MGH Ep.* 1, p. 210; *PL* 77, 649 (lib. III, ep. 53); cf. D. 45, c. 1 (ed. Friedberg, col. 160): « Nova vero atque inaudita est ista praedicatio, quae verberibus exigit fidem ».

CONC. TOLET. IV, c. 57: MANSI 10, 633; cf. D. 45, c. 5 (ed. Friedberg, col. 161-162): « De Iudaeis hoc praecepit sancta synodus, nemini deinceps ad credendum vim inferre; *cui enim vult Deus misereretur, et quem vult indurare.* Non enim tales inviti salvandi sunt, sed volentes, ut integra sit forma iustitiae: sicut enim homo proprii arbitrii voluntate serpenti oboediens periit, sic vocante gratia [325] Dei, propriae mentis conversione homo quisque credendo salvatur. Ergo non vi, sed libera arbitrii facultate, ut convertantur suadendi sunt, non potius impellendi . . . ».

to her only on the condition that they are fully conscious of the significance and consequences of the act they wish to make." Cf. also the Encyclical Letter *Mystici Corporis*, 29 June 1943: AAS 35 (1943), 243: "Though we desire this unceasing prayer to rise to God from the whole mystical body in common, that all the straying sheep may hasten to enter the one fold of Jesus Christ, we still recognize that this must be done of their own free will; for no one believes unless he wills to believe. Hence they are most certainly not genuine Christians who against their belief are forced to go into a church, to approach the altar and to receive the sacraments; for the 'faith without which it is impossible to please God' (Heb 11:6) is an entirely free 'submission of intellect and will' (First Vatican Council, *Constitution on the Catholic Faith*, ch. 3). Therefore, whenever it happens, despite the constant teaching of this apostolic see, that anyone is compelled to embrace the Catholic faith against his will, our sense of duty demands that we condemn the act."

[8] Lactantius, *Divinarum Institutionum*, bk. V, 19: ed. S. Brandt and G. Laubmann, *CSEL* 19, p. 463; *PL* 6, 614 (ch. 20): "There is no need for violence or injury, for religion cannot be forced; the whole matter should be carried on with words rather than whips, in order that there might be free will."

Op. cit.: *CSEL* 19, p. 464; *PL* 6, 614: "Therefore we hold no one back against his will—for anyone who is without devotion and faith is of no use to God—and yet no one departs who is held fast by the truth itself."

Op. cit.: *CSEL* 19, p. 465; *PL* 6, 616: "For nothing is so voluntary as religion; once the spirit of the one offering sacrifice has turned away, religion is already destroyed, is itself already nothing."

St. Ambrose, *Epistola ad Valentinianum Imp.*, Ep. 21, *PL* 16, 1047: "God's law taught us what to strive for; human laws cannot teach this. Such laws are merely accustomed to extorting a change from the faint of heart; they cannot inspire faith."

St. Augustine, *Contra litteras Petiliani*, bk. II, ch. 83: ed. M Petschenig, *CSEL* 52, p. 112; *PL* 43, 315; cf. C. 23, q. 5, ch. 33 (ed. Friedberg, col. 939): "Augustine replied: No one, indeed, is forced to embrace the faith against his will; but through the severity of God, or rather through his mercy, faithlessness is usually punished by the lashes of tribulation."

St. Gregory the Great, *Epistola ad Virgilium et Theodorum Episcopos Massilliae Galliarium*, Registrum Epistolarum, I, 45: ed. P. Ewald and L.M. Hartmann, *MGH Ep.* 1, p. 72; *PL* 77, 510-11 (bk. I, ep. 47): "For if anyone should have come to the holy baptismal font, not through the persuasion of preaching, but out of compulsion, when he returns to the place of his former superstition he will die the worse for it, having come from a place where he only seemed to have been reborn."

Epistola ad Iohannem Episcopum Constantinopolitanum, Registrum Epistolarum, III, 52: *MGH Ep.* 1, p. 210; *PL* 77, 649 (bk. III, ep. 53); cf. D. 45, ch. 1 (ed. Friedberg, col. 160): "That preaching is indeed new and unheard of, that exacts faith by means of lashing."

Fourth Council of Toledo, ch. 57: Mansi 10, 633; cf. D. 45, ch. 5 (ed. Friedberg, col. 161-162); "Concerning the Jews, the holy synod declared that henceforth force is not to be applied to anyone in order to make them believe; *for God has mercy on whom he wishes, and hardens whom he wishes*. For such men are to be saved not unwillingly but willingly, in order that justice may be perfect: for just as man perished by obeying the serpent through his own free-will, so at the call of [325] God's grace, each man is saved by believing through the conversion of his own mind. Therefore, not by force, but by the free judgment of their own free will are they to be persuaded to convert, rather than compelled . . ."

CLEMENS III, *Litterae Decretales*: X, V, 6, 9, ed. Friedberg col. 774: «... Statuimus enim ut nullus Christianus invitos vel nolentes Iudaeos ad baptismum (per violentiam) venitre compellat. Si quis autem ad Christianos causa fidei confugerit, postquam voluntas eius fuerit patefacta, Christianus absque calumnia efficiatur; quippe Christi fidem habere non creditur, qui ad Christianorum baptismum non spontaneus, sed invitus cogitur pervenire ... ».

INNOCENTIUS III, *Epistola ad Arelatensem Archiepiscopum*, X, III, 42, 3: ed. Friedberg, col. 646: «... Verum id est religioni Christianae contrarium, ut semper invitus et penitus contradicens ad recipiendam et servandam Christianitatem aliquis compellatur ... ».

«Ad amplexandam fidem catholicam nemo invitus cogatur » *C.I.C.*, c. 1351. Ut patet ex textu supra citato, haec norma canonica ex S. Augustino provenit. Inde excerpta in *Decretum* et postea in *Codicem* translata est.

[9] Cf. *Io.* 6, 44.

[10] Cf. IOANNES XXIII, Litt. Encycl. *Pacem in terris*, 11 aprilis 1963: *A.A.S.*, 55 (1963), pp. 260-261: «In hominis iuribus hoc quoque numerandum est, ut et Deum, ad rectam conscientiae suae normam, venerari possit, et religionem privatim publice profiteri ». Cf. PIUS XII, *Nuntius radiophonicus*, 24 dec. 1942: *A.A.S.*, 35 (1943), p. 19, ubi inter « iura fundamentalia personae» hoc etiam collocatur: « il diritto al culto di Dio privato e pubblico, compresa l'azione caritativa religiosa ». Cf. PIUS XI, Litt. Encycl. *Mit brennender Sorge*, 14 martii 1937: *A.A.S.*, 29 (1937), p. 160: « Der gläubige Mensch hat ein unverlierbares Recht, seinen Glauben zu bekennen und in den ihm gemässen Formen zu betätigen. Gesetze, die das Bekenntnis und die Betätigung dieses Glaubens unterdrücken oder erschweren, stehen in Widerspruch mit einem Naturgesetz ». Cf. LEO XIII, Litt. Encycl. *Libertas praestantissimum*, 20 iunii 1888: *Acta Leonis XIII*, 8 (1888), pp. 237-238: « Illa quoque magnopere praedicatur, quam conscientiae libertatem nominant; quae si ita accipiatur ut suo cuique arbitratu aeque liceat Deum colere, non colere, argumentis, quae supra allata sunt, satis convincitur. Sed potest etiam in hanc sententiam accipi, ut homini ex conscientia officii Dei voluntatem sequi et iussa facere, nulla re impediente, in civitate liceat. Haec quidem vera, haec digna filiis Dei libertas, quae humanae dignitatem personae honestissime tuetur, est omni vi iniuriaque maior, eademque Ecclesiae semper optata ac praecipue cara ».

[11] Commemoranda est hoc loco expositio constitutionalismi, qui dicitur, a IOANNE XXIII data in Litt. Encycl. *Pacem in terris*, 11 aprilis 1963, cf. *A.A.S.*, 55 (1963), pp. 278-279, in contextu totius documenti. Est enim huiusmodi constitutionalismus, qui sane religioni christianae plurimum debet, doctrina de iuridiciali et politica civitatis compositione secundum quam «potestas publica suapte natura ad tutandum communitatis bonum spectat, cuius princeps officium est agnoscere honestos libertatis fines eiusque iura sarta tecta servare » (*ibid.*, pp. 285-286). Immo ad constitutionalismum vero sensu christianum pertinet illud quod praedicavit LEO XIII, Litt. Encycl. *Sapientiae christianae*, 10 ianuarii 1890: *A.S.S.*, 22 (1889-90), p. 396: «Dubitari vero salva fide non potest, istiusmodi regimen animorom Ecclesiae esse assignatum uni, nihil ut in eo sit politicae potestati loci; non enim Caesari, sed Petro claves regni caelorum Iesus Christus commendavit ». Agit **[326]** igitur ultra vires, et rem sacram, quae homo est, maxime violat potestas publica, quando sese regimini animorum vel curae animarum immiscet.

[12] Cf. IOANNES XXIII, Litt. Encycl. *Mater et Magistra*, 15 maii 1961: *A.A.S.*, 53 (1961),

Schema 2: Prior Declaration

Clement III, *Litterae Decretales*: X, V, 6, 9, ed. Friedberg col. 774: ". . . For we have decreed that no Christian is to force Jews reluctantly or against their will to approach baptism (by violence). If, however, someone has recourse to Christians on account of his faith, after he has made known his will, let him be made a Christian without dispute; since one who is forced to approach Christian baptism not voluntarily but against his will is not considered to have the faith of Christ . . ."

Innocent III, *Epistola ad Arelatensem Archiepiscopum*, X, III, 42, 3: ed. Friedberg, col. 646: ". . . Truly it is contrary to the Christian religion that anyone ever be forced, against his will and while interiorly opposing it, to receive and keep the Christian faith . . ."

Code of Canon Law [1917], c. 1351: "No one may be forced to embrace the Catholic faith against his will." As is clear from the text cited above, this canonical rule has its origin in St. Augustine. From there it was carried over into the *Decretum* and afterward into the *Code of Canon Law*.

[9] Cf. Jn 6:44.

[10] Cf. John XXIII, Encyclical Letter *Pacem in terris*, 11 April 1963: AAS 55 (1963), 260-61 "Also among man's rights is that of being able to worship God in accordance with the right dictates of his own conscience, and to profess his religion both in private and in public." Cf. Pius XII, Radio message, 24 December 1942: AAS 35 (1943), 19, where among "the fundamental rights of the person" is also included "the right to worship God privately and publicly, including religious charitable activity." Cf. Pius XI, Encyclical Letter *Mit brennender Sorge*, 14 March 1937: AAS 29 (1937), 160: "The believer has an absolute right to profess his faith and live according to its dictates. Laws that impede this profession and practice of faith are against natural law." Cf. Leo XIII, Encyclical Letter *Libertas praestantissimum*, 20 June 1888: Acta Leonis XIII, 8 (1888), 237-38: "Another freedom is widely advocated, namely, freedom of conscience. If by this is meant that everyone may, as he chooses, worship God or not, it is sufficiently refuted by the arguments already adduced. But it may also be taken to mean that every man in the state may follow the will of God and, from a consciousness of duty and free from every obstacle, obey his commands. This, indeed, is true freedom, a freedom worthy of the sons of God, which nobly maintains the dignity of man and is stronger than all violence or wrong—a freedom which the Church has always desired and held most dear."

[11] One must keep in mind here the explanation of constitutionalism provided by John XXIII, in the Encyclical Letter *Pacem in terris*, 11 April 1963: cf. AAS 55 (1963), 278-79, within the context of the entire document. This kind of constitutionalism, which in fact owes much to the Christian religion, is a doctrine that concerns the juridical and political composition of the state, according to which "the whole raison d'être of the public power is to safeguard the interests of the community. Its sovereign duty is to recognize the noble realm of freedom and protect its rights" (*ibid.*, 285-86). Indeed, Leo XIII's statements in the Encyclical Letter *Sapientiae christianae*, 10 January 1890: ASS 22 (1889-1890), 396, concern Christian constitutionalism in the true sense: "No one can, however, without risk to faith, foster any doubt as to the Church alone having been invested with such power of governing souls as to exclude altogether the civil authority. In truth, it was not to Caesar but to Peter that Jesus Christ entrusted the keys of the kingdom of heaven." [326] The public power therefore exceeds its powers and completely violates sacred matters, of which man himself is a part, when it involves itself in the governing of minds or the care of souls.

[12] Cf. John XXIII, Encyclical Letter *Mater et Magistra*, 15 May 1961: AAS 53 (1961), 417:

p. 417: «... debent qui publicae rei praesunt compertam habere rectam de communi omnium bono notionem, quae summam complectitur earum vitae socialis condicionum, quibus homines suam ipsorum perfectionem possint plenius atque expeditius consequi». Cf. etiam IOANNES XXIII, Litt. Encycl. *Pacem in terris,* 11 aprilis 1963: *A.A.S.,* 55 (1963), p. 273.

[13] Quod attinet ad intolerantiam religiosam ex parte potestatis publicae, suprema principia tradit PIUS XII, Alloc. *Ci riesce,* 6 dec. 1953: *A.A.S.,* 45 (1953), pp. 798-799: Può darsi che in determinate circostanze Egli (Dio) non dia agli uomini nessun mandato, non imponga nessun dovere, non dia persino nessun diritto d'impedire e di reprimere ciò che è erroneo e falso? Uno sguardo alla realtà dà una risposta affermativa». Et, allato exemplo divinae providentiae, pergit: « Quindi l'affermazione: Il traviamento religioso e morale deve essere sempre impedito, quanto è possibile, perchè la sua tolleranza è in se stessa immorale, non può valere nella sua incondizionata assolutezza. D'altra parte, Dio non ha dato nemmeno all'autorità umana un siffatto precetto assoluto e universale, nè in campo della fede nè in quello della morale. Non conosco un tale precetto ne la comune convinzione degli uomini, nè la coscienza cristiana, nè le fonti della rivelazione, nè la prassi della Chiesa ».

[14] Cf. IOANNES XXIII, Litt. Encycl. *Pacem in terris,* 11 aprilis 1963: *A.A.S.,* 55 (1963), pp. 295-296, ubi, quibusdam defectibus non obstantibus, commendatur Professio Universalis Iurium Humanorum, die 10 dec. 1948 a Foederatarum Nationum Coetu Generali rata habita: «Nihilominus Professionem eamdem habendam esse censemus quemdam quasi gradum atque aditum ad iuridicialem politicamque ordinationem constituendam omnium populorum, qui in mundo sunt. Siquidem ea universis prorsus hominibus solemniter agnoscitur humanae dignitas personae, atque iura cuivis homini asseruntur veritatem libere quaerendi, honestatis sequendi normas, iustitiae officia usurpandi, vitam exigendi homine dignam, alia deinceps cum hisce coniuncta».

[15] Iuri ad libertatem religiosam, sicut ceteris naturae iuribus, respondet officium in aliis hominibus: cf. IOANNES XXIII, Litt. Encycl. *Pacem in terris,* 11 aprilis 1963: *A.A.S.,* 55 (1963), p. 264: « Quibus probatis, consequens est etiam, ut in hominum consortione unius hominis naturali cuidam iuri officium aliorum hominum respondeat; officium videlicet ius illud agnoscendi et colendi ». Hoc officio praecipue tenetur potestas publica: « Verum cum nostra hac aetate commune bonum maxime in humanae personae servatis iuribus et officiis consistere putetur, tum praecipue in eo sint oportet curatorum rei publicae partes, ut hinc iura agnoscantur, colantur, inter se componantur, defendantur, provehantur, illinc suis quisque officiis facilius fungi possit » (*ibid.,* pp. 273-274). Et citatur PIUS XII, *Nuntius radiophonicus,* 1 iunii 1941: *A.A.S.,* 33 (1941), p. 200: « Inviolabilia iura tueri, hominum propria, atque curare, ut facilius quisque suis muneribus defungatur, hoc cuiusvis publicae potestatis officium est praecipuum ».

[16] Quod pertinet ad dignitatem illam civilem, secundum quam dignitas humana in publicum prodit, cf. PIUS XII, *Nuntius radiophonicus,* 24 dec. 1944: *A.A.S.,* 37 (1945), p. 14: « In un popolo degno di tal nome il cittadino sente in se stesso la coscienza della sua personalità, dei suoi doveri e dei suoi diritti, della [327] propria libertà congiunta col rispetto della libertà e della dignità altrui ». Hoc loco commendat Romanus Pontifex etiam illud « ideale di libertà e di uguaglianza » (*loc. cit.*), quod in Statu democratico, iuxta sana rationis principia ordinato, obtineat necesse est, quodque postulat, ut hominis ius in societate ad liberum exercitium religionis plene agnoscatur, colatur, defendatur, provehatur.

[17] Cf. Pius XII, Alloc. ad Praelatos auditores ceterosque bfficiales administros Tribunalis S. Romanae Rotae, 6 oct. 1946: *A.A.S.,* 38 (1946), p. 393: « I sempre più frequenti contatti e la

"... those in public power should have a secure and proper concept of the common good of all, one which embraces the sum of those conditions of social life by which men can pursue their own perfection more fully and without impediment." Cf. also John XXIII, Encyclical Letter *Pacem in terris*, 11 April, 1963: AAS 55 (1963), 273.

[13] Concerning religious intolerance on the part of the public power, the primary principles were indicated by Pius XII, Allocution *Ci riesce*, 6 December 1953; AAS 45 (1953), 798-99: "Is it possible that in certain circumstances God may not give men any mandate, may not impose any duty, may not even communicate the right to impede or to repress what is erroneous and false? One glance at reality indicates that the answer is yes." After giving an example of divine providence, the pope continues: "Hence the assertion: 'religious and moral error should always be impeded as much as possible, because tolerating them is in itself immoral,' cannot be valid absolutely and unconditionally. God has not granted to human authority such an absolute and universal command in matters of faith or morals. I know of no such command, nor does the common conviction of mankind, the Christian conscience, the sources of revelation, or the practice of the Church."

[14] Cf. John XXIII, Encyclical Letter *Pacem in terris*, 11 April 1963: AAS 55 (1963), 295-96, where, certain defects notwithstanding, the pope commends the Universal Declaration of Human Rights, ratified by the General Assembly of the United Nations on December 10, 1948: "Nevertheless, we think the document should be considered a step in the right direction, an approach toward the establishment of a juridical and political ordering of the world community. It is a solemn recognition of the personal dignity of every human being; an assertion of everyone's right to be free to seek out the truth, to follow moral principles, to discharge the duties imposed by justice, and to lead a fully human life. It also recognized other rights connected with these."

[15] As with the other rights of nature, there corresponds to the right to religious freedom a duty toward other men: cf. John XXIII, Encyclical Letter *Pacem in terris*, 11 April 1963: AAS 55 (1963), 264: "Once this is admitted, it follows that in human society one man's natural right gives rise to a corresponding duty in other men; the duty, that is, of recognizing and respecting that right." The public power is especially bound by this duty: "It is generally accepted today that the common good is best safeguarded when personal rights and duties are guaranteed. The chief concern of civil authorities must therefore be to ensure that these rights are recognized, respected, co-ordinated, defended and promoted, and that each individual is enabled to perform his duties more easily" (*ibid.*, 273-274). Here there is a reference to Pius XII, Radio message, 1 June 1941, AAS 33 (1941), 200: "To safeguard the inviolable rights of the human person, and to facilitate the performance of his duties, is the principal duty of every public power."

[16] Concerning man's civil dignity, by which human dignity is extended into the public sphere, cf. Pius XII, Radio message, 24 December 1944: AAS 37 (1945), 14: "In a people worthy of the name, the citizen feels within himself a consciousness of his personhood, of his duties and rights, of [**327**] his own freedom together with respect for the freedom and dignity of others." Here the pope commends also the "ideal of freedom and equality" (*loc. cit.*) that it is necessary to maintain in a democratic state organized according to sound principles of reason, which demands that man's right to the free exercise of religion in society be fully acknowledged, cultivated, defended, and promoted.

[17] Cf. Pius XII, "Allocution to prelate auditors and other officials and administrators of the Tribunal of the Sacred Roman Rota," 6 October 1946: AAS 38 (1946), 393: "The increas-

promiscuità delle diverse confessioni religiose entro i confini di un medesimo popolo hanno condotto i tribunali civili a seguire il principio della "tolleranza" e della "libertà di coscienza". Anzi vi è una tolleranza politica, civile e sociale verso i seguaci delle altre confessioni, che in tali circostanze è anche per i cattolici un dovere morale ».

Insuper, ad Communitatem internationalem quod attinet, cf. PIUS XII, Alloc. *Ci riesce*, 6 dec. 1953: *A.A.S.*, 45 (1953), p. 797: « Gli interessi religiosi e morali esigeranno per tutta la estensione della Comunità (dei popoli) un regolamento ben definito, che valga per tutto il territorio dei singoli Stati sovrani membri di tale Comunità delle nazioni. Secondo le probabilità e le circostanze, è prevedibile che questo regolamento di diritto positivo verrà enunciato così: Nell'interno del suo territorio e per i suoi cittadini ogni Stato regolerà gli affari religiosi e morali con una propria legge; nondimeno in tutto il territorio della Comunità degli Stati sarà permesso ai cittadini di ogni Stato-membro l'esercizio delle proprie credenze e pratiche etiche e religiose, in quanto queste non contravvengano alle leggi penali dello Stato in cui essi soggiornano ». Secundum Romanum Pontificem, cives catholici et Status catholici moderatores possunt ex conscientia eiusmodi legi consentire.

ingly frequent contact and co-mingling of different religious confessions within the borders of the same nation have led civil courts to follow the principles of 'tolerance' and 'freedom of conscience.' There is, in fact, a political, civil and social tolerance toward those of other faiths which in certain circumstances is a moral obligation for Catholics also."

In addition, regarding the international community, cf. Pius XII, Allocution *Ci riesce*, 6 December 1953: AAS 45 (1953), 797: "The interests of religion and morality will require for the whole extent of the community of nations a well-defined rule, one that will hold throughout the territory of each individual sovereign member state of the community of nations. Depending on the circumstances, it is likely that this rule of positive law will be set forth as follows: within its own territory and for its own citizens, each state will regulate religious and moral affairs according to its own laws; nevertheless, throughout the whole territory of the community of states, the citizens of every member state will be allowed to exercise their own beliefs and ethical and religious practices, as long as they do not contravene the penal laws of the state in which they are residing." According to the pope, Catholic citizens and leaders of Catholic states can in good conscience consent to such a law.

SCHEMA DECLARATIONIS DE LIBERTATE RELIGIOSA

Textus emendatus

(Acta Synodalia III/8, 426-49)

DE IURE PERSONAE ET COMMUNITATUM AD LIBERTATEM IN RE RELIGIOSA

I. LIBERTATIS RELIGIOSAE GENERALIS RATIO

1. (*Rerum status hodiernus*). Dignitatis personae humanae hac nostra aetate homines magis magisque conscii fiunt.[1] Exigunt libertates civiles, ut possint in societate vitam agere homine dignam. Itemque postulant iuridicam limitationem potestatis publicae, ne fines honestae libertatis personalis nimis circumscribantur. Quae libertatis postulatio maxime ea respicit, quae ad religionem spectant. In permultis publicis civitatum constitutionibus civium libertas in re religiosa instituta est tamquam stabile regimen.[2]

Libertas religiosa communiter hodie intelligitur esse verum ius, in dignitate humana fundatum, quod debet in iuridica et politica compositione societatis ita agnosci, ut ius civile [427] evadat. Percipitur insuper esse ius, secundum quod homines debent liberi seu immunes esse a coercitione ex parte hominum et cuiusvis potestatis mere humanae, non solum in sua conscientia efformanda de re religiosa, sed etiam in religionis libero exercitio. Quod quidem exercitium religionis agnoscitur liberum esse debere duplici sensu, ut scilicet in re religiosa nemo cogatur ad agendum contra suam conscientiam, neque impediatur quominus iuxta suam conscientiam agat, intra limites qui certa norma morali et iuridica determinantur. Denique intelligitur tutelam huius iuris tum ad singulos homines tum maxime ad potestates publicas pertinere.

Per hanc igitur iuridicam libertatis religiosae notionem, quae nostra aetate generatim agnoscitur, nullatenus significatur hominem nulla obligatione in re religiosa teneri aut a Dei potestate emancipari. Non enim concip-

DRAFT OF THE DECLARATION ON RELIGIOUS FREEDOM

Emended Text

(*Acta Synodalia* III/8, 426-49)

ON THE RIGHT OF THE PERSON AND OF COMMUNITIES
TO FREEDOM IN RELIGIOUS MATTERS

I. THE GENERAL PRINCIPLE OF RELIGIOUS FREEDOM

1. (*Present state of affairs*). Men and women of our time are becoming more and more conscious of the dignity of the human person.[1] They demand civil liberties, in order that they may be able to lead a life in society that is worthy of man. They also demand that juridical limits be set to the public power, in order that rightful personal freedom not be excessively restricted. This demand for freedom is chiefly concerned with those things that concern religion. In numerous state constitutions the freedom of citizens in religious matters has already been instituted as a fixed practice.[2]

Religious freedom is commonly understood today to be a true right, having its foundation in human dignity, a right that should be acknowledged in the juridical and political structure of society, so that it [427] becomes a civil right. It is understood as a right according to which men and women should be free or immune from coercion on the part of other men or of any merely human power, not only in forming their conscience in religious matters, but also in the free exercise of their religion. Indeed, it is acknowledged that the exercise of religion should be free in a twofold sense, namely, that in religious matters no one may be forced to act against his conscience, nor prevented from acting according to his conscience, within the limits determined by established moral and juridical norms. Finally, it is understood that the protection of this right is the responsibility of both individuals and especially public powers.

This juridical conception of religious freedom, therefore, which is generally acknowledged today, in no way implies that man has no obligations in religious matters, or that he is set free from God's authority. It is not

285

itur ac si persona humana falsum et verum possit aeque aestimare, vel ipsi officium non incumbat formandi veram sibi de rebus religiosis sententiam vel arbitrario statuere valeat utrum, in qua religione et quanam ratione Deo servire velit.[3]

2. (*Quaestio historica*). Patet igitur libertatem religiosam hodie non eodem modo ac olim considerari. Revera saeculo decimo nono in multis nationibus invalere coepit ideologia, laicismus nuncupata.[4] Nitebatur in placito rationalistico de absoluta autonomia individualis rationis humanae, secundum quod homo est sibi ipsi lex et Deo nullatenus subiicitur.[5] Ex hoc placito philosophico derivata est quaedam notio libertatis religiosae, in qua omnimodus relativismus atque indifferentismus in re religiosa [428] latebat.[6] Hanc libertatis religiosae notionem eiusque praemissam philosophicam Ecclesia reprobavit. Componi enim non potest notio haec cum dignitate humana, quae maxime consistit in eo, quod homo, ad imaginem Dei factus, Deum vivum et verum cognoscat Eique soli serviat.[7]

Porro cum placito philosophico laicismi cohaerebat placitum politicum de omnipotentia status etiam in re religiosa.[8] Hoc placito innixi, non pauci tunc temporis moderatores reipublicae legale libertatis religiosae regimen statuebant, quo Ecclesia Catholica intra ipsum ordinem temporalem ita a statu concludebatur, ut esset omnipotenti status potestati subiecta.[9] Reprobavit Ecclesia hoc regimen eiusque praemissam politicam. Gravissime enim violant Ecclesiae nativam libertatem. Praeterea componi cum hominis libertate in societate non potest affirmatio totalis autonomiae potestatis publicae sine modo sine lege, cum quo totalitarismus hodiernus intime connectitur.[10]

Utraque haec damnatio, olim lata, hodie manet integra et immutabilis.[11] Mutantur tamen tempora et ideologiae. Etenim his nostris diebus hoc rude rationalismi genus, quod saeculo decimo nono proprium fuit, iam gravioribus erroribus locum fere cessit. Quod maius est, ex eo tempore totalitarismus status, libertati humanae prorsus infensus, in multis orbis regionibus praevalere coepit. Praeterea Ecclesia, novis problematibus exsurgentibus et perspectis, e principiis, quae semper eadem manent in suo sensu et sua sententia, ampliorem doctrinam de re sociali et civili continuo evolvit, de thesauro suo proferens nova et vetera. In hac doctrina firmius in dies persona humana asseritur esse et esse debere totius vitae socialis fundamentum, finis, subiectum.[12] Itemque [429] in luce ponitur hominem, prout est persona, officiis teneri iuribusque gaudere, quae exsurgunt e suiipsius natura.[13] Hoc

understood to mean that the human person can equally value what is false and what is true, that he no longer has the duty to form for himself a true judgment about religious matters, or that he can determine at will whether or in which religion and in what way he wishes to serve God.

2. (*The historical question*). It is clear, then, that religious freedom is not regarded today in the same way as it once was. In the nineteenth century, the ideology known as 'laicism' began to prevail in many nations.[4] This ideology was grounded in the rationalist principle of the absolute autonomy of individual human reason, according to which man is a law unto himself and is in no way subject to God.[5] From this philosophical principle, a certain conception of religious freedom was derived, in which all kinds of relativism and indifferentism in religious matters [428] were concealed.[6] The Church condemned this conception of religious freedom and its philosophical premise; for it cannot be reconciled with human dignity, which chiefly consists in this, that man, made in the image of God, may know the living and true God and serve him alone.[7]

Closely connected with the philosophical principle of laicism was a political principle concerning the omnipotence of the state, even in religious matters.[8] With the support of this principle, not a few government leaders of the time established a legal practice of religious freedom, according to which the Catholic Church was circumscribed by the state within the temporal order itself, so that the Church was made subject to the omnipotent power of the state.[9] The Church condemned this practice and its political premise as gravely violating the native freedom of the Church. Furthermore, the freedom of man in society cannot be reconciled with such an assertion of the absolute autonomy of the public power, as unlimited and beyond the law, an assertion with which the totalitarianism of today is not unconnected.[10]

Each of these condemnations, leveled of old, remains firm and unchangeable today.[11] Nevertheless, the times and ideologies have changed. Indeed, the coarse kind of rationalism proper to the nineteenth century has today given way to more serious errors. What is more, since that time a state totalitarianism totally hostile to human freedom has begun to prevail in many areas of the world. Furthermore, with the development of new problems and perspectives, the Church has continued to unfold a more ample teaching on social and civil matters, from principles that remain always the same in their meaning and purpose, bringing forth from out of her treasury things both new and old. The fact that the human person is and must be the foundation, end, and subject of all social life is asserted more strongly today in the teaching of the Church.[12] [429] This teaching also sheds light on the

valet in omnibus partibus vitae atque activitatis humanae, ac praecipue in iis, quae ad religionem spectant.[14] Tandem clarius in dies affirmatur, praecipuum potestatis publicae munus in eo esse quod omnium civium naturalia iura tueatur, colat, vindicet.[15]

Cum historiae decursu igitur exorta est nova quaedam quaestio de libertate religiosa. Hodie enim agitur de observanda conservandaque dignitate personae humanae ac proinde de efficaciter tuendis eius iuribus, quorum primum est hominis ius, ut sit in re religiosa immunis a coercitione, praesertim ex parte potestatis publicae.[16]

3. (*Declaratio*). His positis, haec Sacra Synodus hac sua Declaratione exponere intendit quid de hodierno libertatis religiosae regimine sentiat. Primo affirmat et docet, iuxta constantem Ecclesiae doctrinam, non liberum esse unicuique homini quam quisque maluerit sequi in vita religiosa sententiam, sed unam religionem veram esse, quam Deus et Pater Domini nostri Iesu Christi per Filium suum incarnatum revelavit atque Ecclesiae custodiendam et omnibus hominibus evangelizandam tradidit; homines vero gravi teneri officio veritatem in re religiosa inquirendi et cognitam sectandi. Insuper declarat haec Sacra Synodus, hanc catholicam de unica vera religione doctrinam nullatenus adversari libertati humanae et civili in vita religiosa ducenda. Veritas enim evangelica est in societate humana fermentum, quod plura honestae libertatis beneficia per saecula protulit; praeterea Ecclesiae [430] doctrina de hominis dignitate, quatenus ex ipso rationis fonte depromitur, libertatem civilem in re religiosa firmiter sustentat et commendat.

Cum igitur Ecclesiae incumbat munus, ut honestae hominis in civitate libertati patrocinetur eamque sua doctrina atque auctoritate roboret, haec Sacra Synodus declarat regimen iuridicum hodiernum libertatis religiosae, quippe quod principiis rationis humanae fulcitur, esse in se honestum et vere necessarium ad custodiendam in societate hodierna hominis dignitatem et personalem et civilem. Affirmat insuper libertatem religiosam, sensu iam descripto, esse verum ius, in ipsa dignitate personae humanae fundatum, quod omnes homines omnesque communitates religiosae possunt sibi legitime vindicare.[17]

fact that man, as a person, is bound by certain duties and enjoys certain rights, which duties and rights arise from his own nature.[13] This applies in all areas of life and human activity, but especially in those that concern religion.[14] Finally, it is more clearly affirmed today that the chief function of the public power consists in protecting, cultivating, and defending the natural rights of all citizens.[15]

In the course of history, then, a new kind of question has arisen in regard to religious freedom. For religious freedom today is concerned with observing and upholding the dignity of the human person, and thus with effectively protecting his rights, the first of which is man's right to be free from coercion in religious matters, especially on the part of the public power.[16]

3. (*Declaration*) Presupposing these things, this sacred Council intends with this Declaration to set forth its judgment on the practice of religious freedom today. First of all, it declares and teaches, according to the constant teaching of the Church, that each man is not free to follow whatever opinion in religious life he may prefer, but that there is one true religion, which God the Father of our Lord Jesus Christ through his incarnate Son revealed and handed over to the Church to preserve and preach to all people; men and women are in fact bound by a serious duty to seek the truth in religious matters and to follow it once it is known. In addition, this sacred Council declares that this Catholic teaching on the one true religion is in no way opposed to human and civil freedom in the practice of religious life. The truth of the Gospel is a leaven in society that has brought about many benefits of genuine freedom throughout the ages; the teaching of the Church [430] about man's dignity, moreover, insofar as it is drawn from the font of reason itself, firmly supports and commends civil freedom in religious matters.

Therefore, since it is incumbent upon the Church to protect the genuine civil freedom of man and to strengthen it with her teaching and authority, this sacred Council declares that the current juridical practice of religious freedom, which is supported by principles of human reason, is in itself noble and truly necessary for the protection of man's dignity, both personal and civil, in today's society. In addition, it declares that religious freedom, in the sense just described, is a true right, having its foundation in the very dignity of the human person, a right that all men and all religious communities can legitimately claim for themselves.[17]

II. DOCTRINA DE LIBERTATE RELIGIOSA
EX RATIONE DESUMPTA

4. (*Fundamenta libertatis religiosae*).

a) (*Integritas personae*). Homo, qui persona est, natura sua est socialis. Proinde in eius activitate aspectus socialis inseparabiliter connectitur cum aspectu interiore. Ergo iniuria homini fit, si quis interiorem hominis personalem libertatem in re religiosa agnoscat, simulque ei liberum in societate religionis exercitium deneget. Hoc modo enim violaretur ipsa integritas personae. Nexus inter libertatem interiorem et eius manifestationem socialem est omnino indissolubilis. Libertas religiosa est una, indivisa et indivisibilis, uni subiecto integre sumpto inhaeret, et ad duo simul spectat: nempe ad libertatem interiorem seu conscientiae et ad liberum exercitium religionis.

[431] *b*) (*Inquisitio veritatis*). Homo habet officium et ius quaerendi veritatem. Veritatem autem quaerere, eique iam inventae firmiter adhaerere tenetur humano modo, libera scilicet inquisitione atque assensu personali. Insuper, cum homo sit natura sua socialis, veritas quaeritur et invenitur per magisterium seu institutionem et per communicationem inter homines, in qua alii aliis exponunt veritatem quam invenerunt vel se invenisse iudicaverint.[18] Quae omnia maxime valent de veritatibus in re religiosa. Quare ad debitam hominis libertatem religiosam pertinet ut non impediatur in suis persuasionibus de re religiosa in dialogo exponendis.

c) (*Indoles religionis*). Ex ipsa religionis indole, exercitium eius consistit primario in actibus interioribus prorsus voluntariis atque liberis, quibus homo sese ad Deum directe ordinat, eo quidem animo ut suam necessitudinem ad Deum agnoscat et debita oboedientia adhaereat voluntati divinae. Actus autem religionis interiores sua ipsorum indole, quae cum natura sociali hominis cohaeret, in actus exteriores prodeunt. Exinde sequitur quod homo ius habet, ut in sua religione publice exercenda immunis sit a coercitione sive legali sive sociali.

d) (*Conscientia humana*). Suprema humanae vitae norma est lex divina, quae est aeterna, absoluta, obiectiva, universalis. Homo autem legi divinae obtemperare tantummodo potest, secundum quod illam sui ipsius conscientiae dictamine percipit. Neque finem suum ultimum consequi potest, nisi certa conscientiae iudicia, mediis adhibitis idoneis, sibi prudenter [432] efformet et his dictaminibus fideliter oboediat. Inde sequitur principium morale absolutum, quod vetat, ne quis in re religiosa cogatur ad agen-

II. THE TEACHING ON RELIGIOUS FREEDOM
DERIVED FROM REASON

4. (*The foundations of religious freedom*)

a) (*The integrity of the person*). Man, as a person, is by his very nature social. In all his actions, this social dimension of man is inseparably joined to his interior dimension. It is therefore an injustice for anyone to recognize man's personal freedom in religious matters and simultaneously deny him the free exercise of religion in society, since this would violate the very integrity of the person. The connection between interior freedom and its social manifestation is wholly indissoluble. Religious freedom is one, undivided and indivisible, and it inheres in one integral subject; at the same time, it refers to two different dimensions: namely, to interior freedom or freedom of conscience, on the one hand, and to the free exercise of religion, on the other.

[**431**] *b*) (*The search for truth*). Man has the duty and the right to seek the truth. He is bound to seek the truth and to adhere to it firmly once it is found, however, in a way that is proper to man, namely, by means of free inquiry and personal assent. Moreover, since man is by his nature social, the truth must be sought and found through instruction or education and by communication between persons, in which men and women share with one another the truth they have found or judged they have found.[18] All of this applies especially to truth in religious matters. For this reason, it belongs to man's due religious freedom that he not be prevented from expressing his own convictions on religious matters in dialogue with others.

c) (*The nature of religion*). By the very nature of religion, its exercise consists primarily in interior acts that are entirely voluntary and free, by which man orders himself directly toward God, with the intention of acknowledging his relationship to God and holding fast to the divine will with all due obedience. These interior acts of religion, however, by their intrinsic nature—which is closely connected to the social nature of man—give rise to exterior actions. It follows that man has the right, in the public exercise of his religion, to be immune from legal or social coercion.

d) (*Human conscience*). The highest norm of human life is the divine law, which is eternal, absolute, objective, and universal. Man can only obey the divine law, however, insofar as he perceives it by means of the dictates of his own conscience. He cannot achieve his final end unless he prudently forms sure judgments of conscience for himself, using all suitable means, [**432**] and faithfully follows these dictates. From this the absolute moral principle follows, that it is prohibited to force anyone to act against his conscience

dum contra suam conscientiam.[19] Hisce autem nostris diebus, aucto sensu dignitatis humanae, personalis et civilis, aliud insuper exigitur, ne scilicet quis in societate humana impediatur, maxime a potestate publica, quominus agat in re religiosa secundum suam conscientiam, salvo ordine publico, qui partem essentialem totius boni communis constituit. Quae quidem exigentia est prorsus rationi consentanea et homine digna.[20]

e) (*Moderatio civitatis*). Actus religiosi, quibus homines privatim et publice sese ad Deum ex intima sententia personali ordinant, temporalem et terrestrem rerum ordinem transcendunt. Ideo in his actibus ponendis homo non subest potestati civili, cuius competentia ob ipsum eius finem ad ordinem terrestrem et temporalem restringitur,[21] et cuius potestas legifera solummodo ad actus exteriores extenditur.[22] Potestas ergo publica, quae de interioribus actibus religiosis nequit iudicare, nequit pariter publicum religionis exercitium coercere aut impedire, salvis tamen exigentiis ordinis publici. Libertas debet homini agnosci quam maxima fieri potest ac non restringenda est nisi in quantum est necessarium.[23] Ipsa omnino limites suos excedit, si in regimen animorum aut in curam animarum sese quovis modo immisceat.[24]

5. (*Limites libertatis religiosae*).

a) (*Norma moralis*). Ius ad libertatem in re religiosa exercetur in societate humana, ideoque quibusdam normis limitantibus obnoxium [433] est. Quarum prima est principium morale responsabilitatis personalis erga alios. Etenim in iuribus suis exercendis unusquisque debet rationem habere iurium aliarum personarum suorumque officiorum erga alios, quibuscum est ei agendum secundum iustitiam et humanitatem.

b) (*Norma iuridica*). Societas civilis ius habet sese protegendi contra abusus, qui perpetrari possint adducto titulo libertatis religiosae. Pertinet praecipue ad potestates publicas huiusmodi protectionem praestare, non tamen modo arbitrario, sed secundum normas iuridicas, quae constituuntur exigentiis ordinis publici. Qui ordo publicus est illa pars essentialis boni communis, quae committitur potestati publicae, ut praecipue vi coercitiva legis protegatur. Exercitium religionis in societate a coercitiva interventione status immune esse debet, nisi quando exercitium religionis graviter noceat ordini publico sive per perturbationem pacis publicae, sive per violationem moralitatis publicae, sive per laesionem iurium civilium aliorum.

in religious matters.[19] In our day, however, given the growing awareness of both personal and civil human dignity, a further demand is made: namely, that no one in society be prevented from acting according to his conscience in religious matters, especially by the public power, provided that public order, which constitutes an essential part of the whole common good, is preserved. This demand is entirely consistent with reason and is worthy of man.[20]

e) (*State governance*). Religious acts, in which men and women privately and publicly order themselves toward God out of a personal, intimate conviction, transcend the temporal and earthly order of things. In performing these acts, therefore, man is not subject to the civil power, whose competence, on account of its end, is restricted to the earthly and temporal order,[21] and whose legislative power extends only to external actions.[22] The public power, therefore, since it cannot pass judgment on interior religious acts, likewise cannot coerce or impede the public exercise of religion, provided that the demands of public order are preserved. Man's freedom should be acknowledged as far as possible and should not be restricted except insofar as it is necessary.[23] The public power completely exceeds its limits if it involves itself in any way in the governing of minds or the care of souls.[24]

5. (*The limits of religious freedom*)

a) (*The moral norm*). The right to freedom in religious matters is exercised in human society, and is therefore subject to certain limiting norms. [433] The first of these is the moral principle of personal responsibility toward others. In exercising his rights, each person should keep in mind both the rights of other persons and his duties toward others. He should act toward them with justice and humanity.

b) (*The juridical norm*). Civil society has the right to protect itself against abuses that could be committed in the name of religious freedom. It belongs especially to the public power to afford protection of this sort, not in an arbitrary fashion, but according to juridical norms determined by the requirements of public order. Public order is that essential part of the common good that is entrusted to the public power, in order to be protected especially by the coercive power of the law. The exercise of religion in society should be immune from the coercive intervention of the state, except when such exercise seriously harms the public order, either by disturbing the public peace, by violating public morality, or by offending the civil rights of others.

III. CONSEQUENTIAE PRACTICAE

6. (*Cura libertatis religiosae*). Inviolabilia hominis iura tueri praecipuum est cuiusvis potestatis publicae officium. Debet igitur potestas publica, per iustas leges, efficaciter suscipere tutelam curamque libertatis religiosae omnium civium. Itemque a potestate publica providendum est, ne civium aequalitas in ordinatione iuridica laedatur propter rationes religiosas.

Ex quibus sequitur nefas esse potestati publicae, per vim vel metum civibus imponere [434] professionem aut reiectionem cuiusvis religionis. Eo magis contra voluntatem Dei et contra sacra personae et familiae gentium iura agitur, quando vis adhibeatur ad religionem ipsam delendam vel cohibendam sive in toto genere humano sive in aliqua regione sive in determinato coetu religioso. Immo vero huic Sacrae Synodo in votis est, ut ius personae humanae ad libertatem religiosam in omnibus per orbem terrarum civitatibus agnoscatur et efficaci tutela iuridica muniatur.[25] Quo magis enim societas civilis propitias suppeditat condiciones ad veritatem divulgandam vitamque religiosam fovendam, eo magis ipsa fruetur bonis, quae undequaque proveniunt ex fidelitate hominum erga Deum Eiusque sanctam voluntatem.[26]

7. (*Libertas communitatum religiosarum*). Libertas religiosa, quae singulis personis competit, etiam communitatibus agnoscenda est. Hae namque a sociali natura tum hominis, tum ipsius religionis requiruntur.

[435] Illis igitur iure debentur independentia et immunitas, ut secundum proprias leges sese regant, Deum cultu publico honoret, membra sua in vita religiosa exercenda adiuvent et doctrina sustentent atque eas institutiones promoveant, in quibus membra cooperentur ad vitam propriam secundum sua principia religiosa ordinandam.

Communitatibus religiosis pariter competit ius, ne mediis legalibus vel actione administrativa status impediantur in suis propriis ministris seligendis atque educandis, in communicando cum auctoritatibus religiosis in aliis orbis terrarum partibus degentibus, necnon in bonis acquirendis et fruendis.

Communitates religiosae ius etiam habent, ne impediantur in sua fide, ore et scripto, publice docenda atque testanda. In fide autem religiosa spargenda et usibus inducendis abstinendum semper est ab omni actionis genere, quod coercitionem vel suasionem inhonestam aut minus rectam sapere videatur, praesertim quando de pueris vel rudioribus agitur.

III. PRACTICAL CONSEQUENCES

6. (*The care of religious freedom*). It is the chief duty of every public power to protect the inviolable rights of man. The public power should
therefore effectively undertake to protect and care for the religious freedom
of all citizens through just laws. The public power should also see to it that
the equality of citizens before the law is never violated for religious reasons.

It follows that it is wrong for the public power to impose by force or
fear the [434] profession or rejection of any religion on its citizens. All the
more is it against God's will and the sacred rights of the person and of the
family of nations to use force in order to destroy or repress religion itself,
either in the human race as a whole or in a particular region or in a specific
religious group. This sacred Council prays that the right of the human person
to religious freedom be acknowledged in all the nations of the world and
be secured by effective juridical protection.[25] For the more that civil society
provides favorable conditions for spreading the truth and fostering religious
life, the more it will enjoy those goods that come forth everywhere from
men's fidelity to God and his holy will.[26]

7. (*The freedom of religious communities*). The religious freedom that
belongs to individual persons must be recognized for communities as well.
These communities are called for by the social nature of man and of religion
itself.

[435] Independence and immunity are therefore due to these communities by right, so that they may govern themselves according to their own
laws, honor God with public worship, assist their members in their practice
of religious life, strengthen them by instruction, and promote institutions in
which members can join together to order their own life according to their
religious principles.

Religious communities likewise have the right not to be impeded, either
by legal measures or by administrative action on the part of the state, in selecting and educating their own ministers, in communicating with religious authorities in other parts of the world, or in acquiring and making use of goods.

Religious communities also have the right not to be prevented from
publicly teaching about or witnessing to their faith in speech or in writing.
In spreading their religious faith and introducing their practices, however,
they must always refrain from any kind of activity that would seem to suggest
any hint of coercion or dishonest or less than proper persuasion, especially
in regard to children or those less educated.

Tandem ad libertatem religiosam spectat quod communitates religiosae libere possint ostendere singularem valorem veritatis religiosae in ordinanda societate et in tota activitate humana dirigenda.

8. (*Libertas religiosa familiae*). Cuique familiae, utpote quae est societas proprio iure gaudens, competit ius ad libere ordinandam religiosam vitam suam domesticam, sub moderatione parentum. Parentibus autem competit ius ad determinandam rationem institutionis [436] religiosae liberis tradendae. Parentibus insuper a publicis potestatibus agnoscendum est ius eligendi, vera cum libertate, scholas vel alia educationis media. Propter hanc autem electionis libertatem non sunt eis iniusta onera imponenda.

9. (*Libertas associationis religiosae*). Personae humanae ius inest ne a potestate civili impediatur quominus communitatem religiosam ingrediatur aut relinquat. Praeterea in natura hominis sociali atque in ipsa natura religionis fundatur ius, quo homines possint, salvis iuribus aliorum, conventus vel associationes ad fines religiosos, educativos, culturales, caritativos, sociales prosequendos sibi libere constituere.

IV. DOCTRINA LIBERTATIS RELIGIOSAE SUB LUCE REVELATIONIS

10. (*Libertas Ecclesiae*). In bonis Ecclesiae, quae ubique semperque conservanda sunt ab omnique iniuria defendenda, illud certe praestantissimum est, tanta ipsam perfrui agendi liberate, quantam salus hominum curanda requirat. Haec enim est libertas divina, ab Unigenito Dei Filio auctore profecta, qui Ecclesiam sanguine fuso excitavit. Atque adeo propria est Ecclesiae, ut qui contra eam faciunt libertatem, iidem contra Deum faciunt. Iuxta totam traditionem catholicam, libertas Ecclesiae est principium fundamentale in iis, quae spectant ad relationem inter Ecclesiam et ordinem civilem vitae humanae.[27]

Ecclesia sibi in societate humana et coram quavis potestate publica vindicat libertatem, [437] utpote quae est auctoritas spiritualis, a Christo Domino constituta, cui soli ex divino mandato incumbit officium, ut in mundum universum eat atque evangelium praedicet omni creaturae (cf. *Mc.* 16, 15; *Mt.* 28, 10-20).[28] Pariter libertatem sibi vindicat Ecclesia, prout est etiam societas hominum divinitus convocata, quorum omnes et singuli in societate civili iure gaudent vivendi ad rationis conscientiaeque christianae praescripta.[29]

Finally, religious freedom entails that religious communities freely be able to show the unique value of religious truth for ordering society and directing all human activity.

8. (*The religious freedom of the family*). Each family, as a society in its own right, has the right to order freely its own domestic religious life, under the guidance of the parents. Parents also have the right to determine the way in which religious instruction [436] will be handed on to their children. In addition, public powers must acknowledge the right of parents to choose with true freedom among schools or other means of education. Unjust burdens must not be placed upon them on account of this freedom of choice.

9. (*The freedom of religious association*). The human person has the right not to be prevented by the civil power from entering or leaving a religious community. Furthermore, there is in man's social nature and in the very nature of religion the foundation for the right by which men and women can freely hold meetings and establish associations for the pursuit of religious, educational, cultural, charitable, or social ends, provided the rights of others are preserved.

IV. THE TEACHING ON RELIGIOUS FREEDOM IN THE LIGHT OF REVELATION

10. (*The freedom of the Church*). Preeminent among the goods of the Church that must always and everywhere be preserved and defended against all harm is to enjoy as much freedom in acting as the care of man's salvation may demand. This is a divine freedom, accomplished by the only begotten Son of God, who gave life to the Church through the shedding of his blood. This freedom is so proper to the Church that whoever acts against it acts against God. According to the whole Catholic tradition, the freedom of the Church is a fundamental principle among those that concern the relationship between the Church and the civil order of human life.[27]

The Church claims for herself freedom in human society and before every public power [437] insofar as she is a spiritual authority, constituted by Christ the Lord, upon whom alone rests, by divine command, the duty to go throughout the whole world preaching the Gospel to every creature (cf. Mk 16:15; Mt 28:10-20).[28] The Church likewise claims for herself freedom as a society of men and women called together by God, who as a whole and individually enjoy the right to live in civil society according to the precepts of reason and a Christian conscience.[29]

Iamvero ubi reapse viget hodiernum regimen libertatis religiosae, ipsa Ecclesia stabilem obtinet condicionem et iuris et facti plenamque independentiam in missione divina exsequenda, quae ei soli ex mandato Christi committitur.[30] Praeterea Christifideles iure civili gaudent ne impediantur in vita ducenda iuxta fidem catholicam. Concordia igitur datur inter libertatem, quam Ecclesia sibi mandato Christi vindicat, et libertatem religiosam illam quam Ecclesia postulat pro omnibus hominibus et communitatibus ut verum ius, ipsius rationis lumine comprobatum.

11. (*Libertas fidei*). Doctrina fundamentalis catholica est, in verbo Dei contenta et a Patribus constanter praedicata,[31] hominem habere veram responsabilitatem in credendo, neminem tamen invitum esse cogendum ad amplexandam fidem catholicam.[32] Etenim ipsa sua natura actus fidei christianae liber est. Namque homo, a Christo Salvatore redemptus et in adoptionem filiorum per Iesum Christum vocatus (*Eph.* 1, 5), Deo sese revelanti adhaerere non potest, nisi Pater traxerit eum (*Io.* 6, 44) et rationabile liberumque Deo praestiterit fidei obsequium. Unde etiam sequitur, [438] quod fides eo magis est genuina, quo magis libera est et personalis.

Indoli ergo fidei christianae oppositum est quodvis in re religiosa genus coercitionis ex parte humanae potestatis. Ideo in regimine libertatis religiosae condiciones dantur, in quibus exigentiae doctrinae catholicae in hac materia observantur.

12. (*Doctrina evangelica*). Libertas religiosa, prout hodie intelligitur, altas radices habet in verbo Dei. Libertas, quam Christus praedicavit, donum Dei est quo homo, liberatus a lege peccati (*Rom.* 8, 2), directe ordinatur ad Deum Patrem per Iesum Christum (*1 Cor.* 8, 6). Libertas autem religiosa a societate postulata innititur in dignitate personae, ad quam Christus semper spectavit in conducendis hominibus ad perfectam libertatem filiorum Dei.

Etenim Iesus, qui Christus et Dominus est (*Act.* 2, 36) idemque mitis et humilis corde (*Mt.* 11, 29), in ministerio suo peragendo discipulos allexit quidem et invitavit, numquam vero coegit (*Mt.* 4, 19; 11, 28-30; 19, 16-22; *Io.* 6, 68). Miracula fecit ut auditores fide verbo suo adhaererent; tamen consulto prodigia illa patrare iterum iterumque renuit, quibus homines ad assentiendum quodammodo cogerentur (*Mt.* 12, 38-39; *Io.* 6, 30-33). Revera Satanas huiusmodi prodigia proposuit Christo, tentans Eum (*Mt.* 4, 5-7);[33] Iudaei pariter talia signa petebant (*Lc.* 11, 16; *Io.* 2, 18): quae omnia recusavit Iesus (*Lc.* 11, 16 ss.; *Io.* 4, 48). Respuit prodigia illa quae violentiam redolerent, ut quando Apostoli, a Samaritanis non recepti, Ei proposuerunt: « Domine,

Indeed, where the practice of religious freedom truly thrives today, the Church maintains a stable condition both in law and in fact, and full independence in carrying out the divine mission entrusted to her alone by Christ's command.[30] Furthermore, the Christian faithful enjoy the civil right of not being prevented from leading a life according to the Catholic faith. A harmony therefore exists between the freedom that the Church claims for herself by Christ's command, and the religious freedom that the Church claims for all men and communities as a true right, one that is confirmed by the light of reason itself.

11. (*The freedom of faith*). It is a fundamental Catholic teaching, contained in the word of God and constantly proclaimed by the Fathers, that man has a true responsibility to believe, but that no one may be forced to embrace the Catholic faith against his will.[32] The act of Christian faith is of its very nature a free act. For man, redeemed by Christ the Savior and called to be an adopted son through Jesus Christ (Eph 1:5), cannot hold fast to God as he reveals himself unless he is drawn by the Father (Jn 6:44) and offers to God a rational and free submission of faith. Thus it follows [**438**] that the more genuine faith is, the more free and personal it is.

Any kind of coercion in religious matters on the part of human power is therefore opposed to the very nature of the Christian faith. In the practice of religious freedom, then, there are conditions under which the demands of Catholic teaching in this matter are observed.

12. (*The teaching of the Gospel*). Religious freedom, as it is understood today, has deep roots in the word of God. The freedom that Christ preached is a gift of God by which man, freed from the law of sin (Rom 8:2) is directly ordered to God the Father through Jesus Christ (1 Cor 8:6). The religious freedom demanded by society, however, rests upon the dignity of the person, a dignity to which Christ always looked in leading men and women to the perfect freedom of the children of God.

For Jesus, who is Christ and Lord (Acts 2:36) and at the same time meek and humble of heart (Mt 11:29), certainly attracted and invited disciples as he went about his ministry, but he never forced them (Mt 4:19; 11:28-30; 19:16-22; Jn 6:68). He performed miracles so that his listeners would hold fast to his word by faith; but he deliberately refused again and again to perform wonders that might force men in some way to assent (Mt 12:38-39; Jn 6:30-33). Satan in fact tempted Christ by proposing wonders of this sort (Mt 4:5-7),[33] and the Jews likewise sought such signs (Lk 11:16; Jn 2:18), but Jesus refused them all (Lk 11:16 ff.; Jn 4:48). He rejected those wonders that suggested violence in any way, as when the apostles, turned away by the Sa-

vis dicimus ut descendat ignis de caelo et consumat illos? », quemadmodum tempore Eliae prophetae factum est. Severe eos [439] increpavit Dominus dicens: « Nescitis cuius spiritus estis. Filius hominis non venit animas perdere, sed salvare » (Lc. 9, 54-56). Christus semper fuit ille perfectus Servus Yahweh (Is. 42, 1-4) qui harundinem quassatam non confringit neque linum fumigans extinguit (Mt. 12, 20). Venit ut ministraret (Mc. 10, 45) et ut testimonium perhiberet veritati (Io. 18, 37), quod tandem summopere praestitit sanguine suo. Exaltatus a terra, omnes vi amoris traxit ad seipsum.

Quod Christus fecit et docuit, Apostoli secuti sunt. Ab ipso Ecclesiae initio discipuli Christi laboraverunt ut homines ad Deum converterent non per actionem coercitivam nec per artificia inhonesta, sed per virtutem verbi Dei. Sicuti Christus, Apostoli quoque intenti fuerunt, ut testimonium redderent veritati Dei, abundantius audentes coram populo et principibus « sine timore verbum Dei loqui » (Phil. 1, 14; Act. 4, 13-20). Firma fiducia tenebant, ipsum evangelium revera esse virtutem Dei in salutem omni credenti (Rom. 1, 16). Omnibus ergo spretis « armis carnalibus », exemplum mansuetudinis et modestiae Christi sequentes, verbum Dei praedicaverunt plene confisi in divina huius verbi virtute ad potestates Deo adversas destruendas et homines ad fidem et obsequium Christi reducendos (2 Cor. 10, 3-5).

Iuxta mentem ergo Christi Eiusque principia agit Ecclesia, quando hodie, aucto in hominibus sensu propriae dignitatis, regimen libertatis religiosae tuetur, eique fovet pro pastorali sua erga libertatem humanam sollicitudine.

[440] 13. (Munus Ecclesiae). Ecclesia Catholica, ut divino obtemperet mandato: « docete omnes gentes . . . docentes eos servare omnia quaecumque mandavi vobis » (Mt. 28, 19-20), impensa cura adlaborare debet « ut sermo Dei currat et clarificetur » (2 Thess. 3, 1) et omnes uno animo et ore honorificent Deum et Patrem Domini nostri Iesu Christi.

Obsecrat igitur Ecclesia, a filiis suis « primum omnium fieri obsecrationes, orationes, postulationes, gratiarum actiones pro omnibus hominibus . . . Hoc enim bonum est et acceptum coram Salvatore nostro Deo, qui omnes homines vult salvos fieri et ad agnitionem veritatis venire » (1 Tim. 2, 1-4).

Christifideles in sua efformanda conscientia diligenter attendere debent ad sacram certamque Ecclesiae doctrinam.[34] Dei enim voluntate Ecclesia Catholica magistra est veritatis, eiusque munus est, ut veritatem, quae

maritans, asked: "Lord, do you want us to bid fire come down from heaven and consume them?", as had happened in the time of Elijah the prophet. The Lord severely [439] rebuked them, saying: "You do not know what manner of spirit you are of; for the Son of man came not to destroy men's lives but to save them" (Lk 9:54-56). Christ was always that perfect Servant of Yahweh (Is 42:1-4) who does not break a bruised reed nor quench a smoldering wick (Mt 12:20). He came to serve (Mk 10:45) and to bear witness to the truth (Jn 18:37), a witness that he finally rendered to the highest degree with his own blood. When he was lifted up from the earth, he drew all men to himself by the power of his love.

The apostles followed what Christ did and taught. From the very beginning of the Church they strove to convert men and women to God, not through coercion or by dishonest means, but by the power of the word of God. Like Christ, the apostles were intent to bear witness to the truth of God, daring "to speak the word of God without fear" (Phil 1:14; Acts 4:13-20) and in full before the people and their leaders. With firm faith they held that the Gospel itself is truly the power of God for the salvation of all who believe (Rom 1:16). Rejecting all "worldly weapons," therefore, and following the example of Christ's meekness and modesty, they preached the word of God, fully trusting in the divine power of this word to destroy the powers that are opposed to God and to lead men and women to the faith and allegiance of Christ (2 Cor 10:3-5).

The Church, therefore, acts according to the mind of Christ and his principles when today, given the growing awareness in men and women of their own dignity, she upholds and supports the practice of religious freedom, in keeping with her pastoral concern for human freedom.

[440] 13. (*The task of the Church*). In order to obey the divine command: "Go and make disciples of all nations . . . teaching them to observe all that I have commanded you" (Mt 28:19-20), the Catholic Church should strive with great care "that the word of the Lord may speed on and triumph" (2 Thes 3:1) and that all with one mind and voice may glorify God the Father of our Lord Jesus Christ.

The Church therefore entreats her children, "First of all that supplications, prayers, intercessions, and thanksgivings be made for all men . . . This is good and it is acceptable in the sight of God our Savior, who desires all men to be saved and to come to the knowledge of the truth" (1 Tim 2:1-4).

In forming their conscience, the Christian faithful should carefully attend to the sacred and certain teaching of the Church.[34] For by the will of God the Catholic Church is the teacher of truth, and it is her duty to

Christus est, explicet atque authentice doceat, simulque principia ordinis moralis, ex ipsa natura humana profluentia, auctoritate sua declaret atque confirmet. Insuper Christiani, in sapientia ambulantes ad eos qui foris sunt, « in Spiritu Sancto, in caritate non ficta, in verbo veritatis » (2 Cor. 6, 6-7), lumen vitae cum omni fiducia (Act. 4, 29) et fortitudine apostolica, ad sanguinis usque effusionem, diffundere [441] satagant auxiliis naturae et gratiae, quibus ipse Dominus usus est, praedicatione nempe doctrinae, exemplo vitae et testimonio perhibito veritati.

Etenim discipulus gravi adstringitur officio erga veritatem Christi, ut eam nimirum plenius in dies cognoscat, fideliter annuntiet, strenue defendat. Simul tamen caritas Christi urget eum ut amanter prudenter patienter agat cum hominibus, qui in errore circa fidem versantur.[35] Adhibendus est modus suavis et humanae naturae aptatus, quo ipse Deus et Pater Domini nostri Iesu Christi homines sensim ad suum amorem allicit. Respiciendum igitur est tum ad officia erga verbum vivificans quod praedicandum est, tum ad humanae iura personae, tum ad mensuram gratiae a Deo per Christum tributam homini, qui ad fidem libere accipiendam et profitendam invitatur. Error reiiciendus est, veritas praedicanda, intellectus illustrandus, persona humana debita reverentia prosequenda.

14. (*Conclusio*). Constat igitur praesentis aetatis homines, quacumque cultura imbuantur, magis in dies optare ut libere possint religionem privatim publiceque profiteri; patet etiam libertatem religiosam in plerisque constitutionibus iam ut ius civile declarari.

Non desunt tamen regimina in quibus, etsi in ipsa eorum constitutione ius ad cultum Deo praestandum agnoscitur, tamen ipsae publicae potestates conantur cives a religione profitenda removere et communitatibus religiosis vitam perdifficilem ac periclitantem reddere.

Illa fausta huius temporis signa laeto animo salutans, haec vera deploranda facta cum moerore denuntians, Sacra Synodus christifideles [442] adhortatur et huius aetatis homines universos adprecatur ut perattente considerent quantopere libertas religiosa necessaria sit in praesentibus potissimum vitae humanae adiunctis.

Manifestum est enim cunctas gentes magis magisque in dies unum fieri, homines diversae culturae et religionis arctioribus inter se devinciri relationibus, augeri conscientiam propriae cuiusque responsabilitatis. Proinde ut pacificae relationes et concordia in genere humano instaurentur et firmentur, omnino requiritur ut ubique terrarum libertas religiosa efficaci tutela

proclaim and authoritatively teach the truth that is Christ, and likewise to declare and confirm with her authority the principles of the moral order that flow from human nature. In addition, as Christians conduct themselves in wisdom toward those outside, "in the Holy Spirit, in genuine charity, in truthful speech" (2 Cor 6:6-7), let them be diligent in diffusing the light of life with all boldness (Acts 4:29) and apostolic courage, even to the shedding of their blood, [441] using the resources of nature and grace that the Lord himself employed, namely, the preaching of doctrine, the example of their life, and bearing witness to the truth.

The disciple is bound by a grave duty to the truth of Christ, to know it more fully each day, to proclaim it faithfully, and to defend it vigorously. At the same time, the love of Christ urges him to deal lovingly, prudently, and patiently with those who dwell in error about the faith.[35] He should act in the same way, gentle and adapted to human nature, in which God the Father of our Lord Jesus Christ gradually attracts men to his love. He must therefore consider not only his duties toward the life-giving word that must be preached, but also the rights of the human person, and the measure of grace that God has bestowed through Christ upon those who are invited freely to receive and profess the faith. Error is to be rejected, the truth to be preached, man's intellect to be enlightened, and the human person to be regarded with all the reverence that is due to him.

14. (*Conclusion*). It is well known that men and women of today, no matter what culture they belong to, desire more every day to be able to profess their religion freely in private and in public; it is also clear that religious freedom has already been declared to be a civil right in most constitutions.

Governments are not lacking, however, in which, although the right to worship God is acknowledged in their very constitutions, the public powers themselves still endeavor to prevent citizens from professing their religion and to make life very difficult and dangerous for religious communities.

Welcoming the former with joy as a favorable sign of the times, while denouncing the latter with sorrow as something to be deplored, this sacred Council urges the Christian faithful [442] and implores all men and women of our time to consider carefully how necessary religious freedom is, especially in the present circumstances of human life.

It is clear that all nations are becoming more and more united every day, that men and women of different cultures and religions are being bound to one another with closer ties, and that there is a growing consciousness of the responsibility proper to each person. Hence, in order that peaceful relations and harmony may be established and strengthened among mankind,

iuridica muniatur et suprema hominum officia et iura ad vitam religiosam libere in societate ducendam observentur. Faxit igitur Deus et Pater omnium ut familia humana, diligenter servato regimine libertatis religiosae in societate, per gratiam Christi et virtutem Spiritus Sancti adducatur ad sublimiorem illam ac perennem libertatem « qua Christus nos liberavit » (*Gal.* 5, 1)

NOTAE

[1] Cf. IOANNES XXIII, Litt. Encycl. *Pacem in terris,* 11 aprilis 1963: *A.A.S.,* 55 (1963), p. 279, ubi Summus Pontifex ad realitates hodiernas animadvertit: « At hae, de quibus diximus, animorum appetitiones illud etiam manifesto testantur, nostro hoc tempore homines magis magisque fieri dignitatis suae conscios, atque adeo incitari cum ad reipublicae administrationem participandam, tum ad poscendum, ut propria inviolabiliaque iura in publica civitatis disciplina serventur. Neque haec satis; nam homines nunc illud insuper poscunt, ut nempe civitatis auctoritates et ad normam publicae constitutionis creentur, et sua munera intra eiusdem terminos obeant ». Cf. *ibid.,* p. 265: « Illud praeterea humanae dignitas personae exigitur, ut in agendo homo proprio consilio et libertate fruatur. Quocirca, si de civium coniunctione agitur, est profecto cur ipse iura colat, officia servet, atque, in innumeris operibus exercendis, aliis sociam tribuat operam, suo praesertim impulsu [443] et consulto; ita scilicet ut suo quisque instituto, iudicio, officiique conscientia agat, iam non commotus coercitione vel sollicitatione extrinsecus plerumque adductis; quandoquidem, si qua hominum societas una ratione virium est instituta, ea nihil humani in se habere dicenda est, utpote in qua homines a libertate cohibeantur, qui contra ad vitae progressus, ad perfectionemque assequendam apte ipsi incitandi sunt ».

Quod pertinet ad dignitatem illam civilem, secundum quam dignitas humana in publicum prodit, cf. PIUS XII, *Nuntius radiophonicus,* 24 dec. 1944: *A.A.S.,* 37 (1945) p. 14: «In un popolo degno di tal nome il cittadino sente in se stesso la coscienza della sua personalità, dei suoi doveri e dei suoi diritti, della propria libertà congiunta col rispetto della libertà e della dignità altrui ». Hoc loco commendat Romanus Pontifex etiam illud « ideale di libertà e di uguaglianza » (*loc. cit.*), quod in Statu democratico, iuxta sana rationis principia ordinato, obtineat necesse est, quodque postulat, ut hominis ius in societate ad liberum exercitium religionis plene agnoscatur, colatur, defendatur.

[2] GIANNINI A., *Le Costituzioni degli Stati del Vicino Oriente,* Roma 1931; PEASLEE AMOS S., *Constitutions of Nations,* New Jersey (USA) 1950; MIRKINE-GUETZEVITCH B., *Le Costituzioni Europee,* Milano 1954; ZAMORA A., *Digesto Constitutional Americano,* Buenos Aires 1958; LAVROFF D. G. ET PEISER G., *Les Constitutions Africaines,* Paris 1963; STRAMACCI M., *Le Costituzioni degli Stati Africani,* Milano 1963.

[3] De conceptu libertatis religiosae, ut ab aliis Christianis intelligitur cf. documenta Consilii Mundialis Ecclesiarum (World Council of Churches): « *Declaration on Religious Liberty* » (Assembly Amsterdam, 1948), « *Statement on Religious Liberty* » (Assembly New Delhi, 1961).

religious freedom must be secured by effective juridical protection throughout the world, and the highest duties and rights of men and women to lead a religious life freely in society must be observed. May God the Father of all therefore grant that the human family, having diligently upheld the practice of religious freedom in society, be led by the grace of Christ and the power of the Holy Spirit to that sublime and everlasting freedom "for which Christ has set us free" (Gal 5:1).

NOTES

¹ Cf. John XXIII, Encyclical Letter *Pacem in terris*, 11 April 1963: AAS 55 (1963), 279, where the pope makes the following observations on present-day realities: "But the aspirations we have mentioned are a clear indication of the fact that men, increasingly aware nowadays of their personal dignity, have found the incentive to enter government service and demand constitutional recognition for their own inviolable rights. Not content with this, they are also demanding the observance of constitutional procedures in the appointment of public authorities, and are insisting that they exercise their office within this constitutional framework." Cf. *ibid.*, 265: "Man's personal dignity requires besides that he enjoy freedom and be able to make up his own mind when he acts. In his association with his fellows, therefore, there is every reason why his recognition of rights, observance of duties, and many-sided collaboration with other men, should be primarily a matter of his own personal decision. [**443**] Each man should act on his own initiative, conviction, and sense of responsibility, not under the constant pressure of external coercion or enticement. There is nothing human about a society that is welded together by force. Far from encouraging, as it should, the attainment of man's progress and perfection, it is merely an obstacle to his freedom."

Concerning man's civil dignity, by which human dignity is extended into the public sphere, cf. Pius XII, Radio message, 24 December 1944: AAS 37 (1945), 14: "In a people worthy of the name, the citizen feels within himself a consciousness of his personhood, of his duties and rights, of his own freedom together with respect for the freedom and dignity of others." Here the pope commends also the "ideal of freedom and equality" (*loc. cit.*) that it is necessary to maintain in a democratic state organized according to sound principles of reason, which demands that man's right to the free exercise of religion in society be fully acknowledged, cultivated, and defended.

² A. Giannini, *Le Costituzioni degli Stati del Vicino Oriente*, Roma 1931; Amos S. Peaslee, *Constitutions of Nations*, New Jersey (USA) 1950; B. Mirkine-Guetzevitch, *Le Costituzioni Europee*, Milano 1954; A. Zamora, *Digesto Constitutional Americano*, Buenos Aires 1958; D. G. Lavroff and G. Peiser, *Les Constitutions Africaines*, Paris 1963; M. Stramacci, *Le Costituzioni degli Stati Africani*, Milano 1963.

³ For an overview of how the concept of religious freedom is understood by other Christians, cf. the documents of the World Council of Churches: "Declaration on Religious Liberty" (Amsterdam Assembly, 1948), and "Statement on Religious Liberty" (New Delhi Assembly, 1961).

⁴ Istiusmodi ideologiam brevius exposuit LEO XIII in Litt. Encycl. *Immortale Dei*, 1 nov. 1885: *A.S.S.*, 18 (1885), pp. 170-171, dein fusius in Litt. Encycl. *Libertas praestantissimum*, 20 iunii 1888: *A.S.S.*, 20 (1887), pp. 600-609.

⁵ Cf. PIUS IX, *Syllabus*, 8 dec. 1864, DENZINGER-BANNWART, *Enchiridion Symbolorum*, n. 1703: « Humana ratio, nullo prorsus Dei respectu habito, unicus est veri et falsi, boni et mali arbiter, sibi ipsi est lex et naturalibus suis viribus ad hominum ac populorum bonum curandum sibi sufficit ». Cf. LEO XIII, Litt. Encycl. *Libertas praestantissimum*, 20 iunii 1888: *A.S.S.*, 20 (1887), p. 600: « Iamvero totius rationalismi humanae principatus rationis caput est: quae oboedientiam divinae aeternaeque rationi debitam recusans, suique se iuris esse decernens, ipsa sibi sola efficitur summum principium et fons et iudex veritatis. Ita illi, quos diximus, liberalismi sectatores in actione vitae nullam contendunt esse, cui parendum sit, divinam potentiam, sed sibi quemque esse legem ».

⁶ Cf. PIUS IX, *Syllabus*, 8 dec. 1864, DENZINGER-BANNWART, *Enchiridion Symbolorum*, n. 1715: « Liberum cuique homini est eam amplecti ac profiteri religionem, quam rationis lumine quis ductus veram putaverit ». Cf. *ibid.*, n. 1716.

⁷ Cf. LEO XIII, Litt. Encycl. *Libertas praestantissimum*, 20 iunii 1888: *A.S.S.*, 20 (1887), p. 603: « Ac primo illud in singulis personis videamus, quod est tantopere virtuti religionis contrarium, scilicet de libertate uti loquuntur, cultus. Quae hoc est veluti fundamento constituta, integrum cuique esse, aut quam libuerit aut omnino nullam profiteri religionem. Contra vero ex omnibus hominum officiis illud est sine dubitatione maximam ac sanctissimam, quo pie religioseque Deum colere homines iubemur ».

⁸ [444] Cf. PIUS IX, *Syllabus*, 8 dec. 1864, DENZINGER-BANNWART, *Enchiridion Symbolorum*, n. 1739: « Reipublicae status, utpote omnium iurium origo et fons, iure quodam pollet nullis circumscripto limitibus ». Ad vitium totalitarismi in ideologia laicistica saepius attendit LEO XIII; cf., e. g., Litt. Encycl. *Humanum genus*, 20 aprilis 1884: *A.S.S.*, 16 (1906), p. 426: « Fontes omnium iurium officiorumque civilium vel in multitudine inesse vel in potestate gubernante civitatem, eaque novissimis informata disciplinis ».

⁹ Cf. LEO XIII, Litt. Encycl. *Immortale Dei*, 1 nov. 1885: *A.S.S.*, 18 (1885), p. 171: « Ad summam sic agunt cum Ecclesia ut societatis perfectae genere et iuribus opinione detractis, plane similem habeant ceterarum communitatum, quas res publica continet. Ob eamque rem si quid illa iuris, si quid possidet facultatis ad agendum legitimae, possidere dicitur concessu beneficioque principum civitatis . . . Ita Ecclesia in hoc rerum publicarum statu, qui nunc a pluribus adamatur, mos et voluntas est, aut prorsus de medio pellere Ecclesiam aut vinctam adstrictamque imperio tenere ».

¹⁰ Cf. LEO XIII, Litt. Encycl. *Libertas praestantissimum*, 20 iunii 1888: *A.S.S.*, 20 (1887), p. 609: «Contra Liberalismi fautores, qui herilem atque infinite potentem faciunt principatum, vitamque nullo ad Deum respectu degendam praedicant, hanc de quo loquimur coniunctam cum honestate religioneque libertatem minime agnoscunt. Cuius conservandae causa si quid fiat, iniuria et contra rempublicam factum criminantur. Quod si vere dicerent, nullus esset tam immanis dominatus, cui subesse et quem ferre non oporteret ».

¹¹ Cf. PIUS XI, Epist. Encycl. *Maximam gravissimamque*, 18 ianuarii 1924: *A.A.S.*, 16 (1924), p. 10: « Ea enim, quae Pius X damnavit, Nos pariter damnamus. Quotiescumque autem in "laicitate", ut dicunt, sensus inest vel propositum Deo et religioni infestum adversumque, a Deo et a religione alienum, "laicitatem" ipsam omnino improbamus atque improbandam esse aperte declaramus ».

[4] Leo XIII dealt briefly with this kind of ideology in the Encyclical Letter *Immortale Dei*, 1 November 1885: ASS 18 (1885), 170-171, and afterwards more fully in the Encyclical Letter *Libertas praestantissimum*, 20 June 1888: ASS 20 (1887), 600-609.

[5] Cf. Pius IX, *Syllabus*, 8 December 1864, Denzinger-Bannwart, *Enchiridion Symbolorum*, n. 1703: "Human reason, with absolutely no respect for God, is the sole arbiter of what is true and false, good and evil, a law unto itself that by its own native power suffices to care for the good of man and of peoples." Cf. Leo XIII, Encyclical Letter *Libertas praestantissimum*, 20 June 1888: ASS 20 (1887), 600: "The fundamental doctrine of rationalism is the supremacy of human reason, which, refusing due submission to the divine and eternal reason, proclaims its own independence, and constitutes itself as the supreme principle and source and judge of truth. Hence, these followers of liberalism deny the existence of any divine authority to which obedience is due, and proclaim that every man is a law unto himself."

[6] Cf. Pius IX, *Syllabus*, 8 December 1864, Denzinger-Bannwart, *Enchiridion Symbolorum*, n. 1715: "Each man is free to embrace and profess that religion which he judges to be true by the light of reason." Cf. *ibid.*, n. 1716.

[7] Cf. Leo XIII, Encyclical Letter *Libertas praestantissimum*, 20 June 1888: ASS 20 (1887), 603: "First, let us examine that freedom of individuals which is so opposed to the virtue of religion, namely, *freedom of worship*, as it is called. This is based on the principle that every man is free to profess as he may choose any religion or none. But, assuredly, of all the duties which man has to fulfill, that, without doubt, is the greatest and most sacred which commands him to worship God with devotion and piety."

[8] [444] Cf. Pius X, *Syllabus*, 8 December 1864, Denzinger-Bannwart, *Enchiridion Symbolorum*, n. 1739: "The state, as the origin and source of all rights, is endowed with a certain right not circumscribed by any limits." Leo XIII frequently drew attention to the error of totalitarianism hidden in the ideology of laicism; cf., e.g., Encyclical Letter *Humanum genus*, 20 April 1884: ASS 16 (1906), 426: "The source of all rights and civil duties is either in the multitude or in the governing authority, when this is constituted according to the latest doctrines."

[9] Cf. Leo XIII, Encyclical Letter *Immortale Dei*, 1 November 1885: ASS 18 (1885), 171: "Lastly, they treat the Church with such arrogance that, rejecting entirely her title to the nature and rights of a perfect society, they hold that she differs in no respect from other societies in the state, and for this reason possesses no right nor any legal power of action, save that which she holds by the concession and favor of the government. . . . Accordingly, it has become the practice and determination under this condition of public polity (now so much admired by many) either to forbid the action of the Church altogether, or to keep her in check and bondage to the state."

[10] Cf. Leo XIII, Encyclical Letter *Libertas praestantissimum*, 20 June 1888: ASS 20 (1887), 609: "By the patrons of liberalism, however, who make the state absolute and omnipotent, and proclaim that man should live altogether independently of God, the liberty of which we speak, which goes hand in hand with virtue and religion, is not admitted; and whatever is done for its preservation is accounted an injury and an offense against the state. Indeed, if what they say were really true, there would be no tyranny, no matter how monstrous, which we should not be bound to endure and submit to."

[11] Cf. Pius XI, Encyclical Epistle *Maximam gravissimamque*, 18 January 1924: ASS 16 (1924), 10: "Whatever Pius X condemned, we condemn; wherever and as often as the term 'laicism' is understood in the sense of a feeling or ideal inimical or foreign to God and to religion, we absolutely condemn such a thing and declare moreover to the whole world that such 'laicism' must be condemned."

[12] Cf. IOANNES XXIII, Litt. Encycl. *Pacem in terris,* 11 aprilis 1963: *A.A.S.,* 55 (1963), p. 263: « Nam, quemadmodum Decessor noster fel. rec. Pius XII ait, tantum abest ut homo, uti talis, habendus tamquam vitae socialis obiectum vel iners quoddam elementum, ut magis eiusdem sit existimandus subiectum, fundamentum, finis ». Cf. PIUS XII, *Nuntius radiophonicus,* 24 dec. 1944: *A.A.S.,* 37 (1945), p. 12.

[13] Cf. IOANNES XXIII, Litt. Encycl. *Pacem in terris,* 11 aprilis 1963: *A.A.S.,* 55 (1963), p. 259.

[14] Cf. IOANNES XXIII, Litt. Encycl. *Pacem in terris,* 11 aprilis 1963: *A.A.S.,* 55 (1963), pp. 260-261: « In hominis iuribus hoc quoque numerandum est, ut et Deum, ad rectam conscientiae suae normam, venerari possit, et religionem privatim publice profiteri ». Cf. PIUS XII, *Nuntius radiophonicus,* 24 dec. 1942: *A.A.S.,* 35 (1943), p. 19, ubi inter « iura fundamentalia personae » hoc etiam collocatur: « il diritto al culto di Dio privato e pubblico, compresa l'azione caritativa religiosa ». Cf. PIUS XI, Litt. Encycl. *Mit brennender Sorge,* 14 martii 1937: *A.A.S.,* 29 (1937), p. 160: «Der gläubige Mensch hat ein unverlierbares Recht, seinen Glauben zu bekennen und in den ihm gemässen Formen zu betätigen. Gesetze, die das Bekenntnis und die Betätigung dieses Glaubens unterdrücken oder erschweren, stehen in Widerspruch mit einem Naturgesetz ». Cf. LEO XIII, Litt. Encycl. *Libertas praestantissimum,* 20 iunii 1888: *Acta Leonis XIII,* 8 (1888), pp. 237-238: « Illa quoque magnopere praedicatur, quam conscientiae libertatem [445] nominant; quae si ita accipiatur ut suo cuique arbitratu aeque liceat Deum colere, non colere, argumentis, quae supra allata sunt, satis convincitur. Sed potest etiam in hanc sententiam accipi, ut homini ex conscientia officii Dei voluntatem sequi et iussa facere, nulla re impediente, in civitate liceat. Haec quidem vera, haec digna filiis Dei libertas, quae humanae dignitatem personae honestissime tuetur, est omni vi iniuriaque maior, eademque Ecclesiae semper optata ac praecipue cara ».

[15] Cf. IOANNES XXIII, Litt. Encycl. *Pacem in terris,* 11 aprilis 1963: *A.A.S.,* 55 (1963), pp. 273-274: « Verum cum nostra hac aetate commune bonum maxime in humanae personae servatis iuribus et officiis consistere putetur, tum praecipue in eo sint oportet curatorum rei publicae partes, ut hinc iura agnoscantur, colantur, inter se componantur, defendantur, provehantur, illinc suis quisque officiis facilius fungi possit. Etenim "inviolabilia iura tueri, hominum propria, atque curare, ut facilius quisque suis muneribus defungatur, hoc cuiusvis publicae potestatis officium est praecipuum" ». Cf. PIUS XII, *Nuntius radiophonicus,* 1 iunii 1941: *A.A.S.,* 33 (1941), p. 200.

[16] Hoc loco memoranda est distinctio, facta a IOANNE XXIII, Litt. Encycl. *Pacem in terris,* 11 aprilis 1963: *A.A.S.,* 55 (1963), p. 300: « Inde deinceps par omnino est, a falsis philosophorum placitis de natura, de origine, de fine mundi et hominis plane incepta distinguere, quae sive res oeconomicas et sociales, sive ingenii cultum, sive civitatis temporationem contingunt, etiamsi incepta hoc genus ab illis placitis originem et incitamentum ducant; quoniam dum formula disciplinae, postquam definite descripta est, iam non mutatur, incepta illa, utpote quae in mutabilibus rerum condicionibus versentur, his non possunt quin sint admodum sane obnoxia. De reliquo quis eat infitias, in hisce inceptis, quatenus videlicet cum rectae rationis praeceptis congruant, et iustas hominis appetitiones referant, posse aliquid boni et probandi inesse? ». Quod valet in praesenti materia. Distinctio potest et debet iam nunc fieri inter ipsum regimen libertatis religiosae et placita laicismi, unde regimen quondam originem suam duxit in quibusdam civitatibus.

[17] Recentius de hac materia scripserunt G. DE BROGLIE, S. I., *Le Droit naturel à la liberté religieuse* (Paris, Beauchesne, 1964); L. JANSSENS, *Liberté de conscience et liberté religieuse* (Paris, Desclée de Brouwer, 1964).

[12] Cf. John XXIII, Encyclical Letter *Pacem in terris*, 11 April 1963: AAS 55 (1963), 263: "As Pope Pius XII said, 'man as such, far from being an object or, as it were, an inert element in society, is rather its subject, its basis and its purpose; and so must he be esteemed.'" Cf. Pius XII, Radio message, 24 December 1944: AAS 37 (1945), 12.

[13] Cf. John XXIII, Encyclical Letter *Pacem in terris,* 11 April 1963: AAS 55 (1963), 259.

[14] Cf. John XXIII, Encyclical Letter *Pacem in terris*, 11 April 1963: AAS 55 (1963), 260-61 "Also among man's rights is that of being able to worship God in accordance with the right dictates of his own conscience, and to profess his religion both in private and in public." Cf. Pius XII, Radio message, 24 December 1942: AAS 35 (1943), 19, where among "the fundamental rights of the person" is also included "the right to worship God privately and publicly, including religious charitable activity." Cf. Pius XI, Encyclical Letter *Mit brennender Sorge*, 14 March 1937: AAS 29 (1937), 160: "The believer has an absolute right to profess his faith and live according to its dictates. Laws that impede this profession and practice of faith are against natural law." Cf. Leo XIII, Encyclical Letter *Libertas praestantissimum*, 20 June 1888: *Acta Leonis XIII*, 8 (1888), 237-38: "Another freedom is widely advocated, namely, freedom of conscience. [445] If by this is meant that everyone may, as he chooses, worship God or not, it is sufficiently refuted by the arguments already adduced. But it may also be taken to mean that every man in the state may follow the will of God and, from a consciousness of duty and free from every obstacle, obey his commands. This, indeed, is true freedom, a freedom worthy of the sons of God, which nobly maintains the dignity of man and is stronger than all violence or wrong—a freedom which the Church has always desired and held most dear."

[15] Cf. John XXIII, Encyclical Letter *Pacem in terris*, 11 April 1963: AAS 55 (1963), 273-74: "It is generally accepted today that the common good is best safeguarded when personal rights and duties are guaranteed. The chief concern of civil authorities must therefore be to ensure that these rights are recognized, respected, co-ordinated, defended and promoted, and that each individual is enabled to perform his duties more easily. For 'to safeguard the inviolable rights of the human person, and to facilitate the performance of his duties, is the principal duty of every public power.'" Cf. Pius XII, Radio message, 1 June 1941: AAS 33 (1941), 200.

[16] Here one must keep in mind the distinction made by John XXIII in the Encyclical Letter *Pacem in terris*, 11 April 1963: AAS 55 (1963), 300: "Again it is perfectly legitimate to make a clear distinction between a false philosophy of the nature, origin and purpose of men and the world, and economic, social, cultural, and political undertakings, even when such undertakings draw their origin and inspiration from that philosophy. True, the philosophic formula does not change once it has been set down in precise terms, but the undertakings clearly cannot avoid being influenced to a certain extent by the changing conditions in which they have to operate. Besides, who can deny the possible existence of good and commendable elements in these undertakings, elements which do indeed conform to the dictates of right reason, and are an expression of man's lawful aspirations?" This statement applies also in the present matter. We can and should distinguish today between the practice of religious freedom itself, on the one hand, and the principles of laicism, on the other, recognizing that in certain states the former had its origin in the latter.

[17] This question has been treated recently by G. De Broglie, S.J., *Le Droit naturel à la liberté religieuse* (Paris: Beauchesne, 1964) and L. Janssens, *Liberté de conscience et liberté religieuse* (Paris: Descelée de Brouwer, 1964).

[18] De dialogo seu colloquio circa veritates religiosas, cf. PAULUS VI, Litt. Encycl. *Ecclesiam suam*, 6 aug. 1964, Typis Polyglottis Vaticanis, 1964, pp. 35-45.

[19] Perdurante aevo post Reformationem, eo usque tandem pervenit communis hominum sensus, ut agnoscat, neminem esse a potestate publica cogendum, ut agat contra conscientiam, neminemve esse propter conscientiam puniendum; cf. J. LECLER, S. I., *Histoire de la tolérance religieuse au siècle de la Réforme*, Paris, Aubier, Editions Montaigne, 1955, tom. II, *fere passim*. Nova tamen nostris temporibus exorta est quaestio, utrum homo quavis vi prohibeatur, quin agat in societate civili iuxta conscientiam.

[20] Cf. IOANNES XXIII, Litt. Encycl. *Pacem in terris*, 11 aprilis 1963: *A.A.S.*, 55 (1963), p. 289: « Quin et illud accedit quod mutuae rerum publicarum rationes ad libertatis normam sunt ordinandae ». Cf. *ibid.*, pp. 266, 297.

[21] Cf. LEO XIII, Epist. Encycl. *Cum multa*, 8 dec. 1882: *A.S.S.*, 15 (1898), pp. 242-43: « Igitur oportet rem sacram remque civilem, quae sunt genere naturaque distincta, etiam opinione iudicioque secernere. Nam hoc genus de rebus civilibus, quantumvis in honestum et grave, si spectetur in se, vitae huius, quae in terris degitur, fines nequaquam praetergreditur. Contra vero religio, nata Deo et ad Deum [**446**] referens omnia, altius se pandit caelumque contingit . . . Quapropter religionem et quidquid est singulari quodam vinculo cum religione colligatum, rectum est superioris ordinis ducere ». Traditionem iteravit PIUS XI, Litt. Encycl. *Non abbiamo bisogno*, 29 iunii 1931: *A.A.S.*, 23 (1931), p. 303: « La Chiesa di Gesù Cristo non ha mai contestato i diritti e i doveri dello Stato circa l'educazione dei cittadini e Noi stessi li abbiamo ricordati e proclamati nella recente Nostra Lettera Enciclica sulla educazione cristiana della gioventù; diritti e doveri incontestabili finché rimangono nei confini delle competenze proprie dello Stato; competenze che sono alla loro volta chiaramente fissate dalle finalità dello Stato; finalità certamente non soltanto corporee e materiali, ma di per se stesse necessariamente contenute nei limiti del naturale, del terreno, del temporaneo ».

[22] Cf. S. THOMAS, *Summa theologica*, I-II, q. 91, a. 4 c: « De his potest homo legem ferre de quibus potest iudicare. Iudicium autem hominis esse non potest de interioribus actibus, qui latent, sed solum de exterioribus actibus, qui apparent »; cf. II-II, q. 104, a. 5 c: « In his quae pertinent ad interiorem motum voluntatis, homo non tenetur homini oboedire sed solum Deo ». Cf. IOANNES XXIII, Litt. Encycl. *Pacem in terris*, 11 aprilis 1963: *A.A.S.*, 55 (1963), p. 270: « Sed quoniam omnes homines in naturali dignitate sunt inter se pares, tum nemo valet alium ad aliquid intimis animi sensibus efficiendum cogere; quod quidem unus Deus potest, utpote qui unus arcana pectoris consilia scrutetur ac iudicet ».

[23] Sic redditur aliis verbis nota regula iuris canonici, ex iure romano quoad sensum deprompta, « Odia restringi et favores convenit ampliari ». Cf. V. BARTOCCETTI, *De regulis iuris canonici* (Angelo Belardetti Editore, Roma 1955), p. 73.

[24] Cf. LEO XIII, Litt. Encycl. *Sapientiae christianae*, 10 ianuarii 1890: *A.S.S.*, 22 (1889-90), p. 396: « Dubitari vero salva fide non potest, istiusmodi regimen animorum Ecclesiae esse assignatum uni, nihil ut in eo sit politicae potestati loci; non enim Caesari, sed Petro claves regni caelorum Iesus Christus commendavit ».

[25] Cf. IOANNES XXIII, Litt. Encycl. *Pacem in terris*, 11 aprilis 1963: *A.A.S.*, 55 (1963), pp. 295-296, ubi, quibusdam defectibus non obstantibus, commendatur Professio Universalis Iurium Humanorum, die 10 dec. 1948 a Foederatarum Nationum Coetu Generali rata habita:

Schema 3: Emended Text

[18] Regarding dialogue or colloquia on religious truths, cf. Paul VI, Encyclical Letter *Ecclesiam suam*, 6 August 1964, Vatican Polyglot Press, 1964, 35-45.

[19] During the period following the Reformation, the general opinion among men reached the point of acknowledging that no one should be forced by the public power to act against his conscience, or be punished on account of his conscience; cf. J. Lecler, S.J., *Histoire de la tolérance religieuse au siècle de la Réforme* (Paris: Aubier, Editions Montaigne, 1955), vol. II, *passim*. A new question has arisen in our times, however, namely, whether men and women may be prohibited by the use of force from acting in civil society according to their conscience.

[20] Cf. John XXIII, Encyclical Letter *Pacem in terris*, 11 April 1963: AAS 55 (1963), 289: "Furthermore, relations between states must be regulated by the principle of freedom." Cf. *ibid.*, 266, 297.

[21] Cf. Leo XIII, Encyclical Epistle *Cum multa*, 8 December 1882: ASS 15 (1898), 242-43: "The sacred and civil orders being, therefore, distinct in their origin and in their nature, should be conceived and judged of as such. For matters of the civil order—however lawful, however important they be—do not extend, when considered in themselves, beyond the limits of that life which we live on this our earth. But religion, born of God, and [**446**] referring all things to God, takes a higher flight and touches heaven. . . . It is, then, right to look on religion, and whatever is connected in any particular way with it, as belonging to a higher order." Pius XI repeated this teaching in the Encyclical Letter *Non abbiamo bisogno*, 29 June 1931: AAS 23 (1931), 303: "The Church of Jesus Christ has never contested the rights and the duties of the state concerning the education of its citizens; indeed, we ourselves have recalled and proclaimed them in our recent encyclical on the 'Christian Education of Youth.' Such rights and duties are unchallengeable as long as they remain within the limits of the state's proper competency, a competence which in its turn is clearly indicated and determined by the end of the state, an end which, though certainly not only bodily and material, is by its very nature limited to the natural, the terrestrial and the temporal."

[22] Cf. St. Thomas, *Summa theologica*, I-II, q. 91, a. 4, c: "Man can make laws in those matters of which he is competent to judge. But man is not competent to judge of interior movements, which are hidden, but only of exterior acts, which are apparent." Cf. II-II, q. 104, a. 5, c: "In matters touching on the interior movement of the will man is not bound to obey his fellow man, but God alone." Cf. John XXIII, Encyclical Letter *Pacem in terris*, 11 April 1963: AAS 55 (1963), 270: "But since all men are equal in natural dignity, no man has the capacity to force internal compliance on another. Only God can do that, for he alone scrutinizes and judges the secret counsels of the heart."

[23] This statement expresses in different words the following well-known rule of canon law, which derives its meaning from Roman law: "Whatever is burdensome should be restricted; whatever is favorable should be increased." Cf. V. Bartoccetti, *De regulis iuris canonici* (Rome: Angelo Belardetti, 1955), 73.

[24] Cf. Leo XIII, Encyclical Letter *Sapientiae christianae*, 10 January 1890: ASS 22 (1889-90), 396: "No one can, however, without risk to faith, foster any doubt as to the Church alone having been invested with such power of governing souls as to exclude altogether the civil authority. In truth, it was not to Caesar but to Peter that Jesus Christ entrusted the keys of the kingdom of heaven."

[25] Cf. John XXIII, Encyclical Letter *Pacem in terris*, 11 April 1963: AAS 55 (1963), 295-96, where, certain defects notwithstanding, the pope commends the Universal Declaration of Human Rights, ratified by the General Assembly of the United Nations on December 10,

« Nihilominus Professionem eandem habendam esse censemus quemdam quasi gradum atque aditum ad iuridicialem politicamque ordinationem constituendam omnium populorum, qui in mundo sunt. Siquidem ea universis prorsus hominibus solemniter agnoscitur humanae dignitas personae, atque iura cuivis homini asseruntur veritatem libere quaerendi, honestatis sequendi normas, iustitiae officia usurpandi, vitam exigendi homine dignam, alia deinceps cum hisce coniuncta ».

[26] Cf. LEO XIII, Litt. Encycl. *Immortale Dei*, 1 nov. 1885: *A.S.S.*, 18 (1885), p. 161: « Immortale Dei miserenti opus, quod est Ecclesia, quamquam per se et natura sua salutem spectat animorum adipiscendamque in caelis felicitatis, tamen in ipso etiam rerum mortalium genere tot ac tantas ultro parit utilitates, ut plures maioresve non posset, si in primis et maxime esset ad tuendam huius vitae, quae in terris agitur, prosperitatem institutum ». Quod quidem thema, e S. Augustino derivatum, saepe saepius evolvere solebat Leo XIII.

[27] Cf. LEO XIII, Litterae *Officio sanctissimo*, 22 dec. 1887: *A.S.S.*, 22 (1887), p. 269: «In bonis autem Ecclesiae, quae Nobis ubique semperque conservare debemus, ab omnique iniuria defendere, illud certe praestantissimum est, tantam ipsam perfrui agendi libertate, quantam salus hominum curanda requirat. Haec [447] nimirum est libertas divina, ab Unigenito Dei Filio auctore profecta, qui Ecclesiam sanguine fuso excitavit; qui eam perpetuam in hominibus statuit; qui voluit ipsi ipse praeesse. Atque adeo propria est Ecclesiae, perfecti divinique operis, ut qui contra eam faciunt libertatem, iidem contra Deum et contra officium ». Ut olim Gregorius VII, sic temporibus modernis exstabat LEO XIII propugnator libertatis Ecclesiae. Cf. Litterae *Ex litteris*, 7 aprilis 1887: *A.S.S.*, 19 (1886), p. 465: «Nos quidem vel ab initio nostri pontificatus multo et serio cogitare de vobis instituimus, atque, ut ratio Nostri ferebat officii, consilium cepimus omnia conari, si qua ratione liceat, pacatam tranquillitatem cum libertate legitima catholico nomini restituere ». In sexaginta fere documentis, quae relationes inter rem sacram remque civilem tractant, octoginta vices occurrit formula verborum, « libertas Ecclesiae », vel formula aequipollens. Ipsi enim Leoni XIII, sicut toti traditioni catholicae, libertas Ecclesiae principium est fundamentale in iis, quae spectant ad relationem inter Ecclesiam et instituta omnia ordinis civilis.

[28] Cf. PIUS XII, Litt. Encycl. *Summi Pontificatus*, 20 oct. 1939: *A.A.S.*, 31 (1939), pp. 445-46: « Quamobrem Nos, ut eius in terris vices gerimus, qui a sacro vate "Princeps pacis" appellatur (*Is.* 9, 6), civitatum rectores eosque omnes, e quorum opera quovis modo publica res pendet, compellamus vehementerque obtestamur ut Ecclesia plena semper libertate fruatur debita, qua suam possit educationis operam exsequi, ac veritatem impertire mentibus, animis inculcare iustitiam, eosque divina Iesu Christi refovere caritate ».

[29] Cf. PIUS XI, Litterae *Firmissimam constantiam*, 28 martii 1937: *A.A.S.*, 29 (1937), p. 196: « Proposita eiusmodi aestimandarum rerum mensura, concedendum sane est, ad christianam vitam explicandam externa quoque praesidia, quae sensibus percipiuntur, esse necessaria, pariterque Ecclesiae tamquam hominum societati opus omnino esse, ad vitae usuram atque incrementum, iusta agendi libertate, ipsosque fideles iure gaudere in societate civili vivendi ad rationis conscientiaeque praescripta ».

[30] Cf. PIUS XII, Allocutio *Ci riesce*, 6 dec. 1953: *A.A.S.*, 45 (1953), p. 802, ubi fines clare definiuntur, quos Ecclesia prae oculis habet in ineundis Concordatis: « I Concordati debbono quindi assicurare alla Chiesa una stabile condizione di diritto e di fatto nello Stato, con cui sono conclusi, e garantire ad essa la piena indipendenza nell'adempimento della sua divina missione ». Exinde insuper constat, nihil esse in doctrina de libertate religiosa, quod cum praxi hodierna Concordatorum quovis modo pugnat.

1948: "Nevertheless, we think the document should be considered a step in the right direction, an approach toward the establishment of a juridical and political ordering of the world community. It is a solemn recognition of the personal dignity of every human being; an assertion of everyone's right to be free to seek out the truth, to follow moral principles, to discharge the duties imposed by justice, and to lead a fully human life. It also recognized other rights connected with these."

[26] Cf. Leo XIII, Encyclical Letter *Immortale Dei,* 1 November 1885: ASS 18 (1885), 161: "The Catholic Church, that imperishable handiwork of our all-merciful God, has for her immediate and natural purpose the saving of souls and securing our happiness in heaven. Yet, in regard to things temporal, she is the source of benefits as manifold and great as if the chief end of her existence were to ensure the prospering of our earthly life." This idea, which derives from St. Augustine, was increasingly developed by Leo XIII throughout his pontificate.

[27] Cf. Leo XIII, Encyclical *Officio sanctissimo,* 22 December 1887: ASS 22 (1887), 269: "Of the goods of the Church that it is our duty everywhere and always to maintain and defend against all injustice, the first is certainly that of enjoying the full freedom of action she may need in working for the salvation of souls. This [447] is a divine liberty, having as its author the only Son of God, who by the shedding of his blood gave birth to the Church, who established it until the end of time, and chose himself to be its head. This liberty is so essential to the Church, a perfect and divine institution, that they who attack this liberty at the same time offend against God and their duty." Like Gregory VII before him, Leo XIII stands out in the modern period as a great defender of the freedom of the Church. Cf. the Encyclical *Ex litteris,* 7 April 1887: ASS 19 (1886), 465: "Indeed, from the beginning of our pontificate we have given much serious thought toward you, and, bearing in in mind our office, we resolved to attempt all things possible to restore to the Catholic name peaceful tranquility with lawful freedom." In almost sixty documents that deal with relations between sacred and civil affairs, the phrase "freedom of the Church," or its equivalent, occurs eighty times. Indeed, for Leo XIII himself, as for the whole Catholic tradition, the freedom of the Church is a fundamental principle among those that concern the relationship between the Church and all the institutions of the civil order.

[28] Cf. Pius XII, Encyclical Letter *Summi Pontificatus,* 20 October 1939: AAS 31 (1939), 445-46: "Accordingly we, as representatives on earth of him who was proclaimed by the prophet 'Prince of Peace' (Is 9:6) appeal to and vigorously implore the leaders of nations, and those who can in any way influence public life, to let the Church have full liberty to fulfill her role as educator by teaching men truth, by inculcating justice and by inflaming hearts with the divine love of Christ."

[29] Cf. Pius XI, Encyclical *Firmissimam constantiam,* 28 March 1937: AAS 29 (1937), 196: "Once this gradation of values and activities is established, it must be admitted that for Christian life to develop it must have recourse to external and sensible means; that the Church, being a society of men, cannot exist or develop if it does not enjoy liberty of action, and that its members have the right to find in civil society the possibility of living according to the dictates of reason and their conscience."

[30] Cf. Pius XII, Allocution *Ci riesce,* 6 December 1953: AAS 45 (1953), 802, where the limits that the Church has in mind when entering into concordats are clearly defined: "Concordats should therefore assure to the Church a stable condition in right and in fact within the state with which they are concluded, and guarantee to her full independence in fulfilling her divine mission." From this it is evident that there is nothing in the teaching on religious freedom that is at odds in any way with the current practice of concordats.

³¹ LACTANTIUS, *Divinarum Institutionum,* lib. V, 19: ed. S. Brandt et G. Laubmann, *CSEL* 19, p. 463; *PL* 6, 614 (cap. 20): « Non est opus vi et iniuria, quia religio cogi non potest, verbis potius quam verberibus res agenda est, ut sit voluntas ».

Op. cit.: CSEL 19, p. 464; *PL* 6, 614: «Itaque nemo a nobis retinetur invitus—inutilis est enim Deo qui devotione ac fide caret—et tamen nemo discedit ipsa veritate retinente ».

Op. cit.: CSEL 19, p. 465; *PL* 6, 616: « Nihil est enim tam voluntarium quam religio, in qua si animus sacrificantis aversus est, iam sublata, iam nulla est ».

S. AMBROSIUS, *Epistola ad Valentinianum Imp., Ep.* 21: *PL* 16, 1047: « Dei lex nos docuit quid sequamur, humanae leges hoc docere non possumus. Extorquere solent timidis commutationem fidem inspirare non possunt ».

S. AUGUSTINUS, *Contra litteras Petiliani,* lib. II, cap. 83: ed. M. Petschenig, **[448]** *CSEL* 52, p. 112; *PL* 43, 315; cf. C. 23, q. 5, c. 33 (ed. Friedberg, col. 939): « Augustinus respondit: Ad fidem quidem nullus est cogendus invitus; sed per severitatem, immo et per misericordiam Dei tribulationum flagellis solet perfidia castigari ».

S. GREGORIUS MAGNUS, *Epistola ad Virgilium et Theodorum Episcopos Massilliae Galliarum,* Registrum Epistolarum, I, 45: ed. P. Ewald et L. M. Hartmann, *MGH Ep.* 1, p. 72; *PL* 77, 510-11 (lib. I, ep. 47): « Dum enim quispiam ad baptismatis fontem non praedicationis suavitate, sed necessitate pervenerit, ad pristinam superstitionem remeans in de deterius moritur, unde renatus esse videbatur ».

Epistola ad Iohannem Episcopum Constantinopolitanum, Registrum Epistolarum, III, 52: *MGH Ep.* 1, p. 210; *PL* 77, 649 (lib. III, ep. 53); cf. D. 45, c. 1 (ed. Friedberg, col. 160): « Nova vero atque inaudita est ista praedicatio, quae verberibus exigit fidem ».

CONC. TOLET. IV, c. 57: MANSI 10, 633; cf. D. 45, c. 5 (ed. Friedberg, col. 161-162): « De Iudaeis hoc praecepit sancta synodus, nemini deinceps ad credendum vim inferre; *cui enim vult Deus misereatur, et quem vult indurat.* Non enim tales inviti salvandi sunt, sed volentes, ut integra sit forma iustitiae: sicut enim homo proprii arbitrii voluntate serpenti oboediens periit, sic vocante gratia Dei, propriae mentis conversione homo quisque credendo salvatur. Ergo non vi, sed liberi arbitrii facultate, ut convertantur suadendi sunt, non potius impellendi . . . ».

CLEMENS III, Litterae Decretales: X, V, 6, 9, ed. Friedberg, col. 774: « . . . Statuimus enim ut nullus Christianus invitos vel nolentes Iudaeos ad baptismum (per violentiam) venire compellat. Si quis autem ad Christianos causa fidei confugerit, postquam voluntas eius fuerit patefacta, Christianus absque calumnia efficiatur: quippe Christi fidem habere non creditur, qui ad Christianorum baptismum non spontaneus, sed invitus cogitur pervenire . . . ».

INNOCENTUS III, *Epistola ad Arelatensem Archiepiscopum,* X, III, 42, 3: ed. Friedberg, col. 646: « . . . Verum id est religioni Christianae contrarium, ut semper invitus et penitus contradicens ad recipiendam et servandam Christianitatem aliquis compellatur . . . ».

³² Cf. *C.I.C.,* c. 1351; cf. PIUS XII, Alloc. ad Praelatos auditores ceterosque officiales et administros Tribunalis S. Romanae Rotae, 6 oct. 1946: *A.A.S.,* 38 (1946), p. 394, ubi citatur a R. P. *Pro Memoria* Secretarius Status ad Legationem Yugoslaviae ad Sanctam Sedem: « D'après les

[31] Lactantius, *Divinarum Institutionum*, bk. V, 19: ed. S. Brandt and G. Laubmann, *CSEL* 19, p. 463; *PL* 6, 614 (ch. 20): "There is no need for violence or injury, for religion cannot be forced; the whole matter should be carried on with words rather than whips, in order that there might be free will."

Op. cit.: *CSEL* 19, p. 464; *PL* 6, 614: "Therefore we hold no one back against his will—for anyone who is without devotion and faith is of no use to God—and yet no one departs who is held fast by the truth itself."

Op. cit.: *CSEL* 19, p. 465; *PL* 6, 616: "For nothing is so voluntary as religion; once the spirit of the one offering sacrifice has turned away, religion is already destroyed, is itself already nothing."

St. Ambrose, *Epistola ad Valentinianum Imp.*, Ep. 21, *PL* 16, 1047: "God's law taught us what to strive for; human laws cannot teach this. Such laws are merely accustomed to extorting a change from the faint of heart; they cannot inspire faith."

St. Augustine, *Contra litteras Petiliani*, bk. II, ch. 83: ed. M Petschenig, **[448]** *CSEL* 52, p. 112; *PL* 43, 315; cf. C. 23, q. 5, ch. 33 (ed. Friedberg, col. 939): "Augustine replied: No one, indeed, is forced to embrace the faith against his will; but through the severity of God, or rather through his mercy, faithlessness is usually punished by the lashes of tribulation."

St. Gregory the Great, *Epistola ad Virgilium et Theodorum Episcopos Massilliae Galliarium*, Registrum Epistolarum, I, 45: ed. P. Ewald and L.M. Hartmann, *MGH Ep.* 1, p. 72; *PL* 77, 510-11 (bk. I, ep. 47): "For if anyone should have come to the holy baptismal font, not through the persuasion of preaching, but out of compulsion, when he returns to the place of his former superstition he will die the worse for it, having come from a place where he only seemed to have been reborn."

Epistola ad Iohannem Episcopum Constantinopolitanum, Registrum Epistolarum, III, 52: *MGH Ep.* 1, p. 210; *PL* 77, 649 (bk. III, ep. 53); cf. D. 45, ch. 1 (ed. Friedberg, col. 160): "That preaching is indeed new and unheard of, that exacts faith by means of lashing."

Fourth Council of Toledo, ch. 57: Mansi 10, 633; cf. D. 45, ch. 5 (ed. Friedberg, col. 161-162); "Concerning the Jews, the holy synod declared that henceforth force is not to be applied to anyone in order to make them believe; *for God has mercy on whom he wishes, and hardens whom he wishes.* For such men are to be saved not unwillingly but willingly, in order that justice may be perfect: for just as man perished by obeying the serpent through his own free-will, so at the call of God's grace, each man is saved by believing through the conversion of his own mind. Therefore, not by force, but by the free judgment of their own free will are they to be persuaded to convert, rather than compelled . . ."

Clement III, *Litterae Decretales*: X, V, 6, 9, ed. Friedberg col. 774: ". . . For we have decreed that no Christian is to force Jews reluctantly or against their will to approach baptism (by violence). If, however, someone has recourse to Christians on account of his faith, after he has made known his will, let him be made a Christian without dispute; since one who is forced to approach Christian baptism not voluntarily but against his will is not considered to have the faith of Christ . . ."

Innocent III, *Epistola ad Arelatensem Archiepiscopum*, X, III, 42, 3: ed. Friedberg, col. 646: ". . . Truly it is contrary to the Christian religion that anyone ever be forced, against his will and while interiorly opposing it, to receive and keep the Christian faith . . ."

[32] Cf. *Code of Canon Law* [1917], c. 1351; cf. Pius XII, "Allocution to prelate auditors and other officials and administrators of the Tribunal of the Sacred Roman Rota," 6 October 1946: AAS 38 (1946), 394, where the pope cites the *pro memoria* of the Secretariat of State to the

principes de la doctrine catholique, la conversion doit être le résultat, non pas de contraintes extérieures mais de l'adhésion de l'âme aux verités enseignées par l'Eglise catholique. C'est pour cela que l'Eglise catholique n'admet pas dans son sein les adultes, qui demandent à y entrer ou à y faire retour, qu'à la condition qu'ils soient pleinement conscients de la portée et des conséquences de l'acte qu'ils veulent accomplir ». Idem, Litt. Encycl. *Mystici Corporis*, 29 iunii 1943: *A.A.S.*, 35 (1943), p. 243: «At si cupimus non intermissam eiusmodi totius mystici Corporis conprecationem admoveri Deo, ut aberrantes omnes in unum Iesu Christi ovile quam primum ingrediantur, profitemur tamen omnino necessarium esse id sponte libenterque fieri, cum nemo credat nisi volens. Quamobrem si qui, non credentes, eo reapse compelluntur ut Ecclesiae aedificium intrent, ut ad altare accedant, sacramentaque suscipiant, ii procul dubio veri christifideles non fiunt; fides enim, sine qua "impossibile [449] est placere Deo" (*Hebr.* 11, 6), liberrimum esse debet "obsequium intellectus et voluntatis" (CONC. VAT., *Const. de fide catholica*, cap. 3). Si igitur aliquando contingat, ut contra constantem Apostolicae huius Sedis doctrinam, ad amplexandam catholicam fidem aliquis adigatur invitus, id Nos facere non possumus quin, pro officii nostri conscientia, reprobamus ».

[33] Tentationes Christo a Satana propositae simul ac petitiones prodigiorum a Iudaeis oblatae provenerunt ex aestimatione populari Messiae tamquam regis fortis et mirabilis. Si Christus his consiliis acquievisset, dereliquisset consilio Patris Eum iubentis ut munus messianicum exsequeretur per indolem mitem et humilem Servi Yahweh.

[34] Cf. PIUS XII, *Nuntius radiophonicus*, 28 martii 1952: *A.A.S.*, 44 (1952), pp. 270-78, de conscientia christiana efformanda.

[35] Cf. IOANNES XXIII, Litt. Encycl. *Pacem in terris*, 11 aprilis 1963: *A.A.S.*, 55 (1963), pp. 299-300: « Omnino errores ab iis qui opinione labuntur semper distinguere aequum est, quamvis de hominibus agatur, qui aut errore veritatis aut impari rerum cognitione capti sint, vel ad sacra vel ad optimam vitae actionem attinentium. Nam homo ad errorem lapsus iam non humanitate instructus esse desinit, neque suam umquam personae dignitatem amittit, cuius ratio est semper habenda. Praeterea in hominis natura numquam facultas perit et refragandi erroribus et viam ad veritatem quaerendi. Neque umquam hac in re providentissimi Dei auxilia hominem deficiunt. Ex quo fieri potest, ut si quis hodie vel perspicuitate egeat, vel in falsas discesserit sententias, possit postmodum, Dei collustratus lumine veritatem amplecti ».

Yugoslavian Embassy to the Holy See: "In accordance with the principles of Catholic teaching, conversion should be the result not of external constraints but of the soul's adherence to the truths taught by the Catholic Church. This is why the Catholic Church admits to herself adults who seek to enter or return to her only on the condition that they are fully conscious of the significance and consequences of the act they wish to make." Cf. also the Encyclical Letter *Mystici Corporis*, 29 June 1943: AAS 35 (1943), 243: "Though we desire this unceasing prayer to rise to God from the whole mystical body in common, that all the straying sheep may hasten to enter the one fold of Jesus Christ, we still recognize that this must be done of their own free will; for no one believes unless he wills to believe. Hence they are most certainly not genuine Christians who against their belief are forced to go into a church, to approach the altar and to receive the sacraments; for the 'faith without which it is impossible [449] to please God' (Heb 11:6) is an entirely free 'submission of intellect and will' (First Vatican Council, *Constitution on the Catholic Faith*, ch. 3). Therefore, whenever it happens, despite the constant teaching of this apostolic see, that anyone is compelled to embrace the Catholic faith against his will, our sense of duty demands that we condemn the act."

[33] The temptations that Satan suggested to Christ, like the demands for miracles made by the Jews, derived from a popular conception that the Messiah would be a strong and miraculous king. Had Christ agreed to these suggestions, he would have forsaken the plan of his Father, which directed him to carry out the messianic mission in the meek and humble manner of the Servant of Yahweh.

[34] On the formation of a Christian conscience, cf. Pius XII, Radio message, 28 March 1952: AAS 44 (1952), 270-78.

[35] Cf. John XXIII, Encyclical Letter *Pacem in terris*, 11 April 1963: AAS 55 (1963), 299-300: "It is always perfectly justifiable to distinguish between error as such and the person who falls into error—even in the case of men who err regarding the truth or are led astray as a result of their inadequate knowledge, in matters either of religion or of the highest ethical standards. A man who has fallen into error does not cease to be a man. He never forfeits his personal dignity; and that is something that must always be taken into account. Besides, there exists in man's very nature an undying capacity to break through the barriers of error and seek the road to truth. God, in his great providence, is ever present with his aid. Today, maybe, a man lacks faith and turns aside into error; tomorrow, perhaps, illumined by God's light, he may indeed embrace the truth."

SCHEMA DECLARATIONIS DE LIBERTATE RELIGIOSA

Textus reemendatus

(Acta Synodalia IV/1, 146-67*)*

DE IURE PERSONAE ET COMMUNITATUM
AD LIBERTATEM IN RE RELIGIOSA

1. Dignitatis humanae personae homines hac nostra aetate magis in dies conscii fiunt.[1] Postulat haec dignitas, ut in agendo homo proprio suo consilio et libertate fruatur, sitque non coercitione commotus sed officii conscientia. Quae libertatis postulatio in societate humana ea maxime respicit, quae ad religionem spectant. Ad has animorum appetitiones diligenter attendens, Ecclesia sibi proponit discernere, quantum sint veritati et iustitiae conformes. Simulque ad suam doctrinam divinitus traditam denuo animadvertens, de thesauro suo vetera profert et nova, quae ad iustas hominum appetitiones confirmandas inserviunt.

I. DECLARATIO

2. Itaque haec Vaticana Synodus declarat ius ad libertatem religiosam esse revera fundatum [147] in ipsa dignitate personae humanae, qualis et ratione et maxime verbo Dei revelato cognoscitur.[2] Huiusmodi autem libertas in eo consistit quod homines debent immunes esse a coercitione sive hominum singulorom sive coetuum socialium et cuiusvis potestatis humanae, et ita quidem ut in re religiosa neque aliquis cogatur ad agendum contra suam conscientiam, neque impediatur, quominus iuxta suam conscientiam privatim et publice agat intra debitos limites.

Insuper declarat huiusmodi ius in iuridica societatis ordinatione ita esse agnoscendum, ut ius civile evadat, quod omnes homines omnesque communitates religiosae legitime sibi possint vindicare. Cura autem huius iuris tum ad cives tum ad potestates publicas pertinet modo unicuique proprio.[3]

Declarat denique, ex hac libertatis religiosae aflirmatione non sequi

DRAFT OF THE DECLARATION ON RELIGIOUS FREEDOM

Re-emended Text

(*Acta Synodalia* IV/1, 146-67)

ON THE RIGHT OF THE PERSON AND OF COMMUNITIES
TO FREEDOM IN RELIGIOUS MATTERS

1. Men and women of our time are becoming more conscious every day of the dignity of the human person.[1] This dignity demands that in acting man enjoy his own counsel and freedom, not impelled by coercion but moved by a sense of duty. This demand for freedom in human society is chiefly concerned with those things that concern religion. Carefully attending to these desires of men's hearts, the Church proposes to discern to what degree they are in conformity with truth and justice. At the same time, attending anew to her divinely inspired tradition of teachings, she draws forth from out of her treasury things both old and new that serve to confirm the just desires of men.

I. DECLARATION

2. This Vatican Council declares that the right to religious freedom has its foundation [147] in the very dignity of the human person, as known from both reason and especially the revealed word of God.[2] Such freedom consists in this, that men and women should be immune from coercion on the part of individuals, social groups, or any human power, so that no one is forced to act against his conscience in religious matters, or prevented from acting according to his conscience, in private or in public, within due limits.

In addition, this Council declares that this right must be acknowledged in the juridical order of society, so that it becomes a civil right, one that all persons and all religious communities can legitimately claim for themselves. Care for this right is the responsibility of both citizens and public powers, in the way that is proper to each.[3]

Finally, this Council declares that it does not follow from this affirma-

hominem nulla obligatione in re religiosa teneri aut esse a Dei auctoritate emancipatum. Libertas enim religiosa non implicat personam humanam falsum ac verum posse aeque aestimare, aut dispensari officio formandi sibi veram de rebus religiosis sententiam, aut posse arbitrario statuere, utrum et in qua religione et quanam ratione [148] Deo servire velit. Porro ratio libertatis religiosae intactam relinquit doctrinam catholicam de unica vera religione et de unica Christi Ecclesia.

II. DOCTRINA DE LIBERTATE RELIGIOSA EX RATIONE DESUMPTA

3. Suprema humanae vitae norma est lex divina, aeterna atque universalis, qua Deus consilio sapientiae et dilectionis suae mundum universum viasque communitatis humanae ordinat, dirigit, gubernat.[4] Deus autem huius suae legis hominem participem reddit, eam veluti quadam irradiatione ipsi naturae humanae imprimens, ut homo, providentia divina suaviter disponente, veritatem incommutabilem magis magisque cognoscere possit.[5]

Dictamina vero huius legis divinae homo semper percipit et agnoscit mediante conscientia sua; hoc autem ad ipsam personae humanae dignitatem pertinet. Quapropter tenetur quisque in universa activitate sua conscientiam sequi fideliter, ut ad Deum, finem suum, perveniat.

Ideo homo officium et ius quoque habet veritatem in re religiosa quaerendi, ut sibi mediis adhibitis idoneis certa conscientiae iudicia prudenter efformet. Veritas autem est humano modo inquirenda, libera scilicet inquisitione, eique inventae firmiter est adhaerendum, assensu nempe personali. Insuper, cum homo sit natura sua socialis, veritas quaeritur et invenitur [149] per magisterium seu institutionem et per communicationem atque dialogum, quibus alii aliis exponunt veritatem quam invenerunt vel invenisse putant, ut sese invicem in veritate quaerenda adiuvent.

Sollemne ergo est principium morale, quod vetat, ne quis in re religiosa cogatur ad agendum contra suam conscientiam.[6]

Nostris autem diebus, aucto sensu dignitatis humanae personalis et civilis, exigitur insuper ne quis in societate humana, ulla vi adhibita vel a singulis hominibus vel a coetibus socialibus aut a potestate publica, impediatur

tion of religious freedom that man has no obligations in religious matters or that he is set free from God's authority. Religious freedom does not imply that the human person can equally value what is false and what is true, that he no longer has the duty to form for himself a true judgment about religious matters, or that he can determine at will whether or in which religion and in what way [148] he wishes to serve God. The principle of religious freedom thus leaves intact the Catholic teaching on the one true religion and the one Church of Christ.

II. THE TEACHING ON RELIGIOUS FREEDOM DERIVED FROM REASON

3. The highest norm of human life is the divine law, eternal and universal, by which God, in the providence of his wisdom and love, orders, directs, and governs the whole world and the ways of the human community.[4] God grants man a share in this law, imprinting it on human nature itself by a kind of illumination, as it were, so that man, under the gentle direction of divine providence, can come to know more and more the truth that is itself unchanging.[5]

It is always through the mediation of his conscience that man perceives and recognizes the precepts of this divine law; this belongs to the very dignity of the human person. Each person is therefore bound in all his actions to follow his conscience faithfully, so that he may come to God, his end.

Man therefore has the duty and the right to seek the truth in religious matters, so that he may prudently form sure judgments of conscience for himself, using all suitable means. The truth, however, must be sought in a way proper to man, namely, by means of free inquiry, and it must be firmly adhered to once it is found, by means of personal assent. Moreover, since man is by his nature social, the truth must be sought and found [149] through instruction or education and by communication and dialogue, in which men and women share with one another the truth they have found or think they have found, so as to assist each other in seeking the truth.

It is therefore a traditional moral principle that it is prohibited to force anyone to act against his conscience in religious matters.[6]

In our day, however, given the growing awareness of both personal and civil human dignity, a further demand is made, that no one in society be prevented by any use of force, whether on the part of individuals, social

quominus privatim et publice agat in re religiosa iuxta suam conscientiam, intra videlicet debitos limites. Quae quidem exigentia est rationi prorsus consentanea et homine digna.

Etenim natura socialis personae humanae necessario sese exhibet in rebus quoque ad religionem pertinentibus. Exercitium namque religionis, ex ipsa eius indole, consistit primario in actibus internis prorsus voluntariis et liberis, quibus homo sese ad Deum directe ordinat, eo nempe animo, ut suam necessitudinem ad Deum agnoscat et debita oboedientia adhaereat voluntati divinae. Sed praeterea ipsa socialis hominis natura exigit, ut homo internos religionis actus socialiter manifestet, seu actibus externis, quibus in societate cum aliis communicet. Iniuria ergo homini fit, si quis internam cuiusque libertatem in re religiosa agnoscat quidem at simul ei deneget liberum in societate religionis exercitium debitos limites non excedens.

[150] Praeterea actus religiosi, quibus homines privatim et publice sese ad Deum ex animi sententia ordinant, natura sua terrestrem et temporalem rerum ordinem transcendunt. Competentia vero potestatis civilis ob ipsum eius finem proprium, qui exactius his diebus perspicitur atque describitur secundum exigentias dignitatis personae eiusque iura, ad ordinem terrestrem et temporalem eo consilio restringitur,[7] ut personae humanae expeditiore libertate ad finem suum ultimum secundum conscientiam suam tendere possint. Potestas igitur civilis limites suos excedere dicenda est, si in ea, quae ipsam ordinationem hominis ad Deum respiciunt, sese immisceat. Neque ideo ullo modo e naturali sua dignitate excidere dicenda est, si suas erga communitatem partes agat, sese ad res huius saeculi restringendo, atque ita personam humanam agnoscat eique inserviat.

Dignitas ergo personae humanae exigit, ne quis impediatur, etiam a potestate publica, quominus in re religiosa tum privatim tum publice agat, intra debitos limites, iuxta suam conscientiam.

4. (*Limites libertatis religiosae*).

a) (*Norma moralis*). Ius ad libertatem in re religiosa exercetur in societate humana, ideoque eius usus quibusdam normis moderantibus obnoxius est. Quarum prima est principium legis moralis observandae. In vita autem sociali eminet principium responsabilitatis [151] personalis et socialis. Etenim in iuribus suis exercendis singuli homines coetusque sociales debent rationem habere et iurium aliorum et suorum officiorum erga alios; cum omnibus enim secundum iustitiam et humanitatem agendum est.

b) (*Norma iuridica*). Societas civilis ius habet sese protegendi contra

groups or the public power, from acting according to his conscience in religious matters, in private or in public, within due limits. This demand is entirely consistent with reason and is worthy of man.

Indeed, the social nature of the human person is necessarily exhibited also in those things that concern religion. By its very nature the exercise of religion consists primarily in interior acts that are entirely voluntary and free, by which man orders himself directly toward God, with the intention of acknowledging his relationship to God and holding fast to the divine will with all due obedience. But man's social nature itself demands that he manifest these interior religious acts socially, in external actions, by which he communicates with others in society. It is therefore an injustice for anyone to recognize man's interior freedom in religious matters and at the same time deny him the free exercise of religion in society, provided this exercise does not exceed due limits.

[150] Furthermore, religious acts, in which men and women privately and publicly order themselves toward God out of a sense of inner conviction, by their nature transcend the earthly and temporal order of things. The competence of the civil power, however, on account of its proper end—which today is more accurately perceived and described in terms of the demands of the dignity of the person and his rights—is restricted in its purpose to the earthly and temporal order,[7] in order that human persons can strive toward their final end more easily and freely, according to their conscience. The civil power must therefore be said to exceed its limits if it involves itself in those matters that concern the very ordination of man to God. Nor can it be said to be deprived in any way of its inherent worth, provided it performs its duty toward the community, restricting itself to secular matters, and in this way acknowledging and serving the human person.

The dignity of the human person therefore demands that no one be prevented, not even by the public power, from acting according to his conscience in religious matters, in private or in public, within due limits.

4. (*The limits of religious freedom*).

a) (*The moral norm*). The right to freedom in religious matters is exercised in human society, and its use is therefore subject to certain governing norms. The first of these is the principle that the moral law must be observed. In social life, however, the principle [151] of personal and social responsibility is preeminent. In exercising their rights, individuals and social groups should keep in mind both the rights of others and their duties toward others; they should act toward all with justice and humanity.

b) (*The juridical norm*). Civil society has the right to protect itself

abusus, qui haberi possint, invocato titulo libertatis religiosae. Pertinet praecipue ad potestatem civilem huiusmodi protectionem praestare, non tamen
modo arbitrario, sed secundum normas iuridicas, quas necessitates ordinis
publici postulant. Illud autem societatis bonum, quod est ordo publicus,
requirit sufficientem pacis publicae curam, debitam custodiam publicae
moralitatis, et pacificam compositionem atque efficacem aequalium iurium
tutelam pro omnibus civibus. Quod quidem bonum est universae societati
adeo necessarium, ut actus, qui grave damnum ei inferant, sint reprimendi.
Exercitium ergo religionis in societate legitime non potest prohiberi coercitiva interventione potestatis civilis nisi vel perturbet pacem publicam vel
publicam violet moralitatem vel iura laedat aliorum. Ceterum servanda est
regula iuris ex qua libertas debet quam maxime homini agnosci nec restringenda est nisi quando et prout est necessarium.[8]

5. (*Cura libertatis religiosae*). Inviolabilia hominis iura tueri ac promovere est praecipuum cuiusvis potestatis civilis officium.[9] Debet igitur potestas
civilis per iustas leges efficaciter suscipere tutelam curamque libertatis religiosae omnium civium. Eidem providendum [152] est, ne civium aequalitas
iuridica unquam laedatur propter rationes religiosas.

Hinc sequitur nefas esse potestati publicae, per vim vel metum aut
alia iniusta media civibus imponere professionem aut reiectionem cuiusvis
religionis, vel impedire,quominus quisquam communitatem religiosam aut
ingrediatur aut relinquat. Eo magis contra voluntatem Dei et contra sacra
personae et familiae gentium iura agitur, quando vis quocumque modo adhibeatur ad religionem ipsam delendam vel cohibendam sive in toto genere
humano sive in aliqua regione sive in determinato coetu religioso.

Huic Vaticanae Synodo in votis est, ut ius personae humanae ad libertatem religiosam in omnibus per orbem terrarum civitatibus agnoscatur,
efficaci tutela iuridica muniatur et aptis mediis consulatur ut cives revera ipsa
religionis iura exercere eiusdemque officia adimplere valeant. Ceterum, quo
magis societas civilis propitias suppeditabit condiciones ad vitam religiosam
fovendam, eo magis ipsa fruetur bonis, quae undequaque proveniunt ex
fidelitate hominum erga Deum Eiusque sanctam voluntatem.[10]

Hoc vero libertatis religiosae regimen non impedit, quominus, attentis
populorum circumstantiis historicis, uni communitati religiosae specialis
agnitio in iuridica civitatis ordinatione tribuatur, eo tamen pacto, ut simul
omnibus civibus et communitatibus religiosis ius ad libertatem in re religiosa
agnoscatur et observetur.

[153] 6. (*Libertas communitatum religiosarum*). Libertas religiosa,

against abuses that could be committed in the name of religious freedom. It belongs especially to the civil power to afford protection of this sort, not in an arbitrary fashion, but according to juridical norms that are required by the needs of public order. Public order is that good of society that concerns the adequate care of public peace, the due preservation of public morality, and the effective protection of the equal rights of all citizens and the peaceful settlement of conflict of rights. This good is in fact so necessary to the whole society that any acts that inflict serious injury upon it must be suppressed. The exercise of religion in society, therefore, cannot be legitimately prohibited by the coercive intervention of the civil power unless such exercise disturbs the public peace, violates public morality, or offends the rights of others. For the rest, that rule of law should be upheld which holds that man's freedom should be acknowledged as far as possible, and should not be restricted except when and insofar as necessary.[8]

5. (*The care of religious freedom*). It is the chief duty of every civil power to protect and promote the inviolable rights of man.[9] The civil power should therefore effectively undertake to protect and care for the religious freedom of all citizens through just laws. It should also see to it [152] that the equality of citizens before the law is never violated for religious reasons.

It follows that it is wrong for the public power to impose by force or fear or any other unjust means the profession or rejection of any religion on its citizens, or to prevent anyone from entering or leaving a religious community. All the more is it against God's will and the sacred rights of the person and the family of nations to use force in any way in order to destroy or repress religion itself, either in the human race as a whole or in a particular region or in a specific religious group.

This Vatican Council prays that the human person's right to religious freedom be acknowledged in all the nations of the world, be secured by effective juridical protection, and be cared for by suitable means, so that citizens may truly be able to exercise their religious rights and fulfill their religious duties. For the rest, the more that civil society provides favorable conditions for fostering religious life, the more it will enjoy those goods that come forth everywhere from men's fidelity to God and his holy will.[10]

This practice of religious freedom does not prevent one religious community from being granted special recognition in the juridical order of the state, in light of the historical circumstances of the people, provided that at the same time the right to freedom in religious matters be acknowledged and observed for all citizens and religious communities.

[153] 6. (*The freedom of religious communities*). The religious freedom

quae singulis personis competit, etiam communitatibus agnoscenda est. Hae namque a sociali natura tum hominis tum ipsius religionis requiruntur.

His igitur communitatibus iure debetur immunitas, ut secundum proprias leges sese regant, Numen supremum cultu publico honorent, membra sua in vita religiosa exercenda adiuvent et doctrina sustentent atque eas institutiones promoveant, in quibus membra cooperentur ad vitam propriam secundum sua principia religiosa ordinandam.

Communitatibus religiosis pariter competit ius, ne mediis legalibus vel actione administrativa potestatis civilis impediantur in suis propriis ministris seligendis atque educandis, in communicando cum auctoritatibus et communitatibus religiosis, quae in aliis orbis terrarum partibus degunt, necnon in bonis congruis acquirendis et fruendis.

Communitates religiosae ius etiam habent, ne impediantur in sua fide ore et scripto publice docenda atque testanda, legitimis exigentiis ordinis publici non violatis. In fide autem religiosa disseminanda et in usibus inducendis abstinendum semper est ab omni actionis genere, quod coercitionem vel suasionem inhonestam aut minus rectam sapere videatur, praesertim quando de rudioribus vel de egenis agitur.

Tandem ad libertatem religiosam spectat quod communitates religiosae libere possint ostendere singularem suae doctrinae virtutem in ordinanda societate ac tota vivificanda activitate humana. Praeterea in sociali hominis natura [154] atque in ipsa indole religionis fundatur ius, quo homines, suo ipsorum sensu religioso moti, libere possunt conventus habere vel associationes educativas, culturales, caritativas, sociales constituere.

7. (*Libertas religiosa familiae*). Cuique familiae, utpote quae est societas proprio ac primordiali iure gaudens, competit ius ad libere ordinandam religiosam vitam suam domesticam sub moderatione parentum. His autem competit ius ad determinandam rationem iustitutionis religiosae suis liberis tradendae. Insuper a civili potestate agnoscendum est ius parentum deligendi, vera cum libertate, scholas vel alia educationis media, neque ob hanc electionis libertatem sunt eis iuiusta onera imponenda. Potestas civilis iura parentum violat, si unicam imponat educationis rationem, ex qua omnis formatio religiosa excludatur.

that belongs to individual persons must be recognized for communities as well. These communities are called for by the social nature of man and of religion itself.

Immunity is therefore due to these communities by right, so that they may govern themselves according to their own laws, honor the Supreme Being with public worship, assist their members in their practice of religious life, strengthen them by instruction, and promote institutions in which members can join together to order their own life according to their religious principles.

Religious communities likewise have the right not to be impeded, either by legal measures or by administrative action on the part of the civil power, in selecting and educating their own ministers, in communicating with religious authorities and communities in other parts of the world, or in acquiring and making use of any necessary goods.

Religious communities also have the right not to be prevented from publicly teaching about or witnessing to their faith in speech or in writing, provided they do not violate the legitimate requirements of public order. In spreading their religious faith and introducing their practices, however, they must always refrain from any kind of activity that would seem to suggest any hint of coercion or dishonest or less than proper persuasion, especially in regard to those less educated or in need.

Finally, religious freedom entails that religious communities freely be able to show the unique value of their doctrine for ordering society and animating all human activity. Furthermore, there is in man's social nature [154] and in the very nature of religion the foundation for the right by which men and women, moved by their own religious sense, can freely hold meetings and establish educational, cultural, charitable, and social associations.

7. (*The religious freedom of the family*). Each family, as a society in its own original right, has the right to order freely its own domestic religious life, under the guidance of the parents. Parents also have the right to determine the way in which religious instruction will be handed on to their children. In addition, the civil power must acknowledge the right of parents to choose with true freedom among schools or other means of education, and must not burden them unjustly on account of this freedom of choice. The civil power violates the rights of parents if it imposes a single system of education that excludes all religious formation.

III. DOCTRINA LIBERTATIS RELIGIOSAE
SUB LUCE REVELATIONIS

8. Quae de iure hominis ad libertatem religiosam declarat haec Vaticana Synodus fundamentum quidem proximum habent in dignitate personae, cuius exigentiae rationi humanae plecius innotuerunt per saeculorum experientiam. Ast haec libertas radices habet in divina revelatione, qua primum humanae personae dignitas in tota sua amplitudine incepit manifestari, et inde eo magis a christianis sancte servanda. Praeterea libertas religiosa in societate plene est cum libertate actus fidei christianae [155] congrua ac cum debita Ecclesiae libertate in sua divina missione exsequenda omnino consona.

9. (*Libertas religiosa in historia salutis radicatur*). Deus enim initio ad imaginem suam constituit hominem eumque in manu consilii sui reliquit (cf. *Gn.* 1, 27; *Sir.* 15, 14; 17, 6). Immo voluit, ut libere sancta societate Ei haereat: cum populo qui Ei oboedientiam spoponderat foedus sanctum inivit (cf. *Ex.* 19, 5-8; 24, 7; *Ios.* 24, 16 ss. 22). Per Prophetas illum paulatim edocuit unumquemque personali devotione ad Deum esse convertendum novumque foedus promisit, quo legem suam in corde et mente inscriberet (cf. *Ier.* 31, 31-33; *Ez.* 36, 26-27).

Ubi ergo venit plenitudo temporis misit Deus Filium suum qui mandatum amoris discipulis suis dedit libere ad Se, trahente Patre, per fidem accedentibus (cf. *Io.* 6, 44). In corda eorumdem Spiritum suum et caritatem effudit, qua non iam servi, sed sicut filii Dei agunt (cf. *Rom.* 5, 5; 8, 14), in libertatem iam vocati (cf. *Gal.* 5, 13), perventuri tandem ad « libertatem gloriae filiorum Dei » (*Rom.* 8, 21). Distinxit insuper Dominus Iesus quae Dei sunt et quae Caesaris, ita ut Christifideles et Caesari propter conscientiam oboediant in iis quae Caesaris sunt (cf. *Rom.* 13, 5), et Deo in iis quae inviolabiliter Dei sunt. Hanc viam secuti sunt innumeri martyres et fideles per saecula et per orbem.

Quae omnia Ecclesia decursu temporum sedulo custodivit et tradidit. Fideles ad maiorem in dies libertatem spiritus instituit, et in iis genuinum oboedientiae sensum excoluit. Potestatum saecularium oppressioni restitit, suique ministerii sacri libertatem propugnavit. Tandem, etsi inter populum Dei in terris peregrinantem [156] non defuerunt qui alias vias, spiritui evangelico minus conformes inierint, inconcussa tamen semper mansit Ecclesiae doctrina, neminem esse ad fidem cogendum.

III. THE TEACHING ON RELIGIOUS FREEDOM
IN THE LIGHT OF REVELATION

8. The declarations of this Vatican Council regarding man's right to religious freedom have their immediate foundation in the dignity of the person, a dignity whose demands have come to be more fully known to human reason through centuries of experience. But this freedom also has roots in divine revelation, through which the dignity of the human person first began to be made manifest in all its fullness; therefore this freedom must be observed by Christians all the more faithfully. Religious freedom in society is in full agreement with the freedom of the act of Christian faith, [155] and wholly consonant with the freedom due to the Church in following out her divine mission.

9. (*Religious freedom is rooted in salvation history*). In the beginning God created man in his own image and left him in the power of his own judgment (cf. Gen 1:27; Sir 15:14; 17:6). Indeed, God wanted man to hold fast to him freely in a holy communion: he entered into a holy covenant with his people, who promised him obedience (cf. Ex 19:5-8; 24:7; Jos 24:16, 22). Through the prophets he gradually taught them that each man must turn to God in personal devotion, and he promised a new covenant in which he would write his law on their hearts and minds (cf. Jer 31:32-33; Ez 36:26-27).

In the fullness of time, therefore, God sent his Son, who gave the commandment of love to his disciples, who came to him freely through faith, drawn by the Father. He poured into their hearts his Spirit and charity, through which they act no longer as servants but as sons of God (cf. Rom 5:5; 8:14), called to freedom even now (cf. Gal 5:13) and in the end called to obtain "the glorious freedom of the children of God" (Rom 8:21). In addition, the Lord Jesus distinguished between what belongs to God and what to Caesar, so that the Christian faithful may in good conscience obey both Caesar in the things that are Caesar's (cf. Rom 13:5) and God in the things that are inviolably God's. This is the way that countless martyrs and faithful have followed through the ages and throughout the world.

Through the ages the Church has carefully protected and handed on all these things. She has built up in the faithful day by day a greater freedom of spirit, and has cultivated in them a genuine sense of obedience. She has resisted the oppression of secular powers, and has fought in defense of the freedom of her sacred ministry. Finally, although among the people of God, as it has made its pilgrim way on earth, [156] there have been those who followed other paths less in keeping with the spirit of the Gospel, the teaching

Evangelicum fermentum in mentibus quoque hominum diu est operatum atque multum contulit ad hoc, ut temporum decursu latius agnosceretur
principium, in re religiosa homines immunes esse servandos in civitate a
quacumque humana coercitione.

10. (*Modus agendi Christi et Apostolorum*). Deus Ipse quidem homines ad inserviendum Sibi vocat, non vero coercet. Rationem enim habet
dignitatis personae humanae ab Ipso conditae, quae proprio consilio duci
et libertate frui debet. Hoc autem summe apparuit in Christo Iesu, in quo
Deus Seipsum ac vias suas tamquam in perfecto humano exemplari manifestavit. Etenim Christus, qui Magister et Dominus est noster (cf. *Io.* 13, 13),
idemque mitis et humilis corde (cf. *Mt.* 11, 29), in ministerio suo peragendo
discipulos patienter allexit et invitavit (cf. *Mt.* 4, 19; 11, 28-30; 19, 16-22; *Io.* 6,
68). Miraculis utique praedicationem suam suffulsit et confirmavit, ut auditores verbo suo fide haererent. At vero ea prodigia semper renuit patrare,
quae violentia quadam assensum fidei ab hominibus non bene dispositis
extorquere viderentur. Auditores quidem eiusmodi signa petebant (cf. *Lc.*
11, 16; *Mt.* 27, 42-43), quae tamen recusavit Iesus (cf. *Lc.* 11, 16 sq.; *Io.* 4, 48).
Ipsos Apostolos increpavit, qui Ei proponebant: « Domine, vis dicimus ut
descendat ignis de caelo et consumat illos? » (cf. *Lc.* 9, 54-56). Christus autem
sese praebuit ut perfectum Servum Yahweh (cf. *Is.* 42, 1-4), qui « harundinem quassatam non confringit et linum fumigans non extinguit » (*Mt.* 12,
20). Regnum eius [**157**] non percutiendo vindicatur (cf. *Mt.* 26, 51-53), sed
stabilitur testificando et audiendo veritatem (cf. *Io.* 18, 37), et crescit amore,
quo homines ad Seipsum trahit (cf. *Io.* 12, 32).

Christi exemplum secuti sunt Apostoli. Ab ipso Ecclesiae exordio discipuli Christi allaborarunt ut homines ad Christum Dominum confitendum
converterent, non actione coercitiva neque artificiis Evangelio indignis, sed
in primis virtute verbi Dei (cf. *1 Cor.* 2, 3-5; *1 Thess.* 2, 3-5). Sicuti Christus,
Apostoli intenti semper fuerunt ad testimonium reddendum veritati Dei,
abundantius audentes coram populo et principibus « sine timore verbum
Dei loqui » (*Phil.* 1, 14; cf. *Act.* 4, 13-20). Firma fiducia tenebant ipsum evangelium revera esse virtutem Dei in salutem omni credenti (cf. *Rom.* 1, 16).
Omnibus ergo spretis « armis carnalibus » (cf. *2 Cor.* 10, 4), exemplum mansuetudinis et modestiae Christi sequentes, verbum Dei praedicaverunt plene

of the Church has nonetheless always remained unshaken, that no one is to be forced to embrace the faith.

The leaven of the Gospel has long been about its quiet work in the minds of men; to this is due, in large measure, the fact that in the course of time the principle has become more widely recognized, that in religious matters men and women are to be kept immune within civil society from any kind of human coercion.

10. (*Christ's and the apostles' way of acting*). God himself calls men and women to serve him, but he does not coerce them. For he has regard for the dignity of the human person whom he himself created, who should be led by his own counsel and enjoy his own freedom. This truth appeared in consummate form in Jesus Christ, in whom God manifested himself and his ways as in a perfect human being. For Christ, who is our Master and Lord (cf. Jn 13:13) and at the same time meek and humble of heart (cf. Mt 11:29), attracted and invited disciples with patience as he went about his ministry (cf. Mt 4:19; 11:28-30; 19:16-22; Jn 6:68). He supported and confirmed his teaching with miracles, so that his listeners would hold fast to his word in faith. But he always refused to work wonders that would seem to extort, by a kind of violence, an assent of faith from men who were not well disposed. His listeners in fact sought signs of this sort (cf. Lk 11:16; Mt. 27:42-43), but Jesus refused them (cf. Lk 11:16 ff.; Jn 4:48). He rebuked the apostles themselves, when they asked him, "Lord, do you want us to bid fire come down from heaven and consume them?" (cf. Lk 9:54-56). Christ showed himself to be the perfect Servant of Yahweh (cf. Is 42:1-4), who "does not break a bruised reed nor quench a smoldering wick" (Mt 12:20). His kingdom [**157**] is not claimed by force of blows (cf. Mt 26:51-53), but is established by bearing witness to and listening to the truth (cf. Jn 18:37), and it grows through the love by which he draws men to himself (cf. Jn 12:32).

The apostles followed Christ's example. From the very beginning of the Church they strove to convert men and women to the confession of Christ as Lord, not through coercion or means unworthy of the Gospel, but foremost by the power of the word of God (cf. 1 Cor 2:3-5; 1 Thes 2:3-5). Like Christ, the apostles were always intent to bear witness to the truth of God, daring "to speak the word of God without fear" (Phil 1:14; cf. Acts 4:13-20) and in full before the people and their leaders. With firm faith they held that the Gospel itself is truly the power of God for the salvation of all who believe (cf. Rom 1:16). Rejecting all "worldly weapons" (cf. 2 Cor 10:3-5), therefore, and following the example of Christ's meekness and modesty, they preached

confisi divina huius verbi virtute ad potestates Deo adversas destruendas et homines ad fidem et obsequium Christi reducendos (cf. *2 Cor.* 10, 3-5).

Ecclesia igitur, evangelicae veritati fidelis,[11] viam Christi et Apostolorum sequitur quando rationem libertatis religiosae ut hominis dignitati consonam agnoscit eamque fovet.

11. (*Libertas actus fidei*). Caput est ex praecipuis doctrinae catholicae, in verbo Dei contentum [158] et a Patribus constanter praedicatum,[12] hominem debere Deo libere respondere credendo; invitum proinde neminem esse cogendum ad amplectendam fidem.[13] Etenim actus fidei ipsa sua natura liber est, cum homo, a Christo Salvatore redemptus et in adoptionem filiorum per Iesum Christum vocatus (cf. *Eph.* 1, 5), Deo sese revelanti adhaerere non possit, nisi Pater traxerit eum (cf. *Io.* 6, 44) et rationabile liberumque Deo praestiterit fidei obsequium. Indoli ergo fidei repugnat ut, in re religiosa, quodvis genus coercitionis ex parte hominum adhibeatur. Ac proinde ratio libertatis religiosae haud parum eo confert ad illum rerum statum efficiendum, quo homines expedite possint invitari ad fidem christianam libere amplectendam eamque in tota vitae ratione actuose confitendam.

12. (*Libertas Ecclesiae*). Inter ea quae ad bonum Ecclesiae spectant et ubique semperque servanda sunt atque ab omni iniuria defendenda, illud certe praestantissimum est, eam tanta perfrui agendi libertate, quauntam salus hominum curanda requirat.[14] Haec enim libertas sacra est, qua Unigenitus Dei Filius ditavit Ecclesiam acquisitam sanguine suo. Ecclesiae autem adeo propria est, ut qui eam impugnent, iidem contra Dei voluntatem agant. Ex catholica traditione libertas Ecclesiae est principium fundamentale in relationibus inter Ecclesiam et ordinem civilem vitae humanae.

In societate humana et coram quavis potestate publica Ecclesia sibi vindicat libertatem, utpote auctoritas spiritualis, a Christo Domino constituta, cui ex divino mandato incumbit [159] officium eundi in mundum universum et evangelium praedicandi omni creaturae (cf. *Mc.* 16, 15; *Mt.* 28, 18-20).[15] Pariter libertatem sibi vindicat Ecclesia prout est etiam societas hominum convocationi divinae libere respondentium, qui iure gaudent vivendi in societate civili secundum fidei christianae praescripta.[16]

Iamvero si reapse viget ratio libertatis religiosae, Ecclesia stabilem obtinet et iuris et facti condicionem plenamque independentiam in missione divina exsequenda, quae ei ex mandato Christi commissa est.[17] Praeterea Christifideles, non minus quam ceteri homines, iure civili gaudent ne impe-

the word of God, fully trusting in the divine power of this word to destroy the powers that are opposed to God and to lead men and women to the faith and allegiance of Christ (cf. 2 Cor 10:3-5).

The Church, therefore, faithful to the truth of the Gospel,[11] is following in the way of Christ and the apostles when she acknowledges and supports the principle of religious freedom as consonant with the dignity of man.

11. (*The freedom of the act of faith*). It is a chief tenet of Catholic teaching, contained in the word of God [158] and constantly proclaimed by the Fathers,[12] that man's response to God in faith should be free; no one is to be forced, therefore, to embrace the faith against his will.[13] The act of faith is of its very nature a free act. For man, redeemed by Christ the Savior and called to be an adopted son through Jesus Christ (cf. Eph 1:5), cannot hold fast to God as he reveals himself unless he is drawn by the Father (cf. Jn 6:44) and offers to God a rational and free submission of faith. It is therefore incompatible with the very nature of faith for men to employ any kind of coercion in religious matters. The principle of religious freedom thus contributes in no small way to bringing about a state of affairs in which men and women can without hindrance be invited to embrace the Christian faith in freedom, and actively profess it in their whole way of life.

12. (*The freedom of the Church*). Preeminent among those things that concern the good of the Church, which must always and everywhere be preserved and defended against all harm, is for the Church to enjoy as much freedom in acting as the care of man's salvation may demand.[14] This is a sacred freedom with which the only begotten Son of God endowed the Church whom he purchased with his blood. This freedom is so proper to the Church that whoever opposes it acts against the will of God. According to the Catholic tradition, the freedom of the Church is a fundamental principle in relations between the Church and the civil order of human life.

The Church claims for herself freedom in human society and before every public power insofar as she is a spiritual authority, constituted by Christ the Lord, upon whom rests, by divine command, [159] the duty to go throughout the whole world preaching the Gospel to every creature (cf. Mk 16:15; Mt 28:10-20).[15] The Church likewise claims for herself freedom as a society of men and women responding freely to the divine call, who enjoy the right to live in civil society according to the precepts of the Christian faith.[16]

Indeed, where the principle of religious freedom truly thrives, the Church maintains a stable condition both in law and in fact, and full independence in carrying out the divine mission entrusted to her by Christ's command.[17] Furthermore, the Christian faithful, no less than other men and

diantur in vita sua iuxta conscientiam agenda. Concordia igitur viget inter libertatem Ecclesiae et libertatem illam religiosam, quae omnibus hominibus et communitatibus est tamquam ius agnoscenda.

13. (*Munus Ecclesiae*). Ecclesia Catholica, ut divino obtemperet mandato: « docete omnes gentes . . . docentes eos servare omnia quaecumque mandavi vobis » (*Mt.* 28, 19-20), impensa cura adlaborare debet « ut sermo Dei curtat et clarilicetur » (2 *Thess.* 3, 1).

Enixe igitur rogat Ecclesia ut a filiis suis « primum omnium fiant obsecrationes, orationes, postulationes, gratiarum actiones pro omnibus hominibus . . . Hoc enim bonum est et acceptum coram Salvatore nostro Deo, qui omnes homines vult salvos fieri et ad agnitionem veritatis venire » (*1 Tim.* 2, 1-4).

Christifideles autem in sua efformanda conscientia diligenter, attendere debent ad sacram [160] certamque Ecclesiae doctrinam.[18] Dei enim voluntate Ecclesia Catholica magistra est veritatis, eiusque munus est, ut veritatem, quae Christus est, enuntiet atque authentice doceat, simulque principia ordinis moralis, ex ipsa natura humana profluentia, auctoritate sua declaret atque confirmet. Insuper Christiani, in sapientia ambulantes ad eos qui foris sunt, « in Spiritu Sancto, in caritate non ficta, in verbo veritatis » (2 *Cor.* 6, 6-7) lumen vitae cum omni fiducia (cf. *Act.* 4, 29) et fortitudine apostolica, ad sanguinis usque effusionem, diffundere satagant.

Etenim discipulus erga inaestimabile donum veritatis Christi gravi adstringitur officio, eam plenius in dies cognoscendi, annuntiandi fideliter, strenue defendendi. Simul tamen caritas Christi urget eum, ut amanter prudenter patienter agat cum hominibus, qui in errore vel ignorantia circa fidem versantur.[19] Respiciendum igitur est tum ad officia erga verbum vivificans quod praedicandum est, tum ad humanae personae iura, tum ad mensuram gratiae a Deo per Christum tributam homini, qui ad fidem libere accipiendam et profitendam invitatur.

IV. CONCLUSIO

14. Constat igitur praesentis aetatis homines optare ut libere possint religionem privatim publiceque profiteri; libertatem autem religiosam in plerisque constitutionibus iam ut [161] ius civile declarari[20] et instrumentis internationalibus agnosci.[21]

women, enjoy the civil right of not being prevented from acting according to their conscience. A harmony therefore exists between the freedom of the Church and the religious freedom that must be acknowledged as a right of all men and communities.

13. (*The task of the Church*). In order to obey the divine command: "Go and make disciples of all nations . . . teaching them to observe all that I have commanded you" (Mt 28:19-20), the Catholic Church should strive with great care "that the word of the Lord may speed on and triumph" (2 Thes 3:1).

The Church therefore earnestly entreats her children, "First of all that supplications, prayers, intercessions, and thanksgivings be made for all men . . . This is good and it is acceptable in the sight of God our Savior, who desires all men to be saved and to come to the knowledge of the truth" (1 Tim 2:1-4).

In forming their conscience, the Christian faithful should carefully attend to the sacred [160] and certain teaching of the Church.[18] For by the will of God the Catholic Church is the teacher of truth, and it is her duty to proclaim and authoritatively teach the truth that is Christ, and likewise to declare and confirm with her authority the principles of the moral order that flow from human nature. In addition, as Christians conduct themselves in wisdom toward those outside, "in the Holy Spirit, in genuine charity, in truthful speech" (2 Cor 6:6-7), let them be diligent in diffusing the light of life with all boldness (cf. Acts 4:29) and apostolic courage, even to the shedding of their blood.

The disciple is bound by a grave duty to the inestimable gift of Christ's truth, to know it more fully each day, to proclaim it faithfully, and to defend it vigorously. At the same time, the love of Christ urges him to deal lovingly, prudently, and patiently with those who dwell in error or ignorance about the faith.[19] He must therefore consider not only his duties toward the life-giving word that must be preached, but also the rights of the human person, and the measure of grace that God has bestowed through Christ upon those who are invited freely to receive and profess the faith.

IV. CONCLUSION

14. It is well known that men and women of today desire to be able to profess their religion freely in private and in public. Religious freedom has already been declared to be [161] a civil right in most constitutions,[20] and is acknowledged in international documents as well.[21]

At non desunt regimina in quibus, etsi in eorum constitutione ius ad cultum Deo praestandum agnoscitur, tamen ipsae publicae potestates conantur cives a religione profitenda removere et communitatibus religiosis vitam perdifficilem ac periclitantem reddere.

Illa fausta huius temporis signa laeto animo salutans, haec vero deploranda facta cum moerore denuntians, Sacra Synodus Christifideles hortatur, exorat autem homines universos, ut perattente considerent quantopere libertas religiosa necessaria sit, in praesentibus potissimum vitae humanae adiunctis.

Manifestum est enim cunctas gentes magis in dies unum fieri, homines diversae culturae et religionis arctioribus inter se devinciri rationibus, augeri denique conscientiam propriae cuiusque responsabilitatis. Proinde ut pacificae relationes et concordia in genere humano instaurentur et firmentur, requiritur ut ubique terrarum libertas religiosa efficaci tutela iuridica muniatur atque observentur suprema hominum officia et iura ad vitam religiosam libere in societate ducendam.

Manifestum praeterea est, cum nostrae aetatis homines varia ratione premantur et in periculum veniant ne proprio libero consilio utantur, Christianis quam maxime incumbere officium veram libertatem in se et in aliis tutandi ac promovendi. Ex altera autem parte non pauci ita propensi videntur, ut specie libertatis omnem subiectionem reiiciant ac debitam oboedientiam parvi faciant. Religiosa igitur libertas ad hoc inservire et ordinari debet, ut homines eam nobilem libertatem expeditius consequi possint, ad quam a Deo vocati sunt.

[162] Quapropter haec Vaticana Synodus omnes hortatur, praesertim vero eos qui curam habent alios educandi, ut homines formare satagant, qui et legitimae auctoritati oboedientes et genuinae libertatis amatores sint; homines nempe, qui proprio consilio res in luce veritatis diiudicent, activitates suas cum sensu responsabilitatis disponant, et quaecumque sunt vera atque iusta persequi nitantur, operam suam libenter cum ceteris consociando.

Faxit Deus et Pater omnium ut familia humana, diligenter servata libertatis religiosae ratione in societate, per gratiam Christi et virtutem Spiritus Sancti adducatur ad sublimem illam ac perennem « libertatem gloriae filiorum Dei » (*Rom.* 8, 21).

Governments are not lacking, however, in which, although the right to worship God is acknowledged in their constitutions, the public powers themselves still endeavor to prevent citizens from professing their religion and to make life very difficult and dangerous for religious communities.

Welcoming the former with joy as a favorable sign of the times, while denouncing the latter with sorrow as something to be deplored, this sacred Council urges the Christian faithful and entreats all men and women to consider carefully how necessary religious freedom is, especially in the present circumstances of human life.

It is clear that all nations are becoming more united every day, that men and women of different cultures and religions are being bound to one another with closer ties, and that there is a growing consciousness of the responsibility proper to each person. Hence, in order that peaceful relations and harmony may be established and strengthened among mankind, religious freedom must be secured by effective juridical protection throughout the world, and the highest duties and rights of men and women to lead a religious life freely in society must be observed.

It is also clear that men and women of our time are subjected to a variety of pressures and are in danger of being unable to make use of their own free counsel; for this reason, the greatest possible duty falls upon Christians to protect and promote true freedom among themselves and among others. On the other hand, not a few seem disposed, under the pretense of freedom, to reject all submission and to make light of the duty of obedience. Religious freedom should therefore be devoted and ordered to this end, that men and women may be able to pursue more easily that noble freedom to which they are called by God.

[162] For this reason, this Vatican Council urges all men and women, especially those who are responsible for educating others, to be diligent in forming human beings who are obedient to legitimate authority and who are lovers of genuine freedom; men and women, that is, who by their own counsel decide matters in the light of truth, who act with a sense of responsibility, and who endeavor to pursue whatever is true and just, cooperating willingly with others in their work.

May God the Father of all grant that the human family, having diligently upheld the principle of religious freedom in society, be led by the grace of Christ and the power of the Holy Spirit to that sublime and everlasting "glorious freedom of the children of God" (Rom 8:21).

NOTAE

[1] Cf. IOANNES XXIII, Litt. Encycl. *Pacem in terris,* 11 aprilis 1963: *A.A.S.,* 55 (1963), p. 279, ubi Summus Pontifex ad realitates hodiernas animadvertit: « At hae, de quibus diximus, animorum appetitiones illud etiam manifesto testantur, nostro hoc tempore homines magis magisque fieri dignitatis suae conscios, atque adeo incitari cum ad reipublicae administratio nem participandam, tum ad poscendum, ut propria inviolabiliaque iura in publica civitatis disciplina serventur. Neque haec satis; nam homines nunc illud insuper poscunt, ut nempe civitatis auctoritates et ad normam publicae constitutionis creentur, et sua munera intra eiusdem terminos obeant ». Cf. *ibid.,* p. 265: « Illud praeterea humanae dignitas personae exigitur, ut in agendo homo proprio consilio et libertate fruatur. Quocirca, si de civium coniunctione agitur, est profecto cur ipse iura colat, officia servet, atque, in innumeris operibus exercendis, aliis sociam tribuat operam, suo praesertim impulsu et consulto; ita scilicet ut suo quisque instituto, iudicio, officiique conscientia agat, iam non commotus coercitione vel sollicitatione extrinsecus plerumque adductis; quandoquidem, si qua hominum societas una ratione virium est instituta, ea nihil humani in se habere dicenda est, utpote in qua homines a libertate cohibeantur, qui contra ad vitae progressus, ad perfectionemque assequendam apte ipsi incitandi sunt ».

[**163**] Quod pertinet ad dignitatem illam civilem, secundum quam dignitas humana in publicum prodit, cf. PIUS XII, *Nuntius radiophonicus,* 24 dec. 1944: *A.A.S.,* 37 (1945) p. 14: «In un popolo degno di tal nome il cittadino sente in se stesso la coscienza della sua personalità, dei suoi doveri e dei suoi diritti, della propria libertà congiunta col rispetto della libertà e della dignità altrui ». Hoc loco commendat Romanus Pontifex etiam illud « ideale di libertà e di uguaglianza » (*loc. cit.*), quod in Statu democratico, iuxta sana rationis principia ordinato, obtineat necesse est, quodque postulat, ut hominis ius in societate ad liberum exercitium religionis plene agnoscatur, colatur, defendatur.

[2] Cf. IOANNES XXIII, Litt. Encycl. *Pacem in terris,* 11 aprilis 1963: *A.A.S.,* 55 (1963), pp. 260-261: « In hominis iuribus hoc quoque numerandum est, ut et Deum, ad rectam conscientiae suae normam, venerari possit, et religionem privatim publice profiteri ». Cf. PIUS XII, *Nuntius radiophonicus,* 24 dec. 1942: *A.A.S.,* 35 (1943), p. 19, ubi inter « iura fundamentalia personae » hoc etiam collocatur: « il diritto al culto di Dio privato e pubblico, compresa l'azione caritativa religiosa ». Cf. PIUS XI, Litt. Encycl. *Mit brennender Sorge,* 14 martii 1937: *A.A.S.,* 29 (1937), p. 160: «Der gläubige Mensch hat ein unverlierbares Recht, seinen Glauben zu bekennen und in den ihm gemässen Formen zu betätigen. Gesetze, die das Bekenntnis und die Betätigung dieses Glaubens unterdrücken oder erschweren, stehen in Widerspruch mit einem Naturgesetz ». Cf. LEO XIII, Litt. Encycl. *Libertas praestantissimum,* 20 iunii 1888: *Acta Leonis XIII,* 8 (1888), pp. 237-238: « Illa quoque magnopere praedicatur, quam conscientiae libertatem nominant; quae si ita accipiatur ut suo cuique arbitratu aeque liceat Deum colere, non colere, argumentis, quae supra allata sunt, satis convincitur. Sed potest etiam in hanc sententiam accipi, ut homini ex conscientia officii Dei voluntatem sequi et iussa facere, nulla re impediente, in civitate liceat. Haec quidem vera, haec digna filiis Dei libertas, quae humanae dignitatem personae honestissime tuetur, est omni vi iniuriaque maior, eademque Ecclesiae semper optata ac praecipue cara ».

[3] De conceptu libertatis religiosae, ut ab aliis Christianis intelligitur cf. documenta Consilii Mundialis Ecclesiarum (World Council of Churches): « *Declaration on Religious Liberty* » (Assembly Amsterdam, 1948), « *Statement on Religious Liberty* » (Assembly New Delhi, 1961).

Schema 4: Re-emended Text

NOTES

[1] Cf. John XXIII, Encyclical Letter *Pacem in terris*, 11 April 1963: AAS 55 (1963), 279, where the pope makes the following observations on present-day realities: "But the aspirations we have mentioned are a clear indication of the fact that men, increasingly aware nowadays of their personal dignity, have found the incentive to enter government service and demand constitutional recognition for their own inviolable rights. Not content with this, they are also demanding the observance of constitutional procedures in the appointment of public authorities, and are insisting that they exercise their office within this constitutional framework." Cf. *ibid.*, 265: "Man's personal dignity requires besides that he enjoy freedom and be able to make up his own mind when he acts. In his association with his fellows, therefore, there is every reason why his recognition of rights, observance of duties, and many-sided collaboration with other men, should be primarily a matter of his own personal decision. Each man should act on his own initiative, conviction, and sense of responsibility, not under the constant pressure of external coercion or enticement. There is nothing human about a society that is welded together by force. Far from encouraging, as it should, the attainment of man's progress and perfection, it is merely an obstacle to his freedom."

[**163**] Concerning man's civil dignity, by which human dignity is extended into the public sphere, cf. Pius XII, Radio message, 24 December 1944: AAS 37 (1945), 14: "In a people worthy of the name, the citizen feels within himself a consciousness of his personhood, of his duties and rights, of his own freedom together with respect for the freedom and dignity of others." Here the pope commends also the "ideal of freedom and equality" (*loc. cit.*) that it is necessary to maintain in a democratic state organized according to sound principles of reason, which demands that man's right to the free exercise of religion in society be fully acknowledged, cultivated, and defended.

[2] Cf. John XXIII, Encyclical Letter *Pacem in terris*, 11 April 1963: AAS 55 (1963), 260-61 "Also among man's rights is that of being able to worship God in accordance with the right dictates of his own conscience, and to profess his religion both in private and in public." Cf. Pius XII, Radio message, 24 December 1942: AAS 35 (1943), 19, where among "the fundamental rights of the person" is also included "the right to worship God privately and publicly, including religious charitable activity." Cf. Pius XI, Encyclical Letter *Mit brennender Sorge*, 14 March 1937: AAS 29 (1937), 160: "The believer has an absolute right to profess his faith and live according to its dictates. Laws that impede this profession and practice of faith are against natural law." Cf. Leo XIII, Encyclical Letter, *Libertas praestantissimum*, 20 June 1888: *Acta Leonis XIII*, 8 (1888), 237-38: "Another freedom is widely advocated, namely, freedom of conscience. If by this is meant that everyone may, as he chooses, worship God or not, it is sufficiently refuted by the arguments already adduced. But it may also be taken to mean that every man in the state may follow the will of God and, from a consciousness of duty and free from every obstacle, obey his commands. This, indeed, is true freedom, a freedom worthy of the sons of God, which nobly maintains the dignity of man and is stronger than all violence or wrong—a freedom which the Church has always desired and held most dear."

[3] For an overview of how the concept of religious freedom is understood by other Christians, cf. the documents of the World Council of Churches: "Declaration on Religious Liberty" (Amsterdam Assembly, 1948), and "Statement on Religious Liberty" (New Delhi Assembly, 1961).

[4] Cf. S. THOMAS, *Summa theol.*, I-II, q. 91, a. 1; q. 93, a. 1.

[5] Cf. *ibid.*, q. 93, a. 2.

[6] Quoad historiam huius quaestionis cf. J. LECLER, S. I., *Histoire de la tolérance religieuse au siècle de la Réforme*, Paris, Aubier, Editions Montaigne, 1955, tom. II, *fere passim*.

[7] Cf. LEO XIII, Epist. Encycl. *Cum multa*, 8 dec. 1882: *A.S.S.*, 15 (1898), pp. 242-43: « Igitur oportet rem sacram remque civilem, quae sunt genere naturaque distincta, etiam opinione iudicioque secernere. Nam hoc genus de rebus civilibus, quantumvis in honestum et grave, si spectetur in se, vitae huius, quae in terris degitur, fines nequaquam praetergreditur. Contra vero religio, nata Deo et ad Deum referens omnia, altius se pandit caelumque contingit . . . Quapropter religionem et quidquid est singulari quodam vinculo cum religione colligatum, rectum est superioris ordinis ducere ». Traditionem iteravit PIUS XI, Litt. Encycl. *Non abbiamo bisogno*, 29 iunii 1931: *A.A.S.*, 23 (1931), p. 303: « La Chiesa di Gesù Cristo non ha mai contestato i diritti e i doveri dello Stato circa l'educazione dei cittadini e Noi stessi li abbiamo ricordati e proclamati nella recente Nostra Lettera Enciclica [164] sulla educazione cristiana della gioventù; diritti e doveri incontestabili finché rimangono nei confini delle competenze proprie dello Stato; competenze che sono alla loro volta chiaramente fissate dalle finalità dello Stato; finalità certamente non soltanto corporee e materiali, ma di per se stesse necessariamente contenute nei limiti del naturale, del terreno, del temporaneo ».

Cf. S. THOMAS, *Summa theologica*, I-II, q. 91, a. 4 c: « De his potest homo legem ferre de quibus potest iudicare. Iudicium autem hominis esse non potest de interioribus actibus, qui latent, sed solum de exterioribus actibus, qui apparent »; cf. II-II, q. 104, a. 5 c: « In his quae pertinent ad interiorem motum voluntatis, homo non tenetur homini oboedire sed solum Deo ». Cf. IOANNES XXIII, Litt. Encycl. *Pacem in terris*, 11 aprilis 1963: *A.A.S.*, 55 (1963), p. 270: « Sed quoniam omnes homines in naturali dignitate sunt inter se pares, tum nemo valet alium ad aliquid intimis animi sensibus efficiendum cogere; quod quidem unus Deus potest, utpote qui unus arcana pectoris consilia scrutetur ac iudicet ».

[8] Sic redditur aliis verbis nota regula iuris canonici, ex iure romano quoad sensum deprompta, « Odia restringi et favores convenit ampliari ». Cf. V. BARTOCCETTI, *De regulis iuris canonici* (Angelo Belardetti Editore, Roma 1955), p. 73.

[9] Cf. IOANNES XXIII, Litt. Encycl. *Pacem in terris*, 11 aprilis 1963: *A.A.S.*, 55 (1963), pp. 273-274: « Verum cum nostra hac aetate commune bonum maxime in humanae personae servatis iuribus et officiis consistere putetur, tum praecipue in eo sint oportet curatorum rei publicae partes, ut hinc iura agnoscantur, colantur, inter se componantur, defendantur, provehantur, illinc suis quisque officiis facilius fungi possit. Etenim "inviolabilia iura tueri, hominum propria, atque curare, ut facilius quisque suis muneribus defungatur, hoc cuiusvis publicae potestatis officium est praecipuum" ». Cf. PIUS XII, *Nuntius radiophonicus*, 1 iunii 1941: *A.A.S.*, 33 (1941), p. 200.

[10] Cf. LEO XIII, Litt. Encycl. *Immortale Dei*, 1 nov. 1885: *A.S.S.*, 18 (1885), p. 161: « Immortale Dei miserenti opus, quod est Ecclesia, quamquam per se et natura sua salutem spectat animorum adipiscendamque in caelis felicitatis, tamen in ipso etiam rerum mortalium genere tot ac tantas ultro parit utilitates, ut plures maioresve non posset, si in primis et maxime esset ad tuendam huius vitae, quae in terris agitur, prosperitatem institutum ». Quod quidem thema, e S. Augustino derivatum, saepe saepius evolvere solebat Leo XIII.

[11] Cf. PAULUS VI, Litt. Encycl. *Ecclesiam suam*, 6 aug. 1964: *A.A.S.*, 56 (1964), pp. 642-43.

[4] Cf. St. Thomas, *Summa theologica*, I-II, q. 91, a. 1; q. 93, a. 1.

[5] Cf. *ibid.*, q. 93, a. 2.

[6] On the history of this question, cf. J. Lecler, S.J., *Histoire de la tolérance religieuse au siècle de la Réforme* (Paris: Aubier, Editions Montaigne, 1955), vol. II, *passim*.

[7] Cf. Leo XIII, Encyclical Epistle *Cum multa*, 8 December 1882: ASS 15 (1898), 242-43: "The sacred and civil orders being, therefore, distinct in their origin and in their nature, should be conceived and judged of as such. For matters of the civil order—however lawful, however important they be—do not extend, when considered in themselves, beyond the limits of that life which we live on this our earth. But religion, born of God, and referring all things to God, takes a higher flight and touches heaven. . . . It is, then, right to look on religion, and whatever is connected in any particular way with it, as belonging to a higher order." Pius XI repeated this teaching in the Encyclical Letter *Non abbiamo bisogno*, 29 June 1931: AAS 23 (1931), 303: "The Church of Jesus Christ has never contested the rights and the duties of the state concerning the education of its citizens; indeed, we ourselves have recalled and proclaimed them in our recent encyclical [**164**] on the 'Christian Education of Youth.' Such rights and duties are unchallengeable as long as they remain within the limits of the state's proper competency, a competence which in its turn is clearly indicated and determined by the end of the state, an end which, though certainly not only bodily and material, is by its very nature limited to the natural, the terrestrial and the temporal."

Cf. St. Thomas, *Summa theologica*, I-II, q. 91, a. 4, c: "Man can make laws in those matters of which he is competent to judge. But man is not competent to judge of interior movements, which are hidden, but only of exterior acts, which are apparent." Cf. II-II, q. 104, a. 5, c: "In matters touching the interior movement of the will man is not bound to obey his fellow man, but God alone." Cf. John XXIII, Encyclical Letter *Pacem in terris*, 11 April 1963: AAS 55 (1963), 270: "But since all men are equal in natural dignity, no man has the capacity to force internal compliance on another. Only God can do that, for he alone scrutinizes and judges the secret counsels of the heart."

[8] This statement expresses in different words the following well-known rule of canon law, which derives its meaning from Roman law: "Whatever is burdensome should be restricted; whatever is favorable should be increased." Cf. V. Bartoccetti, *De regulis iuris canonici* (Rome: Angelo Belardetti, 1955), 73.

[9] Cf. John XXIII, Encylical Letter *Pacem in terris*, 11 April 1963: AAS 55 (1963), 273-74: "It is generally accepted today that the common good is best safeguarded when personal rights and duties are guaranteed. The chief concern of civil authorities must therefore be to ensure that these rights are recognized, respected, co-ordinated, defended and promoted, and that each individual is enabled to perform his duties more easily. For 'to safeguard the inviolable rights of the human person, and to facilitate the performance of his duties, is the principal duty of every public power.'" Cf. Pius XII, Radio message, 1 June 1941: AAS 33 (1941), 200.

[10] Cf. Leo XIII, Encyclical Letter *Immortale Dei*, 1 November 1885: ASS 18 (1885), 161: "The Catholic Church, that imperishable handiwork of our all-merciful God, has for her immediate and natural purpose the saving of souls and securing our happiness in heaven. Yet, in regard to things temporal, she is the source of benefits as manifold and great as if the chief end of her existence were to ensure the prospering of our earthly life." This idea, which derives from St. Augustine, was increasingly developed by Leo XIII throughout his pontificate.

[11] Cf. Paul VI, Encyclical Letter *Ecclesiam suam,* 6 August 1964: AAS 56 (1964), 642-43.

¹² LACTANTIUS, *Divinarum Institutionum,* lib. V, 19: ed. S. Brandt et G. Laubmann, *CSEL* 19, p. 463; *PL* 6, 614 (cap. 20): « Non est opus vi et iniuria, quia religio cogi non potest, verbis potius quam verberibus res agenda est, ut sit voluntas ».

Op. cit.: CSEL 19, p. 464; *PL* 6, 614: «Itaque nemo a nobis retinetur invitus—inutilis est enim Deo qui devotione ac fide caret—et tamen nemo discedit ipsa veritate retinente ».

Op. cit.: CSEL 19, p. 465; *PL* 6, 616: « Nihil est enim tam voluntarium quam religio, in qua si animus sacrificantis aversus est, iam sublata, iam nulla est ».

S. AMBROSIUS, *Epistola ad Valentinianum Imp., Ep.* 21: *PL* 16, 1047: « Dei lex nos docuit quid sequamur, humanae leges hoc docere non possumus. Extorquere solent timidis commutationem fidem inspirare non possunt ».

S. AUGUSTINUS, *Contra litteras Petiliani,* lib. II, cap. 83: ed. M. Petschenig, [165] *CSEL* 52, p. 112; *PL* 43, 315; cf. C. 23, q. 5, c. 33 (ed. Friedberg, col. 939): « Augustinus respondit: Ad fidem quidem nullus est cogendus invitus; sed per severitatem, immo et per misericordiam Dei tribulationum flagellis solet perfidia castigari ».

S. GREGORIUS MAGNUS, *Epistola ad Virgilium et Theodorum Episcopos Massilliae Galliarum,* Registrum Epistolarum, I, 45: ed. P. Ewald et L. M. Hartmann, *MGH Ep.* 1, p. 72; *PL* 77, 510-11 (lib. I, ep. 47): « Dum enim quispiam ad baptismatis fontem non praedicationis suavitate, sed necessitate pervenerit, ad pristinam superstitionem remeans in de deterius moritur, unde renatus esse videbatur ».

Epistola ad Iohannem Episcopum Constantinopolitanum, Registrum Epistolarum, III, 52: *MGH Ep.* 1, p. 210; *PL* 77, 649 (lib. III, ep. 53); cf. D. 45, c. 1 (ed. Friedberg, col. 160): « Nova vero atque inaudita est ista praedicatio, quae verberibus exigit fidem ».

CONC. TOLET. IV, c. 57: MANSI 10, 633; cf. D. 45, c. 5 (ed. Friedberg, col. 161-162): « De Iudaeis hoc praecepit sancta synodus, nemini deinceps ad credendum vim inferre; *cui enim vult Deus misereri, et quem vult indurat.* Non enim tales inviti salvandi sunt, sed volentes, ut integra sit forma iustitiae: sicut enim homo proprii arbitrii voluntate serpenti oboediens periit, sic vocante gratia Dei, propriae mentis conversione homo quisque credendo salvatur. Ergo non vi, sed liberi arbitrii facultate, ut convertantur suadendi sunt, non potius impellendi . . . ».

CLEMENS III, Litterae Decretales: X, V, 6, 9, ed. Friedberg, col. 774: « . . . Statuimus enim ut nullus Christianus invitos vel nolentes Iudaeos ad baptismum (per violentiam) venire compellat. Si quis autem ad Christianos causa fidei confugerit, postquam voluntas eius fuerit patefacta, Christianus absque calumnia efficiatur: quippe Christi fidem habere non creditur, qui ad Christianorum baptismum non spontaneus, sed invitus cogitur pervenire . . . ».

INNOCENTIUS III, *Epistola ad Arelatensem Archiepiscopum,* X, III, 42, 3: ed. Friedberg, col. 646: « . . . Verum id est religioni Christianae contrarium, ut semper invitus et penitus contradicens ad recipiendam et servandam Christianitatem aliquis compellatur . . . ».

¹³ Cf. *C.I.C.,* c. 1351; cf. PIUS XII, Alloc. ad Praelatos auditores ceterosque officiales et administros Tribunalis S. Romanae Rotae, 6 oct. 1946: *A.A.S.,* 38 (1946), p. 394, ubi citatur a R. P. *Pro Memoria* Secretarius Status ad Legationem Yugoslaviae ad Sanctam Sedem: « D'après les

[12] Lactantius, *Divinarum Institutionum*, bk. V, 19: ed. S. Brandt and G. Laubmann, *CSEL* 19, p. 463; *PL* 6, 614 (ch. 20): "There is no need for violence or injury, for religion cannot be forced; the whole matter should be carried on with words rather than whips, so that there might be free will."

Op. cit.: *CSEL* 19, p. 464; *PL* 6, 614: "Therefore we hold no one back against his will—for anyone who is without devotion and faith is of no use to God—and yet no one departs who is held fast by the truth itself."

Op. cit.: *CSEL* 19, p. 465; *PL* 6, 616: "For nothing is so voluntary as religion; once the spirit of the one offering sacrifice has turned away, religion is already destroyed, is itself already nothing."

St. Ambrose, *Epistola ad Valentinianum Imp.*, Ep. 21, *PL* 16, 1047: "God's law taught us what to strive for; human laws cannot teach this. Such laws are merely accustomed to extorting a change from the faint of heart; they cannot inspire faith."

St. Augustine, *Contra litteras Petiliani*, bk. II, ch. 83: ed. M Petschenig, **[165]** *CSEL* 52, p. 112; *PL* 43, 315; cf. C. 23, q. 5, ch. 33 (ed. Friedberg, col. 939): "Augustine replied: No one, indeed, is forced to embrace the faith against his will; but through the severity of God, or rather through His mercy, faithlessness is usually punished by the lashes of tribulation."

St. Gregory the Great, *Epistola ad Virgilium et Theodorum Episcopos Massilliae Galliarium*, Registrum Epistolarum, I, 45: ed. P. Ewald and L.M. Hartmann, *MGH Ep.* 1, p. 72; *PL* 77, 510-11 (bk. I, ep. 47): "For if anyone should have come to the holy baptismal font, not through the persuasion of preaching, but out of compulsion, when he returns to the place of his former superstition he will die the worse for it, having come from a place where he only seemed to have been reborn."

Epistola ad Iohannem Episcopum Constantinopolitanum, Registrum Epistolarum, III, 52: *MGH Ep.* 1, p. 210; *PL* 77, 649 (bk. III, ep. 53); cf. D. 45, ch. 1 (ed. Friedberg, col. 160): "That preaching is indeed new and unheard of, that exacts faith by means of lashing."

Fourth Council of Toledo, ch. 57: Mansi 10, 633; cf. D. 45, ch. 5 (ed. Friedberg, col. 161-162); "Concerning the Jews, the holy synod declared that henceforth force is not to be applied to anyone in order to make them believe; *for God has mercy on whom he wishes, and hardens whom he wishes.* For such men are to be saved not unwillingly but willingly, in order that justice may be perfect: for just as man perished by obeying the serpent through his own free-will, so at the call of God's grace, each man is saved by believing through the conversion of his own mind. Therefore, not by force, but by the free judgment of their own free will are they to be persuaded to convert, rather than compelled . . ."

Clement III, *Litterae Decretales*: X, V, 6, 9, ed. Friedberg col. 774: ". . . For we have decreed that no Christian is to force Jews reluctantly or against their will to approach baptism (by violence). If, however, someone has recourse to Christians on account of his faith, after he has made known his will, let him be made a Christian without dispute; since one who is forced to approach Christian baptism not voluntarily but against his will is not considered to have the faith of Christ . . ."

Innocent III, *Epistola ad Arelatensem Archiepiscopum*, X, III, 42, 3: ed. Friedberg, col. 646: ". . . Truly it is contrary to the Christian religion that anyone ever be forced, against his will and while interiorly opposing it, to receive and keep the Christian faith . . ."

[13] Cf. *Code of Canon Law* [1917], c. 1351; cf. Pius XII, "Allocution to prelate auditors and other officials and administrators of the Tribunal of the Sacred Roman Rota," 6 October 1946: *AAS* 38 (1946), 394, where the pope cites the *pro memoria* of the Secretariat of State to the

principes de la doctrine catholique, la conversion doit être le résultat, non pas de contraintes extérieures mais de l'adhésion de l'âme aux verités enseignées par l'Eglise catholique. C'est pour cela que l'Eglise catholique n'admet pas dans son sein les adultes, qui demandent à y entrer ou à y faire retour, qu'à la condition qu'ils soient pleinement conscients de la portée et des conséquences de l'acte qu'ils veulent accomplir ». Idem, Litt. Encycl. *Mystici Corporis*, 29 iunii 1943: *A.A.S.*, 35 (1943), p. 243: «At si cupimus non intermissam eiusmodi totius mystici Corporis conprecationem admoveri Deo, ut aberrantes omnes in unum Iesu Christi ovile quam primum ingrediantur, profitemur tamen omnino necessarium esse id sponte libenterque fieri, cum nemo credat nisi volens. Quamobrem si qui, non credentes, eo reapse compelluntur ut Ecclesiae aedificium intrent, ut ad altare accedant, sacramentaque suscipiant, [**166**] ii procul dubio veri christifideles non fiunt; fides enim, sine qua "impossibile est placere Deo" (*Hebr.* 11, 6), liberrimum esse debet "obsequium intellectus et voluntatis" (CONC. VAT., *Const. de fide catholica*, cap. 3). Si igitur aliquando contingat, ut contra constantem Apostolicae huius Sedis doctrinam, ad amplexandam catholicam fidem aliquis adigatur invitus, id Nos facere non possumus quin, pro officii nostri conscientia, reprobamus ».

[14] Cf. LEO XIII, Litterae *Officio sanctissimo*, 22 dec. 1887: *A.S.S.*, 22 (1887), p. 269: «In bonis autem Ecclesiae, quae Nobis ubique semperque conservare debemus, ab omnique iniuria defendere, illud certe praestantissimum est, tantam ipsam perfrui agendi libertate, quantam salus hominum curanda requirat. Haec nimirum est libertas divina, ab Unigenito Dei Filio auctore profecta, qui Ecclesiam sanguine fuso excitavit; qui eam perpetuam in hominibus statuit; qui voluit ipsi ipse praeesse. Atque adeo propria est Ecclesiae, perfecti divinique operis, ut qui contra eam faciunt libertatem, iidem contra Deum et contra officium ». Ut olim Gregorius VII, sic temporibus modernis exstabat LEO XIII propugnator libertatis Ecclesiae. Cf. Litterae *Ex litteris*, 7 aprilis 1887: *A.S.S.*, 19 (1886), p. 465: «Nos quidem vel ab initio nostri pontificatus multo et serio cogitare de vobis instituimus, atque, ut ratio Nostri ferebat officii, consilium cepimus omnia conari, si qua ratione liceat, pacatam tranquillitatem cum libertate legitima catholico nomini restituere ». In sexaginta fere documentis, quae relationes inter rem sacram remque civilem tractant, octoginta vices occurrit formula verborum, « libertas Ecclesiae », vel formula aequipollens. Ipsi enim Leoni XIII, sicut toti traditioni catholicae, libertas Ecclesiae principium est fundumentale in iis, quae spectant ad relationem inter Ecclesiam et instituta omnia ordinis civilis.

[15] Cf. PIUS XII, Litt. Encycl. *Summi Pontificatus*, 20 oct. 1939: *A.A.S.*, 31 (1939), pp. 445-46: « Quamobrem Nos, ut eius in terris vices gerimus, qui a sacro vate "Princeps pacis" appellatur (*Is.* 9, 6), civitatum rectores eosque omnes, e quorum opera quovis modo publica res pendet, compellamus vehementerque obtestamur ut Ecclesia plena semper libertate fruatur debita, qua suam possit educationis operam exsequi, ac veritatem impertire mentibus, animis inculcare iustitiam, eosque divina Iesu Christi refovere caritate ».

[16] Cf. PIUS XI, Litterae *Firmissimam constantiam*, 28 martii 1937: *A.A.S.*, 29 (1937), p. 196: « Proposita eiusmodi aestimandarum rerum mensura, concedendum sane est, ad christianam vitam explicandam externa quoque praesidia, quae sensibus percipiuntur, esse necessaria, pariterque Ecclesiae tamquam hominum societati opus omnino esse, ad vitae usuram atque incrementum, iusta agendi libertate, ipsosque fideles iure gaudere in societate civili vivendi ad rationis conscientiaeque praescripta ».

[17] Cf. PIUS XII, Allocutio *Ci riesce*, 6 dec. 1953: *A.A.S.*, 45 (1953), p. 802, ubi fines clare definiuntur, quos Ecclesia prae oculis habet in ineundis Concordatis: « I Concordati debbono quindi assicurare alla Chiesa una stabile condizione di diritto e di fatto nello Stato, con cui

Yugoslavian Embassy to the Holy See: "In accordance with the principles of Catholic teaching, conversion should be the result not of external constraints but of the soul's adherence to the truths taught by the Catholic Church. This is why the Catholic Church admits to herself adults who seek to enter or return to her only on the condition that they are fully conscious of the significance and consequences of the act they wish to make." Cf. also the Encyclical Letter *Mystici Corporis*, 29 June 1943: AAS 35 (1943), 243: "Though we desire this unceasing prayer to rise to God from the whole mystical body in common, that all the straying sheep may hasten to enter the one fold of Jesus Christ, we still recognize that this must be done of their own free will; for no one believes unless he wills to believe. Hence they are most certainly not genuine Christians who against their belief are forced to go into a church, to approach the altar and to receive the sacraments; [**166**] for the 'faith without which it is impossible to please God' (Heb 11:6) is an entirely free 'submission of intellect and will' (First Vatican Council, *Constitution on the Catholic Faith*, ch. 3). Therefore, whenever it happens, despite the constant teaching of this apostolic see, that anyone is compelled to embrace the Catholic faith against his will, our sense of duty demands that we condemn the act."

¹⁴ Cf. Leo XIII, Enyclical *Officio sanctissimo*, 22 December 1887: ASS 22 (1887), 269: "Of the goods of the Church that it is our duty everywhere and always to maintain and defend against all injustice, the first is certainly that of enjoying the full freedom of action she may need in working for the salvation of souls. This is a divine liberty, having as its author the only Son of God, who by the shedding of his blood gave birth to the Church, who established it until the end of time, and chose himself to be its head. This liberty is so essential to the Church, a perfect and divine institution, that they who attack this liberty at the same time offend against God and their duty." Like Gregory VII before him, Leo XIII stands out in the modern period as a great defender of the freedom of the Church. Cf. the Encyclical *Ex litteris*, 7 April 1887: ASS 19 (1886), 465: "Indeed, from the beginning of our pontificate we have given much serious thought toward you, and, bearing in mind our office, we resolved to attempt all things possible to restore to the Catholic name peaceful tranquility with lawful freedom." In almost sixty documents that deal with relations between sacred and civil affairs, the phrase "freedom of the Church," or its equivalent, occurs eighty times. Indeed, for Leo XIII himself, as for the whole Catholic tradition, the freedom of the Church is a fundamental principle among those that concern the relationship between the Church and all the institutions of the civil order.

¹⁵ Cf. Pius XII, Encyclical Letter *Summi Pontificatus*, 20 October 1939: AAS 31 (1939), 445-46: "Accordingly we, as representatives on earth of him who was proclaimed by the prophet 'Prince of Peace' (Is 9:6) appeal to and vigorously implore the leaders of nations, and those who can in any way influence public life, to let the Church have full liberty to fulfill her role as educator by teaching men truth, by inculcating justice and by inflaming hearts with the divine love of Christ."

¹⁶ Cf. Pius XI, Encyclical *Firmissimam constantiam*, 28 March 1937: AAS 29 (1937), 196: "Once this gradation of values and activities is established, it must be admitted that for Christian life to develop it must have recourse to external and sensible means; that the Church, being a society of men, cannot exist or develop if it does not enjoy liberty of action, and that its members have the right to find in civil society the possibility of living according to the dictates of their consciences."

¹⁷ Cf. Pius XII, Allocution *Ci riesce*, 6 December 1953: AAS 45 (1953), 802, where the limits that the Church has in mind when entering into concordats are clearly defined: "Concordats should therefore assure to the Church a stable condition in right and in fact within

sono conclusi, e garantire ad essa la piena indipendenza nell'adempimento della sua divina missione ». Exinde insuper constat, nihil esse in doctrina de libertate religiosa, quod cum praxi hodierna Concordatorum quovis modo pugnat.

[18] Cf. PIUS XII, *Nuntius radiophonicus*, 28 martii 1952: *A.A.S.*, 44 (1952), pp. 270-78, de conscientia christiana efformanda.

[19] Cf. IOANNES XXIII, Litt. Encycl. *Pacem in terris*, 11 aprilis 1963: *A.A.S.*, 55 (1963), [167] pp. 299-300: « Omnino errores ab iis qui opinione labuntur semper distinguere aequum est, quamvis de hominibus agatur, qui aut errore veritatis aut impari rerum cognitione capti sint, vel ad sacra vel ad optimam vitae actionem attinentium. Nam homo ad errorem lapsus iam non humanitate instructus esse desinit, neque suam umquam personae dignitatem amittit, cuius ratio est semper habenda. Praeterea in hominis natura numquam facultas perit et refragandi erroribus et viam ad veritatem quaerendi. Neque umquam hac in re providentissimi Dei auxilia hominem deficiunt. Ex quo fieri potest, ut si quis hodie vel perspicuitate egeat, vel in falsas discesserit sententias, possit postmodum, Dei collustratus lumine veritatem amplecti ».

[20] GIANNINI A., *Le Costituzioni degli Stati del Vicino Oriente*, Roma 1931; PEASLEE AMOS S., *Constitutions of Nations*, New Jersey (USA) 1950; MIRKINE-GUETZEVITCH B., *Le Costituzioni Europee*, Milano 1954; ZAMORA A., *Digesto Constitutional Americano*, Buenos Aires 1958; LAVROFF D. G. ET PEISER G., *Les Constitutions Africaines*, Paris 1963; STRAMACCI M., *Le Costituzioni degli Stati Africani*, Milano 1963.

[21] Cf. IOANNES XXIII, Litt. Encycl. *Pacem in terris*, 11 aprilis 1963: *A.A.S.*, 55 (1963), pp. 295-296, ubi, quibusdam defectibus non obstantibus, commendatur Professio Universalis Iurium Humanorum, die 10 dec. 1948 a Foederatarum Nationum Coetu Generali rata habita: « Nihilominus Professionem eandem habendam esse censemus quemdam quasi gradum atque aditum ad iuridicialem politicamque ordinationem constituendam omnium populorum, qui in mundo sunt. Siquidem ea universis prorsus hominibus solemniter agnoscitur humanae dignitas personae, atque iura cuivis homini asseruntur veritatem libere quaerendi, honestatis sequendi normas, iustitiae officia usurpandi, vitam exigendi homine dignam, alia deinceps cum hisce coniuncta ».

the state with which they are concluded, and guarantee to her full independence in fulfilling her divine mission." From this it is evident that there is nothing in the teaching on religious freedom that is at odds in any way with the current practice of concordats.

[18] On the formation of a Christian conscience, cf. Pius XII, Radio message, 28 March 1952: AAS 44 (1952), 270-78.

[19] Cf. John XXIII, Encyclical Letter *Pacem in terris*, 11 April 1963: AAS 55 (1963), [**167**] 299-300: "It is always perfectly justifiable to distinguish between error as such and the person who falls into error—even in the case of men who err regarding the truth or are led astray as a result of their inadequate knowledge, in matters either of religion or of the highest ethical standards. A man who has fallen into error does not cease to be a man. He never forfeits his personal dignity; and that is something that must always be taken into account. Besides, there exists in man's very nature an undying capacity to break through the barriers of error and seek the road to truth. God, in his great providence, is ever present with his aid. Today, maybe, a man lacks faith and turns aside into error; tomorrow, perhaps, illumined by God's light, he may indeed embrace the truth."

[20] A. Giannini, *Le Costituzioni degli Stati del Vicino Oriente,* Roma 1931; Amos S. Peaslee, *Constitutions of Nations,* New Jersey (USA) 1950; B. Mirkine-Guetzevitch, *Le Costituzioni Europee,* Milano 1954; A. Zamora, *Digesto Constitutional Americano,* Buenos Aires 1958; D. G. Lavroff and G. Peiser, *Les Constitutions Africaines,* Paris 1963; M. Stramacci, *Le Costituzioni degli Stati Africani,* Milano 1963.

[21] Cf. John XXIII, Encyclical Letter *Pacem in terris*, 11 April 1963: AAS 55 (1963), 295-96, where, certain defects notwithstanding, the pope commends the Universal Declaration of Human Rights, ratified by the General Assembly of the United Nations on December 10, 1948: "Nevertheless, we think the document should be considered a step in the right direction, an approach toward the establishment of a juridical and political ordering of the world community. It is a solemn recognition of the personal dignity of every human being; an assertion of everyone's right to be free to seek out the truth, to follow moral principles, to discharge the duties imposed by justice, and to lead a fully human life. It also recognized other rights connected with these."

SCHEMA DECLARATIONIS DE LIBERTATE RELIGIOSA

Textus recognitus

(*Acta Synodalia* IV/5, 77-98)

DE IURE PERSONAE ET COMMUNITATUM AD LIBERTATEM SOCIALEM ET CIVILEM IN RE RELIGIOSA

1. Dignitatis humanae personae homines hac nostra aetate magis in dies conscii fiunt,[1] atque numerus eorum crescit qui exigunt ut in agendo homines proprio suo consilio et libertate responsabili[2] fruantur et utantur, non coercitione commoti, sed officii conscientia ducti. Quae libertatis exigentia in societate humana ea maxime respicit quae sunt animi humani bona, imprimis quidem ea, quae ad religionem spectant. Ad has animorum appetitiones diligenter attendens, sibique proponens declarare quantum sint veritati et iustitiae conformes, haec Vaticana Synodus sacram Ecclesiae traditionem doctrinamque scrutatur, in quibus nova et vetera indesinenter invenit.

Primum itaque profitetur et asseverat Sacra Synodus Deum Ipsum vias generi humano notas fecisse per quas, Ipsi inserviendo, homines in Christo salvi et beati fieri possint. Hanc unicam veram Religionem subsistere credimus in catholica et apostolica Ecclesia, cui Dominus Iesus munus concredidit eam ad universos homines diffundendi, dicens Apostolis: « Euntes ergo docete omnes gentes baptizantes eos in [78] nomine Patris et Filii et Spiritus Sancti, docentes eos servare omnia quaecumque mandavi vobis » (*Mt.* 28, 19-20). Proinde cum homines cuncti teneantur veritatem, praesertim in iis quae cultum Dei respiciunt, quaerere eamque agnitam amplecti ac servare, sacro quoque officio vinciuntur catholicam fidem, prout eam agnoscere potuerunt, amplectendi profitendique.

Pariter vero profitetur Sacra Synodus officia haec hominum conscientiam tangere ac vincire, nec aliter Veritatem sese imponere nisi vi ipsius Veritatis, quae suaviter simul ac fortiter mentibus illabitur. Itaque, quum libertas religiosa, quam homines, in exsequendo officio Deum colendi, exigunt et de qua mentem suam declarare Ecclesia catholica intendit, immunitatem a coercitione in societate civili respiciat, constat eam integram relinquere

DRAFT OF THE DECLARATION ON RELIGIOUS FREEDOM

Authorized Text

(*Acta Synodalia* IV/5, 77-98)

ON THE RIGHT OF THE PERSON AND OF COMMUNITIES TO SOCIAL AND CIVIL FREEDOM IN RELIGIOUS MATTERS

1. Men and women of our time are becoming more conscious every day of the dignity of the human person.[1] Increasing numbers demand that in acting they enjoy and make use of their own counsel and a responsible freedom,[2] not impelled by coercion but moved by a sense of duty. This demand for freedom in human society is chiefly concerned with the goods of the human spirit, first of all those that concern religion. Carefully attending to these desires of men's hearts, and proposing to declare to what degree they are in conformity with truth and justice, this Vatican Council searches the sacred tradition and teaching of the Church, in which it continually discovers things new and old.

The sacred Council first professes and asserts that God himself has made known to mankind the ways in which men are to serve him, and so be saved in Christ and come to blessedness. We believe that this one true religion subsists in the Catholic and apostolic Church, to whom the Lord Jesus committed the task of spreading it among all people, saying to the apostles: "Go, therefore, and make disciples of all nations, baptizing them in [78] the name of the Father and of the Son and of the Holy Spirit, teaching them to observe all that I have commanded you" (Mt 28:19-20). Since all men and women are bound to seek the truth, especially in those things concerning the worship of God, and to embrace and hold fast to it once it is known, they are also bound by a sacred duty to embrace and profess the Catholic faith, insofar as they are able to acknowledge it.

The sacred Council likewise professes that these duties touch on and bind the conscience of man. In no other way does truth impose itself than by the strength of truth itself, entering the mind at once gently and with power. Therefore, since the religious freedom which men and women demand in order to fulfill their duty to worship God, and about which the Catholic Church intends to declare her mind, regards immunity from coercion in

doctrinam catholicam de unica vera religione, de unica Christi Ecclesia et de morali hominum erga ipsam officio. Insuper, hanc libertatem ut ius humanae personae proprium agnoscendo, Sacra Synodus, Summorum Pontificum doctrinam de inviolabilibus humanae personae iuribus necnon de iuridica ordinatione societatis evolvere intendit.

I. LIBERTATIS RELIGIOSAE RATIO GENERALIS

2. (*Libertatis religiosae obiectum et fundamentum*). Haec Vaticana Synodus declarat personam humanam ius habere ad libertatem religiosam. Huiusmodi libertas in eo consistit quod omnes homines debent immunes esse a coercitione [79] sive singulorum sive coetuum socialium et cuiusvis potestatis humanae, et ita quidem ut in re religiosa neque aliquis cogatur ad agendum contra suam conscientiam neque impediatur, quominus iuxta suam conscientiam agat privatim et publice, vel solus vel aliis consociatus, intra debitos limites. Hoc ius personae humanae ad libertatem religiosam in iuridica societatis ordinatione ita est agnoscendum ut ius civile evadat. Insuper declarat ius ad libertatem religiosam esse revera fundatum in ipsa dignitate personae humanae, qualis et verbo Dei revelato et ipsa ratione cognoscitur.[3]

Secundum dignitatem enim suam homines omnes, quia personae sunt, ratione scilicet et libera voluntate praediti ideoque personali responsabilitate aucti, sua ipsorum natura impelluntur necnon morali tenentur obligatione ad veritatem quaerendam, illam imprimis, quae religionem spectat. Tenentur quoque veritati cognitae adhaerere atque totam vitam suam iuxta exigentias veritatis ordinare. Huic autem obligationi satisfacere homines, modo suae propriae naturae consentaneo, non possunt nisi libertate psychologica simulatque immunitate a coercitione externa fruantur. Non tamen in dispositione subiectiva sed in ipsa natura personae humanae libertas religiosa fundatur. Quamobrem ius ad immunitatem perseverat etiam in iis qui obligationi quaerendi veritatem eique adhaerendi non satisfaciunt, dummodo legitimo ordine publico servato, aliorum iura non laedant.

3. (*Libertas religiosa et necessitudo hominis ad Deum*). Quae clarius adhuc patent consideranti [80] supremam humanae vitae normam esse ipsam legem divinam, aeternam, obiectivam atque universalem, qua Deus, consilio sapientiae et dilectionis suae mundum universum viasque communitatis

civil society, it is clear that it leaves intact the Catholic teaching on the one true religion, the one Church of Christ, and the moral duty individuals have toward the Church. In addition, in acknowledging this freedom as a right that is proper to the human person, this sacred Council intends to develop the teaching of the popes on the inviolable rights of the human person and the juridical order of society.

I. THE GENERAL PRINCIPLE OF RELIGIOUS FREEDOM

2. (*The object and foundation of religious freedom*). This Vatican Council declares that the human person has a right to religious freedom. Such freedom consists in this, that all men and women should be immune from coercion [79] on the part of individuals, social groups, or any human power, so that no one is forced to act against his conscience in religious matters, or prevented from acting according to his conscience, in private or in public, whether alone or in association with others, within due limits. This right of the human person to religious freedom must be acknowledged in the juridical order of society, so that it becomes a civil right. In addition, this Council declares that the right to religious freedom has its foundation in the very dignity of the human person, as known from both the revealed word of God and reason itself.[3]

It is in accord with their dignity that all men and women, because they are persons, endowed with reason and free will and therefore privileged with personal responsibility, are impelled by their nature and bound by a moral obligation to seek the truth, especially the truth concerning religion. They are also bound to hold fast to the truth once it is known, and to order their whole life in accord with its demands. They cannot satisfy this obligation in a way that is in keeping with their own nature, however, unless they enjoy psychological freedom as well as immunity from external coercion. Nevertheless, religious freedom does not have its foundation in a subjective disposition, but in the very nature of the human person. Consequently, the right to immunity persists even for those who do not satisfy their obligation to seek the truth and to hold fast to it, provided that legitimate public order is preserved, and that the rights of others are not violated.

3. (*Religious freedom and man's relationship to God*). This becomes even clearer when one considers that [80] the highest norm of human life is the divine law, eternal, objective, and universal, by which God, in the providence of his wisdom and love, orders, directs, and governs the whole world and the

humanae ordinat, dirigit, gubernat.[4] Huius suae legis Deus hominem particiipem reddit, ita ut homo, providentia divina suaviter disponente, veritatem incommutabilem magis magisque agnoscere possit.[5] Quapropter unusquisque officium ideoque et ius habet veritatem in re religiosa quaerendi ut sibi, mediis adhibitis idoneis, recta conscientiae iudicia prudenter efformet.

Veritas autem inquirenda est modo dignitati humanae personae eiusque naturae sociali proprio, libera scilicet inquisitione, per magisterium seu institutionem, per communicationem atque dialogum, quibus alii aliis exponunt veritatem quam invenerunt vel invenisse putant, ut sese invicem in veritate inquirenda adiuvent; veritati autem cognitae firmiter adhaerendum est assensu personali.

Dictamina vero legis divinae homo percipit et agnoscit mediante conscientia sua; quam tenetur fideliter sequi in universa sua activitate, ut ad Deum, finem suum, perveniat. Non est ergo cogendus ut contra suam conscientiam agat.[6] Sed neque impediendus est, quominus iuxta suam conscientiam operetur, praesertim in re religiosa. Exercitium namque religionis, ex ipsa eius indole, consistit primario in actibus internis prorsus voluntariis et liberis, quibus homo sese ad [81] Deum directe ordinat: huiusmodi actus a potestate mere humana nec imperari nec prohiberi possunt.[7] Ipsa autem socialis hominis natura exigit ut homo internos religionis actus externe manifestet, cum aliis in re religiosa communicet, ipsam sui ipsius religionem modo communitario profiteatur.

Iniuria ergo humanae personae et ipsi ordini hominibus a Deo statuto fit, si homini denegetur liberum in societate religionis exercitium, vero ordine publico servato.

Praeterea actus religiosi, quibus homines privatim et publice sese ad Deum ex animi sententia ordinant, natura sua terrestrem et temporalem rerum ordinem transcendunt. Potestas igitur civilis limites suos excedere dicenda est, si ea, quae natura sua terrestrem et temporalem rerum ordinem transcendunt, vel impediat vel dirigat.

4. (*Libertas communitatum religiosarum*). Libertas seu immunitas a coercitione [82] in re religiosa, quae singulis personis competit, etiam communitatibus agnoscenda est, quippe quae a sociali natura tum hominis tum ipsius religionis requiruntur.

His igitur communitatibus iure debetur immunitas, ut secundum pro-

ways of the human community.[4] God grants man a share in this law, so that man, under the gentle direction of divine providence, can acknowledge more and more the truth that is itself unchanging.[5] For this reason, each person has the duty, and therefore the right, to seek the truth in religious matters, so that he may prudently form right judgments of conscience for himself, using all suitable means.

The truth, however, must be sought in a way proper to the dignity of the human person and his social nature, namely, by means of free inquiry, through instruction or education, and by communication and dialogue, in which men and women share with one another the truth they have found or think they have found, so as to assist each other in seeking the truth. Once known, however, the truth must be firmly adhered to by means of personal assent.

It is through the mediation of his conscience that man perceives and recognizes the precepts of the divine law; he is bound in all his actions to follow his conscience faithfully, so that he may come to God, his end. He is therefore not to be forced to act against his conscience.[6] Nor is he to be prevented from acting according to his conscience, especially in religious matters. For by its very nature the exercise of religion consists primarily in interior acts that are entirely voluntary and free, through which man [81] orders himself directly toward God: acts of this kind cannot be commanded or prohibited by any merely human power.[7] Man's social nature itself, however, demands that he manifest these interior religious acts externally, participating with others in religious matters and professing his religion in a communal way.

It is therefore an injustice to the human person, and to the very order of human existence established by God, for men to be denied the free exercise of religion in society when true public order is preserved.

Furthermore, religious acts, in which men and women privately and publicly order themselves toward God out of a sense of inner conviction, by their nature transcend the earthly and temporal order of things. The civil power, therefore, must be said to exceed its limits if it either impedes or directs those matters that by their nature transcend the earthly and temporal order of things.

4. (*The freedom of religious communities*). The freedom or immunity from coercion [82] in religious matters that belongs to individual persons must be recognized for communities as well; these communities are called for by the social nature of man and of religion itself.

Immunity is therefore due to these communities by right, so that they

prias leges sese regant, Numen supremum cultu publico honorent, membra sua in vita religiosa exercenda adiuvent et doctrina sustentent atque eas institutiones promoveant, in quibus membra cooperentur ad vitam propriam secundum sua principia religiosa ordinandam.

Communitatibus religiosis pariter competit ius, ne mediis legalibus vel actione administrativa potestatis civilis impediantur in suis propriis ministris seligendis, educandis, nominandis atque transferendis, in communicando cum auctoritatibus et communitatibus religiosis, quae in aliis orbis terrarum partibus degunt, in aedificiis religiosis erigendis, necnon in bonis congruis acquirendis et fruendis.

Communitates religiosae ius etiam habent, ne impediantur in sua fide ore et scripto publice docenda atque testanda, legitimis exigentiis ordinis publici non violatis. In fide autem religiosa disseminanda et in usibus inducendis abstinendum semper est ab omni actionis genere, quod coercitionem vel suasionem inhonestam aut minus rectam sapere videatur, praesertim quando de rudioribus vel de egenis agitur.

Praeterea ad libertatem religiosam spectat quod communitates religiosae libere possint ostendere singularem suae doctrinae virtutem in ordinanda societate ac tota vivificanda activitate humana. Tandem in sociali hominis natura atque in ipsa indole religionis fundatur ius, quo homines, suo ipsorum sensu religioso moti, libere possunt conventus habere vel associationes [83] educativas, culturales, caritativas, sociales constituere.

5. (*Libertas religiosa familiae*). Cuique familiae, utpote quae est societas proprio ac primordiali iure gaudens, competit ius ad libere ordinandam religiosam vitam suam domesticam sub moderatione parentum. His autem competit ius ad detetminandam rationem institutionis religiosae suis liberis tradendae. Insuper a civili potestate agnoscendum est ius parentum deligendi, vera cum libertate, scholas vel alia educatiouis media, neque ob hanc electionis libertatem sunt eis iniusta onera imponenda. Potestas civilis iura parentum violat, si liberi ad frequentandas lectiones scholares cogantur quae parentum persuasioni religiosae non correspondeant vel si unica imponatur educationis ratio, ex qua formatio religiosa omnino excludatur.

6. (*Cura libertatis religiosae*). Cura huius iuris ad libertatem religiosam tum ad cives tum ad coetus sociales tum ad Ecclesiam aliasque communitates religiosas, modo unicuique proprio, spectat.

Inviolabilia hominis iura tueri ac promovere ad cuiusvis potestatis civilis officium essentialiter pertinet.[8] Debet igitur potestas civilis per iustas

may govern themselves according to their own laws, honor the Supreme Being with public worship, assist their members in their practice of religious life, strengthen them by instruction, and promote institutions in which members can join together to order their own life according to their religious principles.

Religious communities likewise have the right not to be impeded, either by legal measures or by administrative action on the part of the civil power, in selecting, educating, appointing, and transferring their own ministers; in communicating with religious authorities and communities in other parts of the world; in erecting religious buildings; or in acquiring and making use of any necessary goods.

Religious communities also have the right not to be prevented from publicly teaching about or witnessing to their faith in speech or in writing, provided they do not violate the legitimate requirements of public order. In spreading their religious faith and introducing their practices, however, they must always refrain from any kind of activity that would seem to suggest any hint of coercion or dishonest or less than proper persuasion, especially in regard to those less educated or in need.

Furthermore, religious freedom entails that religious communities freely be able to show the unique value of their doctrine for ordering society and animating all human activity. Finally, there is in man's social nature and in the very nature of religion the foundation for the right by which men and women, moved by their own religious sense, can freely hold meetings and [83] establish educational, cultural, charitable, and social associations.

5. (*The religious freedom of the family*). Each family, as a society in its own original right, has the right to order freely its own domestic religious life, under the guidance of the parents. Parents also have the right to determine the way in which religious instruction will be handed on to their children. In addition, the civil power must acknowledge the right of parents to choose with true freedom among schools or other means of education, and must not unjustly burden them on account of this freedom of choice. The civil power violates the rights of parents if it forces their children to attend lessons that are at odds with the religious beliefs of their parents, or if a single system of education is imposed that excludes all religious formation.

6. (*The care of religious freedom*). Care for this right to religious freedom is the responsibility of citizens, social groups, the Church and other religious communities, in the way that is proper to each.

It belongs to the essential duties of every civil power to protect and promote the inviolable rights of man.[8] The civil power should therefore ef-

leges et per alia media apta efficaciter suscipere tutelam libertatis religiosae omnium civium, ac propitias suppeditare condiciones ad vitam religiosam fovendam, ut cives revera religionis iura exercere eiusdemque officia adimplere valeant et ipsa societas fruatur bonis iustitiae et pacis quae proveniunt ex fidelitate hominum erga Deum Eiusque sanctam voluntatem.[9]

[84] Si attentis populorum circumstantiis historicis, uni communitati religiosae specialis civilis agnitio in iuridica civitatis ordinatione tribuitur, necesse est ut simul omnibus civibus et communitatibus religiosis ius ad libertatem in re religiosa agnoscatur et observetur.

Denique a potestate civili providendum est, ne civium aequalitas iuridica unquam, sive aperte sive occulte, laedatur propter rationes religiosas, necnan inter eos discriminatio fiat.

Hinc sequitur nefas esse potestati publicae, per vim vel metum aut alia media civibus imponere professionem aut reiectionem cuiusvis religionis, vel impedire, quominus quisquam communitatem religiosam aut ingrediatur aut relinquat. Eo magis contra voluntatem Dei et contra sacra personae et familiae gentium iura agitur, quando vis quocumque modo adhibeatur ad religionem quamlibet delendam vel cohibendam sive in toto genere humano sive in aliqua regione sive in determinato coetu.

7. (*Limites libertatis religiosae*). Ius ad libertatem in re religiosa exercetur in societate humana, ideoque eius usus quibusdam normis moderantibus obnoxius est.

In societate observandum est principium morale responsabilitatis personalis et socialis: in iuribus suis exercendis singuli homines coetusque sociales lege morali obligantur et in vita sociali praesertim tenentur rationem habere et iurium aliorum et suorum [85] erga alios officiorum et boni omnium communis. Cum omnibus secundum iustitiam et humanitatem agendum est.

Praeterea societas civilis ius habet sese protegendi contra abusus, qui haberi possint, sub praetextu libertatis religiosae. Pertinet praecipue ad potestatem civilem huiusmodi protectionem praestare, non tamen modo arbitrario aut uni parti inique favendo, sed secundum normas iuridicas quas postulant necessitates ordinis publici in ordine morali obiectivo fundati. Illud autem societatis bonum, quod est ordo publicus, requirit efficacem iurium tutelam pro omnibus civibus eorumque pacificam compositionem, sufficientem curam istius honestae pacis publicae, quae est ordinata conviventia in vera iustitia, et debitam custodiam publicae moralitatis. Quod

fectively undertake to protect the religious freedom of all citizens through just laws and other appropriate means, and to provide favorable conditions for fostering religious life, so that citizens may truly be able to exercise their religious rights and fulfill their religious duties, and so that society itself may enjoy the goods of justice and peace that come from men's fidelity to God and his holy will.[9]

[84] If, in light of a people's historical circumstances, special civil recognition is granted to one religious community in the juridical order of the state, it is necessary at the same time that the right to freedom in religious matters be acknowledged and observed for all citizens and religious communities.

Finally, the civil power should see to it that the equality of citizens before the law is never violated for religious reasons, whether openly or covertly, and that there is no discrimination among citizens.

It follows that it is wrong for the public power to impose by force or fear or any other means the profession or rejection of any religion on its citizens, or to prevent anyone from entering or leaving a religious community. All the more is it against God's will and the sacred rights of the person and the family of nations to use force in any way in order to destroy or repress religion, either in the human race as a whole or in a particular region or in a specific religious group.

7. (*The limits of religious freedom*). The right to freedom in religious matters is exercised in human society, and its use is therefore subject to certain governing norms.

Within society, the moral principle of personal and social responsibility must be observed: in exercising their rights, individuals and social groups are bound by the moral law, and in social life especially are bound to keep in mind both the rights of others and their [85] duties toward others, as well as the common good of all. They should act toward all with justice and humanity.

In addition, civil society has the right to protect itself against abuses that could be committed under the pretext of religious freedom. It belongs especially to the civil power to afford protection of this sort, not in an arbitrary fashion or by unjustly favoring one particular group, but according to juridical norms that are required by the needs of a public order grounded in the objective moral order. Public order is that good of society that concerns the effective protection of the rights of all citizens and the peaceful settlement of conflict of rights, the adequate care of that genuine public peace that is obtained when men live and work together in true justice, and the proper

quidem bonum est fundamentalis pars boni communis et universae societati adeo necessarium ut actus qui grave damnum ei inferant sint a potestate civili reprimendi. Ceterum servanda est integrae libertatis consuetudo in societate, secundum quam libertas debet quam maxime homini agnosci, nec restringenda est nisi quando et prout est necessarium.[10]

8. (*Educatio ad libertatem exercendam*). Nostrae aetatis homines varia ratione premuntur et in periculum veniunt ne proprio libero consilio destituantur. Ex altera autem parte non pauci ita propensi videntur, ut specie libertatis omnem subiectionem reiiciant ac debit oboedientiam parvi faciant.

[86] Quapropter haec Vaticana Synodus omnes hortatur, praesertim vero eos qui curam habent alios educandi, ut homines formare satagant, qui ordini morali obsequentes legitimae auctoritati oboediant et genuinae libertatis amatores sint; homines nempe, qui proprio consilio res in luce veritatis diiudicent, activitates suas cum sensu responsabilitatis disponant, et quaecumque sunt vera atque iusta persequi nitantur, operam suam libenter cum ceteris consociando.

Religiosa igitur libertas ad hoc inservire et ordinari debet, ut homines in suis ipsorum officiis adimplendis in vita sociali maiore cum responsabilitate agant.

II. LIBERTAS RELIGIOSA SUB LUCE REVELATIONIS

9. (*Doctrina de libertate religiosa in revelatione radices tenet*). Quae de iure hominis ad libertatem religiosam declarat haec Vaticana Synodus, fundamentum habent in dignitate personae, cuius exigentiae rationi humanae plenius innotuerunt per saeculorum experientiam. Immo haec doctrina de libertate radices habet in divina revelatione, quapropter eo magis a christianis sancte servanda est. Quamvis enim revelatio non expresse affirmet ius ad immunitatem ab externa coercitione in re religiosa, tamen humanae personae dignitatem in tota eius amplitudine patefacit, observantiam Christi erga hominis libertatem in exsequendo officio credendi verbo Dei demonstrat, atque de spiritu nos edocet, quem discipuli talis Magistri debent in omnibus agnoscere et sequi. Quibus omnibus principia generalia illustrantur super quae fundatur doctrina huius Declarationis de libertate religiosa. Praesertim libertas religiosa in societate plene est cum libertate actus fidei christianae congrua.

guardianship of public morality. This good is in fact a fundamental part of the common good, and it is so necessary to the whole society that any acts that inflict serious injury upon it must be suppressed by the civil power. For the rest, the customary practice of the fullness of freedom in society should be upheld, according to which man's freedom should be acknowledged as far as possible, and should not be restricted except when and insofar as necessary.[10]

8. (*Education in the use of freedom*). Men and women of our time are subjected to a variety of pressures and are in danger of losing the use of their own free counsel. On the other hand, not a few seem disposed, under the pretense of freedom, to reject all submission and to make light of the duty of obedience.

[86] For this reason, this Vatican Council urges all men and women, especially those who are responsible for educating others, to be diligent in forming human beings who respect the moral order and are obedient to legitimate authority, and who are lovers of genuine freedom; men and women, that is, who by their own counsel decide matters in the light of truth, who act with a sense of responsibility, and who endeavor to pursue whatever is true and just, cooperating willingly with others in their work.

Religious freedom should therefore be devoted and ordered to this end, that men and women may come to act with greater responsibility in fulfilling their duties in social life.

II. RELIGIOUS FREEDOM IN THE LIGHT OF REVELATION

9. (*The teaching on religious freedom has its roots in revelation*). The declarations of this Vatican Council regarding man's right to religious freedom have their foundation in the dignity of the person, a dignity whose demands have come to be more fully known to human reason through centuries of experience. What is more, this teaching on freedom has its roots in divine revelation, and for this reason must be observed by Christians all the more faithfully. For although revelation does not expressly affirm the right to immunity from external coercion in religious matters, it nonetheless brings to light the dignity of the human person in all its fullness. It manifests the respect Christ showed for the freedom with which man is to fulfill his duty of believing the word of God, and it educates us in the spirit that the disciples of such a Master should adopt and follow in all things. All of this casts light on the general principles which ground the teaching of this Declaration on

[87] 10. (*Libertas actus fidei*). Caput est ex praecipuis doctrinae catholicae, in verbo Dei contentum et a Patribus constanter praedicatum,[11] hominem debere Deo voluntarie respondere credendo; invitum proinde neminem esse cogendum ad amplectendam fidem.[12] Etenim actus fidei ipsa sua natura voluntarius est, cum homo, a Christo Salvatore redemptus et in adoptionem filiorum per Iesum Christum vocatus,[13] Deo sese revelanti adhaerere non possit, nisi Pater traxerit eum,[14] et homo rationabile liberumque Deo praestiterit fidei obsequium. Indoli ergo fidei plene consonum est ut, in re religiosa, quodvis genus coercitionis ex parte hominum excludatur. Ac proinde, ratio libertatis religiosae haud parum confert ad illum rerum statum fovendum, quo homines expedite possint invitari ad fidem christianam sponte amplectendam eamque in tota vitae ratione actuose confitendam.

11. (*Modus agendi Christi et Apostolorum*). Deus quidem homines ad inserviendum Sibi in spiritu et veritate vocat, unde ipsi in conscientia vinciuntur non vero coercentur. Rationem enim habet dignitatis personae humanae ab Ipso conditae, quae proprio consilio duci et libertate frui debet. Hoc autem apparuit in Christo Iesu, in quo Deus Seipsum ac vias suas perfecte manifestavit. Etenim Christus, qui Magister et Dominus est noster,[15] idemque mitis et humilis corde,[16] discipulos patienter allexit et invitavit.[17] Miraculis utique praedicationem suam suffulsit et confirmavit, ut fidem auditorum comprobaret, non ut in eos coercitionem exerceret.[18] Incredulitatem audientium certe exprobravit, sed vindictam Deo in diem Iudicii relinquendo.[19] Mittens Apostolas in mundum dixit eis: « Qui crediderit et baptizatus fuerit salvus erit; qui [88] vero non crediderit condemnabitur » (*Mc.* 16, 16). Ipse vero agnoscens zizaniam cum tritico seminatam, iussit sinere utraque crescere usque ad messem quae fiet in consummatione saeculi.[20] Nolens esse Messias politicus et vi dominans,[21] maluit se dicere Filium Hominis qui venit « ut ministraret et daret animam suam redemptionem pro multis » (*Mc.* 10, 45). Sese praebuit ut perfectum Servum Dei,[22] qui, « harundinem quassatam non confringit et linum fumigans non extinguit » (*Mt.* 12, 20). Potestatem civilem eiusque iura agnovit, iubens censum dari Caesari, clare autem monuit servanda esse iura superiora Dei: « Reddite quae sunt Caesaris Caesari, et quae sunt Dei, Deo » (*Mt.* 22, 21). Tandem in opere redemptionis super crucem complendo, quo salutem et veram libertatem hominibus acquireret, revelationem suam perfecit. Testimonium enim perhibuit veritati,[23] eam tamen contradicentibus vi imponere noluit: « qui

religious freedom. Above all, religious freedom in society is fully consonant with the freedom of the act of Christian faith.

[87] 10. (*The freedom of the act of faith*). It is a chief tenet of Catholic teaching, contained in the word of God and constantly proclaimed by the Fathers,[11] that man's response to God in faith should be voluntary; no one is to be forced, therefore, to embrace the faith against his will.[12] The act of faith is of its very nature a voluntary act. For man, redeemed by Christ the Savior and called to be an adopted son through Jesus Christ,[13] cannot hold fast to God as he reveals himself unless he is drawn by the Father,[14] and offers to God a rational and free submission of faith. It is therefore fully consonant with the nature of faith that in religious matters every kind of coercion on the part of men be excluded. The principle of religious freedom thus contributes in no small way to fostering a state of affairs in which men and women can without hindrance be invited to embrace the Christian faith of their own free will, and actively profess it in their whole way of life.

11. (*Christ's and the apostles' way of acting*). God calls men and women to serve him in spirit and in truth, so that they are bound in conscience but are not coerced. For he has regard for the dignity of the human person whom he himself created, who should be led by his own counsel and enjoy his own freedom. This truth appeared in Jesus Christ, in whom God perfectly manifested himself and his ways. For Christ, who is our Master and Lord,[15] and at the same time meek and humble of heart,[16] attracted and invited disciples with patience.[17] He supported and confirmed his teaching with miracles in order to strengthen the faith of his listeners, not to exercise coercion over them.[18] He certainly denounced the unbelief of his listeners, but he left the verdict to God in anticipation of the day of judgment.[19] As he sent the apostles into the world, he said to them: "He who believes and is baptized will be saved; but he who [88] does not believe will be condemned" (Mk 16:16). But he himself, acknowledging that weeds have been sown amid the wheat, ordered that both be allowed to grow until the harvest time that will come at the end of the world.[20] He did not want to be a political Messiah or to rule by force,[21] but preferred to call himself the Son of Man who came "to serve and to give his life as a ransom for many" (Mk 10:45). He showed himself to be the perfect Servant of God,[22] who "does not break a bruised reed nor quench a smoldering wick" (Mt 12:20). He acknowledged civil power and its rights when he instructed that tribute be given to Caesar, but he clearly warned that the higher rights of God must be upheld: "Render to Caesar the things that are Caesar's, and to God the things that are God's" (Mt 22:21). In the end, when he completed on the cross the work of redemption by which

cum malediceretur, non maledicebat, cum pateretur, non comminabatur »
(*1 Pt.* 2, 23). Regnum enim eius non percutiendo vindicatur,[24] sed stabilitur
testificando et audiendo veritatem, crescit autem amore, qui manifestatus in
cruce homines ad Ipsum trahit.[25]

Apostoli, Christi verbo et exemplo edocti, eamdem viam secuti sunt.
Ab ipsis Ecclesiae exordiis discipuli Christi adlaborarunt ut homines ad
Christum Dominum confitendum converterent, non actione coercitiva
neque artificiis Evangelio indignis, sed in primis virtute verbi Dei.[26] Fortiter omnibus nuntiabant propositum Salvatoris Dei, « qui omnes homines
vult salvos fieri, et ad agnitionem veritatis venire » (*1 Tim.* 2, 4); simul autem
verebantur debiles etiamsi in errore versabantur, sic ostendentes quomodo
« unusquisque nostrum pro se [89] rationem reddet Deo » (*Rom.* 14, 12)[27]
et intantum teneatur conscientiae suae oboedire. Sicuti Christus, Apostoli
intenti semper fuerunt ad testimonium reddendum veritati Dei, abundantius
audentes coram populo et principibus « loqui verbum cum fiducia » (*Act.* 4,
31).[28] Firma enim fide tenebant ipsum evangelium revera esse virtutem Dei
in salutem omni credenti.[29] Omnibus ergo spretis « armis carnalibus »,[30]
exemplum mansuetudinis et modestiae Christi sequentes, verbum Dei praedicaverunt plene confisi divina huius verbi virtute ad potestates Deo adversas
destruendas[31] atque homines ad fidem et obsequium Christi reducendos.[32]
Sicut Magister ita et Apostoli auctoritatem legitimam civilem agnoverunt:
« Non est enim potestas nisi a Deo » docet Apostolus, qui exinde iubet:
« Omnis anima potestatibus sublimioribus subdita sit . . . ; qui resistit potestati, Dei ordinationi resistit » (*Rom.* 13, 1-5).[33] Simul autem non timuerunt
contradicere potestati publicae se sanctae Dei voluntati opponenti: « Oboedire oportet Deo magis quam hominibus » (*Act.* 5, 29).[34] Hanc viam secuti
sunt innumeri martyres et fideles per saecula et per orbem.

12. (*Ecclesia vestigia Christi et Apostolorum sequitur*). Ecclesia igitur
evangelicae veritati fidelis, viam Christi et Apostolorum sequitur quando
rationem libertatis religiosae tamquam dignitati hominis et Dei revelationi consonam agnoscit eamque fovet. Doctrinam a Magistro et ab
Apostolis acceptam, decursu temporum, custodivit et tradidit. Etsi in vita
Populi Dei, per vicissitudines historiae humanae peregrinantis, interdum
exstitit modus agendi, spiritui evangelico minus conformis, immo con-

he achieved for men salvation and true freedom, he brought his revelation to perfect completion. For he bore witness to the truth,[23] yet refused to impose it by force on those who contradicted it: "When he was reviled, he did not revile in return; when he suffered, he did not threaten" (1 Pt 2:23). For his kingdom is not claimed by force of blows,[24] but is established by bearing witness to and listening to the truth, and it grows through the love that he manifested on the cross, drawing men to himself.[25]

Taught by Christ's word and example, the apostles followed the same way. From the very beginnings of the Church they strove to convert men and women to the confession of Christ as Lord, not through coercion or means unworthy of the Gospel, but foremost by the power of the word of God.[26] They steadfastly announced to all the plan of God our Savior, "who desires all men to be saved and to come to the knowledge of the truth" (1 Tim 2:4); at the same time, however, they showed respect for the weak, even though they dwelled in error, thus showing how "each of us shall give [89] account of himself to God" (Rom 14:12)[27] and so far is bound to obey his conscience. Like Christ, the apostles were always intent to bear witness to the truth of God, daring "to speak the word of God with boldness" (Acts 4:31) and in full before the people and their leaders.[28] For with firm faith they held that the Gospel itself is truly the power of God for the salvation of all who believe.[29] Rejecting all "worldly weapons,"[30] therefore, and following the example of Christ's meekness and modesty, they preached the word of God, fully trusting in the divine power of this word to destroy the powers that are opposed to God[31] and to lead men and women to the faith and allegiance of Christ.[32] Like their Master, the apostles also recognized legitimate civil authority: "For there is no authority except from God," the apostle teaches, and for this reason instructs: "Let every person be subject to the governing authorities . . . ; he who resists the authorities resists what God has appointed" (Rom 13:1-5).[33] At the same time, however, the apostles were not afraid to speak out against public powers that opposed the holy will of God: "We must obey God rather than men" (Acts 5:29).[34] This is the way that countless martyrs and faithful have followed through the ages and throughout the world.

12. (*The Church follows in the footsteps of Christ and the apostles*). The Church, therefore, faithful to the truth of the Gospel, is following in the way of Christ and the apostles when she acknowledges and supports the principle of religious freedom as consonant with the dignity of man and the revelation of God. Through the ages the Church has carefully protected and handed on the teaching she has received from her Master and the apostles. Although in the life of the people of God as it has made its pilgrim way through the vi-

trarius, semper tamen mansit Ecclesiae doctrina neminem esse ad fidem cogendum.

[90] Evangelicum fermentum in mentibus hominum sic diu est operatum atque multum contulit, ut homines temporum decursu latius agnoscerent dignitatem personae suae, atque maturesceret persuasio in re religiosa ipsam immunem servandam esse in civitate a quacumque humana coercitione.

13. (*Libertas Ecclesiae*). Inter ea quae ad bonum Ecclesiae, immo ad bonum ipsius terrenae civitatis, spectant et ubique semperque servanda sunt atque ab omni iniuria defendenda, illud certe praestantissimum est, Ecclesiam tanta perfrui agendi libertate, quantam salus hominum curanda requirat.[35] Haec enim libertas sacra est, qua Unigenitus Dei Filius ditavit Ecclesiam acquisitam sanguine suo. Ecclesiae autem adeo propria est, ut qui eam impugnent, iidem contra Dei voluntatem agunt. Libertas Ecclesiae est principium fundamentale in relationibus inter Ecclesiam et ordinem civilem vitae humanae.

In societate humana et coram quavis potestate publica Ecclesia sibi vindicat libertatem, utpote auctoritas spiritualis, a Christo Domino constituta, cui ex divino mandato incumbit officium eundi in mundum universum et evangelium praedicandi omni creaturae.[36] Pariter libertatem sibi vindicat Ecclesia prout est etiam societas hominum, qui iure gaudent vivendi in societate civili secundum fidei christianae praescripta.[37]

Iamvero si viget ratio libertatis religiosae non solum verbis proclamata neque solum [91] legibus sancita, sed etiam cum sinceritate in praxim deducta, tunc demum Ecclesia stabilem obtinet et iuris et facti condicionem ad necessariam independentiam in missione divina exsequenda, quam auctoritates ecclesiasticae in societate presse pressiusque vindicarunt.[38] Simulque Christifideles, sicut et ceteri homines iure civili gaudent ne impediantur in vita sua iuxta conscientiam agenda. Concordia igitur viget inter libertatem Ecclesiae et libertatem illam religiosam, quae omnibus hominibus et communitatibus est tanquam ius agnoscenda et in ordinatione iuridica sancienda.

14. (*Munus Ecclesiae*). Ecclesia Catholica, ut divino obtemperet mandato: « docete omnes gentes » (*Mt.* 28, 19-20), impensa cura adlaborare debet « ut sermo Dei currat et clarificetur » (2 *Thess.* 3, 1).

cissitudes of human history, there have at times appeared ways of acting less in keeping with the spirit of the Gospel, or even opposed to it, the teaching of the Church has nonetheless always stood firm, that no one is to be forced to embrace the faith.

[90] The leaven of the Gospel has long been about its quiet work in the minds of men; to this is due, in large measure, the fact that in the course of time men and women have come to recognize more widely their dignity as persons, and the conviction has grown that in religious matters the person is to be kept immune within civil society from any kind of human coercion.

13. (*The freedom of the Church*). Preeminent among those things that concern the good of the Church and indeed the good of civil society itself on earth, which must always and everywhere be preserved and defended against all harm, is for the Church to enjoy as much freedom in acting as the care of man's salvation may demand.[35] This is a sacred freedom with which the only begotten Son of God endowed the Church whom he purchased with his blood. This freedom is so proper to the Church that whoever opposes it acts against the will of God. The freedom of the Church is a fundamental principle in relations between the Church and the civil order of human life.

The Church claims for herself freedom in human society and before every public power insofar as she is a spiritual authority, constituted by Christ the Lord, upon whom rests, by divine command, the duty to go throughout the whole world preaching the Gospel to every creature.[36] The Church likewise claims for herself freedom as a society of men and women who enjoy the right to live in civil society according to the precepts of the Christian faith.[37]

Indeed, where the principle of religious freedom is not only proclaimed in words or [91] sanctioned by law but also given sincere and practical application, there the Church maintains a stable condition both in law and in fact, as well as the independence necessary to carry out her divine mission, which is what Church authorities claim in society, ever more insistently.[38] At the same time the Christian faithful, like other men and women, enjoy the civil right of not being prevented from acting according to their conscience. A harmony therefore exists between the freedom of the Church and the religious freedom that must be acknowledged as a right of all men and communities and sanctioned by juridical law.

14. (*The task of the Church*). In order to obey the divine command: "make disciples of all nations" (Mt 28:19-20), the Catholic Church should strive with great care "that the word of the Lord may speed on and triumph" (2 Thes 3:1).

Enixe igitur rogat Ecclesia ut a filiis suis « primum omnium fiant obsecrationes, orationes, postulationes, gratiarum actiones pro omnibus hominibus . . . Hoc enim bonum est et acceptum coram Salvatore nostro Deo, qui omnes homines vult salvos fieri et ad agnitionem veritatis venire » (*1 Tim.* 2, 1-4).

Christifideles autem in sua efformanda conscientia diligenter attendere debent ad sacram certamque Ecclesiae doctrinam.[39] Christi enim voluntate Ecclesia Catholica magistra est veritatis, eiusque munus est, ut veritatem, quae Christus est, enuntiet atque authentice doceat, simulque principia ordinis moralis, ex ipsa natura humana profluentia, auctoritate sua declaret atque confirmet. Insuper Christiani, in sapientia ambulantes ad eos qui foris sunt, « in Spiritu Sancto, in caritate non ficta, in verbo veritatis » (*2 Cor.* 6, 6-7), lumen vitae cum omni [92] fiducia[40] et fortitudine apostolica, ad sanguinis usque effusionem, diffundere satagant.

Etenim discipulus erga Christum Magistrum gravi adstringitur officio, donum veritatis ab eo receptae plenius in dies cognoscendi, annuntiandi fideliter, strenueque defendendi, evangelicis mediis adhibitis. Simul tamen caritas Christi urget eum, ut amanter prudenter patienter agat cum hominibus, qui in errore vel ignorantia circa fidem versantur.[41] Respiciendum igitur est tum ad officia erga Christum Verbum vivificans quod praedicandum est, tum ad humanae personae iura, tum ad mensuram gratiae a Deo per Christum tributam homini, qui ad fidem sponte accipiendam et profitendam invitatur.

15. (*Conclusio*). Constat igitur praesentis aetatis homines optare ut libere possint religionem privatim publiceque profiteri; libertatem autem religiosam in plerisque Constitutionibus iam ut ius civile declarari[42] et documentis internationalibus agnosci.[43]

At non desunt regimina in quibus, etsi in eorum Constitutione libertas cultus religiosi agnoscitur, tamen ipsae publicae potestates conantur cives a religione profitenda removere et communitatibus religiosis vitam perdifficilem ac periclitantem reddere.

Illa fausta huius temporis signa laeto animo salutans, haec vero deploranda facta cum moerore denuntians, Sacra Synodus Catholicos hortatur, exorat autem homines universos, ut perattente considerent quantopere libertas religiosa necessaria sit, in praesentibus potissimum vitae humanae adiunctis.

Manifestum est enim cunctas gentes magis in dies unum fieri, homines diversae culturae [93] et religionis arctioribus inter se devinciri rationibus,

The Church therefore earnestly entreats her children, "First of all that supplications, prayers, intercessions, and thanksgivings be made for all men ... This is good and it is acceptable in the sight of God our Savior, who desires all men to be saved and to come to the knowledge of the truth" (1 Tim 2:1-4).

In forming their conscience, the Christian faithful should carefully attend to the sacred and certain teaching of the Church.[39] For by the will of Christ the Catholic Church is the teacher of truth, and it is her duty to proclaim and authoritatively teach the truth that is Christ, and likewise to declare and confirm with her authority the principles of the moral order that flow from human nature. In addition, as Christians conduct themselves in wisdom toward those outside, "in the Holy Spirit, in genuine charity, in truthful speech" (2 Cor 6:6-7), let them be diligent in diffusing the light of life with al [92] boldness[40] and apostolic courage, even to the shedding of their blood.

The disciple is bound by a grave duty to Christ his Teacher, to know more fully each day the gift of truth received from him, to proclaim it faithfully, and to defend it vigorously, making use of the means of the Gospel. At the same time, the love of Christ urges him to deal lovingly, prudently, and patiently with those who dwell in error or ignorance about the faith.[41] He must therefore consider not only his duties toward Christ, the life-giving Word that must be preached, but also the rights of the human person, and the measure of grace that God has bestowed through Christ upon those who are invited freely to receive and profess the faith.

15. (*Conclusion*). It is well known that men and women of today desire to be able to profess their religion freely in private and in public. Religious freedom has already been declared to be a civil right in most constitutions,[42] and is acknowledged in international documents as well.[43]

Governments are not lacking, however, in which, although freedom of religious worship is acknowledged in their constitutions, the public powers themselves still endeavor to prevent citizens from professing their religion and to make life very difficult and dangerous for religious communities.

Welcoming the former with joy as a favorable sign of the times, while denouncing the latter with sorrow as something to be deplored, this sacred Council urges Catholics and entreats all men and women to consider carefully how necessary religious freedom is, especially in the present circumstances of human life.

It is clear that all nations are becoming more united every day, that men and women of different cultures [93] and religions are being bound to

augeri denique conscientiam propriae cuiusque responsabilitatis. Proinde ut pacificae relationes et concordia in genere humano instaurentur et firmentur, requiritur ut ubique terrarum libertas religiosa efficaci tutela iuridica muniatur atque observentur suprema hominum officia et iura ad vitam religiosam libere in societate ducendam.

Faxit Deus et Pater omnium ut familia humana, diligenter servata libertatis religiosae ratione in societate, per gratiam Christi et virtutem Spiritus Sancti adducatur ad sublimem illam ac perennem « libertatem gloriae filiorum Dei » (*Rom.* 8, 21).

NOTAE

[1] Cf. IOANNES XXIII, Litt. Encycl. *Pacem in terris*, 11 aprilis 1963: *A.A.S.*, 55 (1963), p. 279, ubi Summus Pontifex ad realitates hodiernas animadvertit: « At hae, de quibus diximus, animorum appetitiones illud etiam manifesto testantur, nostro hoc tempore homines magis magisque fieri dignitatis suae conscios, atque adeo incitari cum ad reipublicae administrationem participandam, tum ad poscendum, ut propria inviolabiliaque iura in publica civitatis disciplina serventur. Neque haec satis; nam homines nunc illud insuper poscunt, ut nempe civitatis auctoritates et ad normam publicae constitutionis creentur, et sua munera intra eiusdem terminos obeant ». Cf. *ibid.*, p. 265: « Illud praeterea humanae dignitas personae exigitur, ut in agendo homo proprio consilio et libertate fruatur. Quocirca, si de civium coniunctione agitur, est profecto cur ipse iura colat, officia servet, atque, in innumeris operibus exercendis, aliis sociam tribuat operam, suo praesertim impulsu et consulto; ita scilicet ut suo quisque instituto, iudicio, officiique conscientia agat, iam non commotus coercitione vel sollicitatione extrinsecus plerumque adductis; quandoquidem, si qua hominum societas una ratione virium est instituta, ea nihil humani in se habere dicenda est, utpote in qua homines a libertate cohibeantur, qui contra ad vitae progressus, ad perfectionemque assequendam apte ipsi incitandi sunt ».

Quod pertinet ad dignitatem illam civilem, secundum quam dignitas humana in publicum prodit, cf. PIUS XII, *Nuntius radiophonicus*, 24 dec. 1944: *A.A.S.*, 37 (1945) p. 14: «In un popolo degno di tal nome il cittadino sente in se stesso la [94] coscienza della sua personalità, dei suoi doveri e dei suoi diritti, della propria libertà congiunta col rispetto della libertà e della dignità altrui ». Hoc loco commendat Romanus Pontifex etiam illud « ideale di libertà e di uguaglianza » (*loc. cit.*), quod in Statu democratico, iuxta sana rationis principia ordinato, obtineat necesse est, quodque postulat, ut hominis ius in societate ad liberum exercitium religionis plene agnoscatur, colatur, defendatur.

[2] Cf. PAULUS VI, *Homilia* Dom. XIV post Pent., *L'Oss. Rom.*, 13-14 sept. 1965.

[3] Cf. IOANNES XXIII, Litt. Encycl. *Pacem in terris*, 11 aprilis 1963: *A.A.S.*, 55 (1963), pp. 260-261: « In hominis iuribus hoc quoque numerandum est, ut et Deum, ad rectam conscientiae suae normam, venerari possit, et religionem privatim publice profiteri ». Cf. PIUS XII, *Nuntius radiophonicus*, 24 dec. 1942: *A.A.S.*, 35 (1943), p. 19, ubi inter « iura fundamentalia personae »

one another with closer ties, and that there is a growing consciousness of the responsibility proper to each person. Hence, in order that peaceful relations and harmony may be established and strengthened among mankind, religious freedom must be secured by effective juridical protection throughout the world, and the highest duties and rights of men and women to lead a religious life freely in society must be observed.

May God the Father of all grant that the human family, having diligently upheld the principle of religious freedom in society, be led by the grace of Christ and the power of the Holy Spirit to that sublime and everlasting "glorious freedom of the children of God" (Rom 8:21).

NOTES

[1] Cf. John XXIII, Encyclical Letter *Pacem in terris*, 11 April 1963: AAS 55 (1963), 279, where the pope makes the following observations on present-day realities: "But the aspirations we have mentioned are a clear indication of the fact that men, increasingly aware nowadays of their personal dignity, have found the incentive to enter government service and demand constitutional recognition for their own inviolable rights. Not content with this, they are also demanding the observance of constitutional procedures in the appointment of public authorities, and are insisting that they exercise their office within this constitutional framework." Cf. *ibid.*, 265: "Man's personal dignity requires besides that he enjoy freedom and be able to make up his own mind when he acts. In his association with his fellows, therefore, there is every reason why his recognition of rights, observance of duties, and many-sided collaboration with other men, should be primarily a matter of his own personal decision. Each man should act on his own initiative, conviction, and sense of responsibility, not under the constant pressure of external coercion or enticement. There is nothing human about a society that is welded together by force. Far from encouraging, as it should, the attainment of man's progress and perfection, it is merely an obstacle to his freedom."

Concerning man's civil dignity, by which human dignity is extended into the public sphere, cf. Pius XII, Radio message, 24 December 1944: AAS 37 (1945), 14: "In a people worthy of the name, the citizen feels within himself a **[94]** consciousness of his personhood, of his duties and rights, of his own freedom together with respect for the freedom and dignity of others." Here the pope commends also the "ideal of freedom and equality" (*loc. cit.*) that it is necessary to maintain in a democratic state organized according to sound principles of reason, which demands that man's right to the free exercise of religion in society be fully acknowledged, cultivated, and defended.

[2] Cf. Paul VI, Homily, 14th Sunday after Pentecost, *L'Osservatore Romano*, 13-14 September 1965.

[3] Cf. John XXIII, Encyclical Letter *Pacem in terris*, 11 April 1963: AAS 55 (1963), 260-61 "Also among man's rights is that of being able to worship God in accordance with the right dictates of his own conscience, and to profess his religion both in private and in public." Cf. Pius XII, Radio message, 24 December 1942: AAS 35 (1943), 19, where among "the fundamental

hoc etiam collocatur: « il diritto al culto di Dio privato e pubblico, compresa l'azione caritativa religiosa ». Cf. PIUS XI, Litt. Encycl. *Mit brennender Sorge*, 14 martii 1937: *A.A.S.*, 29 (1937), p. 160: «Der gläubige Mensch hat ein unverlierbares Recht, seinen Glauben zu bekennen und in den ihm gemässen Formen zu betätigen. Gesetze, die das Bekenntnis und die Betätigung dieses Glaubens unterdrücken oder erschweren, stehen in Widerspruch mit einem Naturgesetz ». Cf. LEO XIII, Litt. Encycl. *Libertas praestantissimum*, 20 iunii 1888: *Acta Leonis XIII*, 8 (1888), pp. 237-238: « Illa quoque magnopere praedicatur, quam conscientiae libertatem nominant; quae si ita accipiatur ut suo cuique arbitratu aeque liceat Deum colere, non colere, argumentis, quae supra allata sunt, satis convincitur. Sed potest etiam in hanc sententiam accipi, ut homini ex conscientia officii Dei voluntatem sequi et iussa facere, nulla re impediente, in civitate liceat. Haec quidem vera, haec digna filiis Dei libertas, quae humanae dignitatem personae honestissime tuetur, est omni vi iniuriaque maior, eademque Ecclesiae semper optata ac praecipue cara ».

[4] Cf. S. THOMAS, *Summa theologica*, I-II, q. 91, a. 1; q. 93, a. 1.

[5] Cf. *ibid.*, q. 93, a. 2.

[6] Quoad historiam huius quaestionis cf. J. LECLER, S. I., *Histoire de la tolérance religieuse au siècle de la Réforme*, Paris, Aubier, Editions Montaigne, 1955, tom. II, *fere passim*.

[7] Cf. S. THOMAS, *Summa theologica*, I-II, q. 91, a. 4 c: « De his potest homo legem ferre de quibus potest iudicare. Iudicium autem hominis esse non potest de interioribus actibus, qui latent, sed solum de exterioribus actibus, qui apparent »; cf. II-II, q. 104, a. 5 c: « In his quae pertinent ad interiorem motum voluntatis, homo non tenetur homini oboedire sed solum Deo ». Cf. IOANNES XXIII, Litt. Encycl. *Pacem in terris*, 11 aprilis 1963: *A.A.S.*, 55 (1963), p. 270: « Sed quoniam omnes homines in naturali dignitate sunt inter se pares, tum nemo valet alium ad aliquid intimis animi sensibus efficiendum cogere; quod quidem unus Deus potest, utpote qui unus arcana pectoris consilia scrutetur ac iudicet ». Cf. PAULUS VI, *Nuntius Radiophonicus*, 22 decembris 1964: *A.A.S.*, 57 (1965), p. 181.

[8] Cf. IOANNES XXIII, Litt. Encycl. *Pacem in terris*, 11 aprilis 1963: *A.A.S.*, 55 (1963), pp. 273-274: « Verum cum nostra hac aetate commune bonum maxime in humanae personae servatis iuribus et officiis consistere putetur, tum praecipue in eo sint oportet curatorum rei publicae partes, ut hinc iura agnoscantur, colantur, inter se componantur, defendantur, provehantur, illinc suis quisque officiis facilius fungi possit. Etenim "inviolabilia iura tueri, hominum propria, atque curare, ut [95] facilius quisque suis muneribus defungatur, hoc cuiusvis publicae potestatis officium est praecipuum" ». Cf. PIUS XII, *Nuntius radiophonicus*, 1 iunii 1941: *A.A.S.*, 33 (1941), p. 200.

[9] Cf. LEO XIII, Litt. Encycl. *Immortale Dei*, 1 nov. 1885: *A.S.S.*, 18 (1885), p. 161: « Immortale Dei miserenti opus, quod est Ecclesia, quamquam per se et natura sua salutem spectat animorum adipiscendamque in caelis felicitatis, tamen in ipso etiam rerum mortalium genere tot ac tantas ultro parit utilitates, ut plures maioresve non posset, si in primis et maxime esset ad tuendam huius vitae, quae in terris agitur, prosperitatem institutum ». Quod quidem thema, e S. Augustino derivatum, saepe saepius evolvere solebat Leo XIII.

[10] Sic redditur aliis verbis nota regula iuris canonici, ex iure romano quoad sensum deprompta, « Odia restringi et favores convenit ampliari ». Cf. V. BARTOCCETTI, *De regulis iuris canonici* (Angelo Belardetti Editore, Roma 1955), p. 73.

[11] LACTANTIUS, *Divinarum Institutionum*, lib. V, 19: ed. S. Brandt et G. Laubmann, *CSEL* 19, p. 463; *PL* 6, 614 (cap. 20): « Non est opus vi et iniuria, quia religio cogi non potest, verbis potius quam verberibus res agenda est, ut sit voluntas ».

rights of the person" is also included "the right to worship God privately and publicly, including religious charitable activity." Cf. Pius XI, Encyclical Letter *Mit brennender Sorge*, 14 March 1937: AAS 29 (1937), 160: "The believer has an absolute right to profess his faith and live according to its dictates. Laws that impede this profession and practice of faith are against natural law." Cf. Leo XIII, Encyclical Letter *Libertas praestantissimum*, 20 June 1888: *Acta Leonis XIII*, 8 (1888), 237-38: "Another freedom is widely advocated, namely, freedom of conscience. If by this is meant that everyone may, as he chooses, worship God or not, it is sufficiently refuted by the arguments already adduced. But it may also be taken to mean that every man in the state may follow the will of God and, from a consciousness of duty and free from every obstacle, obey his commands. This, indeed, is true freedom, a freedom worthy of the sons of God, which nobly maintains the dignity of man and is stronger than all violence or wrong—a freedom which the Church has always desired and held most dear."

[4] Cf. St. Thomas, *Summa theologica*, I-II, q. 91, a. 1; q. 93, a. 1.

[5] Cf. *ibid.*, q. 93, a. 2.

[6] On the history of this question, cf. J. Lecler, S.J., *Histoire de la tolérance religieuse au siècle de la Réforme* (Paris: Aubier, Editions Montaigne, 1955), vol. II, *passim*.

[7] Cf. St. Thomas, *Summa theologica*, I-II, q. 91, a. 4, c: "Man can make laws in those matters of which he is competent to judge. But man is not competent to judge of interior movements, which are hidden, but only of exterior acts, which are apparent." Cf. II-II, q. 104, a. 5, c: "In matters touching the interior movement of the will man is not bound to obey his fellow man, but God alone." Cf. John XXIII, Encyclical Letter *Pacem in terris*, 11 April 1963: AAS 55 (1963), 270: "But since all men are equal in natural dignity, no man has the capacity to force internal compliance on another. Only God can do that, for he alone scrutinizes and judges the secret counsels of the heart." Cf. Paul VI, Radio message, 22 December 1964: AAS 57 (1965), 181.

[8] Cf. John XXIII, Encylical Letter *Pacem in terris*, 11 April 1963: AAS 55 (1963), 273-74: "It is generally accepted today that the common good is best safeguarded when personal rights and duties are guaranteed. The chief concern of civil authorities must therefore be to ensure that these rights are recognized, respected, co-ordinated, defended and promoted, and that each individual is enabled to perform his duties more easily. For 'to safeguard the inviolable rights of the human person, and to [**95**] facilitate the performance of his duties, is the principal duty of every public power.'" Cf. Pius XII, Radio message, 1 June 1941: AAS 33 (1941), 200.

[9] Cf. Leo XIII, Encyclical Letter *Immortale Dei*, 1 November 1885: ASS 18 (1885), 161: "The Catholic Church, that imperishable handiwork of our all-merciful God, has for her immediate and natural purpose the saving of souls and securing our happiness in heaven. Yet, in regard to things temporal, she is the source of benefits as manifold and great as if the chief end of her existence were to ensure the prospering of our earthly life." This idea, which derives from St. Augustine, was increasingly developed by Leo XIII throughout his pontificate.

[10] This statement expresses in different words the following well-known rule of canon law, which derives its meaning from Roman law: "Whatever is burdensome should be restricted; whatever is favorable should be increased." Cf. V. Bartoccetti, *De regulis iuris canonici* (Rome: Angelo Belardetti, 1955), 73.

[11] Lactantius, *Divinarum Institutionum*, bk. V, 19: ed. S. Brandt and G. Laubmann, *CSEL* 19, p. 463; *PL* 6, 614 (ch. 20): "There is no need for violence or injury, for religion cannot be forced; the whole matter should be carried on with words rather than whips, so that there might be free will."

Op. cit.: CSEL 19, p. 464; *PL* 6, 614: «Itaque nemo a nobis retinetur invitus—inutilis est enim Deo qui devotione ac fide caret—et tamen nemo discedit ipsa veritate retinente ».

Op. cit.: CSEL 19, p. 465; *PL* 6, 616: « Nihil est enim tam voluntarium quam religio, in qua si animus sacrificantis aversus est, iam sublata, iam nulla est ».

S. AMBROSIUS, *Epistola ad Valentinianum Imp., Ep.* 21: *PL* 16, 1047: « Dei lex nos docuit quid sequamur, humanae leges hoc docere non possumus. Extorquere solent timidis commutationem fidem inspirare non possunt ».

S. AUGUSTINUS, *Contra litteras Petiliani,* lib. II, cap. 83: ed. M. Petschenig, *CSEL* 52, p. 112; *PL* 43, 315; cf. C. 23, q. 5, c. 33 (ed. Friedberg, col. 939): « Augustinus respondit: Ad fidem quidem nullus est cogendus invitus; sed per severitatem, immo et per misericordiam Dei tribulationum flagellis solet perfidia castigari ».

S. GREGORIUS MAGNUS, *Epistola ad Virgilium et Theodorum Episcopos Massilliae Galliarum,* Registrum Epistolarum, I, 45: ed. P. Ewald et L. M. Hartmann, *MGH Ep.* 1, p. 72; *PL* 77, 510-11 (lib. I, ep. 47): « Dum enim quispiam ad baptismatis fontem non praedicationis suavitate, sed necessitate pervenerit, ad pristinam superstitionem remeans in de deterius moritur, unde renatus esse videbatur ».

Epistola ad Iohannem Episcopum Constantinopolitanum, Registrum Epistolarum, III, 52: *MGH Ep.* 1, p. 210; *PL* 77, 649 (lib. III, ep. 53); cf. D. 45, c. 1 (ed. Friedberg, col. 160): « Nova vero atque inaudita est ista praedicatio, quae verberibus exigit fidem ».

CONC. TOLET. IV, c. 57: MANSI 10, 633; cf. D. 45, c. 5 (ed. Friedberg, col. 161-162): « De Iudaeis hoc praecepit sancta synodus, nemini deinceps ad credendum vim inferre; *cui enim vult Deus misereretur, et quem vult indurat.* Non enim tales inviti salvandi sunt, sed volentes, ut integra sit forma iustitiae: sicut enim homo proprii arbitrii voluntate serpenti oboediens periit, sic vocante gratia Dei, propriae mentis conversione homo quisque credendo salvatur. Ergo non vi, [96] sed liberi arbitrii facultate, ut convertantur suadendi sunt, non potius impellendi . . . ».

CLEMENS III, Litterae Decretales: X, V, 6, 9, ed. Friedberg, col. 774: « . . . Statuimus enim ut nullus Christianus invitos vel nolentes Iudaeos ad baptismum (per violentiam) venire compellat. Si quis autem ad Christianos causa fidei confugerit, postquam voluntas eius fuerit patefacta, Christianus absque calumnia efficiatur: quippe Christi fidem habere non creditur, qui ad Christianorum baptismum non spontaneus, sed invitus cogitur pervenire . . . ».

INNOCENTUS III, *Epistola ad Arelatensem Archiepiscopum,* X, III, 42, 3: ed. Friedberg, col. 646: « . . . Verum id est religioni Christianae contrarium, ut semper invitus et penitus contradicens ad recipiendam et servandam Christianitatem aliquis compellatur . . . ».

[12] Cf. *C.I.C.,* c. 1351; cf. PIUS XII, Alloc. ad Praelatos auditores ceterosque officiales et administros Tribunalis S. Romanae Rotae, 6 oct. 1946: *A.A.S.,* 38 (1946), p. 394, ubi citatur a R. P. *Pro Memoria* Secretarius Status ad Legationem Yugoslaviae ad Sanctam Sedem: « D'après les principes de la doctrine catholique, la conversion doit être le résultat, non pas de contraintes extérieures mais de l'adhésion de l'âme aux vérités enseignées par l'Eglise catholique. C'est pour cela que l'Eglise catholique n'admet pas dans son sein les adultes, qui demandent à y entrer ou à y faire retour, qu'à la condition qu'ils soient pleinement conscients de la portée et

Op. cit.: CSEL 19, p. 464; *PL* 6, 614: "Therefore we hold no one back against his will—for anyone who is without devotion and faith is of no use to God—and yet no one departs who is held fast by the truth itself."

Op. cit.: CSEL 19, p. 465; *PL* 6, 616: "For nothing is so voluntary as religion; once the spirit of the one offering sacrifice has turned away, religion is already destroyed, is itself already nothing."

St. Ambrose, *Epistola ad Valentinianum Imp.*, Ep. 21, *PL* 16, 1047: "God's law taught us what to strive for; human laws cannot teach this. Such laws are merely accustomed to extorting a change from the faint of heart; they cannot inspire faith."

St. Augustine, *Contra litteras Petiliani*, bk. II, ch. 83: ed. M Petschenig, *CSEL* 52, p. 112; *PL* 43, 315; cf. C. 23, q. 5, ch. 33 (ed. Friedberg, col. 939): "Augustine replied: No one, indeed, is forced to embrace the faith against his will; but through the severity of God, or rather through his mercy, faithlessness is usually punished by the lashes of tribulation."

St. Gregory the Great, *Epistola ad Virgilium et Theodorum Episcopos Massilliae Galliarium*, Registrum Epistolarum, I, 45: ed. P. Ewald and L.M. Hartmann, *MGH Ep.* 1, p. 72; *PL* 77, 510-11 (bk. I, ep. 47): "For if anyone should have come to the holy baptismal font, not through the persuasion of preaching, but out of compulsion, when he returns to the place of his former superstition he will die the worse for it, having come from a place where he only seemed to have been reborn."

Epistola ad Iohannem Episcopum Constantinopolitanum, Registrum Epistolarum, III, 52: *MGH Ep.* 1, p. 210; *PL* 77, 649 (bk. III, ep. 53); cf. D. 45, ch. 1 (ed. Friedberg, col. 160): "That preaching is indeed new and unheard of, that exacts faith by means of lashing."

Fourth Council of Toledo, ch. 57: Mansi 10, 633; cf. D. 45, ch. 5 (ed. Friedberg, col. 161-162); "Concerning the Jews, the holy synod declared that henceforth force is not to be applied to anyone in order to make them believe; *for God has mercy on whom he wishes, and hardens whom he wishes*. For such men are to be saved not unwillingly but willingly, in order that justice may be perfect: for just as man perished by obeying the serpent through his own free-will, so at the call of God's grace, each man is saved by believing through the conversion of his own mind. Therefore, not by force, **[96]** but by the free judgment of their own free will are they to be persuaded to convert, rather than compelled . . ."

Clement III, *Litterae Decretales*: X, V, 6, 9, ed. Friedberg col. 774: ". . . For we have decreed that no Christian is to force Jews reluctantly or against their will to approach baptism (by violence). If, however, someone has recourse to Christians on account of his faith, after he has made known his will, let him be made a Christian without dispute; since one who is forced to approach Christian baptism not voluntarily but against his will is not considered to have the faith of Christ . . ."

Innocent III, *Epistola ad Arelatensem Archiepiscopum*, X, III, 42, 3: ed. Friedberg, col. 646: ". . . It is in truth contrary to the Christian religion that anyone ever be forced, against his will and while interiorly opposing it, to receive and keep the Christian faith . . ."

[12] Cf. *Code of Canon Law* [1917], c. 1351; cf. Pius XII, "Allocution to prelate auditors and other officials and administrators of the Tribunal of the Sacred Roman Rota," 6 October 1946: AAS 38 (1946), 394, where the pope cites the *pro memoria* of the Secretariat of State to the Yugoslavian Embassy to the Holy See: "In accordance with the principles of Catholic teaching, conversion should be the result not of external constraints but of the soul's adherence to the truths taught by the Catholic Church. This is why the Catholic Church admits to herself adults who seek to enter or return to her only on the condition that they are fully conscious of the

des conséquences de l'acte qu'ils veulent accomplir ». Idem, Litt. Encycl. *Mystici Corporis*, 29 iunii 1943: *A.A.S.*, 35 (1943), p. 243: «At si cupimus non intermissam eiusmodi totius mystici Corporis conprecationem admoveri Deo, ut aberrantes omnes in unum Iesu Christi ovile quam primum ingrediantur, profitemur tamen omnino necessarium esse id sponte libenterque fieri, cum nemo credat nisi volens. Quamobrem si qui, non credentes, eo reapse compelluntur ut Ecclesiae aedificium intrent, ut ad altare accedant, sacramentaque suscipiant, ii procul dubio veri christifideles non fiunt; fides enim, sine qua "impossibile est placere Deo" (*Hebr.* 11, 6), liberrimum esse debet "obsequium intellectus et voluntatis" (CONC. VAT., *Const. de fide catholica*, cap. 3). Si igitur aliquando contingat, ut contra constantem Apostolicae huius Sedis doctrinam, ad amplexandam catholicam fidem aliquis adigatur invitus, id Nos facere non possumus quin, pro officii nostri conscientia, reprobamus ».

¹³ Cf. *Eph.* 1, 5.

¹⁴ Cf. *Io.* 6, 44.

¹⁵ Cf. *Io.* 13, 13.

¹⁶ Cf. *Mt.* 11, 29.

¹⁷ Cf. *Mt.* 11, 28-30; *Io.* 6, 68.

¹⁸ Cf. *Mt.* 9, 28-29; *Mc.* 9, 23-24; 6, 5-6.

Cf. PAULUS VI, Litt. Encycl. *Ecclesiam suam*, 6 aug. 1964: *A.A.S.*, 56 (1964), pp. 642-43: «Adeo afuit ut quisquam vi cogeretur venire ad colloquium salutis, ut is magis amoris impulsione invitaretur. Qua invitatione, quamquam grave onus eius animo impositum est, ad quem pertinuit (cf. *Mt.* 11, 21), relicta tamen est ipsi potestas aut veniendi ad colloquium, aut illud fugiendi; quin immo Christus, sive miraculorum numerum (ib. 12, 38 s.), sive eorumdem vim probativam cum ad condiciones tum ad voluntatem audientium aptavit (ib. 13, 13 s.); eo nimirum consilio, ut iidem iuvarentur ad libere assentiendum divinae revelationi, neque exinde suae assensionis praemio carerent ».

¹⁹ [97] Cf. *Mt.* 11, 20-24.

²⁰ Cf. *Mt.* 13, 30 et 40-41.

²¹ Cf. *Mt.* 4, 8-10; *Io.* 6, 15.

²² Cf. *Is.* 42, 1-4.

²³ Cf. *Io.* 18, 37.

²⁴ Cf. *Mt.* 26, 51-53; *Io.* 18, 36.

²⁵ Cf. *Io.* 12, 32.

²⁶ Cf. *1 Cor.* 2, 3-5; *1 Thess.* 2, 3-5.

²⁷ Cf. *Rom.* 14, 1-23; *1 Cor.* 8, 9-13; 10, 23-33.

²⁸ Cf. *Eph.* 6, 20.

²⁹ Cf. *Rom.* 1, 16.

³⁰ Cf. *2 Cor.* 10, 4; *1 Thess.* 5, 8-9.

³¹ Cf. *Eph.* 6, 11-17.

³² Cf. *2 Cor.* 10, 3-5.

³³ Cf. *1 Pt.* 2, 13-17.

³⁴ Cf. *Act.* 4, 19-20.

³⁵ Cf. LEO XIII, Litterae *Officio sanctissimo*, 22 dec. 1887: *A.S.S.*, 22 (1887), p. 269: «In bonis autem Ecclesiae, quae Nobis ubique semperque conservare debemus, ab omnique iniuria defendere, illud certe praestantissimum est, tantam ipsam perfrui agendi libertate, quantam sàlus hominum curanda requirat. Haec nimirum est libertas divina, ab Unigenito Dei Filio auctore profecta, qui Ecclesiam sanguine fuso excitavit; qui eam perpetuam in hominibus sta-

significance and consequences of the act they wish to make." Cf. also the Encyclical Letter *Mystici Corporis*, 29 June 1943: AAS 35 (1943), 243: "Though we desire this unceasing prayer to rise to God from the whole mystical body in common, that all the straying sheep may hasten to enter the one fold of Jesus Christ, we still recognize that this must be done of their own free will; for no one believes unless he wills to believe. Hence they are most certainly not genuine Christians who against their belief are forced to go into a church, to approach the altar and to receive the sacraments; for the 'faith without which it is impossible to please God' (Heb 11:6) is an entirely free 'submission of intellect and will' (First Vatican Council, *Constitution on the Catholic Faith*, ch. 3). Therefore, whenever it happens, despite the constant teaching of this apostolic see, that anyone is compelled to embrace the Catholic faith against his will, our sense of duty demands that we condemn the act."

[13] Cf. Eph 1:5.

[14] Cf. Jn 6:44.

[15] Cf. Jn 13:13.

[16] Cf. Mt 11:29.

[17] Cf. Mt 11:28-30; Jn 6:68.

[18] Cf. Mt 9:28-29; Mk 9:23-24; 6:5-6.

Cf. Paul VI, Encyclical Letter *Ecclesiam suam*, 6 August 1964: AAS 56 (1964), 642-43: "No physical pressure was brought on anyone to accept the dialogue of salvation; far from it. It was an appeal of love. True, it imposed a serious obligation on those toward whom it was directed (cf. Mt 11:21) but it left them free to respond to it or to reject it. Christ adapted the number of his miracles (*ibid.*, 12:38ff.) and their demonstrative force to the dispositions and good will of his hearers (*ibid.*, 13:13ff.) so as to help them to consent freely to the revelation they were given and not to forfeit the reward for their consent."

[19] **[97]** Cf. Mt 11:20-24.

[20] Cf. Mt 13:30 and 40-41.

[21] Cf. Mt 4:8-10; Jn 6:15.

[22] Cf. Is 42:1-4.

[23] Cf. Jn 18:37.

[24] Cf. Mt 26:51-53; Jn 18:36.

[25] Cf. Jn 12:32.

[26] Cf. 1 Cor 2:3-5; 1 Thes 2:3-5.

[27] Cf. Rom 14:1-23; 1 Cor 8:9-13; 10:23-33.

[28] Cf. Eph 6:20.

[29] Cf. Rom 1:16.

[30] Cf. 2 Cor 10:4; 1 Thes 5:8-9.

[31] Cf. Eph 6:11-17.

[32] Cf. 2 Cor 10:3-5.

[33] Cf. 1 Pt 2:13-17.

[34] Cf. Acts 4:19-20.

[35] Cf. Leo XIII, Enyclical *Officio sanctissimo*, 22 December 1887: ASS 22 (1887), 269: "Of the goods of the Church that it is our duty everywhere and always to maintain and defend against all injustice, the first is certainly that of enjoying the full freedom of action she may need in working for the salvation of souls. This is a divine liberty, having as its author the only Son of God, who by the shedding of his blood gave birth to the Church, who established it

tuit; qui voluit ipsi ipse praeesse. Atque adeo propria est Ecclesiae, perfecti divinique operis, ut qui contra eam faciunt libertatem, iidem contra Deum et contra officium ». Ut olim Gregorius VII, sic temporibus modernis exstabat LEO XIII propugnator libertatis Ecclesiae. Cf. Litterae *Ex litteris*, 7 aprilis 1887: A.S.S., 19 (1886), p. 465: «Nos quidem vel ab initio nostri pontificatus multo et serio cogitare de vobis instituimus, atque, ut ratio Nostri ferebat officii, consilium cepimus omnia conari, si qua ratione liceat, pacatam tranquillitatem cum libertate legitima catholico nomini restituere ». In sexaginta fere documentis, quae relationes inter rem sacram remque civilem tractant, octoginta vices occurrit formula verborum, « libertas Ecclesiae », vel formula aequipollens. Ipsi enim Leoni XIII, sicut toti traditioni catholicae, libertas Ecclesiae principium est fundumentale in iis, quae spectant ad relationem inter Ecclesiam et instituta omnia ordinis civilis.

[36] Cf. *Mc.* 16, 15; *Mt.* 28, 18-20.

Cf. PIUS XII, Litt. Encycl. *Summi Pontificatus*, 20 oct. 1939: A.A.S., 31 (1939), pp. 445-46: « Quamobrem Nos, ut eius in terris vices gerimus, qui a sacro vate "Princeps pacis" appellatur (*Is.* 9, 6), civitatum rectores eosque omnes, e quorum opera quovis modo publica res pendet, compellamus vehementerque obtestamur ut Ecclesia plena semper libertate fruatur debita, qua suam possit educationis operam exsequi, ac veritatem impertire mentibus, animis inculcare iustitiam, eosque divina Iesu Christi refovere caritate ».

[37] Cf. PIUS XI, Litterae *Firmissimam constantiam*, 28 martii 1937: A.A.S., 29 (1937), p. 196: « Proposita eiusmodi aestimandarum rerum mensura, concedendum sane est, ad christianam vitam explicandam externa quoque praesidia, quae sensibus percipiuntur, esse necessaria, pariterque Ecclesiae tamquam hominum societati opus omnino esse, ad vitae usuram atque incrementum, iusta agendi libertate, [98] ipsosque fideles iure gaudere in societate civili vivendi ad rationis conscientiaeque praescripta ».

[38] Cf. PIUS XII, Allocutio *Ci riesce*, 6 dec. 1953: A.A.S., 45 (1953), p. 802, ubi fines clare definiuntur, quos Ecclesia prae oculis habet in ineundis Concordatis: « I Concordati debbono quindi assicurare alla Chiesa una stabile condizione di diritto e di fatto nello Stato, con cui sono conclusi, e garantire ad essa la piena indipendenza nell'adempimento della sua divina missione ». Exinde insuper constat, nihil esse in doctrina de libertate religiosa, quod cum praxi hodierna Concordatorum quovis modo pugnat.

[39] Cf. PIUS XII, *Nuntius radiophonicus*, 28 martii 1952: A.A.S., 44 (1952), pp. 270-78, de conscientia christiana efformanda.

[40] Cf. *Act.* 4, 29.

[41] Cf. IOANNES XXIII, Litt. Encycl. *Pacem in terris*, 11 aprilis 1963: A.A.S., 55 (1963), pp. 299-300: « Omnino errores ab iis qui opinione labuntur semper distinguere aequum est, quamvis de hominibus agatur, qui aut errore veritatis aut impari rerum cognitione capti sint, vel ad sacra vel ad optimam vitae actionem attinentium. Nam homo ad errorem lapsus iam non humanitate instructus esse desinit, neque suam umquam personae dignitatem amittit, cuius ratio est semper habenda. Praeterea in hominis natura numquam facultas perit et refragandi erroribus et viam ad veritatem quaerendi. Neque umquam hac in re providentissimi Dei auxilia hominem deficiunt. Ex quo fieri potest, ut si quis hodie vel perspicuitate egeat, vel in falsas discesserit sententias, possit postmodum, Dei collustratus lumine veritatem amplecti ».

[42] GIANNINI A., *Le Costituzioni degli Stati del Vicino Oriente*, Roma 1931; PEASLEE AMOS S., *Constitutions of Nations*, New Jersey (USA) 1950; MIRKINE-GUETZEVITCH B., *Le Costituzioni Europee*, Milano 1954; ZAMORA A., *Digesto Constitutional Americano*, Buenos

until the end of time, and chose himself to be its head. This liberty is so essential to the Church, a perfect and divine institution, that they who attack this liberty at the same time offend against God and their duty." Like Gregory VII before him, Leo XIII stands out in the modern period as a great defender of the freedom of the Church. Cf. the Encyclical *Ex litteris*, 7 April 1887: ASS 19 (1886), 465: "Indeed, from the beginning of our pontificate we have given much serious thought toward you, and, bearing in mind our office, we resolved to attempt all things possible to restore to the Catholic name peaceful tranquility with lawful freedom." In almost sixty documents that deal with relations between sacred and civil affairs, the phrase "freedom of the Church," or its equivalent, occurs eighty times. Indeed, for Leo XIII himself, as for the whole Catholic tradition, the freedom of the Church is a fundamental principle among those that concern the relationship between the Church and all the institutions of the civil order.

[36] Cf. Mk 16:15; Mt 28:18-20.

Cf. Pius XII, Encyclical Letter *Summi Pontificatus*, 20 October 1939: AAS 31 (1939), 445-46: "Accordingly we, as representatives on earth of him who was proclaimed by the prophet 'Prince of Peace' (Is 9:6) appeal to and vigorously implore the leaders of nations, and those who can in any way influence public life, to let the Church have full liberty to fulfill her role as educator by teaching men truth, by inculcating justice and by inflaming hearts with the divine love of Christ."

[37] Cf. Pius XI, Encyclical *Firmissimam constantiam*, 28 March 1937: AAS 29 (1937), 196: "Once this gradation of values and activities is established, it must be admitted that for Christian life to develop it must have recourse to external and sensible means; that the Church, being a society of men, cannot exist or develop if it does not enjoy liberty of action, [**98**] and that its members have the right to find in civil society the possibility of living according to the dictates of their consciences."

[38] Cf. Pius XII, Allocution *Ci riesce*, 6 December 1953: AAS 45 (1953), 802, where the limits that the Church has in mind when entering into concordats are clearly defined: "Concordats should therefore assure to the Church a stable condition in right and in fact within the state with which they are concluded, and guarantee to her full independence in fulfilling her divine mission." From this it is evident that there is nothing in the teaching on religious freedom that is at odds in any way with the current practice of concordats.

[39] On the formation of a Christian conscience, cf. Pius XII, Radio message, 28 March 1952: AAS 44 (1952), 270-78.

[40] Cf. Acts 4:29.

[41] Cf. John XXIII, Encyclical Letter *Pacem in terris*, 11 April 1963: AAS 55 (1963), 299-300: "It is always perfectly justifiable to distinguish between error as such and the person who falls into error—even in the case of men who err regarding the truth or are led astray as a result of their inadequate knowledge, in matters either of religion or of the highest ethical standards. A man who has fallen into error does not cease to be a man. He never forfeits his personal dignity; and that is something that must always be taken into account. Besides, there exists in man's very nature an undying capacity to break through the barriers of error and seek the road to truth. God, in his great providence, is ever present with his aid. Today, maybe, a man lacks faith and turns aside into error; tomorrow, perhaps, illumined by God's light, he may indeed embrace the truth."

[42] A. Giannini, *Le Costituzioni degli Stati del Vicino Oriente*, Roma 1931; Amos S. Peaslee, *Constitutions of Nations*, New Jersey (USA) 1950; B. Mirkine-Guetzevitch, *Le Costituzioni Europee*, Milano 1954; A. Zamora, *Digesto Constitutional Americano*, Buenos Aires 1958; D. G.

Aires 1958; LAVROFF D. G. ET PEISER G., *Les Constitutions Africaines,* Paris 1963; STRA-MACCI M., *Le Costituzioni degli Stati Africani,* Milano 1963; PAVAN P., *Libertà Religiosa e Pubblici Poteri,* Milano 1965.

[43] Cf. IOANNES XXIII, Litt. Encycl. *Pacem in terris,* 11 aprilis 1963: *A.A.S.,* 55 (1963), pp. 295-296, ubi, quibusdam defectibus non obstantibus, commendatur Professio Universalis Iurium Humanorum, die 10 dec. 1948 a Foedaratarum Nationum Coetu Generali rata habita: « Nihilominus Professionem eandem habendam esse censemus quemdam quasi gradum atque aditum ad iuridicialem politicamque ordinationem constituendam omnium populorum, qui in mundo sunt. Siquidem ea universis prorsus hominibus solemniter agnoscitur humanae dignitas personae, atque iura cuivis homini asseruntur veritatem libere quaerendi, honestatis sequendi normas, iustitiae officia usurpandi, vitam exigendi homine dignam, alia deinceps cum hisce coniuncta ».

Lavroff and G. Peiser, *Les Constitutions Africaines,* Paris 1963; M. Stramacci, *Le Costituzioni degli Stati Africani,* Milano 1963; P. Pavan, *Libertà Religiosa e Pubblici Poteri,* Milano 1965.

[43] Cf. John XXIII, Encyclical Letter *Pacem in terris,* 11 April 1963: AAS 55 (1963), 295-96, where, certain defects notwithstanding, the pope commends the Universal Declaration of Human Rights, ratified by the General Assembly of the United Nations on December 10, 1948: "Nevertheless, we think the document should be considered a step in the right direction, an approach toward the establishment of a juridical and political ordering of the world community. It is a solemn recognition of the personal dignity of every human being, an assertion of everyone's right to be free to seek out the truth, to follow moral principles, to discharge the duties imposed by justice, and to lead a fully human life. It also recognized other rights connected with these."

v.

Schema 3 and the Final Text

⟨⟨DRAFT OF⟩⟩* THE DECLARATION ON RELIGIOUS FREEDOM

Emended Text

ON THE RIGHT OF THE PERSON AND OF COMMUNITIES TO FREEDOM IN RELIGIOUS MATTERS

I. THE GENERAL PRINCIPLE OF RELIGIOUS FREEDOM†

1.1 (*Present state of affairs*). Men and women of our time are becoming more <u>and more</u> conscious of the dignity of the human person.[1] ⟨⟨They demand civil liberties, in order that they may be able to lead a life in society that is worthy of man.⟩⟩ They also demand that juridical limits be set to the public power, in order that rightful <u>personal</u> freedom not be excessively restricted. This demand for freedom is chiefly concerned with <u>those things that concern religion</u>. ⟨⟨In numerous state constitutions the freedom of citizens in religious matters has already been instituted as a fixed practice.[2]⟩⟩

---

* The following markers indicate the changes made between schema 3 and the final Declaration:

Double brackets indicate words or phrases that have been ⟨⟨removed⟩⟩.

Italics indicate words or phrases that have been *added*.

Underlining indicates words or phrases that have been <u>modified</u>, sometimes significantly, while still remaining comparable.

Plain, unmarked text indicates that no change has been made.

(Note that the italicized subject headings, located at the beginning of each article, in parentheses, are not part of this system.)

The paragraphs which make up each article have been numbered for the sake of comparison and reference. 1.2, for example, refers to paragraph 2 of article 1.

The final Declaration is presented in its original format, while the paragraphs of schema 3 have been rearranged to match the order of the final. The original paragraphs of both documents have been kept whole and intact. Any phrases or sentences within a paragraph that have been moved elsewhere in the text, or that are comparable to other passages, have been highlighted and footnoted.

Where there is no corresponding paragraph on the opposing page, this indicates that the entire paragraph has either been removed (if found on the left-hand page) or added (if found on the right-hand page).

† Cf. the final text, 2.1 (p. 387)

THE DECLARATION ON RELIGIOUS FREEDOM

Dignitatis Humanae

ON THE RIGHT OF THE PERSON AND OF COMMUNITIES TO
SOCIAL AND CIVIL FREEDOM IN RELIGIOUS MATTERS

1.1 Men and women of our time are becoming more conscious <u>every day</u> of the dignity of the human person.[1] *Increasing numbers demand that in acting they enjoy and make use of their own counsel and a responsible freedom,*[2] *not impelled by coercion but moved by a sense of duty.* They also demand that juridical limits be set to the public power, in order that the rightful freedom <u>of persons</u> *and associations* not be excessively restricted. This demand for freedom *in human society* is chiefly concerned with *the goods of the human spirit, first of all* <u>those that concern the free exercise of religion in society.</u> *Carefully attending to these desires of men's hearts, and proposing to declare to what degree they are in conformity with truth and justice,* *this Vatican Council searches the sacred tradition and teaching of the Church,* <u>from which it draws forth new things that are always in harmony with the old.</u>†

---

* Cf. schema 3, 3.1 (p. 384)
† Cf. schema 3, 2.3 (p. 388)

3.1 (*Declaration*). ⟨⟨Presupposing these things, this sacred Council intends with this Declaration to set forth its judgment on the practice of religious freedom today.*⟩⟩ First of all, it declares and teaches, ⟨⟨according to the constant teaching of the Church, that each man is not free to follow whatever opinion in religious life he may prefer, but that⟩⟩ there is one true religion, which God the Father of our Lord Jesus Christ through his incarnate Son revealed and handed over to the Church to preserve and preach to all people; men and women are in fact bound ⟨⟨by a serious duty⟩⟩ to seek the truth in religious matters and to follow it once it is known. ⟨⟨In addition, this sacred Council declares that this Catholic teaching on the one true religion is in no way opposed to human and civil freedom in the practice of religious life. The truth of the Gospel is a leaven in society ⟨⟨that has brought about many benefits of genuine freedom throughout the ages;⟩⟩† the teaching of the Church about man's dignity, moreover, insofar as it is drawn from the font of reason itself, firmly supports and commends civil freedom in religious matters.⟩⟩

3.2 Therefore, since it is incumbent upon the Church to protect the genuine civil freedom of man and to strengthen it with her teaching and authority, this sacred Council declares that the current juridical practice of religious freedom, which is supported by principles of human reason, is in itself noble and truly necessary for the protection of man's dignity, both personal and civil, in today's society. In addition, it declares that religious freedom, in the sense just described, is a true right, having its foundation in the very dignity of the human person, a right that all men and all religious communities can legitimately claim for themselves.[17]

---

* Cf. the final text, 1.1 (p. 383)
† Cf. the final text, 12.2 (pp. 405-407)

1.2 <u>The sacred Council first professes</u> *that God himself has made known to mankind the way in which men are to serve him, and so be saved in Christ and come to blessedness. We believe that* <u>this one true religion subsists in the Catholic and apostolic Church, to whom the Lord Jesus committed the task of spreading it among all people,</u> *saying to the apostles: "Go, therefore, and make disciples of all nations, baptizing them in the name of the Father and of the Son and of the Holy Spirit, teaching them to observe all that I have commanded you" (Mt 28:19-20). All* men and women are in fact bound to seek the truth, *especially* <u>in those things concerning God and his Church,</u> and to <u>embrace and hold fast to it</u> once it is known.

1.3 The sacred Council likewise professes that these duties touch on and bind the conscience of man. In no other way does truth impose itself than by the strength of truth itself, entering the mind at once gently and with power. Further, since the religious freedom which men and women demand in order to fulfill their duty to worship God concerns immunity from coercion in civil society, it leaves intact the traditional Catholic teaching on the moral duty individuals and society have toward the true religion and the one Church of Christ. In addition, in taking up this issue of religious freedom, the sacred Council intends to develop the teaching of the recent popes on the inviolable rights of the human person and the juridical order of society.

1.2 Religious freedom is ⟨⟨commonly understood today to be⟩⟩ a ⟨⟨true⟩⟩ right, having its foundation in human dignity, a right that should be acknowledged in the juridical and political structure of society, so that it becomes a civil right. ⟨⟨It is understood as a right according to which⟩⟩ men and women should be ⟨⟨free or⟩⟩ immune from coercion on the part of other men or of any ⟨⟨merely⟩⟩ human power, ⟨⟨not only in forming their conscience in religious matters, but also in the free exercise of their religion. Indeed, it is acknowledged that the exercise of religion should be free in a twofold sense, namely,⟩⟩ that in religious matters no one may be forced to act against his conscience, nor prevented from acting according to his conscience, within the limits determined by established moral and juridical norms. ⟨⟨Finally, it is understood that⟩⟩ the protection of this right is the responsibility of both individuals and ⟨⟨especially⟩⟩ public powers.*

1.3 This juridical conception of religious freedom, therefore, which is generally acknowledged today, in no way implies that man has no obligations in religious matters, or that he is set free from God's authority. It is not understood to mean that the human person can equally value what is false and what is true, that he no longer has the duty to form for himself a true judgment about religious matters, or that he can determine at will whether or in which religion and in what way he wishes to serve God.

2.1 (*The historical question*). It is clear, then, that religious freedom is not regarded today in the same way as it once was. In the nineteenth century, the ideology known as laicism began to prevail in many nations.[4] This ideology was grounded in the rationalist principle of the absolute autonomy of individual human reason, according to which man is a law unto himself and is in no way subject to God.[5] From this philosophical principle, a certain conception of religious freedom was derived, in which all kinds of relativism and indifferentism in religious matters were concealed.[6] The Church condemned this conception of religious freedom and its philosophical premise; for it cannot be reconciled with human dignity, which chiefly consists in this, that man, made in the image of God, may know the living and true God and serve him alone.[7]

2.2 Closely connected with the philosophical principle of laicism was a political principle concerning the omnipotence of the state, even in religious matters.[8] With the support of this principle, not a few government leaders of the time established a legal practice of religious freedom, according to which the Catholic Church was circumscribed by the state within the temporal

---

* Cf. the final text, 6.1 (p. 397)

I. THE GENERAL PRINCIPLE OF RELIGIOUS FREEDOM*

2.1 (*The object and foundation of religious freedom*). *This Vatican Council declares that the human person has a right to religious freedom.* Such freedom consists in this, that *all* men and women should be immune from coercion on the part of <u>individuals</u>, *social groups* or any human power, so that no one is forced to act against his conscience in religious matters, or prevented from acting according to his conscience, *in private or in public, whether alone or in association with others,* <u>within due limits</u>. *In addition, this Council declares that* <u>the right to religious freedom has its foundation in the very dignity of the human person,</u> *as known from both the revealed word of God and from reason itself.*[3] This right of the human person to religious freedom must be acknowledged <u>in the juridical order of society</u>, so that it becomes a civil right.

---

* Cf. schema 3, 1.1 (p. 382)

order itself, so that the Church was made subject to the omnipotent power of the state.[9] The Church condemned this practice and its political premise as gravely violating the native freedom of the Church. Furthermore, the freedom of man in society cannot be reconciled with such an assertion of the absolute autonomy of the public power, as unlimited and beyond the law, an assertion with which the totalitarianism of today is not unconnected.[10]

2.3 Each of these condemnations, leveled of old, remains firm and unchangeable today.[11] Nevertheless, the times and ideologies have changed. Indeed, the coarse kind of rationalism proper to the nineteenth century has today given way to more serious errors. What is more, since that time a state totalitarianism totally hostile to human freedom has begun to prevail in many areas of the world. ⟨⟨Furthermore, with the development of new problems and perspectives, the Church has continued to unfold a more ample teaching on social and civil matters, from principles that remain always the same in their meaning and purpose,⟩⟩ bringing forth from out of her treasury things both new and old.* The fact that the human person is and must be the foundation, end, and subject of all social life is asserted more strongly today in the teaching of the Church.[12] This teaching also sheds light on the fact that man, as a person, is bound by certain duties and enjoys certain rights, which duties and rights arise from his own nature.[13] This applies in all areas of life and human activity, but especially in those that concern religion.[14] Finally, it is more clearly affirmed today that the chief function of the public power consists in protecting, cultivating, and defending the natural rights of all citizens.[15]

2.4 In the course of history, then, a new kind of question has arisen in regard to religious freedom. For religious freedom today is concerned with observing and upholding the dignity of the human person, and thus with effectively protecting his rights, the first of which is man's right to be free from coercion in religious matters, especially on the part of the public power.[16]

---

* Cf. the final text, 1.1 (p. 383)

2.2 It is in accord with their dignity that all men and women, because they are persons, endowed with reason and free will and therefore privileged with personal responsibility, are impelled by their nature and bound by a moral obligation to seek the truth, especially the truth concerning religion. They are also bound to hold fast to the truth once it is known, and to order their whole life in accord with its demands. They cannot satisfy this obligation in a way that is in keeping with their own nature, however, unless they enjoy psychological freedom as well as immunity from external coercion. The right to religious freedom does not have its foundation in the subjective disposition of the person, therefore, but rather in his very nature. Consequently, the right to this immunity persists even for those who do not satisfy their obligation to seek the truth and

II. THE TEACHING ON RELIGIOUS FREEDOM
DERIVED FROM REASON

4. (*The foundations of religious freedom*)

4*a*) (*The integrity of the person*). Man, as a person, is by his very nature social. In all his actions, this social dimension of man is inseparably joined to his interior dimension. It is therefore an injustice for anyone to ⟨⟨recognize man's personal freedom in religious matters and simultaneously⟩⟩ deny him the free exercise of religion in society,* since this would violate the very integrity of the person. The connection between interior freedom and its social manifestation is wholly indissoluble. Religious freedom is one, undivided and indivisible, and it inheres in one integral subject; at the same time, it refers to two different dimensions: namely, to interior freedom or freedom of conscience, on the one hand, and to the free exercise of religion, on the other.

4*b*) (*The search for truth*). Man has the duty and the right to seek the truth.† He is bound to seek the truth and to adhere to it firmly once it is found, however, in a way that is proper to man, namely, by means of free inquiry and personal assent. ⟨⟨Moreover, since⟩⟩ man is by his nature social, ⟨⟨the truth must be sought and found⟩⟩ through instruction or education and by communication ⟨⟨between persons,⟩⟩ in which men and women share with one another the truth they have found or judged they have found.[18] ⟨⟨All of this applies especially to truth in religious matters. For this reason, it belongs to man's due religious freedom that he not be prevented from expressing his own convictions on religious matters in dialogue with others.⟩⟩

* Cf. the final text, 3.4 (p. 393)
† Cf. the final text, 3.1 (p. 391)

to hold fast to it; the exercise of this right is not to be impeded, provided that just public order is preserved.

3.1 (*Religious freedom and man's relationship to God*). This becomes even clearer when one considers that the highest norm of human life is the divine law, eternal, objective, and universal,* by which God, in the providence of his wisdom and love, orders, directs, and governs the whole world and the ways of the human community.[4] God grants man a share in this law, so that man, under the gentle direction of divine providence, can acknowledge more and more the truth that is itself unchanging.[5] For this reason, each person has the duty, and *therefore* the right, to seek the truth† in religious matters, so that he may prudently form right *and true* judgments of conscience for himself, using all suitable means.‡

3.2 The truth, however, must be sought in a way proper to *the dignity of* the human person *and* his social nature, namely, by means of free inquiry, with the help of instruction or education, communication *and dialogue*, in which men and women share with one another the truth they have found or think they have found, *so as to assist each other in seeking the truth*. Once known, however, the truth must be firmly adhered to by means of personal assent.

* Cf. schema 3, 4d (p. 392)
† Cf. schema 3, 4b (p. 390)
‡ Cf. schema 3, 4d (p. 392)

4c) (*The nature of religion*). By the very nature of religion, its exercise consists <u>primarily</u> in interior acts that are ⟨⟨entirely⟩⟩ voluntary and free, by which man orders himself directly toward God, ⟨⟨with the intention of acknowledging his relationship to God and holding fast to the divine will with all due obedience.⟩⟩ These interior acts of religion, however, by their intrinsic nature—which is closely connected to the social nature of man—give rise to exterior actions.* ⟨⟨It follows that man has the right, in the public exercise of his religion, to be immune from legal or social coercion.⟩⟩

4d) (*Human conscience*). The highest norm of human life is the divine law, which is eternal, ⟨⟨absolute,⟩⟩ objective, and universal.† <u>Man can only obey the divine law, however, insofar as he perceives it by means of the dictates of his own conscience. He cannot achieve his final end unless he prudently forms <u>sure</u> judgments of conscience for himself, using all suitable means,‡ ⟨⟨and⟩⟩ <u>faithfully follows these dictates. From this</u> ⟨⟨the absolute moral principle⟩⟩ <u>follows, that it is prohibited to force anyone to act against his conscience</u> ⟨⟨in religious matters.[19] In our day, however, given the growing awareness of both personal and civil human dignity, a further demand is made: namely, that no one in society be⟩⟩ prevented from acting according to his conscience in religious matters, ⟨⟨especially by the public power, provided that public order, which constitutes an essential part of the whole common good, is preserved. This demand is entirely consistent with reason and is worthy of man.[20]⟩⟩

4e) (*State governance*). Religious acts, in which men and women privately and publicly order themselves toward God out of a <u>personal, intimate</u> conviction, transcend the temporal and earthly order of things. ⟨⟨In performing these acts, therefore, man is not subject to⟩⟩ the civil power, <u>whose competence, on account of its end, is restricted to the earthly and temporal order,</u>[21] ⟨⟨and whose legislative power extends only to external actions.[22] The public power, therefore, since it cannot pass judgment on interior religious acts, likewise⟩⟩ <u>cannot coerce or impede the public exercise of religion,</u> provided that ⟨⟨the demands of⟩⟩ public order are preserved.§ Man's freedom should be acknowledged as far as possible and should not be

* Cf. the final text, 3.3 (p. 393)
† Cf. the final text, 3.1 (p. 391)
‡ Cf. the final text, 3.1 (p. 391)
§ Cf. the final text, 3.4 (p. 393)

3.3 It is through the mediation of his conscience that man perceives and acknowledges the precepts of the divine law; *he is bound in all his actions to follow his conscience faithfully, so that he may come to God, his end.* He is therefore not to be forced to act against his conscience.[6] *Nor is he to be* prevented from acting according to his conscience, *especially* in religious matters. For by its very nature the exercise of religion consists first of all in interior acts that are voluntary and free, through which man orders himself directly toward God: *acts of this kind cannot be commanded or prohibited by any merely human power.*[7] Man's social nature itself, however, demands that he express these interior religious acts externally, *participating with others in religious matters and professing his religion in a communal way.**

3.4 It is therefore an injustice to the human person, *and to the very order of human existence established by God,* for men to be denied the free exercise of religion in society† when *just* public order is preserved.‡

3.5 *Furthermore,* religious acts, in which men and women privately and publicly order themselves toward God out of a sense of inner conviction, *by their nature* transcend the earthly and temporal order of things. The civil power, *therefore,* whose proper end is the care of the temporal common good, *should in fact acknowledge and show favor to the religious life of its citizens; but* this power must be said to exceed its limits if it presumes either to direct or to impede religious acts.

* Cf. schema 3, 4c (p. 392)
† Cf. schema 3, 4a (p. 390)
‡ Cf. schema 3, 4e (p. 392)

restricted except insofar as it is necessary.*²³ The public power completely exceeds its limits if it ⟨⟨involves itself in any way in the governing of minds or the care of souls.²⁴⟩⟩

III. PRACTICAL CONSEQUENCES

7.1 (*The freedom of religious communities*). The religious freedom that belongs to individual persons must be recognized for communities as well. These communities are called for by the social nature of man and of religion itself.

7.2 ⟨⟨Independence and⟩⟩ immunity are therefore due to these communities by right, so that they may govern themselves according to their own laws, honor God with public worship, assist their members in their practice of religious life, strengthen them by instruction, and promote institutions in which members can join together to order their own life according to their religious principles.

7.3 Religious communities likewise have the right not to be impeded, either by legal measures or by administrative action on the part of the state, in selecting and educating their own ministers, in communicating with religious authorities in other parts of the world, or in acquiring and making use of goods.

7.4 Religious communities also have the right not to be prevented from publicly teaching about or witnessing to their faith in speech or in writing. In spreading their religious faith and introducing their practices, however, they must always refrain from any kind of activity that would seem to suggest any hint of coercion or dishonest or less than proper persuasion, especially in regard to children or those less educated.

7.5 Finally, religious freedom entails that religious communities freely be able to show the unique value of religious truth for ordering society and directing all human activity.

---

* Cf. the final text, 7.3 (pp. 399-401)

4.1 (*The freedom of religious communities*). The freedom *or immunity from coercion* in religious matters that belongs to individual persons must also be recognized for them when they act together in community. Religious communities are called for by the social nature of man and of religion itself.

4.2 Immunity is therefore due to these communities by right, *provided they do not violate the just requirements of public order,* so that they may govern themselves according to their own norms, honor the Supreme Being with public worship, assist their members in their practice of religious life, strengthen them by instruction, and promote institutions in which members can join together to order their own life according to their religious principles.

4.3 Religious communities likewise have the right not to be impeded, either by legal measures or by administrative action on the part of the civil power, in selecting, educating, *appointing, and transferring* their own ministers; in communicating with religious authorities *and communities* in other parts of the world; *in erecting religious buildings*; or in acquiring and making use of *any necessary* goods.

4.4 Religious communities also have the right not to be prevented from publicly teaching about or witnessing to their faith in speech or in writing. In spreading their religious faith and introducing their practices, however, they must always refrain from any kind of activity that would seem to suggest any hint of coercion or dishonest or less than proper persuasion, especially in regard to those less educated or in need. *To act in such a way should be considered an abuse of one's own right and a violation of the right of others.*

4.5 Furthermore, religious freedom entails that religious communities not be prohibited from freely showing the unique value of their doctrine for ordering society and animating all human activity. Finally, there is in man's social nature and in the very nature of religion the foundation for the right by which men and women, *moved by their own religious sense,* can freely hold meetings and establish educational, cultural, charitable, and social associations.*

* Cf. schema 3, 9.1 (p. 396)

8.1 (*The religious freedom of the family*). Each family, as a society in its own right, has the right to order freely its own domestic religious life, under the guidance of the parents. Parents also have the right to determine the way in which religious instruction will be handed on to their children. In addition, public powers must acknowledge the right of parents to choose with true freedom among schools or other means of education. Unjust burdens must not be placed upon them on account of this freedom of choice.

9.1 (*The freedom of religious association*). The human person has the right not to be prevented by the civil power from entering or leaving a religious community.* Furthermore, there is in man's social nature and in the very nature of religion the foundation for the right by which men and women can freely hold meetings and establish associations for the pursuit of religious, educational, cultural, charitable, or social ends, ⟨⟨provided the rights of others are preserved.⟩⟩†

6.1 (*The care of religious freedom*). It is the chief duty of every public power to protect the inviolable rights of man. The public power should therefore effectively undertake to protect ⟨⟨and care for⟩⟩ the religious freedom of all citizens through just laws. The public power should ⟨⟨also⟩⟩ see to it that the equality of citizens before the law is never violated for religious reasons.‡

* Cf. the final text, 6.5 (p. 399)
† Cf. the final text, 4.5 (p. 395)
‡ Cf. the final text, 6.4 (p. 399)

5.1 (*The religious freedom of the family*). Each family, as a society in its own *original* right, has the right to order freely its own domestic religious life, under the guidance of the parents. Parents also have the right to determine the way in which religious instruction will be handed on to their children, *in accord with their own religious beliefs.* The civil power must therefore acknowledge the right of parents to choose with true freedom among schools or other means of education, and must not unjustly burden them on account of this freedom of choice, *whether directly or indirectly. Furthermore, the rights of parents are violated if their children are forced to attend lessons that are at odds with the religious beliefs of their parents, or if a single system of education is imposed that excludes all religious formation.*

6.1 (*The care of religious freedom*). Since the common good of society consists in the sum of those conditions of social life by which men can pursue their own perfection more fully and with greater ease, it chiefly consists in the protection of the rights and duties of the human person.[8] Care for the right *to religious freedom* is the responsibility of citizens, *social groups,* civil powers, *the Church, and other religious communities, in virtue of their duty toward the common good, and in the way that is proper to each.**

6.2 It belongs to the essential duties of every civil power to protect *and promote* the inviolable rights of man.[9] The civil power should therefore effectively undertake to protect the religious freedom of all citizens through just laws *and other appropriate means, and* to provide favorable conditions for fostering religious life, *so that citizens may truly be able to exercise their religious rights and fulfill their religious duties, and* so that society itself may enjoy the goods *of justice and peace* that come from men's fidelity to God and his holy will.†[10]

6.3 If, in light of a people's particular circumstances, special civil recognition is granted to one religious community in the juridical order of the state, it is necessary at the same time that the right to freedom in reli-

---

* Cf. schema 3, 1.2 (p. 386)
† Cf. schema 3, 6.2 (p. 398)

6.2 It follows that it is wrong for the public power to impose by force or fear the profession or rejection of any religion on its citizens. All the more is it against God's will and the sacred rights of the person and of the family of nations to use force in order to destroy or repress religion ⟨⟨itself,⟩⟩ either in the human race as a whole or in a particular region or in a specific religious group. ⟨⟨This sacred Council prays that the right of the human person to religious freedom be acknowledged in all the nations of the world and be secured by effective juridical protection.[25]⟩⟩ ⟨⟨For the more that civil society⟩⟩ provides favorable conditions for ⟨⟨spreading the truth and⟩⟩ fostering religious life, the more it will enjoy those goods that come ⟨⟨forth everywhere⟩⟩ from men's fidelity to God and his holy will.[*][26]

5. (*The limits of religious freedom*)[†]

5a) (*The moral norm*). The right to freedom in religious matters is exercised in human society, and is therefore subject to certain limiting norms. ⟨⟨The first of these is⟩⟩ the moral principle of personal responsibility ⟨⟨toward others.⟩⟩ In exercising his rights, each person should keep in mind both the rights of other ⟨⟨persons⟩⟩ and his duties toward others. He should act toward them with justice and humanity.

5b) (*The juridical norm*). Civil society has the right to protect itself against abuses that could be committed in the name of religious freedom. It belongs especially to the public power to afford protection of this sort, not in an arbitrary fashion, but according to juridical norms determined by the requirements of public order. Public order is that essential part of the common good ⟨⟨that is entrusted to the public power, in order to be protected especially by the coercive power of the law. The exercise of religion in society should be immune from the coercive intervention of the state, except when such exercise seriously harms the public order, either by disturbing⟩⟩ the public peace, ⟨⟨by violating⟩⟩ public morality, ⟨⟨or by offending⟩⟩ the civil rights of others.

---

[*] Cf. the final text, 6.2 (p. 397)

[†] This article, which comprises paragraphs 5a and 5b, below, was originally located in section II of schema 3, "The teaching on religious freedom derived from reason."

gious matters be acknowledged and observed for all citizens and religious communities.

6.4 *Finally,* the <u>civil</u> power should see to it that the equality of citizens before the law, *itself part of the common good of society,* is never violated for religious reasons, *whether openly or covertly,** and that there is no discrimi-nation among citizens.

6.5 It follows that it is wrong for the public power to impose by force or fear *or any other means* the profession or rejection of any religion on its citizens, <u>or to prevent anyone</u> from entering or leaving a religious commu-nity.† All the more is it against God's will and the sacred rights of the person and the family of nations to use force *in any way* in order to destroy or repress religion, either in the human race as a whole or in a particular region or in a specific religious group.

7.1 (*The limits of religious freedom*). The right to freedom in religious matters is exercised in human society, and *its use* is therefore subject to certain <u>governing</u> norms.

7.2 *In the use of all freedoms,* the moral principle of personal *and social* responsibility *must be observed*: in exercising <u>their</u> rights, <u>individuals</u> *and so-cial groups* <u>are bound</u> *by the moral law* to keep in mind both the rights of others and <u>their</u> duties toward others, *as well as the common good of all.* <u>They</u> should act toward <u>all</u> with justice and humanity.

7.3 *In addition,* since civil society has the right to protect itself against abuses that could be committed <u>under the pretext</u> of religious freedom, it belongs especially to the <u>civil</u> power to afford protection of this sort. *This protection should* not *be provided* in an arbitrary fashion, *however, or by unjustly favoring one particular group,* but according to juridical norms <u>that conform to the objective moral order.</u> *Such norms are necessary for the ef-fective protection of* <u>the rights of all citizens</u> *and the peaceful settlement of conflicts of rights, for the adequate care of that genuine* public peace *that is obtained when men live and work together in true justice, and for the proper guardianship of* public morality. <u>All of these constitute a fundamental part of the common good, and come under the category of public order.</u> *For the rest,*

---

* Cf. schema 3, 6.1 (p. 396)
† Cf. schema 3, 9.1 (p. 396)

IV. ⟨⟨THE TEACHING ON⟩⟩ RELIGIOUS FREEDOM
IN THE LIGHT OF REVELATION

12.1 (*The teaching of the Gospel*). <u>Religious freedom</u>, ⟨⟨as it is understood today,⟩⟩ <u>has deep roots in the word of God.</u> ⟨⟨The freedom that Christ preached is a gift of God by which man, freed from the law of sin (Rom 8:2) is directly ordered to God the Father through Jesus Christ (1 Cor 8:6).⟩⟩ <u>The religious freedom demanded by society, however, rests upon the dignity of the person,</u> a dignity to which Christ always looked in leading men and women to the perfect freedom of the children of God.

the customary practice of the fullness of freedom in society should be upheld, according to which man's freedom should be acknowledged as far as possible, and should not be restricted except when and insofar as necessary.*[11]

8.1 (*Education in the use of freedom*). Men and women of our time are subjected to a variety of pressures and are in danger of losing the use of their own free counsel. On the other hand, not a few seem disposed, under the pretense of freedom, to reject all submission and to make light of the duty of obedience.

8.2 For this reason, this Vatican Council urges all men and women, especially those who are responsible for educating others, to be diligent in forming human beings who respect the moral order and are obedient to legitimate authority, and who are lovers of genuine freedom; men and women, that is, who by their own counsel decide matters in the light of truth, who act with a sense of responsibility, and who endeavor to pursue whatever is true and just, cooperating willingly with others in their work.

8.3 Religious freedom should therefore also be devoted and ordered to this end, that men and women may come to act with greater responsibility in fulfilling their duties in social life.

II. RELIGIOUS FREEDOM
IN THE LIGHT OF REVELATION

9.1 (*The teaching on religious freedom has its roots in revelation*). The declarations of this Vatican Council regarding man's right to religious freedom have their foundation in the dignity of the person, *a dignity whose demands have come to be more fully known to human reason through centuries of experience. What is more,* this teaching on freedom has its roots in divine revelation, *and for this reason must be observed by Christians all the more faithfully. For although revelation does not expressly affirm the right to immunity from external coercion in religious matters, it nonetheless brings to light the dignity of the human person in all its fullness.* It manifests the respect Christ showed for the freedom with which man is to fulfill his duty of believing the word of God, *and it educates us in the spirit that the disciples of such a Master should adopt and follow in all things. All of this casts light on the general principles which ground the teaching of this Declaration on religious freedom. Above all, religious freedom in society is fully consonant with the freedom of the act of Christian faith.*

---

* Cf. schema 3, 4e (pp. 392-94)

11.1 (*The freedom of faith*). It is a <u>fundamental</u> Catholic teaching, contained in the word of God and constantly proclaimed by the Fathers, that ⟨⟨man has a true responsibility to believe, but that⟩⟩ no one may be forced to embrace the ⟨⟨Catholic⟩⟩ faith against his will.³² The act of ⟨⟨Christian⟩⟩ faith is of its very nature a <u>free</u> act. For man, redeemed by Christ the Savior and called to be an adopted son through Jesus Christ (Eph 1:5), cannot hold fast to God as he reveals himself <u>unless he is drawn by the Father</u> (Jn 6:44) and offers to God a rational and free submission of faith. ⟨⟨Thus it follows that the more genuine faith is, the more free and personal it is.⟩⟩

11.2 <u>Any kind of coercion in religious matters on the part of human power is therefore opposed to the very nature of the Christian faith.</u> ⟨⟨In the practice of religious freedom, then, there are conditions under which the demands of Catholic teaching in this matter are observed.⟩⟩

12.2 For <u>Jesus</u>, who is <u>Christ</u> and Lord (Acts 2:36) and at the same time meek and humble of heart (Mt 11:29), ⟨⟨certainly⟩⟩ attracted and invited disciples ⟨⟨as he went about his ministry, but he never forced them (Mt 4:19; 11:28-30; 19:16-22; Jn 6:68).⟩⟩ <u>He performed miracles so that his listeners would hold fast to his word by faith;</u> ⟨⟨but he deliberately refused again and again to perform wonders that might force men in some way to assent (Mt 12:38-39; Jn 6:30-33). Satan in fact tempted Christ by proposing wonders of this sort (Mt 4:5-7),³³ and the Jews likewise sought such signs (Lk 11:16; Jn 2:18), but Jesus refused them all (Lk 11:16 ff.; Jn 4:48). He rejected those wonders that suggested violence in any way, as when the apostles, turned away by the Samaritans, asked: "Lord, do you want us to bid fire come down from heaven and consume them?", as had happened in the time of Elijah the prophet. The Lord severely rebuked them, saying: "You do not know what manner of spirit you are of; for the Son of man came not to destroy men's lives but to save them" (Lk 9:54-56).⟩⟩ <u>Christ was always that perfect Servant of Yahweh</u> (Is 42:1-4) who does not break a bruised reed nor quench a smoldering wick (Mt 12:20). ⟨⟨He came to serve (Mk 10:45) and⟩⟩ to bear witness to the truth (Jn 18:37), ⟨⟨a witness that he finally rendered to the highest degree with his own blood.⟩⟩ <u>When he was lifted up from the earth, he drew all men to himself by the power of his love.</u>

10.1 (*The freedom of the act of faith*). It is <u>a chief tenet of</u> Catholic teaching, contained in the word of God and constantly proclaimed by the Fathers,[12] that *man's response to God in faith should be voluntary*; no one is to be forced, *therefore*, to embrace the faith against his will.[13] The act of faith is of its very nature a <u>voluntary</u> act. For man, redeemed by Christ the Savior and called to be an adopted son through Jesus Christ,[14] cannot hold fast to God as he reveals himself <u>unless, drawn by the Father</u>,[15] he offers to God a rational and free submission of faith. <u>It is therefore fully consonant with the nature of faith that in religious matters every kind of coercion on the part of men be excluded</u>. *The principle of religious freedom thus contributes in no small way to fostering a state of affairs in which men and women can without hindrance be invited to the Christian faith, embrace it of their own free will, and actively profess it in their whole way of life.*

11.1 (*Christ's and the apostles' way of acting*). *God calls men and women to serve him in spirit and in truth, so that they are bound in conscience but are not coerced. For he has regard for the dignity of the human person whom he himself created, who should be led by his own counsel and enjoy his own freedom. This truth appeared in consummate form in Jesus Christ, in whom God perfectly manifested himself and his ways.* For <u>Christ</u>, who is our <u>Master</u> and Lord,[16] and at the same time meek and humble of heart,[17] attracted and invited disciples *with patience.*[18] <u>He supported and confirmed his teaching with miracles in order to awaken and strengthen the faith of his listeners</u>, *not to exercise coercion over them.*[19] *He certainly denounced the unbelief of his listeners, but he left the verdict to God in anticipation of the day of judgment.*[20] *As he sent the apostles into the world, he said to them:* "He who believes and is baptized will be saved; but he who does not believe will be condemned" (Mk 16:16). *But he himself, acknowledging that weeds have been sown amid the wheat, ordered that both be allowed to grow until the harvest time that will come at the end of the world.*[21] *He did not want to be a political Messiah or to rule by force,*[22] *but preferred to call himself the Son of Man who came* "to serve and to give his life as a ransom for many" (Mk 10:45). <u>He showed himself to be the perfect Servant of God</u>,[23] who "does not break a bruised reed nor quench a smoldering wick" (Mt 12:20). *He acknowledged civil power and its rights when he instructed that tribute be given to Caesar, but he clearly warned that the higher rights of God must be upheld:* "Render to Caesar the things that are Caesar's, and to God the things that are God's" (Mt 22:21). *In the end, when he completed on the cross the work of redemption by which he achieved for men salvation and true freedom, he brought his revelation to perfect completion. For* he bore witness to the truth,[24] *yet*

12.3 The apostles followed what Christ did and taught. From the very beginning of the Church they strove to convert men and women to God, not through coercion or by dishonest means, but by the power of the word of God. Like Christ, the apostles were intent to bear witness to the truth of God, daring "to speak the word of God without fear" (Phil 1:14; Acts 4:13-20) and in full before the people and their leaders. With firm faith they held that the Gospel itself is truly the power of God for the salvation of all who believe (Rom 1:16). Rejecting all "worldly weapons," therefore, and following the example of Christ's meekness and modesty, they preached the word of God, fully trusting in the divine power of this word to destroy the powers that are opposed to God and to lead men and women to the faith and allegiance of Christ (2 Cor 10:3-5).

12.4 The Church, therefore, acts according to the mind of Christ and his principles when ⟨⟨today, given the growing awareness in men and women of their own dignity,⟩⟩ she upholds and supports the practice of religious freedom, ⟨⟨in keeping with her pastoral concern for human freedom.⟩⟩

refused to impose it by force on those who contradicted it. For his kingdom is not claimed by force of blows,[25] *but is established by bearing witness to and listening to the truth, and it grows through* <u>the love by which Christ, lifted up on the cross, draws men to himself.</u>[26]

11.2 <u>Taught by Christ's word and example, the apostles followed the same way.</u> From the very <u>beginnings</u> of the Church they strove to convert men and women to <u>the confession of Christ as Lord,</u> not through coercion or <u>means unworthy of the Gospel,</u> but *foremost* by the power of the word of God.[27] *They steadfastly announced to all the plan of God our Savior, "who desires all men to be saved and to come to the knowledge of the truth" (1 Tim 2:4); at the same time, however, they showed respect for the weak, even though they dwelled in error, thus showing how "each of us shall give account of himself to God" (Rom 14:12)*[28] *and so far is bound to obey his conscience.* Like Christ, the apostles were *always* intent to bear witness to the truth of God, daring to speak "the word of God <u>with boldness</u>" (Acts 4:31) and in full before the people and their leaders.[29] *For* with firm faith they held that the Gospel itself is truly the power of God for the salvation of all who believe.[30] Rejecting all "worldly weapons,"[31] therefore, and following the example of Christ's meekness and modesty, they preached the word of God, fully trusting in the divine power of this word to destroy the powers that are opposed to God[32] and to lead men and women to the faith and allegiance of Christ.[33] *Like their Master, the apostles also recognized legitimate civil authority: "For there is no authority except from God," the apostle teaches, and for this reason instructs: "Let every person be subject to the governing authorities; . . . he who resists the authorities resists what God has appointed" (Rom 13:1-5).*[34] *At the same time, however, the apostles were not afraid to speak out against public powers that opposed the holy will of God: "We must obey God rather than men" (Acts 5:29).*[35] *This is the way that countless martyrs and faithful have followed through the ages and throughout the world.*

12. (*The Church follows in the footsteps of Christ and the apostles*). The Church, therefore, *faithful to the truth of the Gospel,* <u>is following in the way of Christ</u> *and the apostles* when she <u>acknowledges</u> and supports the <u>principle</u> of religious freedom *as consonant with the dignity of man and the revelation of God. Through the ages the Church has carefully protected and handed on the teaching she has received from her Master and the apostles. Although in the life of the people of God as it has made its pilgrim way through the vicissitudes of human history, there have at times appeared ways of acting less in keeping with the spirit of the Gospel, or even opposed to it, the teaching of the Church has nonetheless always stood firm, that no one is to be forced to embrace the faith.*

12.2 <u>The leaven of the Gospel has long been about its quiet work in the</u>

10.1 (*The freedom of the Church*). Preeminent among the goods of the Church that must always and everywhere be preserved and defended against all harm is to enjoy as much freedom in acting as the care of man's salvation may demand. This is a <u>divine</u> freedom, <u>accomplished by the only begotten Son of God, who gave life to the Church through the shedding of his blood.</u> This freedom is so proper to the Church that whoever <u>acts against</u> it acts against God. ⟨⟨According to the whole Catholic tradition,⟩⟩ the freedom of the Church is a fundamental principle <u>among those that concern the relationship between the Church and the civil order of human life.</u>[27]

10.2 The Church claims for herself freedom in human society and before every public power insofar as she is a spiritual authority, constituted by Christ the Lord, upon whom ⟨⟨alone⟩⟩ rests, by divine command, the duty to go throughout the whole world preaching the Gospel to every creature (cf. Mk 16:15; Mt 28:10-20).[28] The Church likewise claims for herself freedom as a society of men and women ⟨⟨called together by God,⟩⟩ who ⟨⟨as a whole and individually⟩⟩ enjoy the right to live in civil society according to the precepts <u>of reason and a Christian conscience.</u>

10.3 Indeed, where the <u>practice</u> of religious freedom <u>truly thrives</u> ⟨⟨today,⟩⟩ the Church maintains a stable condition both in law and in fact, <u>and full independence in carrying out the divine mission entrusted to her</u> ⟨⟨alone by Christ's command.[30]⟩⟩ <u>Furthermore,</u> the Christian faithful enjoy the civil right of not being prevented from <u>leading a life according to the Catholic faith.</u> A harmony therefore exists between the freedom <u>that the Church claims for herself</u> ⟨⟨by Christ's command,⟩⟩ and the religious freedom that <u>the Church claims for all men and communities as a true right,</u> ⟨⟨one that is confirmed by the light of reason itself.⟩⟩

13.1 (*The task of the Church*). In order to obey the divine command: ⟨⟨"Go and⟩⟩ make disciples of all nations ⟨⟨ . . . teaching them to observe all that I have commanded you"⟩⟩ (Mt 28:19-20), the Cathoic Church should strive with great care "that the word of the Lord may speed on and triumph" (2 Thes 3:1) ⟨⟨and that all with one mind and voice may glorify God the Father of our Lord Jesus Christ.⟩⟩

minds of men;* to this is due, in large measure, the fact that in the course of time men and women have come to recognize more widely their dignity as persons, and the conviction has grown that in religious matters the person is to be kept immune within civil society from any kind of human coercion.

13.1 (*The freedom of the Church*). Preeminent among those things that concern the good of the Church *and indeed the good of civil society itself on earth*, which must always and everywhere be preserved and defended against all harm, is *for the Church* to enjoy as much freedom in acting as the care of man's salvation may demand.[36] This is a sacred freedom, with which the only begotten Son of God endowed the Church whom he purchased with his blood. *Indeed*, this freedom is so proper to the Church that whoever opposes it acts against *the will of* God. The freedom of the Church is a fundamental principle in relations between the Church and the public powers and the whole civil order.

13.2 The Church claims for herself freedom in human society and before every public power insofar as she is a spiritual authority, constituted by Christ the Lord, upon whom rests, by divine command, the duty to go throughout the whole world preaching the Gospel to every creature.[37] The Church likewise claims for herself freedom as a society of men and women who enjoy the right to live in civil society according to the precepts of the Christian faith.[38]

13.3 Indeed, where the principle of religious freedom is not only proclaimed in words or sanctioned by law but also given sincere and practical application, *there* the Church maintains a stable condition both in law and in fact, as well as the independence necessary to carry out her divine mission, *which is what Church authorities claim in society, ever more insistently*.[39] At the same time the Christian faithful, *like other men and women*, enjoy the civil right of not being prevented from acting according to their conscience. A harmony therefore exists between the freedom of the Church and the religious freedom that must be acknowledged as a right of all persons and communities *and sanctioned by juridical law*.

14.1 (*The task of the Church*). In order to obey the divine command: "make disciples of all nations" (Mt 28:19), the Catholic Church should strive with great care "that the word of the Lord may speed on and triumph" (2 Thes 3:1).

---

* Cf. schema 3, 3.2 (p. 384)

13.2 The Church therefore entreats her children, "First of all that supplications, prayers, intercessions, and thanksgivings be made for all men . . . This is good and it is acceptable in the sight of God our Savior, who desires all men to be saved and to come to the knowledge of the truth" (1 Tim 2:1-4).

13.3 In forming their conscience, the Christian faithful should carefully attend to the sacred and certain teaching of the Church.[34] For by the will of <u>God</u> the Catholic Church is the teacher of truth, and it is her duty to proclaim and authoritatively teach the truth that is Christ, and likewise to declare and confirm with her authority the principles of the moral order that flow from human nature. In addition, as Christians conduct themselves in wisdom toward those outside, "in the Holy Spirit, in genuine charity, in truthful speech" (2 Cor 6:6-7), let them be diligent in diffusing the light of life with all boldness (Acts 4:29) and apostolic courage, even to the shedding of their blood, ⟨⟨using the resources of nature and grace that the Lord himself employed, namely, the preaching of doctrine, the example of their life, and bearing witness to the truth.⟩⟩

13.4 The disciple is bound by a grave duty <u>to the truth of Christ</u>, to know <u>it</u> more fully each day, to proclaim it faithfully, and to defend it vigorously. At the same time, the love of Christ urges him to deal lovingly, prudently, and patiently with those who dwell in error about the faith.[35] ⟨⟨He should act in the same way, gentle and adapted to human nature, in which God the Father of our Lord Jesus Christ gradually attracts men to his love.⟩⟩ He must therefore consider not only his duties toward the life-giving <u>word</u> that must be preached, but also the rights of the human person, and the measure of grace that God has bestowed through Christ upon those who are invited freely to receive and profess the faith. ⟨⟨Error is to be rejected, the truth to be preached, man's intellect to be enlightened, and the human person to be regarded with all the reverence that is due to him.⟩⟩

14.1 (*Conclusion*). It is well known that men and women of today, ⟨⟨no matter what culture they belong to,⟩⟩ desire ⟨⟨more every day⟩⟩ to be able to profess their religion freely in private and in public; <u>it is also clear that</u> religious freedom has already been declared to be a civil right in most constitutions.

14.2 Governments are not lacking, however, in which, although <u>the right to worship God</u> is acknowledged in their ⟨⟨very⟩⟩ constitutions, the public powers themselves still endeavor to prevent citizens from professing their religion and to make life very difficult and dangerous for religious communities.

14.2 The Church therefore *earnestly* entreats her children, "First of all that supplications, prayers, intercessions, and thanksgivings be made for all men . . . This is good and it is acceptable in the sight of God our Savior, who desires all men to be saved and to come to the knowledge of the truth" (1 Tim 2:1-4).

14.3 In forming their conscience, the Christian faithful should carefully attend to the sacred and certain teaching of the Church.[40] For by the will of Christ the Catholic Church is the teacher of truth, and it is her duty to proclaim and authoritatively teach the truth that is Christ, and likewise to declare and confirm with her authority the principles of the moral order that flow from human nature. In addition, as Christians conduct themselves in wisdom toward those outside, "in the Holy Spirit, in genuine charity, in truthful speech" (2 Cor 6:6-7), let them be diligent in diffusing the light of life with all boldness[41] and apostolic courage, even to the shedding of their blood.

14.4 The disciple is bound by a grave duty to Christ his Teacher, to know more fully each day the truth received from him, to proclaim it faithfully, and to defend it vigorously, *excluding all means contrary to the spirit of the Gospel*. At the same time, the love of Christ urges him to deal lovingly, prudently, and patiently with those who dwell in error *or ignorance* about the faith.[42] He must therefore consider not only his duties toward *Christ*, the life-giving Word that must be preached, but also the rights of the human person, and the measure of grace that God has bestowed through Christ upon those who are invited freely to receive and profess the faith.

15.1 (*Conclusion*). It is well known that men and women of today desire to be able to profess their religion freely in private and in public. Indeed, religious freedom has already been declared to be a civil right in most constitutions,[43] *and is solemnly acknowledged in international documents as well.*[44]

15.2 Governments are not lacking, however, in which, although freedom of religious worship is acknowledged in their constitutions, the public powers themselves still endeavor to prevent citizens from professing their religion and to make life very difficult and dangerous for religious communities.

14.3 Welcoming the former with joy as a favorable sign of the times, while denouncing the latter with sorrow as something to be deplored, this sacred Council urges the Christian faithful and implores all men and women ⟨⟨of our time⟩⟩ to consider carefully how necessary religious freedom is, especially in the present circumstances of human life.

14.4 It is clear that all nations are becoming more ⟨⟨and more⟩⟩ united every day, that men and women of different cultures and religions are being bound to one another with closer ties, and that there is a growing consciousness of the responsibility proper to each person. Hence, in order that peaceful relations and harmony may be established and strengthened among mankind, religious freedom must be secured by effective juridical protection throughout the world, and the highest duties and rights of men and women to lead a religious life freely in society must be observed. May God the Father of all ⟨⟨therefore⟩⟩ grant that the human family, having diligently upheld the practice of religious freedom in society, be led by the grace of Christ and the power of the Holy Spirit to that sublime and everlasting freedom "for which Christ has set us free" (Gal 5:1).

NOTES

[1] Cf. John XXIII, Encyclical Letter *Pacem in terris*, 11 April 1963: AAS 55 (1963), 279, where the pope makes the following observations on present-day realities: "But the aspirations we have mentioned are a clear indication of the fact that men, increasingly aware nowadays of their personal dignity, have found the incentive to enter government service and demand constitutional recognition for their own inviolable rights. Not content with this, they are also demanding the observance of constitutional procedures in the appointment of public authorities, and are insisting that they exercise their office within this constitutional framework." Cf. *ibid.*, 265: "Man's personal dignity requires besides that he enjoy freedom and be able to make up his own mind when he acts. In his association with his fellows, therefore, there is every reason why his recognition of rights, observance of duties, and many-sided collaboration with other men, should be primarily a matter of his own personal decision. Each man should act on his own initiative, conviction, and sense of responsibility, not under the constant pressure of external coercion or enticement. There is nothing human about a society that is welded together by force. Far from encouraging, as it should, the attainment of man's progress and perfection, it is merely an obstacle to his freedom."

Concerning man's civil dignity, by which human dignity is extended into the public sphere, cf. Pius XII, Radio message, 24 December 1944: AAS 37 (1945), 14: "In a people worthy of the name, the citizen feels within himself a consciousness of his personhood, of his duties and rights, of his own freedom together with respect for the freedom and dignity of others." Here the pope commends also the "ideal of freedom and equality" (*loc. cit.*) that it is necessary to maintain in a democratic state organized according to sound principles of reason, which

15.3 Welcoming the former with joy as a favorable sign of the times, while denouncing the latter with sorrow as something to be deplored, this sacred Council urges <u>Catholics</u> and <u>entreats</u> all men and women to consider carefully how necessary religious freedom is, especially in <u>the present condition of the human family</u>.

15.4 It is clear that all nations are becoming more united every day, that men and women of different cultures and religions are being bound to one another with closer ties, and that there is a growing consciousness of the responsibility proper to each person. Hence, in order that peaceful relations and harmony may be established and strengthened among mankind, religious freedom must be secured by effective juridical protection throughout the world, and the highest duties and rights of men and women to lead a religious life freely in society must be observed.

15.5 May God the Father of all grant that the human family, having diligently upheld the <u>principle</u> of religious freedom in society, be led by the grace of Christ and the power of the Holy Spirit to that sublime and everlasting <u>"glorious freedom of the children of God"</u> (Rom 8:21).

NOTES

[1] Cf. John XXIII, Encyclical Letter *Pacem in terris*, 11 April 1963: AAS 55 (1963), 279, where the pope makes the following observations on present-day realities: "But the aspirations we have mentioned are a clear indication of the fact that men, increasingly aware nowadays of their personal dignity, have found the incentive to enter government service and demand constitutional recognition for their own inviolable rights. Not content with this, they are also demanding the observance of constitutional procedures in the appointment of public authorities, and are insisting that they exercise their office within this constitutional framework." Cf. *ibid.*, 265: "Man's personal dignity requires besides that he enjoy freedom and be able to make up his own mind when he acts. In his association with his fellows, therefore, there is every reason why his recognition of rights, observance of duties, and many-sided collaboration with other men, should be primarily a matter of his own personal decision. Each man should act on his own initiative, conviction, and sense of responsibility, not under the constant pressure of external coercion or enticement. There is nothing human about a society that is welded together by force. Far from encouraging, as it should, the attainment of man's progress and perfection, it is merely an obstacle to his freedom."

Concerning man's civil dignity, by which human dignity is extended into the public sphere, cf. Pius XII, Radio message, 24 December 1944: AAS 37 (1945), 14: "In a people worthy of the name, the citizen feels within himself a consciousness of his personhood, of his duties and rights, of his own freedom together with respect for the freedom and dignity of others." Here the pope commends also the "ideal of freedom and equality" (*loc. cit.*) that it is necessary to maintain in a democratic state organized according to sound principles of reason, which demands that man's right to the free exercise of religion in society be fully acknowledged, cultivated, and defended.

[14] Cf. John XXIII, Encyclical Letter *Pacem in terris*, 11 April 1963: AAS 55 (1963), 260-61: "Also among man's rights is that of being able to worship God in accordance with the right dictates of his own conscience, and to profess his religion both in private and in public." Cf. Pius XII, Radio message, 24 December 1942: AAS 35 (1943), 19, where among "the fundamental rights of the person" is also included "the right to worship God privately and publicly, including religious charitable activity." Cf. Pius XI, Encyclical Letter *Mit brennender Sorge*, 14 March 1937: AAS 29 (1937), 160: "The believer has an absolute right to profess his faith and live according to its dictates. Laws that impede this profession and practice of faith are against natural law." Cf. Leo XIII, Encyclical Letter *Libertas praestantissimum*, 20 June 1888: *Acta Leonis XIII*, 8 (1888), 237-38: "Another freedom is widely advocated, namely, freedom of conscience. If by this is meant that everyone may, as he chooses, worship God or not, it is sufficiently refuted by the arguments already adduced. But it may also be taken to mean that every man in the state may follow the will of God and, from a consciousness of duty and free from every obstacle, obey his commands. This, indeed, is true freedom, a freedom worthy of the sons of God, which nobly maintains the dignity of man and is stronger than all violence or wrong—a freedom which the Church has always desired and held most dear."

[3] For an overview of how the concept of religious freedom is understood by other Christians, cf. the documents of the World Council of Churches: "Declaration on Religious Liberty" (Amsterdam Assembly, 1948), and "Statement on Religious Liberty" (New Delhi Assembly, 1961).

[19] ⟨⟨During the period following the Reformation, the general opinion among men reached the point of acknowledging that no one should be forced by the public power to act against his conscience, or be punished on account of his conscience;⟩⟩ cf. J. Lecler, S.J., *Histoire de la tolérance religieuse au siècle de la Réforme* (Paris: Aubier, Editions Montaigne, 1955), vol. II, *passim*. ⟨⟨A new question has arisen in our times, however, namely, whether men and women may be prohibited by the use of force from acting in civil society according to their conscience.⟩⟩

[22] Cf. St. Thomas, *Summa theologica*, I-II, q. 91, a. 4, c: "Man can make laws in those matters of which he is competent to judge. But man is not competent to judge of interior movements, which are hidden, but only of exterior acts, which are apparent." Cf. II-II, q. 104, a. 5, c: "In matters touching on the interior movement of the will man is not bound to obey his fellow man, but God alone." Cf. John XXIII, Encyclical Letter *Pacem in terris*, 11 April 1963: AAS 55 (1963), 270: "But since all men are equal in natural dignity, no man has the capacity to force internal compliance on another. Only God can do that, for he alone scrutinizes and judges the secret counsels of the heart."

[15] Cf. John XXIII, Encyclical Letter *Pacem in terris*, 11 April 1963: AAS 55 (1963), 273-74: "It is generally accepted today that the common good is best safeguarded when personal rights

demands that man's right to the free exercise of religion in society be fully acknowledged, cultivated, and defended.

[2] Cf. Paul VI, Homily, 14th Sunday after Pentecost, *L'Osservatore Romano*, 13-14 September 1965.

[3] Cf. John XXIII, Encyclical Letter *Pacem in terris*, 11 April 1963: AAS 55 (1963), 260-61: "Also among man's rights is that of being able to worship God in accordance with the right dictates of his own conscience, and to profess his religion both in private and in public." Cf. Pius XII, Radio message, 24 December 1942: AAS 35 (1943), 19, where among "the fundamental rights of the person" is also included "the right to worship God privately and publicly, including religious charitable activity." Cf. Pius XI, Encyclical Letter *Mit brennender Sorge*, 14 March 1937: AAS 29 (1937), 160: "The believer has an absolute right to profess his faith and live according to its dictates. Laws that impede this profession and practice of faith are against natural law." Cf. Leo XIII, Encyclical Letter *Libertas praestantissimum*, 20 June 1888: *Acta Leonis XIII*, 8 (1888), 237-38: "Another freedom is widely advocated, namely, freedom of conscience. If by this is meant that everyone may, as he chooses, worship God or not, it is sufficiently refuted by the arguments already adduced. But it may also be taken to mean that every man in the state may follow the will of God and, from a consciousness of duty and free from every obstacle, obey his commands. This, indeed, is true freedom, a freedom worthy of the sons of God, which nobly maintains the dignity of man and is stronger than all violence or wrong—a freedom which the Church has always desired and held most dear."

For an overview of how the concept of religious freedom is understood by other Christians, cf. the documents of the World Council of Churches: "Declaration on Religious Liberty" (Amsterdam Assembly, 1948), and "Statement on Religious Liberty" (New Delhi Assembly, 1961).

[4] Cf. St. Thomas, *Summa theologica*, I-II, q. 91, a. 1; q. 93, a. 1.

[5] Cf. *ibid.*, q. 93, a. 2.

[6] *On the history of this question*, cf. J. Lecler, S.J., *Histoire de la tolérance religieuse au siècle de la Réforme* (Paris: Aubier, Editions Montaigne, 1955), vol. II, *passim*.

[7] Cf. St. Thomas, *Summa theologica*, I-II, q. 91, a. 4, c: "Man can make laws in those matters of which he is competent to judge. But man is not competent to judge of interior movements, which are hidden, but only of exterior acts, which are apparent." Cf. II-II, q. 104, a. 5, c: "In matters touching the interior movement of the will man is not bound to obey his fellow man, but God alone." Cf. John XXIII, Encyclical Letter *Pacem in terris*, 11 April 1963: AAS 55 (1963), 270: "But since all men are equal in natural dignity, no man has the capacity to force internal compliance on another. Only God can do that, for he alone scrutinizes and judges the secret counsels of the heart." Cf. Paul VI, Radio message, 22 December 1964: AAS 57 (1965), 181.

[8] This description of the common good is found in John XXIII, Encyclical Letter *Mater et Magistra*, 15 May 1961: AAS 53 (1961), 417; *Pacem in terris*, 11 April 1963: AAS 55 (1963), 273.

The words which follow ("it chiefly consists in the protection of the rights and duties of the human person") are also taken from the Encyclical Letter *Pacem in terris*, 273.

[9] Cf. John XXIII, Encylical Letter *Pacem in terris*, 11 April 1963: AAS 55 (1963), 273-74: "It is generally accepted today that the common good is best safeguarded when personal rights

and duties are guaranteed. The chief concern of civil authorities must therefore be to ensure that these rights are recognized, respected, co-ordinated, defended and promoted, and that each individual is enabled to perform his duties more easily. For 'to safeguard the inviolable rights of the human person, and to facilitate the performance of his duties, is the principal duty of every public power.'" Cf. Pius XII, Radio message, 1 June 1941: AAS 33 (1941), 200.

[26] Cf. Leo XIII, Encyclical Letter *Immortale Dei*, 1 November 1885; ASS 18 (1885), 161: "The Catholic Church, that imperishable handiwork of our all-merciful God, has for her immediate and natural purpose the saving of souls and securing our happiness in heaven. Yet, in regard to things temporal, she is the source of benefits as manifold and great as if the chief end of her existence were to ensure the prospering of our earthly life." This idea, which derives from St. Augustine, was increasingly developed by Leo XIII throughout his pontificate.

[23] This statement expresses in different words the following well-known rule of canon law, which derives its meaning from Roman law: "Whatever is burdensome should be restricted; whatever is favorable should be increased." Cf. V. Bartoccetti, *De regulis iuris canonici* (Rome: Angelo Belardetti, 1955), 73.

[31] Lactantius, *Divinarum Institutionum*, bk. V, 19: ed. S. Brandt and G. Laubmann, CSEL 19, p. 463; PL 6, 614 (ch. 20): "There is no need for violence or injury, for religion cannot be forced; the whole matter should be carried on with words rather than whips, in order that there might be free will."

Op. cit.: CSEL 19, p. 464; PL 6, 614: "Therefore we hold no one back against his will—for anyone who is without devotion and faith is of no use to God—and yet no one departs who is held fast by the truth itself."

Op. cit.: CSEL 19, p. 465; PL 6, 616: "For nothing is so voluntary as religion; once the spirit of the one offering sacrifice has turned away, religion is already destroyed, is itself already nothing."

St. Ambrose, *Epistola ad Valentinianum Imp.*, Ep. 21, PL 16, 1047: "God's law taught us what to strive for; human laws cannot teach this. Such laws are merely accustomed to extorting a change from the faint of heart; they cannot inspire faith."

St. Augustine, *Contra litteras Petiliani*, bk. II, ch. 83: ed. M Petschenig, CSEL 52, p. 112; PL 43, 315; cf. C. 23, q. 5, ch. 33 (ed. Friedberg, col. 939): "Augustine replied: No one, indeed, is forced to embrace the faith against his will; but through the severity of God, or rather through his mercy, faithlessness is usually punished by the lashes of tribulation."

St. Gregory the Great, *Epistola ad Virgilium et Theodorum Episcopos Massilliae Galliarium*, Registrum Epistolarum, I, 45: ed. P. Ewald and L.M. Hartmann, MGH Ep. 1, p. 72; PL 77, 510-11 (bk. I, ep. 47): "For if anyone should have come to the holy baptismal font, not through the persuasion of preaching, but out of compulsion, when he returns to the place of his former superstition he will die the worse for it, having come from a place where he only seemed to have been reborn."

Epistola ad Iohannem Episcopum Constantinopolitanum, Registrum Epistolarum, III, 52: MGH Ep. 1, p. 210; PL 77, 649 (bk. III, ep. 53); cf. D. 45, ch. 1 (ed. Friedberg, col. 160): "That preaching is indeed new and unheard of, that exacts faith by means of lashing."

Fourth Council of Toledo, ch. 57: Mansi 10, 633; cf. D. 45, ch. 5 (ed. Friedberg, col. 161-162); "Concerning the Jews, the holy synod declared that henceforth force is not to be applied to anyone in order to make them believe; *for God has mercy on whom he wishes, and hardens whom he wishes.* For such men are to be saved not unwillingly but willingly, in order that justice may be perfect: for just as man perished by obeying the serpent through his own free-will, so

and duties are guaranteed. The chief concern of civil authorities must therefore be to ensure that these rights are recognized, respected, co-ordinated, defended and promoted, and that each individual is enabled to perform his duties more easily. For 'to safeguard the inviolable rights of the human person, and to facilitate the performance of his duties, is the principal duty of every public power.'" Cf. Pius XII, Radio message, 1 June 1941: AAS 33 (1941), 200.

[10] Cf. Leo XIII, Encyclical Letter *Immortale Dei*, 1 November 1885: ASS 18 (1885), 161: "The Catholic Church, that imperishable handiwork of our all-merciful God, has for her immediate and natural purpose the saving of souls and securing our happiness in heaven. Yet, in regard to things temporal, she is the source of benefits as manifold and great as if the chief end of her existence were to ensure the prospering of our earthly life." This idea, which derives from St. Augustine, was increasingly developed by Leo XIII throughout his pontificate.

[11] This statement expresses in different words the following well-known rule of canon law, which derives its meaning from Roman law: "Whatever is burdensome should be restricted; whatever is favorable should be increased." Cf. V. Bartoccetti, *De regulis iuris canonici* (Rome: Angelo Belardetti, 1955), 73.

[12] Lactantius, *Divinarum Institutionum*, bk. V, 19: ed. S. Brandt and G. Laubmann, *CSEL* 19, p. 463; *PL* 6, 614 (ch. 20): "There is no need for violence or injury, for religion cannot be forced; the whole matter should be carried on with words rather than whips, so that there might be free will."

Op. cit.: *CSEL* 19, p. 464; *PL* 6, 614: "Therefore we hold no one back against his will—for anyone who is without devotion and faith is of no use to God—and yet no one departs who is held fast by the truth itself."

Op. cit.: *CSEL* 19, p. 465; *PL* 6, 616: "For nothing is so voluntary as religion; once the spirit of the one offering sacrifice has turned away, religion is already destroyed, is itself already nothing."

St. Ambrose, *Epistola ad Valentinianum Imp.*, Ep. 21, *PL* 16, 1047: "God's law taught us what to strive for; human laws cannot teach this. Such laws are merely accustomed to extorting a change from the faint of heart; they cannot inspire faith."

St. Augustine, *Contra litteras Petiliani*, bk. II, ch. 83: ed. M Petschenig, *CSEL* 52, p. 112; *PL* 43, 315; cf. C. 23, q. 5, ch. 33 (ed. Friedberg, col. 939): "Augustine replied: No one, indeed, is forced to embrace the faith against his will; but through the severity of God, or rather through his mercy, faithlessness is usually punished by the lashes of tribulation."

St. Gregory the Great, *Epistola ad Virgilium et Theodorum Episcopos Massilliae Galliarium*, Registrum Epistolarum, I, 45: ed. P. Ewald and L.M. Hartmann, *MGH Ep.* 1, p. 72; *PL* 77, 510-11 (bk. I, ep. 47): "For if anyone should have come to the holy baptismal font, not through the persuasion of preaching, but out of compulsion, when he returns to the place of his former superstition he will die the worse for it, having come from a place where he only seemed to have been reborn."

Epistola ad Iohannem Episcopum Constantinopolitanum, Registrum Epistolarum, III, 52: *MGH Ep.* 1, p. 210; *PL* 77, 649 (bk. III, ep. 53); cf. D. 45, ch. 1 (ed. Friedberg, col. 160): "That preaching is indeed new and unheard of, that exacts faith by means of lashing."

Fourth Council of Toledo, ch. 57: Mansi 10, 633; cf. D. 45, ch. 5 (ed. Friedberg, col. 161-162); "Concerning the Jews, the holy synod declared that henceforth force is not to be applied to anyone in order to make them believe; *for God has mercy on whom he wishes, and hardens whom he wishes.* For such men are to be saved not unwillingly but willingly, in order that justice may be perfect: for just as man perished by obeying the serpent through his own free-will, so at the call of God's grace, each man is saved by believing through the conversion of his own mind. Therefore, not by force, but by the free judgment of their own free will are they to be persuaded to convert, rather than compelled . . ."

Clement III, *Litterae Decretales*: X, V, 6, 9, ed. Friedberg col. 774: ". . . For we have decreed that no Christian is to force Jews reluctantly or against their will to approach baptism (by violence). If, however, someone has recourse to Christians on account of his faith, after he has made known his will, let him be made a Christian without dispute; since one who is forced to approach Christian baptism not voluntarily but against his will is not considered to have the faith of Christ . . ."

Innocent III, *Epistola ad Arelatensem Archiepiscopum*, X, III, 42, 3: ed. Friedberg, col. 646: ". . . Truly it is contrary to the Christian religion that anyone ever be forced, against his will and while interiorly opposing it, to receive and keep the Christian faith . . ."

[32] Cf. *Code of Canon Law* [1917], c. 1351; cf. Pius XII, "Allocution to prelate auditors and other officials and administrators of the Tribunal of the Sacred Roman Rota," 6 October 1946: AAS 38 (1946), 394, where the pope cites the *pro memoria* of the Secretariat of State to the Yugoslavian Embassy to the Holy See: "In accordance with the principles of Catholic teaching, conversion should be the result not of external constraints but of the soul's adherence to the truths taught by the Catholic Church. This is why the Catholic Church admits to herself adults who seek to enter or return to her only on the condition that they are fully conscious of the significance and consequences of the act they wish to make." Cf. also the Encyclical Letter *Mystici Corporis*, 29 June 1943: AAS 35 (1943), 243: "Though we desire this unceasing prayer to rise to God from the whole mystical body in common, that all the straying sheep may hasten to enter the one fold of Jesus Christ, we still recognize that this must be done of their own free will; for no one believes unless he wills to believe. Hence they are most certainly not genuine Christians who against their belief are forced to go into a church, to approach the altar and to receive the sacraments; for the 'faith without which it is impossible to please God' (Heb 11:6) is an entirely free 'submission of intellect and will' (First Vatican Council, *Constitution on the Catholic Faith*, ch. 3). Therefore, whenever it happens, despite the constant teaching of this apostolic see, that anyone is compelled to embrace the Catholic faith against his will, our sense of duty demands that we condemn the act."

[18] ⟨⟨Regarding dialogue or colloquia on religious truths,⟩⟩ cf. Paul VI, Encyclical Letter *Ecclesiam suam*, 6 August 1964, <u>Vatican Polyglot Press, 1964, 35-45</u>.

at the call of God's grace, each man is saved by believing through the conversion of his own mind. Therefore, not by force, but by the free judgment of their own free will are they to be persuaded to convert, rather than compelled . . ."

Clement III, *Litterae Decretales:* X, V, 6, 9, ed. Friedberg col. 774: ". . . For we have decreed that no Christian is to force Jews reluctantly or against their will to approach baptism (by violence). If, however, someone has recourse to Christians on account of his faith, after he has made known his will, let him be made a Christian without dispute; since one who is forced to approach Christian baptism not voluntarily but against his will is not considered to have the faith of Christ . . ."

Innocent III, *Epistola ad Arelatensem Archiepiscopum,* X, III, 42, 3: ed. Friedberg, col. 646: ". . . It is in truth contrary to the Christian religion that anyone ever be forced, against his will and while interiorly opposing it, to receive and keep the Christian faith . . ."

[13] Cf. *Code of Canon Law* [1917], c. 1351; cf. Pius XII, "Allocution to prelate auditors and other officials and administrators of the Tribunal of the Sacred Roman Rota," 6 October 1946: AAS 38 (1946), 394, where the pope cites the *pro memoria* of the Secretariat of State to the Yugoslavian Embassy to the Holy See: "In accordance with the principles of Catholic teaching, conversion should be the result not of external constraints but of the soul's adherence to the truths taught by the Catholic Church. This is why the Catholic Church admits to herself adults who seek to enter or return to her only on the condition that they are fully conscious of the significance and consequences of the act they wish to make." Cf. also the Encyclical Letter *Mystici Corporis,* 29 June 1943: AAS 35 (1943), 243: "Though we desire this unceasing prayer to rise to God from the whole mystical body in common, that all the straying sheep may hasten to enter the one fold of Jesus Christ, we still recognize that this must be done of their own free will; for no one believes unless he wills to believe. Hence they are most certainly not genuine Christians who against their belief are forced to go into a church, to approach the altar and to receive the sacraments; for the 'faith without which it is impossible to please God' (Heb 11:6) is an entirely free 'submission of intellect and will' (First Vatican Council, *Constitution on the Catholic Faith,* ch. 3). Therefore, whenever it happens, despite the constant teaching of this apostolic see, that anyone is compelled to embrace the Catholic faith against his will, our sense of duty demands that we condemn the act."

[14] Cf. Eph 1:5.

[15] Cf. Jn 6:44.

[16] Cf. Jn 13:13.

[17] Cf. Mt 11:29.

[18] Cf. Mt 11:28-30; Jn 6:68.

[19] Cf. Mt 9:28-29; Mk 9:23-24; 6:5-6.

Cf. Paul VI, Encyclical Letter *Ecclesiam suam,* 6 August 1964: AAS 56 (1964), 642-43: "No physical pressure was brought to bear on anyone to accept the dialogue of salvation; far from it. It was an appeal of love. True, it imposed a serious obligation on those toward whom it was directed (cf. Mt 11:21), but it left them free to respond to it or to reject it. Christ adapted the number of his miracles (*ibid.,* 12:38ff.) and their demonstrative force to the dispositions and good will of his hearers (*ibid.,* 13:13ff.) so as to help them to consent freely to the revelation they were given and not to forfeit the reward for their consent."

[20] Cf. Mt 11:20-24.

[21] Cf. Mt 13:30 and 40-41.

[22] Cf. Mt 4:8-10; Jn 6:15.

[27] Cf. Leo XIII, Enyclical *Officio sanctissimo,* 22 December 1887: ASS 22 (1887), 269: "Of the goods of the Church that it is our duty everywhere and always to maintain and defend against all injustice, the first is certainly that of enjoying the full freedom of action she may need in working for the salvation of souls. This is a divine liberty, having as its author the only Son of God, who by the shedding of his blood gave birth to the Church, who established it until the end of time, and chose himself to be its head. This liberty is so essential to the Church, a perfect and divine institution, that they who attack this liberty at the same time offend against God and their duty." Like Gregory VII before him, Leo XIII stands out in the modern period as a great defender of the freedom of the Church. Cf. the Encyclical *Ex litteris,* 7 April 1887: ASS 19 (1886), 465: "Indeed, from the beginning of our pontificate we have given much serious thought toward you, and, bearing in mind our office, we resolved to attempt all things possible to restore to the Catholic name peaceful tranquility with lawful freedom." In almost sixty documents that deal with relations between sacred and civil affairs, the phrase "freedom of the Church," or its equivalent, occurs eighty times. Indeed, for Leo XIII himself, as for the whole Catholic tradition, the freedom of the Church is a fundamental principle among those that concern the relationship between the Church and all the institutions of the civil order.

[28] Cf. Pius XII, Encyclical Letter *Summi Pontificatus,* 20 October 1939: AAS 31 (1939), 445-46: "Accordingly we, as representatives on earth of him who was proclaimed by the prophet 'Prince of Peace' (Is 9:6) appeal to and vigorously implore the leaders of nations, and those who can in any way influence public life, to let the Church have full liberty to fulfill her role as educator by teaching men truth, by inculcating justice and by inflaming hearts with the divine love of Christ."

[29] Cf. Pius XI, Encyclical *Firmissimam constantiam,* 28 March 1937: AAS 29 (1937), 196: "Once this gradation of values and activities is established, it must be admitted that for Christian life to develop it must have recourse to external and sensible means; that the Church, being a society of men, cannot exist or develop if it does not enjoy liberty of action, and that its members have the right to find in civil society the possibility of living according to the dictates of reason and their conscience."

[30] Cf. Pius XII, Allocution *Ci riesce,* 6 December 1953: AAS 45 (1953), 802, where the limits that the Church has in mind when entering into concordats are clearly defined: "Concordats should therefore assure to the Church a stable condition in right and in fact within the state with which they are concluded, and guarantee to her full independence in fulfilling

[23] Cf. Is 42:1-4.

[24] Cf. Jn 18:37.

[25] Cf. Mt 26:51-53; Jn 18:36.

[26] Cf. Jn 12:32.

[27] Cf. 1 Cor 2:3-5; 1 Thes 2:3-5.

[28] Cf. Rom 14:1-23; 1 Cor 8:9-13; 10:23-33.

[29] Cf. Eph 6:20.

[30] Cf. Rom 1:16.

[31] Cf. 2 Cor 10:4; 1 Thes 5:8-9.

[32] Cf. Eph 6:11-17.

[33] Cf. 2 Cor 10:3-5.

[34] Cf. 1 Pt 2:13-17.

[35] Cf. Acts 4:19-20.

[36] Cf. Leo XIII, Enyclical *Officio sanctissimo,* 22 December 1887: ASS 22 (1887), 269: "Of the goods of the Church that it is our duty everywhere and always to maintain and defend against all injustice, the first is certainly that of enjoying the full freedom of action she may need in working for the salvation of souls. This is a divine liberty, having as its author the only Son of God, who by the shedding of his blood gave birth to the Church, who established it until the end of time, and chose himself to be its head. This liberty is so essential to the Church, a perfect and divine institution, that those who attack this liberty at the same time offend against God and their duty." Like Gregory VII before him, Leo XIII stands out in the modern period as a great defender of the freedom of the Church. Cf. the Encyclical *Ex litteris,* 7 April 1887: ASS 19 (1886), 465: "Indeed, from the beginning of our pontificate we have given much serious thought toward you, and, bearing in mind our office, we resolved to attempt all things possible to restore to the Catholic name peaceful tranquility with lawful freedom." In almost sixty documents that deal with relations between sacred and civil affairs, the phrase "freedom of the Church," or its equivalent, occurs eighty times. Indeed, for Leo XIII himself, as for the whole Catholic tradition, the freedom of the Church is a fundamental principle among those that concern the relationship between the Church and all the institutions of the civil order.

[37] Cf. Mk 16:15; Mt 28:18-20.

Cf. Pius XII, Encyclical Letter *Summi Pontificatus,* 20 October 1939: AAS 31 (1939), 445-46: "Accordingly we, as representatives on earth of him who was proclaimed by the prophet 'Prince of Peace' (Is 9:6) appeal to and vigorously implore the leaders of nations, and those who can in any way influence public life, to let the Church have full liberty to fulfill her role as educator by teaching men truth, by inculcating justice and by inflaming hearts with the divine love of Christ."

[38] Cf. Pius XI, Encyclical *Firmissimam constantiam,* 28 March 1937: AAS 29 (1937), 196: "Once this gradation of values and activities is established, it must be admitted that for Christian life to develop it must have recourse to external and sensible means; that the Church, being a society of men, cannot exist or develop if it does not enjoy liberty of action, and that its members have the right to find in civil society the possibility of living according to the dictates of their consciences."

[39] Cf. Pius XII, Allocution *Ci riesce,* 6 December 1953: AAS 45 (1953), 802, where the limits that the Church has in mind when entering into concordats are clearly defined: "Concordats should therefore assure to the Church a stable condition in right and in fact within the state with which they are concluded, and guarantee to her full independence in fulfilling

her divine mission." From this it is evident that there is nothing in the teaching on religious freedom that is at odds in any way with the current practice of concordats.

[34] On the formation of a Christian conscience, cf. Pius XII, Radio message, 28 March 1952: AAS 44 (1952), 270-78.

[35] Cf. John XXIII, Encyclical Letter *Pacem in terris*, 11 April 1963: AAS 55 (1963), 299-300: "It is always perfectly justifiable to distinguish between error as such and the person who falls into error—even in the case of men who err regarding the truth or are led astray as a result of their inadequate knowledge, in matters either of religion or of the highest ethical standards. A man who has fallen into error does not cease to be a man. He never forfeits his personal dignity; and that is something that must always be taken into account. Besides, there exists in man's very nature an undying capacity to break through the barriers of error and seek the road to truth. God, in his great providence, is ever present with his aid. Today, maybe, a man lacks faith and turns aside into error; tomorrow, perhaps, illumined by God's light, he may indeed embrace the truth."

[2] A. Giannini, *Le Costituzioni degli Stati del Vicino Oriente,* Roma 1931; Amos S. Peaslee, *Constitutions of Nations,* New Jersey (USA) 1950; B. Mirkine-Guetzevitch, *Le Costituzioni Europee,* Milano 1954; A. Zamora, *Digesto Constitutional Americano,* Buenos Aires 1958; D. G. Lavroff and G. Peiser, *Les Constitutions Africaines,* Paris 1963; M. Stramacci, *Le Costituzioni degli Stati Africani,* Milano 1963.

[25] Cf. John XXIII, Encyclical letter *Pacem in terris*, 11 April 1963: AAS 55 (1963), 295-96, where, certain defects notwithstanding, the pope commends the Universal Declaration of Human Rights, ratified by the General Assembly of the United Nations on December 10, 1948: "Nevertheless, we think the document should be considered a step in the right direction, an approach toward the establishment of a juridical and political ordering of the world community. It is a solemn recognition of the personal dignity of every human being; an assertion of everyone's right to be free to seek out the truth, to follow moral principles, to discharge the duties imposed by justice, and to lead a fully human life. It also recognized other rights connected with these."

[4] Leo XIII dealt briefly with this kind of ideology in the Encyclical Letter *Immortale Dei,* 1 November 1885: ASS 18 (1885), 170-71, and afterwards more fully in the Encyclical Letter *Libertas praestantissimum,* 20 June 1888: ASS 20 (1887), 600-609.

[5] Cf. Pius IX, *Syllabus,* 8 December 1864, Denzinger-Bannwart, *Enchiridion Symbolorum,* n. 1703: "Human reason, with absolutely no respect for God, is the sole arbiter of what is true and false, good and evil, a law unto itself that by its own native power suffices to care for the good of man and of peoples." Cf. Leo XIII, Encyclical Letter *Libertas praestantissimum,* 20 June 1888: ASS 20 (1887), 600: "The fundamental doctrine of rationalism is the supremacy of human reason, which, refusing due submission to the divine and eternal reason, proclaims its own independence, and constitutes itself as the supreme principle and source and judge of truth. Hence, these followers of liberalism deny the existence of any divine authority to which obedience is due, and proclaim that every man is a law unto himself."

[6] Cf. Pius IX, *Syllabus,* 8 December 1864, Denzinger-Bannwart, *Enchiridion Symbolorum,* n. 1715: "Each man is free to embrace and profess that religion which he judges to be true by the light of reason." Cf. *ibid.,* n. 1716.

[7] Cf. Leo XIII, Encyclical Letter *Libertas praestantissimum,* 20 June 1888: ASS 20 (1887), 603: "First, let us examine that freedom of individuals which is so opposed to the virtue of

her divine mission." From this it is evident that there is nothing in the teaching on religious freedom that is at odds in any way with the current practice of concordats.

[40] On the formation of a Christian conscience, cf. Pius XII, Radio message, 28 March 1952: AAS 44 (1952), 270-78.

[41] Cf. Acts 4:29.

[42] Cf. John XXIII, Encyclical Letter *Pacem in terris*, 11 April 1963: AAS 55 (1963), 299-300: "It is always perfectly justifiable to distinguish between error as such and the person who falls into error—even in the case of men who err regarding the truth or are led astray as a result of their inadequate knowledge, in matters either of religion or of the highest ethical standards. A man who has fallen into error does not cease to be a man. He never forfeits his personal dignity; and that is something that must always be taken into account. Besides, there exists in man's very nature an undying capacity to break through the barriers of error and seek the road to truth. God, in his great providence, is ever present with his aid. Today, maybe, a man lacks faith and turns aside into error; tomorrow, perhaps, illumined by God's light, he may indeed embrace the truth."

[43] A. Giannini, *Le Costituzioni degli Stati del Vicino Oriente*, Roma 1931; Amos S. Peaslee, *Constitutions of Nations*, New Jersey (USA) 1950; B. Mirkine-Guetzevitch, *Le Costituzioni Europee*, Milano 1954; A. Zamora, *Digesto Constitutional Americano*, Buenos Aires 1958; D. G. Lavroff and G. Peiser, *Les Constitutions Africaines*, Paris 1963; M. Stramacci, *Le Costituzioni degli Stati Africani*, Milano 1963; P. Pavan, *Libertà Religiosa e Pubblici Poteri*, Milano 1965.

[44] Cf. John XXIII, Encyclical Letter *Pacem in terris*, 11 April 1963: AAS 55 (1963), 295-96, where, certain defects notwithstanding, the pope commends the Universal Declaration of Human Rights, ratified by the General Assembly of the United Nations on December 10, 1948: "Nevertheless, we think the document should be considered a step in the right direction, an approach toward the establishment of a juridical and political ordering of the world community. It is a solemn recognition of the personal dignity of every human being, an assertion of everyone's right to be free to seek out the truth, to follow moral principles, to discharge the duties imposed by justice, and to lead a fully human life. It also recognized other rights connected with these."

religion, namely, *freedom of worship*, as it is called. This is based on the principle that every man is free to profess as he may choose any religion or none. But, assuredly, of all the duties which man has to fulfill, that, without doubt, is the greatest and most sacred which commands him to worship God with devotion and piety."

[8] Cf. Pius X, *Syllabus*, 8 December 1864, Denzinger-Bannwart, *Enchiridion Symbolorum*, n. 1739: "The state, as the origin and source of all rights, is endowed with a certain right not circumscribed by any limits." Leo XIII frequently drew attention to the error of totalitarianism hidden in the ideology of laicism; cf., e.g., Encyclical Letter *Humanum genus*, 20 April 1884: ASS 16 (1906), 426: "The source of all rights and civil duties is either in the multitude or in the governing authority, when this is constituted according to the latest doctrines."

[9] Cf. Leo XIII, Encyclical Letter *Immortale Dei*, 1 November 1885: ASS 18 (1885), 171: "Lastly, they treat the Church with such arrogance that, rejecting entirely her title to the nature and rights of a perfect society, they hold that she differs in no respect from other societies in the state, and for this reason possesses no right nor any legal power of action, save that which she holds by the concession and favor of the government. . . . Accordingly, it has become the practice and determination under this condition of public polity (now so much admired by many) either to forbid the action of the Church altogether, or to keep her in check and bondage to the state."

[10] Cf. Leo XIII, Encyclical Letter *Libertas praestantissimum*, 20 June 1888: ASS 20 (1887), 609: "By the patrons of liberalism, however, who make the state absolute and omnipotent, and proclaim that man should live altogether independently of God, the liberty of which we speak, which goes hand in hand with virtue and religion, is not admitted; and whatever is done for its preservation is accounted an injury and an offense against the state. Indeed, if what they say were really true, there would be no tyranny, no matter how monstrous, which we should not be bound to endure and submit to."

[11] Cf. Pius XI, Encyclical Epistle *Maximam gravissimamque*, 18 January 1924: AAS 16 (1924), 10: "Whatever Pius X condemned, we condemn; wherever and as often as the term 'laicism' is understood in the sense of a feeling or ideal inimical or foreign to God and to religion, we absolutely condemn such a thing and declare moreover to the whole world that such 'laicism' must be condemned."

[12] Cf. John XXIII, Encyclical Letter *Pacem in terris*, 11 April 1963: AAS 55 (1963), 263: "As Pope Pius XII said, 'man as such, far from being an object or, as it were, an inert element in society, is rather its subject, its basis and its purpose; and so must he be esteemed.'" Cf. Pius XII, Radio message, 24 December 1944: AAS 37 (1945), 12.

[13] Cf. John XXIII, Encyclical Letter *Pacem in terris*, 11 April 1963: AAS 55 (1963), 259.

[16] Here one must keep in mind the distinction made by John XXIII in the Encyclical Letter *Pacem in terris*, 11 April 1963: AAS 55 (1963), 300: "Again it is perfectly legitimate to make a clear distinction between a false philosophy of the nature, origin and purpose of men and the world, and economic, social, cultural, and political undertakings, even when such undertakings draw their origin and inspiration from that philosophy. True, the philosophic formula does not change once it has been set down in precise terms, but the undertakings clearly cannot avoid being influenced to a certain extent by the changing conditions in which they have to operate. Besides, who can deny the possible existence of good and commendable elements in these undertakings, elements which do indeed conform to the dictates of right reason, and are an expression of man's lawful aspirations?" This statement applies also in the present matter. We can and should distinguish today between the practice of religious

Final Text: The Declaration on Religious Freedom

freedom itself, on the one hand, and the principles of laicism, on the other, recognizing that in certain states the former had its origin in the latter.

[17] This question has been treated recently by G. De Broglie, S.J., *Le Droit naturel à la liberté religieuse* (Paris: Beauchesne, 1964) and L. Janssens, *Liberté de conscience et liberté religieuse* (Paris: Descelée de Brouwer, 1964).

[20] Cf. John XXIII, Encyclical Letter *Pacem in terris*, 11 April 1963: AAS 55 (1963), 289: "Furthermore, relations between states must be regulated by the principle of freedom." Cf. *ibid.*, 266, 297.

[21] Cf. Leo XIII, Encyclical Epistle *Cum multa*, 8 December 1882: ASS 15 (1898), 242-43: "The sacred and civil orders being, therefore, distinct in their origin and in their nature, should be conceived and judged of as such. For matters of the civil order—however lawful, however important they be—do not extend, when considered in themselves, beyond the limits of that life which we live on this our earth. But religion, born of God, and referring all things to God, takes a higher flight and touches heaven. . . . It is, then, right to look on religion, and whatever is connected in any particular way with it, as belonging to a higher order." Pius XI repeated this teaching in the Encyclical Letter *Non abbiamo bisogno*, 29 June 1931: AAS 23 (1931), 303: "The Church of Jesus Christ has never contested the rights and the duties of the state concerning the education of its citizens; indeed, we ourselves have recalled and proclaimed them in our recent encyclical on the 'Christian Education of Youth.' Such rights and duties are unchallengeable as long as they remain within the limits of the state's proper competency, a competence which in its turn is clearly indicated and determined by the end of the state, end which, though certainly not only bodily and material, is by its very nature limited to the natural, the terrestrial and the temporal."

[24] Cf. Leo XIII, Encyclical Letter *Sapientiae christianae*, 10 January 1890: ASS 22 (1889-90), 396: "No one can, however, without risk to faith, foster any doubt as to the Church alone having been invested with such power of governing souls as to exclude altogether the civil authority. In truth, it was not to Caesar but to Peter that Jesus Christ entrusted the keys of the kingdom of heaven."

[33] The temptations that Satan suggested to Christ, like the demands for miracles made by the Jews, derived from a popular conception that the Messiah would be a strong and miraculous king. Had Christ agreed to these suggestions, he would have forsaken the plan of his Father, which directed him to carry out the messianic mission in the meek and humble manner of the Servant of Yahweh.

The Conciliar Interventions of Karol Wojtyła

Translated by Patrick T. Brannan, S.J., and Michael Camacho

ANIMADVERSIONES SCRIPTO EXHIBITAE CIRCA SCHEMA DECRETI DE OECUMENISMO

(*Acta Synodalia* III/3, 766-68)

EXC.MUS P. D. CAROLUS WOJTYŁA
Episcopus tit. Ombitanus, vic. ap. Cracoviensis

1. Cap. V schematis *de Oecumenismo*, cui titulus: « De libertate religiosa », sub duplici aspectu, scil. ethico et iuridico, hanc quaestionem tractare videtur. Isti duo aspectus intime connectuntur. Libertas enim in sensu iuridico eandem in sensu ethico supponit. Pro nostro schemate maioris momenti sensus ethicus habetur. Agitur enim de fratribus separatis, qui veritatem christianam aliter concipiunt et aliter vivunt ac nos catholici. Non raro tamen in hoc cap. V sensus ethicus libertatis religiosae cum sensu iuridico, in Codicibus nonnullarum nationum accepto, confunditur, ut patet ex ipsa definitione libertatis ab auctoribus schematis propositae. Affirmant enim (pag. 4 in medio) libertatem religiosam esse immunitatem ab externa coactione. In pag. vero 5 definitur « libertas religiosa seu ius personae ne ab aliis impediatur quominus observet et proclamet officia sua publica et privata erga Deum et erga homines, singulariter vel collective sumptos, prout conscientia manifestantur ». Utraque definitio videtur partialis et negativa, respicit enim potius tolerantiam religiosam quam libertatem. Utique, unicuique licet sequi conscientiam certam, etsi sit invincibiliter erronea, sed huic principio anteponatur aliud, quod sonat: debemus sequi conscientiam certam et veram.

Unde *propono,* ut haec definitio et conceptus libertatis in nostro schemate saltem suppleatur per talem definitionem et conceptionem libertatis, in qua magis appareat momentum ipsius veritatis obiectivae—non solum subiectivae—pro libertate. Retinendo ergo principium de conscientia invinciliter erronea, quod tamquam principium tolerantiae religiosae considerari potest, valorem ipsius veritatis obiectivae vindicare oportet, praesertim in re tanti momenti ut est oecumenismus et libertas religiosa. Nonne dictum est a Domino: « Veritas liberabit vos! ».

Ipsum momentum libertatis est in electione, non autem in electione

1. Written Observations on Schema 1:
On Ecumenism, Chapter 5: On Religious Freedom

WRITTEN OBSERVATIONS ON THE DRAFT OF THE DECREE ON ECUMENISM

(*Acta Synodalia* III/3, 766-68)

MOST REV. KAROL WOJTYŁA
Titular Bishop of Ombi, Auxiliary Bishop of Kraków

1. Chapter 5 of the schema *On Ecumenism*, "On Religious Freedom," appears to deal with this theme under two different aspects: the ethical and the juridical. These two aspects are intimately connected, since freedom in the juridical sense presupposes freedom in the ethical sense. The latter is more important for this schema, since the document deals with Christians who understand and live the Christian truth differently than we do as Catholics. Nevertheless, it is not uncommon in this chapter for the ethical sense of religious freedom to be confused with the juridical sense found in the legislation of various nations; this is evident from the definition of freedom which the authors of the schema propose. They state (in the middle of p. 4) that religious freedom is immunity from external coercion. Again, on page 5, they give the following definition: "religious freedom, or the person's right not to be prevented by others from observing and proclaiming his public and private duties to God and to men, both individually and collectively, as these duties are manifested by conscience." Both of these definitions seem to be partial and negative, and concerned with religious tolerance rather than with freedom. To be sure, everyone is permitted to follow a sure conscience, even if it is invincibly erroneous; but there is another principle that should be set before this one, namely: we should follow a sure and true conscience.

Thus I propose that this definition and understanding of freedom in our schema be supplemented with a definition and understanding in which the importance for freedom of the objective truth itself—not only of subjective truth—is made more clear. While maintaining the principle of an invincibly erroneous conscience, therefore—which can be considered a principle of religious tolerance—we must defend the value of the objective truth itself, especially in a matter of such importance as ecumenism and religious freedom. Did not the Lord say, "The truth will set you free"?

The whole weight of freedom lies in choice: not, however, in the choice

427

boni cuiuslibet, sed veri boni. Oportet ergo, ut in capite « de libertate religiosa » praesertim sub aspectu oecumenico iura personae iuribus ipsius veritatis melius componantur. Persona humana perfectionem sibi propriam obtinet in veritate, quae naturae eius rationali correspondet et etiam verae libertatis certissimum fundamentum constituit. In quaestione oecumenica oritur inde principium sincerissimae investigationis ipsius veritatis christianae.

Si autem agitur de libertate religiosa in sensu civico, *tunc proponere audeo,* ut quaestio haec in schemate *de Oecumenismo* cap. V tractetur magis distincte, in speciali paragrapho—postea autem, ut ponatur in schemate *de praesentia Ecclesiae in mundo hodierno* tamquam problema fundamentale. Pro exsistentia enim et labore Ecclesiae in mundo hodierno maximi est momenti, ut ius civicum cuiuslibet personae ad religionem colendam strenue observetur, et ut parentes catholici vi eiusdem iuris liberos suos in veritate christiana educare possint. Istud autem civicum ius fundatur non solum in principia tolerantiae, sed etiam in naturali iure cuiuslibet personae ad veritatem cognoscendam, cui ius Ecclesiae ad veritatem tradendam componatur oportet.

2. In n. 6 legimus: « ut omnes homines bonae voluntatis, sive credentes, sive nullam religionem profitentes, simul operam dent ad ordinandam societatem [767] secundum normas morales ex ipsa dignitate personae humanae profluentes ». Postea n. 7 additur: « Quae normae quamvis fundamentum commune ad instaurandum ordinem vere humanum praebeant, a christifidelibus tamen non ut unica et suprema norma considerandae sunt. Fide constat hominem . . . regi posse ac debere praecepto caritatis . . . ». Videtur in tali textu ordo moralis christianus in caritate supernaturali consistens ordini pure naturali ex ipsa dignitate personae humanae in ordine naturae profluenti superaedificari. Oportet igitur exprimere potius, quod ordo moralis christianus ordinem moralem naturae et omnia iura personae humanae in se continet et tamen elevat, vivificat et sanctificat, ut patet ex Encyclica *Pacem in terris* Papae Ioannis XXIII. Libertas enim non in hoc habetur, « ut simus parvuli fluctuantes et circumferamur omni vento doctrinae in nequitia hominum, in astutia ad circumventionem erroris » ut dicit S. Paulus, sed in hoc, quod « veritatem facientes in caritate, crescamus in illo per omnia, qui est caput Christus » (*Eph.* 4, 14-15). Ipse vero Christus dixit: « Si vos manseritis in sermone meo, . . . cognoscetis veritatem et veritas liberabit vos. Omnis qui facit peccatum, servus peccati est. Si ergo

of any good whatsoever, but in the choice of the true good. In the chapter "On religious freedom," therefore, especially in its ecumenical dimensions, we need to bring together in a better way the rights of the person and the rights of the truth itself. It is in the truth that the human person achieves his own proper perfection, for the truth corresponds to his rational nature and constitutes the firmest foundation for true freedom. In this way, the question of ecumenism gives rise to the beginning of a sincere investigation into Christian truth itself.

When dealing with religious freedom in the civil sense, however, I would venture to suggest that in the schema *On ecumenism*, chapter 5, this question be dealt with separately, in a special paragraph—and that afterwards it be included in the schema *On the presence of the Church in the modern world* as a fundamental issue. It is of the utmost importance for the existence and work of the Church in the modern world that the civil right of every person to practice their religion be vigorously observed, and that Catholic parents be able to educate their children in the truth of Christianity, by virtue of the same right. This civil right has its foundation not only in the principle of tolerance, however, but also in the natural right of every person to know the truth, to which must be joined the right of the Church to hand on the truth.

2. In article 6 we read: "that all men and women of good will, whether believers or those who profess no religion, may work together to order society [767] according to the moral norms that flow from the very dignity of the human person." Afterwards, in article 7, the following is added: "Although such norms offer a common foundation for building up a truly human order, the Christian faithful should nonetheless not consider them to be the sole and supreme norm. By faith we know that man . . . can and ought to be governed by the rule of charity. . . ." In this passage, it seems that the Christian moral order, consisting in supernatural charity, is superimposed upon the purely natural order, which flows from the dignity of the human person in the order of nature. It would be better to say: the Christian moral order contains within itself the moral order of nature and all the rights of the human person; at the same time, it elevates, animates, and sanctifies these, as is clear from Pope John XXIII's Encyclical *Pacem in terris*. For freedom does not consist in "being like children, tossed to and fro and carried about with every wind of doctrine, by the cunning of men, by their craftiness in deceitful wiles," as St. Paul says, but in "doing the truth in love, so that we grow up in every way into him who is the head, into Christ" (Eph 4:14-15). Indeed, Christ himself said: "If you remain in my word, . . . you will know

vos Filius liberaverit, vere liberi estis ». In his verbis optima notio libertatis religiosae continetur.

3. Redactio cap. V nostri schematis claritate et praecisione caret et non raro confusionem patit. Proponendae videntur emendationes sequentes:

a) Pag. 4, n. 2, lin. 15 verba: « assensus ne detur nisi cum plena libertate » substituatur per expressionem: « assensus detur cum plena pro posse libertate », hoc enim melius correspondet conditioni diversorum hominum et in diversis circumstantiis.

b) In nn. 3 et 4 affirmatur voluntatem Dei a persona humana tantummodo adimpleri posse, « prout lex divina mediante dictamine conscientiae percipitur ». Sed dictamen conscientiae non est id, mediante quo lex divina cognoscitur, ut schema affirmat, sed non nisi id, quo lex haec ad actum applicatur. Lex moralis enim cognoscitur synderesi et scientia, non vero conscientia, quae non nisi applicat principia synderesis et conclusiones scientiae moralis ad concretum actum.

c) In propositione prima pag. 5 auctores schematis affirmant: « In unoquoque actu morali ponendo homo observare debet duas sequentes exigentias: 1. Unica datur veritas quae est ipse Deus. Iura Dei sunt absoluta et unusquisque homo semper et ubique sese submittere debet sacrae voluntati Dei. 2. Deus . . . petit submissionem liberam, i. e. ex perspecta voluntate divini (forsan: divina?) imperatam obedientiam ». Praetermisso enim facto valde confusae redactionis harum potius quattuor quam duarum « exigentiarum », notare oportet, quod verbum « observare » sensu proprio significat aut implere praecepta, aut actualiter et exacte inspicere aliquam rem. Si sumatur in primo sensu, scil. pro impletione praecepti, tunc non est ad rem, si agitur de prima, secunda et quarta propositione, quia haec sunt speculativa et ideo ab homine impleri nequeunt. Impleri enim non possunt nisi exigentiae et praecepta, non vero talis propositio theoretica, quod « unica datur Veritas quae est ipse Deus », quod « iura Dei sunt absoluta », quod « Deus qui hominem ad imaginem suam liberum creavit, ab ipso petit submissionem liberam ». Si vero verbum « observare » sumitur in sensu proprio pro actuali et exacta inspectione alicuius rei seu veritatis, tunc a fortiori est impossibile, ut « *in unoquoque actu* morali ponendo homo observare », seu actualiter et exacte inspicere teneatur, sed sufficit saltem virtualiter illas admittere vel non negare.

the truth, and the truth will make you free. Everyone who commits sin is a slave to sin. So if the Son makes you free, you will be free indeed." In these words is contained the most perfect conception of religious freedom there is.

3. The composition of chapter 5 of our schema lacks clarity and precision, and at times gives rise to confusion. It seems necessary to suggest the following:

a) On page 4, article 2, line 15, the words: "give their assent with full freedom" should be replaced with the expression: "give their assent with as much freedom as possible," since this corresponds better to the situation of different people in different circumstances.

b) In articles 3 and 4, it is said that God's will can be fulfilled by the human person "only to the extent that he perceives the divine law by means of the dictates of his conscience." But the dictates of one's conscience do not reveal the divine law, as the text maintains, but rather apply this law to a given action. The moral law is known by synderesis and knowledge, not by conscience, which only applies the principles of synderesis and the conclusions of moral knowledge to the concrete action.

c) In the first statement on page 5, the authors of the schema state: "In every moral act that he performs, man should observe the following two demands: 1) There is only one truth which is God himself. The rights of God are absolute, and every single man, always and everywhere, should submit himself to the sacred will of God. 2) God . . . seeks from man free submission, that is, the obedience that comes from a clear perception of the will of the divine (perhaps: of the divine will?)." Apart from the fact that the composition here is somewhat confused, since there are four "demands" to be taken into account, rather than two, "to observe" in its proper sense means either to fulfill a precept, or to examine something in fact and exactly. If it is taken in the first sense, as the fulfillment of a precept, then it does not apply here, in regard to the first, second or fourth statements, since these are speculative propositions, which as such cannot literally be fulfilled by man. Only a demand or a precept can be fulfilled, not a theoretical proposition such as "there is only one truth which is God himself," or "the rights of God are absolute," or "God, who created man free in his own image, seeks from him free submission." But if "to observe" is taken in its proper sense, that is, as the actual and exact examination of some object or truth, then it is all the more impossible that "*in every moral act* that he performs, man should observe" these demands, that is, that he is bound to examine them in fact and exactly every single time. It is enough simply to admit them virtually, or not to deny them.

Unde *propono,* ut loco verborum: « In unoquoque actu morali ponendo homo [768] observare debet duas exigentias », ponatur: « Fides docet nos: 1. Unica datur veritas », etc.

d) Verba quae sequuntur, quod scil., « si . . . persona humana erroneam solutionem admittit, nec ullus homo, nec ulla humana potestas ius habet sese huic conscientiae erranti substituendi a. v. in ipsam coercitionem exercendi » distinctione indigent: nullus homo, nec ulla potestas humana ius habet coercitionem exercendi in personam humanam erroneam solutionem admittentem, si haec erronea solutio neque bono communi, neque bono alieno, neque bono ipsius errantis opponitur. Si vero opponitur, tunc certum est, quod legitimi superiores, ut parentes et vigiles boni communis, quandam coercitionem in errantem exercere possunt, ne iste errorem suum sequendo sive aliis, sive sibimetipsi proportionate grave malum non causet.

e) Inexacta et confusa esset propositio sehematis (pag. 6 in medio): « Sacra Synodus solemniter affirmat ius ad libertatem conscientiae in re religiosa externe exercendam, *salvo bono communi,* semper et ubique valere et ab omnibus agnoscendum esse », nisi excludatur falsa notio boni communis. Saepe saepius enim in societate et vita sociali, ubi magis vel minus aperte utilitarismus viget, pro bono communi substituitur id quod sub aliquo aspectu vel pro aliqua factione utile tantum est.

Thus I propose that in place of the words: "In every moral act that he performs, man [768] should observe the following two demands," there be put: "Our faith teaches us: 1) There is only one truth," etc.

d) The following statement requires a distinction to be made: "if . . . the human person arrives at an erroneous conclusion, no human being and no human power has the right to take the place of this erring conscience, or in other words to exercise coercion over it." No human being or human power has the right to use coercion on a person who arrives at an erroneous conclusion, if this erroneous conclusion is not itself opposed either to the common good, or to another's good, or to the good of the person in error. If it is, in fact, opposed to one or more of these, then it is clear that legitimate superiors, such as parents or those responsible for the common good, can exercise a kind of coercion on the one in error, lest by acting on his error he cause proportionately grave evil either to others or to himself.

e) Regarding the following statement of the schema (middle of page 6), "This sacred Council solemnly declares that the right to exercise freedom of conscience in religious matters in an external way is always and everywhere valid, *provided the common good is secured*, and that it must be acknowledged by all people": this statement remains inexact and confused, unless a false understanding of the common good is precluded. For more and more often in society and in social life, where utilitarianism more or less openly reigns, the common good is exchanged for things that are only useful in some particular way or for some particular group.

PATRUM ORATIONES DE LIBERTATE RELIGIOSA
[*Declaratio prior*]

(*Acta Synodalia* III/2, 530-32)

25 septembris 1964

EXC.MUS P. D. CAROLUS WOJTYŁA
Archiepiscopus Cracoviensis

Venerabiles Patres et Fratres,

1. Decreto *de Oecumenismo* adnectitur declaratio cui titulus « de libertate religiosa », quae duos fines distinctos habet et duo etiam sunt, respectu quorum scripta est. Primus finis: ut actio oecumenica promoveatur, et propter hunc finem declaratio respicit omnes fratres separatos. Finis secundus: ut libertas personae humanae in civitate hodierna, et praesertim in Statu, observetur, et propter hunc finem declaratio respicit praecipue omnes, qui res publicas moderantur. In genere, documentum nostrum, etsi partes doctrinae catholicae continet et illustrat, non est tamen praesertim pro Ecclesia tantum « ad intra », sed potius « ad extra ». Pertinet ad illum dialogum, de quo Paulus Pp. VI, f. r., [531] in sua prima Encyclica locutus est, ad duos nempe eius ambitus. Oportet ergo propter perspicuitatem totius documenti, ut 1. haec orientatio ad extra clarius appareat, et 2. ut etiam illi, ad quos declaratio vertitur, bene distinguantur. Secus documentum fines suos non obtinebit. Videtur etiam, non esse proficuum in unico documento fines tam diversos inquirere, praesertim autem ad tam diversos collocutores sese vertere. Melius esset illos duos aspectus libertatis in re religiosa vel in duo documenta distincta inserere (aspectus secundus, i. e. civicus posset in schemate *de Ecclesia in mundo huius temporis* suum locum invenire), vel saltem in uno eodemque documento clarius distinguere.

2. Cum agitur de libertate in re religionis, in primo sensu, i. e. oecumenico—tunc oportet ut nexus inter libertatem et veritatem magis sublineatur. Libertas enim una ex parte est propter veritatem, altera tamen ex parte nequit perfici nisi veritatis ope. Unde illa verba Domini nostri, quae tam expresse sonant pro quolibet homine: « veritas liberabit vos » . . . .[1] Non datur libertas sine veritate.

2. Oral Intervention on Schema 2: *Prior Declaration*

CONCILIAR SPEECHES ON RELIGIOUS FREEDOM
[*Prior Declaration*]

(*Acta Synodalia* III/2, 530-32)

25 September 1964

MOST REV. KAROL WOJTYŁA
Archbishop of Kraków

Venerable Fathers and Brothers,

1. The declaration "On Religious Freedom," which is connected to the decree *On Ecumenism,* has two distinct ends, and was written with two different audiences in mind. The first end is to promote ecumenical activity, and for this reason the declaration concerns all other Christians. The second end is to uphold the freedom of the human person in civil society today, especially within the state, and for this reason the declaration concerns in a special way all government leaders. In general, our document, although it concerns and illuminates parts of Catholic teaching, is not especially for the Church *ad intra,* but rather for those *ad extra.* As such, it belongs to that dialogue that Pope Paul VI [**531**] spoke of in his first encyclical, addressing both of these groups. Therefore, for the sake of the clarity of the overall document, it is necessary (1) that this orientation *ad extra* be made more clearly apparent, and (2) that those to whom the declaration is directed be more clearly distinguished. Lacking this, the document will not achieve its ends. It also does not seem advantageous to try to achieve such different ends in a single document, especially when it is directed to such different interlocutors. It would be better either to treat these two dimensions of religious freedom in two distinct documents (the second dimension, i.e., the civil one, could find a place in the schema *On the Church in the modern world*), or at least to distinguish them more clearly within one and the same document.

2. When dealing with religious freedom in the first sense, the ecumenical sense, we need to emphasize more strongly the connection that exists between freedom and truth. On the one hand, freedom exists for the sake of truth; on the other hand, without truth, freedom cannot achieve its own perfection. Hence the words of our Lord, which sound so clearly for every man: "The truth will set you free."[1] There is no freedom without truth.

435

Relatio libertatis ad veritatem maximi est momenti in actione oecumenica. Finis enim huius actionis non est alius nisi liberatio totius christianitatis a scissionibus, quae tamen non potest plene adipisci, nisi quando perficietur unio in veritate. Proinde non sufficit, si principium libertatis religiosae erga fratres separatos appareat ut solum principium tolerantiae; tolerantia enim sensum non tantum positivum, sed etiam aliquo modo negativum habet. Cum hoc principio in actione oecumenica obtinetur tantum aliquod « status quo ». Desiderandus autem est progressus in veritate simul cognoscenda, finaliter enim nihil aliud quam veritas liberabit nos a multimodis separationibus.

3. Quando de libertate religiosa in sensu secundo, i. e. civico, fit sermo, tunc agitur utique de principio tolerantiae. *Principium hoc*[2] constituit ius fundamentale hominis religiosi in societate, quod ab omnibus et praesertim ab illis qui res publicas moderantur, debet strictissime observari. Oportet tamen considerare: 1. quod diversae in mundo hodierno exsistunt res publicae et diversimode etiam leges ab eis statutae ad legem divinam, revelatam et naturalem, se habent. Oportet etiam considerare 2. quod atheistae in omni religione nihil aliud videre cupiunt nisi alienationem mentis humanae, a qua hominem illis etiam mediis, quae Statui competunt, liberare volunt. Docent autem, materialismo innixi, quod liberatio haec simul cum progressu scientifico, praesertim autem technico et oeconomico advenire debet. Loquendo proinde de libertate religiosa oportet omni cum exactitudine praesentare personam humanam, quae nequit tantum considerari ut instrumentum in oeconomia et societate, cum sit eius finis. Oportet, ut persona humana appareat [532] in reali sublimitate suae naturae rationalis, religio autem ut culmen istius naturae. Consistit enim in libera mentis humanae ad Deum adhaesione, quae est omnino personalis et conscientiosa, et ex appetitu oritur veritatis. Talis homo, cultor Dei in veritate . . .[3], veritatique in sua relatione ad Deum sincerrime intentus, libertatem sui ipsius in hac relatione expostulat nec cessat, nisi eam obtineat. Et huic relationi nullum brachium saeculare sese interponat, quia religio ipsa sua natura omnia saecularia transcendit. Concilium ergo, sub lumine fidei et sanae rationis, debet profiteri plenam et solidam veritatem de homine, qui in religione nullo modo alienatur, sed perficit semetipsum. Hanc veritatem exspectant tam credentes quam etiam non credentes.

The relationship of freedom to truth is of the utmost importance for ecumenical activity. For the aim of this activity is nothing less than the liberation of the whole of Christianity from schism, which cannot be fully achieved until the union of Christians is made perfect in truth. For this reason it is not enough, in our interactions with other Christians, to propose the principle of religious freedom as simply a principle of tolerance; for tolerance has not only a positive meaning, but also in some ways a negative one. Given this principle alone, only a kind of "status quo" will be achieved in ecumenical activity. But what we must seek is progress in acknowledging the truth together, since in the end nothing but the truth will free us from our manifold separations.

3. When the discussion concerns religious freedom in the second sense, the civil sense, then, to be sure, the principle of tolerance enters into the question. *This principle*[2] constitutes the fundamental right of religious man in society, a right that must be strictly observed by all individuals and especially by government leaders. Nonetheless, we should consider (1) that in today's world there are different states with different laws, which are situated differently with respect to the divine law, both revealed and natural. We should also consider (2) that atheists are inclined to see in all religion nothing more than the alienation of human reason, an alienation from which they intend to liberate man, even by means that properly belong only to the state. Beginning from a materialist standpoint, they advocate that this liberation be achieved together with scientific progress, especially technological and economic progress. When speaking about religious freedom, therefore, we must present the human person with complete accuracy, as someone who cannot be considered only a means in the economy or in society, since the person is their end. The human person must appear [532] in the real grandeur of his rational nature, and religion must appear as this nature's crown and summit. For religion consists in the human mind holding fast to God in freedom, in a way that is wholly personal and conscientious, arising from a desire for the truth. A human being of this sort, a worshipper of God in truth,[3] one who in his relationship with God is sincerely intent on the truth, demands freedom for himself in this relationship, and will not cease to do so until he obtains it. No secular arm may insert itself into this relationship, because religion of its very nature transcends all secular matters. The Council, therefore, in the light of faith and sound reason, should declare the full and genuine truth about man, who in religion is in no way alienated, but rather achieves his own perfection. Not only believers but nonbelievers also await this truth.

Ius ad libertatem religionis exercendae connectitur cum illis iuribus personae, quae respiciunt veritatem—i. e. ius ad eam cognoscendam, ad eam aliis tradendam et cum illis communicandam, unde problema instructionis religiosae in diversis gradibus a schola primaria usque ad seminaria, universitates et academias. Praeterea—ius ad vitam, non solum personalem et privatam, sed etiam communitariam et publicam, in luce veritatis, quam profitemur, instituendam in diversis ambitibus . . . .[4] Omnia ista, quae in particulari multum valent, consectaria videntur illius veritatis, quae in hac re est prima et fundamentalis. Oportet ergo, ut Concilium Vaticanum II veritatem istam in suo dialogo cum mundo hodierno fortiter et efficaciter inculcet. Dixi. Gratias.

In textu scriptu tradito:
   [1] (*Io.* 8, 32).
   [2] quae.
   [3] (*Io.* 4, 23).
   [4] et sub diverso aspectu.

2. Oral Intervention on Schema 2

The right to freedom in the exercise of one's religion is connected with those rights of the person which concern the truth: the right to acknowledge the truth, to hand it on to others and to communicate it to them, which leads to the issue of religious instruction on different levels, from primary school to seminaries, universities, and academies. Moreover, the right to life in the light of the truth that we profess, not only the right to personal and private life, but also to communal and public life, must be established in these different areas . . . .[4] All of these things, which are each important in their own ways, appear to be consequences of that truth which is first and most fundamental in this matter. It is therefore necessary for the Second Vatican Council, in its dialogue with the modern world, to insist strongly and effectively on the truth. Thank you.

In the submitted written text:

   [1] (Jn 8:32).

   [2] which.

   [3] (Jn 4:23).

   [4] under their different aspects.

ANIMADVERSIONES SCRIPTO EXHIBITAE QUOAD SCHEMA DECLARATIONIS DE LIBERTATE RELIGIOSA
[*Textus emendatus*]

(*Acta Synodalia,* Appendix, 606-607)

EXC.MUS P. D. CAROLUS WOJTYŁA
Archiepiscopus Crocoviensis

N. 1, p. 3, lin. 14. Ubi dictum est « Libertas religiosa communiter hodie intellegitur esse verum ius, in dignitate humana fundatum . . . », dicatur potius « . . . *dignitatem personae humanae respiciens* ». *Ratio* autem est, quia dignitas humana non est ipsum fundamentum libertatis religiosae, potius rationabilitas naturae humanae (similiter etiam p. 6 in fine).

N. 3, p. 6, lin. 8. Post verba « quid de hodierno libertatis religiosae regimine sentiat », talis proponitur mutatio in ordine textus: « Prima affirmat et docet, iuxta constantem Ecclesiae doctrinam, unam religionem vetam esse, quam Deus et Pater Domini nostri Iesu Christi per Filium suum incarnatum revelavit atque Ecclesiae custodiendam et omnibus hominibus evangelizandam tradidit; homines vero gravi teneri officio veritatem in re religiosa inquirendi et cognitam sectandi, liberum autem non esse unicuique homini quam quisque maluerit seqni in vita religiosa sententiam. Simul tamen declarat haec Sacra Synodus, hanc catholicam de unica vera religione doctrinam nullatenus adversari libertati humanae; non enim obstat libero personae humanae arbitrio necessitas sequendi veritatem cognitam. Immo, in hoc monstratur vera eiusdem personae dignitas, quae doctrinae evangelicae intime correspondet, simul autem ex ipso rationis fonte depromitur. Cum proinde Ecclesiae incumbat munus . . . » etc. (ut in textu).

N. 3, p. 6, linn. 40-41. Verba « omnesque communitates religiosae » omittantur. *Ratio*: assertio sumi posset eo sensu ut omnes communitates religiosae, verae et falsae, haberent eadem *iura,* quod Ecclesia merito damnavit, ut dictum manet in animadv. generali 2.

N. 3, p. 6, lin. 42. Post ultima huius numeri verba addatur: « Nec con-

3. Written Observations on Schema 3: *Emended Text*

WRITTEN OBSERVATIONS ON THE DRAFT OF THE
DECLARATION ON RELIGIOUS FREEDOM
[*Emended text*]

(Acta Synodalia, Appendix, 606-607)

MOST REV. KAROL WOJTYŁA
Archbishop of Kraków

Article 1, page 3, line 14. Where the text reads, "Religious freedom is commonly understood today to be a true right, having its foundation in human dignity . . ." it should say instead: " . . . *a right that concerns the dignity of the human person.*" The reason is that the foundation of religious freedom is not human dignity itself, but rather the rationality of human nature (likewise on page 6, at the end).

Article 3, page 6, line 8. After the words, "to set forth its judgment on the practice of religious freedom today," I suggest a change such as the following in the order of the text: "First of all, the Council declares and teaches, according to the constant teaching of the Church, that there is one true religion, which God the Father of our Lord Jesus Christ through his incarnate Son revealed and handed over to the Church to preserve and preach to all people; men and women are in fact bound by a serious duty to seek the truth in religious matters, and to follow it once it is known, but no man is free to follow whatever religious opinion he may prefer. At the same time, this sacred Council declares that this Catholic teaching on the one true religion is in no way opposed to human freedom; for the human person's obligation to follow the truth, once it is known, is not opposed to his free will. On the contrary, it is here that the true dignity of the human person is made manifest, which corresponds intimately to the teaching of the Gospel, and is at the same time drawn from the font of reason itself. Since it is therefore incumbent on the Church . . . " etc. (as in the text).

Article 3, page 6, lines 40-41. The words "and all religious communities" should be omitted. The reason is that this statement could be taken to mean that all religious communities, both true and false, have the same *rights*, which the Church has already with good reason condemned, as stated in general observation 2.

Article 3, page 6, line 42. After the final words of this section, the fol-

tradicere laudandae agnitioni verae religionis ex parte Status ». *Ratio*: exposita in animadv. generali 1.

N. 4, p. 7, linn. 8-9 (sub *a*). Loco « Hoc modo violaretur ipsa integritas personae » melius dicatur: « Hoc modo violaretur summum ius personae ipsa graviter offenderetur ».

P. 7, lin. 19 (sub *b*). Loco « libera scil. inquisitione » ponatur « libera scil. decisione », quia ex contextu patet de effectu inquisitionis iam agi.

[607] P. 8 (sub *d*). Res tali modo proponitur ac si quilibet homo habeat conscientiam certam et veram in re religiosa. Multi tamen habent conscientiam dubiam de hac re, multi etiam invincibiliter erroneam. Potestas publica, de qua in capite « Moderatio Civitatis » fit sermo « de interioribus actibus religiosis nequit iudicare ». Unde oritur principium tolerantiae. Tolerantiae tamen principiis non contradicit nostra sollicitudo, ut alii in conscientiae suae secundum verum bonum morale formatione adiuventur. In casu conscientiae erroneae, etiam invincibiliter, respectus personae possibilitatem non excludit persuadendi ei de veritate argumentis eam probantibus. Excluditur tamen pressio physica mediata vel immediata atque coactio physica vel sociologica. Haec omnia principio responsabilitatis erga alios, de quo in n. 5, p. 9, forsitan componenda sunt.

N. 5, p. 9, in capite *b*) « De norma iuridica » nonnulla inveniuntur, *quae atheistis militantibus interpretationem anti-religiosam facilem reddant.* Faciliter ergo omnem actionem anti-religiosam tanquam exercitium iuris societatis civilis « sese protegendi contra abusus qui perpetrantur adducto titulo libertatis religiosae » considerari possunt.

Mutantur ergo verba praedicta. Praesertim autem supprimantur ultima in hoc capite: « . . . sive per perturbationem pacis publicae, sive per violationem moralitatis publicae, sive per laesionem civium aliorum» (linn. 34-35).

Nec haec verba instrumentum persecutionis Ecclesiae vel saltem limitationis eius cultus externi in manibus atheistarum fiant. Ipsi enim saepe proclamant omnem religiosam manifestationem nocivam esse bono communi, et sic decretum de libertate religiosa faciliter intellegere possunt in sensu libertatis impugnandi religionem.

lowing should be added: "Let there be no opposition on the part of the state to the recognition that should be given to the true religion." The reason for this is given in general observation 1.

Article 4, page 7, lines 8-9 (under *a*). In place of "Since this would violate the very integrity of the person," it would be better to say: "Since this would violate the person's greatest right, and gravely offend the person himself."

Page 7, line 19 (under *b*). In place of the words "namely, by means of free inquiry," we should put "namely, through a free decision," since it is clear from the context that it is a question of the result of an inquiry that has already been made.

[607] Page 8 (under *d*). The topic is set forth in such a way that it seems as if every man has a sure and true conscience in religious matters. Many have an uncertain conscience in these matters, however, many even an invincibly erroneous conscience. The public power, as stated in the section "State Governance," "cannot pass judgment on interior religious acts." This constitutes the origin of the principle of tolerance. Our own concern, however—that men and women be supported in forming their conscience in a moral way, in accord with the true good—does not contradict this principle of tolerance. In the case of an erroneous conscience, even one that is invincibly erroneous, respect for the person does not exclude the possibility of persuading him of the truth by means of arguments in support of it. Any remote or immediate physical pressure or physical or social coercion, however, is excluded. All of this needs to be reconciled, perhaps, with the principle of responsibility toward others, as discussed in article 5, page 9.

Article 5, page 9, section *b*), "On the juridical norm." Not a few statements can be found in this section *that could easily afford militant atheists an anti-religious interpretation.* It would be easy for them to consider any action taken against religion as an exercise of civil society's right "to protect itself against abuses that could be committed in the name of religious freedom."

The preceding words should therefore be changed. In particular, the final words of this section should be omitted: " . . . either by disturbing the public peace, by violating public morality, or by offending the civil rights of others" (lines 34-35).

Do not let these words become an instrument in the hands of atheists for persecuting the Church, or at the very least for setting limits to her external worship. For atheists will often claim that every manifestation of religion is harmful to the common good, and in this way they could easily interpret the decree on religious freedom as a license to attack religion.

N. 7, p. 11, linn. 32-33. Supprimantur verba: « . . . praesertim quando de pueris vel rudioribus agitur »; propter eandem rationem ne scil. tanquam argumentum contra opus catechisationis assumere possint.

N. 12, p. 14, linn. 28-31. Argumentum, quod scil. Christus « consulto prodigia illa perpetrare lterum iterumque renuit, quibus homines ad assentiendum quodammodo cogerentur » non valet, quia Christus haec miracula patrare recusavit propter malam voluntatem Iudaeorum, non autem ideo quasi per repetitionem miraculorum libertas eorum religiosa diminui posset.

Article 7, page 11, lines 32-33: The words " . . . especially in regard to children or those less educated" should be removed for the same reason as above, namely, lest they be taken to provide an argument against catechesis.

Article 12, page 14, lines 28-31. The argument here, that Christ "deliberately refused again and again to perform wonders that might force men in some way to assent," does not hold. Christ refused to work these miracles on account of the bad will of the Jews. It is not as though their religious freedom could be diminished through the repetition of miracles.

PATRUM ORATIONES DE LIBERTATE RELIGIOSA
[Textus reemendatus]

(Acta Synodalia IV/2, 11-13)

22 septembris 1965

EXC.MUS P. D. CAROLUS WOJTYŁA
Archiepiscopus Cracoviensis

Venerabiles Fratres,

Loquor iterum nomine episcoporum Poloniae . . . .[1] Animadversiones meae *respiciunt*[2] essentialiter maiorem claritatem totius documenti, cuius momentum certo certius magnum est.

1. . . .[3] *Sub aspectu doctrinali.* In titulo documenti vocamus ipsum declarationem, res tamen ipsa, quae tangitur in illo, ad doctrinam moralem Ecclesiae pertinet. In declaratione conciliari non sufficeret tantum repetere illa, quae in civili legislatione plurium nationum et etiam in declarationibus internationalibus iam de libertate religiosa dicta sunt. Oportet illa supponere, quod in textu schematis utique invenitur. In documento conciliari declaramus habitudinem Ecclesiae ad istam libertatem, quae in Ecclesiae doctrina fundamentum suum habet. Ecclesiae autem doctrina est revelata et simul rationi sanae consona in illis, quae rationi ipsi perspicua sunt. In hoc sensu mundus hodiernus et omnes bonae voluntatis homines declarationem Concilii de libertate religiosa exspectant.

En, doctrina illa, quae in cap. II et III invenitur, eadem est doctrina Ecclesiae; in cap. III modo scripturistico i. e. positivo, in cap. autem II modo magis speculativo praesentata. Melius tamen videretur, rationem et revelationem in istis capitibus non tam separare, prout in titulis videtur. Verum enim est in revelatis, immo in ipso facto Revelationis veram et profundam includi doctrinam libertatis religiosae, cuius etiam doctrinae homines eo magis conscii fiunt, quo humanae personae dignitatem theoretice et practice magis agnoscunt. Proinde quaedam mutatio titulorum mihi *videretur*[4] opportuna, i. e. ut cap. II intituletur « Doctrina de libertate religiosa in dignitate humanae personae fundata », et cap. III « Doctrina de libertate religiosa ex Scriptura et Traditione illustrata » . . . .[5]

4. Oral Intervention on Schema 4: *Re-emended Text*

CONCILIAR SPEECHES ON RELIGIOUS FREEDOM
[*Re-emended Text*]

(Acta Synodalia IV/2, 11-13)

22 September 1965

MOST REV. KAROL WOJTYŁA
Archbishop of Kraków

Venerable Fathers,

I speak once again on behalf of the bishops of Poland . . . .[1] My observations in essence *concern*[2] the need for greater clarity in the document as a whole, a document which is certainly of very great importance.

1. . . .[3] *Regarding the doctrinal aspect.* In its title, our document is called a declaration, but the subject matter which it treats belongs to the moral teaching of the Church. In a conciliar declaration, it would not suffice simply to repeat what has already been said about religious freedom in the civil legislation of many nations, and in international declarations as well. We must presuppose these statements, and they can at any rate be found in the text of our draft. In the conciliar document we are declaring the Church's stance toward such conceptions of freedom, a stance that has its foundation in the teaching of the Church. The teaching of the Church, however, is revealed, while at the same time in harmony with sound reason in those matters that are evident to reason itself. In this sense, the modern world and all men and women of good will await the Council's declaration on religious freedom.

See how that teaching that is found in parts II and III is one and the same teaching of the Church; it is presented in part III in a more scriptural or positive way, and in part II in a more speculative way. Still, it would seem better not to separate reason and revelation so much in these sections, at least as they appear to be from their titles. The truth is that it is in what has been revealed, indeed in the very fact of revelation, that the true and profound teaching on religious freedom is contained. Men and women are becoming more conscious of this teaching, the more they acknowledge the dignity of the human person in theory and in practice. For this reason it *would seem*[4] to me that a change in the titles is called for: part II should be titled "The teaching on religious freedom grounded in the dignity of the

447

2. Declaratio de libertate religiosa seu de iure personae et communitatum ad libertatem in re religiosa, respicit utique potestates civiles, [12] sed primario et directe respicit ipsam personam humanam. Eius significatio ethico-socialis significationem ethico-personalem praesupponit. Secundum hanc significationem constituit etiam fundamentum dialogi inter credentes et *inter credentes et*[6] non credentes. Cum tamen illud ius personae ad libertatem in re religiosa a Concilio declaratur, declarari debet etiam responsabilitas in hac re, i. e. in isto iure utendo. Responsabilitas illa autem maxima est, quia res ipsa i. e. religio—relatio ad Deum—maximi est momenti. Et hoc quidem primo, respectu personae cuiuslibet: maximi est momenti pro persona humana qua tali, quomodo ipsa suo iure nativo ad libertatem in re religiosa usa fuerit, quomodo ad Deum sese habuerit. Secundo autem momentum istud responsabilitatis personalis in ordinem socialem transit. Quilibet homo debet vi nostrae conciliaris declarationis etiam ipse declarare posse non tantum suam libertatem sed etiam suam personalem responsabilitatem in re religiosa. Non tantum dicere « in hac re liber sum », sed etiam « responsabilis sum ». Haec est doctrina in viva traditione Ecclesiae confessorum et martyrum fundata. Responsabilitas est quasi culmen et necessarium complementum libertatis. Ipsa debet sublineari, ut declaratio nostra videatur intime personalistica in sensu christiano, non tamen liberalismo vel indifferentismo obnoxia.

Civiles potestates libertatem religiosam tam personalem quam communitariam strictissime et delicatissime observare debent etiam propter responsabilitatem, quae in hae re cuilibet personae humanae incumbit, i. e. pro ipsius religionis humana etiam profunditate.

Notare adhuc vellem, quod sublineando responsabilitatem libertati correlativam, hoc modo etiam—saltem mediate—significationem et vim obiectivam religionis exprimamus. Ius quidem subiectivum est, i. e. ius subiecti scil. personae, immo est ius ad libertatem; sed cum libertati adnexa sit tam magna responsabilitas, et iuri tam gravis obligatio interna, tunc—etsi in perspectiva subiecti, quae nostro schemati aliqualiter connaturalis videtur—optime tamen apparet valor obiectivus religionis, *qui ultimatim ex veritate emanat.*[7]

human person," and part III, "The teaching on religious freedom illuminated by Scripture and Tradition" . . . .[5]

2. The declaration on religious freedom, or on the right of the person and of communities to freedom in religious matters, is concerned of course with civil powers, [12] but it primarily and directly concerns the human person himself. Its social-ethical significance presupposes its personal-ethical significance. In accord with the latter, the declaration also constitutes a foundation for dialogue between believers, *as well as between believers*[6] and non-believers. Still, when the Council declares the person's right to freedom in religious matters, it should also declare the need for responsibility in this matter, that is, in the use of this right. This responsibility, in fact, is paramount, because the matter itself, that is, religion—man's relationship to God—is of the utmost importance. This is the case first for each and every person: it is of the utmost importance for the human person as such how he uses his right to freedom in religious matters, or how he stands before God. Secondly, however, the importance of personal responsibility enters into the social order. By virtue of our conciliar declaration, each and every person should be able to declare for himself not only his freedom in religious matters, but also his personal responsibility. He should be able to say not only "I am free in this matter," but also "I am responsible." This teaching has its foundation in the Church's living tradition of confessors and martyrs. Responsibility is, as it were, the culmination and the necessary complement of freedom. This should be stressed, so that our Declaration may be seen to be deeply personalistic in a Christian sense, yet not subject to liberalism or indifferentism.

Civil powers should strictly and meticulously observe the religious freedom of persons and communities also for this reason, that is, on account of the responsibility incumbent upon each and every human person in this matter, or, in other words, out of respect for the profound significance that religion has for man.

I would like to point out besides that by emphasizing the responsibility that corresponds to freedom, we might also express in this way, at least indirectly, the significance and objective force of religion. The right itself is indeed subjective—that is, the right of a subject, a person—and it is a right to freedom; but since with freedom comes great responsibility, and with a right a serious obligation, then—even within the perspective of the subject, which seems in some ways to be characteristic of our schema—there nevertheless appears most clearly the objective value of religion, *which ultimately comes from the truth itself.*[7]

3. Consequenter *alia*[8] vellem adhuc dicere de limitibus libertatis religiosae determinandis. Ad hanc rem iterum invocandum videtur principium legis moralis observandae, quod quidem in pag. 9, nn. 15 ss. innuitur tamquam prima norma moderans *usum*[9] libertatis religiosae in societate humana, sed non videtur constituere fundamentum ipsius « declarationis » in pag. 5 et 6; immo limites usus libertatis religiosae determinantur « secundum normas iuridicas, quas necessitates ordinis publici postulant » . . .[10] ergo secundum legem positivam tantum *(pag. 9)*.[11] Ad hanc difficilem quaestionem clarificandam oportet dicere, quod ius [13] ad libertatem religiosam tamquam naturale (i.e. in lege naturae ergo divina fundatum) non recipit limites nisi ex parte eiusdem legis moralis. Lex humana positiva limites hic imponere nequit, nisi secundum legem moralem. A. v.: tamquam abusus libertatis religiosae potest considerari tantum actus moraliter malus, i. e. contra legem moralem. Proinde propono, ut in textu « declarationis », pag. 6, lin. 7 in fine, ubi legitur « . . . ut in re religiosa neque aliquis cogatur ad agendum contra suam conscientiam, neque impediatur, quominus iuxta suam conscientiam privatim et publice agat intra debitos limites », loco verborum « intra debitos limites » ponatur: « nisi tamen actus ex alio capite iam a lege morali vel imperati vel prohibiti sunt » . . . .[12]

Secundum idem principium legis moralis observandae revidenda sunt praesertim illa quae pag. 9, linn. 27 ss. de norma iuridica eiusque vi limitandi usum libertatis religiosae, quae adhuc multis in locis non videntur opportuna, immo possunt abusibus contra veram libertatem religiosam occasionem praebere. Dixi. Gracias.

In textu scripto tradito:
  [1] iterum, quia iam exc.mus arch. Posnaniensis hoc nomine locutus est. Schema declarationis *de libertate religiosa* in suo textu praesenti magis nobis placet quam in praecedenti propter multas correctiones quae opportuniorem illum reddiderunt.
  [2] in quibus aliae adhuc correctiones postulabuntur, respiciunt tamen.
  [3] Primo autem.
  [4] videtur.
  [5] Proponerem etiam talem mutationem textus introductorii, ut pag. 1 linn. 8-14 sic sonaret: « quapropter Ecclesia, de concredito sibi thesauro doctrinae divinitus revelatae nova simul et vetera proferens, discernere intendit quantum haec religiosae libertatis postulatio veritati et iustitiae conformis sit ».
  [6] deest.

3. Consequently, I would like to say *a few more things*[8] on determining the limits of religious freedom. In this matter it seems necessary to appeal once again to the principle that the moral law must be observed, which in fact is referred to on page 9, articles 15 ff., as the first norm that governs the *use*[9] of religious freedom in human society, but which does not seem to constitute the foundation for the "declaration" itself, on pages 5 and 6; indeed, limits to the use of religious freedom are said to be determined "according to the juridical norms that are required by the needs of public order" . . . ,[10] and therefore only according to positive law *(page 9).*[11] To shed some light on this difficult question, it must be said that the right [13] to religious freedom, as a natural right (that is, a right having its foundation in natural, and therefore in divine, law) admits of no limitations except on the part of this same moral law. Positive human law cannot impose any limits on this right, except in accord with the moral law. In other words: only a morally evil act, one that is contrary to the moral law, can be considered an abuse of religious freedom. Thus I propose that in the text of the "declaration," on page 6, line 7, at the end, where it reads " . . . so that no one is forced to act against his conscience in religious matters, or prevented from acting according to his conscience, in private or in public, within due limits" in place of the words "within due limits," there be put: "unless his actions are commanded or prohibited already by another source, the moral law" . . . .[12]

In keeping with this same principle, that the moral law must be observed, it is particularly necessary to revise the statements found on page 9, lines 27 ff., on the juridical norm and its power to limit the use of religious freedom, which in many places still do not seem adequate, and which could in fact provide occasion for abuses against true religious freedom. Thank you.

In the submitted written text:
    [1] also on behalf of the Most Rev. Archbishop of Poznań. We find this draft of the declaration *On religious freedom* more acceptable in its present form than the preceding text, due to the many corrections that have made it more suitable.
    [2] among which other corrections are still necessary, nevertheless are concerned.
    [3] The first.
    [4] seems.
    [5] I would also propose a change like this in the introductory text. E.g., page 1, lines 8-14 would read: « for which reason the Church, bringing forth from the treasury of divinely revealed teachings entrusted to her things new and at the same time old, intends to discern to what degree this demand for religious freedom is in conformity with truth and justice."
    [6] omitted.

[7] deest.

[8] aliqua.

[9] usus.

[10] (pag. 9, linn. 32 ss.).

[11] deest.

[12] (sicut imperata est v. g. restitutio obligatoria, et prohibita prostitutio vel occisio sub specie actionis religiosae).

[7] omitted.

[8] some other things.

[9] uses.

[10] (page 9, lines 32 ff.).

[11] omitted.

[12] (as, e.g., obligatory reparation is commanded, and prostitution or murder in the name of religion is prohibited).

ANIMADVERSIONES SCRIPTO EXHIBITAE QUOAD SCHEMA DECLARATIONIS DE LIBERTATE RELIGIOSA
[*Textus reemendatus*]

(Acta Synodalia IV/2, 292-93)

EXC.MUS P. D. CAROLUS WOJTYŁA
Archiepiscopus Cracoviensis

Schema declarationis *de libertate religiosa* placet in suo textu praesenti magis quam in praecedenti; multae enim in eo expressiones inoppor-
tunae feliciter correctae sunt vel evanuerunt. *Sub aspectu doctrinali* tamen
quaedam sunt animadvertenda, quae ad claritatem documenti alicuius videntur esse momenti.

1. Agitur *primo de limitibus libertatis religiosae determinandis.* Etsi in
pag. 9 lin. 15 ss. innuitur, quod *principium legis moralis observandae* est prima
norma moderans usus eiusdem libertatis in societate humana, hoc tamen
principium non invocatur ab initio et non pervadit totum textum. Deficit
praesertim in ipsa « declaratione » pag. 5 et 6, immo limites usus libertatis
religiosae determinantur « secundum normas iuridicas, quas necessitates
ordinis publici postulant » (pag. 9, linn. 32 ss.), ergo secundum legem positivam tantum. *Ius tamen ad libertatem religiosam tamquam naturale et di-*
vinum non recipit limites, nisi ex parte legis moralis, quae etiam naturalis et
divina est. Lex humana positiva in tantum potest limites istas imponere in
quantum ipsa vim legis moralis naturalis et divinae in se habet.

Proinde *propono,* ut in textu declarationis, pag. 6 lin. 7, in fine, ubi legitur « . . . ut in re religiosa neque aliquis cogatur ad agendum contra suam
conscientiam, [293] neque impediator, quominus iuxta suam conscientiam
privatim et publice agat intra debitos limites » loco verborum « intra debitos
limites » ponatur: « nisi tamen actus ex alio capite iam a lege morali vel imperati vel prohibiti sint » (exemplum actus imperati—restitutio obligatoria;
exemplum actus prohibiti—occisio innocentium ad finem religiosum vel
prostitutio sub specie actionis religiosae). In tali casu abusus libertatis religiosae potest esse tantum actus moraliter malus i. e. contra legem moralem.
Praesertim autem iste abusus libertatis religiosae pluribus in locis schematis
aequivocationibus obnoxius est.

5. Written Observations on Schema 4: *Re-emended Text*

WRITTEN OBSERVATIONS ON THE DRAFT OF THE
DECLARATION ON RELIGIOUS FREEDOM
[*Re-emended Text*]

(*Acta Synodalia* IV/2, 292-93)

MOST REV. KAROL WOJTYŁA
Archbishop of Kraków

The draft of the declaration *On religious freedom* is more acceptable in its present form than in the preceding text; many of the more inopportune expressions have happily been corrected or omitted. *Regarding its doctrinal aspect*, however, there are still certain matters that must be attended to, which seem to be of some importance for the overall clarity of the document.

1. *First, on determining the limits of religious freedom.* Although it is said on page 9, lines 15 ff., that *the principle that the moral law must be observed* is the first norm that governs the use of religious freedom in human society, this principle is nonetheless not invoked from the beginning, and is not present throughout the text. It is especially lacking in the "declaration" itself on pages 5 and 6; indeed, limits to the use of religious freedom are said to be determined "according to the juridical norms that are required by the needs of public order" (page 9, lines 32 ff.), and therefore only according to positive law. *Yet the right to religious freedom, as a right at once natural and divine, admits of no limitations except on the part of the moral law, which is itself also natural and divine.* Positive human law can only impose such limits insofar as it contains within itself the force of natural and divine moral law.

Thus I propose that in the text of the declaration, on page 6, line 7, at the end, where it reads, "so that no one is forced to act against his conscience in religious matters, [**293**] or prevented from acting according to his conscience, in private or in public, within due limits," in place of the words "within due limits," there be put: "unless his actions are commanded or prohibited already by another source, the moral law" (an example of a commanded action is obligatory reparation; an example of a prohibited action is the murder of innocents for religious purposes, or prostitution in the name of religion). In this case, the abuse of religious freedom can only be a morally evil act, that is, one that is contrary to the moral law. There are many ambiguous passages in the schema, however, that could give rise to such an abuse of religious freedom.

455

2. Proponendo hanc mutationem textus per invocationem principii legis moralis observandae, proponere auderem ulterius, ut ipse conceptus libertatis religiosae in documento conciliari *praesentaretur substantialiter tamquam doctrina revelata, quae sanae rationi omnino consonat, ab ipsa tamen non distinguitur*, prout in textu videmus. Concilli enim est docere veritatem divinam non tantum humanam. Si veritas haec rationi humanae etiam apparet, sicut in contemporaneo statu quaestionis de libertate religiosa videmus, tanto melius. Mundus tamen doctrinam Ecclesiae i. e. doctrinam revelatam de hac re expectat, non tantum repetitionem eorum, quorum ipse capax est, prout bene scimus. Et hoc etiam propter dialogum cum illis, qui de eadem re i. e. de libertate religiosa sub luce rationis tantum quaedam statuunt, magni videtur esse momenti.

De cetero doctrina, quam in textu sub titulo II Doctrina de libertate religiosa ex ratione desumpta et III Doctrina libertatis religiosae sub luce Revelationis, *eadem est doctrina Ecclesiae*—sub titulo III modo magis scripturistico, sub titulo autem II modo magis speculativo praesentata. Melius ergo videtur in titulis istis rationem et Revelationem non tam distinguere, hoc enim methodo scholastica nimis imbuitur. Verum tamen est in Revelatione vera et profunda inveniri doctrina libertatis religiosae, cuius de cetero homines eo magis conscii fiunt, quo magis personae humanae dignitatem agnoscunt. Melius forsitan esset, ut titulus II sonaret sic « Doctrina de libertate religiosa ex dignitate personae humanae desumpta », quam postea doctrinam ex fontibus S. Scripturae illuminaremus. Proponerem etiam—in eadem linea—ut pag. 1 linn. 8-14 textus sic immutetur: « Quapropter Ecclesia, de concredito sibi thesauro doctrinae divinitus revelatae nova simul et vetera proferens, discernere intendit, quantum hac religiosae libertatis postulatio veritati iustitiaeque conformis sit ».

Mutationibus talibus indoles documenti mutabitur in hoc sensu, quod Concilium doctrinam proferetur revelatam *de re morali et quidem fundamentali, qualis est libertas religiosa*, utendo ad hunc finem argumentis etiam ex ratione desumptis, cum obiectum talia omnino admittit.

2. I propose a change of this sort in the text, then, appealing to the principle that the moral law must be observed. I would venture to make the further proposal that the very concept of religious freedom found in the conciliar document *be presented in essence as a revealed teaching, one that is wholly consonant with sound reason, and yet not separated from it,* as we find in the text. The Council should teach the truth of God, not only the truth of man. If the former is evident to human reason as well, as we see in the contemporary state of affairs in regard to religious freedom, so much the better. Still, the world awaits the Church's teaching on this matter, the revealed teaching, and not simply the repetition of what it is itself already capable of, as we well know. This seems to be of great importance also in matters of dialogue with those who are making decisions about the issue of religious freedom in the light of reason alone.

As for the rest: that teaching which in the text falls under part II, "The teaching on religious freedom derived from reason," and part III, "The teaching on religious freedom in the light of revelation," *is one and the same teaching of the Church*—in part III it is presented in a more scriptural way, in part II in a more speculative way. It seems better, therefore, not to separate reason and revelation so much in the titles of these sections. This kind of separation remains too steeped in scholastic methods. The truth is that it is in revelation that the true and profound teaching on religious freedom is contained. Men and women are becoming more conscious of this teaching, the more they acknowledge the dignity of the human person. It would perhaps be better for the title of part II to read "The teaching on religious freedom derived from the dignity of the human person," and afterwards to illuminate this same teaching from the sources of sacred scripture. I would also propose, along the same lines, that on page 1, lines 8-14, the text be changed as follows: "for which reason the Church, bringing forth from the treasury of divinely revealed teachings entrusted to her things new and at the same time old, intends to discern to what degree this demand for religious freedom is in conformity with truth and justice."

By means of such changes, the overall character of the document will be improved in this sense, that the Council will produce a revealed teaching *on the moral and indeed fundamental issue of religious freedom,* using to this end arguments derived from reason also, since the subject matter fully admits them.

The Conciliar Intervention of Alfred Ancel

Translated by Michael Camacho

PATRUM ORATIONES DE LIBERTATE RELIGIOSA
[*Textus reemendatus*]

(*Acta Synodalia* IV/2, 16-18)

22 septembris 1965

EXC.MUS P. D. ALFREDUS ANCEL
Episcopus tit. Myrinensis, aux. Lugdunensis

Venerabiles Patres et Fratres carissimi,

Aliquid brevissime, post votationem hesternam, vellem afferre. Nomine autem plus quam centum episcoporum Galliae et quorumdam aliorum loquor.

[17] Pluries enim postulatum est ut *fundamentum ontologicum* libertatis religiosae afferretur. Aliquibus enim videtur insufficiens argumentum ex sola dignitate personae humanae *proveniens.*[1]

Insuper nondum ostensum est quis nexus exsistat inter obligationem quaerendi veritatem et ipsam libertatem religiosam. Sane pluries dictum est obligationem inesse homini quaerendi veritatem; pariter dictum est nullam esse obiectionem ex parte libertatis religiosae contra hanc obligationem; sed nunquam, ni fallor, positive manifestatus est nexus inter utramque.

Unde vellem paucis verbis afferre hoc fundamentum ontologicum et, eo ipso, ostendere nexum necessarium qui exsistit inter obligationem quaerendi veritatem obiectivam et ipsam libertatem religiosam.

Ecce autem[2] propositio mea: fundamentum ontologicum libertatis religiosae, qualis in nostro textu proponitur, est ipsa obligatio quaerendi veritatem.

Etenim omnis homo, quia homo est, i. e. ratione et voluntate *libera*[3] praeditus, tenetur quaerere veritatem obiectivam, eique adhaerere et totam vitam suam secundum exigentias veritatis ordinare.

In hoc principio consentire nobiscum possunt omnes qui veritatem et iustitiam toto corde quaerunt, etiamsi credentes non sint.

Ex alia parte, quia non in aliqua dispositione subiectiva, sed in ipsa natura hominis fundatur hoc principium, valore gaudet stricte universali.

Oral Intervention on Schema 4: *Re-emended Text*

CONCILIAR SPEECHES ON RELIGIOUS FREEDOM
[*Re-emended Text*]

(*Acta Synodalia* IV/2, 16-18)

22 September 1965

MOST REV. ALFRED ANCEL
Titular Bishop of Myrina, Auxiliary Bishop of Lyon

Venerable Fathers and dearest Brothers,

I would like to make a very brief proposal, following yesterday's vote. I speak on behalf of more than a hundred bishops of France, and for certain others as well.

[17] Several times the request has been made that the *ontological foundation* of religious freedom be set forth. For the argument *stemming*[1] simply from the dignity of the human person seems to some to be insufficient.

Moreover, the connection that exists between the obligation to seek the truth and religious freedom itself has not yet been made clear. To be sure, we have often heard that man has an obligation to seek the truth; likewise, we have heard that religious freedom presents no obstacle to this obligation; but at no time, unless I am mistaken, has the positive connection between these two been made clear.

Thus, in a few words, I would like to indicate what this ontological foundation is, and in this way to show the necessary connection that exists between the obligation to seek the objective truth and religious freedom itself.

My proposition *is as follows:*[2] the obligation to seek the truth is itself the ontological foundation of religious freedom, as set forth in our text.

For in fact every man, because he is a human being, endowed with reason and *free*[3] will, is bound to seek the objective truth, and to hold fast to it and order his whole life according to its demands.

All those who seek truth and justice with their whole heart, even non-believers, can agree with us on this principle.

On the other hand, because it does not have its foundation in any subjective disposition, but in the very nature of man, this principle has a strictly universal validity.

Saepissime tandem et sub diversis formis, hoc principium a Scriptura explicite affirmatur.

Attamen ut homo huic obligationi satisfacere possit, eo modo quo Deus vult, i. e. modo consentaneo suae naturae, necessarium est ut non solum libertate psychologica fruatur, sed etiam ut immunitate ab omni coercitione gaudeat. Ideoque non solum non datur oppositio inter libertatem religiosam et ipsam obligationem quaerendi veritatem, sed libertas religiosa in hac ipsa obligatione fundatur et obligatio quaerendi veritatem postulat libertatem religiosam.

Notate tandem, venerabiles Patres, plerosque homines sive christianos sive non christianos unice cognituros esse de nostro textu quae in n. 2 enuntiantur. Hic numerus enim nucleum declarationis constituit.

Vellem ergo ut in isto numero ponatur hoc fundamentum ontologicum atque clare affirmetur connexio quae exsistit inter libertatem religiosam et obligationem quaerendi veritatem.

Ex *hoc autem*[4] firmabitur opinio eorum qui libertatem religiosam libenter admittebant, et maior securitas afferetur iis qui, in hoc tempore crescentis indifferentismi et subiectivismi, aliquem timorem, et non sine ratione, patiebantur.

[18] Modum autem quo haec in n. 2 inseri poterunt, exc.mo secretario tradidi. Dixi.

In textu scripto tradito:
[1] desumptum.
[2] En igitur.
[3] deest.
[4] his autem quae dixi.

Ultimately, this principle is explicitly affirmed by Scripture in countless ways and in different forms.

Nevertheless, in order for man to be able to satisfy this obligation in the way God wills, that is, in a way consistent with his nature, he must enjoy not only psychological freedom but also immunity from all coercion. Not only is there no opposition between religious freedom and the obligation to seek the truth, therefore, but in fact religious freedom has its foundation in this obligation itself, and the obligation to seek the truth in turn requires religious freedom.

Finally, venerable Fathers, please note that many people, whether Christians or not, will look especially to what is said in article 2 of our text. Indeed, this article constitutes the very heart of the declaration.

I would therefore like for this ontological foundation to find a place in this article, and for the connection that exists between religious freedom and the obligation to seek the truth to be clearly stated there.

In this way, moreover,[4] the opinion of those who have been more open to religious freedom will be supported, while greater assurance will also be given to those who have been apprehensive in this regard, and not without reason, in this time of growing indifferentism and subjectivism.

[18] I have handed on to the secretary a suggestion for how these items can be inserted into article 2.

In the submitted written text:
  [1] derived.
  [2] Therefore, here is.
  [3] omitted.
  [4] From what I have said, moreover.

Select Bibliography

Alberigo, Giuseppe, Jean-Pierre Jossua, and Joseph A. Komonchak, eds. *The Reception of Vatican II.* Translated by Matthew J. O'Connell. Washington, DC: Catholic University of America Press, 1987.

Alberigo, Giuseppe, and Joseph A. Komonchak, eds. *History of Vatican II.* 5 vols. Maryknoll, NY: Orbis, 1995-2006.

André-Vincent, Philippe. *La liberté religieuse: Droit fondamental.* Paris: Téqui, 1976.

Araujo, Robert J. "John Paul II and the Legacy of *Dignitatis Humanae.*" *Theological Studies* 64, no. 3 (2003): 667-68.

Aubert, Roger. "La liberté religieuse du Syllabus de 1864 à nos jours." In *Essais sur la liberté religieuse,* 13-25. Paris: Fayard, 1965.

Baum, Gregory. "Declaration on Religious Freedom — Development of Its Doctrinal Basis." *The Ecumenist* 4 (1966): 121-26.

Baxter, Michael. "John Courtney Murray." In *Blackwell Companion to Political Theology,* edited by Peter Scott and William Cavanaugh, 150-64. Oxford: Blackwell, 2004.

Bevans, Stephen B., and Jeffrey Gros. *Evangelization and Religious Freedom: Ad gentes, Dignitatis humanae.* New York: Paulist Press, 2008.

Bradley, Gerard V. "Beyond Murray's Articles of Peace and of Faith." In *John Courtney Murray and the American Civil Conversation,* edited by Kenneth L. Grasso and Robert P. Hunt, 181-204. Grand Rapids: Eerdmans, 1992.

―――. "Church Autonomy in the Constitutional Order: The End of Church and State?" *Louisiana Law Review* 49 (1989): 1057-87.

―――. "Dogmatomachy — A 'Privatization' Theory of the Religion Clause Cases." *St. Louis Law Journal* 30 (1986): 275-330.

Broglie, Guy de. *Problèmes chrétiens sur la liberté religieuse.* Paris: Beauchesne, 1965.

For a helpful further bibliography, especially on the writings of John Paul II and John Courtney Murray, see Hermínio Rico, *John Paul II and the Legacy of Dignitatis Humanae* (Washington, DC: Georgetown University Press, 2002), 246-61.

Burghardt, Walter J., ed. *Religious Freedom, 1965 and 1975: A Symposium on a Historic Document.* New York: Paulist Press, 1976.

Burtchaell, James T. "Religious Freedom." In *Modern Catholicism: Vatican II and After,* edited by Adrian Hastings. New York: Oxford University Press, 1991.

Canavan, Francis J. *"Dignitatis Humanae,* the Catholic Conception of the State, and Public Morality." In *Catholicism and Religious Freedom: Contemporary Reflections on Vatican II's Declaration on Religious Liberty,* edited by Kenneth L. Grasso and Robert P. Hunt, 69-85. Lanham: Rowman & Littlefield, 2006.

———. "Murray on Vatican II's *Declaration on Religious Freedom." Communio: International Catholic Review* 9, no. 4 (1982): 404-5.

———. "Religious Freedom: John Courtney Murray and Vatican II." In *John Courtney Murray and the American Civil Conversation,* edited by Kenneth L. Grasso and Robert P. Hunt, 167-80. Grand Rapids: Eerdmans, 1992.

Carbone, Vincenzo. "Il ruolo di Paolo VI nell'evoluzione e nella redazione della dichiarazione *Dignitatis humanae."* In *Paolo VI e il rapporto Chiesa-mondo al Concilio,* 126-73. Brescia: Istituto Paolo VI, 1991.

Carillo de Albornoz, A. F. "The Ecumenical and World Significance of the Vatican Declaration on Religious Liberty." *The Ecumenical Review* 18, no. 1 (1966): 58-84.

———. *Le Concile et la liberté religieuse.* Paris: Éditions du Cerf, 1967.

———. "Religious Liberty and the Second Vatican Council." *The Ecumenical Review* 16, no. 4 (1964): 395-405.

Castelli, Enrico, H. Gouhier, S. Cotta, and H. Panikkar. *L'Herméneutique de la liberté religieuse.* Paris: Montaigne, 1968.

Chinnici, Joseph P. *"Dignitatis humanae personae:* Surveying the Landscape for Its Reception in the United States." *U.S. Catholic Historian* 24, no. 1 (2006): 63-82.

Clifford, Catherine E. "The Ecumenical Context of *Dignitatis humanae:* Forty Years after Vatican II." *Science et Esprit* 59, no. 2-3 (2007): 387-403.

Coste, René. *L'Église et les droits de l'homme.* Tournai: Desclée, 1980.

———. *Théologie de la liberté religieuse: Liberté de conscience, liberté de religion.* Gembloux: Duculot, 1969.

Crawford, David S. "The Architecture of Freedom: John Paul II and John Courtney Murray on Religious Freedom." In *Catholicism and Religious Freedom: Contemporary Reflections on Vatican II's Declaration on Religious Liberty,* edited by Kenneth L. Grasso and Robert P. Hunt, 195-221. Lanham, MD: Rowman & Littlefield, 2006.

Craycraft, Kenneth R., Jr. *The American Myth of Religious Freedom.* Dallas: Spence, 1999.

———. "Religion as Moral Duty and Civil Right: *Dignitatis humanae* on Religious Liberty." In *Catholicism, Liberalism, and Communitarianism,* edited by Kenneth L. Grasso, Gerard V. Bradley, and Robert P. Hunt. Lanham, MD: Rowman & Littlefield, 1995.

Crosby, John F. "On Proposing the Truth and Not Imposing It: John Paul II's Personalism and the Teaching of *Dignitatis Humanae."* In *Catholicism and Religious Freedom: Contemporary Reflections on Vatican II's Declaration on Religious Liberty,* edited by Kenneth L. Grasso and Robert P. Hunt, 135-59. Lanham: Rowman & Littlefield, 2006.

Daniélou, Jean. "Religious Liberty." *Journal of Ecumenical Studies* 2 (1965): 265-71.

Davies, Michael. *The Second Vatican Council and Religious Liberty.* Long Prairie, MN: Neumann Press, 1992.

D'Elia, Donald J., and Stephen M. Krason, eds. *We Hold These Truths and More: Further Catholic Reflections on the American Proposition; The Thought of Fr. John Courtney Murray, S.J. and Its Relevance Today.* Steubenville, OH: Franciscan University Press, 1993.

Doak, Mary. "Resisting the Eclipse of *Dignitatis Humanae.*" *Horizons* 33, no. 1 (2006): 33-53.

Dulles, Avery. "*Dignitatis humanae* and the Development of Catholic Doctrine." In *Catholicism and Religious Freedom: Contemporary Reflections on Vatican II's Declaration on Religious Liberty,* edited by Kenneth L. Grasso and Robert P. Hunt, 43-67. Lanham, MD: Rowman & Littlefield, 2006.

Dupont, Dom Philippe. "La liberté religieuse." *Communio: Revue Catholique Internationale* 13, no. 6 (1988): 75-99.

Essig, Isabelle. "Du primat de la vérité à celui de la dignité de la personne: Le déplacement opéré par la déclaration *Dignitatis humanae.*" In *Imaginer la théologie catholique, permanence et transformations de la foi en attendant Jésus-Christ,* edited by Jeremy Driscol, 437-63. Rome: Centro Studi S. Anselmo, 2000.

Flannery, Kevin. "*Dignitatis Humanae* and the Development of Doctrine." *Catholic Dossier* 6, no. 2 (2000): 31-35.

Fogarty, Gerald. "*Dignitatis humanae personae* and the American Experience." In *Vatican II and Its Legacy,* edited by Mathijs Lamberigts and Leo Kenis, 285. Leuven: Leuven University Press, 2002.

Fuchs, Josef. "Christliche Freiheit, Freiheit der Kirche, Religionsfreiheit." In *Acta Congressus Internationalis de Theologia Concilii Vaticani II,* edited by Adolfus Schönmetzer, 574-84. Vatican: Typis Polyglottis Vaticanis, 1968.

———. "De libertate religiosa et de libertate religionis Christi." *Gregorianum* 47 (1966): 41-52.

George, Robert P., and William L. Saunders. "*Dignitatis Humanae:* The Freedom of the Church and the Responsibility of the State." In *Catholicism and Religious Freedom: Contemporary Reflections on Vatican II's Declaration on Religious Liberty,* edited by Kenneth L. Grasso and Robert P. Hunt, 1-17. Lanham: Rowman & Littlefield, 2006.

Gonnet, Dominique. *La liberté religieuse à Vatican II: La contribution de John Courtney Murray, S.J.* Paris: Éditions du Cerf, 1994.

Gould, William J., Jr. "The Challenge of Liberal Political Culture in the Thought of John Courtney Murray." *Communio: International Catholic Review* 19, no. 1 (1992): 113-44.

Grasso, Kenneth L. "An Unfinished Argument: *Dignitatis Humanae,* John Courtney Murray and the Catholic Theory of the State." In *Catholicism and Religious Freedom: Contemporary Reflections on Vatican II's Declaration on Religious Liberty,* edited by Kenneth L. Grasso and Robert P. Hunt, 161-93. Lanham: Rowman & Littlefield, 2006.

Grasso, Kenneth L., and Robert P. Hunt, eds. *Catholicism and Religious Freedom: Contem-*

porary Reflections on Vatican II's Declaration on Religious Liberty. Lanham, MD: Rowman & Littlefield, 2006.

Grootaers, Jan. "Paul VI et la déclaration conciliaire sur la liberté religieuse *Dignitatis humanae.*" In *Paolo VI e il rapporto Chiesa-mondo al Concilio,* 85-125. Brescia: Istituto Paolo VI, 1991.

Hamer, Jérôme. "Histoire du texte de la Déclaration." In *Vatican II: La liberté religieuse; Déclaration "Dignitatis humanae personae,"* edited by Jérôme Hamer and Yves Congar, 53-110. Paris: Éditions du Cerf, 1967.

Harrison, Brian W. "John Courtney Murray: A Reliable Interpreter of Dignitatis Humanae?" *In We Hold These Truths and More: Further Reflections on the American Proposition,* edited by Donald J. D'Elia and Stephen M. Krason, 134-65. Steubenville, OH: Franciscan University Press, 1993.

———. *Religious Liberty and Contraception.* Melbourne: John XXIII Fellowship, 1988.

Hehir, J. Bryan. "*Dignitatis humanae* in the Pontificate of John Paul II." In *Religious Liberty: Paul VI and Dignitatis humanae,* edited by John T. Ford, 169-83. Brescia: Istituto Paolo VI, 1995.

———. "Vatican II and the Signs of the Times: Catholic Teaching on Church, State, and Society." In *Religion and Politics in the American Milieu,* edited by Leslie Griffin. Notre Dame: Review of Politics, University of Notre Dame, n.d.

Hittinger, Russell. "The Declaration on Religious Liberty, *Dignitatis humanae.*" In *Vatican II: Renewal within Tradition,* edited by Matthew L. Lamb and Matthew Levering, 359-82. New York: Oxford University Press, 2008.

———. "*Dignitatis humanae,* Religious Liberty, and Ecclesiastical Self-Government." In *The First Grace: Rediscovering the Natural Law in a Post-Christian World,* 215-41. Wilmington, DE: ISI Books, 2003.

Hollenbach, David. "The Church's Social Mission in a Pluralistic Society." In *Vatican II: The Unfinished Agenda; A Look to the Future,* edited by Lucien Richard, with Daniel T. Harrington and John W. O'Malley, 113-28. New York: Paulist Press, 1987.

Hooper, J. Leon, and Todd David Whitmore, eds. *John Courtney Murray and the Growth of Tradition.* Kansas City, MO: Sheed & Ward, 1996.

Hunt, Robert P. "Two Concepts of Religious Liberty: *Dignitatis Humanae* v. The U.S. Supreme Court." In *Catholicism and Religious Freedom: Contemporary Reflections on Vatican II's Declaration on Religious Liberty,* edited by Kenneth L. Grasso and Robert P. Hunt, 19-41. Lanham: Rowman & Littlefield, 2006.

Jarczyk, Gwendoline. *La Liberté religieuse: Vingt ans après le Concile.* Paris: Desclée, 1984.

Janssens, Louis. *Freedom of Conscience and Religious Freedom.* Staten Island, NY: Alba House, 1966.

Kasper, Walter. *The Christian Understanding of Freedom and the History of Freedom in the Modern Era.* Milwaukee: Marquette University Press, 1988.

Komonchak, Joseph A. "The American Contribution to *Dignitatis humanae:* The Role of John Courtney Murray, S.J." *U.S. Catholic Historian* 24, no. 1 (2006): 1-20.

———. "The Silencing of John Courtney Murray." In *Cristianesimo nella storia: Saggi in onore di Giuseppe Alberigo,* edited by A. Melloni, D. Menozzi, G. Ruggieri, M. Toschi, 657-702. Bologna: Il Mulino, 1996.

————. "U.S. Bishops' Suggestions for Vatican II." *Cristianesimo nella Storia* 15 (1994): 313-71.

————. "Vatican II and the Encounter between Catholicism and Liberalism." In *Catholicism and Liberalism: Contributions to American Public Philosophy,* edited by R. B. Douglass and D. Hollenbach, 76-99. Cambridge: Cambridge University Press, 1994.

————. "What They Said Before the Council: How the U.S. Bishops Envisioned Vatican II." *Commonweal* 117 (1990): 714-16.

König, Franz Cardinal. "The Right to Religious Freedom: The Significance of *Dignitatis Humanae.*" In *Vatican II Revisited by Those Who Were There,* 283-90. London: Geoffrey Chapman, 1986.

Kupczak, Jaroslaw. "John Paul II and the Legacy of *Dignitatis Humanae.*" *Thomist* 67, no. 4 (2003): 662-65.

Lecler, Joseph. "La déclaration conciliaire sur la liberté religieuse." *Études* 324 (1966): 516-30.

————. "Liberté de conscience: Origines et sens divers de l'expression." *Recherches de Science Religieuse* 54, no. 3 (1966): 370-406.

Lécrivain, Philippe. "La liberté religieuse du concile aux Lumières." *Projet* 213 (1988): 127-37.

Lefebvre, Marcel. *Religious Liberty Questioned.* Kansas City, MO: Angelus Press, 2002.

Littell, Franklin H. "The Significance of the Declaration on Religious Liberty." *Journal of Ecumenical Studies* 5 (1968): 326-37.

Lobkowicz, Nicholas. "Pharaoh Amenhotep and Dignitatis Humanae." *Oasis* 4, no. 8 (2008): 17-23.

Love, Thomas T. "*De Libertate Religiosa:* An Interpretative Analysis." *Journal of Church and State* 8, no. 1 (1966): 30-48.

Madelin, Henri. "La liberté religieuse et la sphère du politique: Pour l'intelligence de la Déclaration *Dignitatis humanae personae.*" *Nouvelle Revue Théologique* 97, no. 2 (1975): 110-26, 914-39.

Margerie, Bertrand de. "Liberté civile et obligation éthique en matière religieuse." *Vie Spirituelle* 144, no. 690 (1990): 355-71.

————. *Liberté religieuse et régne du Christ.* Paris: Éditions du Cerf, 1988.

McGreevy, John T. *Catholicism and American Freedom: A History.* New York: W. W. Norton, 2003.

Mestre, Achille. "L'Église catholique et la liberté religieuse depuis 1975." *Recherches de Science Religieuse* 78, no. 1 (1990): 73-96.

Minnerath, Roland. "La déclaration *Dignitatis Humanae* à la fin du Concile Vatican II." *Revue des sciences religieuses* 74, no. 2 (2000): 226-42.

————. *Le droit de l'Église à la liberté: Du syllabus à Vatican II.* Paris: Beauchesne, 1982.

Mistò, Luigi. "Paul VI and *Dignitatis humanae:* Theory and Practice." In *Religious Liberty: Paul VI and Dignitatis humanae,* edited by John T. Ford, 12-38. Brescia: Publicazzioni dell'Istituto Paolo VI, 1995.

Murray, John Courtney. "Arguments for the Human Right to Religious Freedom." In *Religious Liberty: Catholic Struggles with Pluralism,* edited by J. L. Hooper, 229-

44. Louisville: Westminster/John Knox, 1993. First published as "De argumentis pro iure hominis ad libertatem religiosam." In *Acta Congressus Internationalis de Theologia Concilii Vaticanii II*, edited by A. Schönmetzer, 562-73. Rome: Typis Polyglottis Vaticanis, 1968.

————. "The Church and Totalitarian Democracy." *Theological Studies* 13 (1952): 525-63.

————. "Commentary to 'Declaration on Religious Freedom.'" In *The Documents of Vatican II*, edited by W. M. Abbott, 672-74. New York: America Press, 1966.

————. "The Crisis in Church-State Relationships in the U.S.A." *The Review of Politics* 61, no. 4 (1999): 675-714.

————. "The Declaration on Religious Freedom." In *Bridging the Sacred and the Secular: Selected Writings of John Courtney Murray, SJ*, edited by J. L. Hooper, 187-99. Washington, DC: Georgetown University Press, 1994. First published in *War, Poverty, Freedom: The Christian Response*, 3-16. New York: Paulist Press, 1966.

————. "The Declaration on Religious Freedom." In *Vatican II: An Interfaith Appraisal*, edited by J. H. Miller, 565-85. Notre Dame: University of Notre Dame Press, 1966.

————. "The Declaration on Religious Freedom: A Moment in Its Legislative History." In *Religious Liberty: An End and a Beginning*, edited by J. C. Murray, 15-42. New York: Macmillan, 1966.

————. "Declaration on Religious Freedom: Commentary." In *American Participation at the Second Vatican Council*, edited by V. A. Yzermans, 668-76. New York: Sheed & Ward, 1967.

————. "The Declaration on Religious Freedom: Its Deeper Significance." *America* 114 (1966): 592-93.

————. "For the Freedom and Transcendence of the Church." *The American Ecclesiastical Review* 126 (1952): 28-48.

————. "Freedom, Authority, Community." *America* 115 (1966): 734-41.

————. "Freedom in the Age of Renewal." *The American Benedictine Review* 18 (1967): 319-24.

————. "Governmental Repression of Heresy." *Proceedings of the Catholic Theological Society of America* 3 (1948): 26-98.

————. "The Issue of Church and State at Vatican Council II." In *Religious Liberty: Catholic Struggles with Pluralism*, edited by J. L. Hooper, 199-228. Louisville: Westminster/John Knox, 1993.

————. "Leo XIII and Pius XII: Government and the Order of Religion." In *Religious Liberty: Catholic Struggles with Pluralism*, edited by J. L. Hooper, 49-126. Louisville: Westminster/John Knox, 1993.

————. "Leo XIII: Separation of Church and State." *Theological Studies* 14 (1953): 145-214.

————. "Leo XIII: Two Concepts of Government: II. Government and the Order of Culture." *Theological Studies* 15 (1954): 1-33.

————. "On Religious Liberty." *America* 109 (November 1963): 704-6.

————. "On the Structure of the Church-State Problem." In *The Catholic Church in World Affairs*, edited by W. Gurian and M. A. Fitzsimons, 11-32. Notre Dame: University of Notre Dame Press, 1954.

———. "Osservazioni sulla dichiarazione della libertà religiosa." *La Civiltà Cattolica* 116 (1965): 536-64.

———. "The Problem of Religious Freedom." *Theological Studies* 25 (1964): 503-75.

———. "The Problem of 'the Religion of the State.'" *American Ecclesiastical Review* 124 (1951): 327-52.

———. "Religious Freedom." In *The Documents of Vatican II,* edited by W. M. Abbott, 673-96. New York: America Press, 1966.

———. "Religious Freedom." In *Freedom and Man,* edited by J. C. Murray, 131-40. New York: P. J. Kenedy and Sons, 1965.

———. "Religious Freedom and the Atheist." In *Bridging the Sacred and the Secular: Selected Writings of John Courtney Murray, SJ,* edited by J. L. Hooper, 255-65. Washington, DC: Georgetown University Press, 1994. First published as "La liberta religiosa e l'ateo," *L'Ateismo Contemporaneo* 4 (1970): 109-17.

———. "Religious Liberty and Development of Doctrine." *The Catholic World* 204 (1967): 277-83.

———. "This Matter of Religious Freedom." *America* 112 (1965): 40-43.

———. "Vers une intelligence du développement de la doctrine de l'Église sur la liberté religieuse." In *Vatican II: La liberté religieuse,* edited by J. Hamer and Y. Congar, 111-47. Paris: Éditions du Cerf, 1967.

———. *We Hold These Truths: Catholic Reflections on the American Proposition.* Kansas City, MO: Sheed & Ward, 1960.

Noonan, John T., Jr. *The Lustre of Our Country: The American Experience of Religious Freedom.* Berkeley: University of California Press, 1998.

O'Donnell, Robert J. "The Church Learning and the Church Teaching: Vatican II and the Liberal Tradition of Religious Freedom." *Journal of Ecumenical Studies* 29, no. 3-4 (1992): 399-417.

O'Malley, John W. *Tradition and Transition: Historical Perspectives on Vatican II.* Wilmington, DE: M. Glazier, 1989.

Orsy, Ladislas M. "The Divine Dignity of Human Persons in *Dignitatis Humanae.*" *Theological Studies* 75, no. 1 (2014): 8-22.

Paul VI. "Liberty Rooted in Man's Dignity: General Audience, 18 August 1971." In *The Teachings of Pope Paul VI: 1971.* Washington, DC: United States Catholic Conference, 1972.

———. "Truth Is the Root of Freedom: General Audience, 9 July 1969." In *The Teachings of Pope Paul VI: 1969.* Vatican City: Libreria Editrice Vaticana, 1970.

Pavan, Pietro. "The Declaration on Religious Freedom." In *Commentary on the Documents of Vatican II,* edited by Herbert Vorgrimler, 4:48-62. New York: Herder & Herder, 1968.

———. "*Dignitatis humanae* dans la vie de l'Église." *Conscience et Liberté* (1977): 48-57.

———. "Ecumenism and Vatican II's Declaration on Religious Freedom." In *Religious Freedom, 1965 and 1975: A Symposium on a Historic Document,* edited by Walter J. Burghardt, 29. New York: Paulist Press, 1976.

———. *La dichiarazione conciliare "Dignitatis humanae" a 20 anni dalla pubblicazione.* Casale Monferrato: Piemme, 1986.

————. "Le droit à la liberté religieuse en ses éléments essentiels." In *Vatican II: La liberté religieuse,* edited by J. Hamer and Y. Congar, 149-203. Paris: Éditions du Cerf, 1967.

————. "The Right to Religious Freedom in the Conciliar Declaration." In *Religious Freedom,* 35-46. Concilium 18. New York: Paulist Press, 1966.

Pavlischek, Keith J. *John Courtney Murray and the Dilemma of Religious Toleration.* Kirksville, MO: Thomas Jefferson University Press, 1994.

————. "John Courtney Murray, Civil Religion, and the Problem of Political Neutrality." *Journal of Church and State* 34, no. 4 (1992): 729-50.

Pelotte, Donald E. *John Courtney Murray: Theologian in Conflict.* New York: Paulist Press, 1976.

Pink, Thomas. "The Interpretation of *Dignitatis Humanae:* A Reply to Martin Rhomheimer." *Nova et Vetera* 11 (2013): 77-121.

————. "The Right to Religious Liberty and the Coercion of Belief: A Note on *Dignitatis humanae.*" In *Reason, Morality and Law: The Jurisprudence of John Finnis,* edited by Robert George and John Keown. Oxford: Oxford University Press, 2013.

Portier, William. "Theology of Manners as Theology of Containment: John Courtney Murray and *Dignitatis humanae* Forty Years After." *U.S. Catholic Historian* 24, no. 1 (2006): 83-105.

Rausch, James S. *"Dignitatis humanae:* The Unfinished Agenda." In *Religious Freedom, 1965 and 1975: A Symposium on a Historic Document,* edited by Walter J. Burghardt, 39-51. New York: Paulist Press, 1976.

Regan, Richard J. *Conflict and Consensus: Religious Freedom and the Second Vatican Council.* New York: Macmillan, 1967.

————. "John Courtney Murray: The American Bishops and the Declaration on Religious Liberty." In *Religious Liberty: Paul VI and Dignitatis humanae,* edited by John T. Ford, 51-66. Brescia: Istituto Paolo VI, 1995.

Rico, Hermínio. *John Paul II and the Legacy of Dignitatis Humanae.* Washington, DC: Georgetown University Press, 2002.

Rhonheimer, Martin. "Benedict XVI's 'Hermeneutic of Reform' and Religious Freedom." In *The Common Good of Constitutional Democracy,* edited by William F. Murphy, 429-54. Washington, DC: Catholic University of America Press, 2013.

————. *"Dignitatis Humanae* — Not a Mere Question of Church Policy: A Response to Thomas Pink." *Nova et Vetera* 12, no. 2 (2014): 445-70.

Roche, Jean. *Église et liberté religieuse.* Paris: Desclée, 1966.

Scanlon, Regis. "Did Vatican II Reverse the Church's Teaching on Religious Liberty?" *Homiletic and Pastoral Review* (2011): 61-68.

Scatena, Silvia. *La fatica della libertà: L'elaborazione della dichiarazione "Dignitatis humanae" sulla libertà religiosa del Vaticano II.* Bologna: Il Mulino, 2003.

Schindler, David L. "Civil Community inside the Liberal State: Truth, Freedom, and Human Dignity." In *Ordering Love: Liberal Societies and the Memory of God,* 65-132. Grand Rapids: Eerdmans, 2011.

————. *Heart of the World, Center of the Church: Communio Ecclesiology, Liberalism, and Liberation.* Grand Rapids: Eerdmans, 1996.

Scanlon, Regis. "Did Vatican II Reverse the Church's Teaching on Religious Liberty?" *Homiletic & Pastoral Review* (2011): 61-68.

Scola, Angelo. "Gli interventi di Karol Wojtyla al Concilio Ecumenico Vaticano II: Esposizione ed interpretazione teologica." In *Karol Wojtyla: Filosofo, teologo, poeta: Atti del I Colloquio Internazionale del Pensiero Cristiano organizzato da ISTRA — Istituto di Studi per la Transizione, Roma, 23-25 settembre 1983.* Vatican City: Libreria Editrice Vaticana, 1984.

Sesboüé, Bernard. "La doctrine de la liberté religieuse est-elle contraire à la Révélation chrétienne et à la tradition de l'Église?" *Documents Épiscopat* 15 (1986): 1-19.

Steinfels, Peter. "The Failed Encounter: The Catholic Church and Liberalism in the Nineteenth Century." In *Catholicism and Liberalism: Contributions to American Public Philosophy,* edited by R. B. Douglass and D. Hollenbach, 19-44. Cambridge: Cambridge University Press, 1994.

Storck, Thomas. *Foundations of a Catholic Political Order.* Beltsville, MD: Four Faces Press, 1998.

Stransky, Thomas F. *Declaration on Religious Freedom of Vatican Council II.* New York: Paulist Press, 1967.

Sweeney, James. "Catholicism and Freedom: *Dignitatis Humanae* — The Text and Its Reception." In *Reading Religion in Text and Context,* 17-33. Aldershot: Ashgate, 2006.

Swidler, Leonard, ed. *Religious Liberty and Human Rights in Nations and in Religions.* Philadelphia: Ecumenical Press, 1986.

Thils, Gustave. "Le fondement naturel et universel de la 'liberté religieuse.'" *Revue Théologique de Louvain* 20, no. 1 (1989): 59-66.

Valuet, Basile. *La liberté religieuse et la tradition catholique: Un cas de développement doctrinal homogène dans le magistère authentique.* 3 vols. Le Barroux: Abbaye Sainte-Madeleine, 1998.

Vaucelles, Louis de. "La déclaration de Vatican II sur la liberté religieuse." In *La liberté religieuse dans le Judaïsme, le Christianisme et l'Islam,* edited by E. Poulat, R. Chenu, É. Binet, 129-34. Paris: Éditions du Cerf, 1981.

Vischer, Lukas. "Religious Freedom and the World Council of Churches." In *Religious Freedom,* 53-63. Concilium 18. New York: Paulist Press, 1966.

Wallace, Marilyn. *The Right of Religious Liberty and Its Basis in the Theological Literature of the French Language.* Ann Arbor, MI: University Microfilms International, 1987.

Weigel, George S. *Catholicism and the Renewal of American Democracy.* New York: Paulist Press, 1989.

———. "The Future of the John Courtney Murray Project." In *John Courtney Murray and the American Civil Conversation,* edited by Kenneth L. Grasso and Robert P. Hunt, 273-96. Grand Rapids: Eerdmans, 1992.

———. *Tranquillitas Ordinis: The Present Failure and Future Promise of American Catholic Thought on War and Peace.* New York: Oxford University Press, 1987.

Whitmore, Todd. "Immunity or Empowerment? John Courtney Murray and the Question of Religious Liberty." *Journal of Religious Ethics* 21, no. 2 (1993): 247-73.

Yzermans, Vincent A., ed. *American Participation in the Second Vatican Council.* New York: Sheed & Ward, 1967.

Index